Table of Integrals

ELEMENTARY FORMS

1. $\displaystyle\int u\,dv = uv - \int v\,du$

10. $\displaystyle\int \sec u \tan u\,du = \sec u + C$

2. $\displaystyle\int u^n\,du = \frac{1}{n+1}u^{n+1} + C \quad \text{if } n \neq -1$

11. $\displaystyle\int \csc u \cot u\,du = -\csc u + C$

3. $\displaystyle\int \frac{du}{u} = \ln|u| + C$

12. $\displaystyle\int \tan u\,du = \ln|\sec u| + C$

4. $\displaystyle\int e^u\,du = e^u + C$

13. $\displaystyle\int \cot u\,du = \ln|\sin u| + C$

5. $\displaystyle\int a^u\,du = \frac{a^u}{\ln a} + C$

14. $\displaystyle\int \sec u\,du = \ln|\sec u + \tan u| + C$

6. $\displaystyle\int \sin u\,du = -\cos u + C$

15. $\displaystyle\int \csc u\,du = \ln|\csc u - \cot u| + C$

7. $\displaystyle\int \cos u\,du = \sin u + C$

16. $\displaystyle\int \frac{du}{\sqrt{a^2 - u^2}} = \sin^{-1}\frac{u}{a} + C$

8. $\displaystyle\int \sec^2 u\,du = \tan u + C$

17. $\displaystyle\int \frac{du}{a^2 + u^2} = \frac{1}{a}\tan^{-1}\frac{u}{a} + c$

9. $\displaystyle\int \csc^2 u\,du = -\cot u + C$

18. $\displaystyle\int \frac{du}{a^2 - u^2} = \frac{1}{2a}\left|\frac{u+a}{u-a}\right| + C$

TRIGONOMETRIC FORMS

19. $\displaystyle\int \sin^2 u\,du = \frac{1}{2}u - \frac{1}{4}\sin 2u + C$

23. $\displaystyle\int \sin^3 u\,du = -\frac{1}{3}(2 + \sin^2 u)\cos u + C$

20. $\displaystyle\int \cos^2 u\,du = \frac{1}{2}u + \frac{1}{4}\sin 2u + C$

24. $\displaystyle\int \cos^3 u\,du = \frac{1}{3}(2 + \cos^2 u)\sin u + C$

21. $\displaystyle\int \tan^2 u\,du = \tan u - u + C$

25. $\displaystyle\int \tan^3 u\,du = \frac{1}{2}\tan^2 u + \ln|\cos u| + C$

22. $\displaystyle\int \cot^2 u\,du = -\cot u - u + C$

26. $\displaystyle\int \cot^3 u\,du = -\frac{1}{2}\cot^2 u - \ln|\sin u| + C$

27. $\displaystyle\int \sec^3 u\,du = \frac{1}{2}\sec u \tan u + \frac{1}{2}\ln|\sec u + \tan u| + C$

28. $\displaystyle\int \csc^3 u\,du = -\frac{1}{2}\csc u \cot u + \frac{1}{2}\ln|\csc u - \cot u| + C$

29. $\displaystyle\int \sin au \sin bu\,du = \frac{\sin(a-b)u}{2(a-b)} - \frac{\sin(a+b)u}{2(a+b)} + C \quad \text{if } a^2 \neq b^2$

(Continued on rear endpaper)

DIFFERENTIAL EQUATIONS WITH GRAPHICAL AND NUMERICAL METHODS

DIFFERENTIAL EQUATIONS WITH GRAPHICAL AND NUMERICAL METHODS

BERNARD W. BANKS

California State Polytechnic University

Prentice
Hall

PRENTICE HALL, Upper Saddle River, New Jersey   07458

Library of Congress Cataloging-in-Publication Data

```
Banks, Bernard W.
    Differential equations with graphical and numerical methods/Bernard W. Banks.
      p.  cm.
    Includes index.
    ISBN 0-13-084376-8
    1.  Differential equations.
  QA371.B26   2001
  515'.35--dc21                                                00-0022175
                                                               CIP
```

Acquisitions Editor: *George Lobell*
Production Editor: *Lynn Savino Wendel*
Assistant Vice President of Production and Manufacturing: *David W. Riccardi*
Executive Managing Editor: *Kathleen Schiaparelli*
Senior Managing Editor: *Linda Mihatov Behrens*
Manufacturing Buyer: *Alan Fischer*
Manufacturing Manager: *Trudy Pisciotti*
Director of Marketing: *John Tweeddale*
Marketing Manager: *Angela Battle*
Marketing Assistant: *Vince Jansen*
Associate Editor, Mathematics/Statistics Media: *Audra J. Walsh*
Editorial Assistant: *Gale Epps*
Art Director: *Ann France*
Interior Designer: *Marjory Dressler*
Cover Designer: *Jonathan Boylan*
Composition: *MacroTEX*
Chapter Opening Art: *Marjory Dressler*
Art Editor: *Grace Hazeldine*
Art Manager: *Gus Vibal*
Director of Creative Services: *Paul Belfanti*
Cover image credit: *Melvin L. Prueitt*

 © 2001 by Prentice Hall, Inc.
Upper Saddle River, New Jersey 07458

Printed in the United States of America
10 9 8 7 6 5 4 3 2 1

ISBN 0-13-084376-8

PRENTICE-HALL INTERNATIONAL (UK) LIMITED, LONDON
PRENTICE-HALL OF AUSTRALIA PTY. LIMITED, SYDNEY
PRENTICE-HALL CANADA, INC., TORONTO
PRENTICE-HALL HISPANOAMERICANA, S.A., MEXICO
PRENTICE-HALL OF INDIA PRIVATE LIMITED, NEW DELHI
PRENTICE-HALL OF JAPAN, INC., TOKYO
PEARSON EDUCATION ASIA PTE. LTD.
EDITORA PRENTICE-HALL DO BRASIL, LTDA., RIO DE JANEIRO

To my parents James and Phyllis Banks and my wife Harriet Lord.

CONTENTS

Preface   xi

1 Introduction   1

1.1. What Is a Differential Equation?   1
1.2. Applications of Differential Equations   3
1.3. Approaches to Solving Differential Equations   6
1.4. Reduction to First-Order Systems   7

2 The First-Order Equation $y' = f(x, y)$ 12

2.1. The Graphical Viewpoint (Direction Fields)   12
2.2. Numerical Methods   17
2.3. Analytic Methods of Solution   23
2.4. Autonomous Equations and Critical Points   40
2.5. The Dependence of Solutions on Initial Conditions   44
Supplementary Exercises   46

3 Introduction to First-Order Systems   48

3.1. Solutions to First-Order Systems   48
3.2. Orbit Crossing and Periodic Solutions   56
3.3. Numerical Approximations   58
3.4. Some Qualitative Behavior   64
3.5. The Pendulum   70
3.6. Limit Cycles   74
Supplementary Exercises   78

4 Higher-Order Linear Equations   79

4.1. Introduction   79
4.2. A Strategy for Solving Linear Homogeneous Equations   80
4.3. Linear Homogeneous Equations with Constant Coefficients   88
4.4. NonHomogeneous Equations   97
4.5. Vibration   107
Supplementary Exercises   115

5   First-Order Systems: Linear Methods   117

5.1. Matrices, Independence, and Eigenvectors   117
5.2. Solving 2×2 Linear Systems   131
5.3. The Matrix Exponential Function   138
5.4. Qualitative Behavior of Linear Systems   151
5.5. A Coupled System of Masses and Springs   156
5.6. Linearization of 2×2 Systems   159
Supplementary Exercises   164

6   Series Methods and Famous Functions   166

6.1. A Power Series Method   166
6.2. Famous Functions   181
6.3. Regular Singular Points and the Method of Frobenius   186
6.4. The Exceptional Cases   193
Supplementary Exercises   197

7   Bifurcations and Chaos   198

7.1. Bifurcation   199
7.2. Flows   203
7.3. A Basic Theorem   209
7.4. Some Simple Attractors   213
7.5. The Periodically Driven Pendulum   218
7.6. Chaos   223
Supplementary Exercises   229

8   The Laplace Transform   230

8.1. Introduction   230
8.2. Transforms of Basic Functions   235
8.3. Solving Linear Homogeneous Equations   240
8.4. NonHomogeneous Equations and the Convolution   244
8.5. Discontinuous and Impulsive Forcing Functions   248
8.6. Laplace Transforms and Systems   257
8.7. Poles and Qualitative Behavior   261
Supplementary Exercises   264

9 Partial Differential Equations and Fourier Series 265

9.1. Some General Remarks 265
9.2. The Heat Equation, Wave Equation, and Laplace's Equation 269
9.3. The Heat Equation and Initial Condition 279
9.4. Vector Spaces and Operators 288
9.5. The Heat Equation Revisited 308
9.6. Periodic Functions and Fourier Series 314
9.7. The One-Dimensional Wave Equation 319
9.8. The Convergence of Series 326
9.9. The Two-Dimensional Wave Equation 328
9.10. Laplace's Equation 338
Supplementary Exercises 345

10 The Finite Differences Method 347

10.1. Finite Difference Approximations 347
10.2. An Example 351
10.3. The Heat and Wave Equations 357
10.4. A Backward Method for the Heat Equation 366
10.5. Variable Coefficient and NonLinear Examples 370
10.6. Laplace's Equation 373
10.7. Stability 381
Supplementary Exercises 385

APPENDICES

A Linear Systems, Matrices, and Determinants 387

A.1. Solution of Systems of Equations 387
A.2. Matrices, Inverses, and Determinants 391

B The Two-Variable Taylor Theorem 403

C The Existence and Uniqueness Theorem 405

D   Mathematica, Maple, and MatLab   409

D.1.   Graphing   409
D.2.   Field&Solution   415
D.3.   ERGraphical   420
D.4.   ERNumerical   425
D.5.   2x2System   427
D.6.   2x2Numerical   431
D.7.   Fourier Series   431

E   Answers and Hints to Odd-Numbered Exercises   437

Bibliography   457
Index   459

PREFACE

S ome time ago I searched for a textbook for a sophomore course in differential equations that would combine analytical (algebraic) methods of solution with graphical and numerical methods in a unified way. Some texts made computer graphics the center of the course and left out such topics as variation of parameters and infinite series. Other texts retained the traditional topics, but the graphics seemed to be grafted on as an afterthought. This book is an outgrowth of this failed search. The book retains almost all the traditional canon of differential equations, but it employs graphical and numerical methods from the outset, both as methods of solution and as means of illuminating concepts.

To employ graphical and numerical methods from the start, it was necessary to make first-order systems and reduction to first-order systems the focal point. First-order systems form the core subject matter of Chapters 1 through 5 and Chapter 7. Chapter 6 covers power series solutions, but even here first-order systems make a brief appearance in order to make clear why points at which the leading coefficient of a linear differential equation vanishes must be considered singular. Through first-order systems, solutions can easily be presented graphically with today's computer resources. This opens the way for visual interpretation of solutions and fields. First-order systems also provide the unified means of applying numerical methods to a very wide range of differential equations. Because of this, differential equations can be investigated that could not be considered in times gone by. Models of competing species, the pendulum, and the tunnel diode oscillator are taken up early in the text.

In spite of the emphasis on first-order systems, I have not neglected the basics of analytic solutions. Separable, linear, and exact equations are solved in the study of a single first-order equation in Chapter 2, and higher-order constant coefficient linear equations are treated in Chapter 4. However, the knowledge of first-order systems developed in Chapter 3 is used to establish the strategy for solving higher-order linear equations. Power series methods are also not neglected. Indeed, they cannot be, since they are needed in the solution of partial differential equations, which is the subject of Chapter 9.

Chapter 9 presents the solution of partial differential equations through the method of separation of variables and Fourier series. Chapter 10 introduces the reader to numerical methods of solution for partial differential equations. These two chapters were more difficult to write than the others because there is no unifying theme, such as first-order systems for ordinary differential equations. Nonetheless, graphics and numerical methods have been employed to help clarify ideas and to extend the range of equations solved. Computer algebra systems (CAS) such as Mathematica, Maple or MatLab (the Three M's) are used to advantage to illustrate convergence of Fourier series, graph modes of vibration for drumheads, and animate solutions. The chapter on numerical methods for partial differential equations is, I think, new in a book of this type. However, I believe it is entirely in keeping with the theme of this book and the availability of powerful computing resources. The use of a CAS makes the instability of some of the finite difference methods easy to explore, and it makes possible the exploration of some nonlinear partial differential equations.

Chapter 8 is a traditional treatment of the Laplace transform. The Laplace transform does not call for graphical or numerical methods, but I thought it important to include the Laplace transform because it is such an elegant way of dealing with constant coefficient linear equations and discontinuous forcing functions.

A large proportion of the exercises call for the use of a computer. The necessary software is available at the Prentice Hall web site:

www.prenhall.com/banks

A Note to Instructors

For ordinary differential equations I have written a series of applications specific to the task at hand for the Windows and MacOs operating systems. These require no other support than the operating system. Packages for the entire book are also available at the web site for each of the Three M's. These routines are also listed completely in the instructors manual. If, however, you wish to have your students develop their own packages in one of the Three M's, Appendix D provides a guide to the development of these packages. This does have pedagogical value if you have the time. If you intend to cover the material on partial differential equations, then developing facility with one of the Three M's will be helpful.

The formal abstractions of vector spaces and linear transformations are introduced only in Section 9.4. Admittedly, this is quite late in the text, but it is not until this point that the references to linear combinations and linearity properties have sufficiently motivated the abstractions of a vector space and linear transformation. Together, Appendix A and Section 9.4 provide an introduction to the basic elements of linear algebra. They are self-contained, and Appendix A has exercises also. Thus Appendix A and Section 9.4 can be used at any time as supplementary lectures. If you feel the need to introduce concepts from linear algebra earlier, there is nothing to prevent you doing so. Indeed, if your students lack a good college algebra preparation, I recommend covering the material on solutions of systems of linear equations in Appendix A before going into Chapter 4.

The Supplementary Exercise sections at the end of chapters contain exercises that are of a more challenging nature or develop a topic that was not covered in the chapter. These exercises could be used as projects to be completed in, say, a ten-day period.

I confess to repeatedly abusing notation by referring to $f(x)$ as a function as well as the value of the function. I do this deliberately because I believe that using the precise notation for functions would tend to confuse students who are not yet mathematically very sophisticated. Besides, the precise notation can become quite cumbersome at times. Students will find "consider the function $f(x) = 3x...$" much more palatable than "consider the function $f : R \rightarrow R$ defined by $f(x) = 3x...$."

It is intended that the book be covered in two semesters. The first semester should aim to cover Chapters 1 through 7 and the second Chapters 8 through 10. In one quarter, I have been able to cover Chapters 1 through 4 and Sections 6.1 and 6.2 with the omission of a few nonessential sections. There is no question that the material on partial differential equations is inherently more difficult than the rest of the text. However, this material is accessible if it is covered at a gentle pace. Sections that may be omitted without loss of continuity are 2.5, 3.5, 3.6, and all of Chapters 7, 8, and 10.

Finally, detailed suggestions for teaching sections of the text may be found in the instructors manual for the text. Also included are suggestions for laboratory activities, sample exam questions, and complete listings of the software packages.

Acknowledgments

Several of my colleagues have taught from the text during its preparation. Their contributions have been invaluable. I would like to thank Dr. Weiqing Xie, Dr. Martin Nakashima, Dr. Alan Radnitz, and especially Dr. Harriet Lord for her constant help in the development of this text. I would also like to thank my editor, George Lobell, and his staff for their guidance and help.

Bernard W. Banks
bwbanks@csupomona.edu

CHAPTER 1

INTRODUCTION

Differential equations arise in a wide range of practical problems. Whether you want to send an exploration mission to Mars or model the dynamics of populations of fish, differential equations will emerge as an essential part of the study of these tasks. The aim of this book is to provide you with an introduction to differential equations and the main ways in which differential equations can be studied. This book will describe what differential equations are, how they arise from practical problems, and the tools available for solving them.

This chapter introduces you to the general terms and concepts that are fundamental to the study of differential equations. Examples are given of practical problems that lead to differential equations. This will give you an introduction to the usefulness of the subject. Finally, the chapter closes with the description of a technique that reduces a wide range of differential equations to what can be considered a standard form. It is through this standard form that computing resources may be applied and important general results derived.

1.1 WHAT IS A DIFFERENTIAL EQUATION?

A differential equation may be described as an equation in which there are symbols for some of the derivatives of an unknown function. The order of such a differential equation is the order of the highest derivative in the equation. Differential equations come in two types, ordinary and partial. In an ordinary differential equation the unknown function is of one variable only, and the derivatives are ordinary. On the other hand, in a partial differential equation the unknown function is of several variables, and the derivatives are partial derivatives.

This book gives a brief introduction to the vast subject of partial differential equations, but the main focus is on equations of ordinary type. We shall delay discussing partial differential equations until the necessary groundwork in ordinary differential equations has been laid.

A **solution** to an ordinary differential equation is a function $\phi(x)$ defined on an interval (a, b) such that, if the appropriate derivatives of $\phi(x)$ are substituted for the corresponding symbols for those derivatives in the equation, the equation becomes an identity for all $x \in (a, b)$.

We shall soon drop the adjective "ordinary" unless it is needed. So, unless otherwise stated, all differential equations may be assumed to be ordinary.

Here is an example of the ideas of a differential equation and a solution.

Example 1.1.1 The following is a second-order ordinary differential equation.

$$y'' - y = x.$$

One solution (there are others) is

$$\phi(x) = -x + 2e^x.$$

Indeed, $\phi'(x) = -1 + 2e^x$, and $\phi''(x) = 2e^x$. Therefore,

$$\phi''(x) - \phi(x) = 2e^x - (-x + 2e^x) = x.$$

This is an identity for all x. In this case the interval of x for which the equation holds is $(-\infty, \infty)$. ∎

The square ∎ will indicate the close of examples, definitions, and proofs. Here is another example.

Example 1.1.2 The function $\phi(x) = -1/(x - 1)$ is a solution to the equation

$$y' = y^2.$$

To verify this take the derivative and make the substitutions in the equation. This is the result.

$$\phi'(x) = \frac{1}{(x - 1)^2} = \left(\frac{-1}{x - 1}\right)^2 = (\phi(x))^2.$$

This is an identity for $x > 1$ or for $x < 1$. If we insist that the solution pass through $(0, 1)$, then we choose the solution defined for $x < 1$. The point $(0, 1)$ is called an initial condition, and we will have much more to say about this later. ∎

1.2 APPLICATIONS OF DIFFERENTIAL EQUATIONS

Differential equations can be applied in many diverse areas. A very small sample of the kinds of applications that are possible is given next. At appropriate points in the text, applications will be made and evaluated in detail.

Science in general and physics in particular provide rich sources of differential equations. The reason for this, in physics at least, is that the laws of nature are most often expressed in terms of rates of change. For example Newton's second law relates the rate of change of momentum to force in the equation

$$\frac{dmv}{dt} = F.$$

If the mass is a constant, we have the more familiar equation

$$ma = F,$$

FIGURE 1.1

where a is the acceleration. You will recall that the acceleration is the second derivative of the position as a function of time. A specific example is given by a mass m suspended from a spring (Figure 1.1).

Imagine that the mass is allowed to extend the spring until the force of gravity is balanced out by the spring. If the displacement of the mass is measured from this position, the force of gravity can be ignored. Let $x(t)$ be the displacement of the mass from the rest position, and assume that the spring produces a force that is proportional to the extension of the spring. Suppose that the formula is $F(x) = -kx$; then the second law gives us

$$mx''(t) = -kx(t)$$

or

$$mx''(t) + kx(t) = 0.$$

If we assume, in addition, there is a force of friction proportional to the velocity of the mass, then the equation of the motion is

$$mx''(t) = -cx'(t) - kx(t)$$

or

$$mx''(t) + cx'(t) + kx(t) = 0,$$

where $c > 0$ is the constant of proportionality. We assume this constant is positive because the force of friction is oppositely directed to the direction of motion.

The next example is from electronics. The circuit shown in Figure 1.2 has an inductor, resistor, capacitor, and generator that produces an electromotive force $E(t)$, which is a function of time. Kirchhoff's second law of electricity states that the sum of the voltage drops around the circuit must add up to the

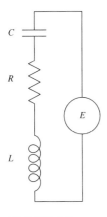

FIGURE 1.2

electromotive force. If $q(t)$ is the charge on the capacitor at time t, then the voltage drop across the capacitor is $q(t)/C$. Here the units for C are faradays and the units for $q(t)$ are coulombs. The current is the rate at which charge passes a point in the wire. Thus $q'(t)$ is the current, and the units are amperes (coulombs per second). Resistance is measured in ohms, so if R is the resistance, then the voltage drop across the resistor is $Rq'(t)$. Finally, the voltage drop across the inductor is proportional to the rate of change of the current. This proportionality constant is the inductance, L, and it is measured in henrys. Thus the voltage drop across the inductor is $Lq''(t)$. Therefore, adding the voltage drops we get

$$Lq''(t) + Rq'(t) + q(t)/C = E(t).$$

Here is yet another example from physics, this one from statics. If a cable hangs from two pins, it assumes a sort of parabolic shape. However, it is not a parabola. What is this shape? Consider Figure 1.3. The figure shows a hanging cable with part of the cable removed and a balance of forces diagram. The cable is hung from two pins at $(-1, 10)$ and $(1, 10)$. At x the remaining cable to $(1, 10)$ has been removed and replaced with the tension force T that the removed cable exerted on the cable to the left of x. Since the cable is flexible, this tension force is tangent to the curve at x, and the force has been resolved into the horizontal and vertical components of magnitudes H and V, respectively. The cable is still in static equilibrium.

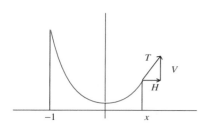

FIGURE 1.3

Since the cable is in static equilibrium, the tension forces in the cable are constant with respect to time. Consider the piece of cable from the bottom of the curve to the point x. The tension force T_0 at $x = 0$ pulls on the piece of cable from 0 to x horizontally and to the left. Thus there is no vertical force at 0. Therefore, the vertical force, V, must equal the weight of this section of the cable in order for it to remain motionless. Thus

$$V = \int_0^x \rho\sqrt{1 + (y')^2}\,dt,$$

where ρ is the weight density of the cable per unit of length, and $y(t)$ is the function whose graph is the hanging cable.

Remember that the tension force T_0 on the left of the cable segment is horizontal; so to maintain the equilibrium of the segment, $H = T_0$. Thus H does not depend on x. Let k be the reciprocal of the constant H.

The differential equation that y must satisfy is found as follows. Note that, from the force triangle, $y'(x) = V/H$. Therefore,

$$y'(x) = \frac{V}{H} = kV = k\int_0^x \rho\sqrt{1 + (y')^2}\,dt.$$

Differentiating gives

$$y''(x) = k\rho\sqrt{1 + (y'(x))^2}.$$

The solution of this differential equation is the curve in which the cable hangs. Solving this equation is required in Supplementary Exercise 5 of Chapter 2.

In biology, a population of bacteria may reasonably be assumed to grow at a rate proportional to the population, provided the population has sufficient space and nutrients and no factors such as antibiotics are introduced. If $P(t)$ is the number of bacteria in the population at time t, then the differential equation is

$$P'(t) = rP(t).$$

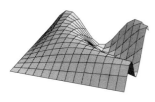

Figure 1.4 shows a portion of a ski area and the corresponding contour map. Running across the middle of the region is a ridge, and just to the "northeast" of that there is a long valley. Recall that contours, or level curves, are curves of constant height on the terrain. Suppose that you wish to ski from the ridge into the valley by the fastest route. What path should you take? You should take the path that is always pointing downhill in the steepest direction, and this means that the path must cut the contours at right angles.

Suppose that the altitude of the mountain over the point (x, y) is given by $z = f(x, y)$. Then a contour is a curve satisfying

$$f(x, y) = c.$$

You will recall that the gradient vector, defined by

$$\frac{\partial f}{\partial x}\vec{i} + \frac{\partial f}{\partial y}\vec{j},$$

FIGURE 1.4

is at right angles to the contour and is the direction of most rapid increase in height. Therefore, to ski down the mountain most rapidly, the skier must always be heading in the direction opposite to the gradient. Suppose also that the path down the mountain has been parameterized by the functions $x = x(t)$, $y = y(t)$, and $z = z(t)$. Then

$$z(t) = f(x(t), y(t)),$$

and so it is $x = x(t)$ and $y = y(t)$ that we need to find. Skiing in a direction opposite to the gradient means that the horizontal velocity

$$\vec{v}(t) = x'(t)\vec{i} + y'(t)\vec{j}$$

must be in the direction

$$-\frac{\partial f}{\partial x}\vec{i} - \frac{\partial f}{\partial y}\vec{j}$$

at $(x(t), y(t))$. If we assume the parameterization is such that the velocity is actually equal to the negative of the gradient, this will be enough to describe the path down the mountain, although it will not necessarily give the correct speed for the skier. After all, the same path down the mountain can be skied making a snow plow all the way or skiing as fast as possible.

The ski area in the Figure 1.4 is described by

$$f(x, y) = \sin(xy),$$

so our discussion leads to the following differential equations that the path must satisfy.

$$x'(t) = -y(t)\cos(x(t)y(t)),$$
$$y'(t) = -x(t)\cos(x(t)y(t)).$$

This is an example of a system of two first-order equations in two unknown functions. A solution is a pair of functions $x = x(t)$ and $y = y(t)$ defined on an interval (a, b) such that the preceding equations become identities on this interval.

Systems of first-order ordinary differential equations are the standard forms mentioned earlier, and they will play an important role in this book. We shall have more to say about systems very shortly.

1.3 APPROACHES TO SOLVING DIFFERENTIAL EQUATIONS

Recall that a solution to a differential equation is a function $\phi(x)$ defined on an interval (a, b) such that when the appropriate derivatives of $\phi(x)$ are inserted in the equation the equation becomes an identity on the interval (a, b).

For a given equation, the first question that comes to mind is whether the equation has any solutions. This is referred to as the **question of existence**.

Once solutions to an equation are known to exist, we can set about discovering their properties. Solutions are, of course, functions, so we might first attempt to solve for these functions. By this we mean that we express the solutions in terms of known functions and familiar mathematical objects, such as integrals, algebraic equations, and power series. This is similar to the situation of finding roots to a polynomial. Sometimes it is possible to solve for the roots in an algebraic formula. For example, quadratic equations can always be solved this way. We shall call this approach the analytic method.

For many equations there is a geometrical connection between the solutions and the equation. With the help of computer graphics, this relation can be drawn and the behavior of solutions visualized. This is analogous to drawing the graph of a polynomial in order to visualize its roots. We shall call this approach to discovering information about the solution the graphical or qualitative approach.

It is natural to want to compute the value of a solution at any point in its domain to any desired degree of accuracy. The fulfillment of this desire almost always demands numerical methods. Resorting to the analogy of polynomial roots again, if we want to calculate a root of a polynomial to ten decimal places, in most cases we shall have to use a numerical method, such as bisection or

Newton's method. We refer to the methods of approximation of solutions as **numerical methods**. We shall see that a combination of these approaches often gives the fullest picture of a solution.

Finally, if an equation has solutions, it is reasonable to ask what additional information will be needed to select just one solution from the set of solutions. This is called the **uniqueness problem**, and the additional information is usually referred to as the **initial condition**.

1.4 REDUCTION TO FIRST-ORDER SYSTEMS

A most important approach to solving a differential equation is to reduce it to a system of first-order equations, because first-order systems lend themselves to graphical interpretation and numerical analysis. Moreover, questions of existence and uniqueness of solutions are usually settled by reducing the equation to a first-order system. This first-order system is the standard form mentioned earlier. The reduction procedure is easily explained through examples.

First the equation is solved for the highest-order derivative that occurs. For example the equation

$$y'' + e^x y' + 3y^2 = 0$$

can be solved for y'' to give

$$y'' = -3y^2 - e^x y'.$$

If we set $u_1 = y$ and $u_2 = y'$, then we can write

$$u_1' = u_2,$$
$$u_2' = -3u_1^2 - e^x u_2.$$

In this way the second-order equation has been traded in for a system of two first-order equations. If y is a function solving

$$y''(x) = -3y^2(x) - e^x y'(x),$$

then $u_1(x) = y(x)$ and $u_2(x) = y'(x)$ solve the system. Conversely, if $\{u_1, u_2\}$ solves the system, in the sense that

$$u_1'(x) = u_2(x),$$
$$u_2'(x) = -3u_1^2(x) - e^x u_2(x),$$

are identities for some interval of x, then $y(x) = u_1(x)$ solves the original second-order equation.

Here is a third-order example.

Example 1.4.1 Consider the equation

$$y^{(3)} - 3y'' + 2y' = 0.$$

If we set $u_1 = y$, $u_2 = y'$, and $u_3 = y''$, then the corresponding first-order system is

$$u_1' = u_2,$$
$$u_2' = u_3,$$
$$u_3' = -2u_2 + 3u_3.$$

The solutions to the third-order equation and the system are related as follows. If $\phi(x)$ is a solution to the third-order equation defined on (a, b), then the functions $u_1(x) = \phi(x)$, $u_2(x) = \phi'(x)$, and $u_3(x) = \phi''(x)$ satisfy the system identically on (a, b). Conversely, if $\{u_1(x), u_2(x), u_3(x)\}$ satisfy the system on and interval (a, b), then the function $\phi(x) = u_1(x)$ satisfies the third-order equation on (a, b).

As a specific example consider $\phi(x) = e^{2x}$. You can quickly verify that this function satisfies

$$y^{(3)} - 3y'' + 2y' = 0$$

for all x. The corresponding solution to the system is $\{u_1 = e^{2x}, u_2 = 2e^{2x}, u_3 = 4e^{2x}\}$. Indeed,

$$u_1' = 2e^{2x} = u_2,$$
$$u_2' = 4e^{2x} = u_3,$$
$$u_3' = 8e^{2x} = -2u_2 + 3u_3.$$

You can also easily verify that $\{u_1 = e^x, u_2 = e^x, u_3 = e^x\}$ satisfy the system for all x, and then verify that $\phi(x) = u_1(x) = e^x$ satisfies the third-order equation for all x. ■

Here are two more examples of reduction to first order.

Examples 1.4.2

1. We reduce the equation $y'' - x^2 y' + 3y = e^x$ as follows. Set $u_1 = y$ and $u_2 = y'$. Then we have the system

$$u_1'(x) = u_2(x),$$
$$u_2'(x) = e^x - 3u_1(x) + x^2 u_2(x).$$

2. Consider $y^{(3)} + y'' - \sin(x)y = 0$. We set $u_1 = y$, $u_2 = y'$, and $u_3 = y''$. Then we get the system

$$u_1'(x) = u_2(x),$$
$$u_2'(x) = u_3(x),$$
$$u_3'(x) = \sin(x)u_1(x) - u_3(x).$$

■

Recall the second-order equation

$$my'' + ky = 0$$

that described the motion of an object of mass m suspended from a spring with spring constant k. Reduction of this equation to a first-order system gives a different way to view the motion. Set $u(t) = y(t)$ and $v(t) = y'(t)$. Then $u(t)$ is displacement of the object as a function of time, and $v(t)$ is the velocity of the object at time t. The first-order system is

$$u' = v,$$
$$v' = -\frac{k}{m}u.$$

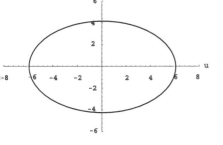

FIGURE 1.5

The functions $u = u(t)$ and $v = v(t)$ parameterize a path in the (u, v)-plane. Figure 1.5 shows a typical path where the mass is 4 units and the spring constant is 2 units.

As time advances the point $(u(t), v(t))$ moves around the ellipse. When it is on the u-axis, the velocity is zero and the displacement is at a maximum of 6 units. As time progresses the velocity increases to a maximum of a little over 4 units when the point is on the v-axis. The path (called an orbit) describes the exchange between displacement and velocity. Therefore, the reduction to the standard form of a first-order system has revealed in graphical terms the relation between displacement and velocity. The (u, v)-plane is often called the **phase plane**.

First-order systems are not only important in applying graphical and numerical methods to higher-order equations, but, as we mentioned at the outset, it is easier to understand the existence and uniqueness problems for first-order systems than it is for nth-order equations. In addition, first-order systems arise naturally in many applications. Thus systems of the form

$$x_1'(t) = f_1(t, x_1(t), \dots, x_n(t)),$$
$$x_2'(t) = f_2(t, x_1(t), \dots, x_n(t)),$$
$$\vdots$$
$$x_n'(t) = f_n(t, x_1(t), \dots, x_n(t))$$

play a primary role in ordinary differential equations. Such systems will be a recurrent theme throughout this book.

Here is one more example of a system and a solution to the system.

Example 1.4.3   The system is

$$u_1'(t) = u_2(t),$$
$$u_2'(t) = -u_1(t).$$

A solution to this is (u_1, u_2), where $u_1(t) = \sin(t)$ and $u_2(t) = \cos(t)$. To see this, we calculate the derivatives and substitute in the equations to see that we get identities. The derivatives are $u_1'(t) = \cos(t)$ and $u_2'(t) = -\sin(t)$. Thus

$$u_1'(t) = \cos(t) = u_2(t),$$
$$u_2'(t) = -\sin(t) = -u_1(t).$$

In the (u_1, u_2) phase plane the path traced out by the parametric functions $u_1(t) = \sin(t)$ and $u_2(t) = \cos(t)$ is a circle.   ∎

Clearly, being able to reduce an nth-order equation to a first-order system depends on being able to solve the equation for $y^{(n)}$. In solving for the highest-order derivative, the usual problems associated with solving equations are sometimes encountered. We may implicitly divide by zero, or squaring both sides may introduce extraneous solutions. The following example gives an indication of the pitfalls one must avoid.

Example 1.4.4   Consider $\sqrt{y'} - x = 0$. Solving for y' gives $y' = x^2$, so the solutions are $y(x) = x^3/3 + c$. So solutions to the second equation are defined for all x. But solutions to the first equation are not defined for negative x. Indeed, squaring both sides introduced extraneous solutions.   ∎

EXERCISES FOR CHAPTER 1

In exercise 21 you are asked to use software for the first time. If you plan to write your own routines in Mathematica, Maple, or MatLab, you will need to turn to Appendix D and work through the appropriate section of the Graphing module. Otherwise, you will need to download the appropriate software from the web site given in the preface.

1. Show that $y = e^x$ is a solution to $y'' - 2y' + y = 0$.
2. Show that $y = \sin(x)$ is a solution to $y'' + y = 0$.
3. Show that $y = \frac{1}{\sqrt{1-2x}}$ is a solution to the first order equation $y' - y^3 = 0$. On what interval is this solution defined?
4. Show that $y = xe^x$ solves the equation $y'' - 2y' + y = 0$
5. Write a short paragraph describing what a differential equation is. What is a solution? Give an example of a differential equation and a solution to it. Do not use examples that have already been given.

For Exercises 6–8, translate each statement into a differential equation.

6. The acceleration of a particle is equal to its displacement.
7. The rate of change of a population of bacteria is proportional to the difference between the population and the square of the population.
8. The acceleration of a falling body is proportional to g minus a constant multiple of the velocity. Only one unknown function must appear.
9. Show that the functions $u_1 = e^x - e^{2x}$ and $u_2 = e^x - 2e^{2x}$ provide a solution to the system

$$u_1'(x) = u_2(x),$$
$$u_2'(x) = -2u_1(x) + 3u_2(x).$$

For Exercises 10–15, reduce each equation to a first-order system.

10. $y'' - 2y' + 3^x y = e^x$.
11. $y^{(3)} + y'' - \sin(x)y = 0$.
12. $e^x y^{(3)} - 2y'' - \sin(x)y = \cos(x)$.
13. $3y'' - 2xy' + 3^x y = e^x$.
14. $y^{(3)} + y'' - \sin(x)y = \sin(x)$.
15. $e^x y^{(4)} - 2y'' - y = \cos(x) + x$.
16. Show that the function $\phi(x) = xe^x$ satisfies the equation

$y'' - 2y' + y = 0$. Reduce this equation to a first-order system, and show that the functions $u_1(x) = xe^x$ and $u_2(x) = e^x + xe^x$ satisfy the system.

17. Explain how the solutions to $y'' - \sin(x)y' + y^4 = 3$ are related to the corresponding system of first-order equations.

18. Let $\phi(x)$ be a solution to a differential equation. Match the following statements with the approaches (A) to (C) to solving the equation.

    (a) $\phi(x) = \sin(x - 2)$.
    (b) Since $\phi'(x)$ satisfies $y' = y^2 + 1$, $\phi(x)$ is always positive, and so it must be increasing.
    (c) Here is a table of values of $\phi(x)$.
    (A) A numerical approach.
    (B) A qualitative or graphical approach.
    (C) An analytic approach.

19. Let $\phi(x)$ be a solution to a differential equation. Match the following statements with the approaches (A) to (C)

to solving the equation.

    (a) $\phi(x) = 3e^x + 2x$.
    (b) Since $\phi'(x)$ satisfies $y' = -e^y$, $\phi(x)$ is always negative, and so it must be decreasing.
    (c) Here is a table of values of $\phi(x)$.
    (A) A numerical approach.
    (B) A qualitative or graphical approach.
    (C) An analytic approach.

20. The equations $y' - e^{-x^2} = 0$ and $y(0) = 0$ have a unique solution. In what sense do you think the solution can be found? Say as much as you can about the solution. *Hint:* Can you express the solution as an integral?

21. This exercise is intended to start you becoming familiar with the support software that you intend to use with this text. Draw graphs of the following functions: (a) $f(x) = \sin(3x)$, (b) $f(x) = x^2/5 - 2\cos(2x)$, (c) $f(x) = \frac{3x}{x^2+1}$, and (d) $f(x) = \arctan(3x)$.

CHAPTER 2

THE FIRST-ORDER EQUATION $Y' = F(X, Y)$

The simplest first-order system consists of just one equation $y' = f(x, y)$ in one unknown function y. This chapter is devoted to the study of this equation. We shall study the equation from a graphical, analytic, and numerical point of view. While we study the equation from the graphical viewpoint, we shall answer the questions of existence and uniqueness. That is, does this equation have any solutions, and under what circumstances is a solution unique?

2.1 THE GRAPHICAL VIEWPOINT (DIRECTION FIELDS)

A great deal of insight can be gained if the equation is interpreted geometrically. If ϕ is a solution to the equation on an interval (a, b), then the identity $\phi'(x) = f(x, \phi(x))$ may be interpreted to say that the tangent line to the graph of ϕ at x must have slope $f(x, \phi(x))$ at the point $(x, \phi(x))$ through which it passes. This may be expressed in a slightly different way. Think of the number $f(x, y)$ as the slope of a short line segment through the point (x, y). Then a solution to the differential equation has a graph that passes through the plane so that, at each point (x, y) through which it passes, the line segment at that point of slope $f(x, y)$ is tangent to the graph. If line segments of slope $f(x, y)$ are plotted at a lattice of points in the plane, then, as we shall see, the eye quickly sees the nature of solutions. We call f, or the lattice of line segments, the **inclination** or **direction field** of the equation. An example of the inclination field of the equation $y' = -y/5$ is given in Figure 2.1.

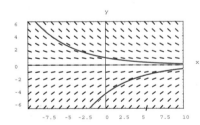

FIGURE 2.1

Notice how the solutions pass through the field tangentially. This is the geometric meaning of the differential equation. Notice also that each point in the plane would appear to uniquely determine a solution. The specification of a point through which the solution must pass is called an initial condition. We make a formal definition of this.

Definition 2.1.1

A point (x_0, y_0) through which a solution to $y' = f(x, y)$ is required to pass is called an initial condition.   ●

A differential equation together with an initial condition is often called an **initial value problem**.

Consider the equation $y' = -y/5$ again. You can easily see that functions of the form

$$y = Ce^{-x/5}$$

are solutions to this equation. Geometrically, this means that the slope of the tangent line to the graph of $y = Ce^{-x/5}$ at (x, y) must be $-y/5$. Moreover, if an initial condition is given, then the C will be determined. For example, if we require that the solution pass through $(0, 2)$, then $2 = Ce^{-0/5} = C$. Therefore, we have $y = 2e^{-x/5}$. Shortly, it will be shown that this is the only solution to this equation through this initial condition.

Consider the pair of fields drawn in Figures 2.2A and 2.2B for the equations $y' = 5y^2$ and $y' = 3y^{2/3}$, respectively. These fields look alike. However, they are by no means similar. Notice that $y \equiv 0$ is a solution of both equations. The other solution drawn in Figure 2.2A is $y = 1/(-4 - 5x)$, and this does not cross the x-axis. In Figure 2.2B, $y = x^3$ is the second solution drawn. It passes through $(0, 0)$, and so we have two solutions passing through the origin. You may have surmised that, if the slopes of the field lines change continuously as (x, y) moves about the plane, there should be at least one solution passing through each point. This is correct, and this was first proved by the Italian mathematician Peano in 1886 [6]. However, the field in Figure 2.2B, which varies continuously, indicates that the continuity of f in $y' = f(x, y)$ is not enough to guarantee that only one solution passes through each point.

You may have noticed that the function $f(x, y) = 3y^{2/3}$ defining the equation having at least two solutions through the origin does not have a partial derivative with respect to y along the x-axis. This suggests that for both existence and uniqueness it may be enough that f and $\frac{\partial f}{\partial y}$ be continuous. This is the case, and we summarize this in a theorem.

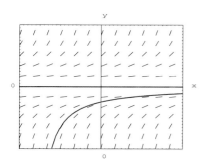

FIGURE 2.2A

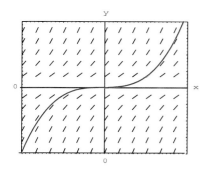

FIGURE 2.2B

Theorem 2.1.2

Suppose that f and $\frac{\partial f}{\partial y}$ are continuous functions on the rectangle $R = \{(x, y) | a \leq x \leq b$ and $c \leq y \leq d\}$. If (x_0, y_0) is a point in the interior of the rectangle, then there is a positive number h and a function ϕ that is defined on $(x_0 - h, x_0 + h)$, such that ϕ is a solution to $y' = f(x, y)$ and $y(x_0) = y_0$, and the graph of ϕ is in R. Moreover, any solution passing through (x_0, y_0) and having its graph in R agrees with any other on the intersection of their domains.   ●

For an outline of the proof of this theorem see Appendix C or [1]. The proof shows where the continuity of $\frac{\partial f}{\partial y}$ comes into play.

Unless otherwise stated, we shall always assume that f and $\frac{\partial f}{\partial y}$ are continuous functions on the rectangle $R = \{(x, y)|a \le x \le b \text{ and } c \le y \le d\}$.

If the hypotheses of the theorem hold, then solutions passing through a given point must agree on the intersection of their domains. This has a simple consequence. Such graphs cannot cross one another; thus graphs of solutions that have points in common join together to form one larger solution. Therefore, if all the graphs of the solutions passing through a given point are combined, one **maximal solution** is formed. For the sake of brevity, we shall refer to this unique maximal solution through a given point as the solution through that point. In a given rectangle where the function and partial derivative are continuous, the maximal solution through a point inside the rectangle is the curve that continues tangentially through the field until the boundary of the rectangle is reached.

The following examples give further illustrations of the meaning of Theorem 2.1.2.

Example 2.1.3 Consider the equation

$$y' = \frac{y^2}{1 + x^2 + y^2}.$$

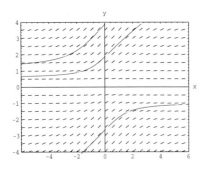

FIGURE 2.3

The field and some solutions are shown in Figure 2.3. Notice that $f(x, 0) = 0$, so the field line segments have slope equal to zero on the x-axis. This agrees with the figure. You should compute some additional field slopes such as $f(0, 1)$, $f(1, 3)$, and $f(-1, 3)$ and then compare them with the field drawn. This is to make sure that you understand how the field line segment slopes are computed from the equation.

The functions $f(x, y) = \frac{y^2}{1+x^2+y^2}$ and $\frac{\partial f}{\partial y} = \frac{2y(1+x^2+y^2)-2y^3}{(1+x^2+y^2)^2}$ are continuous throughout the plane. So, through each point in the plane there is only one (maximal) solution. Examine the field and solutions. As expected there is no crossing of solutions. ∎

In the next example the continuity conditions do not hold. Note the behavior.

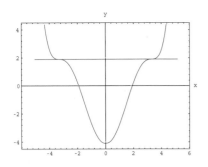

FIGURE 2.4

Example 2.1.4 Let $y' = x(2 - y)^{2/3}$. The partial derivative $\frac{\partial f}{\partial y}$ does not exist along the line $y = 2$. Observe that $y = 2$ is a solution. Figure 2.4 shows the graph of two solutions. Note how the two solutions cross at points on the line $y = 2$.

Warning: You should not fall into the trap of thinking that if the partial derivative is not continuous then there must be multiple solutions through the points of discontinuity. This is not true. ∎

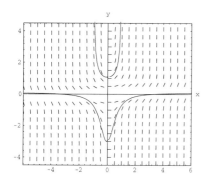

FIGURE 2.5

The final example shows that even if $f(x, y)$ is a very nice function one cannot necessarily expect the maximal solutions to be defined throughout the full horizontal extent of the rectangle.

Example 2.1.5   Let $y' = 2xy^2$. Figure 2.5 shows the graphs of two solutions. One has initial condition $(0, 1)$ and the other $(0, -3)$. The first solution is defined only on the interval $(-1, 1)$, whereas the second is defined for all real numbers.

The moral of this example is that f may have continuous derivatives of all orders, but a maximal solution may only be defined over a small interval. Worse than this is the fact that solutions may be defined for all real numbers or only for an interval of finite length, depending on how you choose the initial condition.   ■

EXERCISES 2.1

For those readers intending to write their own routines in one of the Three M's, you will need to turn to Appendix D and the module Field&Solution. In subsequent exercise sets it will be assumed that readers writing their own routines in the Three M's will know to turn to Appendix D when a new software package is mentioned.

The term **window** *is used to describe the rectangle in which solutions and fields are to be drawn. This is the same as the ranges on the x- and y-axes.*

1. Draw the field of $y' = x - y^2$. Compute field line slopes at three points in the window and compare with the drawn field. Draw solutions through this field with initial conditions $(0, 1)$, $(-1, -3)$, and $(0, 4)$. Use a window $[-6, 6] \times [-4, 4]$. What does Theorem 2.1.2 say about this example. Do the solutions that appear to merge actually do so? Explain! Be careful!

2. Draw the field of $y' = x^2 - y^2$. Compute field line slopes at three points in the window and compare with the drawn field. Draw solutions through this field with initial conditions $(0, 1)$, $(-2, -3)$, and $(0, 3)$. Use a window $[-6, 6] \times [-4, 4]$. What does Theorem 2.1.2 say about this example. Do the solutions that appear to merge actually do so? Explain! Be careful!

3. Draw the field of $y' = x^3 - y$. Compute field line slopes at three points in the window and compare with the drawn field. Draw solutions through this field with initial conditions $(0, 1)$, $(-1, -3)$, and $(0, 4)$. Use a window $[-12, 12] \times [-8, 8]$. What does Theorem 2.1.2 say about this example. Do the solutions that appear to merge actually do so? Explain! Be careful!

4. Draw the field of $y' = \frac{x}{1+y^2}$ in the window $[-6, 6] \times [-6, 6]$. Compute field line slopes at three points in the window and compare with the drawn field. Draw several solutions through this field. Do you expect any solutions to cross? Explain!

5. Draw the field of $y' = y^2$ in the window $[-6, 6] \times [-12, 12]$. Compute field line slopes at three points in the window and compare with the drawn field. Draw the solution through $(0, 1)$ with the x-range for the plot set to 6 and a step size (to be explained soon) of 0.01. Repeat this for windows with larger ranges on the y-axis. Is this solution defined on all of $[-6, 6]$? Describe the solution briefly. Do you think it has a vertical asymptote somewhere?

6. Draw the field of $y' = y^3$ in the window $[-6, 6] \times [-12, 12]$. Compute field line slopes at three points in the window and compare with the drawn field. Draw the solution through $(0, 1)$ with the x-range for the plot set to 6 and a step size (to be explained soon) of 0.01. Repeat this for windows with larger ranges on the y-axis. Is this solution defined on all of $[-6, 6]$? Describe the solution briefly. Do you think it has a vertical asymptote somewhere?

7. Draw the field of $y' = y^{4/3}$ in the window $[-6, 6] \times [-12, 12]$. Draw the solution through $(0, 1)$ with the x-range for the plot set to 6 and a step size (to be explained soon) of 0.01. Repeat this for windows with larger ranges on the y-axis. Is this solution defined on all of $[-6, 6]$? Describe the solution briefly. Do you think it has a vertical asymptote somewhere?

8. Draw the field of $y' = ((xy)^2)^{1/3}$ in the window $[-6, 6] \times [-4, 4]$. Draw a solution through $(0, 0)$ and one through $(0, -1)$. What does Theorem 2.1.2 have to say about this? *Note:* You may have trouble with your program if you do not enter the powers in the strict form shown.

9. Draw the field of $y' = x - y$. Draw solutions through this field with initial conditions $(0, 1)$, $(0, -3)$, and $(0, 4)$. Use a window $[-6, 6] \times [-4, 4]$ and a left-right range of solution of 6. What does Theorem 2.1.2 say about this example. Do the solutions merge together? Explain! Be careful!

10. Draw the field of $y' = \frac{y^2}{1+x^2}$ in the window $[-6, 6] \times [-4, 4]$. Draw several solutions through this field. Do you expect any solutions to cross? Explain!

11. Draw the field of $y' = xy^2$ in the window $[-6, 6] \times [-12, 12]$. Draw the solution through $(0, 1)$ with the x-range for the plot set to 6 and a step size (to be explained soon) of 0.01. Repeat this for windows with larger ranges on the y-axis. Is this solution defined on all of $[-6, 6]$? Describe the solution briefly. Do you think it has a vertical asymptote somewhere?

12. Draw the field of $y' = 2(y^4)^{1/5}$ in the window $[-6, 6] \times [-4, 4]$. Draw a solution through $(0, 0)$ and one through $(-2, -0.1)$. What does Theorem 2.1.2 have to say about this?

· 13. Draw maximal solutions through $(-3, -3)$, $(-3, 0)$, and $(1, 1)$ through the following field. Don't leave the window.

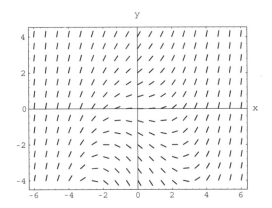

14. Draw several solutions to $y' = |y|$. Observe that solutions do not cross. In this case $\frac{\partial f}{\partial y}$ is not continuous in any rectangle containing the x - axis. Is there any contradiction here? Explain!

15. Explain the terms **solution** and **uniqueness** as they relate to the equation $y' = x + y$. Note that Theorem 2.1.2 does not explain these terms.

16. Example 2.1.5 shows that, whereas the function $f(x, y)$ in the equation $y' = f(x, y)$ can be continuous and have continuous partial derivatives everywhere, a solution may be defined for only a finite interval about the initial point. Find another example and use Field&Solution to confirm your belief.

17. Use Field&Solution to draw solutions through $(0, 0)$ and $(0, -0.1)$ for the equation $y' = f(x, y) = |y|^{1/3}$. Without any calculation, what can you say about $\partial f / \partial y$ and why?

18. Use Field&Solution to draw solutions through $(0, 0)$ and $(0, 1)$ for the equation $y' = f(x, y) = |y|^{2/3}$. Without any calculation, what can you say about $\partial f / \partial y$ and why?

19. Use Field&Solution to draw solutions through $(0, 2)$ and $(0, 1)$ for the equation $y' = f(x, y) = |1 - y|^{1/3}$. Without any calculation, what can you say about $\partial f / \partial y$ and why?

20. Without using the Field&Solution package, describe the behavior of solutions to $y' = y^4$ in general terms. Is there a constant solution? *Hint:* What does the derivative tell you?

21. Without using the Field&Solution package, describe the behaviour of solutions to $y' = 1 + y^2$ in general terms. Is there a constant solution? *Hint:* What does the derivative tell you?

22. Suppose that $f(-x, y) = -f(x, y)$ throughout the plane. Do solutions to $y' = f(x, y)$ have a particular symmetry? Explain by sketching a field with the given property. Do you need to assume that solutions are unique?

23. Suppose that $f(x, -y) = -f(x, y)$ throughout the plane. Do solutions to $y' = f(x, y)$ have a particular reflection property? Explain by sketching a field with the given property.

24. Prove that if $f(-x, y) = -f(x, y)$ and f and $\partial f / \partial y$ are continuous throughout the plane then any solution to $y' = f(x, y)$ passing through the y-axis is y-axis symmetric. To do this, suppose that $\phi(x)$ is a solution. Show that $\psi(x) = \phi(-x)$ is also a solution. Now, using uniqueness, argue that $\psi(x) = \phi(x)$, and so $\phi(x) = \phi(-x)$.

25. Prove that if $f(x, -y) = -f(x, y)$ throughout the plane then the reflection of any solution to $y' = f(x, y)$ across the x-axis is also a solution. Suppose that $\phi(x)$ is a solution. Show that $\psi(x) = -\phi(x)$ is also a solution.

2.2 NUMERICAL METHODS

In the preceding section the graphical viewpoint was introduced. It was used to gain a visual image of solutions to $y' = f(x, y)$ and to make clear the relation between fields and solutions. This graphical view is also an excellent starting point for an explanation of numerical methods, which are introduced next. The numerical methods studied here represent a small portion of a large literature. For further information on the subject you can consult [2].

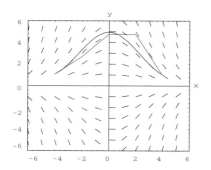

FIGURE 2.6

2.2.1 Euler's Method

Figure 2.6 shows the solution to $y' = -xy/5$, where $y(-4) = 1$. Also shown is the polygonal curve obtained by dividing $[-4, 4]$ into four subdivisions, and, starting at $(-4, 1)$, following the inclination field line segment at that point for two horizontal units, then following the inclination field line at the new point for two horizontal units, and so on.

In the exercises you will be asked to experiment with this procedure using shorter and shorter horizontal steps or increments. Perhaps you can already guess that the polygonal curves with smaller steps approach the solution. This algorithm is called Euler's method, and it will now be described in more detail.

Let h be the increment, and let Δy be the change in y along the field line at (x_0, y_0) due to the change h in x. Then, since $f(x_0, y_0)$ is the slope of that field line, $\Delta y = f(x_0, y_0)h$, and the coordinates of the new point are (x_1, y_1), where $y_1 = y_0 + f(x_0, y_0)h$. In general, to move from (x_n, y_n) to (x_{n+1}, y_{n+1}), we set

$$x_{n+1} = x_n + h,$$

and

$$y_{n+1} = y_n + f(x_n, y_n)h.$$

The increment h is often called the **step size**.

Example 2.2.1   We shall approximate the solution to $y' = xy$ and $y(0) = 1$ at four points on the interval $[0, 1]$. The step size is $h = 0.25$.

$$x_1 = 0 + 0.25 = 0.25,$$

and

$$y_1 = 1 + (0.25)(0)(1) = 1.$$

Next,

$$x_2 = 0.25 + 0.25 = 0.5,$$

and

$$y_2 = 1 + (0.25)(0.25)(1) = 1.0625.$$

Again,
$$x_3 = 0.75,$$

and
$$y_3 = 1.0625 + (0.25)(0.5)(1.0625) = 1.1953125.$$

Finally,
$$x_4 = 1,$$

and
$$y_4 = 1.1953125 + (0.25)(0.75)(1.1953125) = 1.419433594.$$

Clearly, the assistance of a computer would be useful. ∎

We shall now investigate how well Euler's method approximates the true solution. To this end, assume that f and its partial derivatives to the second order are continuous on a rectangle containing the graph of the solution and the points of approximation. This is enough to guarantee that the solution is unique. Let ϕ be the solution defined on $[a, b]$ that is to be approximated. Let $h = (b - a)/n$, $x_0 = a$, $x_i = x_0 + ih$, and $y_{i+1} = y_i + hf(x_i, y_i)$, for $i = 1, \ldots, n$.

First we estimate the error introduced in one step of Euler's method. To do this, apply Taylor's theorem to the solution ϕ to get

$$\phi(x_{i+1}) = \phi(x_i) + \phi'(x_i)h + \phi''(z)\frac{h^2}{2},$$

where $x_i < z < x_{i+1}$. Now $\phi'(x) = f(x, \phi(x))$ on the interval, so

$$\phi''(x) = \frac{\partial f}{\partial x}(x, \phi(x)) + \frac{\partial f}{\partial y}(x, \phi(x))\phi'(x)$$

by the chain rule applied to $f(x, y)$. We have assumed that f and its partial derivatives are continuous on the rectangle, so $\phi(x)$, $\phi'(x)$, and $\phi''(x)$ are continuous on the interval $[a, b]$, provided the graph of the solution lies in the rectangle. But if $\phi''(x)$ is continuous on $[a, b]$, it must have a maximum and minimum value on the interval, and so $|\phi''(x)| \leq M$ for a number M. So if $y_i = \phi(x_i)$, we have

$$|\phi(x_{i+1}) - (\phi(x_i) + \phi'(x_i)h)| = |\phi(x_{i+1}) - (y_i + f(x_i, y_i)h)| \leq Mh^2,$$

for the constant M. Thus the quantity

$$y_{i+1} = y_i + hf(x_i, y_i),$$

which is calculated by Euler's algorithm, approximates the true value $\phi(x_{i+1})$ with error no greater than a constant times h^2. We say that the error introduced in one step of Euler's method is of order h^2. It is possible to deduce a bound on the error over the whole interval of approximation, but we shall content ourselves with the following plausibility argument.

If the error introduced at each step is bounded by Mh^2, and there are $(b - a)/h$ steps required to get from a to b, then it is reasonable to suppose that the error should be bounded by some constant times $\frac{b-a}{h}Mh^2 = Ch$. This is in fact true, and we say that the global error is of order h. To be precise, there is a positive constant C such that

$$|\phi(x_i) - y_i| \leq Ch,$$

for all $i = 0, \ldots n$.

If we choose h small enough, we can get an approximation that is as accurate as we please. However, all is not as satisfactory as it seems. The bound Ch is a purely mathematical error bound between the true value and the value computed in the approximation scheme. It assumes that all values are computed with perfect accuracy. In practice, this is not the case, for there is round-off error in computing the numbers involved in the approximation. Now, if we use very small values of h, we shall have to make many computations, which leads to large round-off errors. Indeed, for each numerical method a balance must be struck between the ideal mathematical error and round-off error. Thus an improved method of approximation with a better mathematical error bound is desirable, if this is not at the expense of a large increase in computation.

You may suggest that if we expand the solution to higher order using Taylor's theorem then we can get higher orders of h into the one-step error bound. This is true, but to employ such an algorithm we would need to calculate partial derivatives of f to the required order. This is inconvenient; but worse is the fact that we may not have a formula for f from which to compute partial derivatives. For this reason a different approach is used to get better accuracy.

2.2.2 Improvements on Euler's Method

A simple improvement on Euler's method is made by averaging slopes of the field segments at the current point (x_i, y_i) and at the next point generated by Euler's method, which is $(x_i + h, y_i + hf(x_i, y_i))$. So if we let $k_1 = f(x_i, y_i)$, then the slope at the next point of the Euler method can be written $k_2 = f(x_i + h, y_i + hk_1)$. Then the next point in this averaging method can be defined to be

$$y_{i+1} = y_i + h\left(\frac{k_1 + k_2}{2}\right).$$

The algorithm looks like this

$$x_{i+1} = x_i + h,$$
$$k_1 = f(x_i, y_i),$$
$$k_2 = f(x_i + h, y_i + hk_1),$$
$$y_{i+1} = \left(y_i + h\frac{k_1 + k_2}{2}\right).$$

It can be shown that this algorithm has a global error bound of order h^2.

This averaging algorithm is not a very practical algorithm for approximating solutions. A practical algorithm is provided by the fourth-order Runge-Kutta method. We shall call this method Runge-Kutta for short. This method employs a weighted average of the slopes of field segments at four points generated near the current point (x_i, y_i). Here are the slopes k_i at the four points followed by the weighted average presented as an algorithm.

$$k_1 = f(x_i, y_i),$$
$$k_2 = f(x_i + h/2, y_i + hk_1/2),$$
$$k_3 = f(x_i + h/2, y_i + hk_2/2),$$
$$k_4 = f(x_i + h, y_i + hk_3),$$
$$y_{i+1} = y_i + h(k_1 + 2k_2 + 2k_3 + k_4)/6.$$

Figure 2.7 shows a diagram of the four points at which the field slopes are calculated and averaged for the field $f(x, y) = (x + y)/2$.

The first slope is that at the current point (x_i, y_i). The second is calculated halfway along the line segment generated by Euler's method. You can easily give descriptions of the last two.

Here is a concrete example of one step of the Runge-Kutta method.

FIGURE 2.7

Example 2.2.2 Here is just one step of the Runge-Kutta method applied to $y' = f(x, y) = xy$ with $y(0) = 1$ and step size $h = 0.25$.

First, $x_0 = 0$ and $y_0 = 1$, and so

$$k_1 = f(0, 1) = 0,$$
$$k_2 = f(0 + 0.125, 1 + (0.25)(0)/2) = (0.125)(1) = 0.125,$$
$$k_3 = f(0 + 0.125, 1 + (0.25)(0.125)/2) = 0.126953125,$$
$$k_4 = f(0 + 0.25, 1 + (0.25)(0.126953125)) = 0.2579345703.$$

Finally,

$$x_1 = 0.25,$$

and

$$y_1 = 1 + (0.25)(0 + (0.125)(2) + (0.126953125)(2) + (0.2579345703))/6$$
$$= 1.031743368.$$

The actual solution is

$$\phi(x) = e^{x^2/2}.$$

This may be verified by differentiating and substituting in the equation. Using a calculator gives $\phi(0.25) = 1.031743407$. Runge-Kutta has done an excellent job here. Compare this with the first step in the preceding example. ∎

Runge-Kutta has a fourth-order global error estimate. This means that the error between the approximate and true values on the interval of approximation is less than Mh^4 for some constant M. Unfortunately, we usually do not know what M is, and so we do not have a formula for the error bound. How can we know if we have chosen h small enough so that the error is as small as we desire? Usually, our only recourse is to take successively smaller values of the step h and examine the decimal places in the approximation data. If the digits are stable out to, say, the third decimal place as the step is made smaller, then we may be reasonably sure that the data are accurate to three places. This is no guarantee, but, along with good engineering intuition, it is often the best we can do.

Example 2.2.3   Consider the equation $y' = x^2 - y^2$. Suppose that we want to approximate the solution using Runge-Kutta on the interval $[0, 1]$ with initial value $y_0 = 1$. Consider the table of values of y that we get at $x = 0.5$ for a decreasing sequence of values of the step size h.

h	0.5	0.1	0.05	0.01	0.005
y	0.70193990	0.70176903	0.70176842	0.70176838	0.70176838

As you look at the values of y as h decreases, notice how the value of y corrected to three decimal place becomes stable, and then to four decimal places, and so on. We can be reasonably confident in the value $y = 0.7017684$ from the table of data. The rule of thumb that we are using is that, if the figures corrected to a given number of decimal places stabilize as the step is made smaller, then those figures are probably good.   ∎

We shall see in the exercises that the Runge-Kutta method is very accurate in many circumstances. However, be warned that all numerical methods of approximating solutions to the equation $y' = f(x, y)$ can fail to give satisfactory approximations. Examples of such unsatisfactory behavior are in the exercises, and the question will be returned to later in the chapter.

EXERCISES 2.2

1. The solution to the initial-value problem $y' = -xy/5$ and $y(0) = 2$ is $y = 2e^{-x^2/10}$. By hand, use Euler's method and the Runge-Kutta method to approximate the solution on $[0, 1]$ using two subdivisions. In both cases compute the actual error at $x = 0.5$ and $x = 1$.

2. The solution to $y' = x + y$ and $y(0) = 3$ is $y = -1 - x + 4e^x$. By hand, use Euler's method and the Runge-Kutta method to approximate the solution on $[0, 1]$ using two subdivisions. In both cases compute the actual error at $x = 0.5$ and $x = 1$.

3. The solution to $y' = x + y$ and $y(0) = 3$ is $y = -1 - x + 4e^x$. By hand, use Euler's method and the Runge-Kutta method to approximate the solution on $[0, 0.5]$ using two subdivisions. In both cases compute the actual error at $x = 0.25$ and $x = 0.5$.

4. The solution to the initial-value problem $y' = -xy/5$ and

$y(0) = 2$ is $y = 2e^{-x^2/10}$. By hand, use Euler's method and the Runge-Kutta method to approximate the solution on $[0, 0.5]$ using two subdivisions. In both cases compute the actual error at $x = 0.25$ and $x = 0.5$.

5. By hand, carry out one step of Euler's method and the Runge-Kutta method where $y' = xy + y^2$, $y(1) = 2$, and the step size is 0.1.

6. By hand, carry out one step of Euler's method and the Runge-Kutta method where $y' = xy - 3y$, $y(-1) = 2$, and the step size is 0.1.

In each of Exercises 7–10, use the package ERGraphical.

7. Consider the equation $y' = x - y$. Approximate the solution on $[-1, 3]$ with initial value $y_0 = 2$ using the Euler and Runge-Kutta methods with step sizes $h = 1, h = 0.5$, and $h = 0.1$. Compare the performance of the two methods.

8. Consider the equation $y' = y^2$. Approximate the solution on $[0, 1]$ with initial value $y_0 = 1$ using the Euler and Runge-Kutta methods with step sizes $h = 0.25$, $h = 0.1$, and $h = 0.01$. Use a tick distance of 0.2 on the x-axis and 20 on the y-axis. Again compare the performance of the methods.

9. Create an example (not from the text) in which the package ERGraphical clearly illustrates how Euler's method follows a field line segment at each step. It is not likely that you will be able to get a perfect match between field segments and polygonal lines drawn by Euler's method, but do your best to get a good illustration. Drawing field segments at unit intervals may help.

10. Consider the equation $y' = x^2 + y$. Approximate the solution on $[-3, 3]$ with initial value $y_0 = 0$ using the ERGraphical package with step sizes $h = 1, h = 0.5$, and $h = 0.1$. Compare the performance of the two methods.

11. 11) Find an equation in which Euler does just as well as Runge-Kutta. Explain in terms of the algorithms why your answer is correct. *Hint:* Don't make it hard!

In each of the Exercises 12–15, use the package ERNumerical.

12. Consider the equation $y' = x - y$. Approximate the solution on $[0, 2]$ with initial value $y_0 = 2$. Run the package for step sizes of $h = 0.1$, $h = 0.05$, $h = 0.02$, and $h = 0.01$. Record the values of both methods at $x = 1$. What approximate value are you confident in for each method and why?

13. Consider the equation $y' = xy$. Approximate the solution on $[0, 1]$ with initial value $y_0 = 1$. Run the package for step sizes of $h = 0.1, h = 0.05, h = 0.02$, and $h = 0.01$. Record the values of both methods at $x = 1$. What ap-

proximate value are you confident in for each method and why?

14. Consider the equation $y' = 3x + y$. Approximate the solution on $[0, 2]$ with initial value $y_0 = 2$. Run the package for step sizes of $h = 0.1, h = 0.05, h = 0.02$, and $h = 0.01$. Record the values of both methods at $x = 1$. What approximate value are you confident in for each method and why?

15. Consider the equation $y' = x^2 - y$. Approximate the solution on $[0, 1]$ with initial value $y_0 = 1$. Run the package for step sizes of $h = 0.1, h = 0.05, h = 0.02$, and $h = 0.01$. Record the values of both methods at $x = 1$. What approximate value are you confident in for each method and why?

16. Consider the initial-value problem $y' = y^2$ and $y(0) = 1$.

   (a) Verify that $\phi(x) = -1/(x - 1)$ is the solution to this initial value problem.

   (b) Run the ERNumerical package on the interval $[0, 2]$ with step sizes of $h = 0.1, h = 0.05$, and $h = 0.01$. What values do you get at $x = 1$? What is the "value" of the actual solution at 1? What is the moral of this example?

17. Consider the initial value problem $y' = y^4/3$ and $y(1) = 1$.

   (a) Verify that $\phi(x) = 1/(2 - x)^{1/3}$ is the solution to this initial-value problem.

   (b) Run the ERNumerical package on the interval $[1, 3]$ with step sizes of $h = 0.1, h = 0.05$, and $h = 0.01$. What values do you get at $x = 2$? What is the "value" of the actual solution at 2? What is the moral of this example?

18. Run the ERGraphical package on the initial value problem $y' = (y^2)^{1/5}$ and $y(-1) = -1$ on the interval $[-1, 6]$. Use step sizes of $h = 1$ and $h = 0.99$. Ignore the black graph and consider only the blue (Euler).

   (a) Describe the two polygonal (blue) curves that you get.

   (b) Carefully explain how this slight change in step size can cause such a radical change in result. *Hint:* Nonuniqueness of solutions is playing a role.

   (c) Could this type of behavior also happen with the Runge-Kutta method?

19. Consider the equation $y' = 2y^{2/5}$.

   (a) Use the Runge-Kutta method on the interval $[-1, 2]$ with step size 0.2 and $y(-1) = -1$, but pretend that you have a poor computer by rounding each y_i computed to one decimal place. This can be done easily by using ERNumerical package to compute one step at a time and rounding each time.

(b) Now use the ERNumerical package to apply the Runge-Kutta method on the whole interval without rounding.

(c) Describe the results in parts a and b.

(d) Carefully explain this phenomenon using results on existence and uniqueness.

(e) Could even a good computer encounter this type of behavior? Explain!

20. In a window $[-12, 12] \times [-8, 8]$, use the package Field&Solution to draw the solution to $y' = \sin(xy)$, where $y(-12) = 1$. Use step sizes of $0.1, 0.05, 0.01$, and 0.001 and a left-right range for the solution of 24. The graphics program merely plots the output of the Runge-Kutta algorithm.

(a) Explain why the solution must be symmetric with respect to the y-axis.

(b) The graphics output is not symmetric. What moral do you draw from this example?

21. Use ERNumerical to approximate the solution to the initial-value problem $y' = 2x + xy^2 - x^5$ and $y(0) = 0$ at $x = 5$. Use the interval $[0, 6]$ and step sizes of $0.2, 0.1, 0.01$, and 0.001. Show that the solution is $\phi(x) = x^2$, and so $\phi(5) = 25$! What conclusion do you draw from this? This type of behavior is considered further in Section 2.5

2.3 ANALYTIC METHODS OF SOLUTION

By analytic methods of solution, we have in mind procedures that express the solution (function) explicitly in terms of known functions and integrals of known functions or implicitly as an implicit solution to an equation in two variables. We present several of these methods in the sections that follow.

2.3.1 Separation of Variables

If a differential equation can be written in the form

$$g(y)\frac{dy}{dx} = h(x),$$

we say that the variables are **separable**, or the variables have been separated. If the variables in an equation can be separated, then a method of solution presents itself. The method will first be demonstrated through an example, and then the method will be justified.

Example 2.3.1   Consider the equation $y' = xy$. This is separable since we can write it in the form $\frac{1}{y}\frac{dy}{dx} = x$. If we "multiply" by dx, we get the expression

$$\frac{1}{y}dy = x\,dx.$$

This expression begs to be integrated on both sides. We do so to get

$$\int \frac{1}{y}dy = \int x\,dx,$$

which yields

$$\ln(|y|) = x^2/2 + c.$$

This equation can be solved for y to give

$$y = e^{x^2/2}e^c = Ae^{x^2/2}.$$

In removing the absolute value we get a plus or minus sign, but this is absorbed in the arbitrary constant A.

If we differentiate with respect to x, it is easily shown that

$$y = Ae^{x^2/2}$$

satisfies the original differential equation. Moreover, specifying an initial condition determines A.   ■

Here is the justification of this method. We start with the equation $g(y)\frac{dy}{dx} = h(x)$ in separated form. Let

$$G(y) = \int g(y)dy$$

and

$$H(x) = \int h(x)dx.$$

Now suppose that ϕ, defined on (a, b), satisfies the equation

$$G(y) = H(x) + c$$

in the sense that

$$G(\phi(x)) = H(x) + c$$

is an identity for all x in (a, b). If we differentiate both sides of this equation, we get

$$G'(\phi(x))\phi'(x) = H'(x).$$

But from the definition of G and H it follows immediately that

$$g(\phi(x))\phi'(x) = h(x).$$

This says that ϕ is a solution to the equation.

A word of warning is in order. If the equation is not already in separated form the process of separation may throw out certain solutions. Here is an example.

Example 2.3.2   Consider the equation $y' = y^2$. Separating, we get

$$\int \frac{1}{y^2}dy = \int dx.$$

Note that y could not be zero here. Integrating we get

$$y = \frac{-1}{x + c}.$$

Solutions of this form are never zero, but $y \equiv 0$ is obviously a solution. In the process of separation we have lost this solution.   ■

The example shows the importance of keeping track of any potential divisions by zero that might exclude solutions.

The following example illustrates the fact that the equation

$$G(y) = H(x) + c$$

may not be solvable in any explicit way for y. When this happens the solution is defined implicitly by the equation, and the solution may well be a restricted portion of the graph of $G(y) = H(x)+c$. Indeed, the graph of $G(y) = H(x)+c$ may not be the graph of a function at all.

Recall that the graph of the equation

$$F(x, y) = c$$

is called a **contour** of the function F. Thus a solution to the differential equation will be a portion of the contour of $G(y) - H(x) = c$.

Here is a simple example in which we cannot solve for y within a single formula.

Example 2.3.3   The equation $y' = (3x^2 - 6x + 2)/(2y - 3y^2)$ is "solved" as follows. We have

$$\int (2y - 3y^2)\, dy = \int (3x^2 - 6x + 2)\, dx,$$

and so

$$y^2 - y^3 = x^3 - 3x^2 + 2x + c.$$

If the initial condition is $(0.5, -0.5)$ then the equation is

$$y^2 - y^3 - x^3 + 3x^2 - 2x = 0.$$

The contour of this equation is shown in Figure 2.8.

The graph of the solution in this case is the bottom of the "bag" extending from about 0 to 1 on the x-axis. Notice that the entire graph does not satisfy the vertical line test, and so the entire graph is not a solution. The point is that the equation we get by carrying out the integrations in the separation of variables may define a curve in the plane that is not a function. The solution is a portion of the graph satisfying the vertical line test and passing through the initial point. ∎

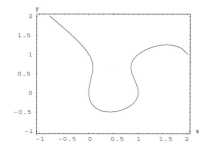

FIGURE 2.8

Mathematical Models

Now that you know a good bit about the equation $y' = f(x, y)$, it is time to apply this knowledge. The process of applying mathematical ideas to practical problems has become known as **modeling**, or creating a mathematical model.

Roughly speaking, a mathematical model is a collection of symbols or variables corresponding to physically measurable quantities, together with relations among these variables expressing physical relationships between the quantities. The usefulness of a mathematical model lies in the hope that, when the symbols and relations are interpreted as statements about objects in the world, these statements will be true. If this is so, further mathematical deduction from these relations should lead to further true statements about the world. Two concrete examples will help clarify the idea.

A Population Model

It is desirable to promote the survival of the elephant. To this end a herd of elephants is transferred to a large lush area where the herd can expand. Unfortunately, ivory poachers continue to decimate the herd, and the number of poachers to be expected is proportional to the size of the herd. We want to know what the future holds for the herd. To this end, we build a mathematical model of the dynamics of the elephant population E as a function of time.

It is not unreasonable to assume that, unmolested, the herd will grow at a rate proportional to the population, since we have said that there is plenty of room for the herd to grow. But the number of poachers is proportional to $E(t)$, so in a unit time interval the number of contacts between poachers and elephants might well be proportional to $E(t)E(t) = (E(t))^2$. After all, the more elephants the more contacts, and the more poachers the more contacts. Thus, as a provisional assumption, it is reasonable to suppose that the number of elephant kills in a unit time interval will be proportional to E^2. These considerations suggest that the rate of change of the elephant population $\frac{dE}{dt}$ should be

$$\frac{dE}{dt} = aE - bE^2,$$

where a and b are positive constants.

The symbol involved in our model is the function E, which is a function of t. We interpret E as the elephant population function and t as time. Our model makes a statement about the rate of change of this population, which, if true, will allow us to deduce the precise form of E.

Before solving this equation it is important to note that our model of the population dynamics of the herd is provisional and open to criticism and improvement. For one thing, it is not likely that the breeding rate of the herd will remain unchanged in the presence of poachers.

To solve the equation, we separate the variables to get

$$\int \frac{1}{E(a - bE)} dE = \int dt.$$

We use partial fractions on the left to get

$$\frac{\ln(E)}{a} - \frac{\ln(a - bE)}{a} = t + c.$$

We can solve for E to get

$$E(t) = \frac{aK e^{at}}{(1 + bK e^{at})},$$

where K is a constant to be determined by the initial size of the herd, say, at time $t = 0$. If we divide top and bottom by e^{at} and let $t \to \infty$, we get

$$E(t) = \frac{aK}{e^{-at} + bK} \to \frac{aK}{bK} = \frac{a}{b}.$$

So in the long run the population approaches a/b. This is called the **carrying capacity**. Note that it does not depend on the initial population. If the proportion of poachers is large, the carrying capacity may be so small that the model no longer applies and the herd is wiped out. Obviously, policing the poachers is important.

Newtons Law of Cooling

Newton's law of cooling asserts that the rate at which the temperature of an object changes is proportional to the difference between the temperature of the object at that instant and the temperature of the surroundings of the object at that instant. If T is the temperature of the object as a function of time and S is the temperature of the surroundings, Newton's law of cooling can be expressed as

$$\frac{dT}{dt} = a(S - T),$$

where a is a positive constant. If S is a constant, the equation is separable, and the solution is left to the exercises.

Several more models will be introduced in the following sections and throughout the rest of the book.

Homogeneous Equations

A differential equation of the form

$$y' = g(y/x)$$

is said to be **homogeneous**. Homogeneous equations can always be reduced to separable equations by using the substitution

$$v = y/x.$$

Indeed, $y = xv$, so

$$y' = v + xv',$$

and so

$$v + xv' = g(v).$$

Therefore,

$$\frac{dv}{dx} = \frac{g(v) - v}{x}.$$

This is clearly separable.

Here is an example of the method.

Example 2.3.4   The equation

$$y' = \frac{x + 2y}{x - y}$$

can be put in the homogeneous form

$$y' = \frac{1 + 2y/x}{1 - y/x}$$

by dividing top and bottom by x. We make the substitution $v = y/x$ to get

$$v + xv' = \frac{1 + 2v}{1 - v}.$$

Now solve for v'. The result is

$$v' = \frac{1 + v + v^2}{x(1 - v)}.$$

The separated integrals are

$$\int \frac{1 - v}{1 + v + v^2}\, dv = \int \frac{dx}{x}.$$

The left-hand integral is a little tricky. We need to complete the square. Here is how it goes.

$$\int \frac{1 - v}{1 + v + v^2}\, dv = \int \frac{1 - v}{\frac{3}{4} + (\frac{1}{4} + v + v^2)}\, dv = \int \frac{1 - v}{\frac{3}{4} + (v + \frac{1}{2})^2}\, dv.$$

Substitute $u = v + \frac{1}{2}$ to arrive at

$$\int \frac{\frac{3}{2} - u}{\frac{3}{4} + u^2}\, du = \frac{3}{2} \int \frac{1}{\frac{3}{4} + u^2}\, du - \int \frac{u}{\frac{3}{4} + u^2}\, du.$$

Evaluating, we get

$$\int \frac{\frac{3}{2} - u}{\frac{3}{4} + u^2}\, du = \sqrt{3}\tan^{-1}(\frac{2}{\sqrt{3}}u) - \frac{1}{2}\ln(\frac{3}{4} + u^2).$$

Returning to v gives

$$\int \frac{1-v}{1+v+v^2}\, dv = \sqrt{3}\tan^{-1}(\frac{2}{\sqrt{3}}(v+\frac{1}{2})) - \frac{1}{2}\ln(1+v+v^2).$$

Finally, returning to y yields

$$\sqrt{3}\tan^{-1}(\frac{2}{\sqrt{3}}(\frac{y}{x}+\frac{1}{2})) - \frac{1}{2}\ln(1+\frac{y}{x}+(\frac{y}{x})^2) = \ln|x| + C.$$

As usual, C must be determined by an initial condition, and then the solution is a portion of the curve determined by the preceding equation.   ∎

EXERCISES 2.3.1

Use separation of variables to solve Exercises 1–10. Get y as a function of x explicitly when possible.

1. Solve $y' = y$ with initial condition $(0, 1)$. Ignoring the initial condition, are any solutions missed by the separation process?

2. Solve $y' = 2xy^2$ with initial condition $(0, 4)$. Is the solution defined for all x? Ignoring the initial condition, are any solutions missed by the separation process?

3. Solve $y' = x(1 + y^2)$ with initial condition $(0, 0)$.

4. Solve $y' = y^2$ with initial condition $(0, 1)$. Ignoring the initial condition, are any solutions missed by the separation process?

5. Solve $y' = 3x^2 y^2$ with initial condition $(0, 4)$. Is the solution defined for all x? Ignoring the initial condition, are any solutions missed by the separation process?

6. Solve $y' = x^2(1 + y^2)$ with initial condition $(0, 0)$.

7. Solve $y' = x\sec(y)$ with initial condition $(0, 0)$. Ignoring the initial condition, are any solutions missed by the separation process?

8. Solve $y' = 2x(1 - y)$ with initial condition $(0, 4)$. Is the solution defined for all x? Ignoring the initial condition, are any solutions missed by the separation process?

9. Solve $y' = xy + xy^2$ with initial condition $(0, -2)$.

10. Solve $y' = e^{x+y}$.

In Exercises 11–17, solve the equation to get $G(y) = H(x) + c$. Then use the package ContourPlot to plot the curve satisfying $G(y) = H(x) + c$. Clearly indicate which portion of the curve is the maximal solution passing through the initial point. Use a $[-6, 6] \times [-4, 4]$ window.

11. $y' = 2x/(4y^3 + 2y)$ with initial condition $(-1, -1)$.

12. $y' = \sin(x)/\cos(y)$ with initial condition $(0, 0)$.

13. $y' = (\cos(x) + 2x)/(\cos(y) + 2y)$ with initial condition $(0, -\pi)$.

14. $y' = (2x - 1)/(y^2 + 2y)$ with initial condition $(-1, -1)$.

15. $y' = \sin(2x)/\cos(3y)$ with initial condition $(0, 0)$. You may need to experiment with the plotter to get a good picture.

16. $y' = xy^2(y - 1)$ with initial condition $(0, 4)$.

17. $y' = [y(x - 2)]/[x(2 - y)]$ with initial condition $(2, 1)$.

18. In Exercise 17, why is the graph bounded in the first quadrant? *Hint:* Experiment with some growing positive values of x and y.

19. Consider the equation $y' = 3y^{2/3}$ with initial condition $(0, 0)$. Solve this by separation of variables. Note that $y \equiv 0$ solves the same initial value problem. Does this contradict the uniqueness theorem?

20. Solve $y' = y/(x + y)$.

21. Solve $y' = (x + y)/x$ with initial condition $y(1) = 1$.

22. Solve $y' = \sin(y/x) + y/x$.

23. Use the package Field&Solution to experiment with the elephant herd model by changing initial populations, breeding rates, and proportions of poachers. Confirm the asymptotic behavior.

24. A friend proposes $E' = (E^2 - 1) - E^3$ as a model for the population of an elephant herd. Explain to your friend where this model fails to fit the facts about elephant populations. *Hint:* Can elephant populations become negative?

25. Is the equation at least a plausible model for an elephant herd. Justify your views.

$$E' = (4 - e^E)E$$

26. In the light of Exercises 24 and 25, propose two criteria that seem reasonable for any population model to satisfy. Justify your views!

27. Equations of the form $y' = ay(b - y)$, where a and b are positive, are called logistic equations, and they are used as a first attempt at modeling population growth.

    (a) Graph several solutions to several examples in the right half-plane, and discover why b is called the carrying capacity.

    (b) Obviously, the carrying capacity for a population will depend on the availability of food. Weather changes from year to year will affect the food supply, so the carrying capacity will change from year to year also. Assume that this change is a simple oscillation about a mean value. Incorporate this in the logistic model in such a way that the population oscillates about this mean. Draw graphs of solutions.

28. Solve Newton's law of cooling assuming that S is constant. What happens as time goes to infinity? Is this expected?

2.3.2 Linear Equations

Here is the definition of a linear equation.

Definition 2.3.5

A first-order differential equation is said to be linear if it has the form

$$y' + a(x)y = b(x),$$

where a and b are continuous functions on some interval.   ●

The nice thing about linear equations is that there is a simple formula for their solution. It is derived as follows.

Suppose that ϕ is a solution to the equation. Then for all x in some interval we have the identity

$$\phi'(x) + a(x)\phi(x) = b(x).$$

Let $A(x) = \int a(x)dx$, so A is simply an antiderivative of a. Now multiply through the differential equation by $e^{A(x)}$ to get

$$\phi'(x)e^{A(x)} + a(x)e^{A(x)}\phi(x) = b(x)e^{A(x)}.$$

You may have noticed that the left-hand side is the derivative of $\phi(x)e^{A(x)}$, and so we have

$$(\phi(x)e^{A(x)})' = b(x)e^{A(x)}.$$

Therefore, integrating gives

$$\phi(x)e^{A(x)} = \int b(x)e^{A(x)}dx + C,$$

and dividing by $e^{A(x)}$ gives the formula for the solution:

$$\phi(x) = e^{-A(x)} \int b(x)e^{A(x)}dx + Ce^{-A(x)}.$$

The arbitrary constant C in this formula will, of course, be determined by the initial condition.

Example 2.3.6   We solve $y' + 2xy = x$ with $y(0) = 2$. Clearly, $A(x) = x^2$, and so

$$y(x) = e^{-x^2} \int x e^{x^2} dx + C e^{-x^2} = \frac{e^{-x^2} e^{x^2}}{2} + C e^{-x^2},$$

and so

$$y(x) = \frac{1}{2} + C e^{-x^2}.$$

But $y(0) = 2$, and so $2 = \frac{1}{2} + C$, so $C = 3/2$. The solution is

$$y(x) = \frac{1}{2} + \frac{3}{2} e^{-x^2}.$$ ∎

A slight modification of this example leads to a problem that must be discussed. If we try to solve $y' + 2xy = 1$, we arrive at

$$y(x) = e^{-x^2} \int e^{x^2} dx + C e^{-x^2},$$

and we cannot evaluate the integral in terms of familiar functions. If the initial condition is $y(x_0) = y_0$, then the solution can be written as

$$y(x) = e^{-x^2} \int_{x_0}^{x} e^{t^2} dt + y_0 e^{x_0^2} e^{-x^2}.$$

But then for any given value of x the integral $\int_{x_0}^{x} e^{t^2} dt$ can be approximated numerically. So the equation can be solved from a practical point of view.

Bernoulli Equations

Close relatives of linear equations are Bernoulli equations. A Bernoulli equation is an equation of the form

$$y' + a(x)y = b(x)y^r.$$

If we divide by y^r, the equation becomes

$$y' y^{-r} + a(x) y^{1-r} = b(x),$$

and if we multiply by $(1 - r)$ we get

$$(1 - r) y' y^{-r} + (1 - r) a(x) y^{1-r} = (1 - r) b(x).$$

It should be noted that the derivative of y^{1-r} is $(1 - r) y^{-r} y'$. Thus the substitution $u = y^{1-r}$ yields the equation

$$u' + (1 - r) a(x) u = (1 - r) b(x).$$

But this equation is linear, so we may solve it by the preceding method and return to the function y at the end. Here is an example.

Example 2.3.7 We solve $y' + \frac{1}{x}y = x^2 y^2$. Dividing by y^2 and multiplying by $(1 - 2) = -1$ gives

$$-y'y^{-2} - \frac{1}{x}y^{-1} = -x^2.$$

But if $u = y^{-1}$, then $u' = -y^{-2}y'$, and so

$$u' - \frac{1}{x}u = -x^2.$$

Solving this linear equation, we have

$$A(x) = \int -\frac{1}{x}dx = -\ln(|x|),$$

and so

$$u(x) = |x| \int -x^2/|x|dx + \overline{C}|x| = x \int -x^2/x dx + Cx = \frac{-x^3}{2} + Cx.$$

Now $y = 1/u$, and so

$$y(x) = \frac{1}{Cx - \frac{x^3}{2}}. \qquad \blacksquare$$

Before concluding this section we should notice four things. First, if $r = 1$ we have multiplied through by 0. This gives the equation $0 = 0$, which is true but is not a linear equation. In this case the original equation is

$$y' + a(x)y = b(x)y,$$

which can be written as

$$y' + (a(x) - b(x))y = 0.$$

But this is linear! Second, when we divide by y^r, we might divide by zero, so we must stay alert to this possibility. Third, if r is negative, initial conditions with $y_0 = 0$ may be impossible. Fourth, in normal form the equation is $y' = -a(x)y + b(x)y^r$, and so if r is negative or fractional, the hypotheses for existence and uniqueness may fail. In this case caution must be exercised.

2.3.3 Three More Mathematical Models

An *RC* Circuit

This model deals with a simple electrical circuit that consists of a resistor in series with a capacitor. We shall connect this to a voltage source of the form $V_0 \sin(\omega t)$, and the question is what will be the current in the circuit and the voltage across the capacitor as a function of time. Let $q(t)$ be the charge on the capacitor at time t. Let the capacitance be C and the resistance R. The current at time t is $i(t) = q'(t)$, since current is the rate of change of charge. The voltage drops around the circuit must add up to the electromotive force, which is $V_0 \sin(\omega t)$. Thus we have the equation

$$Rq'(t) + \frac{1}{C}q(t) = V_0 \sin(\omega t),$$

or in standard form

$$q'(t) + \frac{1}{RC}q(t) = \frac{V_0}{R}\sin(\omega t).$$

To solve this equation, it is convenient to set $a = \frac{1}{RC}$, and $b = \frac{V_0}{R}$. The solution is

$$q(t) = be^{-at}\int e^{at}\sin(\omega t)\,dt + Ke^{-at} = b\frac{a\sin(\omega t) - \omega\cos(\omega t)}{a^2 + \omega^2} + Ke^{-at}.$$

If we assume that the charge on the capacitor at time $t = 0$ is 0, we have

$$q(t) = b\frac{a\sin(\omega t) - \omega\cos(\omega t)}{a^2 + \omega^2} + \frac{b\omega}{a^2 + \omega^2}e^{-at}.$$

Notice that the last term goes to zero as t goes to infinity. It is called the **transient** part of the solution. The first part is called the **steady state**.

Recall from trigonometry that if $C = \sqrt{A^2 + B^2}$, $A = C\cos(\phi)$, and $B = C\sin(\phi)$, then

$$A\sin(\omega t) - B\cos(\omega t) = C(\cos(\phi)\sin(\omega t) - \sin(\phi)\cos(\omega t)) = C\sin(\omega t - \phi).$$

The steady-state part can now be written as follows:

$$b\frac{a\sin(\omega t) - \omega\cos(\omega t)}{a^2 + \omega^2} = \frac{b}{\sqrt{a^2 + \omega^2}}\sin(\omega t - \phi),$$

where $\cos(\phi) = a/\sqrt{a^2 + \omega^2}$ and $\sin(\phi) = \omega/\sqrt{a^2 + \omega^2}$. So we see that the steady state is an oscillation of amplitude $\frac{V_0}{R\sqrt{a^2 + \omega^2}}$ and frequency, which is the same as the driving emf.

A Mixing Problem

This model concerns the flow of a salt solution into a tank from which the well-stirred mixture is allowed to flow out. Suppose initially that the tank contains 200 gal of solution containing 20 lb of salt in solution. A solution containing 3 lb/gal flows in at a rate of 2 gal/min, and the well-stirred mixture flows out at the same rate. How many pounds of salt are in the tank at time t?

Let $A(t)$ be the number of pounds of salt in the tank at time t. The key to the solution of this problem is to study the rate at which salt is coming into the tank and the rate at which it is going out. The format is

$$\frac{dA}{dt} = \text{(lb of salt/min) IN} - \text{(lb of salt/min) OUT}.$$

The number of pounds per minute of salt coming in is 6. The number going out in 1 minute will be the number of pounds of salt in the tank at time t divided by 200 multiplied by 2. So we have

$$\frac{dA}{dt} = 6 - 2\frac{A(t)}{200},$$

or

$$\frac{dA}{dt} + \frac{1}{100}A(t) = 6.$$

This is a linear equation, and the solution is

$$A(t) = 600 + Ce^{-t/100}.$$

Since $A(0) = 20$, $C = -580$, and so

$$A(t) = 600 - 580e^{-t/100}.$$

Notice that the amount of salt in the tank approaches 600 lb. This is to be expected since the concentration of salt is approaching the incoming concentration.

Parachute Jump

Consider a parachutist jumping from a height of 5000 ft. The forces acting on the parachutist are drag and gravity. We shall take "down" as the positive y direction. We shall assume that drag is proportional to velocity, so the drag force is $-cv$, where c is the coefficient of drag. The gravitational force is mg, where m is the mass and g is the acceleration due to gravity. Then Newton's second law says that

$$mv' = mg - cv,$$

or

$$v' + \frac{c}{m}v = g.$$

This is linear, and the solution, where $v(0) = 0$, is

$$v(t) = \frac{mg}{c} - \frac{mg}{c}e^{-ct/m}.$$

As t goes to infinity the velocity approaches mg/c. This velocity is called the terminal velocity.

Some Remarks on Mathematical Models

Most models only approximate the behavior of the real-world system being modeled. In many cases a model may have only a limited range of applicability. The approximate nature of most models usually arises from making simplifying assumptions. The model of a parachute jump is an example. We assume that gravity is constant during the descent, even though it is not. We assume that the drag is given by the formula cv, even though it is well known that this is only valid for a limited range of velocities. In addition, updrafts are not accounted for. You could go on adding to this list of criticisms of the model. These, often unspoken, assumptions are made to make it possible to construct a model of the physical system simple enough to be analyzed. If you try to include every influence on a physical system, you will have to model the entire universe. Since this is impossible, or at least impractical, creating mathematical models can be as much of an art as a science. Because we always have to make limiting assumptions, we cannot speak of the single correct model of a physical system, but only of better or worse models of the system. You should develop the habit of looking at models with a critical eye. Do not ask if the model is correct. Instead, ask where the simplifying assumptions are and whether these are reasonable. Above all, when you create models, jump right in. There is no unique right answer. However, your model will be judged by its effectiveness in describing the physical system that you claim to model.

EXERCISES 2.3.3

1. Solve $y' + 2y = x$, where $y(-1) = 2$. Sketch the solution.

2. Solve $y' + \frac{1}{x}y = x^2$, where $y(-1) = 2$. Sketch the solution.

3. Solve $y' + 2xy = 0$, where $y(0) = 3$. Sketch the solution.

4. Solve $y' + 4xy = x$.

5. Solve $xy' + (x - 2)y = 3x^3 e^{-x}$.

6. Solve $y' + \frac{y}{x} = \sin(x)$.

7. Solve $xy' + y = e^x$.

8. Solve $y' + y = 1/(x^2 + 1)$, where $y(0) = 0$.

9. Solve $y' + y = 1/y$, where $y(0) = 2$. Sketch the solution.

10. Solve $xy' + y = -x^2 y^2 e^x$.

11. Solve $y' + 2xy = y^{5/3}$, $y(0) = 1$. Express the solution as an integral if necessary.

12. In the series circuit of the first application, assume that $R = 10^4$ ohms, $C = 10^{-6}$ farads, $V_0 = 5$ volts, and $\omega = 10$. How long will it take for the transient part of the solution to drop to 1% of the steady-state amplitude?

13. In the series circuit of the first application, assume that $R = 10^5$ ohms, $C = 10^{-7}$ farads, $V_0 = 10$ volts, and $\omega = 20$. How long will it take for the transient part of the solution to drop to 1% of the steady-state amplitude?

14. In the series circuit of the first application, assume that $R = 10^3$ ohms, $C = 10^{-5}$ farads, $V_0 = 5$ volts, and $\omega = 5$. How long will it take for the transient part of the solution to drop to 1% of the steady-state amplitude?

15. In electronics, the voltage drop across a coil is proportional to the rate at which the current through the coil is changing. This proportionality constant is called the **inductance**, and coils are often called inductors. The inductance is often symbolized by L, and it is measured in henrys. Suppose that we have an inductor of inductance L connected in series (one after the other) with a resistor of resistance R. Suppose that a steady voltage V is applied to the ends of the circuit. Write a differential equation that models the current in the circuit as a function of time. Solve the equation.

16. In the salt solution application, assume that the well-stirred solution flows out at a rate of 3 gal/min but the in-flow is still 2 gal/min. The in-flow concentration is

still 3 lb/gal. How many pounds of salt are in the tank at time t?

17. In the salt solution application, assume that the well stirred solution flows out at a rate of 2 gal/min but the in-flow is now 3 gal/min. The in-flow concentration is still 3 lb/gal. How many pounds of salt are in the tank at time t?

18. In the salt solution application, assume that the well-stirred solution flows out at a rate of 2 gal/min but the in-flow is now 4 gal/min. The in-flow concentration is now 2 lb/gal. How many pounds of salt are in the tank at time t?

19. An object weighing 32 lb is dropped from a height of 5000 ft. Assume that the drag on the object is equal to the square of the velocity. Find the velocity as a function of time. What is the terminal velocity? Assume that the acceleration due to gravity is 32 ft/sec/sec.

20. Solve the parachute problem with the assumption that drag is proportional to the square of velocity. What is the terminal velocity?

21. Suppose that you invest $\$A_0$ in a bank account paying an annual interest rate of $r\%$ compounded continuously.

This means that the rate of change of the amount in your account is $rA/100$.

(a) Find the time required as a function of r for your account to double.

(b) What interest rate must be paid in order for your account to double in 10 years?

22. Write a critique of the salt-mixing model. Point to simplifying assumptions.

23. Criticize the elephant population model.

24. The temperature in the desert after sundown in the winter is described by $S(t) = 80 - 60t^2/(1 + t^2)$, where t is the number of hours after sundown. This is reasonably valid until sunrise. A fish bowl is set outside at sundown with an initial temperature of 70°F . Experiment shows that the bowl reaches 40°F in 2 hours. Will the bowl freeze, and if so when? *Hint:* You will run into difficulties; do not be blind to alternate approaches.

25. An ice boat is a sail boat on ice skates. If the ice boat is sailing straight downwind, the boat cannot go faster than the wind. Model the velocity of the ice boat as a function of time. Test the plausibility of your model by plotting solutions.

2.3.4 Exact Equations

In this section we shall consider certain equations of the form

$$M(x, y) + N(x, y)y' = 0.$$

Here is an example of an equation in this form.

$$\sin(xy) + (x^2 + y)y' = 0.$$

We shall assume that all functions of two variables introduced in this section have continuous partial derivatives up to and including the second order in a rectangular region of interest in the xy-plane. We shall say that such functions are smooth on the rectangle. This will not be much of a practical restriction, and it will relieve us of such technical issues as whether the order of partial differentiation makes a difference.

Suppose that the equation $M(x, y) + N(x, y)y' = 0$ is rather special in that there is a function $f(x, y)$ defined in some rectangle of the xy-plane such that $\frac{\partial f}{\partial x}(x, y) = M(x, y)$ and $\frac{\partial f}{\partial y}(x, y) = N(x, y)$ in that rectangle. Suppose that ϕ is a solution to the equation whose graph lies in the rectangle. Then

$$M(x, \phi(x)) + N(x, \phi(x))\phi'(x) = 0,$$

and so

$$\frac{\partial f}{\partial x}(x, \phi(x)) + \frac{\partial f}{\partial y}(x, \phi(x))\phi'(x) = 0.$$

The chain rule tells us that

$$\frac{df(x, \phi(x))}{dx} = \frac{\partial f}{\partial x}(x, \phi(x)) + \frac{\partial f}{\partial y}(x, \phi(x))\phi'(x) = 0,$$

and so

$$f(x, \phi(x)) = c.$$

Thus the solution ϕ satisfies the algebraic equation

$$f(x, y) = c,$$

where c is some constant to be determined by an initial condition.

Conversely, if ϕ is differentiable and satisfies the equation

$$f(x, y) = c$$

in the sense that

$$f(x, \phi(x)) = c$$

is an identity on some interval, then differentiation by the chain rule shows that ϕ must satisfy the original equation.

Here is a very simple example.

Example 2.3.8   Consider the initial value problem $x + yy' = 0$, where $y(0) = -2$. It is not hard to guess that the f that we need is

$$f(x, y) = \frac{x^2 + y^2}{2}.$$

Indeed, $\frac{\partial f}{\partial x}(x, y) = x$ and $\frac{\partial f}{\partial y}(x, y) = y$. Thus any solution must satisfy the algebraic equation

$$\frac{x^2 + y^2}{2} = c.$$

But $y(0) = -2$, and so $c = 2$. Thus the solution must satisfy

$$x^2 + y^2 = 4.$$

It is important to note that this equation is not the solution of the differential equation. However, the solution is an implicit function defined by this equation. Indeed, the solution is

$$\phi(x) = -\sqrt{4 - x^2}$$

with domain $(-2, 2)$.   ■

Definition 2.3.9

We say that the equation $M(x, y) + N(x, y)y' = 0$ is exact in a rectangle Ω if there is a function f defined on Ω such that $\frac{\partial f}{\partial x}(x, y) = M(x, y)$ and $\frac{\partial f}{\partial y}(x, y) = N(x, y)$ in this rectangle.   ●

We remind the reader that M, N, and f in this definition are all assumed to be smooth in the rectangle Ω. The rectangle Ω could be the whole plane or the upper half-plane in certain cases. Thus the rectangle does not have to be finite.

The following theorem summarizes what we have so far.

Theorem 2.3.10

Let $M(x, y) + N(x, y)y' = 0$ be exact in a rectangle Ω. Let $\frac{\partial f}{\partial x}(x, y) = M(x, y)$ and $\frac{\partial f}{\partial y}(x, y) = N(x, y)$ in Ω. Then, if the graph of ϕ lies in Ω, then ϕ is a solution to $M(x, y) + N(x, y)y' = 0$ if and only if ϕ is a solution to $f(x, y) = c$. ●

As with separable equations, a solution to an exact equation is a portion of a contour of a function $f(x, y)$.

With this theorem the main question is how to tell if $M(x, y) + N(x, y)y' = 0$ is exact, and, if so, how can one find f?

Certainly, if $M(x, y) + N(x, y)y' = 0$ is exact in Ω, then

$$\frac{\partial^2 f}{\partial x \partial y} = \frac{\partial M}{\partial y} = \frac{\partial^2 f}{\partial y \partial x} = \frac{\partial N}{\partial x},$$

so

$$\frac{\partial M}{\partial y} = \frac{\partial N}{\partial x}$$

in Ω.

It turns out that this last condition is also sufficient.

Theorem 2.3.11

Suppose that $\frac{\partial M}{\partial y} = \frac{\partial N}{\partial x}$ in the rectangle Ω. Then $M(x, y) + N(x, y)y' = 0$ is exact in Ω. ●

We shall not prove this theorem. However, it is worth pointing out that the theorem does not hold for arbitrary regions in the plane. Indeed, let the region be the plane with the origin removed. Consider

$$M = \frac{-y}{x^2 + y^2} \quad \text{and} \quad N = \frac{x}{x^2 + y^2}.$$

We easily compute that

$$\frac{\partial M}{\partial y} = \frac{\partial N}{\partial x}.$$

Recall that a potential for a vector field is a scalar function whose gradient is the vector field. It is easy to see that $M(x, y) + N(x, y)y' = 0$ being exact is equivalent to the vector field

$$\mathbf{F} = M\vec{\imath} + N\vec{\jmath}$$

having a potential f. But if f is a potential for $\mathbf{F}$, then the line integral around, say, the unit circle must be zero. But direct computation of the line integral using the parameterization $x = \cos(\theta)$ and $y = \sin(\theta)$ shows that this is not so! A simple method for finding f is illustrated in the next example.

Example 2.3.12   Consider the equation $(1 + y\cos(xy)) + (x\cos(xy) + 2y)y' = 0$ with $y(0) = 1$. In the plane, $\frac{\partial M}{\partial y} = \cos(xy) - xy\sin(xy)$ and $\frac{\partial N}{\partial x} = \cos(xy) - xy\sin(xy)$. By Theorem 2.3.11, the equation is exact; so an f exists with $\frac{\partial f}{\partial x}(x, y) = M(x, y)$ and $\frac{\partial f}{\partial y}(x, y) = N(x, y)$. So

$$\frac{\partial f}{\partial x}(x, y) = (1 + y\cos(xy)),$$

and integrating with respect to x gives

$$f(x, y) = \int (1 + y\cos(xy))dx = x + \sin(xy) + g(y).$$

Note that the "constant of integration" $g(y)$ is a function of y, since $g(y) = f(x, y) - (x + \sin(xy))$ is independent of x. We know this is so because the derivative of the right-hand side with respect to x is zero in the rectangle.

Now we have

$$\frac{\partial f}{\partial y}(x, y) = x\cos(xy) + g'(y) = (x\cos(xy) + 2y),$$

and so

$$g'(y) = 2y \quad \text{and} \quad g(y) = y^2.$$

Thus

$$f(x, y) = x + \sin(xy) + y^2.$$

Considering the initial condition the solution must be an implicit solution to

$$x + \sin(xy) + y^2 = 1.$$

Figure 2.9 shows the graph of this equation near the initial condition $(0, 1)$. This is the graph of the contour defined by $x + \sin(xy) + y^2 = 1$, and it is not the graph of a function. But the top portion to the left and above the "tip of the dog's nose" is. This is the graph of a solution through the initial condition.   ■

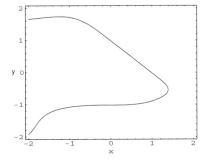

FIGURE 2.9

EXERCISES 2.3.4

In Exercises 1–10, check to see if the equation is exact in the plane. If so, solve it and clearly indicate on a plot of the con- *tour the extent of the solution through the initial condition.*

1. $(x - y) + (y - x)y' = 0$ and $y(0) = 2$.
2. $3x^2y^2 + (2x^3y - 3y^2)y' = 0$ and $y(1) = 2$.

3. $-\sin(x + y) + (2y\cos(x + y) - \sin(x + y))y' = 0$ and $y(0) = 0$.

4. $xy + (y - \frac{x^2}{2})y' = 0$ and $y(0) = 2$.

5. $(4x(x^2 + y^2) - 6xy) + (4y(x^2 + y^2) + 3y^2 - 3x^2)y' = 0$ and $y(\frac{\sqrt{3}}{2}) = \frac{1}{2}$.

6. $x + y^2 + (y + x^2)y' = 0$ and $y(1) = -3$.

7. $(2xy - y) + (x^2 + 3y^2 - x)y' = 0$ and $y(1) = 1$.

8. $(-1 + ye^{xy}) + (xe^{xy} + 1)y' = 0$ and $y(1) = 0$.

9. $(y^4 - 3x^2y) + (4xy^3 - x^3 + 10y)y' = 0$ and $y(1) = 1$.

10. $(\sin(y) + 2x) + (x\cos(y) + 2y)y' = 0$ and $y(1) = 0$.

11. The classification of equations that we have made in this section on analytic methods is not exclusive. To make this point, solve $y + xy' = 0$ by exact, separable, and linear methods.

12. Show that every separable equation is exact.

13. The equation $(y^2 - x) + x^2yy' = 0$ is not exact. Try to solve it using the exact method. What goes wrong?

14. (a) By completing the argument in the text, show that, for $(-y/(x^2+y^2))+(x/(x^2+y^2))y' = 0$, $\partial M/\partial y = \partial N/\partial x$, but that the equation is not exact in any region containing the origin .

    (b) Carry out the exact method, and note that the problem in Exercise 13 does not occur. How can the method fail in this case? This is not easy!

Orthogonal trajectories. *Each equation $y' = f(x, y)$ determines a family of curves in the plane. Exercises 15–20 ask you to find a second family of curves such that each curve of this family intersects the curves of the first family at right angles. Such a family is called the **family of orthogonal trajectories**.*

15. What equation must the orthogonal trajectories satisfy if the original family satisfies $y' = f(x, y)$? *Hint:* how must the slopes of the field segments of each family be related at a point (x, y)?

16. Find the orthogonal trajectories of $y' = -x/y$. Sketch some curves of both families on the same coordinates.

17. Find the orthogonal trajectories of $y' = -2x/y$. Sketch some curves of both families on the same coordinates.

18. Find the orthogonal trajectories of $y' = -x/(x + y)$.

19. Find the orthogonal trajectories of $y' = y$.

20. Find the orthogonal trajectories of $y' = 1/(x + y)$.

21. Consider a flowing river. Assuming that the flow is steady, we can describe the velocity of the water at any point (x, y) on the surface by a vector function $\vec{F}(x, y) = M(x, y)\vec{i} + N(x, y)\vec{j}$. If a cork is thrown in the river, the cork will follow a path such that the velocity of the cork matches the velocity of the flow of the river. Thus, if $\vec{r}(t) = x(t)\vec{i} + y(t)\vec{j}$ parameterizes the path of the cork, then $\vec{r}'(t) = \vec{F}(x(t), y(t))$. If

$$\vec{F}(x, y) = 2x^3/5\vec{i} + y/5\vec{j}$$

Use Field&Solution to draw several paths that the cork could take. *Hint:* This field is the gradient of a scalar function, and the field vectors are at right angles to the level curves.

2.4 AUTONOMOUS EQUATIONS AND CRITICAL POINTS

In this section we shall consider equations of the form

$$y' = f(y).$$

The equation $y' = y$ is a simple example.

Such equations are called **autonomous**. Note that this means that f is independent of x. To ensure the existence and uniqueness of solutions, we shall assume throughout that f and $\frac{\partial f}{\partial y} = f'$ are continuous everywhere.

For the autonomous equation $y' = f(y)$, the zeros of $f(y) = 0$ play a very important role in the qualitative behavior of solutions. The roots of the equation $f(y) = 0$ are called the **critical or equilibrium points** of the equation. Observe that if y_0 is a critical point then $\phi(x) \equiv y_0$ is a solution, because its derivative is identically zero and f is zero along this curve. This solution is a horizontal

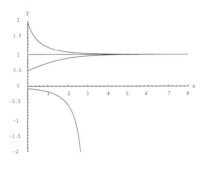

FIGURE 2.10

line through y_0. It is natural to ask how a solution behaves if its initial value is slightly perturbed from an equilibrium or critical initial value. There is no loss of generality in taking the initial conditions at $x_0 = 0$, since f does not depend on x. We shall only be interested in the "future" of solutions, so we concern ourselves only with solutions for which $x \geq 0$. Figure 2.10 and the example illustrate the essentials of the possible behavior.

Example 2.4.1   Figure 2.10 shows solutions to the equation $y' = y(1 - y)$. The critical points are 0 and 1. Any solution with initial condition greater than zero is defined for all $x \geq 0$ and converges to the line $y = 1$. On the other hand, solutions with negative initial conditions, no matter how close that initial condition is to zero, go to infinity in a finite interval of the x-axis. Solutions with initial conditions close to 1 stay close to $y = 1$, but solutions with initial conditions close to 0 stay close to 0 for a while, but they eventually diverge from $y = 0$. ■

Under our assumptions it can be shown that solutions are defined for all $x \geq 0$ or go to $\pm\infty$ in an interval of the form $[0, b)$.

These considerations motivate the following definition.

Definition 2.4.2

Let y_0 be a critical point of the equation $y' = f(y)$. We say y_0 is a stable critical point if for any horizontal band about the solution $y(x) = y_0$ there corresponds an interval about y_0 such that the graphs of all solutions with initial conditions in this interval lie in the band. We say y_0 is unstable otherwise.   ●

In more prosaic terms, a critical point y_0 is stable if it is possible to ensure that solutions stay close to y_0 by choosing their initial conditions close enough to y_0.

For simplicity we consider only critical points that are isolated. A critical point is isolated if it is in an open interval containing no other critical points. Note that if the critical points are isolated the critical points divide the y-axis into open intervals on which f is positive or negative. This observation makes it easy to decide if a critical point is stable or unstable. Here is an example.

Example 2.4.3   Consider $y' = (y - 1)(y + 2)$. The critical points are 1 and -2. Now if $y_1 > 1$ is an initial value, then y' must be positive, since both factors in $(y - 1)(y + 2)$ are. Therefore, if $y(x)$ is the solution with initial value $y(0) = y_1$, then $y(x)$ must be increasing. Moreover, for a given $\epsilon > 0$, as long as $y_1 \leq y \leq y_1 + \epsilon$, y' must be greater than some minimum positive value, say a. In this case the solution with initial condition y_1 must be increasing more rapidly than the line $y = ax + y_1$. But then the solution must get outside the ϵ band $1 \leq y \leq 1 + \epsilon$ as x increases. So $y_0 = 1$ is unstable. Clearly, -2 is stable since solutions below $y = -2$ must increase and those with initial conditions in $(-2, 1)$ must decrease. ∎

An argument such as the one given in the example can be employed to prove the following theorem.

Theorem 2.4.4

Let f and f' be continuous on the real line. Then a critical point y_0 is stable if and only if f is negative on the interval immediately above y_0 and positive on the interval immediately below y_0. ●

2.4.1 The Phase Line

There is another way to describe the qualitative behavior of solutions to an autonomous equation. Consider the equation

$$y'(t) = f(y(t)).$$

The independent variable is explicitly displayed as t because we want to think of solutions as depending on time. In this way we can picture the value $y(t)$ as a point on the real line that moves as time progresses. This real line is the y-axis in the two dimensional graphical representation of the solution. We call this real line the **phase line**. We shall draw phase lines horizontally.

Between critical points on the phase line, the value of the solution moves to the right or the left as $f(y)$ is positive or negative on the interval between critical points. We can indicate this motion by an arrowhead on the phase line. Figure 2.11 shows the phase line for the equation

FIGURE 2.11

$$y' = y(y - 1)(y + 2).$$

The phase line diagram clearly indicates which critical points will be stable and which unstable.

In Chapter 3 the phase line representation will be extended to two dimensions in the form of the phase plane. This will prove very useful in picturing the behavior of solutions to systems of two first-order equations.

2.4.2 The Population Model Continued

An understanding of the behavior of solutions between critical points can be useful in building or modifying models. Recall the elephant population model,

$$\frac{dE}{dt} = aE - bE^2 = E(a - bE).$$

Clearly, 0 and a/b are critical points. The point a/b is stable, and if a population is positive, then the population will grow toward a/b. This is a little unrealistic. If the population is very small to start with, then the population may die out. Perhaps, a minimum population is necessary for successful growth. This is sometimes called a **threshold**.

It is not hard to modify the elephant model to include a threshold. If T is the threshold population, then including the factor $-(T - E)$ will do the job. The model now is

$$\frac{dE}{dt} = -E(T - E)(a - bE),$$

where $0 < T < a/b$. We leave it as an exercise for you to graph solutions that have initial conditions in the intervals determined by the critical points.

EXERCISES 2.4

1. Discuss the critical points of $y' = y(y - 2)(y + 3)$. Draw graphs by hand of solutions starting at initial values of y in each of the open intervals determined by the critical points.

2. Discuss the critical points of $y' = (y + 1)(y - 1)^2(y + 3)$. Draw graphs by hand of solutions starting at initial values of y in each of the open intervals determined by the critical points.

3. Discuss the critical points of $y' = \sin(y)$. Draw graphs by hand of solutions starting at initial values of y in some of the open intervals determined by the critical points.

4. Discuss the critical points of $y' = \cos(y)$. Draw graphs by hand of solutions starting at initial values of y in some of the open intervals determined by the critical points.

5. Discuss the critical points of $y' = (y-1)(y+2)/(y^2+1)$. Draw graphs by hand of solutions starting at initial values of y in each of the open intervals determined by the critical points.

6. Discuss the critical points of $y' = y(y+2)(y-1)(y+3)$. Draw graphs by hand of solutions starting at initial values of y in each of the open intervals determined by the critical points.

7. Discuss the critical points of $y' = (y^3 - 1)(y^4 - y^2 + 1)$. Draw graphs by hand of solutions starting at initial values of y in each of the open intervals determined by the critical points.

8. What are the critical points of $y' = 1 - e^{1-y^2}$? Determine the stability of the critical points without graphing solutions. Explain your reasoning.

9. Graph solutions to the modified elephant herd model for

which $T = 100$, $a = 10^{-3}$, and $b = 10^{-6}$. Describe the behavior of solutions starting on either side of the threshold.

10. Graph solutions to the modified elephant herd model for which $T = 50$, $a = 10^{-4}$, and $b = 10^{-7}$. Describe the behavior of solutions starting on either side of the threshold.

11. Write down an autonomous equation that models the following population behavior. Let $0 < a < b$, and let $P = P(t)$ be the population and P_0 the initial population. If $0 < P_0 < a$, then P goes to zero. If $a < P_0 < b$, then P remains in this interval, but P approaches a. If $b < P_0$, then P goes to infinity.

12. Write down an autonomous equation that models the following population behavior. Let $0 < a < b < c$, and let $P = P(t)$ be the population and P_0 the initial population. If $0 < P_0 < a$, then P goes to zero. If $a < P_0 < b$, then P remains in this interval, but P approaches b. If $b < P_0 < c$, then P approaches b. If $c < P_0$, then P goes to infinity.

13. Create a nonautonomous model with the following properties. Solutions starting between 0 and 1 stay between 0 and 1, and solutions starting above 1 go to infinity.

14. Create a nonautonomous model with the following properties. Solutions starting between -1 and 1 stay between -1 and 1, and solutions starting above 1 go to infinity.

15. Describe the direction of arrows on the phase line on either side of a stable point and on either side of an unstable point.

16. Draw the phase line for $y' = \sin(y)$. Mark the critical

points and arrows.

17. Draw the phase line for $y' = \cos(y)$. Mark the critical points and arrows.

18. Draw the phase line for $y' = (y - 1)(y + 2)/(y^2 + 1)$. Mark the critical points and arrows.

2.5 THE DEPENDENCE OF SOLUTIONS ON INITIAL CONDITIONS

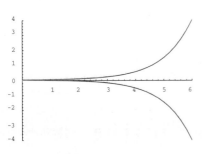

FIGURE 2.12

Consider the first-order equation $y' = f(x, y)$ again. Suppose that f and $\frac{\partial f}{\partial y}$ are continuous throughout a given rectangle. Then, as we know, there is a unique solution through each point inside the rectangle. Suppose that (x_1, y_1) and (x_2, y_2) are two initial conditions within the rectangle. It seems reasonable to suppose that if the initial conditions are close then the unique solutions through these points should be close too. After all, the field is continuous, and so the field about two close points should look about the same. However, as we follow the solutions away from the respective initial conditions, the field may differ in direction. Thus the two solutions start to diverge, and as they diverge the field on each solution may differ in direction more and more. This leads to greater divergence. Indeed, solutions that are, at first, close together may soon diverge from one another rapidly. Figure 2.12 shows this behavior.

The equation is $y' = y$, and the initial conditions are $(0, 0.01)$ and $(0, -0.01)$. The solution for the first condition goes to infinity, whereas the second goes to minus infinity. Certainly, if we choose the initial conditions even closer to the x-axis, the solutions will stay close for a greater range of x; but eventually they will diverge to their separate infinities.

It is true that if an interval $[a, b]$ for x is fixed then, if the initial conditions at a are chosen close enough, the solutions will be as close as we like, where the solutions are both defined in $[a, b]$.

Here is the main theorem on this matter.

Theorem 2.5.1

Suppose that f and $\partial f / \partial y$ are continuous throughout a closed finite rectangle $[a, b] \times [c, d]$; then there is a positive number L such that if y_1 and y_2 are the initial values at x_0 for two solutions $\phi_1(x)$ and $\phi_2(x)$ that lie in the rectangle, then

$$|\phi_1(x) - \phi_2(x)| \leq e^{L|x-x_0|}|y_1 - y_2|$$

on the intersection of their domains. ●

Note that the number L depends only on the function f and the rectangle being considered. Therefore, if y_1 and y_2 are close, then the solutions must be close if x is not allowed to get too large. As x grows, the right-hand side grows exponentially, and the bound on the difference between the solutions grows allowing the solutions to diverge at a possibly exponential rate. Indeed, the constant L can be large, so it is possible for some equations to exhibit extraordinary sensitivity to initial conditions (see Exercise 7).

Note that the inequality above is just that – an inequality. This means that some solutions to some equations may not diverge at an exponential rate. For example, the solutions to the trivial equation $y' = 2x$ have the form $y = x^2 + c$, so if the initial values at 0, say, differ by ϵ, then the solutions differ by ϵ for all $x \geq 0$. On the other hand, solutions to the simple equation $y' = y$ have the form $y = Ce^x$, and so if $\phi_1(0) = y_1$ and $\phi_2(0) = y_2$ then

$$|\phi_1(x) - \phi_2(x)| = |y_1 e^x - y_2 e^x| = e^x |y_1 - y_2|.$$

The divergence is exponential in this case.

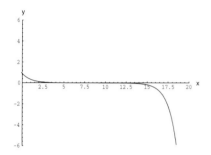

FIGURE 2.13

In summary, solutions with initial values given at a point a can diverge from each other as x increases at most at an exponential rate within a given rectangle or window of observation.

The possibility of exponential divergence has important consequences for numerical methods. Figure 2.13 shows the graph of a numerical solution to the equation $y' - y = -2e^{-x}$ with initial condition $y(0) = 1$.

The numerical method is fourth-order Runge-Kutta and the step size is 0.05. This means that 400 subdivisions were used! One might be tempted to believe that this graph is a good approximation of the true solution. However, the true solution may be easily derived by the method for solving linear equations (see the exercises). It is $y(x) = e^{-x}$. This function decreases asymptotically to the x-axis. How is this to be explained?

First, the general solution to this equation is

$$y(x) = e^{-x} + Ce^x.$$

From this it is easy to see that solutions with different initial values at $x = 0$ will diverge exponentially. Indeed, any solution that is not $y(x) = e^{-x}$ will contain the term Ce^x, where C is not zero. Now Runge-Kutta, in effect, calculates a new initial condition at each step, so if this new initial condition does not fall on $y(x) = e^{-x}$, then the approximation can begin to follow a solution in which the term Ce^x occurs. This approximation will rapidly diverge from the x-axis.

Even the simple equation $y' = y$ is subject to similar numerical approximation errors. However, in the case of this equation, the error is not so noticeable. This is because the approximate solution has the same form as the true solution. The error is also less noticeable in this case because the error as a fraction of the true solution at any point is small.

In both cases the errors stem from the fact that the solutions of these equations are very sensitive to small changes in initial conditions. Close-by initial conditions can have rapidly diverging solutions.

This sensitivity raises another consideration. In practical applications, measurements cannot be made with perfect accuracy, so the initial data for some application may be very slightly different from what was intended. As a result, if the application is modeled by an equation with great sensitivity to initial conditions, the application may respond in a manner that was not intended.

The issue of sensitivity to changes in initial conditions will be taken up again in Chapter 7.

EXERCISES 2.5

1. Solve the equation $y' = x + y$. Let $\phi_1(x)$ and $\phi_2(x)$ be solutions with initial conditions y_1 and y_2 at $x = 0$. Calculate the difference $\phi_1(x) - \phi_2(x)$ and describe the behavior of this difference as x increases. Does this example exhibit similar behavior to that of the example in the text?

2. Solve the equation $y' = y/x$. Consider the difference between solutions for $x > 0$. Does the difference grow exponentially?

3. Solve $y' - y = -2e^{-x}$ and verify the assertions in the text.

4. Use the package Field&Solution on the equation $y' - y = -2e^{-x}$. Draw the field. Use a step size of 0.01. Does the field point to the sensitivity to initial conditions near $(0, 1)$? Explain! Draw the solution through $(0, 1)$ on the interval $[0, 12]$. Experiment with initial conditions $(0, y_0)$ with y_0 close to 1. Briefly describe what you find.

5. (a) Solve $y' = 2xy$.
   (b) Using the package Field&Solution, draw solutions for the initial condition $(0, 0)$ and conditions $(0, y_0)$ for values of y_0 close to 0.
   (c) How does the difference between two solutions grow as x increases? This does not contradict Theorem 2.5.1!
   (d) In Theorem 2.5.1, what value of L will make the conclusion of the theorem true for $y' = 2xy$ on the square $[-1, 1] \times [-1, 1]$?

6. (a) Solve $y' = 3x^2y$.
   (b) Using the package Field&Solution, draw solutions for the initial condition $(0, 0)$ and conditions $(0, y_0)$ for values of y_0 close to 0.
   (c) How does the difference between two solutions grow as x increases? This does not contradict Theorem 2.5.1!
   (d) In Theorem 2.5.1, what value of L will make the conclusion of the theorem true for $y' = 3x^2y$ on the square $[-2, 2] \times [-2, 2]$?

7. Use Field&Solution to experiment with solutions to $y' = \sin(xy)$ with two initial conditions very close to each other and very close to $(5, 1.21)$. The initial conditions should be of the form $(5, y_0)$. How close can you get the y_0 values and still get the solutions to split apart. Place the y-axis at the left for a better picture. Use a step of 0.01.

SUPPLEMENTARY EXERCISES FOR CHAPTER 2

1. You are the ward and heir of the disgustingly rich Rufus P. Greed. You live in the guest house behind the main house on Greed's Bel-Air estate. The butler finds Greed shot in his wine room. The wine room is surrounded by rooms air conditioned to 80°F, and the temperature in the wine room is normally maintained at 40°F. But the bullet that killed Greed smashed the thermostat turning off the air conditioning in the wine room. The medical examiner arrives and measures the body's temperature as 85°F at 10:30 P.M. You can prove that you were on the phone from 8:30 to 9:00 P.M.

Experiment shows that the rate of change of temperature of both the wine room and a body is, at each instant, proportional to the difference between the temperature of the surroundings and the temperature of the object (wine room or body). Forensic experts say the proportionality constant for the body is 0.2, and experiment shows that the wine room warms up to 70°F in 3 hours. Prove your innocence.

2. Return to the parachute model in Section 2.3.2. Assume that the drag coefficient, c, has value 10 when the parachute is open and 1 when it is closed, and the parachutist weighs 150 lb. A wind is blowing out of the north at 20 mph. The jump is made 1 mile north of the touchdown point from a balloon at an altitude of 5000 ft. How long should the parachutist wait before pulling the

rip cord in order to land on the touchdown point?

3. In the autonomous equation $y' = f(y)$, the roots of f are called the critical points of the equation. Solutions often approach some of these critical points asymptotically from one side or the other. This suggests that roots of f might be approximated by using Euler's method.

   (a) Investigate this possibility by experimenting with several choices of f. In particular, experiment with quadratic and cubic polynomials having roots of all possible types. What roots are not approximated by this method?

   (b) What role does step size play in this?

   (c) The equation $y' = -f(y)/f'(y)$ will often have the same critical points as f. If the method is applied to this equation, what advantage does it have?

   (d) Is the method in part c generally faster to a given accuracy?

   (e) Find Newton's method in your calculus book. How does this relate to the method in part c?

   (f) Does using Runge-Kutta offer any advantage?

4. Consider a population that grows according to the law $y' = y(2 - y)$. Now suppose that the population is harvested in a periodic manner so that the equation becomes

$$y' = y(2 - y) - a(1 + \sin(2t)),$$

where a is a positive constant and t (time!) is the independent variable.

   (a) Use Field&Solution to experiment with this harvesting equation with various values of a. Why is this model not satisfactory? Is there such a thing as overharvesting in this model?

   (b) Propose an improvement that gets rid of the objection in part a and makes more sense in terms of real harvesting. Is there such a thing as overharvesting in your new model?

   (c) Critique both models.

5. Solve the hanging cable equation from Chapter 1.

$$y''(x) = k\rho\sqrt{1 + (y'(x))^2}.$$

Assume that $k\rho = 1$. *Hint:* Reduce to a first-order system.

CHAPTER 3

INTRODUCTION TO FIRST-ORDER SYSTEMS

First-order systems play a central role in the study of differential equations for two reasons. First, the majority of differential equations can be reduced to an equivalent first-order system. Thus the questions of existence and uniqueness of solutions to most differential equations can be settled by answering these questions for first-order systems. Second, it is usually most efficient to apply numerical methods to higher-order equations by first reducing them to first-order systems.

In this chapter the basics of first-order systems of differential equations will be introduced. These will include the existence and uniqueness of solutions, numerical approximation methods, and critical points in autonomous systems. Analytic methods will be developed in Chapter 5.

3.1 SOLUTIONS TO FIRST-ORDER SYSTEMS

We shall find vector notation to be useful in discussing systems of first-order equations, so this section begins with a review of vectors and vector-valued functions.

3.1.1 A Brief Review of Vectors

Vectors are mathematical objects used to describe quantities that have both magnitude and direction. We usually represent vectors graphically as arrows. Mathematically, a vector in three dimensions is described by an ordered triple of three real numbers, (x, y, z). The direction of (x, y, z) is the direction of the arrow drawn from the origin to this point in space. The magnitude is the length of this arrow, and this is

$$\sqrt{x^2 + y^2 + z^2}.$$

The vector (x, y, z) is also written in terms of the standard basis vectors $\vec{\imath}$, $\vec{\jmath}$, and $\vec{k}$ as follows:

$$x\vec{\imath} + y\vec{\jmath} + z\vec{k}.$$

The vector corresponding to the arrow from the point (x_1, y_1, z_1) to the point (x_2, y_2, z_2) is

$$(x_2 - x_1)\vec{\imath} + (y_2 - y_1)\vec{\jmath} + (z_2 - z_1)\vec{k}.$$

Vectors are added as follows:

$$(x_1\vec{\imath} + y_1\vec{\jmath} + z_1\vec{k}) + (x_2\vec{\imath} + y_2\vec{\jmath} + z_2\vec{k}) = (x_1 + x_2)\vec{\imath} + (y_1 + y_2)\vec{\jmath} + (z_1 + z_2)\vec{k}.$$

Recall that vector addition corresponds to the addition of arrows by the **parallelogram law**.

If r is a real number then

$$r(x\vec{\imath} + y\vec{\jmath} + z\vec{k}) = rx\vec{\imath} + ry\vec{\jmath} + rz\vec{k}.$$

This is called **scalar multiplication**, and it has the effect of changing the length of the vector by a scale factor of $|r|$ and reversing the direction if r is negative.

Vector-valued functions of a real variable are functions of the form

$$\vec{r}(t) = x(t)\vec{\imath} + y(t)\vec{\jmath} + z(t)\vec{k}.$$

Such functions can be used to describe curves in space (or the plane if $z \equiv 0$). Indeed, if the tail of $\vec{r}(t)$ is placed at the origin, then the tip of $\vec{r}(t)$ sweeps out a curve as t varies over its domain. In this case we call $\vec{r}(t)$ a **position vector**.

The derivative of $\vec{r}(t)$ is defined in the usual way,

$$\vec{r}'(t) = \lim_{\Delta t \to 0} \frac{\vec{r}(t + \Delta t) - \vec{r}(t)}{\Delta t}.$$

Recall that the derivative is a vector tangent to the curve defined by $\vec{r}(t)$ and that the derivative is computed by

$$\vec{r}'(t) = x'(t)\vec{\imath} + y'(t)\vec{\jmath} + z'(t)\vec{k}.$$

Finally, you will recall that a vector field is a function that assigns a vector to each point in the plane, or in space. For example,

$$\vec{F}(x, y) = (x^2 - y)\vec{\imath} + e^{x+y}\vec{\jmath}$$

assigns vectors to points (x, y) in the plane.

3.1.2 Existence and Uniqueness for Systems

The following is the general form of a system of n first-order equations in n unknown functions.

$$x_1'(t) = f_1(t, x_1(t), \ldots, x_n(t)),$$
$$x_2'(t) = f_2(t, x_1(t), \ldots, x_n(t)),$$
$$\vdots$$
$$x_n'(t) = f_n(t, x_1(t), \ldots, x_n(t)).$$

We shall see that the conditions for the existence and uniqueness of solutions to such a system are a straightforward generalization of those for the single equation $y' = f(t, y)$. However, it will be easier to discuss the ideas in the case of a 2×2 system. You will quickly grasp the generalization to the $n \times n$ system.

Consider the system

$$x' = f(t, x, y),$$
$$y' = g(t, x, y).$$

A solution is a pair of functions, $\{x(t), y(t)\}$, defined on an interval (a, b) such that the two equations

$$x'(t) = f(t, x(t), y(t)),$$
$$y'(t) = g(t, x(t), y(t))$$

are identities on (a, b). In the single equation $y' = f(t, y)$ (we have used t for the independent variable for consistency) there is one dependent variable y and one independent variable t. So the graph of a solution is drawn in the plane that has two dimensions or axes. For the 2×2 system there are two dependent variables, x and y, and one independent variable t. The graph of the solution $\{x(t), y(t)\}$ is the set of points $(t, x(t), y(t))$ for t in (a, b), so the graph is a curve in three-dimensional space.

The graph of a solution may be traced out using the position vector function

$$\vec{r}(t) = t\vec{i} + x(t)\vec{j} + y(t)\vec{k}.$$

The derivative of this function is a vector tangent to the graph, and this is the key to the geometrical interpretation. The derivative is

$$\vec{r}'(t) = \vec{i} + x'(t)\vec{j} + y'(t)\vec{k} = \vec{i} + f(t, x(t), y(t))\vec{j} + g(t, x(t), y(t))\vec{k},$$

since $\{x(t), y(t)\}$ is still assumed to be a solution to our system. Thus the graph of a solution passes through the field

$$\vec{i} + f(t, x(t), y(t))\vec{j} + g(t, x(t), y(t))\vec{k}$$

tangentially.

Conversely, suppose that we have a differentiable curve given by

$$\vec{r}(t) = t\vec{i} + x(t)\vec{j} + y(t)\vec{k},$$

that passes through the field

$$\vec{i} + f(t, x, y)\vec{j} + g(t, x, y)\vec{k}$$

tangentially. Then the "velocity" vector $\vec{r}\,'(t)$ at each point, being parallel to the field vector, must be a scalar multiple of the field vector. So

$$\vec{r}\,'(t) = \vec{i} + x'(t)\vec{j} + y'(t)\vec{k} = c(\vec{i} + f(t, x(t), y(t))\vec{j} + g(t, x(t), y(t))\vec{k}).$$

But then $c = 1$, $x'(t) = f(t, x(t), y(t))$, and $y'(t) = g(t, x(t), y(t))$. In short, $\{x(t), y(t)\}$ is a solution to our system. Thus $\{x(t), y(t)\}$ is a solution if and only if the graph of this pair of functions passes through the field $\vec{i} + f(t, x, y)\vec{j} + g(t, x, y)\vec{k}$ tangentially. This is an immediate generalization of the single-equation case.

Figure 3.1 shows a field and some solutions. Notice that the field is represented by line segments, just as in the one-equation case. It is not necessary to add the complication of drawing arrows since only tangency is needed to determine the solution curve.

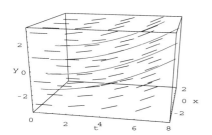

FIGURE 3.1

Now let us consider the question of the existence of solutions. If the functions $f(t, x, y)$ and $g(t, x, y)$ are continuous in a block of three-dimensional space, this means that the field vectors change direction in a continuous fashion. If this is so, it is reasonable to guess that there is a curve through each point inside the block that passes through the field tangentially. This is so, and so solutions exist through each point inside the block. You will recall that for a single equation $y' = f(t, y)$ the continuity of $f(t, y)$ was not enough to guarantee the uniqueness of a solution through a point. The continuity of $\frac{\partial f}{\partial y}(t, y)$ was also needed. Note that this added condition concerns the partial derivative of the field function with respect to the dependent variable. It is also reasonable to guess that uniqueness will be guaranteed if all the partial derivatives of $f(t, x, y)$ and $g(t, x, y)$ with respect to the dependent variables are continuous in the block. This is correct, and we summarize all this in the following theorem.

Theorem 3.1.1

Let $f, g, \frac{\partial f}{\partial x}, \frac{\partial f}{\partial y}, \frac{\partial g}{\partial x}$, and $\frac{\partial g}{\partial y}$ be continuous in the block $[a, b] \times [c_1, d_1] \times [c_2, d_2]$. Let (t_0, x_0, y_0) be a point in the interior of the block. Then there is a positive number h and a pair of functions $\{x(t), y(t)\}$ defined on $(t_0 - h, t_0 + h)$ that satisfy the system

$$x' = f(t, x, y),$$
$$y' = g(t, x, y).$$

Moreover, any two solutions that lie in the block and pass through the point (t_0, x_0, y_0) must agree on the intersection of their domains.   ●

The maximal solution through a point in a block is the solution of maximum domain that lies in the block. Given that the hypotheses of this theorem hold, when we speak of the solution through a point being unique, we shall be referring to this maximal solution.

The point through which a solution is required to pass is called an **initial condition**. If (t_0, x_0, y_0) is an initial condition, the requirement that the solution pass through this point is usually stated in the form $x(t_0) = x_0$ and $y(t_0) = y_0$.

Here is an example of the application of this theorem.

Example 3.1.2   Consider the system

$$x' = \frac{t}{y} + x^2,$$
$$y' = t^2 + xy.$$

We have $f(t, x, y) = \frac{t}{y} + x^2$, $g(t, x, y) = t^2 + xy$, $\frac{\partial f}{\partial x} = 2x$, $\frac{\partial f}{\partial y} = -t/y^2$, $\frac{\partial g}{\partial x} = y$, and $\frac{\partial g}{\partial y} = x$. These functions and partials are continuous in any block that does not include the t,x-plane. So, for a point in the interior of any such block there is only one (maximal) solution passing through it. ∎

In the next example the system is solved explicitly.

Example 3.1.3   The simple system

$$x' = -x + y,$$
$$y' = y$$

can be solved directly. First we solve for y to get $y(t) = c_1 e^t$. Then we solve $x' = -x + c_1 e^t$. This is a first-order linear equation, $x' + x = c_1 e^t$. Thus

$$x(t) = e^{-t} \int e^t c_1 e^t \, dt + c_2 e^{-t} = e^{-t} \int c_1 e^{2t} \, dt + c_2 e^{-t}.$$

Thus

$$x(t) = \frac{1}{2} c_1 e^t + c_2 e^{-t}$$

and

$$y(t) = c_1 e^t.$$

Notice the two arbitrary constants. These are determined by specifying an initial condition, say $x(0) = 1$ and $y(0) = -2$. In this case $c_1 = -2$ and $x(0) = \frac{-2}{2} + c_2 = 1$. So $c_2 = 2$.

The derivation shows that this is the only solution to these equations and the given initial condition. This is, of course, consistent with what the existence and uniqueness theorem says. ∎

If the hypotheses of Theorem 3.1.1 hold, then, as in the single-equation case, solutions cannot cross or even touch tangentially without being identical.

3.1.3 Systems as Vector Equations

The main purpose of the preceding material is to make plausible Theorem 3.1.1. Now return to Figure 3.1. Perhaps you can already see the potential difficulty in interpreting such fields. Projecting a three-dimensional field onto the plane of the page, even in perspective, produces a confusing image. The field in Figure 3.1 is very simple, and so it is not hard to read. More complex fields become unreadable, so we shall not use such fields in an effort to picture the behavior of solutions as we did in the single-equation case. Instead, we will change the way we look at solutions by using vectors to represent a system of equations as a single vector equation.

The system

$$x' = f(t, x, y),$$
$$y' = g(t, x, y)$$

can be expressed as a vector equation by setting

$$\vec{R}(t) = x(t)\vec{i} + y(t)\vec{j}$$

and

$$\vec{F}(t, x, y) = f(t, x, y)\vec{i} + g(t, x, y)\vec{j}.$$

Then $\{x(t), y(t)\}$ is a solution to the system if and only if

$$\vec{R}'(t) = \vec{F}(t, x(t), y(t)) = \vec{F}(t, \vec{R}(t)).$$

When we evaluate $\vec{F}$ at a vector, we evaluate it at the coordinates of that vector.

We now switch from viewing a solution as a pair of functions $\{x(t), y(t)\}$ to viewing a solution as a single function $\vec{R}$ that associates with each t in the interval of definition (a, b) a vector $\vec{R}(t)$ in the xy-plane. You may recall that we call this plane the phase plane of the system.

This vector form of a solution is a function that draws a curve in the phase plane. Put another way, this curve is the range of the vector function solution. This curve or path in the xy-plane is called an **orbit**. It is most important to remember that an orbit is not a solution; it is the range of a solution. As before, the graph of the solution must lie in three dimensions, one for the independent variable and two for the dependent variables. Indeed, the orbit of a solution is the projection of the graph of the solution in (t, x, y) coordinate space onto the xy-plane.

The vector equation and solution can be interpreted physically. Imagine that $\vec{R}(t)$ is describing the motion of a particle in the plane as a function of time. Then the vector equation says that we have a solution if at each instant t

of time the velocity of the particle matches the field vector $\vec{F}(t, \vec{R}(t))$ at that instant and at the point through which the particle is passing. We cannot draw a picture of this because the field vector at any point is not necessarily static. That is, the field may well be constantly changing direction. Therefore, no static geometric interpretation can be given. However, if the system is autonomous, then a geometric picture is possible.

A system is **autonomous** if it has the form

$$x' = f(x, y),$$
$$y' = g(x, y),$$

where f and g do not depend on t.

The right-hand side of the vector equation becomes the static vector field

$$\vec{F}(x, y) = f(x, y)\vec{i} + g(x, y)\vec{j}.$$

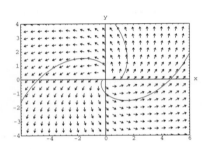

This field can be pictured in the plane. At a suitable lattice of points (x_i, y_i) in the plane we draw the vector $\vec{F}(x_i, y_i)$. Now the derivative of the vector solution is a vector tangent to the orbit, and this is equal to the field vector at the point through which the orbit is passing. Therefore, in this view, it is the orbit of a solution that passes through the field tangentially.

FIGURE 3.2

Figure 3.2 shows the field and the paths or orbits of three solutions to the autonomous system

$$x' = x - y,$$
$$y' = x + y.$$

The field shown here is not quite the field of the system. The reason is that the field vectors in the figure all have the same length. The reason for doing this is to make the nature of the field more transparent. If we drew the field as it really is, the variable lengths of the field vectors would produce a confused picture. When the field is plotted with constant lengths, we say that the field has been **normalized**. We will always use normalized fields in such figures. Note that the orbit of the solution through the field is not affected by normalization because the directions remain unchanged.

EXERCISES 3.1

1. Solve the system

$$x' = 2x,$$
$$y' = y,$$

with $x(0) = 1$ and $y(0) = 3$. *Hint:* Each equation can be solved on its own. Does your solution confirm the conclusions of Theorem 3.1.1? Explain!

2. Solve the system

$$x' = 2x - y,$$
$$y' = y,$$

with $x(0) = 0$ and $y(0) = 2$. *Hint:* Solve one equation and substitute in the other. Does your solution confirm the conclusions of Theorem 3.1.1? Explain!

3. Solve the system

$$x' = x^2 y,$$
$$y' = y,$$

with $x(0) = 1$ and $y(0) = 1$. Is this solution defined for all t? Are any solutions defined for all t? Does your solution confirm the conclusions of Theorem 3.1.1? Explain!

4. Solve the system

$$x' = x^3 y,$$
$$y' = -y,$$

with $x(0) = 1$ and $y(0) = 3$. Is this solution defined for all t? Are any solutions defined for all t? Does your solution confirm the conclusions of Theorem 3.1.1? Explain!

5. Solve the system

$$x' = e^t x + y,$$
$$y' = y,$$

with $x(0) = 1$ and $y(0) = 3$.

6. Given that Theorem 3.1.1 is satisfied by the system

$$x' = f(t, x, y),$$
$$y' = g(t, x, y),$$

could graphs of **solutions** to the system cross at a positive angle in the block?

7. Given that Theorem 3.1.1 is satisfied by the system

$$x' = f(t, x, y),$$
$$y' = g(t, x, y),$$

could an orbit cross itself at a positive angle?

8. Consider the following system

$$x' = x^{2/3} y,$$
$$y' = y.$$

Show that there are two solutions with $x(0) = 0$ and $y(0) = 1$ by exhibiting them explicitly. *Hint:* Solve for y first, and then consider multiple solutions for the x equation. Does Theorem 3.1.1 apply here? Explain!

9. Consider the following system

$$x' = x,$$
$$y' = xy^{2/5}.$$

Show that there are two solutions with $x(0) = 1$ and $y(0) = 0$ by exhibiting them explicitly. *Hint:* Solve for x first, and then consider multiple solutions for the y equation. Does Theorem 3.1.1 apply here? Explain!

10. Use the package 2 × 2System to draw the field of

$$x' = 2x + y,$$
$$y' = x - y$$

in the rectangle $[-6, 6] \times [-4, 4]$. Draw orbits for initial conditions $(1, 1)$, $(-1, 2)$, and $(0, 0)$ at $t = 0$. Explain what is happening with this last initial condition.

11. Use the package 2 × 2System to draw the field of

$$x' = y,$$
$$y' = -x$$

in the rectangle $[-6, 6] \times [-4, 4]$. Draw orbits for initial conditions $(1, 1)$, $(-1, 2)$, and $(0, 0)$ at $t = 0$. Explain what is happening with this last initial condition.

12. Use the package 2 × 2System to draw the field of

$$x' = x + y - 3,$$
$$y' = 2x - y$$

in the rectangle $[-6, 6] \times [-4, 4]$. Draw orbits for initial conditions $(1, 1)$, $(-1, 2)$, and $(1, 2)$ at $t = 0$. Explain what is happening with this last initial condition.

13. Generalize Theorem 3.1.1 to a system of three equations.

14. Generalize Theorem 3.1.1 to a system of four equations.

15. Explain the difference between the graph of a solution and an orbit in the 2 × 2 case.

16. Use the package 2 × 2System to draw the field of

$$x' = y,$$
$$y' = -x.$$

In coordinates, draw the field vectors for this system on paper at $(1, 1)$, $(2, 3)$, and $(-4, -2)$. Compare this with the vectors drawn by 2 × 2System. Comment on lengths and directions.

17. Use the package 2 × 2System to draw the field of

$$x' = x - y^2,$$
$$y' = x + y.$$

In coordinates, draw the field vectors for this system on paper at $(1, 1)$, $(2, 3)$, and $(-4, -2)$. Compare this with the vectors drawn by 2 × 2System. Comment on lengths and directions.

18. Use the package 2 × 2System to draw the field of

$$x' = x - y,$$
$$y' = x^2 + y.$$

In coordinates, draw the field vectors for this system on paper at $(1, 1)$, $(2, 3)$, and $(-4, -2)$. Compare this with the vectors drawn by 2 × 2System. Comment on lengths and directions.

19. Use the package 2 × 2System to draw the field of

$$x' = x - y^2,$$
$$y' = x + y.$$

In coordinates, draw the field vectors for this system on paper at $(1, 1)$, $(2, 3)$, and $(-4, -2)$. Compare this with the vectors drawn by 2 × 2System. Comment on lengths and directions.

3.2 ORBIT CROSSING AND PERIODIC SOLUTIONS

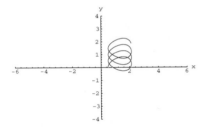

FIGURE 3.3

In this section we discuss how and when orbits of a 2 × 2 system might cross themselves. Throughout this section we shall assume that the hypotheses of the existence and uniqueness theorem hold, so we can assume that through each initial condition there is only one (maximal) solution.

Fields for nonautonomous 2 × 2 systems have the form

$$\vec{F}(t, x, y) = f(t, x, y)\vec{i} + g(t, x, y)\vec{j},$$

where f or g or both depend on t. Because the field depends on t, the field cannot be drawn in the plane. At each point in the plane the field vector is, in general, changing direction as t changes. However, orbits for nonautonomous systems can be drawn, for solutions parameterize curves in the plane whether the system is autonomous or not. Figure 3.3 shows an orbit for the system

$$x'(t) = \sin(t + y),$$
$$y'(t) = \cos(x).$$

Notice that the orbit crosses itself. This kind of behavior is only possible in the nonautonomous case. By the time that the orbit gets back to the point of intersection, the field vector at that point has changed direction thus permitting the orbit to cross itself at an angle.

If the system is autonomous, then an orbit can only "cross" itself in a special way as we now show. Let $\vec{R}(t)$ be the vector form of the solution to the autonomous system

$$x'(t) = f(x(t), y(t)),$$
$$y'(t) = g(x(t), y(t)).$$

Suppose that

$$\vec{R}(t_0) = \vec{R}(t_1),$$

where $t_0 < t_1$. Because the field vectors do not change, the orbit must return to a point from which it started going in the same direction as when it started. This strongly suggests that the motion repeats itself in intervals of $t_1 - t_0$. In short, the motion is periodic. To prove this, let $\vec{R}(t)$ be a solution passing through (x_0, y_0) at $t = t_0$ and at $t = t_1$. Let $\vec{Q}(t) = \vec{R}(t + t_1 - t_0)$. Now

$$\vec{Q}'(t) = \vec{R}'(t + t_1 - t_0) = \vec{F}(\vec{R}(t + t_1 - t_0)) = \vec{F}(\vec{Q}(t)).$$

Recall that by evaluating $\vec{F}$ at a vector we mean that $\vec{F}$ is evaluated at the coordinates of that vector. Thus we have shown that $\vec{Q}(t)$ is a solution of the system also. Moreover, $\vec{Q}(t_0) = \vec{R}(t_1) = x_0\vec{i} + y_0\vec{j}$; so by uniqueness of solutions $\vec{Q}(t) = \vec{R}(t)$, and so

$$\vec{R}(t) = \vec{R}(t + t_1 - t_0).$$

Therefore, the solution is periodic with period $t_1 - t_0$.

Example 3.2.1 If we reduce $y'' + y = 0$ to a first-order system by setting $u = y$ and $v = y'$, we get

$$u' = v,$$
$$v' = -u.$$

In u,v coordinates the field is

$$\vec{F}(u, v) = v\vec{i} - u\vec{j}.$$

This field is always at right angles to the position vector $u\vec{i} + v\vec{j}$, and so the orbits are circles about the origin. Figure 3.4 depicts the situation.

The period of the orbits can be estimated by running 2×2System and either examining the output of each coordinate function of the solution or adjusting the interval for the independent variable until you just obtain the closure of the orbit. This estimate is left to the exercises. We shall obtain precise results in Chapter 4, and the matter will be revisited in Chapter 6. ■

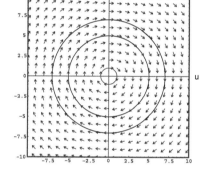

FIGURE 3.4

Periodic solutions have orbits that are simple closed curves or a single point. Clearly, orbits cannot cross at an angle, because this would imply that the field vector at the point of crossing would have to point in two different directions. You may wonder if it is possible to have an orbit of a periodic solution in the form of two circles that are tangent to one another at a point. Interpreted as the motion of a particle, the motion would be around the right circle until the point of tangency is reached, and then around the left circle until the point of tangency is reached again, and so on. The motion is tracing out a figure eight. This is not possible, because upon return to the point of tangency the preceding motion must be repeated as we have shown previously.

EXERCISES 3.2

In Exercises 1–4 use the package 2×2 System to graph the fields and three orbits. Observe how the orbits pass through the fields tangentially.

1. $x' = x - y$
   $y' = x + 2y$

2. $x' = x + 2y$
   $y' = -x + 3y$

3. $x' = x - 2y$
   $y' = x - 3y$

4. $x' = x + y$
   $y' = x - y$

5. Use package 2×2 System to draw the orbit of the solution to the system

$$x' = ty,$$
$$y' = t - x,$$

   with initial condition $(0, 1)$ at $t = 0$. How do you explain the orbit crossing itself? Draw a rough sketch of the graph of the solution in three dimensions.

6. Use package 2×2 System to draw the orbit of the solution to the system

$$x' = \sin(ty),$$
$$y' = \cos(tx),$$

   with initial condition $(2, 0)$ at $t = 0$. How do you explain the orbit crossing itself? Draw a rough sketch of the graph of the solution in three dimensions.

7. Could the following orbit have come from an autonomous system? Explain!

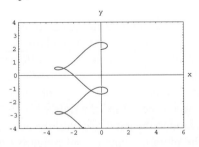

8. Find a 2×2 autonomous system for which some orbits cross. *Hint:* Find solutions to an equation of the form $y' = f(x, y)$ that cross. Then set $x'(t) = 1$ and $y'(t) = f(x(t), y(t))$. Draw the crossing orbits.

9. Reduce the equation $y'' + y = 0$ to a first-order system. Use the package 2×2 System to plot several orbits. If the solutions to $y'' + y = 0$ are periodic, estimate the period.

10. Reduce the equation $y'' + 4y = 0$ to a first-order system. Use the package 2×2 System to plot several orbits. If the solutions to $y'' + 4y = 0$ are periodic, estimate the period.

11. Find the periods of solutions to $y'' + ay = 0$ for several values of a. Make a conjecture relating the periods to the values of a. *Hint:* π and square roots come into it.

12. Suppose that $\{x(t), y(t)\}$ is a solution to an autonomous 2×2 system that satisfies Theorem 3.1.1, and $x(0) = y(0) = x(2) = y(2) = 5$. What is $x(4)$ and why?

13. Suppose that $\{x(t), y(t)\}$ is a solution to an autonomous 2×2 system that satisfies Theorem 3.1.1, and $x(0) = x(3) = -1$ and $y(0) = y(3) = 2$. What is $y(6)$ and why?

14. Find periodic orbits for the system

$$x' = y,$$
$$y' = -\sin(x).$$

   Estimate two different periods. Can you get a period of virtually any length?

15. Find periodic orbits for the system

$$x' = y,$$
$$y' = -4\sin(x).$$

   Estimate two different periods. Can you get a period of virtually any length?

3.3   NUMERICAL APPROXIMATIONS

In this section we shall discuss Euler's method and the Runge-Kutta method for systems of first-order equations.

3.3.1 Euler's Method

Euler's method for systems is a direct extension of the method for a single equation that was introduced in Chapter 2. The idea can most economically be explained in the case of a 2×2 system. Consider the system

$$x'(t) = f(t, x(t), y(t)),$$
$$y'(t) = g(t, x(t), y(t)).$$

For simplicity we shall assume that the f and g together with all the partial derivatives with respect to the x and y are continuous everywhere. In view of this, solutions through any point exist and are unique.

Suppose that a solution exists for $t \in [a, b]$. Let $t_0 = a$, and divide $[a, b]$ into n subdivisions of length $h = (b-a)/n$. Suppose that at t_0 we have the initial point $(x(t_0), y(t_0)) = (x_0, y_0)$; then an approximation to $(x(t_0+h), y(t_0+h))$ can be computed as follows. Since $x'(t_0) = f(t_0, x_0, y_0)$ is the rate of change of x, the approximate change in x in the interval h will be $hf(t_0, x_0, y_0)$. Therefore, an approximate value for x at $t_0 + h$ is $x_1 = x_0 + hf(t_0, x_0, y_0)$. A similar argument applies to y. In general, the approximation (x_{k+1}, y_{k+1}) to the value of the solution $(x(t_0 + (k+1)h), y(t_0 + (k+1)h))$ is obtained by iteration from

$$x_{k+1} = x_k + hf(t_0 + kh, x_k, y_k),$$
$$y_{k+1} = y_k + hg(t_0 + kh, x_k, y_k).$$

Geometrically, at each iteration we calculate the field vector at the last point computed, and then we follow it for the "time interval" h to get to the next point. In vector notation this is

$$\vec{r}_{k+1} = \vec{r}_k + h\vec{F}(t_0 + kh, \vec{r}_k).$$

Here is an example.

Example 3.3.1   Consider the system

$$x'(t) = t + x - y,$$
$$y'(t) = t^2 x,$$

with the initial condition $(1, 2)$ at $t = 1$. We approximate the solution on the interval $[1, 3]$ using four subdivisions. The computation of the x_i values are shown. Then $h = 2/4 = 0.5$. Thus

$t_0 = 1$	$x_0 = 1$	$y = 2$
$t_1 = 1.5$	$x_1 = 1 + 0.5(1 + 1 - 2) = 1$	$y_1 = 2.5$
$t_2 = 2$	$x_2 = 1 + 0.5(1.5 + 1 - 2.5) = 1$	$y_2 = 3.625$
$t_3 = 2.5$	$x_3 = 1 + 0.5(2 + 1 - 3.625) = 0.6875$	$y_3 = 5.625$

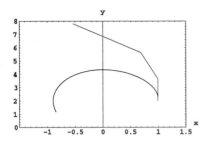

FIGURE 3.5

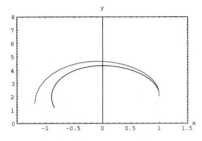

FIGURE 3.6

$$t_4 = 3 \qquad x_4 = 0.69 + 0.5(2.5 + 0.69 - 5.63) = -0.53 \qquad y_4 = 7.77$$

Figure 3.5 shows the points just calculated joined by straight line segments to produce a polygonal approximation of the orbit, which is also shown. This is obviously not very good. ∎

One way to improve the approximation is to increase the number of subdivisions. Figure 3.6 shows the result corresponding to 30 subdivisions in Example 3.3.1.

This is still not very good, and the improvement has been obtained at the price of a great increase in computation. Remember that in any numerical method there are two kinds of errors to be contended with. There is the purely mathematical error between the solution and the mathematical approximation. This is sometimes called the **discretization error**. There is also the computational round-off error due to the inability of the computer to store numbers with perfect accuracy. Euler's method has order of h discretization error, and so accuracy demands many subdivisions; but round-off error then undermines this theoretical accuracy. A much better balance is struck by the fourth-order Runge-Kutta method.

3.3.2 The Runge-Kutta Method

The Runge-Kutta method for a 2×2 system is entirely similar to the single-equation case. As before, the Runge-Kutta method obtains improved accuracy by taking a weighted average of the rates of change of the x and y components calculated from the field at several points "along the way" to the next point to be calculated. The algorithm is as follows. Set $h = (b - a)/n$ as before. If we have calculated (x_k, y_k) at $t_k = t_0 + kh$, we obtain (x_{k+1}, y_{k+1}) at t_{k+1} by computing

$$p_{1k} = f(t_k, x_k, y_k),$$
$$q_{1k} = g(t_k, x_k, y_k),$$
$$p_{2k} = f(t_k + \frac{h}{2}, x_k + \frac{hp_{1k}}{2}, y_k + \frac{hq_{1k}}{2})$$
$$q_{2k} = g(t_k + \frac{h}{2}, x_k + \frac{hp_{1k}}{2}, y_k + \frac{hq_{1k}}{2}),$$
$$p_{3k} = f(t_k + \frac{h}{2}, x_k + \frac{hp_{2k}}{2}, y_k + \frac{hq_{2k}}{2}),$$
$$q_{3k} = g(t_k + \frac{h}{2}, x_k + \frac{hp_{2k}}{2}, y_k + \frac{hq_{2k}}{2}),$$
$$p_{4k} = f(t_k + h, x_k + hp_{3k}, y_k + hq_{3k}),$$
$$q_{4k} = g(t_k + h, x_k + hp_{3k}, y_k + hq_{3k}),$$
$$x_{k+1} = x_k + \frac{h}{6}[p_{1k} + 2p_{2k} + 2p_{3k} + p_{4k}],$$

$$y_{k+1} = y_k + \frac{h}{6}[q_{1k} + 2q_{2k} + 2q_{3k} + q_{4k}].$$

The algorithm can be written down in vector form. Consider

$$\vec{R}'(t) = \vec{F}(t, \vec{R}(t)).$$

Suppose that we are at the point (t_k, x_k, y_k). Set $\vec{v}_k = x_k \vec{\imath} + y_k \vec{\jmath}$. We compute the next point $(t_{k+1}, \vec{v}_{k+1})$ in the approximation as follows. Compute

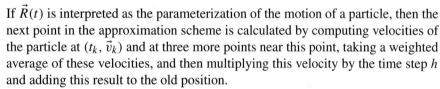

$$\vec{w}_{1k} = \vec{F}(t_k, \vec{v}_k),$$

$$\vec{w}_{2k} = \vec{F}(t_k + \frac{h}{2}, \vec{v}_k + \frac{h\vec{w}_{1k}}{2}),$$

$$\vec{w}_{3k} = \vec{F}(t_k + \frac{h}{2}, \vec{v}_k + \frac{h\vec{w}_{2k}}{2}),$$

$$\vec{w}_{4k} = \vec{F}(t_k + h, \vec{v}_k + h\vec{w}_{3k}).$$

The new point is now given by $t_{k+1} = t_k + h$ and

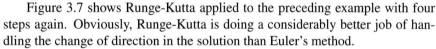

$$\vec{v}_{k+1} = \vec{v}_k + \frac{h}{6}[\vec{w}_{1k} + 2\vec{w}_{2k} + 2\vec{w}_{3k} + \vec{w}_{4k}].$$

If $\vec{R}(t)$ is interpreted as the parameterization of the motion of a particle, then the next point in the approximation scheme is calculated by computing velocities of the particle at $(t_k, \vec{v}_k)$ and at three more points near this point, taking a weighted average of these velocities, and then multiplying this velocity by the time step h and adding this result to the old position.

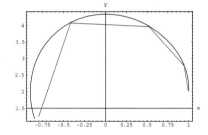

FIGURE 3.7

Figure 3.7 shows Runge-Kutta applied to the preceding example with four steps again. Obviously, Runge-Kutta is doing a considerably better job of handling the change of direction in the solution than Euler's method.

Of course, the Runge-Kutta algorithm can be extended to first-order systems with more than two unknown functions. You are asked to develop the algorithm for the three-function case in the exercises.

3.3.3 Higher-Order Equations

Numerical and graphical methods can be applied to higher-order equations by reducing the equations to a first-order system. However, a word of caution is in order. In using first-order 2×2 system solving packages, you must exercise care so that you do not confuse the variables of the original higher-order equation with those of the 2×2 system. We shall point out the possible confusion in the two examples that follow.

Example 3.3.2 Consider the equation $y'' - t^3 y' - \sin(ty) = 0$ and the initial condition $y(0) = 1$ and $y'(0) = -1$. Set $u = y$ and $v = y'$; then we get the equivalent system

$$u' = v,$$
$$v' = \sin(tu) + t^3 v.$$

We can now apply Runge-Kutta to this system. Here are the approximate values for $u(1)$ generated by the package 2×2Numerical, where the interval is $[0, 2]$ and the step sizes are 0.5, 0.2, 0.1 and 0.05. The values in order are 0.0393632, 0.0383209, 0.0382817, and 0.0382789. Because of the stability of the first four digits, one can be reasonably confident that 0.0382 is correct for the first four places or that 0.0383 is accurate corrected up.

Confusion can arise if your 2×2 system package is set up to accept the field input in the form

$$f(t, x, y) = ?$$
$$g(t, x, y) = ?$$

Now what is x and what is y? Of course, the y of the system is not the y of the original higher-order equation. In the system, $x = u$ and $y = v$. Thus $x(t)$ is the solution to the original differential equation. ■

Example 3.3.3 Consider the equation $y'' - y^2 = t$ with initial condition $y(0) = 1$ and $y'(0) = 0$. The reduction to a first-order system gives

$$u' = v,$$
$$v' = u^2 + t.$$

The 2×2Numerical package yielded for $y(1.5)$ the values 3.61519, 3.61526, and 3.61527 for step sizes of 0.1, 0.05, and 0.01, respectively. We can have reasonable confidence in the value 3.6153. The interval on which the solution was approximated was $[0, 2]$.

Again, if the second dependent variable of a system is y, do not confuse it with the y of the original higher-order equation. ■

EXERCISES 3.3

In Exercises 1–5 apply two steps of Euler's method and the Runge-Kutta method with the step sizes, initial conditions, and intervals provided. Do this by hand, showing your work.

1. The interval is $[1, 5]$ with initial point $(1, 2)$, and the step

size is 2.

$$x' = t + y,$$
$$y' = t^2 - x.$$

2. The interval is $[0, 1]$ with initial point $(1, 1)$, and the step

size is 0.5.

$$x' = 2t + y,$$
$$y' = t + xy.$$

3. The interval is $[0, 1]$ with initial point $(1, 1)$, and the step size is 0.5.

$$x' = t + y^2,$$
$$y' = tx.$$

4. The interval is $[0, 1]$ with initial point $(1, -2)$, and the step size is 0.1.

$$x' = t + x + y,$$
$$y' = t - x.$$

5. The interval is $[2, 3]$ with initial point $(2, 1)$, and the step size is 0.1.

$$x' = xy,$$
$$y' = tx.$$

6. Open package 2×2System and note that it allows both the Euler and Runge-Kutta methods to be used. Apply both methods to the system

$$x' = -y,$$
$$y' = x.$$

What do the true orbits look like and why? Try to get a good approximation to the orbit through $(0, 4)$. Summarize the performance of the Euler and Runge-Kutta methods.

7. Use the package 2×2Numerical on the system

$$x' = -t - y,$$
$$y' = 3t + x,$$

$x(0) = 0$ and $y(0) = 0$. Compute approximations to the solution at $t = 2$. Compare results to the true solution, which is

$$x(t) = -1 - 3t + 3\sin(t) + \cos(t),$$
$$y(t) = 3 - t + \sin(t) - 3\cos(t).$$

8. Use the package 2×2System to draw a field and an Euler method approximation that illustrates the relation between Euler's method and the field. Use this picture to aid in a description of this relation. *Hint:* A larger step size and field lattice may give a better picture.

9. Reduce $y'' + y' + y = 0$ to a first-order system. Let the initial condition at $t = 0$ be $y(0) = 0$ and $y'(0) = 1$. Use the package 2×2Numerical to approximate this solution on $[0, 2]$. Approximate $y(1)$ to four decimal places. What gives you confidence in the accuracy?

10. Reduce $y'' + ty' + \sin(y) = 0$ to a first-order system. Let the initial condition at $t = 0$ be $y(0) = 1$ and $y'(0) = 1$. Use the package 2×2Numerical to approximate this solution on $[0, 2]$. Approximate $y(1.5)$ to four decimal places. What gives you confidence in the accuracy?

11. Consider $y'' + t^2 y' - ty = \sin(t)$ with $y(0) = 2$ and $y'(0) = -1$. Approximate $y(2)$ to two decimal places. What gives you confidence in the accuracy?

12. Reduce $y'' + ty' + 3y = 0$ to a first-order system. Let the initial condition at $t = 1$ be $y(1) = 0$ and $y'(1) = 1$. Use the package 2×2Numerical to approximate this solution on $[1, 3]$. Approximate $y(2)$ to four decimal places. What gives you confidence in the accuracy?

13. Reduce $y'' - 3y' + 2ty = e^t$ to a first-order system. Let the initial condition at $t = 2$ be $y(2) = 1$ and $y'(2) = -1$. Use the package 2×2Numerical to approximate this solution on $[2, 4]$. Approximate $y(3)$ to four decimal places. What gives you confidence in the accuracy?

14. Apply 2×2Numerical to the system

$$x' = y^2,$$
$$y' = x^2$$

on $[0, 4]$ with initial point $(1, 1)$. Explain what happened. Can you draw a diagram of the complete orbit? Why? Why not?

15. Apply 2×2Numerical to the system

$$x' = y^2,$$
$$y' = x^3$$

on $[0, 4]$ with initial point $(1, 1)$. Explain what happened. Can you draw a diagram of the complete orbit? Why? Why not?

16. Reduce $y'' + 10y = 0$ to a first-order system. The solutions are periodic with the same period. Use 2×2Numerical to estimate the period.

17. Write down the Euler algorithm for a first-order system of three equations.

18. Give a geometric description of Euler's method in three dimensions.

19. Write down the Runge-Kutta algorithm for a first-order system of three equations.

20. Show that $\{x(t) = \sqrt{2}\cos(t), y(t) = \sqrt{2}\sin(t)\}$ is a solution to

$$x' = y + 10^t(x^2 + y^2 - 2),$$
$$y' = -x + t^2(x^2 + y^2 - 2).$$

Now run 2 × 2Numerical and try to get good data on the interval [0, 3]. How do you explain this odd behavior?

21. Show that $\{x(t) = \sqrt{2}\cos(t), y(t) = \sqrt{2}\sin(t)\}$ is a solution to

$$x' = y + 4^t(x^2 + y^2 - 2)$$
$$y' = -x + 30^t(x^2 + y^2 - 2).$$

Now run 2 × 2Numerical and try to get good data on the interval [0, 4]. How do you explain this odd behavior?

3.4 SOME QUALITATIVE BEHAVIOR

Throughout this section we shall deal only with 2 × 2 autonomous systems. We shall discuss methods for determining the general behavior of orbits for a 2 × 2 autonomous system.

Throughout this section we shall assume that the functions f and g in the autonomous system

$$x' = f(x, y),$$
$$y' = g(x, y),$$

together with the partial derivatives, are continuous throughout the plane.

The main qualitative question to ask is what the orbits of a given 2 × 2 system look like. A partial answer is given by drawing the field of the system. More information can be obtained by using Runge-Kutta or some other numerical method to draw approximate orbits in the plane. On occasion, we can obtain precise information about the orbits by eliminating the independent variable t as follows:

$$\frac{dy}{dx} = \frac{dy/dt}{dx/dt} = \frac{g(x, y)}{f(x, y)}.$$

Here is a simple example.

Example 3.4.1   From the system

$$x' = y,$$
$$y' = x,$$

we obtain the equation of the orbits

$$\frac{dy}{dx} = \frac{x}{y}.$$

Here the variables separate to give

$$\frac{y^2}{2} = \frac{x^2}{2} + C,$$

and so

$$\frac{y^2}{2} - \frac{x^2}{2} = C.$$

Thus the orbits are hyperbolas.   ∎

If we are lucky, solving the equation $\frac{dy}{dx} = \frac{g(x,y)}{f(x,y)}$ may lead to an equation of the form

$$G(x, y) = C,$$

which the orbits satisfy. It may well be the case that this equation will reveal properties of the orbits that were not apparent in a graphical investigation. In addition, employing a contour plotter to plot the contours (orbits) of $G(x, y) = C$ may prove helpful, but usually this is not as effective as plotting the orbits directly using a differential-equation-solving graphics program.

3.4.1 Critical Points

In Chapter 2 we saw that the critical points of an autonomous equation of the form $y' = f(y)$ played an important role in determining the behavior of solutions. This remains true for 2×2 autonomous systems. We define the notion of a critical point after we make a general point about solutions to autonomous systems.

Consider solutions to the system

$$x' = f(x, y),$$
$$y' = g(x, y),$$

with the initial condition specified at $t = 0$. It will often happen that such a solution is defined for all nonnegative t. If not, then the solution will be defined on an interval of the form $[0, a)$. Moreover, we may take $[0, a)$ to be the largest such (nonnegative) interval on which the solution is defined. If the orbit of such a solution is contained within a circle (the solution is bounded), then it can be shown that the solution can be extended a little further. Figure 3.8 illustrates the situation. This shows a solution whose orbit starts near the origin and stops in the first quadrant in a finite interval of the independent variable. It is not hard to see that we can continue this solution tangentially through the field. This is impossible if $[0, a)$ was already the longest interval on which the solution could be defined. So such a solution cannot be bounded. Indeed, such solutions must go to infinity on the interval $[0, a)$.

There is nothing restrictive in choosing the initial condition at time $t = 0$ for autonomous systems, since we can translate solutions in time at will.

With these remarks in mind, we can now define what is meant by a critical point and what it means for a critical point to be stable.

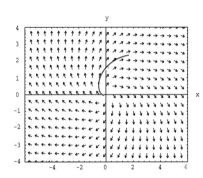

FIGURE 3.8

Definition 3.4.2

1. The point (x_0, y_0) is a critical or equilibrium point of the system

$$x' = f(x, y),$$
$$y' = g(x, y)$$

   if

$$f(x_0, y_0) = 0$$

   and

$$g(x_0, y_0) = 0.$$

2. A critical point (x_0, y_0) is said to be stable if for every disk centered at (x_0, y_0) there is a smaller disk centered at (x_0, y_0) such that all solutions with initial points inside this second disk are defined on $[0, \infty)$ and have their orbits inside the first disk.

3. A stable critical point (x_0, y_0) is said to be asymptotically stable if there is a disk centered at (x_0, y_0) such that each solution with initial point in this disk is defined on $[0, \infty)$ and is such that

$$\lim_{t \to \infty} (x(t), y(t)) = (x_0, y_0). \qquad \bullet$$

In less precise language, a critical point is stable if all solutions starting close enough to the critical point stay close to the critical point. A stable critical point is asymptotically stable if there is a neighborhood of the critical point such that all solutions starting in this neighborhood converge to the critical point.

The graphs of the equations

$$f(x, y) = 0$$

and

$$g(x, y) = 0$$

are called the **nullclines** of the system, and the critical points are the intersection points of the nullclines.

Suppose that (x_0, y_0) is a critical point. Then the constant functions $x(t) = x_0$ and $y(t) = y_0$ form a solution to the system since the derivatives are zero, as is the field vector at the critical point. Thus each critical point is the orbit of the solution through that point.

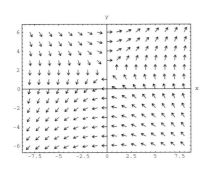

FIGURE 3.9

Example 3.4.3 The system

$$x' = (y - 2),$$
$$y' = x$$

has a critical point at $(0, 2)$. Figure 3.9 strongly suggests that $(0, 2)$ is unstable. The equation of the orbits is

$$\frac{dy}{dx} = \frac{x}{y - 2},$$

and the orbits must satisfy

$$y^2 - 4y - x^2 = C$$

or

$$(y - 2)^2 - x^2 = C'.$$

The orbits are hyperbolas, and one easily sees that, no matter how small a circle is drawn about $(0, 2)$, there are hyperbolic orbits starting inside this circle and leading to infinity. ■

Next we give an example of a stable, but not asymptotically stable critical point.

Example 3.4.4 The system

$$x' = y,$$
$$y' = -36x$$

has a critical point at $(0, 0)$. Solving the orbit equation $dy/dx = -36x/y$ yields

$$x^2 + \frac{y^2}{36} = c.$$

Therefore, the orbits are ellipses centered at the origin. So the origin is stable, but the orbits do not approach the origin as $t \to \infty$, and so the origin is not asymptotically stable. ■

This example also points up the need for the logically complicated $\epsilon - \delta$ definition of stability given previously. In this example the major and minor axes of the ellipses are in the ratio of 6 to 1. It is not possible to find a disk about the origin small enough that orbits with initial conditions in this disk stay in it. Given any disk, we must choose a second disk for the initial conditions one-sixth the radius of the first in order that the corresponding orbits remain in the first disk. Moreover, it is not enough to find just one disk of some radius ϵ

and a corresponding disk of radius δ so that orbits with initial conditions in the δ disk lie in the ϵ disk, for it is not hard to find an example of such a situation in which the orbits are diverging from the origin though contained in the ϵ disk. See Section 3.6 for examples in 2×2 systems. In the single-equation case, it is easy to find a critical point trapped between two close critical points where the inside point is unstable; so while all solutions starting in this interval about the inside critical point stay "close" to the critical point, the critical point is still unstable. Stability must be independent of scale or magnification of the region about the critical point. Therefore, for every ϵ disk (think magnification) we must be able to find the corresponding δ disk so that orbits with initial conditions in the δ disk stay in the ϵ disk.

Generally, solving the orbit equation, as we have in the preceding examples, is hard or impossible. Later we shall provide a test for the stability of critical points that will apply to a fairly wide range of cases. For the time being we must be content with empirical investigation and what we can glean from the orbit equation. Here is another example in the form of an application.

3.4.2 A Competing Species Model

Imagine two species that compete for the same food supply. Let x be the population of one species and y the population of the other. The first species, in the absence of the other, might find its population governed by the differential equation

$$x' = ax(b - x),$$

where a and b are positive constants. For small populations the growth would be approximately exponential, but as the population grows the limited food supply will slow this growth. This type of equation is called a logistic equation. Similar considerations apply to the second species.

When both species compete for the same food supply, each differential equation will have an additional term slowing the exponential growth. The following equations provide a model of the situation.

$$x' = x(a_1 - a_2 x - a_3 y),$$
$$y' = y(b_1 - b_2 x - b_3 y).$$

The nullclines of this system are the x- and y-axes and the lines

$$a_1 - a_2 x - a_3 y = 0$$

and

$$b_1 - b_2 x - b_3 y = 0.$$

How solutions to this system behave depends on the choice of coefficients in the equations. So the behavior depends on the relationship between the two straight lines given. We consider two choices. For each choice we shall plot the field, note the critical points, and draw some orbits.

The first choice is

$$x' = x(4 - x - y),$$
$$y' = y(6 - x - 3y).$$

Figure 3.10 shows the plot.

The critical points are found by solving

$$x(4 - x - y) = 0,$$
$$y(6 - x - 3y) = 0.$$

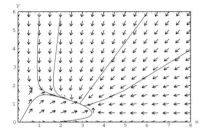

FIGURE 3.10

The critical points are $(0, 0)$, $(0, 2)$, $(4, 0)$, and $(3, 1)$. It appears that all orbits in the first quadrant lead to $(3, 1)$, so it is reasonable to conclude that this point is asymptotically stable. The other points are unstable. For the competing species this means that if some outside influence reduces the populations of the species, but not to zero, then the populations will return to their 3-to-1 balance in due course. The second choice is as follows:

$$x' = x(6 - x - 3y),$$
$$y' = y(4 - x - y).$$

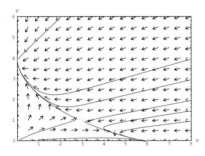

FIGURE 3.11

The critical points are $(0, 0)$, $(0, 4)$, $(6, 0)$, and $(3, 1)$. Figure 3.11 shows that the situation has profoundly changed. The points $(0, 4)$ and $(6, 0)$ are asymptotically stable, and the rest are unstable. Thus the species cannot coexist. Which species survives depends on the initial populations. This model warns us that subtle differences in breeding rates among competing species can lead to completely different environmental dynamics.

EXERCISES 3.4

For the systems in Exercises 1–6, use 2 × 2System to draw the field and several orbits. Find the critical points from the graphical evidence, and decide if they are asymptotically stable, stable, or unstable.

1. $x' = 4y$ and $y' = x$.
2. $x' = 2y$ and $y' = -x$.
3. $x' = y^2$ and $y' = x^2$.
4. $x' = x - y$ and $y' = x + y$.
5. $x' = x(y - 1)$ and $y' = y(x - 2)$.
6. $x' = x(y - 1)(y - 2)$ and $y' = y(x - 3)$.

In Exercises 7–10 use the orbit equation to determine the nature of the orbits. Use this information to decide the stability

of the critical points.

7. $x' = y$ and $y' = -x$.
8. $x' = y$ and $y' = x$.
9. $x' = y^2$ and $y' = x^2$.
10. $x' = y^3$ and $y' = -x^3$.

Study the competing species model in Ecercises 11–14 by finding the critical points and drawing the field and some orbits. Describe the stability of the critical points. Can the species coexist?

11. $x' = x(8 - 2x - y),$
    $y' = y(6 - x - y).$

12. $x' = x(2 - x - y)$,

$y' = y(4 - x - y)$.

13. $x' = x(4 - x - y)$,

$y' = y(2 - x - y)$.

14. $x' = x(4 - x - 4y)$,

$y' = y(4 - x - y)$.

15. What feature of the competing species equations ensures that populations that start out positive cannot become negative in time?

16. Let x be the population of rabbits and y the population of foxes on a certain island. The rabbits have plenty of grass, so, in the absence of foxes, the rabbits would grow according to $x' = ax$. The foxes feed off the rabbits. The number of rabbits killed in a unit of time will be roughly proportional to the product of the populations of rabbits and foxes. Thus $x' = ax - bxy$ seems to be a reasonable description of the rate of change of the rabbit population. In the absence of rabbits, the foxes will die off exponentially. For an individual fox, the food supply for that fox is proportional to the number of rabbits. This adds to this fox's chances of survival and breeding. To apply this to the population of foxes, the addition to the breeding rate will be dxy. Thus $y' = dxy - cy$ is a plausible model of the rate of change of the fox population. These equations are known as the predator–prey or Lotka-Volterra equations. See [1] and [3] for more information on these equations.

Consider the Lotka-Volterra system in the first quadrant only:

$$x' = x(2 - y),$$
$$y' = y(x - 2).$$

(a) Find the critical points.

(b) Use 2 × 2System to investigate this model. What is notable about the orbits?

(c) Are the solutions periodic? If so, is the period dependent on the initial conditions? How does one population vary in relation to the other?

17. In Exercise 16, let us reinterpret the prey as perch and the predator as pike. But now suppose that you have a perch stocking program that adds 2 units of perch per year to the system. Modify the Lotka-Volterra equations in Exercise 16 to accommodate this change, and then answer the following:

(a) Find the critical points.

(b) Use 2 × 2System to investigate this model. Describe the behavior of the solutions.

(c) Can a population ever become negative. Explain!

18. It is not unreasonable to modify the Lotka-Volterra predator–prey equations so that the growth of the prey in the absence of the predators is limited by the food supply. Such an equation would be $x' = x(a - bx)$, where a and b are positive. The carrying capacity is a/b. A typical system with this modification could be

$$x' = x(8 - x - y),$$
$$y' = y(x - 4).$$

Find the critical points, and discuss the nature of orbits in the first quadrant.

19. Suppose that the prey in Exercise 18 are insect pests and the predators are harmless insects to humans. It is decided to use pesticides, but the pesticides kill the helpful predators as well as the prey. The new equations might be

$$x' = x(8 - 1.5x - y),$$
$$y' = y(x - 6).$$

What is the probably unintended consequence of the use of pesticides in this case?

3.5 THE PENDULUM

In this section we shall apply what we have learned about orbits and critical points to the dynamical system that models a pendulum.

A pendulum consists of a mass m on the end of a rigid rod of length l, and the rod is pivoted at the end opposite to the mass. The pivot is placed so that the mass can rotate about the pivot in a vertical plane. Figure 3.12 shows a diagram of the situation.

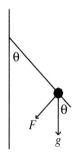

FIGURE 3.12

We assume that the rod is of negligible mass. The external force acting on the pendulum is the force of gravity mg. This force is resolved into two components. One, F, is tangent to the circle of rotation, and the other is in line with the rod. Therefore, the force acting to accelerate the mass is F. Let θ be the angular displacement measured positively counterclockwise; then

$$F = -mg\sin(\theta).$$

The linear velocity of the mass is found as follows. The distance Δs traveled along the circle due to a change $\Delta\theta$ in the angle is

$$\Delta s = l\Delta\theta.$$

Thus the velocity v is

$$v = \frac{ds}{dt} = l\frac{d\theta}{dt}.$$

The acceleration is the derivative of this velocity, so Newton's second law gives

$$m\frac{dv}{dt} = F = -mg\sin(\theta).$$

The following first-order system models the pendulum.

$$\theta' = \frac{v}{l},$$
$$v' = -g\sin(\theta).$$

For simplicity, let $l = 1$ and choose time units so that $g = 1$. We have the system

$$\theta' = v,$$
$$v' = -\sin(\theta).$$

The critical points of this system are $(\pi k, 0)$, where k is any integer. If k is even, then the critical point is stable. This is easy to see from a physical point of view, because these are the points for which the pendulum is pointing straight down and has zero velocity. Small displacements from this will only cause a small oscillation. On the other hand, if k is odd, then the pendulum is pointing straight up and has zero velocity. The smallest disturbance here could cause the pendulum to swing down.

Let us now solve the orbit equation. The equation is

$$\frac{d\theta}{dv} = \frac{v}{-\sin(\theta)},$$

and the solution is

$$\cos(\theta) = \frac{v^2}{2} + c.$$

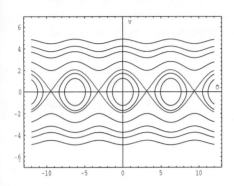

FIGURE 3.13

Notice that c is the cosine of the angular displacement of the pendulum when the velocity is zero.

Figure 3.13 shows a diagram of some of these orbits. Notice that there are some closed orbits indicating periodic solutions and some orbits that are not closed. Again, the physical interpretation is clear. The closed orbits centered on $(0, 0)$ correspond to oscillations that pass through the angle zero and do not have enough energy to go "over the top." The other groups of closed orbits are entirely similar; we need only imagine that the pendulum has been rotated around a few times before it was set oscillating. The nonclosed orbits correspond to situations in which the system has been given enough energy to go over the top. There is no friction in this system, and so the pendulum continues rotating in the same direction, but with a variation in its velocity. Finally, there are those orbits that seem to cross on the θ-axis. Of course, they do not cross. These orbits correspond to the cases where the pendulum is given just enough energy to reach the top and no more. These orbits require infinite time to reach the top of the swing.

Let us now focus on the periodic orbits. With a little manipulation we shall be able to find an integral expression for the period of such an orbit. Consider a closed orbit about the origin. The equation of the orbit is

$$\cos(\theta) = \frac{v^2}{2} + \cos(\alpha),$$

where $0 < \alpha < \pi$ and α is the initial displacement of the pendulum with velocity equal to zero. Physically, it is reasonable to assume that the time taken to traverse the upper half of the orbit is the same as that required to traverse the lower half. Indeed, the only difference is between the motion starting with the pendulum pulled to the right or the left. Similarly, the time required to traverse the portion of the orbit in the first quadrant is the same as for the second quadrant. Thus the time taken to traverse the portion of the orbit in the first quadrant is one-fourth of the period. For this portion, $0 \leq \theta \leq \alpha$. We shall focus on this piece of the orbit.

Now

$$\frac{d\theta}{dt} = v = \sqrt{2(\cos(\theta) - \cos(\alpha))}.$$

We take the positive square root because the piece of the orbit considered is above the θ axis. Therefore,

$$\frac{dt}{d\theta} = \frac{1}{\sqrt{2(\cos(\theta) - \cos(\alpha))}}.$$

Integrating this with respect to θ from 0 to α will give us the time to traverse this quarter of an orbit. Thus the period is

$$4 \int_0^\alpha \frac{1}{\sqrt{2(\cos(\theta) - \cos(\alpha))}} \, d\theta.$$

This is actually an improper integral, but it does converge for $0 < \alpha < \pi$. However, there is no easy way to evaluate this integral, so to find the period of a particular orbit, we need to employ numerical methods. For $\alpha = 1$ the period is approximately 6.68, and for $\alpha = 3$ the period is approximately 16.16. Unlike the simple mass–spring oscillator, the periods here depend on the initial conditions. This might be a slight surprise, but a little more reflection makes it obvious. If the initial angle α is very close to π, it is going to take some time to accelerate away from the "straight up" position. This will take as long as we like if we choose α close enough to π.

We used physical intuition to argue that the times required to traverse the upper and lower halves of a periodic orbit are the same. This actually follows from our integral formula. The time to traverse the top half is

$$\int_{-\alpha}^{\alpha} \frac{1}{\sqrt{2(\cos(\theta) - \cos(\alpha))}}\, d\theta,$$

and for the lower half it is

$$\int_{\alpha}^{-\alpha} \frac{-1}{\sqrt{2(\cos(\theta) - \cos(\alpha))}}\, d\theta.$$

But these integrals are the same.

In Chapter 7 we shall study the driven pendulum, and see that the dependence of the period on the amplitude of the oscillation for a periodically driven pendulum can lead to very interesting behavior.

EXERCISES 3.5

All exercises refer to the system

$$\theta' = v,$$
$$v' = -\sin(\theta).$$

1. Using the given system:
   (a) Use the package 2 × 2System to graph the field of the above system.
   (b) Draw orbits for the initial conditions $(1, 0)$, $(2, 0)$, $(3, 0)$, $(8, 0)$, and $(0, 3)$.
   (c) Describe what is happening to the pendulum with the last two initial conditions.

2. Use the package 2 × 2System to estimate the period of the orbits with initial conditions $(2, 0)$ and $(3.14, 0)$. *Hint:* Experiment with the time range until you just get closure. What statement in the text does this information support?

3. Use the package 2 × 2Numerical to decide what happens to the periods as the initial conditions approach $(0, 0)$.

Make a table of four initial conditions and corresponding periods.

4. Use the package 2 × 2Numerical to approximate the periods calculated in the text. The approximation by Runge-Kutta is not nearly as good as the numerical integration method used in the text.

5. Use the integral formula to show that the time to traverse the upper half-orbit from $-\alpha$ to 0 is the same as from 0 to α.

6. Use the package ContourPlot to reproduce some of the orbits from the orbit equation. Make sure that some are closed and some are not.

7. Use the same procedure as is used in the text to compute the periods of the orbits of the system $x' = y$ and $y' = -x$.

8. Compare Exercises 3 and 7 and explain the agreement. *Hint:* What do you know about $\sin(x)$ and x if x is small?

3.6 LIMIT CYCLES

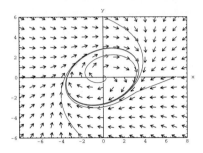

FIGURE 3.14

Consider the field and orbits shown in Figure 3.14. Orbits starting close to the origin move outward, and orbits starting far from the origin move in. All orbits except the critical point at the origin seem to be asymptotic to an elliptically shaped orbit. This is the case, and this elliptical closed periodic orbit is called a **limit cycle**.

Notice that slight perturbations from the limit cycle will return to it. Thus a limit cycle can be thought of as a generalization of the idea of an asymptotically stable critical point to periodic orbits. Periodic orbits can be stable and unstable in much the same way that critical points can be stable and unstable. For instance, a given circular orbit of the system

$$x' = y,$$
$$y' = -x$$

can be regarded as a stable orbit that is not asymptotically stable because orbits with initial conditions close to the given orbit remain close. We will see examples of unstable closed orbits shortly.

What causes limit cycles? The answer to this will have to be intuitive and informal, because a proof is beyond the scope of this text. In essence, limit cycles occur when nonperiodic orbits of solutions are trapped in a closed and bounded region. A region is closed and bounded provided it can be contained in a circle of suitable radius and the region contains all its boundary points.

Suppose that the orbit of a solution is contained in a bounded and closed set. It is a fact that such solutions are defined on $[0, \infty)$. There must be a point (perhaps many) that the solution returns to as close as we please for successive instances of time. More precisely, there must be a point P such that for any $\epsilon > 0$ there are infinitely many values of t such that the solution $(x(t), y(t))$ is inside the circle centered at P and of radius ϵ. The point P might be an asymptotically stable critical point. Indeed, an asymptotically stable critical point can be thought of as the simplest of limit cycles.

Suppose now that there are no critical points in our bounded and closed set. If this is the case, the field vectors will all be longer than a certain positive minimum value. This being the case, the length of the orbit must be infinite or the orbit must be closed. If the orbit is not closed, then, in effect, we must lay out an infinite length of string on the floor of a closed room. Could you lay it out like the graph of $y = \sin(1/x)$ as x approaches zero? No! This is because the field is continuous and cannot change direction like that. You will have to lay out the string in some kind of a spiral. Can the string spiral in to a single point? No! For if it did, the point would have to be a critical point. It would appear that the string must spiral in or out asymptotically to some closed orbit that is not a point. Thus, if an orbit in this closed and bounded region is not a closed orbit, then it must be asymptotic to a closed orbit. Such limiting closed orbits are called **limit cycles**.

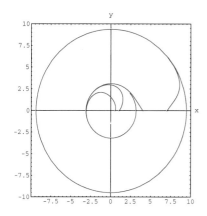

FIGURE 3.15

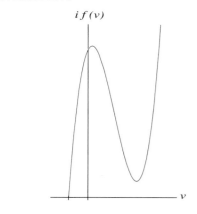

FIGURE 3.16

FIGURE 3.17

It is quite possible to have several limit cycles. Figure 3.15 illustrates this. The system is

$$x' = -y + x \sin(\sqrt{x^2 + y^2}),$$
$$y' = x + y \sin(\sqrt{x^2 + y^2}).$$

This system has closed orbits that are circles centered at the origin and of radii π, 2π, 3π, and so on. However, experiment indicates that only the circles that have radii that are odd multiples of π are limit cycles in the sense that they are the asymptotic limit of other orbits. The circles of radius $2k\pi$ are unstable periodic orbits, and they divide the regions between the limit cycles into two rings. Initial conditions in the smaller ring generate orbits that are asymptotic to the inner limit cycle, and the initial conditions in the outer ring generate orbits that are asymptotic to the outer limit cycle. This is not hard to see from the field equations, and a discussion of this is left to the exercises.

A Tunnel Diode Oscillator

As an application of limit cycles, we shall show how an alternating current can be generated from a direct current source using a tunnel diode.

First recall the basics of circuit analysis. The electrical properties of a circuit can be lumped into three types of circuit elements. They are capacitors, resistors, and inductors. The voltage across a capacitor of capacitance C is given by $V = q/C$, where q is the electric charge on the capacitor. The voltage across a resistor of resistance R is given by $V = iR$, where $i = q'$ is the current flowing through the resistor. The voltage across an inductor of inductance L is given by $V = i'L$, where i' is the rate of change of the current in the inductor. Finally, recall that the sum of the voltage drops around a closed loop must equal the electromotive force in the loop, and the sum of the currents at a junction must be zero.

A tunnel diode is a two-terminal solid-state device such that the current through the device as a function of the voltage across the terminals has the form shown in Figure 3.16. Notice that on a portion of the graph an increase in voltage produces a drop in current. In this region the resistance is negative, and this is the key to the oscillation of the schematic circuit depicted in Figure 3.17.

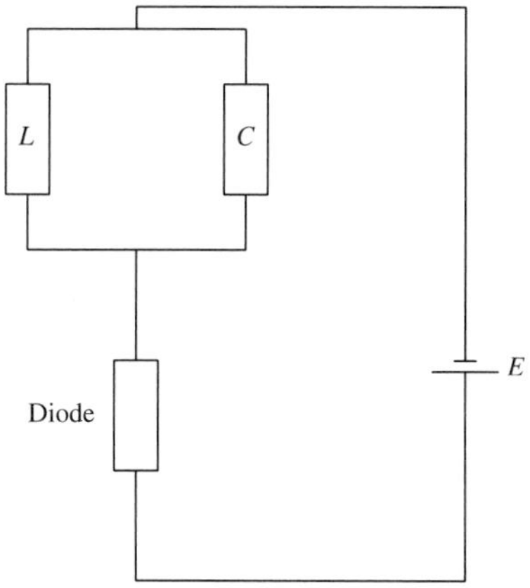

To write down the circuit equations, we must orient some loops. We orient the loop from the battery through the diode and inductor and back to the battery clockwise. We do the same for the simple loop containing the inductor and capacitor.

Let i_1 be the oriented current through the capacitor, i_2 the oriented current through the inductor, and i the oriented current through the battery and diode. Let v be the voltage across the diode.

Since the sum of the currents at a junction must be zero, we have

$$i_2 = i_1 + i.$$

Adding voltage drops around the oriented loops gives

$$L(i_1' + i') + v = E$$

and

$$L(i_1' + i') + q/C = 0,$$

where q is the charge on the capacitor. So subtracting the equations gives

$$v = \frac{q}{C} + E,$$

and since $q' = i_1$ we have

$$i_1 = Cv' \qquad \text{and} \qquad i_1' = Cv''.$$

Now $i = f(v)$, and so

$$i' = f'(v)v'.$$

Therefore,

$$L(Cv'' + f'(v)v') + v = E,$$

and so

$$LCv'' + Lf'(v)v' + v = E.$$

This is a second-order nonlinear equation in v, and it is similar in form to the equation of motion of a mass on a spring with friction introduced in Chapter 1,

$$mx'' + cx' + kx = 0.$$

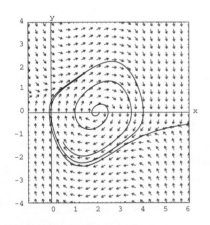

FIGURE 3.18

The two differences are that $E \neq 0$ and the term $Lf'(v)$ is not constant nor even positive. However, we can still use the analogy to the mass–spring system to guess at the behavior of the diode circuit. The introduction of E only shifts the critical point, and it does not affect the behavior materially. For the mass–spring system with friction, the potential energy stored in the spring and the kinetic energy of the mass are constantly being dissipated by the friction. Thus the motion of the mass decays away to zero as time progresses. If we can imagine a mass–spring system with a negative friction, then energy would be put into the system, and the motion would become more extreme with time. For the diode, E is set so that if v is close to E the term $Lf'(v)$ is negative, so the sytem should absorb "energy" and the motion should grow. But as v grows the system switches to dissipating energy, so the system might well be expected to settle down to oscillating between these two poles.

To get a good view of the behavior, consider the reduction of the equation to a first-order system by setting $x = v$ and $y = v'$. We have

$$x' = y,$$

$$y' = \frac{E - x}{LC} - \frac{1}{C}f'(x)y.$$

Figure 3.18 shows the field of an example of this type of system. Notice how the motion starting near $(2, 0)$ builds up as it absorbs energy while the resistance is predominantly negative, and notice how the motion starting at $(6, 6)$ decays toward the limit cycle because the resistance is mostly positive for this motion.

Return to the graph of f. It is roughly cubic, and so its derivative will be approximately quadratic. Suppose that the most negative resistance occurs at 0.15 volt; then f' may reasonably be approximated by something like

$$f'(x) = 0.8(x - 0.15)^2 - 0.023.$$

Figures 3.19 and 3.20 show an orbit converging on the limit cycle and the plot of $x(t) = v(t)$ against time. The nearly periodic nature of the voltage across the diode is very clear here. The circuit values were $L = 0.001$ henry, $C = 0.1 \times 10^{-6}$ farad, and $E = 0.15$ volt.

Figure 3.20 is the graph of the voltage across the diode as a function of time. The period appears to be about 0.00008 second. So the frequency is about $12{,}500$ hertz.

It is very important to understand the difference between the behavior of this circuit and that of a simple circuit composed of a capacitor and inductor. Both oscillate, but if there is any resistance in the LC circuit the oscillation cannot be sustained; it dies away to nothing. The tunnel diode, on the other hand, can have a small amount of resistance in the circuit and sustain oscillation. The tunnel diode can be started with any initial condition, and it will settle into its limit cycle oscillation quickly. In fact, even though $(0.15, 0)$ is a critical point of the diode system, the physical system will go into oscillation. This is because the critical point is unstable, and the thermal agitation of the electrons in the circuit is enough to get things started.

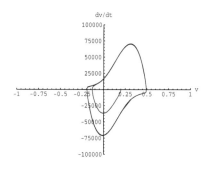

FIGURE 3.19

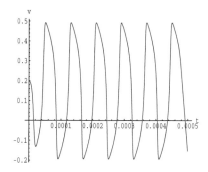

FIGURE 3.20

EXERCISES 3.6

Use the package $2 \times 2System$ *to investigate the periodic orbits of the systems in Exercises 1–3. Decide which orbits are limit cycles. What is the approximate period of each limit cycle? Find all critical points.*

1. $x' = -y + x(4 - x^2 - y^2)$
   $y' = x + y(4 - x^2 - y^2)$

2. $x' = -2y + x(x^2 + y^2 - 3\sqrt{x^2 + y^2} + 2)$
   $y' = 2x + y(x^2 + y^2 - 3\sqrt{x^2 + y^2} + 2)$

3. $x' = y$
   $y' = (2 - x) - 0.5[(x - 2)^2 - 1]y$

4. Is there any relationship between limit cycles and critical points? Make a conjecture based on the preceding examples.

5. Explain the behavior near each of the closed orbits of the system

   $$x' = -y + x\sin(\sqrt{x^2 + y^2}),$$
   $$y' = x + y\sin(\sqrt{x^2 + y^2})$$

   in terms of the directions that the field vectors point near the closed orbits. Use the algebraic expression for the field to justify your statements.

6. Use $2 \times 2System$ to obtain the graphics in the text that

go with the tunnel diode. Note that the period of the solutions is very short, so you will need a very small step size.

7. The equation $y'' - c(1 - y^2)y' + y = 0$, where c is a positive constant, is called van der Pol's equation. It arose in connection with the development of oscillators in the early days of radio. Reduce the equation to a first-order system, and use 2 × 2System to investigate its limit cycle. Draw a typical cycle, and draw a typical periodic solution to van der Pol's equation. Does the period depend on c?

8. Use the package 2 × 2System to investigate the limit cycles of the system

$$x' = y,$$
$$y' = a(5 - x) - b[(x - 5)^2 - 2]y$$

for various choices of a and b. Is the period independent

of a or b? Set $a = 1$. What happens as b approaches zero? Why is this sensible?

9. Draw the field for the system

$$x' = y,$$
$$y' = -x + 3(1 - x^2)y.$$

Draw a closed polygonal curve around the origin so that each field vector on the curve points out. Draw a closed polygonal curve around the preceding curve so that each field vector on the curve points in. Why must orbits stay between the two curves? There is no critical point between the two curves. What do you conclude from this? *Hint:* Drawing the curves takes a few tries to get the hang of it. Changing scales and drawing a reference orbit may help. Print out the field and use a straightedge.

SUPPLEMENTARY EXERCISES FOR CHAPTER 3

1. Use a change to polar coordinates to explain the limit cycles of the system

$$x' = -y + x \sin(\sqrt{x^2 + y^2}),$$
$$y' = x + y \sin(\sqrt{x^2 + y^2}).$$

2. **Hamiltonian Systems**. Certain autonomous systems allow us to find the orbits relatively easily. The system

$$x' = f(x, y),$$
$$y' = g(x, y)$$

is said to be a Hamiltonian system if there is a function $H(x, y)$ such that
$\partial H(x, y)/\partial y = f(x, y)$ and $\partial H(x, y)/\partial x = -g(x, y)$.
We call H the Hamiltonian of the system. A general hint for the problems that follow is to return to exact equations.

(a) Show that the Hamiltonian is constant on the orbits of the system. *Hint:* Differentiate $H(x(t), y(t))$ with respect to t.

(b) How do you test a system to see if it is Hamiltonian?

(c) If a system is Hamiltonian, how do you find the Hamiltonian?

(d) Find the Hamiltonian of the system $x' = y$ and $y' = -x$. What does this tell you about the orbits?

(e) Is the following system Hamiltonian? If so, find the Hamiltonian and plot the level curves.

$$x' = x + y,$$
$$y' = x^2 - y.$$

(f) Show that the pendulum problem is Hamiltonian and find the Hamiltonian.

3. Consider two negatively equally charged fixed spheres centered at -10 and 10 on the x-axis. A third positively charged sphere is free to move on the x-axis in between, but it is constrained by springs that produce a restoring force of $-kx$, where x is the displacement from the origin. Charged spheres produce a force between them of cq_1q_2/r^2, where r is the distance between the centers. Let us assume that the force between one of the fixed spheres and the movable sphere is $200/r^2$. Assume that the spring constant k is 1, and the mass of the movable sphere is also 1.

(a) Using $F = ma$, write the second order differential equation that the displacement x must satisfy.

(b) Convert to a system.

(c) Study the field and solutions. Experiment with various initial conditions. Is there something notable here that is to be expected from the physics?

(d) Make a careful report of your discoveries.

CHAPTER 4

HIGHER-ORDER LINEAR EQUATIONS

4.1 INTRODUCTION

This chapter is devoted primarily to analytic methods for solving higher-order linear differential equations. Unless the equation is linear there is little chance of finding an analytic solution. If necessary, we can use numerical methods on nonlinear and linear equations by reducing them to first-order systems. Here is the definition of a linear differential equation.

Definition 4.1.1

An nth-order linear differential equation is a differential equation of the form

$$a_n(t)y^{(n)} + a_{n-1}(t)y^{(n-1)} + \cdots + a_1(t)y' + a_0(t)y = b(t),$$

where $a_n(t) \neq 0$ for some t. We call the functions $a_i(t)$ the coefficients of the equation. If the coefficients are constant, we say that the equation is a constant-coefficient equation. If b is the zero function, we say that the equation is homogeneous. ●

For example the equation

$$2y^{(3)} - 5y'' + 3y = 0$$

is a third-order constant-coefficient homogeneous linear differential equation.

First we shall use the existence and uniqueness theorem for solutions to systems to establish the corresponding theorem for higher-order linear equations.

Then a strategy for solving higher-order equations will be laid out. We shall then apply this strategy to constant-coefficient homogeneous equations. Following this, we shall show how nonhomogeneous constant-coefficient equations can be solved, and finally how general nonhomogeneous linear equations are solved provided the homogeneous equation has been solved. The solution of homogeneous variable-coefficient equations will be delayed until a later chapter.

4.2   A STRATEGY FOR SOLVING LINEAR HOMOGENEOUS EQUATIONS

This section uses some results from the solution of linear systems of equations. In particular, Cramer's rule and determinants will be used. If you are a little rusty on these topics, it is recommended that you read Sections A.1 and A.2 of Appendix A.

The strategy for solving higher-order linear homogeneous equations to be described in this section will be explained using second-order equations. You will see that the ideas extend to higher orders with ease. Therefore, the equation we shall consider has the form

$$a_2(t)y'' + a_1(t)y' + a_0(t)y = 0.$$

The strategy we shall use to solve this equation is obtained by considering the reduction of this equation to a first-order system. The reduction with $u_1 = y$ and $u_2 = y'$ is

$$u_1' = u_2,$$
$$u_2' = -\frac{a_0(t)}{a_2(t)}u_1 - \frac{a_1(t)}{a_2(t)}u_2.$$

Clearly, $a_2(t)$ had better not be zero. Indeed, if $a_2(t)$ is zero at some value t_0 then this point is called a **singular point** of the equation. Solutions near singular points have to be approached in a different way from the strategy to be developed here, so we shall assume that our equation has the form

$$y'' + a_1(t)y' + a_0(t)y = 0.$$

The system then becomes

$$u_1' = u_2$$
$$u_2' = -a_0(t)u_1 - a_1(t)u_2.$$

Recall that if $y(t)$ is a solution of the second-order equation then $u_1(t) = y(t)$ and $u_2(t) = y'(t)$ is a solution to the system, and if $\{u_1(t), u_2(t)\}$ is a solution to the system, then $y(t) = u_1(t)$ is a solution to the second-order equation.

Suppose that $a_0(t)$ and $a_1(t)$ are continuous functions on some interval $[a, b]$; then the functions on the right-hand side of the system satisfy the existence and uniqueness theorem hypotheses on any block with time interval $[a, b]$. So for any point t_0 in (a, b) and any point (y_0, y_1) in the plane, there is exactly one solution passing through (y_0, y_1) at $t = t_0$. It can be shown that this solution can be defined on the whole interval (a, b). So if $y(t) = u_1(t)$, then $y(t)$ satisfies the equation

$$y'' + a_1(t)y' + a_0(t)y = 0$$

and the conditions $y(t_0) = y_0$ and $y'(t_0) = y_1$.

We shall refer to the problem of solving

$$y'' + a_1(t)y' + a_0(t)y = 0$$

together with the conditions $y(t_0) = y_0$ and $y'(t_0) = y_1$ as an **initial-value problem**.

If $\phi(t)$ is a solution to the initial-value problem

$$y'' + a_1(t)y' + a_0(t)y = 0$$

and $\phi(t_0) = y_0$, and $\phi'(t_0) = y_1$, then $\{u_1 = \phi(t), u_2 = \phi'(t)\}$ satisfy the system, and the orbit passes through the point (y_0, y_1). By uniqueness for systems, this solution is the only one. So there is exactly one solution to

$$y'' + a_1(t)y' + a_0(t)y = 0$$

satisfying the conditions $y(t_0) = y_0$ and $y'(t_0) = y_1$.

We highlight this for equations of any order in a theorem.

Theorem 4.2.1

Let the coefficient functions $a_i(t)$ in the nth-order equation

$$y^{(n)} + a_{n-1}(t)y^{(n-1)} + \cdots + a_1(t)y' + a_0(t)y = 0$$

be continuous on the interval $[a, b]$. Then there is exactly one solution to this equation that satisfies the initial condition $y(t_0) = y_0, y'(t_0) = y_1, \ldots, y^{(n-1)}(t_0) = y_{n-1}$, and $t_0 \in (a, b)$. Moreover, the solution is defined on (a, b).   ●

Before continuing, we stop to discuss the very important notion of linearity. The expression

$$L[y(t)] = y''(t) + a_1(t)y'(t) + a_0(t)y(t)$$

can be thought of as describing a machine for which, if the function $y(t)$ is input, then $L[y(t)]$, which is the function on the right, is output. The name of this machine is L. We call L an **operator**. It is itself a function, but the elements in the domain of L are functions, and the values of L are also functions.

The operator L has two very important properties. If c is any constant, then for a function $\psi(t)$

$$L[c\psi(t)] = c\psi''(t) + a_1(t)c\psi'(t) + a_0(t)c\psi(t) = cL[\psi(t)],$$

and for two functions

$$
\begin{aligned}
L[\psi_1(t) + \psi_2(t)] &= (\psi_1(t) + \psi_2(t))'' \\
&\quad + a_1(t)(\psi_1(t) + \psi_2(t))' + a_0(t)(\psi_1(t) + \psi_2(t)) \\
&= L[\psi_1(t)] + L[\psi_2(t)].
\end{aligned}
$$

If an operator L has these two properties, we say that it is **linear**. What makes the equation

$$a_n(t)y^{(n)} + a_{n-1}(t)y^{(n-1)} + \cdots + a_1(t)y' + a_0(t)y = b(t)$$

linear is that the left-hand side,

$$L[y] = a_n(t)y^{(n)} + a_{n-1}(t)y^{(n-1)} + \cdots + a_1(t)y' + a_0(t)y,$$

defines a linear operator on functions y.

Linearity has a very important consequence for linear homogeneous equations. If $\phi_1(t)$ and $\phi_2(t)$ are solutions of the equation

$$y''(t) + a_1(t)y'(t) + a_0(t)y(t) = 0,$$

then $L[\phi_1(t)] = 0$ and $L[\phi_2(t)] = 0$. So if c_1 and c_2 are any two numbers, then

$$L[c_1\phi_1(t) + c_2\phi_2(t)] = c_1 L[\phi_1(t)] + c_2 L[\phi_2(t)] = 0$$

by linearity. The expression

$$c_1\phi_1(t) + c_2\phi_2(t)$$

is called a **linear combination** of the functions $\phi_1(t)$ and $\phi_2(t)$. So any linear combination of two solutions to the homogeneous equation is also a solution of the equation. This extends immediately to any number of solutions.

The key idea here is that, for a second-order homogeneous equation, if we find two solutions of the "right type," then all other solutions are linear combinations of these two. As you may have guessed, for a third-order equation we need three solutions of the right type, and so on. Do such right type solutions exist? Yes!

To see this, consider Theorem 4.2.1 in the second-order case again. The theorem guarantees unique solutions where the initial conditions are $\{1, 0\}$ and $\{0, 1\}$. Let the solutions with these initial conditions at $t = t_0$ be $\phi_1(t)$ and $\phi_2(t)$, respectively. Then, if we choose the constants c_1 and c_2 to be y_0 and y_1, respectively,

$$\psi(t) = c_1\phi_1(t) + c_2\phi_2(t)$$

solves the homogeneous equation by linearity, and it solves the initial condition because

$$\psi(t_0) = c_1\phi_1(t_0) + c_2\phi_2(t_0) = c_1 1 + c_2 0 = y_0$$

and

$$\psi'(t_0) = c_1\phi_1'(t_0) + c_2\phi_2'(t_0) = c_1 0 + c_2 1 = y_1.$$

What makes this work is the fact that we can solve the equations

$$c_1\phi_1(t_0) + c_2\phi_2(t_0) = y_0,$$
$$c_1\phi_1'(t_0) + c_2\phi_2'(t_0) = y_1.$$

So all we need are two solutions to the homogeneous equation, name them $\phi_1(t)$ and $\phi_2(t)$ again, such that the preceding equations can be solved. But these equations will always be solvable by Cramer's rule, if the following determinant is not zero:

$$\det \begin{bmatrix} \phi_1(t_0) & \phi_2(t_0) \\ \phi_1'(t_0) & \phi_2'(t_0) \end{bmatrix}.$$

A fact that is established in the exercises is that this determinant is either identically zero on the interval (a, b) or never zero. So if it is not zero, then every solution for every initial condition for any t_0 in (a, b) is a linear combination,

$$\psi(t) = c_1\phi_1(t) + c_2\phi_2(t),$$

of these two solutions.

Definition 4.2.2

A set of solutions $\{\phi_1(t), \phi_2(t)\}$ to the homogeneous equation

$$y''(t) + a_1(t)y'(t) + a_0(t)y(t) = 0$$

is called a **fundamental set** if

$$W(t) = \det \begin{bmatrix} \phi_1(t) & \phi_2(t) \\ \phi_1'(t) & \phi_2'(t) \end{bmatrix} \neq 0$$

for all t in the interval (a, b) on which the coefficient functions are continuous. The determinant $W(t)$ is called the Wronskian of the set of solutions.   ●

Here is an example.

Example 4.2.3 We show that $\{e^{-t}, e^{-2t}\}$ is a set of solutions to

$$y'' + 3y' + 2y = 0.$$

Indeed, if $y = e^{-t}$, then

$$y'' + 3y' + 2y = e^{-t} + 3(-e^{-t}) + 2e^{-t} = 0,$$

and if $y = e^{-2t}$, then

$$y'' + 3y' + 2y = 4e^{-2t} - 6e^{-2t} + 2e^{-2t} = 0.$$

Now

$$\det \begin{bmatrix} e^{-t} & e^{-2t} \\ -e^{-t} & -2e^{-2t} \end{bmatrix} = -e^{-3t} \neq 0.$$

So $\{e^{-t}, e^{-2t}\}$ is a fundamental set of solutions, and so every solution is of the form

$$\psi(t) = c_1 e^{-t} + c_2 e^{-2t}.$$

In particular, if we want the unique solution with $\psi(0) = 1$ and $\psi'(0) = 2$, we have the equations

$$c_1 + c_2 = 1,$$
$$-c_1 - 2c_2 = 2.$$

Solving, we get $c_1 = 4$ and $c_2 = -3$. Therefore, the unique solution to this initial-value problem is

$$\psi(t) = 4e^{-t} - 3e^{-2t}.$$

Let us finish this example by seeing the linearity of the equation at work.

$$L[4e^{-t} - 3e^{-2t}] = (4e^{-t} - 3e^{-2t})'' + 3(4e^{-t} - 3e^{-2t})' + 2(4e^{-t} - 3e^{-2t})$$
$$= 4(e^{-t} - 3e^{-t} + 2e^{-t}) - 3(4e^{-2t} + 3(-2)e^{-2t} + 2e^{-2t})$$
$$= 4L[e^{-t}] - 3L[e^{-2t}] = 0 + 0 = 0. \qquad \blacksquare$$

We can summarize by saying that to find all solutions to the equation

$$y^{(n)} + a_{n-1}(t)y^{(n-1)} + \cdots + a_1(t)y' + a_0(t)y = 0$$

we need only find a fundamental set of n solutions, and then every solution is a linear combination of these.

4.2.1 Linear Independence

Fundamental sets of solutions can be described in a slightly different way that makes contact with linear algebra. Let $\{\phi_1, \phi_2, \dots, \phi_n\}$ be a fundamental set of n solutions on (a, b) to the nth-order linear equation

$$y^{(n)} + a_{n-1}(t)y^{(n-1)} + \cdots + a_1(t)y' + a_0(t)y = 0.$$

If we differentiate the equation

$$c_1\phi_1(t) + \cdots + c_n\phi_n(t) = 0$$

$n - 1$ times, we get the set of equations

$$c_1\phi_1(t) + \cdots + c_n\phi_n(t) = 0,$$
$$c_1\phi_1'(t) + \cdots + c_n\phi_n'(t) = 0,$$
$$\vdots$$
$$c_1\phi_1^{(n-1)}(t) + \cdots + c_n\phi_n^{(n-1)}(t) = 0.$$

This set of equations has only the trivial solution $c_1 = \dots c_n = 0$, since the set of solutions is fundamental, and therefore the determinant of this system is nonzero. So if a set of solutions is fundamental, then the only linear combination of these functions that is identically zero on (a, b) is the trivial one.

If a set of solutions has the property that the only linear combination of them that is identically zero is the trivial one, it is natural to ask if the set is fundamental Yes!

We shall prove this by contradiction. That is, we shall suppose that we have a set of solutions $\{\phi_1(x), \dots, \phi_n(x)\}$ with the property that the only linear combination of the solutions that is identically zero is the trivial one, and we shall suppose that this set of solutions has a Wronskian that is zero at some point $t_0 \in (a, b)$. From this we will derive a contradiction. Thus we will have shown that such a set of solutions must be fundamental. The determinant of the equations

$$c_1\phi_1(t_0) + \cdots + c_n\phi_n(t_0) = 0,$$
$$c_1\phi_1'(t_0) + \cdots + c_n\phi_n'(t_0) = 0,$$
$$\vdots$$
$$c_1\phi_1^{(n-1)}(t_0) + \cdots + c_n\phi_n^{(n-1)}(t_0) = 0$$

is the Wronskian, which is assumed to be zero. Therefore, the equations have a nontrivial solution. Assume $\{c_1, c_2, \dots, c_n\}$ is a nontrivial solution. Now set

$$\psi(t) = c_1\phi_1(t) + \cdots + c_n\phi_n(t).$$

This satisfies the equation

$$y^{(n)} + a_{n-1}(t)y^{(n-1)} + \cdots + a_1(t)y' + a_0(t)y = 0$$

and the initial condition $\psi(t_0) = 0$, $\psi'(t_0) = 0$, $\ldots$, and $\psi^{(n-1)}(t_0) = 0$. By uniqueness, $\psi(t) \equiv 0$. This contradicts our assumption that the only linear combination of the set of solutions that is identically zero is the trivial one. Thus the set must be fundamental.

This leads to the following definition.

Definition 4.2.4

A set of functions $\{\phi_1, \phi_2, \ldots, \phi_n\}$ is linearly independent on (a, b) if

$$c_1\phi_1(t) + \cdots + c_n\phi_n(t) = 0$$

for all t in (a, b) implies that $c_1 = c_2 = \cdots = c_n = 0$. ●

The next example shows two ways to test for linear independence.

Example 4.2.5 We show that the set $\{e^t, \sin(t)\}$ is linearly independent on the real line in two ways. In both approaches we start by assuming that

$$c_1 e^t + c_2 \sin(t) = 0$$

on the real line. We then must show that $c_1 = c_2 = 0$. Setting $t = 0$ and $t = \pi/2$ gives $c_1 = 0$ and $c_2 = 0$ respectively. Alternatively, differentiate to get the system

$$c_1 e^t + c_2 \sin(t) = 0,$$
$$c_1 e^t + c_2 \cos(t) = 0.$$

Choose $t = 0$, and solve. ■

In the following example we consider what must be done to show that a set of functions is not linearly independent on an interval.

Example 4.2.6 Consider the set of functions $\{t, t^2, 2t^2 - 3t\}$. If we suspect that this set is linearly dependent on $(-\infty, \infty)$, we must find constants c_1, c_2, and c_3, at least one of which is not zero, such that

$$c_1 t + c_2 t^2 + c_3(2t^2 - 3t) = 0$$

for all t. Collecting the coefficients of the powers of t in this equation yields $c_1 - 3c_3 = 0$ and $c_2 + 2c_3 = 0$. This does not force the c's to be zero. Indeed, we can choose $c_3 = 1$, $c_1 = 3$, and $c_2 = -2$ and satisfy the equation for all t. Thus the set is dependent. ■

We have proved that a set of solutions is fundamental on (a, b) if and only if the set is linearly independent. The argument showed that if the Wronskian of a set of functions was not zero at a point in the interval then the set had to be linearly independent. Note carefully that the proof that if the set was linearly independent then the Wronskian was nonzero in the interval required that the n functions be solutions to an nth-order linear homogeneous differential equation. Therefore, it is illogical to test for linear dependence by trying to show that the Wronskian is zero at a point if we do not know that the functions are solutions to an nth-order equation. Indeed, see Exercise 19 for a demonstration of the fallacy here.

The main result of this section can be summarized in a slightly different way. To find all solutions to the equation

$$y^{(n)} + a_{n-1}(t)y^{(n-1)} + \cdots + a_1(t)y' + a_0(t)y = 0$$

on (a, b), we need only find a linearly independent set of n solutions on (a, b), and then every solution is a linear combination of these.

EXERCISES 4.2

1. Show that $\{e^t, te^t\}$ is a fundamental set of solutions to $y'' - 2y' + y = 0$ on $(-\infty, \infty)$. You must show that they are solutions to begin with. What is the unique solution where $y(0) = 2$ and $y'(0) = -1$?

2. Show that $\{e^t, e^{2t}\}$ is a fundamental set of solutions to $y'' - 3y' + 2y = 0$ on $(-\infty, \infty)$. You must show that they are solutions to begin with. What is the unique solution where $y(0) = 1$ and $y'(0) = -3$?

3. Show that $\{\sin(t), \cos(t)\}$ is a fundamental set of solutions to $y'' + y = 0$ on $(-\infty, \infty)$. You must show that they are solutions to begin with. What is the unique solution where $y(\pi/3) = 1$ and $y'(\pi/3) = -3$?

4. Show that $\{e^t \sin(t), e^t \cos(t)\}$ is a fundamental set of solutions to $y'' - 2y' + 2y = 0$ on $(-\infty, \infty)$. You must show that they are solutions to begin with. What is the unique solution where $y(\pi) = 1$ and $y'(\pi) = 0$?

5. The coefficients of the equation

$$y'' - \frac{3}{t}y' + \frac{3}{t^2}y = 0$$

are continuous, for example, on $(0, \infty)$. Show that $\{t, t^3\}$ is a fundamental set of solutions on this interval. Find the solution satisfying $y(1) = 1$ and $y'(1) = -3$.

6. The coefficients of the equation

$$y'' + \frac{3}{t}y' + \frac{1}{t^2}y = 0$$

are continuous, for example, on $(0, \infty)$. Show that $\{\frac{1}{t}, \frac{\ln(t)}{t}\}$ is a fundamental set of solutions on this interval. Find the solution satisfying $y(1) = 2$ and $y'(1) = 3$.

7. The coefficients of the equation

$$y'' - \frac{1}{t}y' + \frac{1}{t^2}y = 0$$

are continuous, for example, on $(0, \infty)$. Show that $\{t, t \ln(t)\}$ is a fundamental set of solutions on this interval. Find the solution satisfying $y(1) = -1$ and $y'(1) = 2$.

8. What is the generalization of the definition of a fundamental set of solutions to third-order equations?

9. Show that $\{1, e^t, te^t\}$ is a fundamental set of solutions to $y^{(3)} - 2y'' + y' = 0$. What is the unique solution where $y(0) = 2$, $y'(0) = -1$, and $y''(0) = 1$?

10. Show that $\{e^t, te^t, e^{-t}\}$ is a fundamental set of solutions to $y^{(3)} - y'' - y' + y = 0$. What is the unique solution where $y(0) = 1$, $y'(0) = -1$, and $y''(0) = 2$?

11. Use the definition of linear independence to show that $\{1, t, t^2\}$ is a linearly independent set of functions on the real line.

12. Use the definition of linear independence to show that $\{1, t, \sin(t)\}$ is a linearly independent set of functions on the real line.

13. Use the definition of linear independence to show that $\{t, t^2 - 2, t^3 - t\}$ is a linearly independent set of functions on the real line.

14. Use the definition of linear independence to show that $\{1, \sin(t), t^2\}$ is a linearly independent set of functions on the real line.

15. Use the definition of linear independence to show that $\{t, t^2, t^2 - 2t\}$ is not a linearly independent set of functions on the real line.

16. Show that $\{1, \sin^2(t), \cos(2t)\}$ is not a linearly independent set of functions on the real line.

17. Show that $\{1, \cos^2(t), \sin^2(t)\}$ is not a linearly independent set of functions on the real line.

18. Show that the Wronskian

$$W(t) = \det \begin{bmatrix} \phi_1(t) & \phi_2(t) \\ \phi_1'(t) & \phi_2'(t) \end{bmatrix}$$

of solutions $\{\phi_1(t), \phi_2(t)\}$ to

$$y''(t) + a_1(t)y'(t) + a_0(t)y(t) = 0$$

satisfies the equation

$$W'(t) + a_1(t)W(t) = 0.$$

Solve this equation and show that the Wronskian is identically zero or never zero. The equation in W is called Abel's equation. It is still true for an nth-order equation. See Supplementary Exercise 1 at the end of the chapter.

19. Show that $\{t^2, t|t|\}$ is a linearly independent set of functions on the real line, but the Wronskian is **zero**. The latter should be broken into the cases $t < 0$ and $t \geq 0$. There is nothing wrong here. How do you explain this apparent contradiction?

4.3 LINEAR HOMOGENEOUS EQUATIONS WITH CONSTANT COEFFICIENTS

In this section we shall show how to find a fundamental set of solutions for any linear constant-coefficient homogeneous equation of any order. In doing so, we shall have solved all initial-value problems for such equations. We shall see that the method for finding such fundamental sets naturally breaks up into certain cases. In order not to disrupt the natural development of the cases, we will begin by dealing with a technical matter that will arise in due course.

4.3.1 Complex-Valued Functions

Very shortly we shall need to differentiate complex-valued functions of a real variable. A complex-valued function is a function of the form

$$f(t) = u(t) + i\, v(t),$$

where $u(t)$ and $v(t)$ are real-valued functions and $i = \sqrt{-1}$ is the imaginary unit. We call $u(t)$ the **real part** of $f(t)$, and $v(t)$ is called the **imaginary part**. For example,

$$f(t) = t^2 + i\, \sin(t)$$

is a complex-valued function of the real-variable t with real part t^2 and imaginary part $\sin(t)$. Such functions are differentiated by differentiating the real and imaginary parts. So if $f(t) = t^2 + i\, \sin(t)$, then $f'(t) = 2t + i\, \cos(t)$.

A little reflection should make clear that the derivative of the sum or difference of complex-valued functions is the sum or difference of the derivatives. It may be more of a surprise to learn that the product and quotient rules still hold. We verify the product rule.

Let $f(t) = u(t) + i\,v(t)$ and $g(t) = x(t) + i\,y(t)$; then

$$f(t)g(t) = [u(t)x(t) - v(t)y(t)] + i\,[u(t)y(t) + v(t)x(t)].$$

So

$$\begin{aligned}(f(t)g(t))' &= [u'(t)x(t) + u(t)x'(t) - v'(t)y(t) - v(t)y'(t)] \\ &\quad + i\,[u'(t)y(t) + u(t)y'(t) + v'(t)x(t) + v(t)x'(t)].\end{aligned}$$

On the other hand,

$$\begin{aligned}f'(t)g(t) + f(t)g'(t) &= (u'(t) + i\,v'(t))(x(t) + i\,y(t)) \\ &\quad + (u(t) + i\,v(t))(x'(t) + i\,y'(t)) \\ &= [u'(t)x(t) + u(t)x'(t) - v'(t)y(t) - v(t)y'(t)] \\ &\quad + i\,[u'(t)y(t) + u(t)y'(t) + v'(t)x(t) + v(t)x'(t)].\end{aligned}$$

Thus the rules of differentiation for complex-valued functions are the same as for real-valued functions.

A complex-valued function that will be of special interest to us is the exponential function, which is defined as follows. First define the exponential of a complex number by

$$e^{a+bi} = e^a[\cos(b) + i\,\sin(b)].$$

This is Euler's formula. Therefore,

$$e^{(a+i\,b)t} = e^{at + i\,bt} = e^{at}[\cos(bt) + i\,\sin(bt)] = e^{at}\cos(bt) + i\,e^{at}\sin(bt).$$

The derivative of this function is found by differentiating the real and imaginary parts. It is

$$\frac{de^{(a+i\,b)t}}{dt} = (a + i\,b)e^{(a+i\,b)t}.$$

Therefore, a complex exponential is differentiated in the same way as a real exponential. This is all that we shall need.

4.3.2 Distinct Real Roots

Consider the second-order equation

$$y'' + 3y' + 2y = 0.$$

If we set

$$\phi(t) = e^{rt},$$

take the appropriate derivatives, and substitute in the equation, we get

$$\phi''(t) + 3\phi'(t) + 2\phi(t) = r^2 e^{rt} + 3re^{rt} + 2e^{rt}$$
$$= e^{rt}(r^2 + 3r + 2).$$

If we choose r to be a root of the polynomial $x^2 + 3x + 2$, then

$$\phi''(t) + 3\phi'(t) + 2\phi(t) = 0$$

for all t, and so we have a solution. Specifically, the two functions

$$\{e^{-t}, e^{-2t}\}$$

are solutions.

Recall that the operator $L[y] = y'' + 3y' + 2y$ is linear, so we need to check to see if $\{e^{-t}, e^{-2t}\}$ is a fundamental set of solutions. We have seen this set before. The Wronskian is

$$\det \begin{bmatrix} e^{-t} & e^{-2t} \\ -e^{-t} & -2e^{-2t} \end{bmatrix} = -e^{-3t} \neq 0.$$

Therefore, the set is fundamental, and the general solution is

$$y(t) = c_1 e^{-t} + c_2 e^{-2t}.$$

To obtain the unique solution corresponding to the initial condition (y_0, y_1) at $t = t_0$, we solve

$$c_1 e^{-t_0} + c_2 e^{-2t_0} = y_0,$$
$$c_1(-1)e^{-t_0} + c_2(-2)e^{-2t_0} = y_1.$$

Let us consider another example. If we substitute $\phi(t) = e^{rt}$ into the equation

$$y^{(3)} - y'' - 6y' = 0,$$

we get

$$\phi^{(3)}(t) - \phi''(t) - 6\phi'(t) = e^{rt}(r^3 - r^2 - 6r)$$
$$= e^{rt}r(r + 2)(r - 3).$$

Thus, if $r = 0$, $r = -2$, or $r = 3$, we have a solution to the equation. If the set of solutions $\{1, e^{-2t}, e^{3t}\}$ is fundamental, then every solution has the form

$$y(t) = c_1 1 + c_2 e^{-2t} + c_3 e^{3t}.$$

But

$$\det \begin{bmatrix} 1 & e^{-2t} & e^{3t} \\ 0 & (-2)e^{-2t} & 3e^{3t} \\ 0 & 4e^{-2t} & 9e^{3t} \end{bmatrix} = -18e^t - 12e^t = -30e^t \neq 0,$$

and so the set is fundamental.

The method may be summarized as follows. From the equation

$$y^{(n)} + a_{n-1}y^{(n-1)} + \cdots + a_1 y' + a_0 y = 0,$$

obtain the polynomial

$$P(r) = r^n + a_{n-1}r^{n-1} + \cdots + a_1 r + a_0$$

and find its roots. If the roots are $\{r_1, r_2, \ldots, r_n\}$, then $\{e^{r_1 t}, e^{r_2 t}, \ldots, e^{r_n t}\}$ is a set of solutions to the equation.

Definition 4.3.1

For the equation

$$y^{(n)} + a_{n-1}y^{(n-1)} + \cdots + a_1 y' + a_0 y = 0,$$

the polynomial

$$P(r) = r^n + a_{n-1}r^{n-1} + \cdots + a_1 r + a_0$$

is called the **characteristic polynomial** of the equation.   ●

The roots of the characteristic polynomial are often called the **eigenvalues** of the equation. We shall have more to say about eigenvalues in Chapter 5.

If the roots of the characteristic polynomial are real and distinct, this method always produces a fundamental set of solutions for any order constant-coefficient equation. We shall not prove this, but of course we can check any specific case if we want reassurance.

If roots are repeated, then we will not have sufficient solutions to make up a fundamental set. If some roots are complex, then we again will not have a fundamental set of real solutions in strict accordance with the definition of a fundamental set. These difficulties will prove to be minor and will be addressed after we have introduced a useful notation.

EXERCISES 4.3.2

1. Find a fundamental set of solutions for $y'' + 3y' - 4y = 0$. Show that the Wronskian is not zero. Find the unique solution for the initial condition $(1, -2)$ at $t = 0$.

2. Find a fundamental set of solutions for $y'' - 5y' + 6y = 0$. Show that the Wronskian is not zero. Find the unique solution for the initial condition $(2, 1)$ at $t = 0$.

3. Find a fundamental set of solutions for $y^{(3)} - 3y'' - y' + 3y = 0$. Show that the Wronskian is not zero. Find

the unique solution for the initial condition $(1, -2, 0)$ at $t = 0$.

4. Find a fundamental set of solutions for $y'' - 4y' = 0$. Show that the Wronskian is not zero. Find the unique solution for the initial condition $(2, 1)$ at $t = 0$.

5. Find a fundamental set of solutions for $y''' - 2y'' - 3y' = 0$. Show that the Wronskian is not zero. Find the unique solution for the initial condition $(1, 1, -1)$ at $t = 0$.

Find the general solution for Exercises 6–11.

6. $y^{(4)} - 3y'' + 2y = 0$.

7. $y'' - 2y' - 6y = 0$.

8. $y'' - 5y' + 6y = 0$.

9. $y'' - 2y' - 3y = 0$.

10. $y'' + 3y' - 4y = 0$.

11. $y''' - 9y' = 0$.

12. In finding the unique solution to an initial-value problem, what role does the fact that the Wronskian is not zero play?

13. Try to find the general solution to $y'' - 2y' + y = 0$. What difficulty do you encounter? Show that $\{e^t, te^t\}$ is a fundamental set of solutions. What is the general solution?

14. Try to find the general solution to $y'' + 2y' + y = 0$. What difficulty do you encounter? Show that $\{e^{-t}, te^{-t}\}$ is a fundamental set of solutions. What is the general solution?

15. Try to find the general solution to $y'' + y = 0$. What difficulty do you encounter? Can you form combinations of these solutions to get real solutions?

16. Try to find the general solution to $y'' + 9y = 0$. What difficulty do you encounter? Can you form combinations of these solutions to get real solutions?

4.3.3 $P(D)$ Operator Notation

This section introduces a notation that will be useful in the next section and later. Let Df mean the derivative of f, so $Df(t) = f'(t)$. The variable t will often be omitted when it serves no purpose. Naturally, $D^n f$ means the nth derivative of f. By any polynomial expression

$$P(D) = a_n D^n + a_{n-1} D^{n-1} + \cdots + a_1 D + a_0$$

in D applied to a function f, we shall mean

$$P(D)(f) = (a_n D^n + a_{n-1} D^{n-1} + \cdots + a_1 D + a_0)(f)$$
$$= a_n f^{(n)} + a_{n-1} f^{(n-1)} + \cdots + a_1 f' + a_0 f.$$

Thus $P(D)$ is an operator like L, discussed previously. When $P(D)$ is applied to a suitably differentiable function, the result is another function. Moreover, since $D^n(f + g) = D^n f + D^n g$ and $D^n(cf) = cD^n f$, it is easy to see that the operator $P(D)$ is linear. In fact, for the constant-coefficient equation

$$a_n y^{(n)} + a_{n-1} y^{(n-1)} + \cdots + a_1 y' + a_0 y = 0,$$

the corresponding operator defined by

$$P(D)(y) = (a_n D^n + a_{n-1} D^{n-1} + \cdots + a_1 D + a_0)(y)$$

is the operator $L[y]$, defined previously. Such operators are called polynomial operators. Note also that $P(D)$ is the characteristic polynomial of the equation $P(r)$, with r replaced by D. Thus the equation may be succinctly expressed by

$$P(D)(y) = 0.$$

If $P(D)$ and $Q(D)$ are polynomial operators, then the effect of first applying $P(D)$ to f and then applying $Q(D)$ to the result is the same as first multiplying out the product $Q(D)P(D)$, as you would with any polynomials and then applying the result to f. Consider an example.

Example 4.3.2   Let $P(D) = D^2 + 2D$ and $Q(D) = 3D^3 - D^2$. Then

$$\begin{aligned} Q(D)[P(D)(f)] &= (3D^3 - D^2)[D^2 f + 2Df] \\ &= (3D^3 - D^2)[f'' + 2f'] \\ &= 3D^3[f'' + 2f'] - D^2[f'' + 2f'] \\ &= 3D^3 f'' + 6D^3 f' - D^2 f'' - 2D^2 f' \\ &= 3D^5 f + 5D^4 f - 2D^3 f \\ &= (3D^5 + 5D^4 - 2D^3)f. \end{aligned}$$ ∎

In view of this,

$$Q(D)P(D) = P(D)Q(D),$$

since both multiply out to the same polynomial operator. In general, polynomial operators commute, and a proof could be provided along the lines of Example 4.3.2 with a little additional bookkeeping. Because of this we may always factor a polynomial operator into powers of linear factors, just as we can any ordinary polynomial. Moreover, we need not worry about the order of the factors. Here is an example of such a factorization.

$$P(D) = D^3 - 2D^2 + D = D(D-1)^2 = (D-1)^2 D.$$

To factor some polynomials into linear factors, you will need to use the complex numbers.

EXERCISES 4.3.3

1. Apply $D^2 - 3D + 4$ to the function $f(t) = t^3 - \sin(2t)$. What is the resulting function?
2. First apply $D^2 - D$ to $t^6 - 2t^2$ and then apply $D^3 + 2D$ to the result. Now apply the operators in reverse order and compare the result.
3. Factor the operator $D^2 - 5D + 4$ into linear factors.
4. Factor the operator $D^2 + 4$ into linear factors. You will need complex numbers.
5. Factor the operator $D^2 + D + 1$ into linear factors.
6. Factor the operator $[D^2 + D + 1]^3$ into linear factors.
7. Factor the operator $D^2 + 3D + 2$ into linear factors.
8. Show that the operators $(D - t^2)$ and $(D + 2)$ do not commute by applying them in each order to $f(t)$.
9. Show that the operators $(D - t^3)$ and $(D + t)$ do not commute by applying them in each order to $f(t)$.

4.3.4 Repeated and Complex Roots

We have remarked that if roots are repeated or are complex then we do not get a full fundamental set of real solutions. For example, the equation

$$y^{(3)} - 5y'' + 8y' - 4y = 0$$

has characteristic polynomial

$$P(r) = r^3 - 5r^2 + 8r - 4 = (r-1)(r-2)^2,$$

and the root 2 is repeated twice. We say the multiplicity of the root 2 is 2. In operator notation we have

$$P(D)(y) = (D-1)(D-2)^2(y) = 0.$$

If we apply $(D-2)$ to te^{2t}, we get

$$(D-2)(te^{2t}) = D(te^{2t}) - 2te^{2t} = e^{2t} + 2te^{2t} - 2te^{2t} = e^{2t},$$

so if we apply $(D-2)$ to this result, we get zero. Thus

$$(D-2)^2(te^{2t}) = 0,$$

and so te^{2t} is a solution to the equation

$$P(D)(y) = (D-1)(D-2)^2(y) = 0.$$

We now have a fundamental set $\{e^t, e^{2t}, te^{2t}\}$. You can show that the Wronskian is not zero.

Consider the operator $(D-r)$ applied to $t^k e^{rt}$. We have

$$(D-r)(t^k e^{rt}) = D(t^k e^{rt}) - rt^k e^{rt} = kt^{k-1}e^{rt} + rt^k e^{rt} - rt^k e^{rt} = kt^{k-1}e^{rt}.$$

If we apply $(D-r)$ again, we will get $k(k-1)t^{k-2}e^{rt}$. If we apply $(D-r)$ k times, we will get $k!e^{rt}$ and the next application will give zero. Thus, if $m > k$,

$$(D-r)^m(t^k e^{rt}) = 0.$$

Consequently, if $(D-r)^m$ is a factor of $P(D)$ in $P(D)(y) = 0$, then e^{rt}, te^{rt}, $t^2 e^{rt}$, ... , and $t^{m-1}e^{rt}$ are solutions to $P(D)(y) = 0$. But this gives us just the right number of solutions corresponding to each multiplicity to make up a full complement of n solutions for an nth-order equation. Here is an example.

Example 4.3.3   Consider the equation

$$D(D-1)^2(D+2)^3 y = 0.$$

The characteristic polynomial is $P(r) = r(r-1)^2(r+2)^3$, and the roots are 0, 1, and -2 with multiplicities 1, 2, and 3, respectively. Note that the multiplicities add up to the order of the equation. The fundamental set of solutions is

$$\{1, e^t, te^t, e^{-2t}, te^{-2t}, t^2 e^{-2t}\}.$$

Note that the number of solutions is just the order of the equation. The general solution is

$$y(t) = c_1 1 + c_2 e^t + c_3 te^t + c_4 e^{-2t} + c_5 te^{-2t} + c_6 t^2 e^{-2t}. \qquad \blacksquare$$

For each root r we include solutions of the form $t^i e^{rt}$ for $i = 0, 1, 2, \ldots, m-1$, where m is the multiplicity of the root.

All that remains is to deal with complex roots. In operator notation our method of solution is based on the observation that

$$P(D)(e^{rt}) = P(r)e^{rt},$$

and so we will have a solution to the equation $P(D)(y) = 0$ if r is a root of the characteristic polynomial $P(r)$. This still applies even if r proves to be a complex number, for we have seen that the rules for differentiating complex-valued functions are the same as for real-valued functions. In particular, $\frac{de^{rt}}{dt} = re^{rt}$ whether r is real or complex. The problem is how to get real solutions from the complex ones that this method will yield when the roots are complex.

The roots occur in conjugate pairs. For example, the equation

$$y'' - 2y' + 2y = 0$$

has characteristic polynomial $P(r) = r^2 - 2r + 2$, and the roots are $1 + i$ and $1 - i$. The roots will always occur in conjugate pairs if the coefficients of the polynomial are real.

To see this, suppose that z is a root of

$$a_n z^n + a_{n-1} z^{n-1} + \cdots + a_1 z + a_0 = 0,$$

where the coefficients are real. Taking conjugates of both sides, and remembering that the conjugate of a sum or product is the sum or product of the conjugates and the conjugate of a real number is itself, we get

$$0 = \bar{0} = \overline{a_n z^n + a_{n-1} z^{n-1} + \cdots + a_1 z + a_0}$$
$$= a_n \bar{z}^n + a_{n-1} \bar{z}^{n-1} + \cdots + a_1 \bar{z} + a_0.$$

Thus $\bar{z}$ is also a root.

Suppose that a root is $a + bi$ and its conjugate is $a - bi$. These roots yield solutions

$$t^k e^{(a+bi)t} t^k e^{at} \cos(bt) + i\, t^k e^{at} \sin(bt)$$

and

$$t^k e^{(a-bi)t} t^k e^{at} \cos(bt) - i\, t^k e^{at} \sin(bt).$$

If we add the two solutions and divide by 2, we get

$$t^k e^{at} \cos(bt).$$

If we subtract the bottom from the top and divide by $2i$, we get

$$t^k e^{at} \sin(bt).$$

These functions must be solutions to the homogeneous equation from which the complex solutions came, because we obtained them by addition, subtraction, and scalar multiplication, and the operator is linear. So for each pair of complex solutions we get a pair of real solutions. So if the complex solutions are replaced by the real solutions, the number of solutions remains right. The set of solutions obtained in this way can be shown to have a nonzero Wronskian, and so the set is fundamental.

Here is an example of the method.

Example 4.3.4   The characteristic polynomial of the equation

$$y^{(5)} + 4y^{(4)} + 8y^{(3)} + 8y^{(2)} + 4y' = 0$$

is

$$P(r) = r^5 + 4r^4 + 8r^3 + 8r^2 + 4r = r(r^2 + 2r + 2)^2$$
$$= r[r - (-1 + i)]^2[r - (-1 - i)]^2.$$

Thus the real and complex solutions are

$$\{1, e^{(-1+i)t}, te^{(-1+i)t}, e^{(-1-i)t}, te^{(-1-i)t}\}.$$

The fundamental set of real solutions is

$$\{1, e^{-t}\cos(t), te^{-t}\cos(t), e^{-t}\sin(t), te^{-t}\sin(t)\},$$

and the general solution is

$$y(t) = c_1 1 + c_2 e^{-t}\cos(t) + c_3 te^{-t}\cos(t) + c_4 e^{-t}\sin(t) + c_5 te^{-t}\sin(t). \quad \blacksquare$$

Before turning to the exercises it is worth noting that the method of solution that we have applied to higher-order linear constant-coefficient homogeneous equations applies without change to first-order constant-coefficient equations. For example, the characteristic polynomial of

$$y' - 2y = 0$$

is $P(r) = r - 2$, so the solution is $y(t) = ce^{2t}$.

EXERCISES 4.3.4

Solve the initial-value problem in Exercises 1–5

1. $2y'' - y' + y = 0$, where $y(0) = 0$ and $y'(0) = -1$.

2. $y'' - 4y' + 4y = 0$, where $y(0) = 1$ and $y'(0) = 0$.

3. $y'' - y' + 3y = 0$, where $y(0) = -1$ and $y'(0) = 2$.

4. $y'' + 2y' + 3y = 0$, where $y(0) = 0$ and $y'(0) = 2$.

5. $y'' + 4y = 0$, where $y(0) = 2$ and $y'(0) = 2$.

Find the general solution for Exercises 6–14.

6. $y'' + 4y' - 5y = 0$.
7. $y'' + 2y' + 5y = 0$.
8. $y'' - 3y' + 4y = 0$.
9. $2y'' + 4y' = 0$.
10. $D(D^2 + 2D + 2)^3(y) = 0$.
11. $D^3(D^2 + 1)^2(y) = 0$.
12. $D^2(D^2 - 1)^2(y) = 0$.
13. $(D^2 + D + 1)^2(y) = 0$.
14. $(D^3 - 1)(D^2 + 1)^2(y) = 0$.

15. Solve the initial-value problem $y^{(4)} + 3y^{(3)} = 0$, where $y(0) = -1$, $y'(0) = 2$, $y''(0) = 0$, and $y^{(3)}(0) = 2$.
16. Solve the initial-value problem $y^{(6)} - 3y^{(4)} + 3y^{(2)} - y = 0$, with $y_0 = 0$, $y_1 = 1$, $y_2 = -1$, $y_3 = 0$, $y_4 = 0$, and $y_5 = 0$ at $t = 0$.
17. Solve the initial-value problem $y^{(4)} + 4y^{(3)} - 2y^{(2)} - 12y' + 9y = 0$, with $y_0 = 0$, $y_1 = 1$, $y_2 = -1$, and $y_3 = 0$ at $t = 0$.
18. Show that the conjugate of a sum or product of complex numbers is the sum or product of the conjugates.

4.4 NONHOMOGENEOUS EQUATIONS

The general nonhomogeneous equation may be represented in operator notation by

$$L[y(t)] = b(t).$$

Suppose that we have two solutions to this equation, $\psi_1(t)$ and $\psi_2(t)$. Then, by the linearity of L, we have

$$L[\psi_1(t) - \psi_2(t)] = L[\psi_1(t)] - L[\psi_2(t)] = b(t) - b(t) = 0.$$

Thus the difference of solutions to the nonhomogeneous equation is a solution to the homogeneous equation. Now, if $\psi(t)$ is a particular solution to the nonhomogeneous equation, then any other solution $y(t)$ has the form

$$y(t) = \psi(t) + \phi(t),$$

where $\phi(t)$ is a solution to the homogeneous equation. Schematically, all solutions may be expressed in the following form.

general nonhomogeneous = particular nonhomogeneous + homogeneous

Therefore, the strategy for solving a linear nonhomogeneous equation is to solve the homogeneous equation and, by hook or by crook, find one nonhomogeneous solution.

Example 4.4.1   Consider the equation

$$y'' - 2y' + y = 2.$$

It is easy to see that

$$\psi(t) = 2$$

is a solution to the nonhomogeneous equation. The general homogeneous solution is

$$\phi(t) = c_1 e^t + c_2 t e^t,$$

and so the general nonhomogeneous solution is

$$y(t) = 2 + c_1 e^t + c_2 t e^t. \qquad \blacksquare$$

We shall first demonstrate a method for finding a particular solution to a nonhomogeneous equation that applies to a large class of constant-coefficient nonhomogeneous linear equations, and then we shall introduce a method that is applicable to all linear nonhomogeneous equations, constant coefficient or not.

4.4.1 The Methods of Undetermined Coefficients

Consider the nonhomogeneous constant-coefficient linear equation

$$P(D)(y) = a_n y^{(n)} + \cdots + a_1 y' + a_0 y = b(t).$$

Suppose that we have found an operator $Q(D)$ such that

$$Q(D)(b(t)) = 0.$$

If $\psi(t)$ is a solution to $P(D)(\psi(t)) = b(t)$, then

$$Q(D)P(D)(\psi(t)) = Q(D)(b(t)) = 0.$$

Thus solutions to the nonhomogeneous equation

$$P(D)(y(t)) = b(t)$$

are among the solutions to the homogeneous equation

$$Q(D)P(D)(y(t)) = P(D)Q(D)(y(t)) = 0.$$

But we know how to find all solutions to this latter equation, and so, perhaps, it will not be too hard to pick out a solution to the nonhomogeneous equation.

In fact, the strategy is simple. First, find the operator (if possible) of lowest degree $Q(D)$ such that $Q(D)(b(t)) = 0$. We say that $Q(D)$ annihilates or is the **annihilator** of $b(t)$. Second, solve the equation $P(D)Q(D)(\psi(t)) = 0$. Third, substitute the general solution to this homogeneous equation into $P(D)(y(t)) = b(t)$ and determine the constants.

This method is called the **method of annihilators**. Here is an example.

Example 4.4.2   We solve

$$P(D)(y) = (D^2 - 3D + 2)(y) = e^{-t}.$$

The annihilator of e^{-t} is $(D + 1)$, and $P(D) = (D - 1)(D - 2)$. So

$$P(D)Q(D)(y) = (D - 1)(D - 2)(D + 1)y = 0$$

has the general solution

$$\psi(t) = a_1 e^{-t} + a_2 e^t + a_3 e^{2t}.$$

We apply $P(D)$ to this and set it equal to e^{-t}. We have

$$P(D)(\psi(t)) = a_1 P(D)(e^{-t}) + a_2 P(D)(e^t) + a_3 P(D)(e^{2t}) = e^{-t}.$$

But $P(D)(e^t) = 0$ and $P(D)(e^{2t}) = 0$ (why?). So

$$a_1 P(D)(e^{-t}) = a_1[e^{-t} + 3e^{-t} + 2e^{-t}] = 6a_1 e^{-t} = e^{-t}.$$

Therefore, $a_1 = 1/6$, and a particular solution to the homogeneous equation is

$$\psi(t) = e^{-t}/6,$$

and the general solution is

$$y(t) = \frac{e^{-t}}{6} + c_1 e^t + c_2 e^{2t}. \qquad \blacksquare$$

A few remarks about the method and this example are in order. If $b(t)$ can be annihilated by a polynomial operator $Q(D)$, then $b(t)$ is a solution to a constant-coefficient homogeneous equation. So $b(t)$ must be a combination of powers of t times exponentials, or powers of t times exponentials times sines or cosines, or both. Thus, $2t^3 e^{4t} + t \sin(3t)$ has an annihilator, but $\ln(t)$ does not.

The reader should note that we dropped the last two terms from

$$\psi(t) = a_1 e^{-t} + a_2 e^t + a_3 e^{2t}.$$

This was because they are solutions to $P(D)(y) = 0$, and so they would drop out anyway. Dropping them at the start saves a great deal of computation. From the general solution to $P(D)Q(D)(y) = 0$, we can drop any solution to $P(D)(y) = 0$. **Beware**: This does not mean that the particular solution is always to be found among the solutions to $Q(D)(y) = 0$!

Example 4.4.3   We solve

$$P(D)(y) = (D^2 - 3D + 2)(y) = 3e^t.$$

The annihilator is $Q(D) = (D - 1)$. We must solve

$$P(D)Q(D)(y) = (D - 1)^2(D - 2)y = 0.$$

The solution is

$$\psi(t) = a_1 e^t + a_2 t e^t + a_3 e^{2t}.$$

We can throw out the first and last terms because they are solutions to $P(D)y = 0$. Our candidate for a particular solution is

$$\psi(t) = a_2 t e^t.$$

We substitute this in the original differential equation to get

$$a_2(2e^t + te^t) - 3a_2(e^t + te^t) + 2a_2 t e^t = -a_2 e^t = 3e^t.$$

So $a_2 = -3$, and

$$\psi(t) = -3te^t.$$

The general solution is

$$y(t) = -3te^t + c_1 e^t + c_2 e^{2t}. \qquad\blacksquare$$

Introducing the annihilator had two purposes. It showed us that the particular solution that we seek is a solution to $P(D)Q(D)y = 0$, and it alerted us to the need to consider the possible repetition of roots created by the product $P(D)Q(D)$. For example, suppose that $b(t) = t^2 e^{2t}$ and that the characteristic polynomial of $P(D)$ has the root 2 repeated twice. Then the root 2 is repeated three times in $Q(D)$ and twice in $P(D)$. We write down the particular solution by writing down each of the terms belonging to the root 2 up to the multiplicity that is now 5 and throwing out those that belong to $P(D)y = 0$ Thus we have

$$y_p = a_0 t^2 e^{2t} + a_1 t^3 e^{2t} + a_2 t^3 e^{2t} + a_3 t^4 e^{2t}.$$

This all boils down to a simple rule. To the multiplicity of the root determined by $b(t)$, add the multiplicity of the root in $P(D)$; then write out the solution starting at one above the multiplicity in $P(D)$ and continuing to the sum of multiplicities.

Example 4.4.4   Consider

$$y'' - 5y' + 6y = te^{2t}.$$

The root is 2, and $P(D) = (D - 2)(D - 3)$. The multiplicity in $P(D)$ is 1, and the multiplicity in te^{2t} is 2, so the total multiplicity is 3. The form of the particular solution is

$$y_p = a_0 t e^{2t} + a_1 t^2 e^{2t}.$$

The rest of the solution is handled as usual. $\qquad\blacksquare$

This method is often called the **method of undetermined coefficients**. Here are two more examples illustrating the method.

Example 4.4.5   Consider

$$D^2(D + 2)y = 3t^3.$$

The root is 0, and the multiplicity from $P(D)$ is 2. The multiplicity from $3t^3$ is 4, so the total is 6. The particular solution is

$$y_p = a_0 t^2 + a_1 t^3 + a_2 t^4 + a_4 t^5. \qquad \blacksquare$$

Example 4.4.6   Even if the roots are complex, the procedure is the same. Consider

$$(D^2 + 4)y = 2\sin(2t).$$

The roots are the conjugates $\pm 2i$. So the annihilator for both of them is $D^2 + 4$; and so the total multiplicity for both roots is 2, and the multiplicity for both roots in $P(D)$ is 1. Therefore, we can handle both roots at once and write down a real solution. The solution is

$$y_p = a_0 t \sin(2t) + a_1 t \cos(2t). \qquad \blacksquare$$

We need to consider what to do if there is more than one term in $b(t)$. First, consider a group of terms belonging to the same root. For example, let $b(t) = 2te^{3t} - t^3 e^{3t}$. The annihilator is $(D - 3)^4$. Thus the multiplicity introduced by $b(t)$ is the highest multiplicity produced by any of the terms belonging to the same root. We then continue as usual. Second, terms belonging to different roots (not conjugate though) are simply treated separately, and their particular solutions are added to get the grand particular solution. This is possible because the equation is linear.

Here is a final example as a grand finale.

Example 4.4.7   We solve

$$y'' - 3y' + 2y = \sin(2t) + 2\cos(2t) + e^t - 3te^t.$$

The roots of the characteristic polynomial are 1 and 2. The roots on the right are $\pm 2i$ and 1.

We start with $\pm 2i$. These roots do not occur on the left, so the particular solution associated with $\sin(2t) + 2\cos(2t)$ is

$$\psi_1(t) = a_1 \sin(2t) + a_2 \cos(2t).$$

Taking derivatives, we have

$$\psi_1'(t) = 2a_1 \cos(2t) - 2a_2 \sin(2t)$$

$$\psi_1''(t) = -4a_1 \sin(2t) - 4a_2 \cos(2t).$$

Putting these derivatives in the equation

$$y'' - 3y' + 2y = \sin(2t) + 2\cos(2t)$$

and collecting coefficients yields

$$(2a_1 + 6a_2 - 4a_1)\sin(2t) + (2a_2 - 6a_1 - 4a_2)\cos(2t) = \sin(2t) + 2\cos(2t).$$

Equating coefficients yields the system

$$-2a_1 + 6a_2 = 1,$$
$$-6a_1 - 2a_2 = 2.$$

Solving we get $a_1 = -7/20$ and $a_2 = 1/20$. Thus the particular solution is

$$\psi_1(t) = \frac{-7}{20}\sin(2t) + \frac{1}{20}\cos(2t).$$

Now we consider the root 1. This does occur on the left-hand side, so the total multiplicity is 3. The solution corresponding to this root is

$$\psi_2(t) = b_1 t e^t + b_2 t^2 e^t.$$

Taking derivatives, we get

$$\psi_2'(t) = b_1(e^t + t e^t) + b_2(2t e^t + t^2 e^t)$$

and

$$\psi_2''(t) = b_1(2e^t + t e^t) + b_2(2e^t + 4t e^t + t^2 e^t).$$

Inserting these derivatives in the equation

$$y'' - 3y' + 2y = e^t - 3t e^t$$

and collecting coefficients gives

$$(-3b_1 + 2b_1 + 2b_2)e^t + (2b_1 - 3b_1 - 6b_2 + b_1 + 4b_2)t e^t$$
$$+ (2b_2 - 3b_2 + b_2)t^2 e^t = e^t - 3t e^t.$$

From this we get the equations

$$-b_1 + 2b_2 = 1,$$
$$-2b_2 = -3.$$

The solution is $b_1 = 2$ and $b_2 = 3/2$. Therefore, the second particular solution is

$$\psi_2(t) = 2t e^t + \frac{3}{2}t^2 e^t.$$

Finally, the complete particular solution is the sum of these. Thus

$$\psi(t) = -\frac{7}{20}\sin(2t) + \frac{1}{20}\cos(2t) + 2t e^t + \frac{3}{2}t^2 e^t.$$

To this we add the homogeneous solution to get the general solution. ∎

If you have wondered why it is that we can equate the unknown coefficients of the functions on the left with the known ones on the right, it is because the functions that we are working with are fundamental solutions to a constant coefficient homogeneous equation, and so they are linearly independent. Therefore, if all the functions are combined on one side and set equal to zero, the coefficients of each function must be zero.

EXERCISES 4.4.1

Use the method of undetermined coefficients to solve the equations in Exercises 1–15.

1. $y'' + y = 2$ with $y(0) = 1$ and $y'(0) = 2$
2. $y'' - 5y' + 6y = 3e^{2t}$
3. $y'' + y' - 6y = t^2 + 2e^{-3t}$ with $y(0) = -1$ and $y'(0) = 1$
4. $y'' + 2y' + y = 2e^{-t}$
5. $y'' - 2y' = 3t^2 + 1$ with $y(0) = 1$ and $y'(0) = 2$
6. $y'' + y = \sin(t)$
7. $y'' + 3y' + 2y = \cos(t)$
8. $y^{(3)} + y' = t^3$
9. $y'' + y' + y = \sin(t)$
10. $y'' - 4y' + 4y = e^{2t} + e^t$
11. $y'' - y = \sin(t)$
12. $y'' + y = \sin(t)$
13. $y'' + y' + y = 2t + t^2$
14. $y''' + y' = t^2 + 2e^{-3t}$ with $y(0) = -1$, $y'(0) = 1$, and $y''(0) = 1$
15. $y^{(4)} - 4y'' = t + 3e^{2t}$
16. Does the method of undetermined coefficients apply to the following? Explain!
    (a) $y'' + ty' - y = e^t$
    (b) $y'' - 2y' + y = t^{1/3}$

4.4.2 Variation of Parameters

The method of undetermined coefficients does not apply to functions $b(t)$ that are not already solutions to some linear constant-coefficient homogeneous differential equation, nor to equations with variable coefficients. In this section a universal method will be described that applies to all linear equations. It is called the **method of variation of parameters**. The method will be explained for second-order equations only, though the extension to higher-order equations is immediate.

Let $\{\phi_1(t), \phi_2(t)\}$ be a fundamental set of solutions to the equation

$$y'' + a_1(t)y' + a_0(t)y = 0$$

on an interval where the coefficients are continuous. We go about solving the equation

$$y'' + a_1(t)y' + a_0(t)y = b(t)$$

as follows. Set

$$\psi(t) = u_1(t)\phi_1(t) + u_2(t)\phi_2(t).$$

For economy of notation we shall omit the variable t. Differentiating, we have

$$\psi' = u_1'\phi_1 + u_1\phi_1' + u_2'\phi_2 + u_2\phi_2'.$$

We set

$$u_1'\phi_1 + u_2'\phi_2 = 0.$$

Be patient, and you will shortly see why. We now have

$$\psi' = u_1\phi_1' + u_2\phi_2'.$$

We now differentiate this to get

$$\psi'' = u_1\phi_1'' + u_2\phi_2'' + u_1'\phi_1' + u_2'\phi_2'.$$

Now substitute ψ and its derivatives into the equation to get

$$\begin{aligned}
\psi'' + a_1\psi' + a_0\psi &= u_1\phi_1'' + u_2\phi_2'' + u_1'\phi_1' + u_2'\phi_2' \\
&\quad + a_1(u_1\phi_1' + u_2\phi_2') \\
&\quad + a_0(u_1\phi_1 + u_2(t)\phi_2) \\
&= b
\end{aligned}$$

Collecting together all the terms with u_1 as a coefficient, and likewise with u_2, and recalling that ϕ_1 and ϕ_2 are solutions to the homogeneous equation, the preceding simplifies to

$$u_1'\phi_1' + u_2'\phi_2' = b.$$

So if we are to have a solution to the nonhomogeneous equation we must be able to choose the $u_1(t)$ and $u_2(t)$ so that

$$u_1'(t)\phi_1(t) + u_2'(t)\phi_2(t) = 0,$$

and

$$u_1'(t)\phi_1'(t) + u_2'(t)\phi_2'(t) = b(t).$$

These equations can be solved by Cramer's rule. So

$$u_1'(t) = \frac{\begin{vmatrix} 0 & \phi_2 \\ b & \phi_2' \end{vmatrix}}{\begin{vmatrix} \phi_1 & \phi_2 \\ \phi_1' & \phi_2' \end{vmatrix}}$$

and

$$u_2'(t) = \frac{\begin{vmatrix} \phi_1 & 0 \\ \phi_1' & b \end{vmatrix}}{\begin{vmatrix} \phi_1 & \phi_2 \\ \phi_1' & \phi_2' \end{vmatrix}}.$$

Note that it is here that we need our homogeneous solutions to be a fundamental set. The $u_1(t)$ and $u_2(t)$ can now be found by integration.

Example 4.4.8   Consider $y'' + y = \tan(t)$. A fundamental set of solutions to the homogeneous equation is $\{\sin(t), \cos(t)\}$. The particular solution to the nonhomogeneous equation has the form

$$\psi(t) = u_1(t)\sin(t) + u_2(t)\cos(t).$$

Now solve the equations

$$u_1'(t)\sin(t) + u_2'(t)\cos(t) = 0,$$
$$u_1'(t)\cos(t) - u_2'(t)\sin(t) = \tan(t)$$

by any method you like to get $u_1'(t) = \sin(t)$ and $u_2'(t) = \cos(t) - \sec(t)$. These are then integrated to give

$$u_1(t) = -\cos(t)$$

and

$$u_2(t) = \sin(t) - \ln|\sec(t) + \tan(t)|.$$

Thus the particular solution is

$$\psi(t) = -\cos(t)\sin(t) + [\sin(t) - \ln|\sec(t) + \tan(t)|]\cos(t)$$
$$= -\cos(t)\ln|\sec(t) + \tan(t)|.$$

The general solution is

$$y(t) = -\cos(t)\ln|\sec(t) + \tan(t)| + c_1\sin(t) + c_2\cos(t). \qquad \blacksquare$$

The following example shows the method applied to an equation with variable coefficients.

Example 4.4.9   We solve

$$y'' - \frac{2}{t^2}y = 3 - \frac{1}{t^2}, \quad \text{where } t > 0.$$

You should show that $\{t^2, t^{-1}\}$ is a fundamental set of solutions to the homogeneous equation.

The form of the particular solution is

$$\psi(t) = u_1 t^2 + u_2 t^{-1}.$$

We must solve the system

$$u_1' t^2 + u_2' t^{-1} = 0,$$

$$2u_1't - u_2't^{-2} = 3 - \frac{1}{t^2}.$$

Solving these equations yields

$$u_1' = \frac{1}{t} - \frac{1}{3t^3}, \qquad \text{and} \qquad u_2' = \frac{1}{3} - t^2.$$

Integrating then gives

$$u_1 = \ln(t) + \frac{t^{-2}}{6} \qquad \text{and} \qquad u_2 = \frac{t}{3} - \frac{t^3}{3}.$$

Therefore, the particular solution is

$$\psi(t) = t^2 \ln(t) + \frac{1}{6} + \frac{1}{3} - \frac{t^2}{3} = \frac{1}{2} - \frac{t^2}{3} + t^2 \ln(t).$$

The general solution is

$$y(t) = \frac{1}{2} + t^2 \ln(t) + c_1 t^2 + c_2 t^{-1}.$$

Notice how the term $t^2/3$ has been absorbed in the homogeneous solution. ∎

EXERCISES 4.4.2

Use variation of parameters to solve Exercises 1–9.

1. $y'' + 3y' + 2y = e^{3t}$

2. $y'' - 3y' + 2y = e^t$

3. $y'' + y = \sec^2(t)$ on $(-\pi/4, \pi/4)$

4. $y'' + 4y' + 4y = t^{-2}e^{-2t}$ for $t > 0$

5. $y'' + y = \sin(t)$, $y(\pi) = 1$, and $y'(\pi) = 0$

6. $y'' + 3y' = t$

7. Show that $\{t, t^3\}$ is a fundamental set of solutions to $y'' - \frac{3}{t}y' + \frac{3}{t^2}y = 0$ on $(0, \infty)$. Find the general solution to $y'' - \frac{3}{t}y' + \frac{3}{t^2}y = t^2$ on $(0, \infty)$.

8. Show that $\{\frac{1}{t}, \frac{\ln(t)}{t}\}$ is a fundamental set of solutions to $y'' + \frac{3}{t}y' + \frac{1}{t^2}y = 0$ on $(0, \infty)$. Find the solution to $y'' + \frac{3}{t}y' + \frac{1}{t^2}y = 2t$ satisfying $y(1) = 2$ and $y'(1) = 3$.

9. Solve $2y'' + 4y' + 2y = e^{3t}$. How do you deal with the fact that the leading coefficient is not 1?

10. Solve $y'' + y = \csc(t)$. On what intervals is the solution

valid?

11. Show that $\{e^t, t\}$ is a fundamental set of solutions to $(1 - t)y'' + ty' - y = 0$ on $(0, 1)$. Find a particular solution to $(1 - t)y'' + ty' - y = (t - 1)^2 e^{-t}$ using variation of parameters. Is the equation in the correct form for the method?

12. Show that $\{t^2, t^2 \ln(t)\}$ is a fundamental set of solutions to $t^2 y'' - 3ty' + 4y = 0$ on $(0, \infty)$. Find a particular solution to $t^2 y'' - 3ty' + 4y = t^2 \ln(t)$ using variation of parameters. Be sure to get the equation in the right form to apply the method.

13. Find the general solution to $y'' + 9y = f(t)$. The result will involve an integral with $f(t)$ in the integrand.

14. Find the general solution to $y'' + 2y' + y = f(t)$. The result will involve an integral with $f(t)$ in the integrand.

15. Go through the derivation of the method of variation of parameters for third-order equations.

16. Use variation of parameters to solve $y''' - y' = e^t$.

4.5 VIBRATION

The world is full of systems that vibrate. The air vibrates with sound; light is a vibration of the electromagnetic field; bells and drums and violin strings vibrate. The study of vibrating systems is one of the major areas of mathematics, and in this section we will study the simplest of these systems.

In the case of a violin string, the string can store energy in two ways. It can store potential energy when it is slightly stretched, and it can store kinetic energy when it is moving. What makes the analysis of a violin string complicated is the fact that the matter in motion is not concentrated at a point but is spread out as a string. We shall consider the simpler case for which the mass is concentrated at a point and the potential energy is stored in a simple spring.

Before deriving the equations of motion for the mass–spring system we should review two common systems of physical units. The meter-kilogram - second (mks) system measures distance in meters, mass in kilograms, and time in seconds. The unit of force in this system is called the newton, and it is the force that accelerates 1 kilogram at 1 meter per second per second. The old British system still hangs on. In this system, distance is measured in feet, mass is measured in slugs, and time is measured in seconds. The unit of force is the pound. It is important to distinguish between mass and weight. A mass of 1 kilogram is the amount of matter that balances against a standard kilogram maintained at a bureau of standards. On the other hand, weight is the force exerted by gravity on a given mass, and so a given mass will have a different weight on the Moon than it will have on Earth. Since the acceleration due to gravity on Earth is approximately 32 ft/sec^2, a mass of 1 slug weighs approximately 32 lb on Earth.

Consider, then, a mass suspended by a spring. We allow the mass to gently extend the spring until the resistance of the spring exactly balances out the force of gravity. This position of the mass will be $y = 0$, where y is the displacement of the mass from this balanced position, and down will be taken to be positive. Because gravity has been "balanced out," we can ignore it from now on. Since we assume that the spring is an ideal one, we may assume that the force that counters a displacement is proportional to the displacement. Thus

$$F = -ky.$$

Note the minus sign. This is necessary because the force is oppositely directed to the displacement. This relation is called **Hooke's law**. To practically determine the spring constant k, apply a given force and measure the extension of the spring; then divide the force by the extension. For example, if a force of 2 newtons extends the spring 0.5 meter, the spring constant is $2/0.5 = 4$, and the units are newtons /meter.

By Newton's second law, the mass m times the acceleration $y''(t)$ must equal the force $F = -ky$. So

$$my'' = -ky,$$

and

$$my'' + ky = 0.$$

The general solution to this equation is immediately found to be

$$y(t) = c_1 \sin((\sqrt{k/m})t) + c_2 \cos((\sqrt{k/m})t).$$

A simple trick from trigonometry will help us see how these solutions behave. Set $A = \sqrt{c_1^2 + c_2^2}$. We can always find an angle θ such that $\cos(\theta) = c_1/A$ and $\sin(\theta) = c_2/A$. So

$$y(t) = A \cos(\theta) \sin((\sqrt{k/m})t) + A \sin(\theta) \cos((\sqrt{k/m})t)$$
$$= A \sin((\sqrt{k/m})t + \theta).$$

Therefore, the motion is a simple sinusoidal vibration with amplitude A, and period $2\pi/\sqrt{k/m}$, shifted by $\theta\sqrt{m/k}$.

If we trade in this second-order equation for a system of first-order equations, we get an alternative view of the behavior. Set $u = y$ and $v = y'$; then

$$u' = v,$$
$$v' = -\frac{ku}{m}.$$

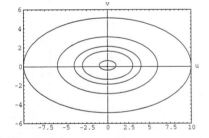

FIGURE 4.1

Here $u(t)$ is the displacement and $v(t)$ is the velocity. As we have seen, the solution is $u(t) = A \sin(\sqrt{k/m}t + \theta)$, and so $v(t) = \sqrt{k/m}A \cos(\sqrt{k/m}t + \theta)$. What does the orbit look like? We eliminate the parameter to get

$$\frac{u^2}{A^2} + \frac{mv^2}{kA^2} = \sin^2(\sqrt{k/m}t + \theta) + \cos^2(\sqrt{k/m}t + \theta) = 1.$$

So the orbits are ellipses. The orbits are closed curves, and this is consistent with the periodic nature of the solutions.

Recall that the u, v-plane is often called the phase plane. Figure 4.1 shows some orbits of solutions to $my'' + ky = 0$ in this phase plane.

4.5.1 Friction

As the mass of our system moves up and down, it is subject to a drag force due to air resistance. We include this in our equation by assuming that the drag is proportional to the velocity of the mass, but oppositely directed to the direction of motion of the mass. The equation now becomes

$$my'' = -ky - cy',$$

where $c > 0$, and so

$$my'' + cy' + ky = 0.$$

The roots of the characteristic polynomial are

$$r = \frac{-c \pm \sqrt{c^2 - 4mk}}{2m},$$

and the nature of the solution depends crucially on the quantity $c^2 - 4mk$. This quantity is often called the **discriminant**.

If $c^2 - 4mk > 0$, then the roots r_1 and r_2 are real and negative. In this case the solution has the form

$$y(t) = c_1 e^{r_1 t} + c_2 e^{r_2 t}.$$

This solution will converge to zero exponentially, and no oscillation occurs. This is called the **overdamped** case.

Depending on the initial condition, the solution may or may not cross the t-axis for positive t. To see this factor out $e^{r_1 t}$ to get

$$y(t) = e^{r_1 t}(c_1 + c_2 e^{(r_2 - r_1)t}).$$

The only way this can be zero is if

$$c_1 + c_2 e^{(r_2 - r_1)t} = 0$$

or

$$e^{(r_2 - r_1)t} = -\frac{c_1}{c_2}.$$

Taking the logarithm gives

$$t = \frac{\ln(-c_1/c_2)}{r_2 - r_1}.$$

We can assume that $r_1 < r_2 < 0$ without changing the generality of our argument. In this case, for t to be positive we need

$$-\frac{c_1}{c_2} > 1 \tag{$*$}$$

Now consider the initial conditions $y(0) = y_0$ and $y'(0) = y_1$. We have

$$c_1 + c_2 = y_0,$$
$$r_1 c_1 + r_2 c_2 = y_1.$$

We can solve for c_1 and c_2 in terms of y_0 and y_1 and then get

$$-\frac{c_1}{c_2} = \frac{y_1 - y_0 r_2}{y_1 - y_0 r_1}.$$

Remember that $r_1 < r_2 < 0$, so in order for $(*)$ to hold it is necessary that y_0 and y_1 be of opposite signs. But this is not sufficient to guarantee that $(*)$ holds, as you can show by experimenting. Indeed, the magnitude of y_1 must be made sufficiently large.

Physically, this is the situation when there is so much friction that displacement alone is not enough to have the mass pass the neutral position; kinetic energy must be added in the direction of the neutral position to have the mass pass this position. Note that the mass can only pass the neutral position at most once.

If $c^2 - 4mk = 0$, then there is one negative root r, but it is a double root. In this case the solution is

$$y(t) = c_1 e^{rt} + c_2 t e^{rt}.$$

The exponential decay overwhelms the factor of t, and so this solution converges to zero also. This is called the **critically damped** case.

This case is entirely similar in behavior to the overdamped case. For the solution to cross the positive t-axis, we must have

$$c_1 e^{rt} + c_2 t e^{rt} = e^{rt}(c_1 + c_2 t) = 0$$

or

$$t = -\frac{c_1}{c_2} > 0.$$

In terms of the initial conditions we have

$$-\frac{c_1}{c_2} = \frac{-y_0}{y_1 - y_0 r}.$$

The derivation of this is actually easier than the argument in the overdamped case, and it is left as an exercise. To cross the positive t-axis, it is again necessary that the initial conditions be of opposite signs. However, it is not sufficient, as a little experiment will show.

Finally, if $c^2 - 4mk < 0$, then the roots are of the form $\lambda \pm \mu i$, where $\lambda < 0$. In this case the solution has the form

$$y(t) = c_1 e^{\lambda t} \sin(\mu t) + c_2 e^{\lambda t} \cos(\mu t).$$

Using the trick from trigonometry again, we can write this as

$$y(t) = A e^{\lambda t} \sin(\mu t + \theta).$$

This solution oscillates, but the amplitude dies away exponentially. This is called the **underdamped** case. Figure 4.2 shows a few orbits in the underdamped case.

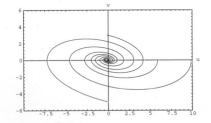

FIGURE 4.2

4.5.2 External Forces

We now consider the effect of forces applied to the mass. If a force $F(t)$ is applied to the mass the equation becomes

$$my''(t) + cy'(t) + ky(t) = F(t).$$

Here we consider the case when $F(t) = F_0 \sin(\omega t)$. The solution has the general form $y(t) = y_p(t) + y_h(t)$, where y_p is the particular nonhomogeneous solution, and y_h is the general homogeneous solution.

Since the drag coefficient c is positive, y_h will contain factors of the form e^{at}, where the a is negative. Therefore, the homogeneous solution will rapidly die out. In the context of vibrations, y_h is called the **transient** solution. On the other hand, if we use the method of undetermined coefficients, the particular solution will have the form

$$y_p(t) = A \sin(\omega t) + B \cos(\omega t),$$

and this does not die out. It is called the **steady-state** solution.

The steady-state solution will depend on ω; that is, it will depend on the frequency of the impressed force. To analyze this dependence it will be useful to introduce the following notation. Set $\lambda = \frac{c}{2m}$, $a^2 = \frac{k}{m}$, and $F_1 = \frac{F_0}{m}$. The equation becomes

$$y''(t) + 2\lambda y'(t) + a^2 y(t) = F_1 \sin(\omega t).$$

The computation of the particular solution takes a bit of effort, so take a deep breath. We differentiate and substitute in the equation. This is how it goes.

$$y_p' = A\omega \cos(\omega t) - B\omega \sin(\omega t),$$

and

$$y_p'' = -A\omega^2 \sin(\omega t) - B\omega^2 \cos(\omega t).$$

Thus

$$-A\omega^2 \sin(\omega t) - B\omega^2 \cos(\omega t) + A2\lambda\omega \cos(\omega t) - B2\lambda\omega \sin(\omega t)$$
$$+ a^2 A \sin(\omega t) + a^2 B \cos(\omega t)$$
$$= F_1 \sin(\omega t).$$

Equating the coefficients of $\sin(\omega t)$ and $\cos(\omega t)$ on both sides gives the system

$$(a^2 - \omega^2)A - 2\lambda\omega B = F_1,$$
$$2\lambda\omega A + (a^2 - \omega^2)B = 0.$$

Solving this system gives

$$A = \frac{F_1(a^2 - \omega^2)}{4\lambda^2\omega^2 + (\omega^2 - a^2)^2}$$

and

$$B = \frac{-2\lambda\omega F_1}{4\lambda^2\omega^2 + (\omega^2 - a^2)^2}.$$

To get the solution, $y_p(t) = A\sin(\omega t) + B\cos(\omega t)$, into a more usable form we use the trick from trigonometry to get

$$y_p(t) = \sqrt{A^2 + B^2}\sin(\omega t - \theta).$$

Substituting for A and B and simplifying yields

$$y_p(t) = \frac{F_1}{\sqrt{4\lambda^2\omega^2 + (\omega^2 - a^2)^2}}\sin(\omega t - \theta).$$

Aside from phase shifts, the solution is determined by the amplitude factor

$$f(\omega) = \frac{1}{\sqrt{4\lambda^2\omega^2 + (\omega^2 - a^2)^2}}.$$

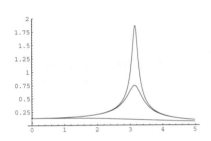

FIGURE 4.3

Figure 4.3 shows three graphs of $f(\omega)$ for different choices of λ and a^2. The bottom graph is the response of a system in which there is a lot of drag. Note that there is no tendency of the amplitude to peak at a certain frequency of the applied force. In the other two graphs there is a definite peak near 3. The sharper peak occurs for the system with the lower drag. The frequency at which the amplitude has a maximum is called the **resonant frequency** and the peaking phenomenon is called **resonance**.

To find the maximum (if it occurs), we differentiate f and set it equal to zero and solve for ω. We have

$$f'(\omega) = \frac{1}{2}(4\lambda^2\omega^2 + (\omega^2 - a^2)^2)^{-1/2}[8\lambda^2\omega + 2(\omega^2 - a^2)2\omega] = 0.$$

Thus

$$2\lambda^2\omega + (\omega^2 - a^2)\omega = 0,$$

and so $\omega = 0$ or $\omega = \sqrt{a^2 - 2\lambda^2}$. A frequency of zero is of no interest, so

$$\omega_{max} = \sqrt{a^2 - 2\lambda^2}.$$

The maximum value of f is

$$f(\omega_{max}) = \frac{1}{2\lambda\sqrt{a^2 - \lambda^2}}.$$

One way to measure the extent of the resonance effect is to consider the ratio of the steady state maximum response amplitude to the driving force amplitude. This ratio is

$$\frac{F_1 f(\omega_{max})}{F_0} = f(\omega_{max})/m = \frac{1}{c\sqrt{\omega_{max}^2 + \lambda^2}}.$$

Unless the resonant frequency is very small, the friction coefficient c is the quantity that most affects the resonant response.

4.5.3 The Undamped Driven System

The mass–spring system with no friction has the equation

$$my'' + ky = F_0 \sin(\omega t)$$

or

$$y'' + a^2 y = F_1 \sin(\omega t),$$

where $a^2 = k/m$ and $F_1 = F_0/m$. A system with no friction is a somewhat ideal case, but there are situations in which the friction is so low that it is easier to treat the system as having no friction at all. Indeed, the general solution when friction is small has the form

$$y(t) = A \sin(\omega t) + B \sin(\omega t) + c_1 e^{-ct/2m} \sin(\gamma t) + c_2 e^{-ct/2m} \cos(\gamma t).$$

But if c is very small relative to m, then $e^{-ct/2m}$ will be close to 1 for an appreciable time period, and so the solution will be approximately

$$y(t) = A \sin(\omega t) + B \sin(\omega t) + c_1 \sin(\gamma t) + c_2 \cos(\gamma t).$$

However, this is very nearly the solution to the equation with no friction at all, provided $\omega \neq a$. The only difference is that $\gamma = \sqrt{(4mk - c^2)}/2m$ is not quite equal to $a = \sqrt{k/m}$. Thus it is worth studying the undamped system as the limiting case of low friction.

If $\omega \neq a$, then the general solution is easily computed to be

$$y(t) = -\frac{F_1}{\omega^2 - a^2} \sin(\omega t) + c_1 \sin(at) + c_2 \cos(at).$$

We see that the amplitude of the particular solution goes to infinity as ω approaches a. To get a better feel for the behavior of the solution, we combine the second and third terms using the trick from trigonometry to get

$$y(t) = -\frac{F_1}{\omega^2 - a^2} \sin(\omega t) + R \sin(at + \delta).$$

If ω is close to a, we have two sine functions of nearly equal frequency, so they will alternately move into step with one another and then fall out of step.

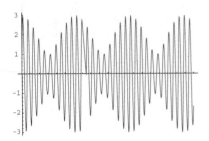

FIGURE 4.4

Thus at times their values will add, and at other times their values will subtract. The net effect is an oscillation that varies in amplitude, which is called **beating**. Figure 4.4 illustrates the beating together of two sine waves. If you listen to two musical notes of very nearly the same frequency, you will hear this beating as an unpleasant wobbling of the tone.

We have noted that as ω approaches a the amplitude of the response grows. At $\omega = a$ we have resonance behavior again, only in this case the response grows to infinity with time. To see this, note that the particular solution to the equation will correspond to a multiplicity of 2 for the roots $\pm ai$; thus the solution has the form

$$y_p(t) = At\sin(at).$$

Therefore, as $t \to \infty$ the solution will go to infinity as well.

EXERCISES 4.5

1. For the mass-spring system described in the text, determine the motion of the mass if the mass is 2 kg, the spring constant is 4 N/m, and the friction constant is 1 N/(m/s). The initial displacement of the mass is 0 m, and the initial velocity is 5 m/s. (The units are m = meters, kg = kilograms, N = newtons, and s = seconds.)

2. For the mass–spring system described in the text, determine the motion of the mass if the mass is 1 kg, the spring constant is 2 N/m, and the friction constant is 3 N/(m/s). The initial displacement of the mass is 1 m, and the initial velocity is -2 m/s.

3. For the mass–spring system described in the text, determine the motion of the mass if the mass is 2 kg, the spring is extended 0.5 m by a force of 1 N, and the friction constant is 1 kg/(m/s). The initial displacement of the mass is 0.5 m, and the initial velocity is 1 m/s.

4. For the mass–spring system described in the text, determine the motion of the mass if the mass is 1 kg, the spring is extended 0.25 m by a force of 1 N, and the friction constant is 0.1 kg/(m/s). The initial displacement of the mass is 0.5 m, and the initial velocity is 0 m/s.

In Exercises 5–10, first predict the behavior of the solution to the initial-value problem using $c^2 - 4mk$. Calculate whether the solution crosses the positive t-axis. Then use 2 × 2System to draw the solution and verify your predictions.

5. $y'' + 3y' + y = 0$, $y(0) = 1$, and $y'(0) = -2$

6. $2y'' + 2y' + y = 0$, $y(0) = 1$, and $y'(0) = 0$

7. $2y'' + 5y' + 2y = 0$, $y(0) = 1$, and $y'(0) = 2$

8. $2y'' + 5y' + 2y = 0$, $y(0) = 2$, and $y'(0) = -5$

9. $y'' + 2y' + y = 0$, $y(0) = 1$, and $y'(0) = -2$

10. $y'' + 2y' + y = 0$, $y(0) = -3$, and $y'(0) = -2$

11. In the phase plane picture, how do you recognize crossing of the t-axis by the solution?

12. Discuss and explain the form of the graphs of all possible solutions in the critically damped case. Assume that the outside force is zero. Be sure to derive the formula for deciding if and when the solutions can cross the t-axis in terms of the initial conditions.

In Exercises 13–17, draw response curves of $f(\omega)$ for the equations using the Graphing package. If you do not move the origin to the lower left, remember that it is only the graph in the first quadrant that has meaning. Calculate the resonant frequency and the ratio of the maximum response amplitude to driving amplitude in each problem when possible. Compare with the graphical results. The indicated ranges for x and y will help.

13. $2y''(t) + 4y'(t) + 5y(t) = 6\sin(\omega t)$, $[0, 6]$, $[0, 0.5]$

14. $3y''(t) + 2y'(t) + y(t) = 10\sin(\omega t)$, $[0, 6]$, $[0, 10]$

15. $2y''(t) + 0.1y'(t) + 4y(t) = 2\sin(\omega t)$, $[0, 6]$, $[0, 20]$

16. 16) $y''(t) + 0.01y'(t) + 10y(t) = 6\sin(\omega t)$, $[0, 6]$, $[0, 40]$

17. $2y''(t) + 0.02y'(t) + 10y(t) = 6\sin(\omega t)$, $[0, 6]$, $[0, 50]$

18. Solve the initial-value problem $y'' + 100y = 2\sin(12t)$, $y(0) = 1$, and $y'(0) = 0$. Graph your solution and observe the beats.

19. Solve the initial-value problem $y'' + 81y = 2\sin(10t)$, $y(0) = -1$, and $y'(0) = 0$. Graph your solution and observe the beats.

20. What is the resonant frequency for the mass/spring system with a mass of 0.02 kg, spring constant of 4 N/m, and

no friction? What happens to solutions driven at such a frequency?

21. What is the resonant frequency for the mass/spring system with a mass of .01 kg, spring constant of 5 N/m, and no friction? What happens to solutions driven at such a frequency?

22. Apply numerical methods to $y'' + y = 0$ to approximate $\sin(1)$ and $\cos(1)$ to three decimal places. What gives you confidence in your accuracy?

23. Consider an inductor of inductance $L = 4 \times 10^{-2}$, a capacitor of capacitance $C = 10^{-2}$, and a resistor of resistance $R = 0.01$ connected in series to a generator with voltage given by $E(t) = \sin(50t) + \sin(60t)$. Recall that if $q(t)$ is the charge on the capacitor at time t then $q(t)$ satisfies

$$Lq'' + Rq' + q/C = E(t).$$

(a) What is the resonant frequency of this circuit? Graph the resonance curve for this circuit.

(b) Use 2 × 2System to graph the solution. Find the frequency of the steady state as closely as you can. What is the frequency of $\sin(50t)$? Note that the transient takes a bit of time. Use $(0, 0)$ for an initial condition.

(c) Repeat part b with the term $\sin(60t)$ removed from $E(t)$. Compare parts b and c.

(d) Try to repeat part b with $\sin(50t)$ removed from $E(t)$. What do you see?

(e) Explain this phenomenon.

(f) What do you think this might have to do with tuning your radio?

SUPPLEMENTARY EXERCISES FOR CHAPTER 4

1. Consider the equation

$$y''' + a_2 y'' + a_1 y' + a_0 y = 0.$$

Let W be the Wronskian of three solutions to this equation.

(a) Prove that

$$W' + a_1 W = 0$$

and that W is identically zero or never zero. *Hint:* Show that the derivative of W is the sum of three determinants each obtained by differentiating a row of W.

(b) Generalize to the nth-order case and prove it. You will need to review facts about determinants.

2. Consider the equation

$$x^2 y'' + 2xy' + y = 0.$$

(a) Find a change of the variable x that will convert this equation to a constant coefficient equation. Solve it, and convert back to a solution to the original equation.

(b) Generalize!

3. The general form of the equation of one-dimensional motion of a mass m subject to a force that may depend on time, displacement and velocity, is

$$my'' = F(t, y, y').$$

(a) A friend suggests that, for a mass on a spring, if the force of friction is proportional to the square of the velocity, then the form of the equation might be

$$y'' = -(y')^2 - y.$$

Examine this graphically, and explain to your friend why this is not a good model. Give an explanation of the behavior of the solutions in terms of the physics that this equation implies. In particular, how do you explain the periodic orbits?

(b) Propose a modified model that does have friction proportional to the square of the velocity. Study the orbits graphically, and explain why your modification does the job.

4. Consider two masses suspended from the ceiling as follows. The first mass is suspended by a spring of constant 4 lb/ft. The second mass is suspended from the first by a spring of constant 5 lb/ft. The first mass weighs 3 lb and the second 2 lb. The masses are allowed to hang down and reach equilibrium. The displacements of the masses are measured from these equilibrium positions. Thus gravity can be ignored. Take "down" to be positive.

(a) Find a system of two second-order equations in the displacement functions that models the dynamics of this system.

(b) Solve the system. *Hint:* Eliminate one of the unknowns to arrive at an equation in one unknown and then solve this. Substitute the result in one of the original equations and solve to complete the task.

(c) Are all solutions periodic?

5. In the mass–spring system we assumed that the spring was perfectly linear, so the restoring force had the form $F(y) = -ky$. Real springs are better modeled by a restoring force of the form $F(y) = -ky + by^3$, where $k > 0$ and b positive or negative.

(a) Draw graphs of the possible restoring forces $F(y) = -ky + by^3$ for $b > 0$ and $b < 0$. Springs for which $b < 0$ are called hard, and springs for which $b > 0$ are called soft. Give a rationale for this terminology. Criticize these spring models.

(b) For both types of springs, reduce to a first-order system and study the fields and orbits. Neglect friction. Describe and explain the behavior.

(c) Discuss when the orbits are closed.

(d) Using 2×2System, experiment with hard springs and driving forces of the form $\sin(\omega t)$. Is there any indication of a resonance phenomenon?

CHAPTER 5

FIRST-ORDER SYSTEMS: LINEAR METHODS

In Chapter 3 the basics of first-order systems were introduced. The conditions for the existence and uniqueness of solutions were discussed, and graphical and numerical methods were developed. In this chapter we consider first-order systems that are linear with constant coefficients. For these special systems we shall be able to find analytic solutions. The 2×2 case will be treated first using the usual approach of eigenvectors and generalized eigenvectors. Solutions found this way will then be used to point the way to a very elegant method for solving these and higher-order systems. This will also lead to a simple way to decide on the stability or instability of the critical points of linear systems.

We shall also use linear systems as approximations to general first-order systems, much as the tangent line is a local approximation to the graph of a function. In this way the critical points of general first-order systems can be tested for stability by referring the question to the stability of the critical point of the approximating linear system.

This chapter draws on some topics from linear algebra. While knowledge of linear algebra is not a prerequisite for this chapter, some knowledge of vector spaces, bases, and linear transformations provides a broader framework in which to view the topics of this chapter. Indeed, the notions of linear combinations, independence, and linearity of operators touched on in Chapter 4, and to be revisited here, can be thought of as motivating the study of linear algebra. Section 9.4 and Appendix A provide a brief survey of basic concepts in linear algebra, and you are encouraged to turn to these if you feel the need for unifying definitions of such concepts as linearity and independence.

5.1 MATRICES, INDEPENDENCE, AND EIGENVECTORS

Matrices can be used to express linear systems in a most economical way. But

117

matrices are not only important for the economy that they provide. The eigenvalues and eigenvectors of these matrices, which we will define in this section, play a pivotal role in solving the systems. For these reasons, we begin this chapter with a discussion of matrices.

5.1.1 Matrices

Matrix Operations and Definitions

A matrix is a rectangular array of numbers. The general form of a matrix is

$$\begin{bmatrix} a_{11} & a_{12} & \cdots & a_{1n} \\ a_{21} & a_{22} & \cdots & a_{2n} \\ & & \vdots & \\ a_{m1} & a_{m2} & \cdots & a_{mn} \end{bmatrix}.$$

Such a matrix is said to be $m \times n$ since it has m rows and n columns.

Here is an example of a 4×3:

$$\begin{bmatrix} 2 & -3 & 5 \\ 0 & 1 & 4 \\ -2 & 3 & 7 \\ 1 & 1 & -6 \end{bmatrix}.$$

Matrices are often symbolized by expressions of the form

$$(a_{ij})_{m \times n}.$$

For example

$$((-1)^{i+j})_{4 \times 3} = \begin{bmatrix} 1 & -1 & 1 \\ -1 & 1 & -1 \\ 1 & -1 & 1 \\ -1 & 1 & -1 \end{bmatrix}.$$

This notation is useful in defining the basic operations that can be performed on matrices. There are three basic operations: addition, multiplication, and multiplication of a matrix by a scalar. This is how they are defined. Matrices are added as follows:

$$(a_{ij})_{m \times n} + (b_{ij})_{m \times n} = (a_{ij} + b_{ij})_{m \times n}.$$

To add two matrices, simply add the entries in a given location. Notice that one can only add matrices of the same dimensions.

The matrix product is defined by

$$(a_{ij})_{m \times n} (b_{ij})_{n \times p} = \left(\sum_{k=1}^{n} a_{ik} b_{kj} \right)_{m \times p}.$$

The matrix product is more complicated. To get the ij entry in the product matrix, take the ith row of the first matrix and lay it against the jth column of the second matrix; then multiply the numbers that are adjacent and add the products. Here is an example.

$$\begin{bmatrix} 2 & -3 & 5 \\ 0 & 1 & 4 \\ -2 & 3 & 7 \\ 1 & 1 & -6 \end{bmatrix} \begin{bmatrix} 1 & -2 \\ 0 & 1 \\ -2 & 4 \end{bmatrix} = \begin{bmatrix} -8 & 13 \\ -8 & 17 \\ -16 & 35 \\ 13 & -25 \end{bmatrix}.$$

Note that in the multiplication of matrices the column number of the first matrix must match the row number of the second. The order of the factors here cannot be reversed, because the dimensions do not match up to perform the multiplication. Even if the factors in the product can be reversed, there is no guarantee that the products will be the same. For example,

$$\begin{bmatrix} 2 & -3 \\ 1 & 1 \end{bmatrix} \begin{bmatrix} 1 & -2 \\ 1 & 2 \end{bmatrix} = \begin{bmatrix} -1 & -10 \\ 2 & 0 \end{bmatrix},$$

and

$$\begin{bmatrix} 1 & -2 \\ 1 & 2 \end{bmatrix} \begin{bmatrix} 2 & -3 \\ 1 & 1 \end{bmatrix} = \begin{bmatrix} 0 & -5 \\ 4 & -1 \end{bmatrix}.$$

We say that matrix multiplication is not commutative.

Multiplication by a scalar is defined by

$$r(a_{ij}) = (ra_{ij}).$$

To multiply by a scalar, simply multiply every entry in the matrix by the scalar. Note that we may drop the dimensions from the matrix symbol when it is not needed or is obvious from context.

In later sections we will want to allow scalar multiplication on the right. The only reason for doing this is that the resulting equations will be more appealing to the eye. Thus Ar is the same as rA.

A matrix consisting of all zeros is called a zero matrix and is denoted by 0.

A square ($n \times n$) matrix that has 1s down the diagonal from the a_{11} position to the a_{nn} position (called the main diagonal) and zeros elsewhere is called the $n \times n$ identity matrix. The reader can quickly verify that the product of the identity matrix with any matrix of the correct dimension for multiplying leaves that matrix unchanged. The identity matrix is a little like the number 1 in the real number system. We use I to denote an identity matrix. Here is a 3×3 identity matrix:

$$I = \begin{bmatrix} 1 & 0 & 0 \\ 0 & 1 & 0 \\ 0 & 0 & 1 \end{bmatrix}.$$

If A and B are $n \times n$ matrices, we say that B is an **inverse matrix** of A if

$$AB = BA = I.$$

For a given matrix A, the inverse matrix B, if it exists, is unique. In this case we use the notation $B = A^{-1}$. It is not true that every nonzero square matrix has an inverse. Indeed, the matrix

$$\begin{bmatrix} 1 & 0 \\ 0 & 0 \end{bmatrix}$$

has no inverse, because if it had we would have

$$\begin{bmatrix} 1 & 0 \\ 0 & 0 \end{bmatrix} \begin{bmatrix} a & b \\ c & d \end{bmatrix} = \begin{bmatrix} a & b \\ 0 & 0 \end{bmatrix} = \begin{bmatrix} 1 & 0 \\ 0 & 1 \end{bmatrix}.$$

Matrices that are single columns are often called **column vectors** or just vectors. Such matrices usually denote a point in the plane or space or higher-dimensional space. For example, the vector $\begin{bmatrix} x \\ y \end{bmatrix}$ may be interpreted in just the same way as $x\vec{i} + y\vec{j}$. When it is convenient, we shall write column vectors horizontally as rows in order not to take up as much space on the page.

Matrix Algebra

The rules of matrix algebra are not much different from the algebra of numbers. There are two notable exceptions: multiplication is not commutative, and many nonzero matrices do not have inverses. Here are some of the rules that can be easily proved by appealing to the definitions of the matrix operations. We assume that the dimensions of the matrices are appropriate for the operations. Let A, B, and C be matrices and r and s scalars.

1. $A + B = B + A$ (addition commutes)
2. $A + (B + C) = (A + B) + C$ (associative law of addition)
3. For any matrix A there is a matrix $-A$ such that $A + (-A) = 0$.
4. $A(BC) = (AB)C$ (associative law of multiplication)
5. $r(sA) = (rs)A$ (associative law of scalars)
6. $(r + s)A = rA + sA$ (distributive law)
7. $r(A + B) = rA + rB$ (distributive law)

In the pages that follow, if you are uncertain of a step in matrix algebra, simply go back to the definitions of the operations involved and verify the statement. Here is an example. In several places we shall have need to conclude that if $rA = 0$ then $r = 0$ or $A = 0$. Now $rA = 0$ means $r(a_{ij}) = (ra_{ij}) = 0$. This last 0 is the zero matrix. So, $ra_{ij} = 0$ for all i and j. If $r = 0$, we are done. If not, then $a_{ij} = 0$ for all i and j, but this means that A is the zero matrix.

Matrix-Valued Functions

Many of our matrices will be matrices of functions such as

$$A(t) = \begin{bmatrix} a_{11}(t) & a_{12}(t) & \cdots & a_{1n}(t) \\ a_{21}(t) & a_{22}(t) & \cdots & a_{2n}(t) \\ & & \vdots & \\ a_{m1}(t) & a_{m2}(t) & \cdots & a_{mn}(t) \end{bmatrix}.$$

By definition the derivative of such a matrix is the matrix of the derivatives of the function entries. Thus,

$$A'(t) = \begin{bmatrix} a'_{11}(t) & a'_{12}(t) & \cdots & a'_{1n}(t) \\ a'_{21}(t) & a'_{22}(t) & \cdots & a'_{2n}(t) \\ & & \vdots & \\ a'_{m1}(t) & a'_{m2}(t) & \cdots & a'_{mn}(t) \end{bmatrix}.$$

The differentiation rules for matrix-valued functions are the same as for ordinary functions. Clearly, the derivative of a sum is the sum of the derivatives, but what about the product rule? Suppose that

$$F(t) = (a_{ij}(t))_{m \times n}(b_{ij}(t))_{n \times p} = \left(\sum_{k=1}^{n} a_{ik}(t)b_{kj}(t) \right)_{m \times p}.$$

Then

$$F'(t) = \left(\sum_{k=1}^{n} a'_{ik}(t)b_{kj}(t) + a_{ik}(t)b'_{kj}(t) \right)$$

$$= \left(\sum_{k=1}^{n} a'_{ik}(t)b_{kj}(t) \right) + \left(\sum_{k=1}^{n} a_{ik}(t)b'_{kj}(t) \right)$$

$$= (a_{ij}(t))'(b_{ij}(t)) + (a_{ij}(t))(b_{ij}(t))'.$$

The pattern of the product rule is unchanged for matrices. The only warning is that the order of the matrices must be maintained.

Matrix Representation of Systems

We are now ready to express systems of first-order linear equations in matrix form. For the system

$$x'_1(t) = a_{11}x_1(t) + \cdots + a_{1n}x_n(t),$$
$$x'_2(t) = a_{21}x_1(t) + \cdots + a_{2n}x_n(t),$$
$$\vdots$$
$$x'_n(t) = a_{n1}x_1(t) + \cdots + a_{nn}x_n(t),$$

set

$$A = \begin{bmatrix} a_{11} & a_{12} & \cdots & a_{1n} \\ a_{21} & a_{22} & \cdots & a_{2n} \\ & & \vdots & \\ a_{n1} & a_{n2} & \cdots & a_{nn} \end{bmatrix},$$

and

$$X(t) = \begin{bmatrix} x_1(t) \\ x_2(t) \\ \vdots \\ x_n(t) \end{bmatrix}.$$

Then the system can be expressed as

$$X'(t) = AX(t).$$

Such a system is called a linear, homogeneous, constant-coefficient, first-order system of differential equations.

Observe that such a system is linear in the sense that if $X_1(t)$ and $X_2(t)$ are solutions then $Y(t) = c_1 X_1(t) + c_2 X_2(t)$ is a solution also. Indeed,

$$Y'(t) = c_1 X_1'(t) + c_2 X_2'(t) = c_1 AX_1(t) + c_2 AX_2(t)$$
$$= A(c_1 X_1(t) + c_2 X_2(t)) = AY(t).$$

The following system is a linear nonhomogeneous system provided not all of the $c_k(t)$ are zero.

$$x_1'(t) = a_{11}x_1(t) + \cdots + a_{1n}x_n(t) + c_1(t),$$
$$x_2'(t) = a_{21}x_1(t) + \cdots + a_{2n}x_n(t) + c_2(t),$$
$$\vdots$$
$$x_n'(t) = a_{n1}x_1(t) + \cdots + a_{nn}x_n(t) + c_n(t).$$

This is easily translated to matrix form by

$$X'(t) = AX(t) + C(t),$$

where $C(t) = \begin{bmatrix} c_1(t) \\ c_2(t) \\ \vdots \\ c_n(t) \end{bmatrix}.$

Surely you will agree that this is a most economical way to write down linear systems, but it is much more than that, because it turns out that the properties of the matrices of systems provide the basis for the solutions of these systems. The concepts that will allow us to solve these systems will now be defined.

5.1.2 Linear Independence

You will recall that to solve an nth-order linear homogeneous equation we had to find a fundamental set of n solutions or, equivalently, find a set of n linearly independent solutions. Then all solutions would be linear combinations of these. We shall need the notion of linear independence in solving linear systems also.

Definition 5.1.1

Let $X_1, X_2, \ldots, X_m$ be column vectors all with the same number of rows, say n. We say that the set of vectors $\{X_1, X_2, \ldots, X_m\}$ is linearly independent if

$$c_1 X_1 + c_2 X_2 + \cdots + c_m X_m = 0$$

implies that $c_1 = c_2 = \cdots = c_m = 0$. We say that the set of vectors is linearly dependent otherwise.   ●

An expression of the form $c_1 X_1 + c_2 X_2 + \cdots + c_m X_m$ is called a **linear combination** of the vectors $X_1, \ldots, X_m$. This definition of a linear combination is virtually the same as that given in Chapter 4. See Section 9.4 for the general definition of a linear combination that applies to all cases. We can now say that a set of vectors is linearly independent if the only linear combination of the vectors that is equal to zero is the one for which all the coefficients c_i are zero.

Example 5.1.2   Is the set of vectors $\{ \begin{bmatrix} 1 \\ 2 \end{bmatrix}, \begin{bmatrix} 3 \\ 4 \end{bmatrix} \}$ linearly independent? To answer this, we must study the possible solutions to

$$c_1 \begin{bmatrix} 1 \\ 2 \end{bmatrix} + c_2 \begin{bmatrix} 3 \\ 4 \end{bmatrix} = 0.$$

As a system of equations, this is

$$1c_1 + 3c_2 = 0,$$
$$2c_1 + 4c_2 = 0.$$

Clearly, the only solution is $c_1 = c_2 = 0$. Therefore, the set of vectors is linearly independent.   ■

Example 5.1.3   The set of vectors $\{ \begin{bmatrix} 1 \\ 2 \\ 3 \end{bmatrix}, \begin{bmatrix} 1 \\ 0 \\ -1 \end{bmatrix}, \begin{bmatrix} 3 \\ 4 \\ 5 \end{bmatrix} \}$ is linearly dependent. To show this, we must find a linear combination of these vectors that is equal to the zero vector, but not all of the three coefficients are zero. If we try to solve for the coefficients from

$$1c_1 + 1c_2 + 3c_3 = 0,$$

$$2c_1 + 0c_2 + 4c_3 = 0,$$
$$3c_1 - 1c_2 + 5c_3 = 0,$$

we quickly discover that one equation is redundant, and the system has nonzero solutions. In fact $c_1 = 2$, $c_2 = 1$, and $c_3 = -1$ will do it. ∎

The coordinate direction vectors $\{\vec{i}, \vec{j}, \vec{k}\}$ in three-dimensional space form a linearly independent set.

If you have a set of m vectors each with n rows and $m > n$, then this set must be linearly dependent. In this case the system of equations to be considered has more unknowns than equations, so the row reduction process of solution must lead to nonzero solutions.

5.1.3 Eigenvalues and Eigenvectors

You will recall that eigenvalues were defined in Chapter 4 as the roots of a certain polynomial called the characteristic polynomial. The eigenvalues of an $n \times n$ matrix are also the roots of a certain polynomial. Note that the definitions of this section only apply to square ($n \times n$) matrices. Here is the formal definition.

Definition 5.1.4

Let A be an $n \times n$ matrix. The polynomial defined by

$$P(\lambda) = \det[A - \lambda I] = \det \begin{bmatrix} a_{11} - \lambda & a_{12} & \cdots & a_{1n} \\ a_{21} & a_{22} - \lambda & \cdots & a_{2n} \\ & & \vdots & \\ a_{n1} & a_{n2} & \cdots & a_{nn} - \lambda \end{bmatrix},$$

where det is the determinant of the matrix, is called the characteristic polynomial of the matrix A. The roots of this polynomial are called the **eigenvalues** of A. ●

Example 5.1.5 Let

$$A = \begin{bmatrix} 1 & 2 & -2 \\ 2 & -2 & 1 \\ 2 & -4 & 3 \end{bmatrix}.$$

Then

$$P(\lambda) = \det \begin{bmatrix} 1 - \lambda & 2 & -2 \\ 2 & -2 - \lambda & 1 \\ 2 & -4 & 3 - \lambda \end{bmatrix}.$$

Expanding this determinant by the top row in the usual way gives

$$P(\lambda) = (1 - \lambda)((-2 - \lambda)(3 - \lambda) + 4) + 2(2(3 - \lambda) - 2)$$

$$- 2(-8 - 2(-2 - \lambda))$$
$$= -\lambda^3 + 2\lambda^2 + \lambda - 2.$$

This factors to give

$$P(\lambda) = -(\lambda - 1)(\lambda + 1)(\lambda - 2).$$

Therefore, the eigenvalues of A are 1, -1, and 2.   ◼

Notice that the characteristic polynomial has the same degree as the dimension of the matrix.

You may be wondering what the relationship is between the characteristic polynomial defined in Chapter 4 and the characteristic polynomial defined here. If you take an nth-order, linear, constant-coefficient equation and reduce it to a first-order system, you will find that the characteristic polynomials of the original equation and the system are the same or differ only by a factor of (-1). This is left as an exercise.

Eigenvalues for matrices can be defined in another way, and this approach is central to solving linear systems. Here is the new definition. Notice that it introduces the notion of an eigenvector as well as eigenvalue.

Definition 5.1.6

Let A be an $n \times n$ matrix. We say that the number λ is an eigenvalue of A if there is a non-zero vector X such that

$$AX = \lambda X.$$

We call X an **eigenvector** corresponding to the eigenvalue λ.   ●

Let us work through an example of finding the eigenvalues and eigenvectors of a matrix according to this new definition.

Example 5.1.7   Let

$$A = \begin{bmatrix} 1 & -2 \\ 1 & 4 \end{bmatrix}.$$

If λ is to be an eigenvalue, we must find a nonzero vector X so that $AX = \lambda X$, or $AX - \lambda X = 0$, or

$$(A - \lambda I)X = 0.$$

Writing this matrix equation out in the form of the system of equations it represents, we have

$$(1 - \lambda)x - 2y = 0,$$
$$x + (4 - \lambda)y = 0.$$

To solve for y, say, we multiply the second equation by $1 - \lambda$ and subtract the resulting equation from the first. The new system is

$$-[(1 - \lambda)(4 - \lambda) + 2]y = 0,$$
$$x + (4 - \lambda)y = 0.$$

The solutions to this system are the same as for the original system. The latter system has the unique solution $(0, 0)$ if and only if

$$(1 - \lambda)(4 - \lambda) + 2 \neq 0.$$

But the left-hand side is the characteristic polynomial of A. Thus we have nonzero solutions, provided the characteristic polynomial of A is zero; that is, λ must be a root of the characteristic polynomial. In this case at least, the eigenvalues according to the new definition are precisely the eigenvalues of the old definition. We shall show later that this holds in general. The eigenvalues are the roots of

$$P(\lambda) = (1 - \lambda)(4 - \lambda) + 2 = \lambda^2 - 5\lambda + 6 = (\lambda - 2)(\lambda - 3).$$

The eigenvalues are $\lambda = 2$ and $\lambda = 3$.

To find the eigenvectors corresponding to these eigenvalues, we replace λ by the eigenvalues in the preceding system of equations and solve for all nonzero solutions. For example, the system corresponding to $\lambda = 2$ is

$$-x - 2y = 0,$$
$$x + 2y = 0.$$

The equations are dependent, as they must be. The set of all solutions (as vectors) is

$$\left\{ \begin{bmatrix} -2t \\ t \end{bmatrix} \middle| t \text{ any real number} \right\}.$$

You should choose any nonzero value of t and check that

$$AX = 2X$$

holds.

Finding the eigenvectors corresponding to $\lambda = 3$ is done in the same way. The set of solutions is

$$\left\{ \begin{bmatrix} -t \\ t \end{bmatrix} \middle| t \text{ any real number} \right\}.$$

It is worth noticing that both sets are straight lines in the plane passing through the origin. Readers who have had a little linear algebra will recognize these lines as one-dimensional subspaces. It is not hard to show that the set of vectors corresponding to a given eigenvalue together with the zero vector form a subspace called the **eigensubspace** corresponding to the eigenvalue.

It is also worth noting for the next section that if we set $t = 1$, say, in each set, we get a set of two linearly independent vectors

$$\left\{ \begin{bmatrix} -2 \\ 1 \end{bmatrix}, \begin{bmatrix} -1 \\ 1 \end{bmatrix} \right\}.$$

Verification is left to you.   ■

We now show that the new definition of eigenvalue is equivalent to the old definition in general.

If $AX = \lambda X$, then $AX - \lambda X = 0$, and

$$(A - \lambda I)X = 0.$$

If $A = (a_{ij})$ and $X = \begin{bmatrix} x_1 \\ x_2 \\ \vdots \\ x_n \end{bmatrix}$, then the preceding equation may be expressed

as

$$(a_{11} - \lambda)x_1 + a_{12}x_2 + \cdots + a_{1n}x_n = 0,$$
$$a_{21}x_1 + (a_{22} - \lambda)x_2 + \cdots + a_{2n}x_n = 0,$$
$$\vdots$$
$$a_{n1}x_1 + a_{n2}x_2 + \cdots + (a_{nn} - \lambda)x_n = 0.$$

There are two possibilities: either the row reduction of this system yields complete diagonalization and a unique solution, or the reduction yields a column or row of zeros, in which case the solution is not unique. In our system the unique solution is $X = 0$, and if the solution is not unique, then there is a nonzero solution. In Appendix A or [4], it is shown that the row operations used to reduce the system do not change whether the determinant of the coefficients of the system at each stage is zero or not. Indeed, the row operations are to interchange rows, multiply a row by a nonzero number, and multiply a row by a number and add to another row. The first operation changes the sign of the determinant, the second multiplies the value of the determinant by that nonzero number, and the third makes no change. Thus solutions are unique if and only if the determinant of the system is not zero. Therefore, we have nonzero solutions to

$$AX = \lambda X$$

precisely when

$$P(\lambda) = \det(A - \lambda I) = 0;$$

but this is precisely when λ is a root of the characteristic polynomial.

In the preceding example, we saw that, if we choose an eigenvector corresponding to the two distinct eigenvalues, the resulting set of vectors is linearly independent. This general principle is summarized in the following theorem.

Theorem 5.1.8

Any set of eigenvectors of a square matrix A, where each eigenvector corresponds to a distinct eigenvalue, is linearly independent. ●

Proof

The proof is by induction on the number of eigenvectors. If the set consists of just one eigenvector X_1 then, since $X_1 \neq 0$, if $cX_1 = 0$, then $c = 0$. Thus a set of one eigenvector is linearly independent. Now suppose that any set of m eigenvectors corresponding to distinct eigenvalues is linearly independent, and consider $m + 1$ such eigenvectors $X_1, X_2, \ldots, X_{m+1}$ corresponding to the eigenvalues $\lambda_1, \lambda_2, \ldots, \lambda_{m+1}$. Suppose that

$$c_1 X_1 + c_2 X_2 + \cdots + c_{m+1} X_{m+1} = 0.$$

We must show that the c_i are zero. We multiply this equation by λ_1, and we also multiply the original equation by A. We get

$$c_1 \lambda_1 X_1 + c_2 \lambda_1 X_2 + \cdots + c_{m+1} \lambda_1 X_{m+1} = 0,$$

and

$$c_1 \lambda_1 X_1 + c_2 \lambda_2 X_2 + \cdots + c_{m+1} \lambda_{m+1} X_{m+1} = 0.$$

Subtracting these equations gives

$$c_2 (\lambda_1 - \lambda_2) X_2 + \cdots + c_{m+1} (\lambda_1 - \lambda_{m+1}) X_{m+1} = 0.$$

By the induction hypothesis the coefficients must be zero, because any m such eigenvectors are assumed to be linearly independent. But, because the eigenvalues are distinct, the terms $(\lambda_1 - \lambda_i)$ are not zero, and so $c_2 = \cdots = c_{m+1} = 0$. Therefore, c_1 is zero also. So the set of $m + 1$ eigenvectors corresponding to distinct eigenvalues is linearly independent. ◆

You may have guessed that if there are no repeated eigenvalues then, as with nth-order, linear, constant-coefficient equations, the general solution to a linear system is going to be easy to write down. You are right! And you will recall that repeated roots required a little extra work. The same is true for systems, and so we shall conclude this section with examples of the two possibilities that arise if an eigenvalue of a 2×2 matrix is repeated.

Example 5.1.9 Consider the matrix

$$A = \begin{bmatrix} 2 & 0 \\ 0 & 2 \end{bmatrix}.$$

The characteristic polynomial is $P(\lambda) = (\lambda - 2)^2$, and so the eigenvalue is $\lambda = 2$ with multiplicity 2.

The system to be solved for the eigenvectors is

$$0x + 0y = 0,$$
$$0x + 0y = 0.$$

Thus every nonzero vector is an eigenvector of this matrix. Moreover, there are innumerable linearly independent sets of pairs of eigenvectors. For example,

$$\left\{ \begin{bmatrix} 1 \\ 0 \end{bmatrix}, \begin{bmatrix} 0 \\ 1 \end{bmatrix} \right\}$$

is such a set. We shall see that this is enough to write down the general solution to the system determined by this matrix.   ■

Contrast this example with the following one.

Example 5.1.10   Consider the matrix

$$A = \begin{bmatrix} 1 & 0 \\ 1 & 1 \end{bmatrix}.$$

The characteristic polynomial is $P(\lambda) = (\lambda - 1)^2$, so the only eigenvalue is $\lambda = 1$, and the multiplicity is 2.

The system to be solved for the eigenvectors is

$$0x + 0y = 0,$$
$$x + 0y = 0.$$

The eigenvectors are all scalar multiples of

$$\begin{bmatrix} 0 \\ 1 \end{bmatrix}.$$

We only get one independent eigenvector, and we shall see in the next section that this will require us to do some additional work before a full solution to the corresponding system can be given.   ■

The case of complex eigenvalues is simple in the 2×2 case. We will always get two distinct conjugate eigenvalues. This will yield two independent complex eigenvectors that are also conjugates. This will lead to a seemingly complex solution that simplifies to a real solution, just as this did in chapter 4.

EXERCISES 5.1

1. Add the matrices, and multiply the matrices in both orders $A = \begin{bmatrix} 3 & 2 \\ -1 & 3 \end{bmatrix}$ and $B = \begin{bmatrix} 2 & 5 \\ 0 & 3 \end{bmatrix}$.

2. Add the matrices, and multiply the matrices in both orders $A = \begin{bmatrix} 3 & 2 & 2 \\ -1 & 3 & 5 \\ 2 & 1 & -4 \end{bmatrix}$ and $B = \begin{bmatrix} 2 & 5 & 2 \\ 0 & 3 & -2 \\ 3 & -1 & 1 \end{bmatrix}$.

3. Differentiate the matrix-valued functions

(a) $A(t) = \begin{bmatrix} 3t & t^2 & 2 \\ -e^{3t} & 2t & 5 \\ t^4 & \sin(t) & -4t^2 \end{bmatrix}$.

(b) $B(t) = \begin{bmatrix} 3 & t^2 & t^3 \\ e^{5t} & -t & 5t^2 \\ t^4 & t-2 & -t^3 \end{bmatrix}$.

Express the following systems in matrix form.

4. $x'(t) = 3x(t) - y(t) + 2z(t),$
$y'(t) = x(t) + 2y(t) - 3z(t),$
$z'(t) = 5x(t) - 2y(t) + 6z(t).$

5. $x'(t) = 3x(t) + 4y(t)$
$y'(t) = -x(t) + 2y(t).$

6. $x'(t) = 3x(t) + 4y(t) + t^3$
$y'(t) = -x(t) + 2y(t) - e^t.$

7. Explain why the product of the $n \times n$ identity matrix I times an $n \times m$ matrix A is A.

8. Explain why the product of the $n \times n$ zero matrix times an $n \times m$ matrix A is the zero matrix.

In Exercises 9–13, decide if the given set is an independent set. Explain!

9. $\{ \begin{bmatrix} 1 \\ 1 \end{bmatrix}, \begin{bmatrix} 3 \\ 1 \end{bmatrix} \}$

10. $\{ \begin{bmatrix} 1 \\ 1 \end{bmatrix}, \begin{bmatrix} 2 \\ 2 \end{bmatrix} \}$

11. $\{ \begin{bmatrix} -1 \\ 2 \end{bmatrix}, \begin{bmatrix} 2 \\ 1 \end{bmatrix} \}$

12. $\{ \begin{bmatrix} 1 \\ 1 \\ 2 \end{bmatrix}, \begin{bmatrix} 3 \\ 3 \\ 5 \end{bmatrix}, \begin{bmatrix} -2 \\ -1 \\ 3 \end{bmatrix} \}$

13. $\{ \begin{bmatrix} 1 \\ 1 \\ 2 \end{bmatrix}, \begin{bmatrix} 3 \\ 3 \\ 6 \end{bmatrix}, \begin{bmatrix} -2 \\ -1 \\ 3 \end{bmatrix} \}$

14. If a set of vectors is linearly dependent, show that one of the vectors can be written as a linear combination of the others.

15. If one vector of a set of vectors can be written as a linear combination of the others, show that the set is dependent.

16. If A and B are square matrices and $AB = 0$, does it follow that $A = 0$ or $B = 0$? Explain!

In Exercises 17–20, find the eigenvalues and as many independent eigenvectors (up to two) as you can for the given matrix. Test the eigenvectors to show that they satisfy $AX = \lambda X$.

17. $A = \begin{bmatrix} 2 & 1 \\ 4 & 2 \end{bmatrix}$

18. $A = \begin{bmatrix} 1 & 1 \\ 4 & 1 \end{bmatrix}$

19. $A = \begin{bmatrix} -3 & \sqrt{2} \\ \sqrt{2} & -2 \end{bmatrix}$

20. $A = \begin{bmatrix} 1 & -1 \\ 1 & 3 \end{bmatrix}$

In Exercises 21 and 22, find the eigenvalues and as many independent eigenvectors (up to three) as you can for the given matrix. Test the eigenvectors to show that they satisfy $AX = \lambda X$.

21.
$$A = \begin{bmatrix} -3 & 0 & 0 \\ 0 & -3 & 0 \\ 0 & 0 & -3 \end{bmatrix}$$

22.
$$A = \begin{bmatrix} -3 & 0 & 0 \\ 1 & -3 & 0 \\ 0 & 0 & 2 \end{bmatrix}.$$

23. Show that the characteristic polynomial of $y'' - 3y' + 2y = 0$ and the characteristic polynomial of linear system obtained by reducing this equation to a first-order system are the same.

5.2 SOLVING 2×2 LINEAR SYSTEMS

In this section we will see how to solve the linear homogeneous system

$$X' = AX,$$

where A is a 2×2 matrix by using eigenvectors.

5.2.1 Two Independent Eigenvectors

We start by considering the case of real eigenvalues. Suppose that λ is a real eigenvalue of the matrix A and X_0 is a corresponding eigenvector. Let

$$X(t) = X_0 e^{\lambda t}.$$

Here we are scalar multiplying on the right, but, as we agreed, this is the same as multiplying on the left.

We claim that $X(t)$ is a solution to our system. Indeed, because X_0 is an eigenvector corresponding to λ, we have

$$X'(t) = X_0 \lambda e^{\lambda t} = \lambda X_0 e^{\lambda t} = A X_0 e^{\lambda t} = A X(t).$$

It is important to take note of the fact that the orbit of this solution is a straight line, since $X(t)$ is a scalar multiple of a fixed vector. The point $X(t)$ moves out along this line if $\lambda > 0$ and in if $\lambda < 0$.

Suppose that we have two eigenvectors X_1 and X_2 corresponding to the real eigenvalues λ_1 and λ_2. Then we have solutions $X_1 e^{\lambda_1 t}$ and $X_2 e^{\lambda_2 t}$. Thus the linear combination

$$X(t) = c_1 X_1 e^{\lambda_1 t} + c_2 X_2 e^{\lambda_2 t}$$

is also a solution, because the system is linear and homogeneous. At $t = 0$ the initial point is

$$X(0) = c_1 X_1 + c_2 X_2.$$

Now, if c_1 and c_2 can be chosen as we please, then we can accommodate all initial conditions provided that

$$c_1 X_1 + c_2 X_2 = \begin{bmatrix} x_0 \\ y_0 \end{bmatrix}$$

can always be solved. If you use Cramer's rule, then the system represented by this equation can be solved uniquely precisely when the determinant of coefficients is nonzero, and this is precisely when the only solution to

$$c_1 X_1 + c_2 X_2 = 0$$

is $c_1 = c_2 = 0$. Thus we can satisfy all possible initial conditions, provided the vectors X_1 and X_2 form an independent set.

Notice that this argument is valid even if the independent eigenvectors belong to the same eigenvalue. Moreover, the argument here applies just as well to an $n \times n$ system as to a 2×2 system. In this case you need n linearly independent eigenvectors of the matrix.

Example 5.2.1   We solve

$$X' = AX,$$

where

$$A = \begin{bmatrix} 1 & -2 \\ 1 & 4 \end{bmatrix}.$$

The characteristic polynomial is $P(\lambda) = \lambda^2 - 5\lambda + 6$, and so the eigenvalues are $\lambda = 2$ and $\lambda = 3$. We now need eigenvectors corresponding to these eigenvalues. Corresponding to $\lambda = 2$, we have

$$-x - 2y = 0,$$
$$x + 2y = 0.$$

Thus $\begin{bmatrix} -2 \\ 1 \end{bmatrix}$ is a corresponding eigenvector. For $\lambda = 3$ we have

$$-2x - 2y = 0,$$
$$x + y = 0,$$

and so $\begin{bmatrix} 1 \\ -1 \end{bmatrix}$ is a corresponding eigenvector. Since the eigenvalues are distinct, these eigenvectors are necessarily linearly independent.

The general solution is

$$X(t) = c_1 \begin{bmatrix} -2 \\ 1 \end{bmatrix} e^{2t} + c_2 \begin{bmatrix} 1 \\ -1 \end{bmatrix} e^{3t}.$$

If the initial condition is that the solution must pass through $(3, -1)$ at $t = 0$, then we must solve

$$-2c_1 + c_2 = 3,$$
$$c_1 - c_2 = -1.$$

We have $c_1 = -2$ and $c_2 = -1$, and so

$$X(t) = -2 \begin{bmatrix} -2 \\ 1 \end{bmatrix} e^{2t} - \begin{bmatrix} 1 \\ -1 \end{bmatrix} e^{3t}.$$

In general, because the exponentials have positive eigenvalues in them, all solutions except the one at the origin will go to infinity. So the origin is unstable. ∎

5.2.2 Complex Eigenvalues

Since the matrix of the system $X' = AX$ has real entries, if the roots are complex, they must be conjugate to one another. So we have distinct eigenvalues, and the eigenvectors corresponding to these eigenvalues must be independent. The only problem is that the eigenvectors will have complex entries. Just as in the case of linear constant-coefficient equations, we can get real solutions by adding and subtracting conjugates.

The conjugate of a matrix with complex entries is obtained by conjugating each of the entries. Thus a real matrix is unchanged by conjugation. We denote the conjugate of a matrix A by $\overline{A}$. Now suppose that we have the eigenvector equation

$$AX_0 = \lambda X_0.$$

Because the conjugate of a product of complex numbers is the product of the conjugates, it is easy to show that the same holds for matrix products and products by scalars. This is left as an exercise. Then, taking conjugates and assuming that A is a real matrix, we get

$$A\overline{X_0} = \overline{\lambda}\,\overline{X_0}.$$

This tells us again that eigenvalues of real matrices occur in conjugate pairs. Moreover, if X_0 is a λ eigenvector, then $\overline{X_0}$ is a $\overline{\lambda}$ eigenvector. For the system

$$X' = AX$$

we have the solution $X(t) = X_0 e^{\lambda t}$ and the conjugate solution $\overline{X}(t) = \overline{X_0} e^{\overline{\lambda} t}$. Just as the sum of a complex number and its conjugate is real, so is the sum of a complex vector and its conjugate. Likewise, the difference of a complex vector and its conjugate all divided by i is real. To see this, just consider what happens at each entry. Since a linear combination of solutions to a linear system is again a solution, the following functions are also solutions:

$$Y_1(t) = \frac{X(t) + \overline{X}(t)}{2}$$

and

$$Y_2(t) = \frac{X(t) - \overline{X}(t)}{2i}.$$

The general solution can now be written in real terms as

$$Y(t) = c_1 Y_1(t) + c_2 Y_2(t).$$

Here is an example illustrating all the steps.

Example 5.2.2   Consider the system

$$x' = x + y,$$
$$y' = -x + y.$$

The matrix of this system is

$$A = \begin{bmatrix} 1 & 1 \\ -1 & 1 \end{bmatrix}.$$

The characteristic polynomial is $P(\lambda) = \lambda^2 - 2\lambda + 2$, and so the eigenvalues are $\lambda = 1 + i$ and $\lambda = 1 - i$.

We find the first eigenvector as before. For $1 + i$ we solve

$$-ix + y = 0,$$
$$-x - iy = 0.$$

These equations are, as always, dependent. Indeed, the first is i times the second. A corresponding eigenvector is $\begin{bmatrix} 1 \\ i \end{bmatrix}$. To get an eigenvector corresponding to $1 - i$, we simply conjugate the one we have already found. Thus the eigenvector corresponding to $1 - i$ is $\begin{bmatrix} 1 \\ -i \end{bmatrix}$.

Using the previous formulas for $Y_1(t)$ and $Y_2(t)$, we get

$$Y_1(t) = e^t \begin{bmatrix} \cos(t) \\ \sin(t) \end{bmatrix}$$

and

$$Y_2(t) = e^t \begin{bmatrix} \sin(t) \\ \cos(t) \end{bmatrix}.$$

The general form of the solution is now

$$Y(t) = e^t [c_1 \begin{bmatrix} \cos(t) \\ \sin(t) \end{bmatrix} + c_2 \begin{bmatrix} \sin(t) \\ \cos(t) \end{bmatrix}].$$

Initial conditions are handled as usual.

Again we can describe solutions in general. Solutions with initial conditions different from the origin will spiral out to infinity. Therefore, the origin is unstable. Had the real part of the eigenvalues been negative, the solutions would have spiraled in, and the origin would have been stable.   ∎

If $(x_0 + ix_1, y_0 + iy_1)$ is an eigenvector corresponding to the eigenvalue $\lambda + i\mu$, it is not hard to show that the general form of the real solution is

$$X(t) = e^{\lambda t} [c_1 \begin{bmatrix} x_0 \cos(\mu t) - x_1 \sin(\mu t) \\ y_0 \cos(\mu t) - y_1 \sin(\mu t) \end{bmatrix} + c_2 \begin{bmatrix} x_0 \sin(\mu t) + x_1 \cos(\mu t) \\ y_0 \sin(\mu t) + y_1 \cos(\mu t) \end{bmatrix}].$$

This is left as an exercise.

It is true that the complex case can be treated in exactly the same manner as the case of distinct real eigenvalues. We carry out the computations with complex numbers just as with real numbers. The real solution that you must get with a real system and real initial data emerges at the end when algebraic simplification is performed. All the imaginary terms will drop out. However, the algebra is cumbersome, and you do not see that you get the second eigenvector for free unless you consider conjugates.

5.2.3 Repeated Eigenvalues

It is in the case of repeated eigenvalues that we begin to see the weakness of the eigenvector approach and the motivation for the method of the next section. Our current method is not too bad for repeated eigenvalues in the 2×2 case, but in higher dimensions the approach we are taking here becomes unwieldy.

Consider the system $X' = AX$ where

$$A = \begin{bmatrix} 2 & 0 \\ 1 & 2 \end{bmatrix}.$$

The characteristic polynomial is $P(\lambda) = (\lambda - 2)^2$, and so the only eigenvalue is $\lambda = 2$. Let us plow ahead in the usual manner and see what happens. We find the eigenvectors of 2 by solving

$$0x + 0y = 0,$$
$$x + 0y = 0.$$

The solutions are all scalar multiples of $\begin{bmatrix} 0 \\ 1 \end{bmatrix}$. Therefore, we get only one independent vector and only one solution,

$$X_1(t) = \begin{bmatrix} 0 \\ 1 \end{bmatrix} e^{2t}.$$

One is tempted to find another solution in the way that we did in Chapter 4. Thus we should try
$$X_2(t) = Vte^{2t}.$$

If this is to be a solution, we must have

$$Ve^{2t} + 2Vte^{2t} = AVte^{2t}.$$

At $t = 0$ we get $V = 0$, so there is no independent solution of this form. On the other hand, if V is an eigenvector of 2 and W is a vector to be determined, and if

$$X_2(t) = Vte^{2t} + We^{2t}$$

is to be a solution, then

$$Ve^{2t} + 2We^{2t} + 2Vte^{2t} = A(Vte^{2t} + We^{2t}) = 2Vte^{2t} + AWe^{2t}.$$

But this is satisfied if W satisfies

$$(A - 2I)We^{2t} = Ve^{2t}.$$

We may divide e^{2t} out of both sides, so the condition for a solution is that V be an eigenvector of the repeated eigenvalue and W satisfy

$$(A - 2I)W = V.$$

We set $V = \begin{bmatrix} 0 \\ 1 \end{bmatrix}$ and solve for W as follows:

$$0w_1 + 0w_2 = 0,$$
$$w_1 + 0w_2 = 1.$$

Thus

$$W = \begin{bmatrix} 1 \\ 0 \end{bmatrix}$$

and the general solution can be written as

$$X(t) = c_1 \begin{bmatrix} 0 \\ 1 \end{bmatrix} e^{2t} + c_2 [\begin{bmatrix} 0 \\ 1 \end{bmatrix} te^{2t} + \begin{bmatrix} 1 \\ 0 \end{bmatrix} e^{2t}].$$

In summary, the procedure for solving a 2×2 system with a repeated eigenvalue is to find a first solution

$$X_1(t) = Ve^{\lambda t},$$

where V is an eigenvector corresponding to λ. Then you solve

$$(A - \lambda I)W = V$$

for W. Then the general solution has the form

$$X(t) = c_1 Ve^{\lambda t} + c_2 [Vte^{\lambda t} + We^{\lambda t}].$$

The vector W is called a **generalized eigenvector**.

Some remarks are in order. First, it is not obvious that we will always be able to solve for W in this procedure. We can, in fact, but the reason for this lies much deeper in linear algebra than we can go here. Second, you can probably see that this approach will not extend to higher-dimensional systems with greater multiplicities in any easy way. This is so. Therefore, a different approach, which is very efficient, is introduced in the next section .

5.2.4 Another Mixing Problem

In Chapter 2 we modeled the amount of salt in a tank as a salt solution flowed in and the well-stirred mixture flowed out. Now we can deal with such mixing problems for which we have two tanks in series. Suppose that there are two tanks and that initially at time $t = 0$ there is 40 lb of salt in 100 gal of solution in the first tank and 15 lb in 100 gal of solution in the second. Fresh water flows into the first tank at a rate of 4 gal/min and the well-stirred mixture flows into the second tank at 5 gal/min. Also, 1 gal/min of the outflow of the second tank is fed back into the first. The well-stirred mixture in the second tank flows out at a rate of 5 gal/min. The question is how much salt is in each tank as time progresses.

Let $x(t)$ be the number of pounds of salt in the first tank at time t. Let $y(t)$ be the number of pounds of salt in the second tank at time t. Using the fact that the rate of change of salt in a tank is equal to the rate in minus the rate out, we have

$$x'(t) = 0 \cdot 4 + 1\frac{y(t)}{100} - 5\frac{x(t)}{100}$$

and

$$y'(t) = 5\frac{x(t)}{100} - 5\frac{y(t)}{100}.$$

This gives us the system

$$x'(t) = -5\frac{x(t)}{100} + 1\frac{y(t)}{100},$$
$$y'(t) = 5\frac{x(t)}{100} - 5\frac{y(t)}{100}.$$

The solution of this system is left to the exercises.

EXERCISES 5.2

In Exercises 1–10, solve the system $X' = AX$ for the given matrix. Use your solution to describe the behavior of solutions as t goes to infinity. Confirm your conclusions using the 2×2 system solver. Note any straight line orbits and relate them to the eigenvalues.

1. $A = \begin{bmatrix} 3 & 1 \\ 2 & 4 \end{bmatrix}$. Also find the unique solution if the solution passes through $(1, 2)$ when $t = 0$.

2. $A = \begin{bmatrix} 0 & 2 \\ -1 & 0 \end{bmatrix}$

3. $A = \begin{bmatrix} -4 & -2 \\ 3 & 1 \end{bmatrix}$

4. $A = \begin{bmatrix} 2 & -2 \\ 2 & -3 \end{bmatrix}$

5. $A = \begin{bmatrix} -2 & -1 \\ 3 & 1 \end{bmatrix}$

6. $A = \begin{bmatrix} 3 & 0 \\ 2 & 3 \end{bmatrix}$. Also find the unique solution if the solution passes through $(-1, 3)$ when $t = 0$.

7. $A = \begin{bmatrix} -4 & 3 \\ -3 & 2 \end{bmatrix}$

8. $A = \begin{bmatrix} -2 & 0 \\ 0 & -2 \end{bmatrix}$

9. $A = \begin{bmatrix} 2 & 1 \\ 4 & 2 \end{bmatrix}$

10. $A = \begin{bmatrix} -2 & 0 \\ 4 & -2 \end{bmatrix}$

11. What condition on the eigenvalues of the 2×2 matrix A guarantees that the origin is asymptotically stable for the system $X' = AX$?

12. What condition on the eigenvalues of the 2×2 matrix A guarantees that the origin is stable for the system $X' = AX$?

13. In terms of the eigenvalues, when is the origin unstable for the system $X' = AX$?

14. Show that the conjugate of the sum and product of matrices is the sum and product of the conjugates. Show that the conjugate of the product of a scalar and a matrix is the product of the conjugates.

Exercises 15 and 16 show that if we have enough distinct eigenvalues then solving higher-dimensional systems is straightforward.

15. In the system $X' = AX$, let $A = \begin{bmatrix} 1 & 0 & 0 \\ -1 & 2 & 0 \\ 2 & 1 & 3 \end{bmatrix}$. Find the general solution.

16. In the system $X' = AX$, let $A = \begin{bmatrix} 0 & -1 & 0 \\ 1 & 0 & 0 \\ 0 & 0 & 3 \end{bmatrix}$. Find the general solution.

17. In the case of complex conjugate eigenvalues, derive the general form of the real solution stated in this section by computing the sum and difference of conjugate solutions and dividing by 2 and $2i$, respectively.

18. Solve the mixing problem given in this section.

19. Fresh water flows into tank A at a rate of 3 gal/min. The well-stirred solution flows into tank B at a rate of 5 gal/min, but 2 gal/min is fed back from tank B to tank A, and an additional 3 gal/min drains from tank B. If tank A contains 50 gal of solution containing 20 lb of salt, and tank B contains 60 gal of solution with 10 lb dissolved at the start, how much salt is in each tank as time progresses?

20. Consider a mass-spring-damper system with a mass of 2 kg, a spring constant of 4 N/m, and a friction constant of 2. Write the first-order 2×2 linear system describing the dynamics of this system and solve it with the methods of this section. Draw some orbits in the phase plane.

21. Consider two 100-gal tanks A and B connected by two pipes. The first pipe empties salt solution from tank A into tank B at a rate of 1 gal/min, and the second pipe empties salt solution from tank B into tank A at the same rate. Initially, tank A holds 20 lb of salt in solution and tank B holds 0 lb. Both tanks are well stirred.

    (a) Set up the system of differential that the amounts of salt in each tank satisfy.

    (b) Without solving, what should be the long-term limit of the solution?

    (c) Solve by finding the eigenvalues and eigenvectors.

    (d) Use 2×2Solution to draw the field and some solutions. Relate what you see to the solution in part (b).

5.3 THE MATRIX EXPONENTIAL FUNCTION*

In the last section we developed a method of solution for 2×2 systems based on eigenvectors and generalized eigenvectors. This method does not generalize well to higher dimensions, nor does it lend itself easily to the use of computer algebra systems. For these reasons it is useful to introduce a new approach to solving linear systems.

    First, let us return to the examples of Section 5.2. If we rewrite the solutions in a different form, a most interesting matrix-valued function of t emerges. The

---

*This section may be omitted without loss of continuity.

first solution was

$$X(t) = c_1 \begin{bmatrix} -2 \\ 1 \end{bmatrix} e^{2t} + c_2 \begin{bmatrix} 1 \\ -1 \end{bmatrix} e^{3t}.$$

Consider a general initial condition (x_0, y_0). We solve

$$-2c_1 + c_2 = x_0,$$
$$c_1 - c_2 = y_0.$$

The solution is $c_1 = -x_0 - y_0$ and $c_2 = -x_0 - 2y_0$. If we put these values of c_1 and c_2 into the general solution, we get

$$X(t) = (-x_0 - y_0) \begin{bmatrix} -2 \\ 1 \end{bmatrix} e^{2t} + (-x_0 - 2y_0) \begin{bmatrix} 1 \\ -1 \end{bmatrix} e^{3t}.$$

This can then be rewritten as a matrix-valued function of t times the initial position vector

$$\begin{bmatrix} x_0 \\ y_0 \end{bmatrix}.$$

The result is

$$X(t) = \begin{bmatrix} 2e^{2t} - e^{3t} & 2e^{2t} - 2e^{3t} \\ e^{3t} - e^{2t} & 2e^{3t} - e^{2t} \end{bmatrix} \begin{bmatrix} x_0 \\ y_0 \end{bmatrix}.$$

The matrix-valued function

$$F(t) = \begin{bmatrix} 2e^{2t} - e^{3t} & 2e^{2t} - 2e^{3t} \\ e^{3t} - e^{2t} & 2e^{3t} - e^{2t} \end{bmatrix}$$

is what we want to focus on.

First observe that

$$F'(t) = \begin{bmatrix} 4e^{2t} - 3e^{3t} & 4e^{2t} - 6e^{3t} \\ 3e^{3t} - 2e^{2t} & 6e^{3t} - 2e^{2t} \end{bmatrix}$$

and

$$AF(t) = \begin{bmatrix} 1 & -2 \\ 1 & 4 \end{bmatrix} \begin{bmatrix} 2e^{2t} - e^{3t} & 2e^{2t} - 2e^{3t} \\ e^{3t} - e^{2t} & 2e^{3t} - e^{2t} \end{bmatrix}$$
$$= \begin{bmatrix} 4e^{2t} - 3e^{3t} & 4e^{2t} - 6e^{3t} \\ 3e^{3t} - 2e^{2t} & 6e^{3t} - 2e^{2t} \end{bmatrix}.$$

The matrix A is the matrix of the system. Also notice that

$$F(0) = \begin{bmatrix} 1 & 0 \\ 0 & 1 \end{bmatrix}.$$

We have the important properties

$$F'(t) = AF(t), \qquad \text{and} \qquad F(0) = I. \tag{$*$}$$

If you carry out the same analysis with the other examples of Section 5.2, you will get the same result. If we could compute $F(t)$ directly from A, we could write down the solution to any initial-value problem in the form

$$X(t) = F(t)X_0,$$

where X_0 is the initial condition. Our task is to find a simple way to compute $F(t)$.

For any linear system with matrix A the function $F(t)$ in (∗) always exists and is unique. The reason is that (∗) is a linear system of, in general, n^2 linear differential equations, and $F(0) = I$ is the initial condition, so our existence and uniqueness theorem guarantees a unique solution. If you differentiate $y(t) = e^{at}$, you get $y'(t) = ae^{at} = ay(t)$, and $y(0) = 1$. The parallel here is so close that we use the notation

$$e^{At} = F(t),$$

and we call e^{At} the **matrix exponential function**. We are not raising e to a matrix power in any literal sense, but both functions share so many properties that the notation is irresistible. Given A, our task is to find an easy way to compute e^{At}.

We can compute e^{at} using the power series

$$e^{at} = \sum_{k=0}^{\infty} \frac{(at)^k}{k!} = 1 + at + \frac{(at)^2}{2!} + \cdots.$$

Perhaps a power series of matrices will also work. We try

$$e^{At} = \sum_{k=0}^{\infty} \frac{(At)^k}{k!} = I + At + \frac{(At)^2}{2!} + \cdots.$$

Do not worry about questions of convergence and the like here; we are just following patterns to see if it will give us a clue. This is a time-honored practice in mathematics. Certainly the series gives

$$e^{A0} = I.$$

What about the derivative? We have

$$\frac{de^{At}}{dt} = \sum_{k=0}^{\infty} \frac{k A^k t^{k-1}}{k!} = A \sum_{k=1}^{\infty} \frac{A^{k-1} t^{k-1}}{(k-1)!} = A \sum_{j=0}^{\infty} \frac{(At)^j}{j!} = Ae^{At}.$$

The series gives the correct differentiation formula also, so the series appears to be a representation of the matrix exponential. However, it is not clear how to boil down this infinite series into a single matrix of functions. There are two ways to do this. The first requires what is called the Jordan form of a matrix. This would require much too much linear algebra to be pursued here. The second approach rests on the fact that if A is an $n \times n$ matrix then A^n can be written as a linear combination of lower powers of A. That is,

$$A^n = c_0 I + c_1 A + c_2 A^2 + \cdots + c_{n-1} A^{n-1}.$$

This is a consequence of the Cayley-Hamilton theorem. A detailed explanation of this is given later in the section.

Since A^n can be written in terms of lower powers of A, so can A^{n+1}. Indeed, $A^{n+1} = AA^n$, so we write A^n in terms of lower powers and multiply by A. Then the resulting A^n in this product is again reduced to lower powers. The same can be done for A^{n+2}, and so on. Ignoring any questions of convergence, we collect all the coefficients of $I, A, A^2, \ldots, A^{n-1}$. The series then becomes

$$e^{At} = \sum_{k=0}^{\infty} \frac{(At)^k}{k!} = \sum_{k=0}^{n-1} b_k(t) A^k = b_0(t)I + b_1(t)A + \cdots + b_{n-1}(t)A^{n-1}.$$

Here $b_k(t)$ is the collected coefficients of A^k in the series. Our sum is now finite, and the task is to find the $b_k(t)$.

Suppose that X_0 is an eigenvector corresponding to the eigenvalue λ of the $n \times n$ matrix A. Then

$$X(t) = e^{At} X_0$$

is the solution to

$$X' = AX$$

with initial value X_0. But we have seen that $X_0 e^{\lambda t}$ solves the same initial-value problem, so

$$e^{At} X_0 = X_0 e^{\lambda t}.$$

Applying both sides of

$$b_0(t)I + b_1(t)A + \cdots + b_{n-1}(t)A^{n-1} = e^{At}$$

to X_0 and noting that $A^k X_0 = \lambda^k X_0$ gives

$$b_0(t)X_0 + b_1(t)\lambda X_0 + b_2(t)\lambda^2 X_0 + \cdots + b_{n-1}(t)\lambda^{n-1} X_0 = e^{\lambda t} X_0$$

or

$$(b_0(t) + b_1(t)\lambda + b_2(t)\lambda^2 + \cdots + b_{n-1}(t)\lambda^{n-1})X_0 = e^{\lambda t} X_0.$$

The vector X_0 is nonzero, so the scalars must be the same. Therefore,

$$b_0(t) + b_1(t)\lambda + b_2(t)\lambda^2 + \cdots + b_{n-1}(t)\lambda^{n-1} = e^{\lambda t}.$$

So now we have one equation involving the n unknown functions $b_k(t)$.

If we have n distinct eigenvalues $\{\lambda_1, \lambda_2, \dots, \lambda_n\}$, then we have n equations in the n unknown functions. Here are the equations in this case.

$$b_0(t) + b_1(t)\lambda_1 + b_2(t)\lambda_1^2 + \cdots + b_{n-1}(t)\lambda_1^{n-1} = e^{\lambda_1 t},$$
$$b_0(t) + b_1(t)\lambda_2 + b_2(t)\lambda_2^2 + \cdots + b_{n-1}(t)\lambda_2^{n-1} = e^{\lambda_2 t},$$

$$\vdots$$

$$b_0(t) + b_1(t)\lambda_n + b_2(t)\lambda_n^2 + \cdots + b_{n-1}(t)\lambda_n^{n-1} = e^{\lambda_n t}.$$

Once these equations have been solved for the functions $b_k(t)$, we can calculate e^{At} from

$$e^{At} = b_0(t)I + b_1(t)A + \cdots + b_{n-1}(t)A^{n-1}.$$

Here is an example illustrating what we have so far.

Example 5.3.1 Consider the system

$$x' = -x - 2y,$$
$$y' = -x.$$

The matrix A is

$$A = \begin{bmatrix} -1 & -2 \\ -1 & 0 \end{bmatrix}.$$

The characteristic polynomial is

$$P(\lambda) = \det \begin{bmatrix} -1-\lambda & -2 \\ -1 & -\lambda \end{bmatrix} = \lambda^2 + \lambda - 2 = (\lambda - 1)(\lambda + 2).$$

The eigenvalues are 1 and -2.

To find the exponential function we must solve

$$b_0(t) + b_1(t)1 = e^{1t},$$
$$b_0(t) + b_1(t)(-2) = e^{-2t}.$$

This is a simple 2×2 system of linear equations in the two unknowns b_0 and b_1. We drop the t in these functions for notational simplicity. These equations can be solved in many ways; for example, simple elimination, Cramer's rule, or matrix row reduction. We use simple elimination here. Subtracting the equations gives

$$3b_1 = e^t - e^{-2t},$$

and so

$$b_1 = \frac{e^t - e^{-2t}}{3}.$$

Thus

$$b_0 = \frac{2e^t + e^{-2t}}{3}.$$

Finally,

$$e^{At} = \frac{2e^t + e^{-2t}}{3} \begin{bmatrix} 1 & 0 \\ 0 & 1 \end{bmatrix} + \frac{e^t - e^{-2t}}{3} \begin{bmatrix} -1 & -2 \\ -1 & 0 \end{bmatrix}$$

$$= \begin{bmatrix} \frac{e^t + 2e^{-2t}}{3} & \frac{-2e^t + 2e^{-2t}}{3} \\ \frac{-e^t + e^{-2t}}{3} & \frac{2e^t + e^{-2t}}{3} \end{bmatrix}.$$

It is easy to verify that

$$\frac{de^{At}}{dt} = \begin{bmatrix} -1 & -2 \\ -1 & 0 \end{bmatrix} \begin{bmatrix} \frac{e^t + 2e^{-2t}}{3} & \frac{-2e^t + 2e^{-2t}}{3} \\ \frac{-e^t + e^{-2t}}{3} & \frac{2e^t + e^{-2t}}{3} \end{bmatrix} = Ae^{At}.$$

Finally, the solution to the system is

$$X(t) = e^{At} X_0$$

or, more explicitly,

$$x(t) = \frac{e^t + 2e^{-2t}}{3} x_0 + \frac{-2e^t + 2e^{-2t}}{3} y_0$$

$$y(t) = \frac{-e^t + e^{-2t}}{3} x_0 + \frac{2e^t + e^{-2t}}{3} y_0.$$

You can check this solution by differentiating and substituting in the original equations. ∎

The next example is a 3×3 system, again with distinct eigenvalues.

Example 5.3.2   The system

$$x' = x + 2y - 2z,$$
$$y' = 2x - 2y + z,$$
$$z' = 2x - 4y + 3z$$

has matrix

$$A = \begin{bmatrix} 1 & 2 & -2 \\ 2 & -2 & 1 \\ 2 & -4 & 3 \end{bmatrix}.$$

The eigenvalues are $1, -1,$ and 2. The equations we must solve are

$$b_0 + b_1 1 + b_2(1)^2 = e^t,$$

$$b_0 + b_1(-1) + b_2(-1)^2 = e^{-t},$$
$$b_0 + b_1 2 + b_2(2)^2 = e^{2t}.$$

This time we solve using Cramer's rule. Recall that determinants of matrices are often symbolized by using straight bars instead of brackets to contain the matrix. We have

$$b_0 = \frac{\begin{vmatrix} e^t & 1 & 1 \\ e^{-t} & -1 & 1 \\ e^{2t} & 2 & 4 \end{vmatrix}}{\begin{vmatrix} 1 & 1 & 1 \\ 1 & -1 & 1 \\ 1 & 2 & 4 \end{vmatrix}}, \qquad b_1 = \frac{\begin{vmatrix} 1 & e^t & 1 \\ 1 & e^{-t} & 1 \\ 1 & e^{2t} & 2 \end{vmatrix}}{\begin{vmatrix} 1 & 1 & 1 \\ 1 & -1 & 1 \\ 1 & 2 & 4 \end{vmatrix}}, \qquad b_2 = \frac{\begin{vmatrix} 1 & 1 & e^t \\ 1 & -1 & e^{-t} \\ 1 & 2 & e^{2t} \end{vmatrix}}{\begin{vmatrix} 1 & 1 & 1 \\ 1 & -1 & 1 \\ 1 & 2 & 4 \end{vmatrix}}.$$

We get

$$b_0 = \frac{3e^t + e^{-t} - e^{2t}}{3}, \qquad b_1 = \frac{-e^{-t} + e^t}{2}, \qquad b_2 = \frac{e^{-t} - 3e^t + 2e^{2t}}{6}.$$

The exponential matrix is

$$e^{At} = b_0 I + b_1 A + b_2 A^2$$

$$= \begin{bmatrix} e^t & -2e^t + 2e^{2t} & 2e^t - 2e^{2t} \\ -e^{-t} + e^t & 2e^{-t} - 2e^t + e^{2t} & -e^{-t} + 2e^t - e^{2t} \\ -e^{-t} + e^t & 2e^{-t} - 2e^t & -e^{-t} + 2e^t \end{bmatrix},$$

and the solution is

$$\begin{bmatrix} x(t) \\ y(t) \\ z(t) \end{bmatrix} = \begin{bmatrix} e^t & -2e^t + 2e^{2t} & 2e^t - 2e^{2t} \\ -e^{-t} + e^t & 2e^{-t} - 2e^t + e^{2t} & -e^{-t} + 2e^t - e^{2t} \\ -e^{-t} + e^t & 2e^{-t} - 2e^t & -e^{-t} + 2e^t \end{bmatrix} \begin{bmatrix} x_0 \\ y_0 \\ z_0 \end{bmatrix}.$$

■

Let us now consider what to do if some of the eigenvalues are repeated or complex. If an eigenvalue is repeated, the present method will not yield enough equations to solve for the $b_i(t)$. Suppose that the eigenvalue λ_0 is repeated, say, m times. Recall that we say that λ_0 has multiplicity m. In this case we supplement the equations of the original method with the equations derived from the equation

$$b_0 + b_1\lambda + \cdots + b_{n-1}\lambda^{n-1} = e^{\lambda t}$$

by differentiating this equation up to $m - 1$ times, treating λ as the variable of differentiation. In each of these new equations we replace λ by the eigenvalue λ_0. This yields the original equation together with $m - 1$ new equations. If each multiplicity is treated in this way, the final number of equations for an $n \times n$ system will be n, and the count will be correct. Once this is done, we proceed exactly as before. A justification for this will be given at the end of this section.

Example 5.3.3   The characteristic polynomial of

$$A = \begin{bmatrix} 2 & 0 & 0 \\ 0 & 2 & 0 \\ -2 & 2 & 1 \end{bmatrix}$$

is

$$P(\lambda) = -(\lambda - 1)(\lambda - 2)^2.$$

So A has eigenvalues 1 and 2, and 2 has multiplicity 2. The first two equations are

$$b_0 + b_1 + b_2 = e^t,$$
$$b_0 + b_1 2 + b_2 2^2 = e^{2t}.$$

To get the third equation, we differentiate

$$b_0 + b_1 \lambda + b_2 \lambda^2 = e^{\lambda t}$$

with respect to λ and then replace λ by 2 to get

$$b_1 + b_2 2 \cdot 2 = t e^{2t}.$$

We now proceed with the following system of equations:

$$b_0 + b_1 + b_2 = e^t,$$
$$b_0 + b_1 2 + b_2 2^2 = e^{2t},$$
$$b_1 + b_2 2 \cdot 2 = t e^{2t},$$

precisely as before.   ∎

As to complex roots, we treat them exactly the same as real roots, including the multiplicities. The exponential matrix may appear to have complex function entries; simplifying using Euler's formula, $e^{(a+bi)} = e^a[\cos(b) + i\sin(b)]$, will always yield the real matrix that it must be.

Once we have the exponential matrix, it is easy to solve nonhomogeneous linear systems. The matrix form is

$$X'(t) = AX(t) + C(t),$$

where $C(t)$ is the column vector of the nonhomogeneous terms $c_i(t)$.

Before solving the nonhomogeneous equation, observe that from the definition of e^{At} it is immediate that

$$Ae^{At} = e^{At}A.$$

Moreover, $e^{At}e^{-At} = I$. To see this, differentiate $e^{At}e^{-At}$ by the product rule, and assume that $\frac{de^{At}}{dt} = Ae^{At}$. We get

$$Ae^{At}e^{-At} + e^{At}(-A)e^{-At} = Ae^{At}e^{-At} - Ae^{At}e^{-At} = 0.$$

Because the derivative of $e^{At}e^{-At}$ is zero, the entries of this matrix must be constants; but $e^{A0}e^{-A0} = I \cdot I = I$, so

$$e^{At}e^{-At} = I.$$

We can rewrite the nonhomogeneous equation as

$$X'(t) - AX(t) = C(t).$$

Now multiply through by e^{-At} to get

$$e^{-At}X'(t) - Ae^{-At}X(t) = e^{-At}C(t).$$

The left-hand side is the product rule of differentiation applied to $e^{-At}X(t)$, so

$$(e^{-At}X(t))' = e^{-At}C(t).$$

Integrating both sides gives

$$e^{-At}X(t) = \int e^{-At}C(t)\,dt + X_1,$$

where integration means to integrate the entries of the column matrix, and X_1 is the collected column of integration constants . Multiplying through by e^{At} yields

$$X(t) = e^{At}\int e^{-At}C(t)\,dt + e^{At}X_1.$$

Thus the method is identical in form to the method of solving linear equations described in Chapter 2.

Example 5.3.4   Consider the nonhomogeneous system

$$x' = -x - 2y + 2,$$
$$y' = -x + t.$$

The matrix A is that of Example 5.3.1, and so the exponential matrix e^{At} is

$$\begin{bmatrix} \frac{e^t + 2e^{-2t}}{3} & \frac{-2e^t + 2e^{-2t}}{3} \\ \frac{-e^t + e^{-2t}}{3} & \frac{2e^t + e^{-2t}}{3} \end{bmatrix}.$$

The matrix e^{-At} is the inverse of e^{At}, and $e^{-At} = e^{A(-t)}$. Therefore, to find e^{-At}, just replace t by $-t$ in e^{At}. Thus

$$e^{-At} = \begin{bmatrix} (2e^{2t} + e^{-t})/3 & (2e^{2t} - 2e^{-t})/3 \\ (e^{2t} - e^{-t})/3 & (e^{2t} + 2e^{-t})/3 \end{bmatrix}.$$

The solution is

$$X(t) = e^{At} \int e^{-At} C(t) \, dt + e^{At} X_1.$$

Now

$$e^{-At} C(t) = \left[\begin{array}{c} 2(2e^{2t} + e^{-t})/3 + (2te^{2t} - 2te^{-t})/3 \\ 2(e^{2t} - e^{-t})/3 + (te^{2t} + 2te^{-t})/3 \end{array} \right],$$

and integration gives

$$\int e^{-At} C(t) \, dt = \left[\begin{array}{c} (te^{2t} + 3e^{2t}/2 + 2te^{-t})/3 \\ (3e^{2t}/4 + te^{2t}/2 - 2te^{-t})/3 \end{array} \right].$$

Thus the general solution is

$$X(t) = \left[\begin{array}{cc} \frac{e^t + 2e^{-2t}}{3} & \frac{-2e^t + 2e^{-2t}}{3} \\ \frac{-e^t + e^{-2t}}{3} & \frac{2e^t + e^{-2t}}{3} \end{array} \right] \left[\begin{array}{c} \frac{te^{2t} + \frac{3e^{2t}}{2} + 2te^{-t}}{3} \\ \frac{\frac{3e^{2t}}{4} + \frac{te^{2t}}{2} - 2te^{-t}}{3} \end{array} \right]$$
$$+ \left[\begin{array}{cc} \frac{e^t + 2e^{-2t}}{3} & \frac{-2e^t + 2e^{-2t}}{3} \\ \frac{-e^t + e^{-2t}}{3} & \frac{2e^t + e^{-2t}}{3} \end{array} \right] \left[\begin{array}{c} x_1 \\ y_1 \end{array} \right].$$

You can multiply out the remaining products if desired.

You should be careful with the initial condition in the nonhomogeneous case. Contrary to what you might assume, $\left[\begin{array}{c} x_1 \\ y_1 \end{array} \right]$ is not the initial condition. Suppose that the initial condition is $(1, 2)$; then $X(0) = \left[\begin{array}{c} 1 \\ 2 \end{array} \right]$ and setting $t = 0$ gives

$$\left[\begin{array}{c} 1 \\ 2 \end{array} \right] = \left[\begin{array}{c} 3/2 \\ 3/4 \end{array} \right] + \left[\begin{array}{c} x_1 \\ y_1 \end{array} \right].$$

So $x_1 = -1/2$ and $y_1 = 5/4$. ∎

5.3.1 The Cayley-Hamilton Theorem

Essential to the collapse of the infinite series for e^{At} into a finite sum was the fact that the nth power of an $n \times n$ matrix A can be expressed in terms of lower powers of A. This is a consequence of the Cayley-Hamilton theorem [4], which we now state and explain.

Theorem 5.3.5

If A is an $n \times n$ matrix and $P(\lambda)$ is the characteristic polynomial of A, then $P(A) = 0$. ●

We cannot prove this in general, but we will prove it in the 2×2 case and give a 3×3 example immediately in order to clarify the theorem.

Example 5.3.6 Let

$$A = \begin{bmatrix} 2 & 0 & 0 \\ 0 & 2 & 0 \\ -2 & 2 & 1 \end{bmatrix}.$$

As we have seen, the characteristic polynomial is

$$P(\lambda) = -(\lambda - 1)(\lambda - 2)^2 = -\lambda^3 + 5\lambda^2 - 8\lambda + 4.$$

Now replace λ by A in the characteristic polynomial. It is always understood that constants multiply the identity matrix of the proper dimension. Thus

$$P(A) = -A^3 + 5A^2 - 8A + 4I,$$

and so

$$P(A) = \begin{bmatrix} -8 & 0 & 0 \\ 0 & -8 & 0 \\ 14 & -14 & -1 \end{bmatrix} + \begin{bmatrix} 20 & 0 & 0 \\ 0 & 20 & 0 \\ -30 & 30 & 5 \end{bmatrix}$$

$$+ \begin{bmatrix} -16 & 0 & 0 \\ 0 & -16 & 0 \\ 16 & -16 & -8 \end{bmatrix} + \begin{bmatrix} 4 & 0 & 0 \\ 0 & 4 & 0 \\ 0 & 0 & 4 \end{bmatrix} = 0.$$

The last 0 here is the zero 3×3 matrix. ∎

We now show that the Cayley-Hamilton theorem holds for any 2×2 matrix. Consider

$$A = \begin{bmatrix} a & b \\ c & d \end{bmatrix}.$$

The characteristic polynomial is

$$P(\lambda) = \begin{vmatrix} a - \lambda & b \\ c & d - \lambda \end{vmatrix} = \lambda^2 - (a + d)\lambda + ad - bc.$$

Therefore,

$$P(A) =$$
$$\begin{bmatrix} a^2 + bc & ab + bd \\ ac + cd & bc + d^2 \end{bmatrix} - (a + d) \begin{bmatrix} a & b \\ c & d \end{bmatrix} + \begin{bmatrix} ad - bc & 0 \\ 0 & ad - bc \end{bmatrix}$$
$$= 0.$$

5.3.2 Justification of the Repeated Eigenvalues Method

A complete justification of the method we have used for dealing with repeated eigenvalues is intricate, and it would not be appropriate to give it here. However, the essentials of the justification can be presented.

Recall that if we have an eigenvalue λ of multiplicity 2 with just one independent eigenvector V, then we have a solution of the form

$$X(t) = Vte^{\lambda t} + We^{\lambda t},$$

where W solves

$$(A - \lambda I)W = V.$$

The initial point of this solution is W, and so by uniqueness of solutions

$$Vte^{\lambda t} + We^{\lambda t} = e^{tA}W = (b_0 + b_1 A + \cdots + b_{n-1}A^{n-1})W.$$

Here we are assuming that

$$e^{tA} = b_0 + b_1 A + \cdots + b_{n-1}A^{n-1}.$$

To keep the notation as simple as possible, assume that $n = 4$. Thus

$$Vte^{\lambda t} + We^{\lambda t} = b_0 W + b_1 A W + b_2 A^2 W + b_3 A^3 W.$$

Since $AW = V + \lambda W$, we can recursively lower the powers on A as follows:

$$Vte^{\lambda t} + We^{\lambda t} = b_0 W + b_1(V + \lambda W) + b_2 A(V + \lambda W) + b_3 A^2(V + \lambda W)$$
$$= b_0 W + b_1(V + \lambda W) + b_2 \lambda V + b_2 \lambda A W + b_3 \lambda^2 + b_3 A^2 \lambda W.$$

Continuing the reduction by replacing AW by $V + \lambda W$, the right-hand side becomes

$$b_0 W + b_1(V + \lambda W) + 2b_2 \lambda V + b_2 \lambda^2 W + b_3 \lambda^2 V + b_3 \lambda^2 V + b_3 \lambda^2(V + \lambda W).$$

Now, if the vectors V and W are independent, then the collected coefficients of each vector on each side must be equal. The coefficients of V give

$$b_1 + 2b_2 \lambda + 3b_3 \lambda^2 = te^{\lambda t}.$$

But this is precisely the equation we would obtain by the rule of differentiation with respect to λ. It can be shown that the vectors V and W are independent.

In higher dimensions there are many different combinations of multiplicities and independent eigenvectors. For example, we could have a single independent eigenvector of multiplicity 3. The form of the solution in this case would be

$$X(t) = V\frac{t^2}{2!}e^{\lambda t} + W_1 te^{\lambda t} + W_2 e^{\lambda t}.$$

Here $(A - \lambda I)V = 0$, $(A - \lambda I)W_1 = V$, and $(A - \lambda I)W_2 = W_1$. Proceeding as before, one can show that the additional equations necessary to solve for the exponential matrix are obtained by the rule of differentiation with respect to λ. A complete justification of the method requires showing that the vector V and the W vectors form an independent set. This is tricky and we cannot go into it here.

The Jordan form of a matrix offers an alternative approach to the exponential matrix and the justification of the approach taken here. A treatment of the Jordan form can be found in [4] or in many upper-division linear algebra books.

EXERCISES 5.3

In Exercises 1–8 solve the system $X'(t) = AX(t)$, where A is as given by finding the exponential matrix. In each case get the unique solution for the initial condition $X_0 = (3, -2)$ at $t = 0$.

1. $A = \begin{bmatrix} 3 & 0 \\ 0 & 3 \end{bmatrix}$

2. $A = \begin{bmatrix} 4 & -2 \\ 1 & 1 \end{bmatrix}$

3. $A = \begin{bmatrix} 1/2 & 1/2 \\ -1/2 & 3/2 \end{bmatrix}$

4. $A = \begin{bmatrix} 3 & -4 \\ 2 & -3 \end{bmatrix}$

5. $A = \begin{bmatrix} 1 & 5 \\ -1 & -1 \end{bmatrix}$

6. $A = \begin{bmatrix} 2 & 0 \\ -1 & 2 \end{bmatrix}$

7. $A = \begin{bmatrix} -4 & -2 \\ 3 & 1 \end{bmatrix}$

8. $A = \begin{bmatrix} 0 & -2 \\ 2 & 0 \end{bmatrix}$

9. Open package 2 × 2System, and draw fields and orbits for the problems in Exercises 1–5. What can you say about orbits and eigenvalues?

10. Solve the system of the mixing problem at the end of Section 5.2 by the method of this section. Graph the functions $x(t)$ and $y(t)$.

11. Suppose that you have two tanks, and that initially at time $t = 0$ there is 60 lb of salt in 100 gal of solution in the first tank and 20 lb in 100 gal of solution in the second. Fresh water flows into the first tank at a rate of 4 gal/min, and the well-stirred mixture flows into the second tank at 4 gal/min. Also, 2 gal/min of the outflow of the second

tank is fed back into the first. The well-stirred mixture in the second tank flows out at 4 gal/min. How much salt is in each tank as time progresses? Use the exponential matrix.

12. Solve $X'(t) = AX(t)$, where $A = \begin{bmatrix} 3 & -1 & 0 \\ 1 & 1 & 0 \\ 1 & 2 & -1 \end{bmatrix}$, by finding the exponential matrix.

13. Solve $X'(t) = AX(t)$, where $A = \begin{bmatrix} 3 & 0 & 0 \\ 2 & 3 & 0 \\ 0 & 0 & -1 \end{bmatrix}$, by finding the exponential matrix.

14. Solve $X'(t) = AX(t)$, where $A = \begin{bmatrix} 3 & 0 & 1 \\ 2 & 3 & 0 \\ 0 & 0 & -1 \end{bmatrix}$, by finding the exponential matrix.

Exercises 15–18 are concerned with tanks that drain from one into the other in a series, with the outflow of the last tank being pumped back into the first. We imagine that each tank drains through a hole in the bottom. It is reasonable to expect that the rate at which a tank drains is proportional to water pressure and thus to the depth of water in the tank. If x is the depth, then $x' = -kx$ is the equation for the draining of a single tank, where k is positive. We assume that the tanks are cylindrical so that depth and volume are proportional.

15. Consider two tanks draining in series, with the outflow of the second tank pumped back into the first. Let $x(t)$ and $y(t)$ be the depths of water at time t in the first and second tanks.

(a) Write down the system of first-order equations describing the dynamics of the water levels. What is the matrix of the system?

(b) If $k_1 = k_2 = 1$, solve the system and describe the behavior of solutions. Do the same if $k_1 = 1$ and

$k_2 = 2$.

16. Compute the characteristic polynomial of the system matrix in Exercise 15(a). Show that one eigenvalue is zero and the other is negative. What does this tell you about the general behavior of solutions? Do either of the water levels oscillate?

17. Consider three tanks draining in series with the outflow of the last tank pumped back into the first.
    (a) Write down the system of first-order equations describing the dynamics of the water levels. What is the matrix of the system?
    (b) If $k_1 = k_2 = k_3 = 1$, solve the system and describe the behavior of solutions. Do the same if $k_1 = 1$, $k_2 = 2$, and $k_3 = 3$.

18. Find the characteristic polynomial for the matrix in Exercise 17a. Discuss the possibility of oscillatory solutions in terms of the eigenvalues. Do all solutions, oscillatory or not, converge to a "steady-state limit"?

For Exercises 19 and 20, if you are familiar with a computer algebra system, you may use it to assist in doing these exercises, but show the notebook or worksheet that you used.

19. Solve the system

$$x' = 4x(t) - 2y(t) + t,$$
$$y' = x(t) + y(t) + e^t.$$

20. Solve the system

$$x' = x(t) + 5y(t) + t,$$
$$y' = -x(t) - y(t) + 1.$$

5.4 QUALITATIVE BEHAVIOR OF LINEAR SYSTEMS

In the exercises of the two preceding sections, we have taken note of the eigenvalues of the system matrix and their relation to the behavior of solutions. In this section we will examine and summarize this relationship. These results extend almost completely to the higher-dimensional cases. We shall begin by examining the stability of the origin in terms of the eigenvalues of the system matrix. Then we will go on to consider the forms of orbits in the phase plane and how these forms relate to the eigenvalues.

Stability

We shall assume that the origin is the only critical point, so there will be no 0 eigenvalue. We leave the case of a 0 eigenvalue to the exercises.

Let us begin by reviewing the forms of solutions to 2×2 systems. If the eigenvalues are real and distinct, we have the solution

$$X(t) = c_1 V_1 e^{\lambda_1 t} + c_2 V_2 e^{\lambda_2 t}.$$

If there is only one real eigenvalue, but there are two independent eigenvectors, the form is

$$X(t) = c_1 V_1 e^{\lambda t} + c_2 V_2 e^{\lambda t}.$$

If there is only one real eigenvalue, and only one independent eigenvector, then the form is

$$X(t) = c_1 V e^{\lambda t} + c_2 (V t e^{\lambda t} + W e^{\lambda t}),$$

where W is a solution to $(A - \lambda I)W = V$. If the eigenvalues are complex conjugates, then the solution, after combining conjugate solutions, has the form

$$X(t) = e^{\lambda t} [c_1 \begin{bmatrix} x_0 \cos(\mu t) - x_1 \sin(\mu t) \\ y_0 \cos(\mu t) - y_1 \sin(\mu t) \end{bmatrix} + c_2 \begin{bmatrix} x_0 \sin(\mu t) + x_1 \cos(\mu t) \\ y_0 \sin(\mu t) + y_1 \cos(\mu t) \end{bmatrix}].$$

In any of the preceding cases, if all the eigenvalues are negative or the real part of the complex eigenvalues is negative, all solutions converge to the origin. In the higher-dimensional cases, this is also true, because each term in the solution will still contain a factor of the form $e^{\lambda t}$, where $\lambda < 0$. Thus, in any dimension, the origin is an asymptotically stable critical point.

If one eigenvalue, say λ, is positive, then the solution $X(t) = cX_0 e^{\lambda t}$, where X_0 is the corresponding eigenvector, has a straight line orbit if $c \neq 0$, and the solution goes to infinity as $t \to \infty$. We can start such solutions as close to the origin as we please by choosing c as small as we please. We see that the origin is unstable.

If the real part of the complex eigenvalues is zero, in the 2×2 case, the solutions are periodic, since only combinations of $\cos(\mu t)$ and $\sin(\mu t)$ appear in the real solutions. Also, it is easy to see that orbits starting close to the origin stay close to the origin. Thus the origin is stable, though it is not asymptotically stable. If the real part of the complex eigenvalues is positive, we see from the form of the solution that it goes to infinity as $t \to \infty$. We shall show very shortly that the orbits in this case spiral out to infinity.

In the $n \times n$ case, if the eigenvalues are all pure imaginary, then, perhaps surprisingly, we cannot conclude that the motion is periodic. This is demonstrated in the next section. Also, it may be mildly surprising to find that with pure imaginary eigenvalues the solutions do not have to remain bounded in the $n \times n$ case. Indeed, repeated roots will introduce factors of type t^k, and so it is possible for solutions to go to infinity.

Let us summarize our results so far in a theorem.

Theorem 5.4.1

Suppose that A is a real $n \times n$ matrix and that the origin is the only critical point. If the real parts of all the eigenvalues are negative, the origin is asymptotically stable. If one eigenvalue has a positive real part, the origin is unstable. If all the real parts are zero, only in the 2×2 case can we conclude that the motion is periodic and that the origin is stable. ●

2 × 2 Orbit Structure

If we draw a number of representative orbits for a variety of 2×2 systems we quickly see that these drawings fall into certain categories that can be identified by the number and type of eigenvalues and eigenvectors of the system. These categories can be discovered by looking a little more carefully at the types of solutions that are possible.

The following general observations will simplify the classification. If both eigenvalues are positive, the form of the orbits is the same as the form of the orbits when both eigenvalues are negative. The difference is in the orientation of the motion. It is outward in the first case and inward in the second. The same can be said for the real parts of complex eigenvalues. If the eigenvalues are of opposite sign, the form of the orbits is the same if the signs are switched. In view of these observations, we need only consider eigenvalues with negative real parts and one case of eigenvalues of opposite sign.

The key to this discussion is the fact that real eigenvalues and eigenvectors determine straight line orbits. Thus, if X_0 is an eigenvector corresponding to the real eigenvalue λ, the orbit of

$$X(t) = X_0 e^{\lambda t}$$

is a straight line containing the vector X_0. We shall also want to examine the way in which other orbits approach the straight lines determined by eigenvectors. To this end, we define the length of $X = \begin{bmatrix} x \\ y \end{bmatrix}$ by $||X|| = \sqrt{x^2 + y^2}$. This definition may be extended to column vectors with any number of entries. We will consider unit tangent vectors to orbits

$$\frac{X'(t)}{||X'(t)||}$$

obtained by dividing tangent vectors by their lengths. The limits of such unit tangent vectors as $t \to \pm\infty$ can tell us about the asymptotic behavior of the orbit.

Let us begin with two distinct negative eigenvalues, say $\lambda_1 < \lambda_2 < 0$. Recall that the form of the solution for real distinct eigenvalues is

$$X(t) = c_1 V_1 e^{\lambda_1 t} + c_2 V_2 e^{\lambda_2 t},$$

where the eigenvectors V_1 and V_2 are independent. These two eigenvectors define two straight lines in the phase plane.

The derivative is

$$X'(t) = e^{\lambda_2 t}[c_1 V_1 \lambda_1 e^{(\lambda_1 - \lambda_2)t} + c_2 V_2 \lambda_2].$$

We have factored out the term $e^{\lambda_2 t}$. Thus the unit tangent vector is

$$\frac{X'(t)}{||X'(t)||} = \frac{[c_1 V_1 \lambda_1 e^{(\lambda_1 - \lambda_2)t} + c_2 V_2 \lambda_2]}{||c_1 V_1 \lambda_1 e^{(\lambda_1 - \lambda_2)t} + c_2 V_2 \lambda_2||}.$$

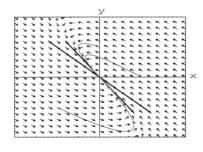

FIGURE 5.1

The exponential multiplying $V_1 \lambda_1$ goes to zero as $t \to \infty$, so the unit tangent vector is asymptotic to a unit vector in the direction of V_2. So orbits that are not the straight lines come in to the origin tangent to the vector V_2. Note that the tangency is to the eigenvector of the eigenvalue that is closer to zero. The same applies to positive distinct eigenvalues. Figure 5.1 is typical of this case. Note the two straight lines and the way in which the orbits approach the origin.

If the eigenvalues are of opposite sign, the orbits are asymptotic to the orbits determined by the eigenvectors. This follows by noting that if $\lambda_1 < 0 < \lambda_2$ then

$$[c_1 V_1 e^{\lambda_1 t} + c_2 V_2 e^{\lambda_2 t}] - c_2 V_2 e^{\lambda_2 t}$$

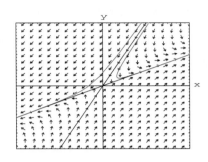

FIGURE 5.2

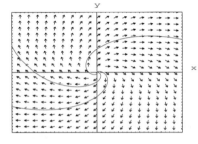

FIGURE 5.3

approaches zero as $t \to \infty$. For the other asymptotic behavior consider

$$[c_1 V_1 e^{\lambda_1 t} + c_2 V_2 e^{\lambda_2 t}] - c_1 V_1 e^{\lambda_1 t}$$

and let $t \to -\infty$. Figure 5.2 shows orbits in this case.

Consider the case of complex conjugate eigenvalues where the real part is not zero. Examine the solution in this case, and note that the "vector part" of the solution

$$c_1 \left[\begin{array}{c} x_0 \cos(\mu t) - x_1 \sin(\mu t) \\ y_0 \cos(\mu t) - y_1 \sin(\mu t) \end{array} \right] + c_2 \left[\begin{array}{c} x_0 \sin(\mu t) + x_1 \cos(\mu t) \\ y_0 \sin(\mu t) + y_1 \cos(\mu t) \end{array} \right]$$

is periodic and it rotates around the origin. This is multiplied by the scalar $e^{\lambda t}$, so this rotating vector expands or contracts as λ is positive or negative. The motion is one of spiraling in or out as $t \to \infty$. Figure 5.3 show a field and solutions where the real part of the eigenvalues is positive.

In the case when the real part of complex eigenvalues is zero, the orbits are closed. In fact it can be shown that the orbits are ellipses centered at the origin.

If we have a repeated real eigenvalue with two independent eigenvectors, the solution has the form

$$X(t) = c_1 V_1 e^{\lambda t} + c_2 V_2 e^{\lambda t} = e^{\lambda t}[c_1 V_1 + c_2 V_2],$$

and so all orbits are straight lines radiating from the origin.

Finally, if we have a repeated real eigenvalue with only one independent eigenvector, the form of the solution is

$$X(t) = c_1 V e^{\lambda t} + c_2 (V t e^{\lambda t} + W e^{\lambda t}).$$

All orbits approach the origin tangent to V. To see the way in which orbits approach the origin, we form the unit tangent vector again. Taking the derivative and factoring out the term $t e^{\lambda t}$ gives

$$X'(t) = t e^{\lambda t} \left[\frac{c_1 \lambda V}{t} + c_2 (\frac{V}{t} + \lambda V + \frac{\lambda W}{t}) \right].$$

The unit tangent vector to an orbit then is

$$\frac{X'(t)}{\|X'(t)\|} = \frac{[\frac{c_1 \lambda V}{t} + c_2 (\frac{V}{t} + \lambda V + \frac{\lambda W}{t})]}{\|\frac{c_1 \lambda V}{t} + c_2 (\frac{V}{t} + \lambda V + \frac{\lambda W}{t})\|}.$$

If $\lambda < 0$, then as t goes to infinity the tangent vector approaches a unit vector in the direction of V. Figure 5.4 illustrates this behavior. The y-axis is the straight line orbit. Notice how the other orbits come in to the origin tangent to the y-axis.

The origin is called a **node** if the eigenvalues are of the same sign. If the eigenvalues are of opposite signs, the origin is called a **saddle**. If the eigenvalues are pure imaginary, the origin is called a **center**, and it is called a **spiral point** if the real parts of complex eigenvalues are not zero.

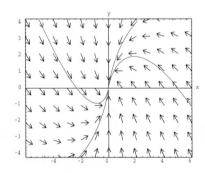

FIGURE 5.4

EXERCISES 5.4

For the linear systems defined by the matrices given in Exercises 1–8, decide if the origin is asymptotically stable, stable, or unstable by finding the eigenvalues.

1. $\begin{bmatrix} 5 & -1 \\ 3 & 1 \end{bmatrix}$.

2. $\begin{bmatrix} -2 & 1 \\ 1 & -2 \end{bmatrix}$.

3. $\begin{bmatrix} -3 & -2 \\ 2 & 2 \end{bmatrix}$.

4. $\begin{bmatrix} 2 & 13 \\ -1 & -2 \end{bmatrix}$.

5. $\begin{bmatrix} 1 & -1 \\ 1 & 1 \end{bmatrix}$.

6. $\begin{bmatrix} 2 & 1 \\ 1 & 1 \end{bmatrix}$.

7. $\begin{bmatrix} -2 & 1 \\ 1 & 2 \end{bmatrix}$.

8. $\begin{bmatrix} 0 & -5 \\ 1 & 0 \end{bmatrix}$.

9. Suppose that a system has matrix $\begin{bmatrix} -1 & 0 & 0 \\ 3 & -1 & 0 \\ 1 & 2 & 3 \end{bmatrix}$.

   Explain that the origin is unstable by exhibiting a straight line solution that starts as close to the origin as you want and goes to infinity. *Hint:* Find an eigenvector.

10. Suppose that a system has matrix $\begin{bmatrix} 3 & 0 & 0 \\ 1 & 3 & 0 \\ 0 & 0 & 2 \end{bmatrix}$. Ex-

    plain that the origin is unstable by exhibiting two straight line solutions that start as close to the origin as you want and go to infinity. *Hint:* Find two eigenvectors.

11. Suppose that a system has matrix $\begin{bmatrix} 1 & 0 & 1 \\ 1 & 1 & 1 \\ 1 & 1 & -1 \end{bmatrix}$. Ex-

    plain that the origin is unstable by exhibiting one straight line solution that starts as close to the origin as you want and goes to infinity.

12. Consider the system $X' = AX$, where

$$\begin{bmatrix} 1 & 2 & -2 \\ 2 & -2 & 1 \\ 2 & -4 & 3 \end{bmatrix}.$$

   Decide if the origin is asymptotically stable, stable, or unstable.

For the orbit diagrams in Exercises 13–16, describe the eigenvalues and how many eigenvectors there were to produce the given diagram.

13.

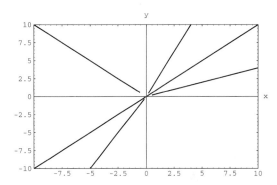

14.

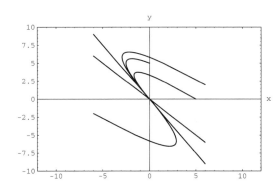

15.

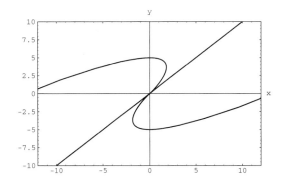

16.

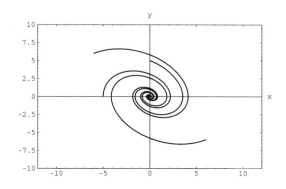

17. If zero is an eigenvalue, explain why there must be in-finitely many critical points.

18. If zero is an eigenvalue, discuss the stability of the critical points in the 2×2 case.

19. What is the minimum dimension of a linear system that has pure imaginary eigenvalues and unbounded solutions? Explain!

20. Solve the differential equation $y^{(4)} + 2y'' + y = 0$. Write down the reduction to a first-order system, and write down the solution to this equation. What point in the text does this illustrate?

5.5 A COUPLED SYSTEM OF MASSES AND SPRINGS

FIGURE 5.5

In this section we shall apply the method of solution of linear systems to a vibrating system having two masses and three springs. In the course of this we shall see that, even if the eigenvalues are pure imaginary, the motion is not necessarily periodic. The arrangement of the masses and springs is shown in the schematic diagram Figure 5.5. The springs are fixed at the left and right extremes, and we assume that the masses slide without friction on a smooth table top.

The constants, k_1, k_2, and k_3 are the spring constants, and m_1 and m_2 are the masses. Assume that the springs are not compressed or stretched. Let the displacement x_1 of the first mass m_1 be measured, say, from the position of the left edge of the mass in this relaxed position. Let x_3 be the displacement of the second mass measured from the position of the left edge of this mass in the relaxed position. Let x_2 and x_4 be the velocities of the first and second masses, respectively. The displacements and velocities are all functions of time, and the task now is to write a system of differential equations describing the dynamics of these quantities.

By the definition of velocity, $x_1'(t) = x_2(t)$ and $x_3'(t) = x_4(t)$. The accelerations of the masses are the derivatives of x_2 and x_4, respectively. Force is mass times acceleration, so we have

$$m_1 x_2'(t) = -k_1 x_1(t) + k_2(x_3(t) - x_1(t)) = -(k_1 + k_2)x_1(t) + k_2 x_3(t)$$

and

$$m_2 x_4'(t) = k_2(x_1(t) - x_3(t)) - k_3 x_3(t) = k_2 x_1(t) - (k_2 + k_3)x_3(t).$$

Dropping the t's and dividing by the masses yields the following linear system of four equations in four unknowns.

$$x_1' = x_2,$$

$$x_2' = -\frac{k_1 + k_2}{m_1}x_1 + \frac{k_2}{m_1}x_3,$$

$$x_3' = x_4,$$

$$x_4' = \frac{k_2}{m_2}x_1 - \frac{k_2 + k_3}{m_2}x_3.$$

To make things concrete, let $m_1 = m_2 = 1$ and $k_1 = k_2 = k_3 = 1$. This is a homogeneous system, and the matrix of the system is

$$A = \begin{bmatrix} 0 & 1 & 0 & 0 \\ -2 & 0 & 1 & 0 \\ 0 & 0 & 0 & 1 \\ 1 & 0 & -2 & 0 \end{bmatrix}.$$

The characteristic polynomial is

$$P(\lambda) = \det \begin{bmatrix} -\lambda & 1 & 0 & 0 \\ -2 & -\lambda & 1 & 0 \\ 0 & 0 & -\lambda & 1 \\ 1 & 0 & -2 & -\lambda \end{bmatrix} = (\lambda^2 + 1)(\lambda^2 + 3).$$

Therefore, the eigenvalues are $\pm i$ and $\pm\sqrt{3}i$. There is no multiplicity, so we solve using the methods of Section 5.2.

To find an eigenvector corresponding to i, we must solve

$$-ix + y + 0z + 0w = 0,$$
$$-2x - iy + z + 0w = 0,$$
$$0x + 0y - iz + w = 0,$$
$$x + 0y - 2z - iw = 0.$$

One solution is the vector $(-i, 1, -i, 1)$. Corresponding to the conjugate root $-i$ is the conjugate vector $(i, 1, i, 1)$. You can show that the other eigenvectors corresponding to the roots $\pm\sqrt{3}i$ can be chosen to be $(\frac{-i}{\sqrt{3}}, -1, \frac{i}{\sqrt{3}}, 1)$ for $\sqrt{3}i$ and $(\frac{i}{\sqrt{3}}, -1, \frac{-i}{\sqrt{3}}, 1)$ for $-\sqrt{3}i$.

We now add and subtract conjugate solutions and divide by 2 and $2i$ respectively to get

$$\frac{\begin{bmatrix} -i \\ 1 \\ -i \\ 1 \end{bmatrix}(\cos(t) + i\sin(t)) + \begin{bmatrix} i \\ 1 \\ i \\ 1 \end{bmatrix}(\cos(t) - i\sin(t))}{2} = \begin{bmatrix} \sin(t) \\ \cos(t) \\ \sin(t) \\ \cos(t) \end{bmatrix},$$

$$\frac{\begin{bmatrix} -i \\ 1 \\ -i \\ 1 \end{bmatrix}(\cos(t)+i\sin(t)) - \begin{bmatrix} i \\ 1 \\ i \\ 1 \end{bmatrix}(\cos(t)-i\sin(t))}{2i} = \begin{bmatrix} -\cos(t) \\ \sin(t) \\ -\cos(t) \\ \sin(t) \end{bmatrix},$$

$$\frac{\begin{bmatrix} -i/\sqrt{3} \\ -1 \\ i/\sqrt{3} \\ 1 \end{bmatrix}(\cos(\sqrt{3}t)+i\sin(\sqrt{3}t)) + \begin{bmatrix} i/\sqrt{3} \\ -1 \\ -i/\sqrt{3} \\ 1 \end{bmatrix}(\cos(\sqrt{3}t)-i\sin(\sqrt{3}t))}{2}$$

$$= \begin{bmatrix} \sin(\sqrt{3}t)/\sqrt{3} \\ -\cos(\sqrt{3}t) \\ -\sin(\sqrt{3}t)/\sqrt{3} \\ \cos(\sqrt{3}t) \end{bmatrix},$$

and

$$\frac{\begin{bmatrix} -i/\sqrt{3} \\ -1 \\ i/\sqrt{3} \\ 1 \end{bmatrix}(\cos(\sqrt{3}t)+i\sin(\sqrt{3}t)) - \begin{bmatrix} i/\sqrt{3} \\ -1 \\ -i/\sqrt{3} \\ 1 \end{bmatrix}(\cos(\sqrt{3}t)-i\sin(\sqrt{3}t))}{2i}$$

$$= \begin{bmatrix} -\cos(\sqrt{3}t)/\sqrt{3} \\ -\sin(\sqrt{3}t) \\ \cos(\sqrt{3}t)/\sqrt{3} \\ \sin(\sqrt{3}t) \end{bmatrix}.$$

The general solution is

$$X(t) = c_1 \begin{bmatrix} \sin(t) \\ \cos(t) \\ \sin(t) \\ \cos(t) \end{bmatrix} + c_2 \begin{bmatrix} -\cos(t) \\ \sin(t) \\ -\cos(t) \\ \sin(t) \end{bmatrix}$$

$$+ c_3 \begin{bmatrix} \sin(\sqrt{3}t)/\sqrt{3} \\ -\cos(\sqrt{3}t) \\ -\sin(\sqrt{3}t)/\sqrt{3} \\ \cos(\sqrt{3}t) \end{bmatrix} + c_4 \begin{bmatrix} -\cos(\sqrt{3}t)/\sqrt{3} \\ -\sin(\sqrt{3}t) \\ \cos(\sqrt{3}t)/\sqrt{3} \\ \sin(\sqrt{3}t) \end{bmatrix}.$$

Then the displacement of the first mass is

$$x_1(t) = c_1 \sin(t) - c_2 \cos(t) + c_3 \sin(\sqrt{3}t)/\sqrt{3} - c_4 \cos(\sqrt{3}t)/\sqrt{3}.$$

By choosing the c_i appropriately, we can get

$$x_1(t) = \sin(t)$$
$$\text{or } x_1(t) = \sin(t) + \sin(\sqrt{3}t).$$

In the first case the motion is obviously periodic, and we shall show that the motion is not periodic in the second case.

In the second case, $x_1(t) = \sin(t) + \sin(\sqrt{3}t)$. Suppose that this function has period p. The derivative is also periodic with the same period. So at $t = p$ we have

$$\cos(p) + \sqrt{3}\cos(\sqrt{3}p) = 1 + \sqrt{3},$$

since

$$\cos(0) + \sqrt{3}\cos(\sqrt{3}0) = 1 + \sqrt{3}.$$

Thus $\cos(\sqrt{3}p) = 1$ and $\cos(p) = 1$, since they have to add to $1 + \sqrt{3}$. But then p and $\sqrt{3}p$ must both be odd multiples of $\pi/2$. This is impossible. Therefore, the solution cannot be periodic.

The periodicity of solutions depends on the choice of initial condition in this example.

EXERCISES 5.5

1. What are the periods of periodic solutions to the system of this section?

2. For the periodic solutions of the system of this section, describe the motion of the masses, and especially describe the way in which the masses move with respect to each other. Do the same for a nonperiodic motion.

3. To the system of this section, add another mass and spring. Write down the system of differential equations

   that models the dynamics of this new system.

4. To the system of this section, add friction proportional to velocity, with coefficient of friction equal to 1, to the first mass. Write down the matrix of this system. On purely physical grounds, how would you describe the general behavior of solutions? In particular, do you expect any periodic motion for either of the masses?

5.6 LINEARIZATION OF 2×2 SYSTEMS

Linear approximation of nonlinear functions is a commonplace in calculus. Indeed, the tangent line is an approximation to the graph of a differentiable function. This tangent line approximation tells us a little about the behavior of the function near the point of tangency. It is not unreasonable to ask if a linear system can be used to approximate the nonlinear autonomous system

$$x' = f(x, y),$$
$$y' = g(x, y).$$

In particular, could we approximate this nonlinear system in a neighborhood of a critical point and thereby discover the stability or instability of the critical point of the nonlinear system? The answer is that this strategy works most of the time. Then how is the nonlinear system approximated?

Suppose that (x_0, y_0) is a critical point of the system

$$x' = f(x, y),$$
$$y' = g(x, y).$$

Then $f(x_0, y_0) = 0$ and $g(x_0, y_0) = 0$.

Now expand f and g in their two-variable Taylor series expansions. For a derivation of the Taylor theorem for functions of two variables, see Appendix B. We have

$$f(x, y) = f(x_0, y_0) + \frac{\partial f}{\partial x}(x_0, y_0)(x - x_0) + \frac{\partial f}{\partial y}(x_0, y_0)(y - y_0)$$

$$+ \text{ higher-order terms,}$$

$$g(x, y) = g(x_0, y_0) + \frac{\partial g}{\partial x}(x_0, y_0)(x - x_0) + \frac{\partial g}{\partial y}(x_0, y_0)(y - y_0)$$

$$+ \text{ higher-order terms.}$$

The higher-order terms are bounded by expressions of the form $M(x - x_0)^h(y - y_0)^k$, where M is a constant and $h + k > 1$. Now, if (x, y) is close to the critical point, the higher-order terms should be small, and the hope is that these terms can be dropped without affecting the form of the behavior of solutions near the critical point. Also, the first terms to the right of the equalities can be dropped because they are zero. Set $\frac{\partial f}{\partial x}(x_0, y_0) = a_{11}, \frac{\partial f}{\partial y}(x_0, y_0) = a_{12},$ $\frac{\partial g}{\partial x}(x_0, y_0) = a_{21},$ and $\frac{\partial g}{\partial y}(x_0, y_0) = a_{22}.$ Then the substitute system is

$$x' = a_{11}(x - x_0) + a_{12}(y - y_0),$$
$$y' = a_{21}(x - x_0) + a_{22}(y - y_0).$$

Finally, if we change coordinates by setting $\bar{x} = x - x_0$ and $\bar{y} = y - y_0$ and note that $\bar{x}' = x'$ and $\bar{y}' = y'$, we get the linear system

$$\bar{x}' = a_{11}\bar{x} + a_{12}\bar{y},$$
$$\bar{y}' = a_{21}\bar{x} + a_{22}\bar{y}.$$

The solutions of this system are just translates of the solutions of the preceding system. Thus the hope is that the behavior of solutions close to the origin of this linear system is similar to the behavior of solutions close to the critical point (x_0, y_0) of the original nonlinear system. This hope is almost completely justified, but there are two exceptional cases that must be considered first.

Example 5.6.1 Consider the system

$$x' = y,$$
$$y' = -x^3.$$

The orbits can be obtained by going to the orbit equation

$$\frac{dy}{dx} = -\frac{x^3}{y}.$$

This separates to give

$$\frac{y^2}{2} + \frac{x^4}{4} = C.$$

Clearly, the origin is stable, for the orbits are bounded since the variables are both to even powers.

On the other hand, the linear approximating system is

$$x' = y,$$
$$y' = 0.$$

Clearly, y is a constant, since its derivative is zero. Therefore, $x(t) = at + b$, and so the origin is unstable. ∎

Therefore, there is an exceptional case if the linear system has zero as an eigenvalue. The reader should not get the idea that in the case of a zero eigenvalue the stability of the nonlinear system and the linear approximation are opposite.

The next example shows that if the eigenvalues are pure imaginary then the behavior of linear system near the critical point does not necessarily reflect the behavior of the nonlinear system near that point.

Example 5.6.2 The system

$$x' = y + (x^2 + y^2)x,$$
$$y' = -x + (x^2 + y^2)y$$

has a critical point at the origin. This critical point is unstable, but this is not immediately clear. If we plot the field and solutions close to the origin, the results are inconclusive. Suffice it to say that solution and field plotters are very useful, but they do not reveal the whole truth. We need to analyze this system more carefully.

To see the truth, we must convert to polar coordinates. This change of coordinates is given by $x = r\cos(\theta)$ and $y = r\sin(\theta)$. Taking derivatives and changing to polar coordinates gives

$$\frac{dx}{dt} = \frac{dr}{dt}\cos(\theta) - r\sin(\theta)\frac{d\theta}{dt} = r\sin(\theta) + r^3\cos(\theta),$$

$$\frac{dy}{dt} = \frac{dr}{dt}\sin(\theta) + r\cos(\theta)\frac{d\theta}{dt} = -r\cos(\theta) + r^3\sin(\theta).$$

In the exercises you are asked to solve for dr/dt. The result is $dr/dt = r^3$. Now r, being the polar radius, is positive. Thus the radius increases to infinity in finite time. To see this, just solve the equation by separation of variables. We conclude that the origin is unstable.

Note, however, that for initial values of r very much smaller than 1 the rate of growth of r will be very small, and the solution will stay close to the origin for a long time.

The linear approximation is

$$x' = y,$$
$$y' = -x,$$

and the orbits are circles. Thus the origin is stable for this linear system. ■

This example shows that if the eigenvalues are pure imaginary then the linear approximation does not say anything about the stability of the critical point of the nonlinear system.

It is, perhaps, not too surprising that the cases of pure imaginary eigenvalues or a zero eigenvalue are exceptional. After all, these cases are very sensitive to any small changes in the coefficients of the system. Indeed, the slightest change can change the form of the solutions completely. If these exceptions are included then the hope that we started this section with can be fulfilled. The following theorem summarizes the situation.

Theorem 5.6.3

Consider the system

$$x' = f(x, y),$$
$$y' = g(x, y).$$

Let (x_0, y_0) be an isolated critical point of this system, and suppose that the second partials of $f(x, y)$ and $g(x, y)$ are all continuous in some disk centered at (x_0, y_0). Let

$$A = \left[\begin{array}{cc} \frac{\partial f}{\partial x}(x_0, y_0) & \frac{\partial f}{\partial y}(x_0, y_0) \\ \frac{\partial g}{\partial x}(x_0, y_0) & \frac{\partial g}{\partial y}(x_0, y_0) \end{array} \right].$$

Then, if no eigenvalue of A is zero and the eigenvalues are not both pure imaginary, the stability of the critical point is the same as the stability of the origin for the linear system defined by A.   ●

The following example illustrates the use of this theorem.

Example 5.6.4   Recall the competing species model. One of the systems we looked at was

$$x' = x(4 - x - y),$$
$$y' = y(6 - x - 3y).$$

Observe that the functions $f(x, y)$ and $g(x, y)$ are continuously differentiable to all orders, so our theorem applies to any critical point. The critical points are $(0, 0)$, $(0, 2)$, $(4, 0)$, and $(3, 1)$, so we have four possible linearizations. Let us start with $(0, 0)$. Since

$$x' = 4x + 0y - x^2 - xy,$$
$$y' = 0x + 6y - xy - 3y^2,$$

the matrix for this critical point is

$$A = \left[\begin{array}{cc} 4 & 0 \\ 0 & 6 \end{array} \right].$$

The eigenvalues are 4 and 6, and so the critical point is unstable, with solutions moving away from the critical point.

Consider $(3, 1)$. The matrix is calculated from

$$A = \left[\begin{array}{cc} \frac{\partial f}{\partial x}(x_0, y_0) & \frac{\partial f}{\partial y}(x_0, y_0) \\ \frac{\partial g}{\partial x}(x_0, y_0) & \frac{\partial g}{\partial y}(x_0, y_0) \end{array} \right],$$

so the matrix is

$$A = \left[\begin{array}{cc} -3 & -3 \\ -1 & -3 \end{array} \right].$$

The characteristic polynomial is $P(x) = x^2 + 6x + 6$. The eigenvalues are both negative, so the critical point is stable. The rest of the critical points can be treated in the same way.   ■

EXERCISES 5.6

In Exercises 1–6 note that the partial derivatives of the system functions are continuous to all orders.

1. Use linearization to decide the stability of the origin for the nonlinear system

$$x' = 2x - y + xy + y^3,$$
$$y' = -3y + y^4.$$

2. Use linearization to decide, if possible, the stability of all the critical points of

$$x' = x(6 - x - 3y),$$
$$y' = y(4 - x - y).$$

3. Use linearization to decide, if possible, the stability of all the critical points of

$$x' = x - xy,$$
$$y' = x + y + x^2.$$

4. Use linearization to decide, if possible, the stability of all the critical points of

$$x' = (x - 1)(y + 2)y,$$
$$y' = x(y - 3).$$

5. Use linearization to decide, if possible, the stability of the origin, where

$$x' = 2x - y + xy - y^2,$$
$$y' = -x + y + x^2.$$

6. Use linearization to decide, if possible, the stability of the origin, where

$$x' = \sin(x + y),$$
$$y' = x.$$

7. Use package 2 × 2System to draw the field and orbits of solutions near the origin for

$$x' = y + (x^2 + y^2)x,$$
$$y' = -x + (x^2 + y^2)y.$$

Estimate the time it takes to leave the unit circle with initial conditions of $(0.1, 0)$ and $(0.01, 0)$.

8. In the system in Exercise 7 change to polar coordinates. That is, derive the differential equations that r and θ satisfy from scratch.

9. If the system in Exercise 7 is converted to polar coordinates, then Exercise 8 shows that the radius satisfies $dr/dt = r^3$. Given the initial conditions $(0.1, 0)$ and $(0.01, 0)$, how long does it actually take for the orbits to leave the unit circle? Do these orbits go to infinity in finite time?

10. Analyze the stability of the origin in the following system by switching to polar coordinates.

(a) $x' = \dfrac{x}{x^2 + y^2 + 1}$,

$y' = \dfrac{y}{x^2 + y^2 + 1}$

(b) Does Theorem 5.6.3 apply? If so, apply it.

SUPPLEMENTARY EXERCISES FOR CHAPTER 5

1. Consider the situation where you have three 1-liter(l) tanks. The first feeds into the second, the second feeds into the third, and the third feeds into the first. The rate of inflow and outflow for all tanks is 1 l/hr. If you start with 10 g of salt in the first tank, 20 g in the second, and 30 g in the third, how much salt is in each tank as time progresses? Does the salt 'even out' to 20 g in each tank in due course? What are the eigenvalues, and how do they relate to the outcome? Run the package 3 × 3 Auton on this problem to see how the orbit looks in three dimensions.

2. To the pendulum model of Chapter 3, add friction pro-

portional to the angular velocity $d\theta/dt$.

(a) Find all the critical points and decide on their stability.

(b) Experiment with values of the friction coefficient, and study the behavior of the solutions about some of the critical points in both the original system and the linearization.

(c) For an asymptotically stable critical point, the set of all points that are initial conditions that define solutions converging to the critical point is called the **basin of attraction** of the critical point. Describe the basins of attraction for the stable critical points of the pendulum with friction.

(d) Write a report on all that you discover.

3. Analyze the application of the eigenvector-generalized eigenvector method to 3×3 systems. Consider all possibilities of eigenvalues and eigenvectors. Take particular care with the question of the number of independent eigenvectors that you might have. Point to difficulties that could arise in trying to find generalized eigenvectors. The following matrix may provide a useful example:

$$
\begin{bmatrix}
2 & 0 & 0 \\
1 & 2 & 0 \\
0 & 0 & 2
\end{bmatrix}.
$$

CHAPTER 6

SERIES METHODS AND FAMOUS FUNCTIONS

So far we have not attempted to analytically solve linear differential equations of higher order with variable coefficients. In this chapter we take up this issue. The method of solution that we shall use expresses the solution as a power series. We shall see that this will often allow more information to be extracted from the solution than would be provided by a numerical method. In addition, the series method will focus our attention on the way in which differential equations can be thought of as defining important functions. We shall see that most of the famous functions of mathematics arise as solutions to differential equations. This will provide a useful perspective from which to view familiar functions and the new functions that will be encountered in mathematics, physics, and engineering.

6.1 A POWER SERIES METHOD

To keep the notation from getting out of hand, we shall discuss the solution of second-order equations. You will easily see how to generalize the method to higher orders. We shall consider equations of the form

$$y'' + a(x)y' + b(x)y = c(x),$$

where $a(x)$, $b(x)$, and $c(x)$ can be expressed as power series. Since the coefficients of the equation can be expressed as power series, it is not unreasonable to guess that the solution may be expressed as a power series also. This is the case, and so we shall first review the basic facts about power series.

6.1.1 Facts about Power Series

Recall that a power series is a series of the form

$$\sum_{k=0}^{\infty} c_k (x - x_0)^k.$$

We call x_0 the center of expansion, and the c_k are called the coefficients.

For each value of x, the series either converges or not. The set of x for which the series converges is an interval centered at x_0. The series may or may not converge at the endpoints of the interval. This depends on the series. We shall not be interested in whether the series converges at the endpoints, so we shall restrict our attention to the open interval on which the series converges. This interval is of the form $(x_0 - R, x_0 + R)$. We call R the radius of convergence. You should keep in mind that this radius may well be infinite. This means that the series converges for all x.

You should recall that the interval of convergence can often be found by applying the ratio or root tests. Here is an example.

Example 6.1.1   Consider the series

$$\sum_{k=0}^{\infty} \frac{(x - 2)^k}{3^k (k + 1)}.$$

We apply the ratio test by computing the limit of the ratio of the absolute values of the $(k + 1)$st term to the kth term as k goes to infinity. We have

$$\rho = \lim_{k \to \infty} \frac{|x - 2|^{k+1}/(3^{k+1}(k + 2))}{|x - 2|^k/(3^k(k + 1))} = \frac{|x - 2|}{3}.$$

You will recall that we have convergence if $\rho < 1$. So for convergence we need

$$|x - 2| < 3.$$

Thus the interval of convergence is $(-1, 5)$.   ■

If the series $\sum_{k=0}^{\infty} c_k (x - x_0)^k$ converges at x, then $\sum_{k=0}^{\infty} c_k (x - x_0)^k$ is a number that we may approximate as closely as we like with a partial sum of the form

$$c_0 + c_1 (x - x_0) + \cdots + c_n (x - x_0)^n$$

by choosing n large enough. The series defines a value for each x in the interval of convergence, so

$$f(x) = \sum_{k=0}^{\infty} c_k (x - x_0)^k$$

defines a function with domain $(x_0 - R, x_0 + R)$.

This function can be differentiated. Indeed,

$$f'(x) = \sum_{k=1}^{\infty} c_k k (x - x_0)^{k-1},$$

and the radius of convergence of the series for f' is the same as the series for f. This means we can differentiate f as many times as we wish. To differentiate f, you differentiate the series for f term by term, just as you would a polynomial.

If $f(x) = \sum_{k=0}^{\infty} c_k (x - x_0)^k$ on the interval of convergence, then there is a simple relation between the coefficients and the derivatives of f at x_0. Since

$$f(x) = c_0 + c_1(x - x_0) + \cdots + c_n(x - x_0)^n + \cdots,$$

we have

$$f(x_0) = c_0.$$

Also,

$$f'(x) = c_1 + c_2 2(x - x_0) + \cdots + c_n n (x - x_0)^{n-1} + \cdots,$$

and so

$$f'(x_0) = c_1.$$

In general,

$$c_k = f^{(k)}(x_0)/k!.$$

Thus the c_k are precisely the Taylor coefficients of f.

An important consequence of this for us is that if

$$\sum_{k=0}^{\infty} a_k (x - x_0)^k = \sum_{k=0}^{\infty} b_k (x - x_0)^k$$

on an interval containing x_0 then the series must be identical. Indeed, if we set

$$f(x) = \sum_{k=0}^{\infty} a_k (x - x_0)^k = \sum_{k=0}^{\infty} b_k (x - x_0)^k$$

on this interval, then

$$a_k = f^{(k)}(x_0)/k! = b_k.$$

Given any infinitely differentiable function g, we may form its Taylor series:

$$\sum_{k=0}^{\infty} \frac{g^{(k)}(x_0)}{k!}(x - x_0)^k.$$

If the series converges at x, is the value of the series the same as $g(x)$? Not necessarily! Not all functions can be represented by their Taylor series.

Definition 6.1.2

If an infinitely differentiable function, g, is defined on an open interval, and at each point, x_0 of the interval, $g(x)$ is equal to the Taylor series of g at x_0 in a neighborhood of x_0, then we say that g is analytic. ●

We shall need to add and multiply power series. The sum is as expected

$$\sum_{k=0}^{\infty} a_k (x - x_0)^k + \sum_{k=0}^{\infty} b_k (x - x_0)^k = \sum_{k=0}^{\infty} [a_k + b_k](x - x_0)^k.$$

The last series converges at least on the intersection of the intervals of convergence of the summands.

The product of power series is computed in the same way that we form the product of two polynomials. We multiply all pairings of terms together and collect all products of the same degree together. It looks like this

$$(a_0 + a_1 (x - x_0) + \cdots + a_n (x - x_0)^n + \cdots)$$

$$\times (b_0 + b_1 (x - x_0) + \cdots + b_n (x - x_0)^n + \cdots)$$

$$= a_0 b_0 + (a_0 b_1 + a_1 b_0)(x - x_0) + (a_0 b_2 + a_1 b_1 + a_2 b_0)(x - x_0)^2 + \cdots.$$

In summation notation, the product is as follows:

$$\left(\sum_{k=0}^{\infty} a_k (x - x_0)^k \right) \left(\sum_{k=0}^{\infty} a_k (x - x_0)^k \right) = \sum_{n=0}^{\infty} \left[\sum_{k=0}^{n} a_k b_{n-k} \right] (x - x_0)^n.$$

The series on the right converges to the product of the series on the left at each point in the intersection of the intervals of convergence.

EXERCISES 6.1.1

Find the interval of convergence of the series in Exercises 1–3.

1. $\displaystyle\sum_{k=0}^{\infty} 2^k (x - 1)^k$

2. $\displaystyle\sum_{k=0}^{\infty} \frac{(x + 2)^k}{k^2 + 1}$

3. $\displaystyle\sum_{k=0}^{\infty} \frac{2^k x^k}{k!}$

Find the derivative of the series in Exercises 4–6 by writing out the sum and differentiating term by term. Use the sigma notation formula for the derivative, and then write out the sum to compare results.

4. $\displaystyle f(x) = \sum_{k=0}^{\infty} 2^k (x - 1)^k$

5. $\displaystyle f(x) = \sum_{k=0}^{\infty} \frac{x^k}{k^2 + 1}$

6. $\displaystyle f(x) = \sum_{k=0}^{\infty} \frac{k x^k}{k + 1}$

7. Find the derivative of the series $f(x) = \sum_{k=2}^{\infty} \frac{2^k x^k}{k-1}$ by writing out the sum and differentiating term by term. What is the appropriate sigma notation formula for this differentiation since the series does not start at $k = 0$?

8. Compute the Taylor series with centers of expansion at $x_0 = 0$ and $x_0 = 1$ of the following functions. (a) $f(x) = x^4$. (b) $f(x) = e^x$.

9. Compute the Taylor series with centers of expansion at $x_0 = 0$ and $x_0 = 1$ of the following functions. (a) $f(x) = x^3 - 3x^2 + 2x - 1$. (b) $f(x) = \sin(x)$.

10. Compute the Taylor series with center of expansion at $x_0 = 0$ and $x_0 = -2$ of $f(x) = x^4 - 3x^3 - 1$.

11. Compute the Taylor series with center of expansion at $x_0 = 0$ and $x_0 = 3$ of $f(x) = x^3 - 3x^2 - x$.

12. What is the Taylor series of any polynomial $P(x) = a_0 + a_1 x + \cdots + a_n x^n$ with center of expansion $x_0 = 0$?

13. Compute the product series of $(2-x+3x^2)(1+x+x^2+x^3+\cdots)$ out to the fifth order.

14. Compute the product series of

$$\sum_{k=0}^{\infty} kx^k \sum_{k=0}^{\infty} \frac{x^k}{k+1}$$

out to the fourth order.

15. Compute the product series of

$$\sum_{k=0}^{\infty} kx^k \sum_{k=0}^{\infty} \frac{x^k}{k!}$$

out to the fourth order.

16. Compute the product series of

$$\sum_{k=0}^{\infty} \frac{x^k}{2^k} \sum_{k=0}^{\infty} \frac{x^k}{k^2+1}$$

out to the fourth order.

17. Use the existence and uniqueness theorem to prove that $f(x) = \sum_{k=0}^{\infty} \frac{x^k}{k!}$ must be e^x by finding a first-order initial-value problem that $f(x)$ satisfies. *Hint:* Differentiate the series for $f(x)$.

18. Show that the series $f(x) = \sum_{k=0}^{\infty} (-1)^k \frac{x^{2k+1}}{(2k+1)!}$ satisfies the initial-value problem $y'' + y = 0$, $y(0) = 0$, and $y'(0) = 1$. By uniqueness of the solution, what must the series be?

6.1.2 A Series Method of Solution

We shall assume that the coefficients and $c(x)$ in

$$y'' + a(x)y' + b(x)y = c(x)$$

are analytic in an interval. It can be proved that the solutions are also analytic in this interval.

We shall see how the series method works by first working through an example. Then we will apply the same procedure to the general equation to get a general formula for the coefficients of the series solution.

Example 6.1.3   Consider the equation

$$y'' - xy = 0.$$

The solution is analytic, so we can assume that it has the form

$$y(x) = \sum_{k=0}^{\infty} y_k x^k.$$

If this is a solution, then taking the appropriate derivatives and substituting in the equation will give the identity

$$\sum_{k=2}^{\infty} y_k k(k-1)x^{k-2} - x\sum_{k=0}^{\infty} y_k x^k = 0.$$

To determine the y_k, we combine the series on the left into a single series. We do this term by term. That is, we find the constant term, then the first-order term, then the second-order term, and so on. Here is the result:

$$y_2 2 \cdot 1 + (y_3 3 \cdot 2 - y_0)x + (y_4 4 \cdot 3 - y_1)x^2 + \cdots$$

$$+(y_{n+2}(n+2)(n+1) - y_{n-1})x^n + \cdots = 0.$$

The only way that the power series on the left can be identically zero is if all the coefficients are zero. This is the key to finding the y_k. We have the following equations:

$$y_2 2 \cdot 1 = 0$$
$$y_3 3 \cdot 2 - y_0 = 0$$
$$y_4 4 \cdot 3 - y_1 = 0$$

and, in general,

$$y_{n+2}(n+2)(n+1) - y_{n-1} = 0.$$

Thus $y_2 = 0$, $y_3 = y_0/(2 \cdot 3)$, and $y_4 = y_1/(3 \cdot 4)$. Now the next equation yields

$$y_5 = \frac{y_2}{4 \cdot 5},$$

but y_2 has already been computed, so we have $y_5 = 0$. The next equation gives

$$y_6 = \frac{y_3}{5 \cdot 6},$$

but we have y_3 in terms of y_1. Thus

$$y_6 = \frac{y_1}{2 \cdot 3 \cdot 5 \cdot 6}.$$

It should be clear that we can compute every y_k in terms of y_0 and y_1. This is because the preceding equations give each y_k in terms of y's with a strictly lower subscript. Thus we can **back substitute** until we have y_k in terms of y_0 or y_1, or possibly both.

It should not surprise you that y_0 and y_1 are not determined by this process. After all, this is a second-order equation, and there will be two arbitrary constants to be determined by the initial conditions.

Here is the solution out to the sixth order.

$$y(x) = y_0 + y_1 x + 0x^2 + \frac{y_0}{2 \cdot 3}x^3 + \frac{y_1}{3 \cdot 4}x^4 + 0x^5 + \frac{y_0}{2 \cdot 3 \cdot 5 \cdot 6}x^6 + \cdots . \blacksquare$$

Let us now carry out the method in general. As we know, the solution is analytic, so we can write it as a power series

$$y(x) = \sum_{k=0}^{\infty} y_k x^k.$$

We have set $x_0 = 0$ simply for notational convenience. You may carry $x - x_0$ through all the calculations that follow if you wish. We differentiate the solution to get

$$y'(x) = \sum_{k=1}^{\infty} y_k k x^{k-1}, \qquad y''(x) = \sum_{k=2}^{\infty} y_k k(k-1) x^{k-2}.$$

We write the coefficients and $c(x)$ as power series. We have

$$a(x) = \sum_{k=0}^{\infty} a_k x^k, \qquad b(x) = \sum_{k=0}^{\infty} b_k x^k, \quad \text{and} \quad c(x) = \sum_{k=0}^{\infty} c_k x^k.$$

Each of the series is substituted in its place in the equation. This is how it looks so far.

$$\sum_{k=2}^{\infty} y_k k(k-1) x^{k-2} + \sum_{k=0}^{\infty} a_k x^k \sum_{k=1}^{\infty} y_k k x^{k-1} + \sum_{k=0}^{\infty} b_k x^k \sum_{k=0}^{\infty} y_k x^k = \sum_{k=0}^{\infty} c_k x^k.$$

We now use addition and multiplication of series to combine the series on the left into a single series. There is, however, a small difficulty. Not all the series start at $k = 0$. To correct this, we re-index the series. Here is an example. We make the change of index by setting $j = k - 2$.

$$\sum_{k=2}^{\infty} y_k k(k-1) x^{k-2} = \sum_{j=0}^{\infty} y_{j+2}(j+2)(j+1) x^j.$$

You should write out a few terms of each of the preceding series to see that they are the same.

We now have

$$\sum_{j=0}^{\infty} y_{j+2}(j+2)(j+1) x^j + \sum_{j=0}^{\infty} a_j x^j \sum_{j=0}^{\infty} y_{j+1}(j+1) x^j + \sum_{j=0}^{\infty} b_j x^j \sum_{j=0}^{\infty} y_j x^j$$

$$= \sum_{j=0}^{\infty} c_j x^j.$$

We can now combine the left as a single series. We get

$$\sum_{n=0}^{\infty} \left[y_{n+2}(n+2)(n+1) + \sum_{j=0}^{n} a_j y_{n-j+1}(n-j+1) + \sum_{j=0}^{n} b_j y_{n-j} \right] x^n$$

$$= \sum_{n=0}^{\infty} c_n x^n.$$

The crucial point has now arrived. If we are to have a solution, the series on the left must equal the series on the right. But this requires that the coefficients be identical. Therefore,

$$y_{n+2}(n+2)(n+1) + \sum_{j=0}^{n} a_j y_{n-j+1}(n-j+1) + \sum_{j=0}^{n} b_j y_{n-j} = c_n,$$

or

$$y_{n+2} = \frac{c_n - \sum_{j=0}^{n} a_j y_{n-j+1}(n-j+1) - \sum_{j=0}^{n} b_j y_{n-j}}{(n+2)(n+1)}.$$

Remember that the a_j, b_j, and c_n are all known and that we are trying to determine the y_k in the solution

$$y(x) = \sum_{k=0}^{\infty} y_k x^k.$$

But this formula gives y_{n+2} in terms of y_r, where r is a strictly lower index. Thus, if y_0 and y_1 are known, then y_2 can be computed. But then y_3 can be computed, and so on. Again, it is no surprise that the first two coefficients are arbitrary. This is a second-order equation, and it requires two initial conditions to specify the solution uniquely. Indeed, since

$$y(x) = \sum_{k=0}^{\infty} y_k x^k,$$

it follows that $y(0) = y_0$ and $y'(0) = y_1$.

The formula defining y_{n+2} in terms of its predecessors is called a **recursion relation**, and we say the y_k are defined recursively. It is the kind of calculation that is perfectly suited to a computer.

Consider another example.

Example 6.1.4   We solve the equation

$$y'' - \frac{1}{1-x} y = 0,$$

with $y(0) = y_0$ and $y'(0) = y_1$. First, all the a_j are zero. Second,

$$\frac{1}{1-x} = 1 + x + x^2 + x^3 + \cdots,$$

and so in the recursion formula we will take $b_j = -1$. Of course, for each n, $c_n = 0$. Thus we have

$$y_{n+2} = \frac{\sum_{j=0}^{n} y_{n-j}}{(n+2)(n+1)}.$$

The y_k can now be computed.

$$y_2 = \frac{y_0}{1 \cdot 2},$$

$$y_3 = \frac{y_0 + y_1}{2 \cdot 3},$$

$$y_4 = \frac{y_0 + y_1 + y_2}{3 \cdot 4} = \frac{y_0 + y_0/2}{3 \cdot 4} + \frac{y_1}{3 \cdot 4} = \frac{3y_0 + 2y_1}{4!},$$

$$y_5 = \frac{y_0 + y_1 + y_2 + y_3}{4 \cdot 5} = \frac{10y_0 + 7y_1}{5!}.$$

Clearly, we can continue to calculate coefficients to any order in terms of y_0 and y_1.

The solution has the form

$$y(x) = y_0 + y_1 x + \frac{y_0}{2!} x^2 + \frac{y_0 + y_1}{3!} x^3 + \frac{3y_0 + 2y_1}{4!} x^4 + \cdots.$$

If the terms containing y_0 are grouped together, and the same with y_1, then the solution can be expressed as a linear combination of two series, as follows:

$$y(x) = y_0 [1 + \frac{1}{2!} x^2 + \frac{1}{3!} x^3 + \frac{3}{4!} x^4 + \cdots] + y_1 [x + \frac{1}{3!} x^3 + \frac{2}{4!} x^4 + \cdots].$$

These two series form a fundamental set of solutions. Therefore, a unique solution is determined by specifying y_0 and y_1. ∎

This example requires further discussion. A neat formula for y_n is not apparent. In fact, for many equations no such formula can be found. Nonetheless, a partial sum of as high a degree as desired may be calculated, and so the solution may be approximated in a neighborhood of the center of expansion. Should we infer from this that the series method merely produces another numerical method? No! Where the series method can be applied, the solution must be infinitely differentiable and not just twice differentiable. This is information we cannot get from, say, the Runge-Kutta method. Furthermore, if a formula for the coefficients can be found, then it is often the case that much more information about the solution can be extracted. The next example provides a simple illustration.

Example 6.1.5 We shall solve

$$y'' - xy' - y = 0,$$

with $y(0) = y_0$ and $y'(0) = y_1$, by the series method. In doing so, we shall find out much more about the solutions of this equation than could be gained from a numerical method.

Because of the location of the initial condition, it is natural to find a series representation of the solution centered at zero.

The reader can easily show that the recursion formula

$$y_{n+2} = \frac{c_n - \sum_{j=0}^{n} a_j y_{n-j+1}(n - j + 1) - \sum_{j=0}^{n} b_j y_{n-j}}{(n + 2)(n + 1)}$$

reduces to

$$y_{n+2} = \frac{y_n}{n + 2}.$$

Thus $y_2 = y_0/2$, $y_3 = y_1/3$, $y_4 = y_2/4 = y_0/2 \cdot 4$, and so on. It is easy to show that

$$y_{2n} = \frac{y_0}{2 \cdot 4 \cdots 2n},$$

and

$$y_{2n+1} = \frac{y_1}{3 \cdot 5 \cdots (2n + 1)}.$$

Therefore, the solution is

$$y(x) = y_0 \sum_{n=0}^{\infty} \frac{1}{2 \cdot 4 \cdots 2n} x^{2n} + y_1 \sum_{n=0}^{\infty} \frac{1}{3 \cdot 5 \cdots (2n + 1)} x^{2n+1}.$$

The series

$$\phi_1(x) = \sum_{n=0}^{\infty} \frac{1}{2 \cdot 4 \cdots 2n} x^{2n}$$

can be rewritten as

$$\phi_1(x) = \sum_{n=0}^{\infty} \frac{1}{2 \cdot 4 \cdots 2n} x^{2n} = \sum_{n=0}^{\infty} \frac{1}{2^n n!} x^{2n} = \sum_{n=0}^{\infty} \frac{1}{n!} \left(\frac{x^2}{2} \right)^n = e^{\frac{x^2}{2}}.$$

This information is not obtainable from a numerical method, so the series method has allowed us to extract much more information than would otherwise have been possible. The second series

$$\phi_2(x) = \sum_{n=0}^{\infty} \frac{1}{3 \cdot 5 \cdots (2n + 1)} x^{2n+1}$$

cannot be boiled down to a familiar function. Nevertheless, the ratio test shows that radius of convergence of this series is infinite, so the solution is infinitely differentiable on the whole real line. The function is odd, that is, $\phi_2(-x) = -\phi_2(x)$. This might be suggested by a numerical method, but how could we be sure? ■

What if the initial condition is not at $x = 0$? If the initial condition is at $x = 1$, say, then the solution procedure is the same as before, except that all series must have center of expansion $x_0 = 1$. Here is an example.

Example 6.1.6 We shall solve the equation

$$y'' + x^2 y' + e^x y = x$$

with initial condition $y(1) = 2$ and $y'(1) = 3$.

First, the power series of coefficient functions must be written in terms of $(x - 1)$. This means calculating the Taylor series of these functions with center of expansion 1.

The expansion for x^2 is

$$1 + \frac{2}{1!}(x - 1) + \frac{2}{2!}(x - 1)^2.$$

The expansion for e^x is

$$e + \frac{e}{1!}(x - 1) + \frac{e}{2!}(x - 1)^2 + \frac{e}{3!}(x - 1)^3 + \cdots,$$

and for x it is

$$1 + (x - 1).$$

The coefficients are $a_0 = 1$, $a_1 = 2$, $a_2 = 1$, $a_3 = 0$, and so on, $b_0 = e$, $b_1 = e$, $b_2 = e/2$, $b_3 = e/6$, and so on, $c_0 = 1$, $c_1 = 1$, $c_2 = 0$, and so on.

Now $y_0 = 2$ and $y_1 = 3$, and so

$$y_2 = \frac{1 - 1 \cdot 2 - e \cdot 2}{2 \cdot 1},$$

and

$$y_3 = \frac{1 - (1 \cdot y_2 \cdot 2 + 2 \cdot 3) - (e \cdot 3 + e \cdot 2)}{3 \cdot 2},$$

and so on .

The solution then has the form

$$y(x) = y_0 + y_1(x - 1) + y_2(x - 1)^2 + y_3(x - 1)^3 + \cdots,$$

where the y_k are calculated as shown.

The calculation of the coefficients is often a very tedious business. A computer algebra system can prove very useful in these calculations. ∎

How does this procedure work for higher-order equations? It is exactly the same. Here is an example.

Example 6.1.7   We solve the initial-value problem

$$y''' - xy' = 0,$$

where $y(0) = 1$, $y'(0) = -1$, and $y''(0) = 2$. The solution and its derivatives are

$$y(x) = \sum_{k=0}^{\infty} y_k x^k, \qquad y'(x) = \sum_{k=1}^{\infty} y_k k x^{k-1},$$

$$y''(x) = \sum_{k=2}^{\infty} y_k k(k-1) x^{k-2}, \qquad \text{and} \qquad y'''(x) = \sum_{k=3}^{\infty} y_k k(k-1)(k-2) x^{k-3}.$$

Substituting in the equation gives

$$\sum_{k=3}^{\infty} y_k k(k-1)(k-2) x^{k-3} - \sum_{k=1}^{\infty} y_k k x^k = 0.$$

Now we write the left-hand side as a single power series, but we write out the series as a sum. Thus

$$y_3 3 \cdot 2 \cdot 1 + (y_4 4 \cdot 3 \cdot 2 - y_1 1)x + (y_5 5 \cdot 4 \cdot 3 - y_2 2)x^2$$
$$+ (y_6 6 \cdot 5 \cdot 4 - y_3 3)x^3 + \cdots = 0.$$

The coefficients of the powers of x in this sum must all be zero. Therefore,

$$y_3 3 \cdot 2 \cdot 1 = 0,$$
$$(y_4 4 \cdot 3 \cdot 2 - y_1 1) = 0,$$
$$(y_5 5 \cdot 4 \cdot 3 - y_2 2) = 0,$$
$$(y_6 6 \cdot 5 \cdot 4 - y_3 3) = 0,$$

and so on. Thus $y_3 = 0$, $y_4 = y_1/4 \cdot 3 \cdot 2 = -1/24$, $y_5 = y_2 2/5 \cdot 4 \cdot 3 = 1/60$, $y_6 = 0$, and so on. **Note very carefully** that $y_2 \neq 2$, but that $y_2 2 = 2$. The partial sum of the solution out to the sixth degree is

$$y(x) \approx 1 - x + x^2 + 0x^3 - \frac{1}{24}x^4 + \frac{1}{60}x^5 + 0x^6.$$

A partial sum of any degree can be calculated, and so the solution in a neighborhood of zero can be computed to any desired accuracy.   ∎

It is important to recognize the limitations of partial sums in approximating solutions. Generally, a partial sum will only give a good approximation to the solution close to the center of expansion. The next example illustrates this.

Example 6.1.8 Let us solve the equation $y'' + y = 0$, where $y(0) = 1$ and $y'(0) = 0$. The solution is, of course, well known to us.

The power series solution at zero is derived in the usual way. Set

$$y(x) = \sum_{n=0}^{\infty} y_n x^n.$$

The coefficients are computed by

$$y_{n+2} = \frac{c_n - \sum_{j=0}^{n} a_j y_{n-j+1}(n-j+1) - \sum_{j=0}^{n} b_j y_{n-j}}{(n+2)(n+1)},$$

which reduces to

$$y_{n+2} = \frac{-y_n}{(n+1)(n+2)}.$$

Since $y_1 = 0$, all the odd terms are zero. We easily compute that

$$y_{2n} = \frac{(-1)^n}{(2n)!},$$

and so

$$y(x) = \sum_{n=0}^{\infty} \frac{(-1)^n}{(2n)!} x^{2n} = \cos(x).$$

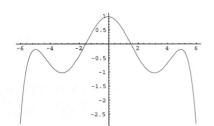

FIGURE 6.1

Figure 6.1 is a graphic of a partial sum of this series.

The partial sum gives a reasonable approximation to the $\cos(x)$ on the interval $(-4, 4)$, but outside this interval the approximation becomes worthless. This is to be expected, because partial sums are polynomials, and polynomials must go to infinity as x goes to infinity. ∎

In defense of series as a numerical method, let it be said that series can give very precise numerical approximations near the center of expansion. Moreover, the error in using a partial sum can often be evaluated in a convenient way. In the last example, the error formula from the alternating series test can be used very effectively.

For example, recall that the error estimate for an alternating series is given by

$$\left| \sum_{k=1}^{n} (-1)^k a_k - L \right| \leq a_{n+1},$$

where L is the limit of the series. Thus, in the preceding case of $\cos(x)$, the partial sum

$$1 - \frac{2^2}{2} + \frac{2^4}{24} - \frac{2^6}{720}$$

approximates $\cos(2)$ with error less than $\frac{2^8}{8!} \approx 6.35 \times 10^{-3}$.

This section concludes with an example that is important in physics and engineering.

Example 6.1.9   The equation

$$(1 - x^2)y'' - 2xy' + \alpha(\alpha + 1)y = 0$$

is called **Legendre's equation**. It occurs in the solution of a number of problems ranging from quantum mechanics to temperature distributions.

Notice that $1/(1 - x^2)$ is analytic on the interval $(-1, 1)$, so we will solve this equation in power series centered at zero. The best approach to solving Legendre's equation is to substitute the series solution directly into the equation. We have

$$(1 - x^2) \sum_{k=2}^{\infty} y_k k(k-1)x^{k-2} - 2x \sum_{k=1}^{\infty} y_k k x^{k-1} + \alpha(\alpha + 1) \sum_{k=0}^{\infty} y_k x^k = 0.$$

The left-hand side is rewritten as a single series. The result is

$$[\alpha(\alpha + 1)y_0 + 2y_2] + [(\alpha(\alpha + 1) - 2)y_1 + 2 \cdot 3y_3]x$$
$$+ [(\alpha(\alpha + 1) - 6)y_2 + 3 \cdot 4y_4]x^2$$
$$+ \cdots + [(\alpha(\alpha + 1) - k(k + 1))y_k + (k + 2)(k + 1)y_{k+2}]x^k + \cdots = 0.$$

Equating the coefficients to zero and writing the recursion relations gives

$$y_2 = -\frac{\alpha(\alpha + 1)}{2}y_0,$$

$$y_3 = -\frac{\alpha(\alpha + 1) - 2}{3 \cdot 2}y_1,$$

and, in general,

$$y_{k+2} = -\frac{\alpha(\alpha + 1) - k(k + 1)}{(k + 2)(k + 1)}y_k.$$

A little experimenting then yields the following formulas for the even and odd coefficients:

$$y_{2m} = (-1)^m \frac{\alpha(\alpha - 2) \cdots (\alpha - 2m + 2)(\alpha + 1)(\alpha + 3) \cdots (\alpha + 2m - 1)}{(2m)!}y_0,$$

and

$$y_{2m+1} =$$
$$(-1)^m \frac{(\alpha - 1)(\alpha - 3) \cdots (\alpha - 2m + 1)(\alpha + 2)(\alpha + 4) \cdots (\alpha + 2m)}{(2m + 1)!}y_1.$$

These are valid for $m \geq 1$. If we alternately set $y_0 = 1$, $y_1 = 0$, and $y_0 = 0$, $y_1 = 1$, we get the following basis for all the solutions:

$$\phi_1(x) = 1 +$$

$$\sum_{m=1}^{\infty} (-1)^m \frac{\alpha(\alpha-2)\cdots(\alpha-2m+2)(\alpha+1)(\alpha+3)\cdots(\alpha+2m-1)}{(2m)!} x^{2m},$$

and

$$\phi_2(x) = x +$$

$$\sum_{m=1}^{\infty} (-1)^m \frac{(\alpha-1)(\alpha-3)\cdots(\alpha-2m+1)(\alpha+2)(\alpha+4)\cdots(\alpha+2m)}{(2m+1)!} x^{2m+1}.$$

If α is a nonnegative integer then one or the other of the preceding solutions is a polynomial. These polynomials, multiplied by suitable constants, prove to be important in physics and engineering. They are called Legendre polynomials. ∎

The Legendre polynomials qualify as famous functions. We shall discuss the relationship between famous functions and differential equations in the next section, and we will use Legendre polynomials as an example. We shall see that Legendre polynomials have many properties that numerical methods could never have revealed.

EXERCISES 6.1.2

1. Use the power series method to compute power series solutions out to the eighth order for the initial-value problem $y'' + x^2 y = 0$, $y(0) = 1$, and $y'(0) = 2$. Graph the fourth-, fifth-, and eighth-order partial sums. On what interval do you think the eighth order partial sum is doing a reasonable job of approximating the solution? Explain!

2. Use the power series method to compute power series solutions out to the sixth order for the initial-value problem $y'' - xy' - xy = x$, $y(0) = 1$, and $y'(0) = 1$. Graph the third-, fourth-, and sixth-order partial sums. On what interval do you think the sixth-order partial sum is doing a reasonable job of approximating the solution? Explain!

3. Use the power series method to compute power series solutions out to the sixth order for the initial-value problem $y'' + xy' - x^2 y = 1 + x^2$, $y(0) = 1$, and $y'(0) = -1$. Graph the second-, fourth-, and sixth-order partial sums. On what interval do you think the sixth-order partial sum is doing a reasonable job of approximating the solution? Explain!

4. Use the series method to solve $y'' - x^2 y = 0$, where

$y(1) = y_0$ and $y'(1) = y_1$. Collect the y_0 terms and the y_1 terms, and write the solution as a linear combination of two solutions carried out to the fourth order. Note that you must convert x^2 to a series centered at $x_0 = 1$.

5. Use the series method to solve to the fourth order $y'' + x^3 y = x$, where $y(1) = 2$, and $y'(1) = -1$. Note that the center is 1.

6. Use the series method to solve to the fourth order $y'' + x^2 y' - x^2 y = x$, where $y(-1) = 2$ and $y'(-1) = -1$.

7. Use the series method to solve to the fourth order $y'' + xy' + (x^2 + 2x)y = 0$, where $y(2) = 1$ and $y'(2) = 1$.

8. Use the power series method to find the power series solution to $y' - e^x y = x$ and $y(0) = 1$ out to the fourth order. Graph the second-, third-, and fourth-order partial sums. On what interval do you think the fourth-order partial sum is doing a reasonable job of approximating the solution. Explain!

9. Use the power series method to find the power series solution to $y'' - \sin(x)y = 0$, $y(0) = 1$, and $y'(0) = 2$ out to the fourth order.

10. Use the power series method to find the power series solution to $y''' - xy = 0$, $y(0) = 1$, $y'(0) = 2$, and $y''(0) = 2$ out to the sixth order.

11. Use the power series method to find the power series solution to $y^{(4)} - xy = 0$, $y(0) = 1$, $y'(0) = 2$, $y''(0) = -1$, and $y'''(0) = 2$ out to the fifth order.

12. Solve $y'' - xy = 0$. Write the solution as a linear combination of two series. Write the series in sigma notation. You will need to write the first few terms explicitly before writing the series.

13. Solve $y'' + xy' + 2y = 0$. Write the solution as a linear combination of two series. Write the series in sigma notation. Are some solutions even and some odd? Explain!

14. **(a)** Use the power series method to find the power series solution to $y'' + y = 0$, $y(0) = 1$, and $y'(0) = 2$ out to the sixth order. Use this to get approximate values of the solution at 0.1, 0.5, 1, and 2. Also write the solution as a sum of series of odd terms and even terms.

    (b) Use the methods of Chapter 4 to solve the equation in terms of familiar functions. Evaluate this at 0.1, 0.5, 1, and 2. Compare with part a above and comment on the results.

    (c) Do the series in part a allow you to estimate the error in using a particular partial sum? Explain! Without

referring to part b, use the series in part a to compute $y(1)$ with error less than 1/1000. *Hint:* Apply the alternating series test.

15. If $\alpha = n$ is zero or a positive integer in Legendre's equation, then one of the solutions in Example 6.1.7 is a polynomial, P_n. These are called Legendre polynomials if they are multiplied by an appropriate constant to get $P_n(1) = 1$. Find the Legendre polynomials for $\alpha = 0$, $\alpha = 1$, $\alpha = 2$, $\alpha = 3$, and $\alpha = 4$.

16. Show that the two solutions derived in the Legendre example are linearly independent on the interval $(-1, 1)$. *Hint:* Look at the linear combination when $x = 0$.

17. Suppose that $y'' + 3y' + 2y = 0$, $y(0) = 1$, and $y'(0) = -1$. Use the power series method to find $y(1)$ with error less than 1/1000. Note that the series alternates.

18. Explain in your own words where, in the series method, we use the fact that equal power series have identical coefficients.

19. Reduce the equation $y'' + ty' + y = 0$ to a first-order system and use 2 × 2Solution to convince yourself that solutions converge to zero as t goes to infinity. Why is it impossible for a partial sum of a series solution to approximate the solution accurately for all $t > 0$?

6.2 FAMOUS FUNCTIONS

In the course of finding analytic solutions to differential equations, the famous functions e^t, $\sin(t)$, and $\cos(t)$ have appeared on numerous occasions. We can ask why these functions are so famous? Why do they appear on practically every calculator? Consider the function e^{at} first. We know this is a solution to the equation

$$y' = ay,$$

and this equation is fundamental to the description of many kinds of natural growth and decay phenomena. This function is important, in large part, because the equation that it solves is important.

The functions $\sin(t)$ and $\cos(t)$ are important for similar reasons. These functions form the basis for all solutions to the equation

$$y'' + y = 0.$$

This equation describes a simple mass-spring system, and so it describes simple harmonic motion. It is because oscillatory motion is so common in our world that this equation is so important, and because this equation is important the solutions $\sin(t)$ and $\cos(t)$ are important. True, the functions $\sin(t)$ and $\cos(t)$ make their appearance in our lives through trigonometry long before we know that they are solutions to a certain differential equation. However, we shall show that even these trigonometric applications can be derived from the differential equation.

In view of these remarks, it is not unreasonable to give primary importance to the differential equations and to regard these equations as defining their solutions. Consider the equation

$$y' = y$$

with the initial condition $y(0) = 1$. The existence and uniqueness theorem tells us that there is a unique solution. Let us call it $g(t)$. You can think of g as an abbreviation for "growth function." We do not know much about $g(t)$ yet, except that it is its own derivative. But, if we carry out the power series solution of this equation, we immediately get

$$g(t) = \sum_{k=0}^{\infty} \frac{t^k}{k!}.$$

So we can compute approximate values of $g(t)$, and, by the ratio test, we know that $g(t)$ is infinitely differentiable and defined for all t. Now we know a bit more about $g(t)$. What about $g(a+t)$? This function satisfies $y' = y$ and $y(0) = g(a)$, but so does $h(t) = g(a)g(t)$. Solutions to initial-value problems are unique, so

$$g(a + t) = g(a)g(t).$$

Thus we have the **power rule** of exponentials. The point is that we could have defined the exponential function to be the solution to the initial-value problem that we started with, and then we could have discovered its properties until it became as familiar to us as e^t.

Many famous functions come into existence in mathematics in exactly this way. A differential equation is recognized as important in mathematics, physics or engineering, and certain of its solutions play such important roles that they are given names. These named solutions are then investigated until they become as familiar as e^t, $\sin(t)$, or $\cos(t)$.

Let us practice this approach to defining functions by considering the equation

$$y'' + y = 0$$

and the initial conditions $y(0) = 0$ and $y'(0) = 1$. Let $\phi(t)$ be the unique solution. Our goal is to discover so much about this function that it is as familiar to us as e^t. Do not imagine that you know anything about $\phi(t)$ yet!

Let us reduce this equation to a first-order system. We get

$$u' = v,$$
$$v' = -u.$$

The field in vector form is $\vec{F}(u, v) = v\vec{\imath} - u\vec{\jmath}$, and this is at right angles to the position vector $u\vec{\imath} + v\vec{\jmath}$ at any point (u, v). Therefore, the orbits of this system are circles. Now $\phi(t) = u(t)$, and so we know that $\phi(t)$ is periodic. We can even determine the period.

Let the period be p. Then the length of the orbit is 2π because it is a circle, and it is also

$$\int_0^p \sqrt{(v(t))^2 + (-u(t))^2}\, dt = \int_0^p \sqrt{(u(t))^2 + (v(t))^2}\, dt = \int_0^p 1\, dt = p.$$

Thus the period is 2π. Note that this means that we may interpret t as the angle between the radial vector and the positive u-axis. Since the orbit is the unit circle, $\phi(t)$ is the sine of t from trigonometry. By the same token, we know that the graph of $\phi(t)$ is the same as the familiar graph of $\sin(t)$.

If we solve the initial-value problem by using the series method we get

$$\phi(t) = \sum_{k=0}^{\infty} (-1)^k \frac{t^{2k+1}}{(2k+1)!}.$$

This, together with the periodicity, allows for extremely accurate approximation of the values of $\phi(t)$.

This is enough to make the point that differential equations can be used to define certain special functions. Let us conclude this section with an example in which the functions are most likely very new to you.

6.2.1 Legendre Polynomials

Return again to Legendre's equation

$$(1 - x^2)y'' - 2xy' + \alpha(\alpha + 1)y = 0.$$

A basis of solutions on $(-1, 1)$ is given by the functions

$$\phi_1(x) = 1 +$$
$$\sum_{m=1}^{\infty} (-1)^m \frac{\alpha(\alpha - 2) \cdots (\alpha - 2m + 2)(\alpha + 1)(\alpha + 3) \cdots (\alpha + 2m - 1)}{(2m)!} x^{2m},$$

and

$$\phi_2(x) = x +$$
$$\sum_{m=1}^{\infty} (-1)^m \frac{(\alpha - 1)(\alpha - 3) \cdots (\alpha - 2m + 1)(\alpha + 2)(\alpha + 4) \cdots (\alpha + 2m)}{(2m + 1)!} x^{2m+1}.$$

Recall again that if α is zero or a positive integer one of these two solutions is a polynomial. These polynomials, except for a constant multiple that makes the value of them 1 at $x = 1$, are defined to be the Legendre polynomials.

It is possible to express the Legendre polynomials in a single finite summation formula. To this end, consider the recursion formula for the coefficients again.

$$y_{k+2} = -\frac{\alpha(\alpha+1) - k(k+1)}{(k+2)(k+1)} y_k = -\frac{(\alpha-k)(\alpha+k+1)}{(k+2)(k+1)} y_k.$$

All coefficients beyond y_n are zero if $\alpha = n$, where n is a positive integer. We compute the coefficients in this case by descent from the highest power occurring. Our recursion then is

$$y_{k-2} = -\frac{k(k-1)}{(n-k+2)(n+k-1)} y_k.$$

Thus

$$y_{n-2} = -\frac{n(n-1)}{2(2n-1)} y_n,$$

and

$$y_{n-4} = \frac{n(n-1)(n-2)(n-3)}{2 \cdot 4(2n-1)(2n-3)} y_n.$$

The next term in the descent is

$$y_{n-6} = -\frac{n(n-1)(n-2)(n-3)(n-4)(n-5)}{2 \cdot 4 \cdot 6(2n-1)(2n-3)(2n-5)} y_n.$$

In general, we have

$$y_{n-2m} = (-1)^m \frac{n(n-1)(n-2)(n-3)(n-4) \cdots (n-(2m-1))}{2 \cdot 4 \cdots 2m(2n-1)(2n-3)(2n-5) \cdots (2n-(2m-1))} y_n$$

for all m such that $2m \le n$. This formula can be expressed entirely in terms of factorials if we set

$$y_n = \frac{(2n)!}{(n!)(n!)}.$$

In this case the fraction is

$$\frac{n(n-1) \cdots (n-(2m-1))2n(2n-1) \cdots (2n-(2m-1))(2n-2m)!}{2 \cdots 2m(2n-1) \cdots (2n-(2m-1))n(n-1) \cdots (n-(2m-1))(n-2m)!(n!)},$$

and after a lot of canceling we get

$$y_{n-2m} = (-1)^m \frac{(2n-2m)!}{m!(n-2m)!(n-m)!}.$$

This is not quite the end of the story. We chose y_n so that the simplification to a formula involving factorials would be as clear as possible. In fact, it is customary to divide this y_n by 2^n as well. The reason for this is to ensure that $P_n(1) = 1$ (see the exercises). Thus

$$y_{n-2m} = (-1)^m \frac{(2n-2m)!}{2^n m!(n-2m)!(n-m)!}.$$

We can now write the Legendre polynomials in the form

$$P_n(x) = \sum_{m=0}^{[n/2]} (-1)^m \frac{(2n - 2m)!}{2^n m!(n - 2m)!(n - m)!} x^{n-2m}$$

where $[n/2]$ is the largest integer less than or equal to $n/2$.

In the next section we shall encounter the famous Bessel functions. These functions also arise as solutions to an important equation.

EXERCISES 6.2

In Exercises 1–3 pretend that you have no prior knowledge of the solution.

1. Define $C(x)$ to be the solution to $y'' + y = 0$, $y(0) = 1$, and $y'(0) = 0$. Find the series solution, and show that the series converges for all x.

2. In Exercise 1, reduce to a first-order system and explain why $C(x)$ is periodic.

3. In Exercise 1, find the period by computing a certain integral.

4. Pretend that the solution to $y'' + 2xy' + 2y = 0$, $y(0) = 1$, and $y'(0) = 0$ is a famous function called fam(x).

   (a) Find the power series solution for this function, and show that it converges for all x.

   (b) Use the series to compute fam$'(x)$ and $2x$fam(x). Use this to show that fam(x) satisfies the equation $y' + 2xy = 0$. Use this to prove that fam(x) is never zero. *Hint:* Solutions are unique through any point, and $y \equiv 0$ is a solution.

   (c) Use 2 × 2System to graph fam(x).

   (d) Can you express fam(x) in terms of familiar functions?

5. Pretend that the solution to $y'' + 4xy' = 0$, $y(0) = 0$, and $y'(0) = 1$ is a famous function, call it $f(x)$.

   (a) Find the series solution and show that it converges for all x.

   (b) Take the derivative of this series and express it as an exponential function.

   (c) Use part b to express $f(x)$ as an integral.

   (d) Get the same result in part c by reducing $y'' + 4xy' = 0$ to a first-order system and solving it directly.

In Exercises 6–10, pretend that you do not know the solution to the simple initial-value problem $y'(x) = 1/x$ and $y(1) = 0$. Let $\phi(x)$ be this unique solution.

6. Show that $\psi_1(x) = \phi(ax)$ and $\psi_2(x) = \phi(a) + \phi(x)$ both satisfy $y'(x) = 1/x$ and $y(1) = \phi(a)$.

7. Why does it follow from Exercise 6 that $\phi(ax) = \phi(a) + \phi(x)$?

8. Show that $\psi_1(x) = \phi(x^r)$ and $\psi_2(x) = r\phi(x)$ both satisfy $y'(x) = r/x$ and $y(1) = 0$.

9. Why does it follow from Exercise 8 that $\phi(x^r) = r\phi(x)$?

10. Use Field&Solution to draw a graph of $\phi(x)$.

11. Show that the Legendre polynomials can be expressed in the form

$$P_n(x) = \frac{1}{2^n n!} \frac{d^n}{dx^n}[(x^2 - 1)^n].$$

This is known as Rodrigues's formula. *Hint:* Expand $(x^2 - 1)^n$ by the binomial theorem and then differentiate the terms.

12. Use Rodrigues's formula to show that $P_n(1) = 1$ for all n. *Hint:* Write $(x^2 - 1)^n = (x - 1)^n(x + 1)^n$, and then use the Leibniz rule for repeated differentiation of products:

$$(fg)^{(n)} = \sum_{k=0}^{n} \binom{n}{k} f^{(n-k)} g^{(k)}.$$

13. The equation $(1 - x^2)y'' - xy' + \alpha^2 y = 0$ is called Chebyshev's equation. Use the series method to find polynomial solutions to this equation. Except for adjustment by a constant, these polynomials are called the Chebyshev polynomials.

6.3 REGULAR SINGULAR POINTS AND THE METHOD OF FROBENIUS

Consider the equation

$$x^2 y'' + 9xy' + 7y = 0.$$

If we attempt to find a power series solution centered at zero by substituting a series for y, we are forced to conclude that all the coefficients are zero. Indeed, the only solution through zero is the trivial solution. You can check that $\{x^{-1}, x^{-7}\}$ is a fundamental set of solutions on $(0, \infty)$, so any solution in a neighborhood of zero must be a linear combination of x^{-1} and x^{-7} on the right side of zero. But then the solution cannot be continuous at zero unless the solution is trivial. If the equation is $x^2 y'' + 9xy' + 7y = 1$, then there is no solution at all that has zero in its domain. We say that we have a singularity at 0.

The nature of this singularity is more readily seen when the preceding equation is converted to a system of first-order equations in matrix form. The coefficient matrix is

$$\begin{bmatrix} 0 & 1 \\ \frac{-7}{x^2} & \frac{-9}{x} \end{bmatrix},$$

and the singular nature of $x = 0$ is now obvious.

Equations of the form

$$a(x)y'' + b(x)y' + c(x)y = 0,$$

where a, b, and c are analytic, are said to have a singularity at each of the points x_0 such that $a(x_0) = 0$. Singularities can be removable, regular, or essential. A removable singularity is one that is only apparent. For example, the singularity at zero in $xy'' - x^2 y = 0$ is removable since we can divide through by x. If the equation can be written in the form

$$(x - x_0)^2 y'' + (x - x_0)b(x)y' + c(x)y = 0,$$

where b and c are analytic in a neighborhood of x_0, then x_0 is a regular singular point. A singularity is essential otherwise.

Solutions near a removable singularity are easily dealt with. Remove the singularity and proceed as in the preceding section.

At a regular or essential singularity we cannot expect to find solutions throughout a neighborhood of the singularity. But we could, of course, move to a nearby nonsingular point and then find power series solutions there. However, such power series will not, in general, extend beyond the singular point. As a consequence, such power series will give very poor information about the solution close to the singularity. To make the point clear, consider the opening example again.

The function $\phi(x) = x^{-1}$ is a solution to

$$x^2 y'' + 9xy' + 7y = 0$$

with initial conditions $\phi(1) = 1$ and $\phi'(1) = -1$. But

$$\frac{1}{x} = \frac{1}{1 + (x - 1)} = \sum_{k=0}^{\infty} (-1)^k (x - 1)^k.$$

So $\sum_{k=0}^{\infty} (-1)^k (x - 1)^k$ is the series solution satisfying the initial data. But this series converges only on $(0, 2)$, and so using this series to evaluate the solution at, say, 0.01, will prove to be very inefficient. The value is, of course, $(0.01)^{-1} = 100$! The point is that there may well be much better solutions near a singularity than are provided by moving to a nearby point and trying a power series solution.

We shall see that at a regular singular point x_0 we shall be able to find solutions of the form

$$\phi(x) = (x - x_0)^r \sum_{k=0}^{\infty} a_k (x - x_0)^k,$$

where r is a root of a quadratic polynomial. The advantage here is that the series part of the solution is centered at the singularity, which is where the series converges most rapidly.

Equations with regular singular points are not mere pathological examples, but occur in nature. Indeed, such equations occur in areas ranging from quantum mechanics to the bending of beams. We now show the method of solution.

6.3.1 The Method of Frobenius

Consider the equation

$$x^2 y'' + x \left(\sum_{k=0}^{\infty} a_k x^k \right) y' + \left(\sum_{k=0}^{\infty} b_k x^k \right) y = 0,$$

where 0 is a regular singular point. For any other regular singular point x_0, replace x by $x - x_0$. We claim that there is a solution of the form

$$y(x) = x^r \sum_{k=0}^{\infty} c_k x^k = \sum_{k=0}^{\infty} c_k x^{r+k}.$$

Differentiating and substituting, we get $y'(x) = \sum_{k=0}^{\infty} (r + k) c_k x^{r+k-1}$ and $y'' = \sum_{k=0}^{\infty} (r + k)(r + k - 1) c_k x^{r+k-2}$, and so

$$x^2 \sum_{k=0}^{\infty} (r + k)(r + k - 1) c_k x^{r+k-2} + x$$

$$\sum_{k=0}^{\infty} a_k x^k \sum_{k=0}^{\infty} (r + k) c_k x^{r+k-1} + \sum_{k=0}^{\infty} b_k x^k \sum_{k=0}^{\infty} c_k x^{r+k} = 0.$$

Therefore, we have

$$\sum_{k=0}^{\infty}(r+k)(r+k-1)c_k x^{r+k} + \sum_{k=0}^{\infty}a_k x^k \sum_{k=0}^{\infty}(r+k)c_k x^{r+k}$$

$$+ \sum_{k=0}^{\infty}b_k x^k \sum_{k=0}^{\infty}c_k x^{r+k} = 0,$$

and dividing by x^r gives

$$\sum_{k=0}^{\infty}(r+k)(r+k-1)c_k x^k + \sum_{k=0}^{\infty}a_k x^k \sum_{k=0}^{\infty}(r+k)c_k x^k + \sum_{k=0}^{\infty}b_k x^k \sum_{k=0}^{\infty}c_k x^k = 0.$$

Recall that power series are multiplied out in the same way that polynomials are. That is,

$$\sum_{k=0}^{\infty}b_k x^k \sum_{k=0}^{\infty}c_k x^k = \sum_{n=0}^{\infty}\left(\sum_{k=0}^{n}b_{n-k}c_k\right)x^n.$$

Therefore, we obtain

$$\sum_{n=0}^{\infty}\left[(r+n)(r+n-1)c_n + \sum_{k=0}^{n}(a_{n-k}(r+k)c_k + b_{n-k}c_k)\right]x^n = 0.$$

But then we must have

$$(r+n)(r+n-1)c_n + \sum_{k=0}^{n}(a_{n-k}(r+k)c_k + b_{n-k}c_k) = 0,$$

for $n \geq 0$. For $n = 0$, we have

$$r(r-1)c_0 + a_0 r c_0 + b_0 c_0 = 0,$$

and without loss of generality we may assume that $c_0 \neq 0$; so

$$I(r) = r(r-1) + a_0 r + b_0 = 0.$$

We call $I(r) = r(r-1) + a_0 r + b_0$, the indicial polynomial, and from now on we will assume that r is a root of I. In the expression

$$(r+n)(r+n-1)c_n + \sum_{k=0}^{n}(a_{n-k}(r+k)c_k + b_{n-k}c_k) = 0$$

if we separate out the c_n term, we get

$$I(r+n)c_n = -\sum_{k=0}^{n-1}(a_{n-k}(r+k)c_k + b_{n-k}c_k),$$

so if $I(r + n)$ is not equal to zero for any $n \geq 1$, we have a recursion formula for the c_n and a solution to the equation with accurate results near the singularity. This is the method of Frobenius.

For a fundamental set of solutions, we need two solutions. If we are lucky the two roots of the indicial polynomial will be real and will not differ by an integer. In this case the method of Frobenius will yield a fundamental set of solutions on an interval $(0, a)$. If the roots do differ by an integer, then the indicial polynomial $I(r_1 + n)$ will be zero for $n = r_2 - r_1$, where r_1 is the lesser root and r_2 is the greater. In this case, we will divide by zero in trying to compute the coefficients of the second solution. The solution corresponding to the largest root is often called a solution of **the first kind** for the given equation. The cases of a single root or roots differing by an integer will be taken up in the next section.

If the roots are complex conjugates, then the difference is pure imaginary, so they do not differ by an integer. Again the method of Frobenius yields a fundamental set. To get real solutions, we can take the sum and difference of the two solutions since the solutions are conjugate to one another.

It is not hard to show that if

$$y = x^r \sum_{n=0}^{\infty} c_n x^n$$

is a solution for $x > 0$, then

$$y = |x|^r \sum_{n=0}^{\infty} c_n x^n$$

is a solution to the left of zero also.

The general recursion formula that we have derived could be useful in writing a program to find the first solution to an equation with a regular singular point. However, it is usually better to carry through the derivation from scratch if you are going to do it by hand. Here is an example.

Example 6.3.1   We solve the equation

$$3x^2 y'' + 2xy' + x^2 y = 0.$$

There is a regular singular point at zero. We try a solution of the form

$$y(x) = x^r \sum_{k=0}^{\infty} c_k x^k = \sum_{k=0}^{\infty} c_k x^{r+k}.$$

Taking derivatives, substituting, and dividing out by x^r gives

$$\sum_{k=0}^{\infty} 3c_k (r + k)(r + k - 1)x^k + \sum_{k=0}^{\infty} 2c_k (r + k)x^k + \sum_{k=0}^{\infty} c_k x^{k+2} = 0.$$

The combined coefficient of x^0 is

$$c_0[3r(r-1)+2r] = c_0 r(3r-1).$$

This must be zero, because the combined power series is equal to zero. Therefore, c_0 is zero or $r(3r-1)$ is zero. If we set $c_0 = 0$, this merely starts the original series at $k = 1$, and since r is, as yet, undetermined, this leaves us with the same problem that we started with. We assume that $c_0 \neq 0$, and thus

$$I(r) = r(3r-1) = 0.$$

This is the indicial polynomial, and it determines r. Indeed, $r = 1/3$ or $r = 0$.
The combined coefficient of x^1 is

$$c_1[3(r+1)(r+1-1)+2(r+1)] = c_1 I(r+1) = 0.$$

Notice that $I(r+n)$ cannot be zero for any positive integer n if r is 0 or 1/3. So, in either case, $c_1 = 0$.
The rest of the coefficients are computed by recursion from

$$c_n = -\frac{c_{n-2}}{I(r+n)}.$$

In either case the odd coefficients are all zero since $c_1 = 0$.
For $r = 1/3$,

$$c_n = -\frac{c_{n-2}}{n(3n+1)},$$

and so it easily follows that

$$c_{2m} = (-1)^m \frac{c_0}{2 \cdot 4 \cdots (2m) \cdot 7 \cdot 13 \cdots (3m+1)}$$

for $m \geq 1$. For $r = 0$,

$$c_n = -\frac{c_{n-2}}{n(3n-1)},$$

and so it easily follows that

$$c_{2m} = (-1)^m \frac{c_0}{2 \cdot 4 \cdots (2m) \cdot 5 \cdot 8 \cdots (3m-1)}$$

for $m \geq 1$.
If we set $c_0 = 1$, the two solutions that we obtain in this manner are

$$\phi_1(x) = x^{1/3} + x^{1/3} \sum_{m=1}^{\infty} (-1)^m \frac{1}{2 \cdot 4 \cdots (2m) \cdot 7 \cdot 13 \cdots (3m+1)} x^{2m},$$

and

$$\phi_2(x) = x^0 + x^0 \sum_{m=1}^{\infty} (-1)^m \frac{1}{2 \cdot 4 \cdots (2m) \cdot 5 \cdot 8 \cdots (3m-1)} x^{2m}$$

$$= 1 + \sum_{m=1}^{\infty} (-1)^m \frac{1}{2 \cdot 4 \cdots (2m) \cdot 5 \cdot 8 \cdots (3m-1)} x^{2m}.$$

It is not hard to show (see the exercises) that these solutions are linearly independent on $x > 0$. To get solutions on $x < 0$, replace $x^{1/3}$ by $|x|^{1/3}$.   ∎

The second example of this section deals with an equation that will be important to us in Chapter 9. It is called **Bessel's equation**. This is another example of an equation whose solutions are so important that they have acquired names and become famous.

Example 6.3.2   Bessel's equation of order α is the equation

$$x^2 y'' + xy' + (x^2 - \alpha^2) y = 0.$$

We shall only deal with Bessel's equation of order zero:

$$x^2 y'' + xy' + x^2 y = 0.$$

We try a solution of the form

$$y(x) = x^r \sum_{k=0}^{\infty} c_k x^k = \sum_{k=0}^{\infty} c_k x^{r+k}.$$

As usual, we differentiate, substitute, and divide out the term x^r to get

$$\sum_{k=0}^{\infty} c_k (r+k)(r+k-1) x^k + \sum_{k=0}^{\infty} c_k (r+k) x^k + \sum_{k=0}^{\infty} c_k x^{k+2} = 0.$$

The indicial polynomial is

$$I(r) = r(r-1) + r = r^2,$$

so the indicial root is 0 with multiplicity 2. Our method will only produce a Bessel function of the zeroth order and first kind.

The recursion relation is

$$c_n = -\frac{c_{n-2}}{n^2},$$

and $c_1 = 0$. Therefore, the odd coefficients are all zero, and

$$c_{2m} = (-1)^m \frac{1}{2^{2m}(m!)^2},$$

if $c_0 = 1$. Bessel functions of order α and the first kind are denoted by J_α. Thus

$$J_0(x) = 1 + \sum_{m=1}^{\infty} (-1)^m \frac{1}{2^{2m}(m!)^2} x^{2m}.$$

The graph of this function is explored in the exercises.   ∎

EXERCISES 6.3

For Exercises 1–6, assume that $x > 0$.

1. Compute a fundamental set of solutions to

$$x^2 y'' - x(\frac{1}{2} + x^2)y' + y/2 = 0$$

out to the fourth order.

2. Find the first four terms of each solution generated by the method of Frobenius applied to the equation

$$x^2 y'' + x(1 + 2x)y' - \frac{1}{9}y = 0.$$

3. Find the first four terms of each solution generated by the method of Frobenius applied to the equation

$$x^2 y'' - x(1/2 + 2x)y' + (1/2)y = 0.$$

4. Find the first three terms of each solution generated by the method of Frobenius applied to the equation

$$x^2 y'' + x(5/3 + x^2)y' - (1/3)y = 0.$$

5. Calculate the formula for the c_n for the two solutions to

$$2x^2 y'' - xy' + (1 + x)y = 0.$$

Find the general solution in sigma notation if possible.

6. Find a solution to

$$x^2 y'' + 4xy' + (2 + x)y = 0.$$

Explain why the method of this section fails to yield a second solution.

7. Find a solution to

$$x^2 y'' + 3xy' + (1 + x)y = 0.$$

Explain why the method of this section fails to yield a second solution.

8. Find a solution to

$$x^2 y'' - x(2 - x^2)y' + 2y = 0.$$

Explain why the method of this section fails to yield a second solution.

9. The equation

$$x^2 y'' + xy' + (x^2 - 1)y = 0$$

is Bessel's equation of order 1. Find J_1.

10. The equation

$$x^2 y'' + xy' + (x^2 - 4)y = 0$$

is Bessel's equation of order 2. Find J_2.

11. The equation

$$x^2 y'' + xy' + (x^2 - 9)y = 0$$

is Bessel's equation of order 3. Find J_3.

12. The equation

$$x^2 y'' + xy' + (x^2 - \frac{1}{9})y = 0$$

is Bessel's equation of order 1/3. Find two independent solutions on $(0, \infty)$. Show that they are independent.

13. Reduce Bessel's equation of order zero to a first-order system, and use 2 × 2System to graph J_0.

   (a) We cannot use initial data at zero, so start the "time" interval from 0.01. Try the interval $[0.01, 50]$ and an initial value of $(0.01, 1)$. Show that this is a good approximation to the true initial data for J_0 at 0.01.

   (b) Do the graphing.

   This suggests that J_0 has an infinite set of zeros. As you go farther out, the distance between zeros seems to approach a constant value of a little over 3. The "amplitude" is decreasing. Perhaps it is not too surprising that it has been shown that $J_0(x)$ is asymptotic to $(\cos(x) + \sin(x))/\sqrt{\pi x}$ as x gets large. This being the case, there are infinitely many zeros for J_0. See the supplementary exercises for more on this.

14. Show that if $y(x) = x^r \sum_{n=0}^{\infty} c_n x^n$ is a solution for $x > 0$ then $y = |x|^r \sum_{n=0}^{\infty} c_n x^n$ is a solution on both sides of zero.

15. Show that if the roots of the indicial polynomial are complex then the corresponding solutions are complex conjugates of one another. Show how a real fundamental set of solutions can be obtained. *Hint:* Assume that c_k and d_k are the coefficients of each solution, respectively, assume that $c_0 = d_0 = 1$, show that c_1 and d_1 are conjugates, and then complete the argument by induction.

16. Show that the solutions of Example 6.3.1 are linearly independent on $[0, \infty)$.

6.4 THE EXCEPTIONAL CASES

We now consider the problem of finding a second solution in the exceptional cases. This section can be skipped without loss of continuity.

6.4.1 Repeated Roots

We suppose that the indicial polynomial has the form

$$I(r) = (r - r_0)^2,$$

where r_0 is the repeated root. In this case the first solution has the form

$$y(x) = x^{r_0} \sum_{n=0}^{\infty} c_n x^n.$$

To find a second solution, it will be convenient to review the way in which the first solution is obtained.

Let L be the linear differential operator defined by

$$L(y)(x) = x^2 y''(x) + x \left(\sum_{k=0}^{\infty} a_k x^k \right) y'(x) + \left(\sum_{k=0}^{\infty} b_k x^k \right) y(x).$$

Then, if

$$y(x) = x^r \sum_{n=0}^{\infty} c_n x^n,$$

then

$$L(y)(x) =$$

$$x^r \sum_{n=0}^{\infty} \left[(r+n)(r+n-1)c_n + \sum_{k=0}^{n} (a_{n-k}(r+k)c_k + b_{n-k}c_k) \right] x^n.$$

Splitting off the $n = 0$ term gives

$$L(y)(x) =$$

$$I(r)x^r c_0 + x^r \sum_{n=1}^{\infty} \left[I(r+n)c_n + \sum_{k=0}^{n} (a_{n-k}(r+k)c_k + b_{n-k}c_k) \right] x^n.$$

It is very important to note that we have not chosen r to be a root of the indicial polynomial yet; it is still a variable. If we choose the c_n recursively, according to the formula

$$c_n(r) = \frac{-\sum_{k=0}^{n-1} (a_{n-k}(r+k)c_k(r) + b_{n-k}c_k(r))}{I(r+n)},$$

then the sum on n is zero, and we are left with

$$L(y)(x) = I(r)x^r c_0 = (r - r_0)^2 x^r c_0.$$

We have emphasized the fact that the c_n are functions of r by writing $c_n(r)$.

If we now choose r to be r_0, we get the first solution as before. To get the second solution, set

$$y(x, r) = x^r \sum_{n=0}^{\infty} c_n(r)x^n,$$

where the $c_n(r)$ are as defined previously. Then

$$L\left(\frac{\partial y(x, r)}{\partial r}\right) = \frac{\partial L(y(x, r))}{\partial r} = c_0[2(r - r_0)x^r + (r - r_0)^2 x^r \ln(x)].$$

Thus, if $r = r_0$, we have a second solution. It can be shown in general that these two solutions make a fundamental set. The second solution is

$$\frac{\partial y}{\partial r}(x, r_0) = x^{r_0} \ln(x) \sum_{n=0}^{\infty} c_n(r_0)x^n + x^{r_0} \sum_{n=0}^{\infty} c_n'(r_0)x^n$$

$$= y_1 \ln(x) + x^{r_0} \sum_{n=0}^{\infty} c_n'(r_0)x^n,$$

where y_1 is the first solution.

6.4.2 Roots That Differ by an Integer

Suppose that r_1 and r_2 are the roots of $I(r)$, and $r_1 - r_2 = n_0$ where n_0 is a positive integer. Therefore,

$$I(r) = (r - r_2)(r - r_1).$$

As before we have the formula

$$L(y)(x) =$$

$$I(r)x^r c_0 + x^r \sum_{n=1}^{\infty} \left[I(r + n)c_n + \sum_{k=0}^{n} (a_{n-k}(r + k)c_k + b_{n-k}c_k) \right] x^n,$$

and the sum on the right can be made zero by the recursion formula for $r = r_1$, but not for $r = r_2$ without modification. The reason is that the recursion formula gives

$$c_n(r) = \frac{-\sum_{k=0}^{n-1} (a_{n-k}(r + k)c_k(r) + b_{n-k}c_k(r))}{I(r + n)}.$$

By induction, it is obvious that c_0 is a factor in each $c_n(r)$. Now the only problem arises when we try to compute $c_{n_0}(r)$, for then the factor $r - r_2$ is in the denominator and it will be zero at $r = r_2$. However, if we set $c_0 = r - r_2$, the dangerous factor will cancel out and the recursion can continue. In this case we have

$$L(y)(x) = x^r (r - r_1)(r - r_2)^2.$$

It seems that we need only set $r = r_2$ to get a solution. However, all we get is a multiple of the first solution.

To see this, we re-index the recursion formula to start at the first nonzero term. Thus

$$c_{n_0+m} = \frac{-\sum_{k=n_0}^{n_0+m-1}(a_{n_0+m-k}(r_2+k)c_k(r_2) + b_{n_0+m-k}c_k(r_2))}{I(r_2 + n_0 + m)}$$

$$= \frac{-\sum_{j=0}^{m-1}(a_{m-j}(r_1+j)c_{n_0+j} + b_{m-j}c_{n_0+j})}{I(r_1 + m)}.$$

This is the same recursion formula as in the first solution. The only difference is that the starting term must be $c_0 = c_{n_0}(r_2)$. The series has the form

$$x^{r_2}\sum_{j=0}^{\infty}c_{n_0+j}x^{n_0+j} = x^{r_1}\sum_{j=0}^{\infty}c_{n_0+j}x^j.$$

Except for the starting term, this is the series of the first solution.

We take the partial derivative with respect to r and evaluate it at r_2 in order to get an independent solution. Indeed,

$$L\left(\frac{\partial y(x, r)}{\partial r}\right) = \frac{\partial L(y(x, r))}{\partial r}$$

$$= x^r \ln(x)(r - r_1)(r - r_2)^2 + x^r[(r - r_2)^2 + 2(r - r_1)(r - r_2)],$$

and if this is evaluated at r_2, we have a solution. We get

$$\frac{\partial y}{\partial r}(x, r_2) = x^{r_2}\ln(x)\sum_{n=0}^{\infty}c_n(r_2)x^n + x^{r_2}\sum_{n=0}^{\infty}c_n'(r_2)x^n$$

$$= c_{n_0}(r_2)y_1(x)\ln(x) + x^{r_2}\sum_{n=0}^{\infty}c_n'(r_2)x^n.$$

We have assumed that the series in y_1 starts with $c_0 = 1$. This solution forms a fundamental set with the first solution.

We give an example of the method.

Example 6.4.1   Consider Bessel's equation of order 1.

$$x^2 y'' + xy' + (x^2 - 1)y = 0.$$

We have $I(r) = r(r - 1) + r - 1 = r^2 - 1$, so the roots are 1 and -1.

We can set up the formulas for the c_n of both solutions by not specifying r or c_0 until needed. For $n = 1$ we have $c_1(r) = 0$. For $n > 1$, we have the general recursion

$$c_n(r) = -\frac{c_{n-2}(r)}{(r + n - 1)(r + n + 1)}.$$

Therefore, all the odd terms are zero. For the even terms we have

$$c_{2m}(r) = \frac{(-1)^m c_0}{(r + 1)(r + 3)^2(r + 5)^2 \cdots (r + 2m - 1)^2(r + 2m + 1)}.$$

For the first solution, set $r = 1$ and $c_0 = 1$. The first solution is found to be

$$J_1(x) = x \sum_{m=0}^{\infty} \frac{(-1)^m x^{2m}}{m!(m + 1)!2^{2m+1}}.$$

To find the second solution, we set $c_0 = (r + 1)$ and use the preceding formulas for the c_n. The odd terms are all zero, and for $c_2(r)$ the factor $r + 1$ cancels out; so we are left with the same coefficients as the first solution except for the constant factor $c_2(-1) = -1/2$.

For this problem, $n_0 = 2$ and $c_2(-1) = -1/2$. Therefore, the second solution is

$$y_2(x) = (-\frac{1}{2}) \ln(x) J_1(x) + x^{-1} \sum_{n=0}^{\infty} c'_n(-1)x^n.$$

Here is the solution with the last sum out to sixth order.

$$y_2(x) = \frac{-1}{2} \ln(x) J_1(x) + x^{-1}[1 + \frac{1}{4}x^2 - \frac{5}{64}x^4 + \frac{5}{1152}x^6 + \cdots]. \quad \blacksquare$$

EXERCISES 6.4

1. Solve $x^2 y'' + (x - 6)y = 0$. Write the first solution in sigma notation. Find the second solution out to the second order. In the second solution, in which coefficient does the cancellation take place that prevents division by zero?

2. Find the first solution to $xy'' - xy' - y = 0$ in sigma notation. Find the second solution out to the third order.

3. Hand check the calculations in Example 6.4.1 out to the second order.

4. Find the Bessel function of order 2 of the second kind out to the fourth order.

5. It is possible for a solution of the second kind to have no logarithmic term. Give an example of an equation with this property. *Hint:* Examine the recursion formula for the $c_n(r)$, and arrange things so that $c_{n_0}(r_2) = 0$.

SUPPLEMENTARY EXERCISES FOR CHAPTER 6

1. This exercise points to another way of calculating series solutions. If

$$y(x) = \sum_{k=0}^{\infty} y_k x^k$$

is the solution to an initial-value problem, then $y_k = y^{(k)}(0)/k!$. So to calculate the coefficients we need only calculate the derivatives of the solution at 0. But the differential equation allows us to do this recursively.

(a) Solve the initial-value problem $y'' - y^2 = 0$, $y(0) = 1$, and $y'(0) = 2$ out to the fourth order using the preceding idea.

(b) Try to solve the initial value problem $(y')^3 - y^2 = 0$, $y(0) = 0$. What goes wrong?

(c) Describe a broad category of differential equations to which this series method can be applied.

2. Show that zero is an essential singularity for

$$x^3 y'' + axy' + by = 0,$$

where a and b are real constants. Investigate the possibility of solutions of the form $x^r \sum_{k=0}^{\infty} c_k x^k$. Consider various values of the ratio b/a, and consider radii of convergence.

3. The gamma function is defined by

$$\Gamma(\alpha) = \int_0^{\infty} e^{-t} t^{\alpha-1} \, dt.$$

(a) Show that $\Gamma(\alpha + 1) = \alpha \Gamma(\alpha)$, and then show that the Gamma Function generalizes the factorial notion. *Hint:* If n is a positive integer, what is $\Gamma(n)$?

(b) For what values of α is the Gamma Function not defined.

(c) Use the gamma function to get a summation formula for all Bessel functions of the first kind.

4. Answer the following Bessel equation problems:

(a) By staying away from the singularity, Bessel's equations can be studied graphically. Graph several solutions to several Bessel equations on $[1, \infty)$. Describe the general behavior of these solutions.

(b) Reduce Bessel's equation

$$t^2 y'' + ty' + (t^2 - \alpha^2) y = 0$$

to a first-order system. Plot the field for $t = 1$, $t = 10$, and $t = 50$. What is happening to the field as $t \to \infty$?

(c) Does the result in part a make sense in the light of the result in part b? Explain!

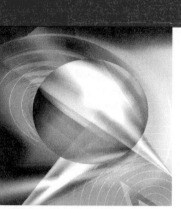

CHAPTER 7

BIFURCATIONS AND CHAOS

This chapter is devoted to an investigation of the long term behavior of solutions to first-order systems. We shall see that the overall behavior of solutions can be greatly affected by small changes in the parameters defining the system and by small changes in initial conditions.

Each system of equations that we have studied can be considered as a member of a family of systems indexed by one or more parameters. For example, the simple equation

$$y' = y$$

can be thought of as a member of the family

$$y' = ay,$$

where a is the parameter. The system

$$x' = x(a_1 - a_2 x - a_3 y),$$
$$y' = y(b_1 - b_2 x - b_3 y),$$

which we used to model two species competing for the same food supply, can be regarded as a family of systems of equations depending on six parameters. The general linear homogeneous system of n equations in n unknowns describes a family of equations indexed by n^2 parameters. It is natural to ask how solutions to these systems of equations might change as the parameters of the family are changed.

If we change one of the parameters in such a family very slightly, it is reasonable to expect that the solutions to the two systems with the same initial conditions will be close initially. This is true under very general conditions. However, it is not necessarily true that the long-term behavior of solutions will be close or even similar.

To make this clear, go back to 2×2 linear homogeneous systems and reflect on the possible solutions we can get by changing the coefficients in the equations. It becomes clear that systems that are only the slightest perturbations of one another can have completely different types of solutions. For example, if the coefficients are changed so that the eigenvalues go from pure imaginary to having a positive real part, the orbits go from closed curves to spirals going to infinity. Certainly, the solutions are close to start with, but they soon diverge rapidly.

Although a small change in a parameter will not much change the initial behavior of solutions, this example shows that it can cause a major change in the long-term behavior of solutions. Such a change is called a **bifurcation**. Thus bifurcation theory is concerned with the way in which the overall qualitative behavior may depend on the parameters of the system. The first part of this chapter is devoted to an investigation of this phenomenon.

In Section 2.5 we briefly discussed the dependence of solutions on initial conditions. In the second part of this chapter we shall revisit this subject. We shall see that the presence of certain subsets of phase space, called **attractors**, can lead the system to be very sensitive to changes in initial conditions. If these attractors are of an especially complicated nature, they are called **strange attractors**, and they cause the system to be hypersensitive to changes in initial conditions. This hypersensitivity makes the prediction of the long-term behavior of a solution impossible. This kind of behavior is called **chaotic**, and the study of this phenomenon has been dubbed **chaos**.

Since both types of sensitivities exhibit themselves in the overall behavior of solutions, we shall find it useful to be able to describe all the solutions of a given system at once. The function that does this is called the **flow** of the system, and we shall investigate this notion after we have discussed bifurcations.

7.1 BIFURCATION

A precise definition of bifurcation is not an easy task, so we shall be content to consider several examples that will give us a feel for the phenomenon. In the process we will arrive at a serviceable working definition of bifurcation.

Let us start with the simplest case of an equation of the form

$$y' = f(a, y),$$

where a is the parameter indexing the family of equations. We have already mentioned the example

$$y' = ay.$$

At first sight it may seem that there is not much to choose between one equation of this family and another. After all, are not the solutions just exponential functions $y_0 e^{at}$ in each case? Yes, but the case $a = 0$ is special. In this case, the solutions are all constant functions, and every value of y is a critical point. But if $a \neq 0$ then only $y = 0$ is a critical point, and all nonzero solutions are proper exponentials. There is a radical change in the nature of the solutions between when $a \neq 0$ and $a = 0$. We say that $a = 0$ is a bifurcation value of the parameter.

It will be helpful to recall the notion of a phase line, which was introduced in Chapter 2. The phase line for the equation

$$y'(t) = f(y(t))$$

FIGURE 7.1

is simply the y-axis. We usually place a little additional information on the phase line. The information we can add is the location of critical points and the direction of motion of the solution in the intervals between the critical points. In effect, the phase line is a one-dimensional version of the phase plane, with critical points and vector field indicating the direction of motion. Figure 7.1 shows the phase line for the equation $y' = y$. Consider the equation

$$y' = y(y^2 - a).$$

Figure 7.2 shows the phase lines for $a = -4$, $a = -1$, $a = 0$, $a = 1$, and $a = 4$ arranged from left to right.

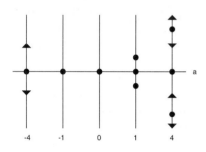

FIGURE 7.2

The direction of motion has been included in the first and last phase lines. The thing to notice is the increase from one critical point to three as a passes through zero. Notice also that the critical point at zero has gone from being unstable to being stable as the other two critical points come into existence. We can infer from this that the nature of solutions radically changes as a passes through zero. In short, we have a bifurcation value. This bifurcation, where one critical point splits into three, has been called a **pitchfork** bifurcation. Incidentally, the word **bifurcation** means a split or fork.

In Figure 7.2 we have plotted some phase lines and critical points at discrete values of the parameter. This was done to emphasize the phase lines, but it can be done continuously just as easily. The diagram we obtain by plotting critical points versus the parameter is often called a **bifurcation diagram**. In the case in hand, the graphs of critical points versus a are the a-axis and the parabola $y^2 = a$. If you sketch this, the pitchfork image becomes very clear.

Examples of bifurcations in the case of 2×2 systems are not hard to find. Consider the system

$$x' = ay + x(9 - x^2 - y^2)/10,$$
$$y' = -ax + y(9 - x^2 - y^2)/10.$$

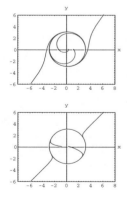

FIGURE 7.3

If $a \neq 0$, you may recognize that this system has a limit cycle, which is the circle of radius 3 centered at the origin. Figure 7.3 shows a sampling of the orbits for $a = 1$ and $a = 0.1$. In both cases, the orbits starting outside the circle spiral in to the circle, and those starting inside spiral out to the circle. This is to be expected because the field is composed of two components. One is at right

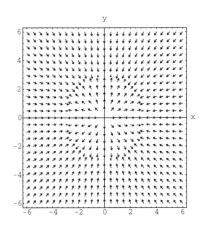

FIGURE 7.4

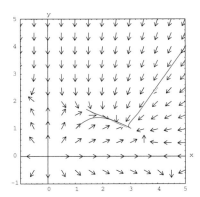

FIGURE 7.5

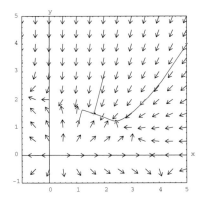

FIGURE 7.6

angles to the radial vector, and the other is parallel to the radius vector, but it points in outside the circle and it points out inside the circle. This circle is a periodic orbit. There is only one critical point, the origin.

However, if $a = 0$, the situation changes dramatically. Now every point on the circle of radius 3 is a critical point. The orbits are now straight lines. This is illustrated in Figure 7.4. Once again, the nature of solutions changes radically in form as the parameter a passes through zero, and so zero is a bifurcation value. In most cases a bifurcation is marked by a change in the number or stability of critical points. However, this is not the only possibility. Consider the equation

$$y' = a^2 y^2 + 1.$$

This equation has no critical points. However, if $a = 0$, then solutions are defined for all t; but if $a \neq 0$, then solutions are defined only for a finite interval for t. There is a dramatic change in the nature of solutions at $a = 0$. Thus $a = 0$ is a bifurcation point. It was mentioned at the begining of the chapter that a proper definition of bifurcation is very difficult. Therefore, we will make do with the intuitive notion of a bifurcation point as a value of the system parameters at which there is a change in the form of solutions to the system.

Harvesting from Competing Species

Let us apply what we have learned about bifurcation to a practical problem. We want to investigate what might happen to two populations of fish competing for the same food supply if we allow harvesting of a proportion of one of the species of fish.

Let us suppose that, without harvesting, the fish populations satisfy the system that was introduced in Section 3.4. Specifically, let us suppose that the populations satisfy

$$x' = x(4 - x - y),$$
$$y' = y(6 - x - 3y).$$

We can suppose that the units are thousands of fish and the time is in years. Figure 7.5 shows the stable situation that holds while there is no harvesting. The equilibrium point is at $(3, 1)$, and this is asymptotically stable.

Now suppose that we harvest a few fish in each time interval from the population represented by $x(t)$. If the rate of harvesting is a in thousands of fish per year, then the system becomes

$$x' = x(4 - x - y) - a,$$
$$y' = y(6 - x - 3y).$$

Figure 7.6 shows the behavior for $a = 1.4$. Notice that the x population of fish has dropped a little and the y population has increased a small amount. Figure 7.7 shows the situation for $a = 1.6$. The situation has radically changed; there is now

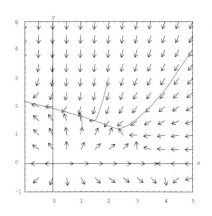

FIGURE 7.7

no critical point in the first quadrant. Moreover, the fish population represented by x has died out. It is not hard to solve for the critical points, and so we leave it as an exercise to show that the nonzero y components of the critical points are given by

$$y = \frac{3 \pm \sqrt{9 - 4(a/6 + 2)}}{2}.$$

The x component is either zero or

$$x = 6 - 3y.$$

Therefore, if $a = 0$, we get $y = 1$ or $y = 2$, in which case the critical points are $(3, 1)$ and $(0, 2)$. If $0 < a < 1.5$, we still have two real values of y and two corresponding critical points in the first quadrant. These critical points merge as a approaches 1.5, and this common point is $(1.5, 1.5)$. They disappear altogether for $a > 1.5$. Thus we have a bifurcation.

All seems reasonably well as we slowly increase our harvesting, but as a reaches 1.5, catastrophe strikes, and the x population is destroyed. Certainly, this is a crude and provisional model, but it is not hard to imagine innumerable systems in nature that could be close to a bifurcation that could lead to disastrous consequences. The loading of a beam comes to mind. If the load exceeds a certain level, the beam fails catastrophically.

Bifurcation and Numerical Methods

Since bifurcation points are values near which the form of solutions may change radically, it is not surprising that bifurcation can have an impact on numerical methods. The following system illustrates how numerical methods may prove unreliable near a bifurcation point.

Example 7.1.1   Consider the following system with parameter a:

$$x' = (x^4 + y^4)ax + y,$$
$$y' = -x + (x^4 + y^4)ay.$$

Clearly, $a = 0$ is a bifurcation point, since at zero the orbits are all circles; but if $a \neq 0$, the orbits spiral in or out. If $a > 0$, the orbits move out rapidly to infinity in finite time. For $a < 0$, the orbits spiral in and are defined for all time. By choosing initial conditions farther from the origin, this radical difference in behavior can be produced for tiny differences in the parameter. Now, if the round-off error of your computer causes it to see $a = 0.00000000001$ as zero, then the numerically computed solution on this machine will be very different from that computed on a more accurate machine.   ∎

EXERCISES 7.1

1. Find the bifurcation value for $y' = ay$. The parameter is a. How do solutions for the equation at the bifurcation value differ from solutions of equations with neighboring values of a. Draw a bifurcation diagram.

2. Find the bifurcation value for $y' = a - y^2$. The parameter is a. Draw a bifurcation diagram, and explain what happens to the solutions as the bifurcation is passed.

3. Find the bifurcation value for $y' = y(a - y^3)$. Draw a bifurcation diagram, and explain what happens to the solutions as the bifurcation value is passed.

4. Find the bifurcation values for $y' = y(a-y)(b-y)$. The parameters are a and b. Give a reason why neighboring equations have radically different solutions.

5. Discuss the bifurcation of the system

$$x' = y + a(9 - x^2 - y^2),$$
$$y' = -x + a(9 - x^2 - y^2).$$

Draw fields for $a = 1$, $a = 0$, and $a = -1$.

6. Discuss the bifurcation of the system

$$x' = x(3(1 + a) - ax - y),$$
$$y' = y(9 - 2x - y).$$

Draw fields showing the orbit structure change as the bifurcation point is crossed.

7. Consider the system

$$x' = ax + y,$$
$$y' = -x + ay.$$

Show that $a = 0$ is a bifurcation point. For any a, how many critical points are there?

8. Imagine an experiment on a system that has a bifurcation in a parameter. The experiment sets this parameter, but the setting is subject to error. Discuss briefly the possibility of two experimenters getting different results.

9. Can a bifurcation diagram for a 2×2 system with a single parameter be drawn. Explain! If you say yes, sketch an example.

10. In the harvesting example of this section, solve for the critical points of the system as a function of the parameter a.

11. If the catfish in a certain pond are left to themselves, the number of fish in hundreds satisfies the equation $y' = y(2 - y)$. If a is the number of fish in hundreds harvested in one unit of time, write the equation governing the harvesting of the fish. Draw a bifurcation diagram, and describe what it means for the fish population.

12. Repeat Exercise 11 for $y' = 0.5y(3 - y)$.

13. Repeat Exercise 11 for $y' = 0.1y(4 - y)$.

7.2 FLOWS

In this chapter, we are concerned with the long-term and overall behavior of solutions to systems, so it will be useful to have a way of expressing all the solutions to a given system in one function. Such a function is called the flow of the system.

We define flows only for autonomous systems for which the existence and uniqueness conditions are satisfied. Each solution is determined uniquely by its initial condition at $t = 0$. Therefore, the family of all solutions, with initial conditions at $t = 0$, can be symbolized by $\phi(t, x)$. For each initial condition x, we get a solution

$$y(t) = \phi(t, x).$$

Note that for $t = 0$

$$\phi(0, x) = x,$$

since all solutions start at the initial condition. Also note that in the case of higher-dimensional systems, x would be an n-tuple, as would $\phi(t, x)$. For a

2×2 system, x would be an ordered pair (x_0, y_0) and $\phi(t, x_0, y_0) = (x(t), y(t))$, where $\{x(t), y(t)\}$ is the solution through (x_0, y_0) at $t = 0$. The function $\phi(t, x)$ is called the **flow** of the differential equation or system.

We have made note of the relation $\phi(0, x) = x$. A second relation that is a direct consequence of the definition of $\phi(t, x)$ is

$$\phi(t + s, x) = \phi(t, \phi(s, x)).$$

To see this, interpret t and s as periods of time. If the solution starts at x and we allow the solution through x to evolve through the time interval $t + s$, we arrive at $\phi(t + s, x)$. Break this down into two steps. First, let time evolve through period s. Then the solution is at $\phi(s, x)$. Now continue the evolution through time interval t. Then the solution is at $\phi(t, \phi(s, x))$. But it is the same solution in both cases, so $\phi(t + s, x) = \phi(t, \phi(s, x))$.

A mathematical proof of this relation, using the vector notation for solutions and systems, is as follows. Let $\vec{R}(t)$ be the solution to the system

$$\vec{R}'(t) = \vec{F}(\vec{R}(t))$$

through $x = \vec{R}(0)$ at $t = 0$. Thus $\vec{R}(t) = \phi(t, x)$. Let $\vec{R}_1(t) = \vec{R}(t + s)$. Then it is immediate that $\vec{R}_1(t)$ is the unique solution through $\vec{R}(s)$ at $t = 0$. But $\vec{R}(t + s)$, as a function of t, is also the unique solution through $\vec{R}(s)$ at $t = 0$. Thus

$$\phi(t + s, x) = \vec{R}(t + s) = \vec{R}_1(t) = \phi(t, \phi(s, x)).$$

It should be mentioned that for solutions that are not defined for all t the preceding relation is only valid if the terms are all defined at t, s, and $t + s$.

Here are two examples of flows.

Example 7.2.1   We can find the flow of

$$y' = y(2 - y)$$

by solving the equation by separation of variables. The result is

$$\phi(t, y_0) = \frac{2y_0 e^{2t}}{2 - y_0 + y_0 e^{2t}}.$$

Observe that $\phi(0, y_0) = y_0$. Showing that $\phi(t + s, x) = \phi(t, \phi(s, x))$ is left as an exercise in algebra.   ∎

Example 7.2.2   The solution to the system

$$x' = 2y,$$
$$y' = -2x$$

with initial condition (x_0, y_0) is

$$x(t) = x_0 \cos(2t) + y_0 \sin(2t),$$
$$y(t) = y_0 \cos(2t) - x_0 \sin(2t).$$

Therefore, the flow is

$$\phi(t, x_0, y_0) = (x_0 \cos(2t) + y_0 \sin(2t),\ y_0 \cos(2t) - x_0 \sin(2t)).$$

Note that $\phi(0, x_0, y_0) = (x_0, y_0)$. Also,

$$\phi(t + s, x_0, y_0) = (x_0 \cos(2(t + s)) + y_0 \sin(2(t + s)),$$
$$y_0 \cos(2(t + s)) - x_0 \sin(2(t + s)),$$

and an application of the sum identities quickly shows that

$$\phi(t + s, x_0, y_0) = \phi(t, \phi(s, x_0, y_0)). \qquad \blacksquare$$

It is important to gain a good visual image of the flow of a system. To this end, consider the flow of the 2×2 system

$$x' = f(x, y),$$
$$y' = g(x, y),$$

where we interpret the independent variable t as time and the dependent variables x and y as the coordinates of a point in the plane. Consider a point (x_0, y_0) in the plane at $t = 0$. The solution through this point is given by the flow function $(x(t), y(t)) = \phi(t, x_0, y_0)$. Thus, as time progresses, the orbit passing through (x_0, y_0) is traced out. If we change the initial point, a different orbit is traced out. Incidentally, orbits are often called **flow lines**. Imagine the phase plane of the system as the surface of a vast river. If we drop a cork in the river, it will follow the flow of the river, and the path it traces out is the flow line or orbit. The flow of the system is capturing in one function the motion of the surface of the river as a whole by describing the motion of every point.

The flow can tell us how patches of the surface of the river behave. Imagine an oil slick on the surface at time $t = 0$. Let this slick be the set of points S_0 in the plane. Consider each point in S_0 as an initial condition. At time t, each point in S_0 has moved along its orbit or flow line to a new position, so the slick as a whole has moved to a new position and form. The new slick S_t at time t is defined by

$$S_t = \{\phi(t, x, y) \mid (x, y) \in S_0\}.$$

Figure 7.8 gives an image of this kind of motion. Flows are exhibited often on the weather section of the news. When you see the atmosphere put in motion by animation, you are watching the flow of the atmospheric system. The motion of cloud masses allows you to visualize the motion of patches of the atmosphere, as well as to get a feel for the motion of individual points.

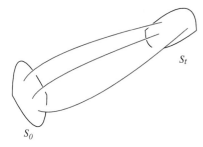

FIGURE 7.8

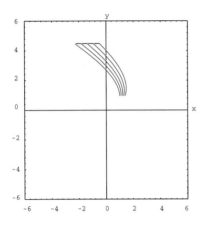

FIGURE 7.9

Example 7.2.3 Figure 7.9 shows the motion of points on a straight line segment as t goes from 0 to 1.5 for the linear system

$$x' = x - y,$$
$$y' = y.$$

In this case, the line segment is transported to a line segment that has been stretched horizontally. ∎

The Divergence of the Field

The fundamental connection between the flow and the field of a system of equations is that the flow lines or orbits pass through the field tangentially. Now that we have the concept of a flow, a little more can be said. Consider a system of three equations in vector form

$$\vec{R}' = \vec{F}(\vec{R}),$$

where

$$\vec{F}(x, y, z) = f_1(x, y, z)\vec{i} + f_2(x, y, z)\vec{j} + f_3(x, y, z)\vec{k}$$

is the field. Recall that the divergence of the field is defined by

$$\text{Div}(\vec{F}) = \frac{\partial f_1}{\partial x} + \frac{\partial f_2}{\partial y} + \frac{\partial f_3}{\partial z}.$$

Imagine that the field describes the velocity of a flow of fluid through space; then recall that the divergence theorem tells us that the volume of fluid that flows through a closed surface in a unit of time is equal to the integral of the divergence of the vector field over the volume enclosed by the surface. Thus the divergence at a point is measuring the rate at which fluid volume is being created in a small region about the point. Put another way, the divergence can be thought of as measuring the rate at which the volume of an initial region of space is expanding. Therefore, it is perhaps not greatly surprising that the divergence of the field is the connection between an initial volume of space and the volume that it becomes as it is swept along by the flow.

More formally, if V_0 is a volume of (x, y, z) space, we define a volume $V(t)$ as follows. Let $\phi(t, x, y, z)$ be the flow of the autonomous system, that is, $\phi(t, x, y, z)$ is the value of the solution to the system at value t of the independent variable when (x, y, z) is the initial condition at $t = 0$. We define

$$V(t) = \{\phi(t, x, y, z) | (x, y, z) \in V_0\}.$$

Intuitively, the points in V_0 move along their orbits as t increases, and so at a given value of t the original volume has been transported through (x, y, z) space to become a new volume of possibly quite different shape. The following fact is known as Liouville's Theorem.

$$\frac{dV(t)}{dt} = \int_{V(t)} \text{Div}(\vec{F}) \, dx \, dy \, dz.$$

Here we are using $V(t)$ on the left to represent the real number that is the volume of space occupied by $V(t)$. This result is very general and applies to any autonomous system and can be restated in two dimensions. In that case, the region is an area in the plane. An outline of the proof will be given in the exercises.

Consider Example 7.2.3 again. The phase space is the plane, and the field is

$$\vec{F}(x, y) = (x - y)\vec{i} + y\vec{j}.$$

Therefore, the divergence is

$$\text{Div}(\vec{F}) = \frac{\partial(x - y)}{\partial x} + \frac{\partial y}{\partial y} = 1 + 1 = 2.$$

Thus if $A(t)$ is the area of a region in the plane, this area satisfies the equation

$$\frac{dA(t)}{dt} = \int_{A(t)} \text{Div}(\vec{F}) \, dx \, dy = 2A(t).$$

Consequently,

$$A(t) = A(0)e^{2t},$$

where $A(0)$ is the area of the initial region at $t = 0$. Thus the area of the region is expanding exponentially.

We shall use Liouville's theorem in the last section of this chapter in the following way. Suppose that the volume $V(t)$ contains a fixed subset A for all t, so $A \subset V(t)$ for all t. Suppose also that the divergence of the system field is $-k$, where $k > 0$. Then we have, as before, $V(t) = V_0 e^{-kt}$. Therefore, the volume $V(t)$ goes to zero as t goes to infinity; but A is trapped inside this shrinking volume, so A must have zero volume. Do not jump to conclusions! The set A could be a point, a curve, a surface, or, as we shall see, a set of far greater complexity.

Example 7.2.4   Consider the system

$$x' = 1 - x^2 - y^2,$$
$$y' = 1 - x^2 - y^2.$$

Since this is a 2×2 system, we consider areas instead of volumes. The field is

$$\vec{F}(x, y) = (1 - x^2 - y^2)\vec{i} + (1 - x^2 - y^2)\vec{j},$$

and so the divergence is

$$\text{Div}(\vec{F}) = -2x - 2y.$$

The divergence is not a constant, but we can work with it anyhow. Consider the initial area to be the triangle bounded by the lines $x + y = 1$, $x = 1$, and $y = 1$. A quick inspection of the field shows that the flow cannot carry points inside the triangle outside it. So if the initial area A_0 is in this triangle, then the area at time t, $A(t)$ must be in this triangle also. Notice that inside the triangle we have

$$\text{Div}(\vec{F}) = -2x - 2y \leq -2.$$

Then Liouville's theorem gives

$$A'(t) = \int_{A(t)} -2x - 2y \, dx \, dy \leq \int_{A(t)} -2 \, dx \, dy = -2A(t).$$

Thus the area $A(t)$ is decreasing at a more rapid rate than if $A'(t) = -2A(t)$. Thus $A(t)$ goes to zero more rapidly than $A_0 e^{-2t}$. Now, if the triangle contains a subset, say S, that is in $A(t)$ for all $t \geq 0$, then the area of S must be zero. Thus S might be a point, a line, a curve, or some more bizarre set of zero area.

Now look in the triangle to see if there is such a set. The arc of the unit circle in the first quadrant is in the triangle A_0. Moreover, each point of the arc is a critical point, so it is stationary under the action of the flow. Thus the arc is a subset of $A(t)$ for all t. Note that this arc has zero area, as we have just proved it must have. ∎

EXERCISES 7.2

1. Find the flow for the equation $y' = y$, and write it in the form "$\phi(t, y) =$". Where has the interval of initial values $(1, 2)$ been moved to by the flow when $t = 3$?

2. Find the flow for the equation $y' = 2y + 1$, and write it in the form "$\phi(t, y) =$". Where has the interval of initial values $(1, 2)$ been moved to by the flow when $t = 3$?

3. Find the flow for the equation $y' = -3y + 5$, and write it in the form "$\phi(t, y) =$". Where has the interval of initial values $(1, 2)$ been moved to by the flow when $t = 1$?

4. Find the flow for the equation $y' = y^2$, and write it in the form "$\phi(t, y) =$". You will need to rearrange the solution so that zero is included as an initial condition. Is $\phi(2, y)$ defined for all y? Explain!

5. Find the flow for the system

$$x' = y,$$
$$y' = x - y,$$

and write it in the form "$\phi(t, x, y) =$". *Hint:* Solve the system by the methods of Chapter 5. Use 2 × 2System to help you describe what happens to the unit disk in the xy-plane as t goes from 0 to 2.

6. Find the flow for the system

$$x' = y,$$

$$y' = -4x,$$

and write it in the form "$\phi(t, x, y) =$". *Hint:* Solve the system by the methods of Chapter 5. Use 2 × 2System to help you describe what happens to the interval $(2, 3)$ on the x-axis in the xy-plane as t goes from 0 to 2.

7. Find the flow for the system

$$x' = -2x + 2y,$$
$$y' = 2x + y,$$

and write it in the form "$\phi(t, x, y) =$". *Hint:* Solve the system by the methods of Chapter 5. Use 2 × 2System to help you describe what happens to the circle $(x - 2)^2 + (y - 2)^2 \leq 1$ in the xy-plane as t goes from 0 to 2.

8. For the system

$$x' = -2x + 2y,$$
$$y' = 2x + y,$$

do areas expand or contract as they are carried along by the flow? Solve for the area as a function of time.

9. For the system

$$x' = x + 2y,$$

$$y' = 2x + 3y,$$

do areas expand or contract as they are carried along by the flow? Solve for the area as a function of time.

10. This exercise outlines the proof of Liouville's theorem. In vector form let the equation be

$$\vec{X}'(s) = \vec{F}(\vec{X}(s)).$$

Fix the independent variable s. The new volume at $s + h$ is $V(s + h)$. So the change is $V(s + h) - V(s)$. If $d\vec{S}$

is a vector element of surface area of the surface of $V(s)$, then this element will sweep out a volume approximately equal to $h\vec{F}(p) \cdot d\vec{S}$, where $\vec{F}$ is evaluated at a point in $d\vec{S}$. Thus the change in volume is approximately

$$V(s + h) - V(s) \approx h \int_{\text{surface } V(s)} \vec{F} \cdot d\vec{S}.$$

Use the divergence theorem and finish the argument.

7.3 A BASIC THEOREM

So far we have been concerned with the sensitivity of solutions to changes in the parameters of a system. Now we turn to the way in which solutions may be sensitive to small changes in initial conditions. Systems can be very sensitive to these changes in ordinary ways, but the intriguing cases involve what are called attractors, especially what are called strange attractors. In this section we shall discuss a basic theorem that places a general limitation on the sensitivity of solutions to changes in initial conditions. However, as we shall see in the following sections, this theorem still allows room enough for some extraordinary things to happen.

As was said at the end of Chapter 2, if initial conditions are close, it is reasonable to expect solutions to be close, at least initially. But, in the long run, there is no reason to expect solutions to remain close. Indeed, in the long run, solutions with close initial conditions can diverge from one another greatly.

Example 7.3.1   Consider $y' = y$. The solutions are $y = Ce^t$. Suppose that y_1 and y_2 are initial values at $t = 0$. Then $y_1(t) = y_1 e^t$ and $y_2(t) = y_2 e^t$. We can compare the distance between these solutions as t increases by

$$|y_1(t) - y_2(t)| = |y_1 e^t - y_2 e^t| = e^t |y_1 - y_2|.$$

We see that if the initial conditions are close then the solutions stay close for a little while, but eventually they diverge at an exponential rate.   ∎

This simple example reflects the way in which solutions generally compare in relation to their initial conditions. To state this general comparison, we will need a new term, which we now define.

Definition 7.3.2

If the function $f(t, y)$ is defined on the rectangle $(a, b) \times (c, d)$, and there is a number L such that

$$|f(t, y_1) - f(t, y_2)| \leq L|y_1 - y_2|$$

for all t in (a, b) and all y_1 and y_2 in (c, d), then we say f satisfies a **Lipschitz condition** on the rectangle. The number L is called a **Lipschitz constant**. The intervals in this definition can be infinite. ●

In the preceding example, a Lipschitz constant is $L = 1$, since

$$|f(t, y_1) - f(t, y_2)| \le |y_1 - y_2|.$$

Consider first a system of just one equation,

$$y' = f(t, y).$$

We shall assume that f and $\frac{\partial f}{\partial y}$ are continuous throughout the plane. This will ensure existence and uniqueness of solutions, as usual.

The following theorem is proved in Appendix C as part of the existence and uniqueness proof.

Theorem 7.3.3

Suppose, in $y' = f(t, y)$, that f satisfies a Lipschitz condition on the rectangle $(a, b) \times (c, d)$ with Lipschitz constant L. Suppose that t_0 is in (a, b) and y_1 and y_2 are in (c, d), and that they are the initial conditions at t_0 of the solutions $y_1(t)$ and $y_2(t)$. Then

$$|y_1(t) - y_2(t)| \le e^{L|t - t_0|}|y_1 - y_2|$$

for all t in (a, b) as long as the graphs of the solutions are in the rectangle. ●

In general terms, this theorem says that the difference between solutions is bounded by an exponential function and that the closer the initial conditions of the solutions, the closer the solutions stay over a given finite interval of time. Note that we cannot expect solutions to stay close for all time.

We cannot do better than this, since this exponential rate of divergence is attained in the simple example given previously.

Example 7.3.4   Consider

$$y' = f(t, y) = 3y + 2.$$

We have

$$|f(t, y_1) - f(t, y_2)| = |3y_1 + 2 - 3y_2 - 2| \le 3|y_1 - y_2|,$$

and so a Lipschitz constant on any rectangle $(a, b) \times (c, d)$ is 3.

The general solution is $y(t) = -2/3 + ce^{3t}$, and so with initial condition y_i at, say $t = 1$, we have

$$y_i = -\frac{2}{3} + ce^3,$$

and so

$$c = e^{-3}(y_i + \frac{2}{3}).$$

Therefore, the solution is

$$y_i(t) = -\frac{2}{3} + e^{-3}(y_i + \frac{2}{3})e^{3t} = -\frac{2}{3} + (y_i + \frac{2}{3})e^{3(t-1)}.$$

Thus we get

$$|y_1(t) - y_2(t)| = |(y_1 + \frac{2}{3})e^{3(t-1)} - (y_2 + \frac{2}{3})e^{3(t-1)}|$$
$$\leq e^{3(t-1)}|y_1 - y_2|.$$

But this is valid on any rectangle, and this is what the theorem predicts.   ■

Example 7.3.5   Consider the equation

$$y' = f(t, y) = 2ty$$

on the rectangle $(a, b) = (-2, 2)$ and $(c, d) = (-\infty, \infty)$. Then

$$|f(t, y_1) - f(t, y_2)| = 2|t||y_1 - y_2| \leq 4|y_1 - y_2|.$$

So 4 is the Lipschitz constant on the rectangle $(-2, 2) \times (-\infty, \infty)$.
The solution with initial condition at $t = 0$ is

$$y(t) = y_0 e^{t^2},$$

and so

$$|y_1(t) - y_2(t)| = e^{t^2}|y_1 - y_2|.$$

At first you may think this does not fit the theorem, for the divergence is at the rate of e^{t^2}. However, if you look more carefully, you will see that $e^{t^2} \leq e^{4t}$ in this rectangle, and so

$$|y_1(t) - y_2(t)| \leq e^{4t}|y_1 - y_2|,$$

as predicted by the theorem.   ■

This last example momentarily gave us pause because it looked as if the rate of divergence was higher than that predicted by the theorem. It is most important to note that the bound on the difference between solutions is only good in the rectangle for which the Lipschitz constant is given. On the other hand, the example does suggest that solutions of one equation may diverge from one another in a different way from solutions of another equation. Theorem 7.3.3 gives an estimate of the maximum distance there can be between solutions in a given interval of t, but it tells us nothing about the potential for the distance between solutions to vary in a violent manner. Indeed, there are other measures of the rate of divergence of solutions that discriminate more sharply between the types of behavior exhibited by different systems of equations. We shall see that, even though the distance between solutions is bounded, the distance between solutions may vary in an unpredictable and chaotic way. These sharper measures of the divergence of solutions from one another are beyond the scope of an introductory text, so we will let the matter rest here.

Theorem 7.3.3 can be restated for higher dimensions. The only difference is that distances are now between vectors instead of real numbers. Here is an example involving a 2×2 system.

Example 7.3.6   The system

$$x' = y,$$
$$y' = x$$

has vector field

$$\vec{F}(t, x, y) = y\vec{i} + x\vec{j}.$$

Therefore,

$$\|\vec{F}(t, x_1, y_1) - \vec{F}(t, x_2, y_2)\| = \|(y_1 - y_2)\vec{i} - (x_1 - x_2)\vec{j}\|$$

$$= \sqrt{(y_1 - y_2)^2 + (x_1 - x_2)^2} = \|(x_1, y_1) - (x_2, y_2)\|.$$

So the Lipschitz constant is 1.

The solution with initial condition at (c, c) is $\vec{R}_1(t) = ce^t(\vec{i} + \vec{j})$; for initial condition $(-c, -c)$ it is $\vec{R}_2(t) = -ce^t(\vec{i} + \vec{j})$. These are two straight line orbits leaving the origin in opposite directions. The difference between them is

$$\|\vec{R}_1(t) - \vec{R}_2(t)\| = 2ce^t\|\vec{i} + \vec{j}\| = 2\sqrt{2}ce^t.$$

But the theorem predicts that

$$\|\vec{R}_1(t) - \vec{R}_2(t)\| \le e^t\|(c, c) - (-c, -c)\| = 2ce^t\|(1, 1)\| = 2\sqrt{2}ce^t.$$

Thus the solutions diverge at an exponential rate.   ∎

It should be noted that the theorem places an upper bound on the divergence of solutions; it does not imply that solutions always diverge at such a rate. Indeed, the system

$$x' = y,$$

$$y' = -x$$

has orbits that are circles centered at the origin, and the solutions have the same period. Consequently, solutions stay at the same distance as the initial conditions for all t.

EXERCISES 7.3

1. Find a Lipschitz constant for the equation $y' = 4y$ that is valid for all t and y. Verify Theorem 7.3.3 for all solutions with initial conditions at $t = 0$.

2. Find a Lipschitz constant for the equation $y' = 3ty$ that is valid for all $t \in (-3, 3)$ and all y. Verify Theorem 7.3.3 for all solutions with initial conditions at $t = 0$.

3. Find a Lipschitz constant for the equation $y' = 3t^2 y$ that is valid for all $t \in (-4, 4)$ and all y. Verify Theorem 7.3.3 for all solutions with initial conditions at $t = 0$.

4. Find a Lipschitz constant for the equation $y' = y^2$ that is valid for all t and all $y \in (-4, 4)$. Use Field&Solution to verify Theorem 7.3.3 for solutions with initial conditions at $t = 0$ by experimenting with initial conditions and measuring the distance between solutions at various values of t.

5. Find a Lipschitz constant for the system

$$x' = x - y,$$
$$y' = x + y$$

that is valid for all t and all x and y. Use 2 × 2System to verify Theorem 7.3.3 for solutions with initial conditions at $t = 0$ by experimenting with initial conditions and measuring the distance between the ends of the orbits for various intervals of t.

6. What can you say about a Lipschitz constant and the variable t for autonomous systems?

7. Consider $y' = y^2$ in the rectangle $[-1, 1] \times [0, 2]$.
    (a) Show that 4 is a Lipschitz constant for this rectangle.
    (b) If $y_1(t)$ and $y_2(t)$ are the solutions corresponding to the initial conditions $(0, 1)$ and $(0, 0.9)$, show that $|y_1(t) - y_2(t)|$ goes to infinity as t approaches 1.
    (c) Why does this not contradict Theorem 7.3.3. *Hint:* Compute the maximum difference between the solutions while they are in the rectangle.

Uniqueness. *Exercises 8 and 9 use Theorem 7.3.3 to prove the uniqueness part of the existence and uniqueness theorem for the equation $y' = f(t, y)$.*

8. It is a fact that if $\dfrac{\partial f}{\partial y}(t, y)$ is continuous on $[a, b] \times [c, d]$ then there is a number L such that

$$|\frac{\partial f}{\partial y}(t, y)| \leq L$$

on that rectangle. Use this and the mean value theorem for $f(t, y)$ considered as a function of y to show that $f(t, y)$ satisfies a Lipschitz condition.

9. Use Theorem 7.3.3 to prove that if $f(t, y)$ and $\dfrac{\partial f}{\partial y}(t, y)$ are continuous on $[a, b] \times [c, d]$ then any solution through an initial point inside the rectangle must be unique.

7.4 SOME SIMPLE ATTRACTORS

Theorem 7.3.3 makes a broad statement about systems in general, but it gives no detailed information about the behavior of solutions. In the last section we mentioned the existence of other measures of the divergence of solutions that can give more detailed information. These measures, as we have said, are beyond the scope of this book. However, we can give examples of systems of equations that illustrate the rich variety of behavior that solutions can exhibit. This is the goal of the rest of this chapter.

In this section you will be introduced to the notion of an attractor. We shall see that attractors can lead to both stable and unstable behaviour of solutions to systems, and that the presence of multiple attractors can lead to solutions being very sensitive to changes in initial conditions. In the last section of this chapter we shall make the acquaintance of a most extraordinary attractor that causes solutions to behave chaotically.

We have encountered very simple attractors already. An asymptotically stable critical point is a simple attractor, as is a limit cycle. Let us refresh our memories with the following examples.

Example 7.4.1 Consider the system

$$x' = x - 2y,$$
$$y' = 2x - 3y.$$

The eigenvalue is -1 with multiplicity equal to 2, so the origin is asymptotically stable. Thus every solution approaches the origin. ∎

Example 7.4.2 Consider the system

$$x' = y + x \sin(\sqrt{x^2 + y^2}),$$
$$y' = -x + y \sin(\sqrt{x^2 + y^2}).$$

Figure 7.10 shows the field and a few orbits for this system.

Notice the attracting limit cycles that are circles of radius πk with k odd. If k is even, the circles are repelling. Notice how the plane is divided into regions of initial conditions where the corresponding solutions move toward an attractor. Such regions are called **attractor basins**. They are somewhat like watersheds draining into the attractor river or lake. The basin for the attractor, which is the circle of radius π, consists of all points inside the circle of radius 2π except the origin.

This example provides the first hint of the kind of sensitivity of solutions to changes in initial conditions that we have in mind. The circle of radius 2π is a periodic orbit; but if initial conditions are chosen very close together, but on opposite sides of this circle, the solutions will head for different limit cycles. So no matter how close the initial conditions, the solutions will eventually be far apart. This circle of radius 2π is a kind of continental divide. Thus multiple attractors can lead to extreme sensitivity to initial conditions along the boundaries of attractor basins. You should experiment with initial conditions lying very close to these boundaries. ∎

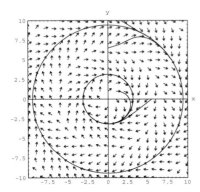

FIGURE 7.10

The next example returns to the forced mass–spring system, but it introduces a trick that will allow us to view the steady-state solution as an attractor.

Example 7.4.3   Consider the equation

$$x'' + 2x' + 2x = \sin(t).$$

This is the equation of a unit mass suspended by a spring of constant 2 with a friction constant of 2 also. The general solution of this equation is

$$x(t) = \frac{1}{5}\sin(t) - \frac{2}{5}\cos(t) + c_0 e^{-t}\sin(t) + c_1 e^{-t}\cos(t).$$

Of course, as $t \to \infty$ the part containing the exponentials goes to zero. Therefore, all solutions approach the steady state solution

$$x(t) = \frac{1}{5}\sin(t) - \frac{2}{5}\cos(t).$$

This steady state is acting as a kind of attractor. However, the attractors we have seen so far are asymptotically stable critical points or limit cycles. These require autonomous systems. Thus, to see the steady-state solution as an attractor, we need to convert the equation

$$x'' + 2x' + 2x = \sin(t)$$

into an equivalent autonomous system. Happily, this is easy to do.

First convert the equation to a first-order system. We have

$$x' = y,$$
$$y' = -2x' - 2x + \sin(t).$$

This is a nonautonomous system because of the $\sin(t)$ on the right-hand side. To get an autonomous system, the trick is to make t a dependent variable and introduce a new independent variable, say s, which is still, in effect, t. We do this by requiring that

$$\frac{dt}{ds} = 1.$$

The resulting autonomous system of three equations is

$$\frac{dx}{ds} = y,$$
$$\frac{dy}{ds} = -2y - 2x + \sin(t),$$
$$\frac{dt}{ds} = 1.$$

The solutions to the autonomous and nonautonomous systems are related as follows. Let $\{x(t), y(t)\}$ be a solution to the nonautonomous system with initial condition (x_0, y_0) at $t = t_0$. The corresponding autonomous solution is $\{\bar{x}(s), \bar{y}(s), t(s)\}$, where $\bar{x}(s) = x(s + t_0)$, $\bar{y}(s) = y(s + t_0)$, and $t(s) = s + t_0$.

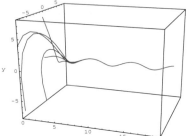

FIGURE 7.11

Note that the initial condition for the autonomous system at $s = 0$ is (x_0, y_0, t_0). Conversely, if $\{\bar{x}(s), \bar{y}(s), t(s)\}$ is a solution to the autonomous system with initial condition (x_0, y_0, t_0) at $s = 0$, then $x(t) = \bar{x}(t-t_0)$ and $y(t) = \bar{y}(t-t_0)$ solve the nonautonomous equation with the corresponding initial conditions. With this trick, in the autonomous system the steady-state solution becomes

$$\{\frac{1}{5}\sin(s + t_0) - \frac{2}{5}\cos(s + t_0), \ \frac{1}{5}\cos(s + t_0) + \frac{2}{5}\sin(s + t_0), s + t_0\}.$$

Regardless of what t_0 is, this is the same curve in (x, y, t)-space. It is a helix. This is an attractor for every point in three space, so the basin for this attractor is all of space. Figure 7.11 is a diagram of this attraction.

This is the only attractor for this system, and its form is so simple that this attractor cannot cause any sensitive behavior. Quite the opposite, every orbit is rapidly indistinguishable from this attractor, which is the autonomous representation of the steady state. ∎

What general properties do the attractors of these examples have? First, an attractor of a system is a subset of the phase space of that system. Second, if an initial condition is chosen in the attractor, the solution stays in the attractor. Third, an attractor has a neighborhood about it such that, if an initial condition is chosen in this neighborhood, the corresponding solution gets asymptotically close to the attractor. We have called the largest such neighborhood the basin of attraction of the attractor. Let us put all this in a definition.

Definition 7.4.4

Let A be a nonempty subset of the phase space of a dynamical system. We say that A is an attractor for this system if:

1. There is a neighborhood U of A, that is, $A \subset U$, such that the solutions corresponding to points in U get asymptotically close to A as $t \to \infty$.

2. The set A is invariant under the action of the flow in the sense that, if x_0 is an initial condition in A, then the corresponding solution stays in A. ●

This definition is perhaps still too broad. According to this definition, the phase space itself is an attractor. The attractors we have considered so far are minimal with respect to the preceding properties. However, Definition 7.4.4 will be serviceable.

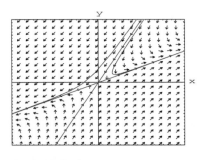

FIGURE 7.12

Example 7.4.5 Figure 7.12 shows the phase portrait for a linear system in which the eigenvalues are of opposite sign. The straight lines are the orbits corresponding to the eigenvectors. The attractor is the line of lower slope. Note that all solutions approach this line asymptotically, so the basin of attraction of this attractor is the whole plane.

However, solutions can show great sensitivity to changes in initial conditions. Consider initial conditions close together but on opposite sides of the straight line of steeper slope in the first quadrant. The solutions eventually head to infinity in opposite directions.   ■

In the next section we shall see the effect that multiple attractors can have on sensitivity.

EXERCISES 7.4

1. Does the system

$$x' = y,$$
$$y' = -x$$

have an attractor other than the whole plane? Explain!

2. What is the minimal attractor of the system

$$x' = -x + y,$$
$$y' = -2y?$$

3. What is the minimal attractor of the system

$$x' = -x + y,$$
$$y' = 2y?$$

Hint: Find the eigenvectors and eigenvalues.

4. Does the system

$$x' = 2x + y,$$
$$y' = y$$

have any attractors that are points or straight lines? Explain!

5. What plane is the minimal attractor of the system

$$x' = x + y + z,$$
$$y' = 2y + z,$$
$$z' = -z?$$

Hint: Find the eigenvalues and eigenvectors.

6. Is it true that if the divergence of the field is negative then the only minimal attractor of a linear system is the origin? Explain and give an example.

7. Is it true that if the divergence of the field is positive then a linear system has no attractor other than the whole plane? Explain and give an example.

8. Describe the minimal attractor of the system

$$x' = -y + x(4 - x^2 - y^2),$$
$$y' = x + y(4 - x^2 - y^2).$$

9. Use 2 × 2System to draw the minimal attractor of the system

$$x' = y,$$
$$y' = -x + 3(1 - x^2)y.$$

10. Find the (minimal) attractor of the system

$$\frac{dx}{ds} = y,$$
$$\frac{dy}{ds} = -2y - 2x + t,$$
$$\frac{dt}{ds} = 1.$$

Show that the attractor is invariant in the sense that any solution that starts on the attractor stays on the attractor. *Hint:* Find the second-order equation that the system came from, and follow the example in the text.

11. Find the (minimal) attractor of the system

$$\frac{dx}{ds} = y,$$
$$\frac{dy}{ds} = -3y - 2x + t^2,$$
$$\frac{dt}{ds} = 1.$$

Show that the attractor is invariant in the sense that any solution that starts on the attractor stays on the attractor. *Hint:* Find the second-order equation that the system came from, and follow the example in the text?

12. Find two initial conditions that are less than 10^{-4} apart that go to different attractors for the system

$$x' = y + x\sin(\sqrt{x^2 + y^2}),$$

$$y' = -x + y\sin(\sqrt{x^2 + y^2}).$$

Give a brief explanation, and do not use any software.

7.5 THE PERIODICALLY DRIVEN PENDULUM

In Section 4.4 the simple free pendulum was discussed in some detail. An equation was found for the orbits, stable and unstable critical points were identified, and the periods of orbits were calculated. To this simple pendulum we shall add a periodic external force and some friction. The specific system is

$$\theta' = v,$$
$$v' = -kv - \sin(\theta) + a\sin(\omega t).$$

In this system, a sinusoidal force of amplitude a and frequency $\omega/2\pi$ is applied to the mass. Friction can be included in the constant k.

For various choices of the parameters, this system exhibits a rich variety of behaviors. For some choices, multiple attractors are present, and there is sensitivity to changes in initial conditions along the attractor boundaries. For other choices of parameters, if the amplitude of the periodic driving force is slowly increased, then the onset of chaotic behavior can be observed. Let us begin with the parameter values $k = 0.5$, $a = 0.4$, and $\omega = 1$.

In the absence of any driving force, the system has asyptotically stable critical points at $(2\pi k, 0)$. For the parameter values that we have chosen, the driving force is relatively small compared to the friction, so the pendulum eventually falls into motion about one of the critical points. Figure 7.13 shows the orbits in the (θ, v)-plane corresponding to initial points $(0, 2.721)$ and $(0, 2.722)$ at $t = 0$. The initial conditions both have the pendulum starting hanging straight down. Only the initial velocities are varied. The first solution orbits about $(0, 0)$, whereas the second, with slightly greater initial velocity, orbits $(2\pi, 0)$. Clearly, solutions can be very sensitive to initial conditions. If we lower the friction constant to $k = 0.1$, we get the remarkable results that the solution with initial point $(0, 1.8)$ falls into orbiting about $(0, 0)$, the solution with initial point $(0, 1.85)$ falls into orbiting about $(3\pi, 0)$, and the solution with initial point $(0, 1.9)$ falls into orbiting about $(2\pi, 0)$. Thus the initial points do not seem to obey any simple pattern as to which point the solutions will eventually orbit. It should be mentioned that the precise results you get will depend on the differential equation solver that you use, as well as step size. However, a little experimentation near the values quoted here will yield similar results.

To get an image of possible attractors that are causing this sensitive behavior, we must write the system as an autonomous 3×3 system. We have

$$\frac{d\theta}{ds} = v,$$

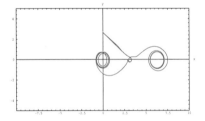

FIGURE 7.13

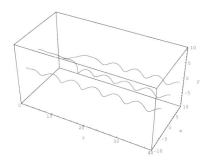

FIGURE 7.14

$$\frac{dv}{ds} = -kv - \sin(\theta) + a\sin(t),$$
$$\frac{dt}{ds} = 1.$$

Figure 7.14 shows helixlike curves winding around lines parallel to the t-axis through the points $(2\pi k, 0)$. Since, for small values of θ, $\sin(\theta) \approx \theta$, the system

$$\frac{d\theta}{ds} = v,$$
$$\frac{dv}{ds} = -kv - \theta + a\sin(t),$$
$$\frac{dt}{ds} = 1$$

approximates the original system. You should recognize this from the preceding section. It is the autonomous version of a forced mass–spring system with friction, and we know that this has a helical attractor. It seems reasonable to tentatively assume that the pseudohelical curves of the driven pendulum are attractors. Even if these curves are not attractors, it is clear from the graphical evidence that solutions become trapped in regions about lines through the points $(2\pi k, 0)$ parallel to the t-axis. Each region has an associated basin of initial points at $t = 0$ whose corresponding solutions eventually get trapped in that region. We will see considerable divergence between solutions whose initial points are close, but are in different basins. By setting $k = 0.1$, we saw that the initial points of solutions that became trapped in different regions were not arranged in any simple pattern. Thus the boundaries of the basins just described must be very complex, and so the overall behavior of the flow of this system is incredibly complex. If we alter the parameters of our system we observe some truly bizarre behavior.

7.5.1 A Hint of Chaos

We add a coil spring to the pendulum so that if the pendulum rotates a restoring force proportional to the rotation is produced. The effect of this will be to keep that bizarre behavior close to the origin of the phase plane. Our system is

$$\theta' = v,$$
$$v' = -kv - \sin(\theta) + a\sin(\omega t) - c\theta.$$

We choose the friction to be zero and $c = 0.1$. If we then increase the amplitude of the driving force a little at a time from $a = 0.1$, an interesting pattern of behavior emerges. At first the motion is confined to oscillation about the stable equilibrium position of $(0, 0)$. At first the oscillation appears to be periodic, or nearly so. But as a is increased the oscillation about the origin becomes more and more complex. To see this, view the functions $\theta(t)$ and $v(t)$ in a differential

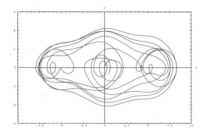

FIGURE 7.15

equation solver. The solution might still be periodic, but this is not clear. At approximately $a = 0.337$ the motion "goes over the top," and the behavior of the solution becomes highly erratic. Figure 7.15 show an image of this chaotic behavior. The pendulum circles about the center, the right, and the left, but when it will switch and how seem completely unpredictable. To get an even better feel for the delicacy of the situation, you should set this system up in 2×2System with a time interval of $[0, 150]$ and experiment. Especially, observe where the orbits end for initial conditions of $(0, 0)$ and $(0.0001, 0)$ and $a = 0.9$.

The graphical evidence does not suggest the presence of any attractors, so how is the sensitivity and apparently random behavior of this system to be accounted for? The discussion that follows proves nothing, but it may shed a little light on the matter. The undriven system has a stable critical point at $(0, 0)$ and two stable and two unstable critical points at the solutions to $\sin(\theta) + 0.1\theta = 0$ and $v = 0$. The magnitude of the values of θ for the unstable points is just a little bigger than π. With the restoring coil spring, it is to be expected that an equilibrium is reached a little beyond the vertical. A quick look at the field for the undriven system shows that all orbits are periodic, and a little experimentation show that the periods of these orbits get longer the larger the orbit (except for the small orbits about the two nonorigin stable points). In the section on vibration in Section 4.5, we applied an external force to the mass in a mass–spring system in which there was no friction. We observed that if the frequency of the driving force was the same as the natural frequency of the mass–spring system then the system continued to absorb energy, and the amplitude of the solution went to infinity. For small oscillations, our undriven pendulum with restoring spring has a period around 6 or 7. This is very close to the period of the driving force, so it is no surprise that small oscillations absorb energy. For orbits of very long period, the driving force only produces a ripple in the overall undriven motion. The pushes and pulls of the driving force average out over long cycles. Clearly, the driving force is initially able to supply enough energy from rest for the pendulum to "go over the top," but it cannot supply enough energy to go into a long period cycle. Thus it is condemned to fall into shorter period cycles, which then lead to the absorptions of more energy and longer cycles. The behavior of this exchange appears to be random and, perhaps, this is understandable.

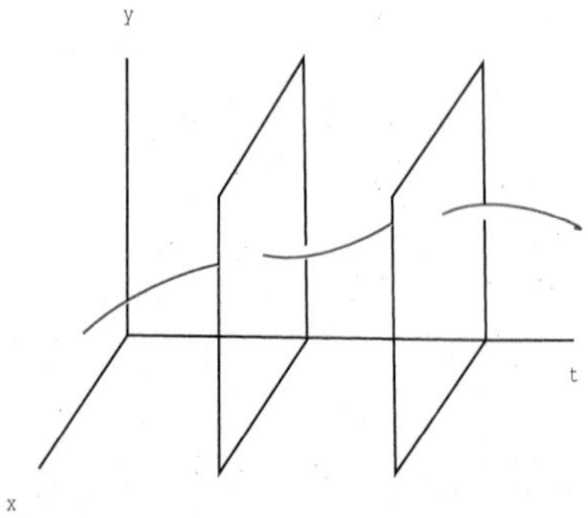

The Poincaré Return Map

The behavior of a periodically driven system such as our pendulum can be viewed in a discrete manner by taking plane cross sections of (x, y, t)-space perpendicular to the t-axis and spaced at intervals of one period of the driving force. Figure 7.16 illustrates the situation. Since the planes are spaced at intervals equal to the period of the driving force, the field between a pair of planes is the same as the field between any other pair. So the motion of a solution between planes is determined by the starting point on the left plane of the pair. If p is the period,

FIGURE 7.16

then the function defined by

$$(x(0), y(0)) \rightarrow (x(p), y(p)),$$

where $(x(0), y(0))$ are the xy-coordinates of the initial point and $(x(p), y(p))$ are the xy-coordinates of the solution after one period, is called the **Poincaré return map**. If we apply the return map to the point $(x(p), y(p))$, we get the xy-coordinates of the point at which the solution will hit the next plane in succession. Repeated application of the return map gives the sequence of intersection points of the planes and the solution. If we project these planes into the xy-plane, the points of intersection will appear as a sequence of points in the xy-plane. This is a kind of discrete orbit that shows the xy-coordinates of the initial point, the point after one period, the point after two periods, and so on. If f is the Poincaré return map and (x_n, y_n) are the xy-coordinates of the solution after n periods, then

$$(x_n, y_n) = f^n((x_0, y_0)),$$

where f^n means apply f to the initial point, then apply f to this result, then apply f to this, and so on n times.

The plot of this sequence of points in the xy-plane can give another view of the behavior of the pendulum. For example, if a point is repeated, that is $(x_0, y_0) = (x_n, y_n)$, for some positive integer n, then, because the field is periodic in the t-axis direction, the sequence of points $(x_0, y_0), (x_1, y_1), \ldots, (x_n, y_n)$ will be repeated over and over. The chaotic behavior reveals itself when you plot points obtained from successive applications of the return map. It becomes clear that predicting the location for the next point to be plotted is impossible. The resulting plot of many applications of the return function produces an image in which there is a great deal of randomness. Figure 7.17 shows such a plot.

If we ignore the system of equations from which it came and consider the Poincaré return map alone, we simply have a function that we may repeatedly apply to a point to generate a sequence of points. This simple arrangement of a function that can be repeatedly applied to a point is called a **discrete dynamical system**. A discrete dynamical system can be represented by

$$x_n = f^n(x_0).$$

So x_n is the result of applying f to x_0, then applying f to that result, then applying f to that, and so on n times. For example, enter a number x_0 into your calculator and then push the sin button repeatedly. If you push the button n times, you get x_n. The sequence that you get can be defined recursively in the form

$$x_{n+1} = f(x_n).$$

The terminology of discrete dynamical systems is close to that of systems of first-order equations. We call x_0 the initial point. The sequence of points $\{x_n\}$ defined by $x_n = f^n(x_0)$ is called the orbit of x_0. An orbit is periodic if $x_n =$

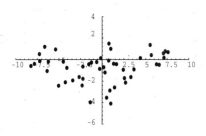

FIGURE 7.17

x_{n+p} for some n and p. If an orbit is periodic, it eventually falls into repeating a finite sequence of points. Discrete dynamical systems can even exhibit random or chaotic behavior, as the return map suggests.

We have actually used discrete dynamical systems earlier. Indeed, Euler's method and the Runge-Kutta method are discrete dynamical systems because they start with an initial value and then repeatedly apply a routine to generate successive values. The last value calculated is the input for the next value to be calculated. But more important is the fact that discrete dynamical systems find their main application in modeling physical systems that have events happening at fixed time intervals. For example, some birds breed once a year, so it would make sense to study the population of a species of bird each year. We shall not go into discrete dynamical systems any further, but an exercise on the subject is provided. This exercise is most interesting for its simplicity of statement and the mysterious complexity of the behavior of orbits.

In the next section we will examine the famous Lorenz attractor and the chaos that it causes.

EXERCISES 7.5

1. Use the package 2×2System to find two initial conditions that are less than 10^{-2} apart that go to different attractors for the system

$$\theta' = v,$$
$$v' = -kv - \sin(\theta) + a\sin(\omega t),$$

where $k = 0.2$, $a = 0.4$, and $\omega = 0.5$.

2. Use the package 2×2System to find two initial conditions that are less than 10^{-2} apart that go to different attractors for the system

$$\theta' = v,$$
$$v' = -kv - \sin(\theta) + a\sin(\omega t),$$

where $k = 0.3$, $a = 0.2$, and $\omega = 1$.

3. Use the package 2 × 2System to find three initial conditions of the form $(0, v)$ that exhibit the "out-of-order" behavior described in the section for the system

$$\theta' = v,$$
$$v' = -kv - \sin(\theta) + a\sin(\omega t),$$

where $k = 0.1$, $a = 0.45$, and $\omega = 1$.

4. Use the package 2 × 2System to find three initial conditions of the form $(0, v)$ that exhibit the "out-of-order" behavior described in the section for the system

$$\theta' = v,$$

$$v' = -kv - \sin(\theta) + a\sin(\omega t),$$

where $k = 0.1$, $a = 0.35$, and $\omega = 1$.

5. In the system

$$\theta' = v,$$
$$v' = -\sin(\theta) - 0.15x + a\sin(t)$$

find the value of a at which you first detect chaotic motion if the initial point is $(0, 0)$.

6. In the system

$$\theta' = v,$$
$$v' = -\sin(\theta) - 0.09x + a\sin(t)$$

find the value of a at which you first detect chaotic motion if the initial point is $(0, 0)$.

Period Doubling and Chaos. *Exercises 7–11 use* 2×2System *to introduce you to the phenomenon of period doubling and the ensuing chaotic behavior that can follow.*

Consider a ball attached to the end of a flexible rod. The rod is clamped in the vertical position with the ball at the top. If the ball is displaced from the vertical a small amount, the force of gravity will tend to pull it farther away from the vertical until the restoring force of the rod increases sufficiently. This a little like a spring whose restoring force is positive initially and only becomes negative with further extension. If x is the displacement from the vertical, the restoring force might be $F = x - x^3$.

7. In the absence of an external force, the equation of this system is $x'' + x' - x + x^3 = 0$, assuming unit values of mass and friction. Reduce this to a 2×2 system and show that there are three equilibrium points. Use 2×2 System to draw the field and a few orbits and decide on the stability of the equilibrium points. Give the physical interpretation of these points.

8. Imagine that the table to which the rod is clamped is being shaken back and forth sinusoidally. This could be modeled as an external force $F_0 \cos(t)$, say, applied to the ball. Write down the nonautonomous 2×2 system that models the motion of the ball.

9. Open your version of 2×2 System and set the initial condition to $(1.5, 0)$, the time interval to $[0, 100]$, and the

step to 0.05. Start with $F_0 = 0.5$. Study the orbit and the component solutions and see that they are asymptotic to periodic functions with period about 6. Increase F_0 by 0.05 at a time and make careful observations of the orbits and solutions. At about $F_0 = 0.7$, notice that the orbit form has changed into two loops. The functions do not look very different, but examine them carefully, and note that the period is now about 12.

10. Continue increasing F_0 as in Exercise 16, and report carefully on what you see. Does the word **chaotic** seem reasonable?

11. Consider the function defined by $f(x) = ax(1 - x)$. In one of the three M's, write a loop to compute $x_{n+1} = f(x_n)$. For various choices of x_0, compute out to x_{200} and plot the results. Do this while increasing a from $a = 2$ to $a = 4$. Report on what you see. Note especially what happens between 3 and 4.

7.6 CHAOS

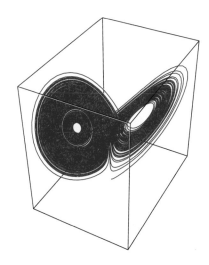

FIGURE 7.18

One of the strangest phenomena associated with systems of first-order differential equations is chaotic behavior. All first-order systems are deterministic in the sense that the initial condition determines the solution. Yet some systems exhibit random and totally unpredictable behavior in spite of the determination of the solution by the initial condition. The chaotic behavior that we have in mind is created by the presence of attractors of very complex form. In this section we will investigate the Lorenz attractor. This attractor was discovered by the American meteorologist E. Lorenz in the 1960s during his studies of atmospheric dynamics.

In the last section we saw that multiple attractors must produce sensitivity to changes in initial conditions near the boundaries between basins of attraction. Imagine now that there is just one attractor, but it is not a simple point or curve. Imagine that the attractor is like some incredibly tangled collection of curves. As a solution approaches this tangle, its behavior becomes more and more like the curves in the tangle. Being a tangle, the orbit is completely unpredictable. Moreover, the slightest change in initial condition would have the solution follow a radically different path near the attractor.

This would be an act of imagination only if it were not for the fact that such complex attractors exist. Figure 7.18 is an orbit of the laLorenz equations.

$$
\begin{aligned}
x' &= -10x + 10y, \\
y' &= 28x - y - xz, \\
z' &= -\frac{8}{3}z + xy.
\end{aligned}
$$

This orbit gives an indication of the existence and shape of an attractor for this system. If more orbits are drawn, it will be seen that they come very close to the orbit already drawn. They seem to fill out a kind of butterfly shape. Indeed, this attractor has been called the butterfly attractor.

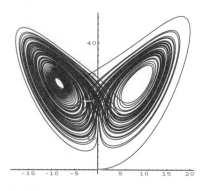

FIGURE 7.19

Figure 7.19 shows a projection of this orbit into the (x, z)-plane. It reveals a little more of the structure of the orbit and the approximate structure of the attractor. Note the extreme tangling of the orbit as it crosses from one wing of the butterfly to the other. Now compound this by all the possible orbits for all initial conditions! Any particular orbit is completely lost in the maze of all the other orbits, and so the future of any particular orbit is completely unpredictable, even though it is deterministic.

You should note the implications of this for numerical computation. Numerical methods repeatedly round off data, which has the effect of altering values for the next step in the algorithm. This is like repeatedly altering initial conditions. In view of this, numerical methods applied to the Lorenz system cannot predict the future of a solution, except that it will approach the attractor.

This is not a mere curiosity, for many complex systems in nature, such as the dynamics of the atmosphere, exhibit such attractors. This implies limits on our ability to make long-range weather forecasts if we intend to use systems of differential equations to model the dynamics.

7.6.1 Some Results on the Lorenz System

The system we have been examining is one member of the parameterized family

$$x' = a(-x + y),$$
$$y' = bx - y - xz,$$
$$z' = -cz + xy,$$

where the parameters a, b, and c are assumed positive. This is called the **Lorenz system**. It was this system that Lorenz was studying in connection with motions in the atmosphere. We shall now analyze this system in a little more detail.

Recall that the divergence of the field of an autonomous system can tell us something about the nature of the flow of the system. For the Lorenz system the divergence is the negative constant $k = -a - 1 - c$, and so Liouville's theorem gives

$$\frac{dV(t)}{dt} = \int_{V(t)} \text{Div}(\vec{F}) \, dx \, dy \, dz = kV(t).$$

But this gives the first-order differential equation

$$\frac{dV(t)}{dt} = kV(t),$$

and the solution is

$$V(t) = V_0 e^{kt}.$$

Remember that k is negative, so as the initial volume V_0 is swept along by the flow the volume is compressed to zero as t goes to infinity.

If the Lorenz attractor is contained in a finite volume, as it appears to be, then the attractor must have zero volume. We have remarked earlier that there are incredibly complex sets that have zero volume. The Lorenz attractor is one of these.

We are now going to show that the orbit of any solution is contained in a sufficiently large ellipsoid. This is sufficient to conclude that an attractor must exist, though we shall not prove this. However, it is plausible, because the volume of this ellipsoid must shrink to zero while staying inside the ellipsoid. Since the orbits cannot escape to infinity, they must converge to some set of zero volume, even if it is only a single point. However, in this case we can see that the attractor is much more complex than that.

Consider the ellipsoid

$$G(x, y, z) = bx^2 + ay^2 + a(z - 2b)^2 = d.$$

We shall show that, if k is sufficiently large, then the field

$$\vec{F} = a(-1x + 1y)\vec{i} + (bx - y - xz)\vec{j} + (-cz + xy)\vec{k}$$

must point into the ellipsoid. In this case no solution starting inside the ellipsoid can leave the ellipsoid. To show that the field points inward, we take the dot product of the field with the gradient of G. The gradient of G gives an outward pointing normal vector to the ellipsoid. Here is the dot product.

$$\vec{F} \cdot \nabla G = -2a[bx^2 + y^2 + c(z - b)^2 - b^2 c].$$

This will be negative provided that the term in brackets is positive. Consider the new ellipsoid

$$bx^2 + y^2 + c(z - b)^2 = b^2 c.$$

If d is large enough, this new ellipsoid will be inside the old ellipsoid

$$bx^2 + ay^2 + a(z - 2b)^2 = d.$$

Therefore, if (x, y, z) is a point on the old ellipsoid, then

$$bx^2 + y^2 + c(z - b)^2 > b^2 c.$$

But this is what we set out to prove.

Therefore, if d is chosen large enough, all orbits starting inside the ellipsoid

$$bx^2 + ay^2 + a(z - 2b)^2 = d$$

must stay inside. Therefore, we know that there is an attractor inside this ellipsoid, and we know it has zero volume.

Next we look at the critical points of the Lorenz system. The equations to be solved for the critical points are

$$a(-x + y) = 0,$$
$$bx - y - xz = 0,$$
$$-cz + xy = 0.$$

Clearly, $x = y$. If $x = 0$, then $y = z = 0$ also, and so the origin is a critical point. If $x \neq 0$, then from the second and third equations

$$z = b - 1$$

and

$$cz = x^2.$$

Thus b must be greater than 1 if $x \neq 0$. If $0 < b \leq 1$, the only critical point is the origin. If $b > 1$, then $x = y = \pm\sqrt{c(b - 1)}$ and $z = b - 1$, so in this case there are three critical points. Let us call them P_0, P_1, and P_2. Notice the bifurcation that takes place as b passes 1. With $0 < b \leq 1$, there is only one critical point, but for b greater than 1, this critical point has split into two more, $(\pm\sqrt{c(b - 1)}, \pm\sqrt{c(b - 1)}, b - 1)$.

Now consider the linearization of this system in a neighborhood of each of the critical points. We start with the origin. To get the linearization near the origin just throw away the non-linear terms. We have

$$x' = a(-x + y),$$
$$y' = bx - y,$$
$$z' = -cz.$$

The matrix of this linear system is

$$\begin{bmatrix} -a & a & 0 \\ b & -1 & 0 \\ 0 & 0 & -c \end{bmatrix}.$$

The characteristic polynomial of this matrix is

$$P(\lambda) = (-c - \lambda)[(-a - \lambda)(-1 - \lambda) - ab],$$

and the eigenvalues are

$$\lambda = -c,$$
$$\lambda = \frac{-(a + 1) \pm \sqrt{(a + 1)^2 - 4a(1 - b)}}{2}.$$

For $0 < b < 1$, the eigenvalues have negative real parts, and so the origin is an asymptotically stable critical point. If $b = 1$, one eigenvalue is zero, and the linear system has infinitely many critical points. But, again, the origin is stable. If $b > 1$, then one eigenvalue is positive, and so there are solutions that move away from the origin. So the origin becomes unstable as the bifurcation value is passed.

To study the other two critical points that come into being when $b > 1$ is somewhat complicated in the general case. Because of this we will restrict our attention to the case where $a = 10$ and $c = 8/3$. The system is

$$x' = 10(-x + y),$$
$$y' = bx - y - xz,$$
$$z' = -\frac{8}{3}z + xy.$$

The critical points are the origin and $(\pm\sqrt{8(b-1)/3}, \pm\sqrt{8(b-1)/3}, b-1)$. We have called these points P_0, P_1, and P_2. We shall linearize at P_1. The situation for P_2 is the same. To linearize, the partial derivatives of

$$f_1(x, y, z) = -10x + 10y,$$
$$f_2(x, y, z) = bx - y - xz,$$

and

$$f_3(x, y, z) = -\frac{8}{3}z + xy$$

must be computed at P_1. The matrix of the linearization is

$$\begin{bmatrix} -10 & 10 & 0 \\ 1 & -1 & -\sqrt{8(b-1)/3} \\ \sqrt{8(b-1)/3} & \sqrt{8(b-1)/3} & -8/3 \end{bmatrix}.$$

The eigenvalues of this matrix are the roots of the following polynomial:

$$P(\lambda) = 3\lambda^3 + 41\lambda^2 + 8(b+10)\lambda + 160(b-1).$$

There is always one real root. If there is more than one real root, the leftmost one is negative if, as we assume, $b > 1$. A little work with an equation solver shows that b has bifurcation values at $b_1 \approx 1.3457$ and $b_2 \approx 24.737$. This is because at b_1 two of the roots become complex with negative real parts, and so the critical point remains stable. At b_2 the complex roots change to having positive real parts, so the critical point becomes unstable. Since one root is still negative in this latter case, there are initial conditions that have solutions that converge to the critical point P_1. But the volume of such initial points is zero, and so the vast majority of solutions diverge from the critical point. Nevertheless, all solutions must stay inside the ellipsoid discussed previously. Exactly the same conclusions hold for P_2.

For values of b greater than b_2, we must have some kind of attractor that is not a point, for we have examined all the critical points and they are unstable. The attractor could be, and sometimes is, a periodic orbit. On the other hand, the attractor may be a much more complex set. This is the case for $b = 28$. Another indication of the complexity of this attractor is given by plotting one of the components of a solution that is approaching the attractor. Figure 7.20 shows the graph of $x(t)$ for one such solution. Notice the chaotic nature of this behavior. When $x(t)$ crosses the t-axis seems random, and the number of oscillations on either side before crossing seems random also. It is conceivable that this image is a part of some immensely complex periodic behavior. It is beyond the scope of this book to prove that a given attractor is or is not a periodic orbit, so we shall be content with what we have been able to uncover using our graphical, numerical, and analytical tools.

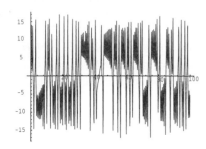

FIGURE 7.20

EXERCISES 7.6

Exercises 1–4 refer to the system

$$x' = 10(-x + y),$$
$$y' = bx - y - xz,$$
$$z' = -\frac{8}{3}z + xy$$

and the 3 × 3Auton package.

1. Use the initial conditions $(2, 2, 2)$, $(2, -2, 2)$, and $(-2, -2, -2)$ and the interval $[0, 30]$ for t. With these conditions, plot the orbits for the following values of the parameter b: 0.1, 0.5, 0.9, and 1.1. What part of the discussion of the Lorenz system does this reflect?

2. Use the initial conditions $(2, 2, 2)$, $(2, -2, 2)$, and $(-2, -2, -2)$ and the interval $[0, 30]$ for t. With these conditions, plot the orbits for the following values of the parameter b: 1.2, 1.3, 1.5, and 3. What part of the discussion of the Lorenz system does this reflect? Does the graphing suggest the emergence of complex eigenvalues with negative real parts at the critical points P_1 and P_2?

3. Use the initial conditions $(2, 2, 2)$, $(2, -2, 2)$, and $(-2, -2, -2)$ and the interval $[0, 50]$ for t. With these conditions, plot the orbits for the following values of the parameter b: 22, 23, 24, and 28. What part of the discussion of the Lorenz system does this reflect?

4. Derive the linearizations of the given Lorenz system at

the points P_1 and P_2, where $b > 1$.

5. Verify that the characteristic polynomial of the linear system for P_1 is as stated in the text.

The following exercises explore the system

$$x' = -y - z,$$
$$y' = x + ay,$$
$$z' = 3 + z(x - 6)$$

using 3 × 3Auton. This is called the Rossler system. For certain values of the parameter a, it has an interesting attractor. You will need to play with scales and viewpoints to get a good idea of the behavior. Use a step of at least 0.05 and a time interval of $[0, 200]$ or even longer.

6. Draw orbits for values $a = 0.2$ and 0.25 and initial condition $(0, 0, 0)$. What causes you to believe that the solutions are approaching a periodic solution?

7. Draw and compare orbits for values $a = 0.2$ and 0.3 using the initial condition $(0, 0, 0)$. Do these appear to approach closed (periodic) orbits? If so, how do you think the periods are related approximately?

8. Slowly increase a from 0.3 to 0.5. Describe what happens. Describe the attractor approached by the orbits with initial conditions $(0, 0, 0)$ and $(1, 1, 1)$.

9. In your favorite computer algebra system, write a Runge-Kutta routine to approximate solutions to the Rossler sys-

tem. Make plots of the $x(t)$ component as you increase a from 0.2. Confirm that the period appears to double be-

fore a more chaotic behavior ensues.

SUPPLEMENTARY EXERCISES FOR CHAPTER 7

1. Show that for the equation $y' = y(a - y^2)$ the flows are equivalent for $a = 1$ and $a = 2$.

2. It is a fact that a 2×2 autonomous system cannot exhibit chaotic behavior. Justify this! *Hint:* Compare the way that orbits can behave in the plane with the way that

orbits can behave in three dimensions or higher.

3. Find (library?) an autonomous 3×3 system different from the Lorenz or Rossler systems that exhibits chaotic behavior. Carry out an analysis of this system similar to the one carried out in the text for the Lorenz system.

CHAPTER 8

THE LAPLACE TRANSFORM

8.1 INTRODUCTION

In this chapter you will be introduced to an alternative method for solving constant-coefficient linear differential equations and linear systems. The method is called the Laplace transform. Why another method for problems that we already know how to solve? The Laplace transform method allows us to deal with discontinuous forcing functions in mechanical and electrical applications in an elegant way. In addition, it will provide an easy way to find particular solutions for nonhomogeneous equations. It will take a little preparation before the usefulness of the Laplace transform will be apparent.

Imagine, if you will, the following scenario. Might it be possible to take a differential equation and transform it into some kind of algebraic equation, solve that equation, and transform back to the solution to the differential equation? We have in mind a transformation machine that takes a function $g(t)$ and produces a new function of s, say $\hat{g}(s)$. We want this machine to take derivatives of $g(t)$ and turn them into expressions in s and $\hat{g}(s)$. Moreover, it is desirable that the machine should transform the sum of functions into the sum of the transforms of these functions, and it should transform $cg(t)$ into $c\hat{g}(s)$. In short, the machine should be linear. Given these conditions, if the transform machine is applied to a linear constant-coefficient differential equation in the function $g(t)$, the result will be an equation in s and $\hat{g}(s)$.

For example, suppose that $g'(t)$ is transformed into $s\hat{g}(s) - g(0)$, and the transformation is also linear. Then the differential equation

$$g'(t) + 2g(t) = 0$$

would transform into

$$s\hat{g}(s) - g(0) + 2\hat{g}(s) = 0.$$

But this could be solved algebraically for $\hat{g}(s)$ to get

$$\hat{g}(s) = \frac{g(0)}{s+2}.$$

If we assume that our transformation machine works in reverse, then we could reverse it to get $g(t)$.

To understand where we might find such a machine, recall the method of integration by parts. The product differentiation formula is

$$(fg)' = f'g + fg',$$

so

$$fg' = (fg)' - f'g.$$

Integrating, we get the integration by parts formula

$$\int fg' \, dt = fg - \int f'g \, dt.$$

The key observation is that integration by parts has the effect of moving the derivative on one function in a product onto the other. If g is the function that we want to transform and $f(t) = e^{-st}$, then we have the formula

$$\int e^{-st} g'(t) \, dt = e^{-st} g(t) + s \int e^{-st} g(t) \, dt.$$

However, the result still involves terms containing the variable t. This is resolved by using an improper integral instead of just the antiderivative. We try integrating over $[0, \infty)$. The result is

$$\int_0^\infty e^{-st} g'(t) \, dt = e^{-st} g(t)|_0^\infty + s \int_0^\infty e^{-st} g(t) \, dt.$$

The first term on the right is

$$e^{-st} g(t)|_0^\infty = \lim_{t \to \infty} e^{-st} g(t) - g(0),$$

and if we assume $s > 0$, the limit will be zero if $g(t)$ does not grow too rapidly. Assuming this, we have the formula

$$\int_0^\infty e^{-st} g'(t) \, dt = s \int_0^\infty e^{-st} g(t) \, dt - g(0).$$

The transformation machine is defined by

$$g(t) \to \hat{g}(s),$$

where

$$\hat{g}(s) = \int_0^\infty e^{-st} g(t) \, dt.$$

Think of $g(t)$ as the input to the machine and $\hat{g}(s)$ as the output. This machine does just what we want with the derivative of a function as input. The output is an expression in s and $\hat{g}(s)$.

Here is the formal definition of the Laplace transform.

Definition 8.1.1

Let $g(t)$ be a continuous function on $[0, \infty)$. The Laplace transform of g, $\mathcal{L}(g)(s)$ or $\hat{g}(s)$, is defined by

$$\mathcal{L}(g)(s) = \hat{g}(s) = \int_0^\infty e^{-st} g(t) \, dt. \qquad\bullet$$

If the function g increases too rapidly, the Laplace transform of it will not exist because the integral will not be defined. However, suppose that

$$|g(t)| \le M e^{at}$$

for some constant M and some positive a. Then

$$|\hat{g}(s)| = \left| \int_0^\infty e^{-st} g(t) \, dt \right| \le \int_0^\infty e^{-st} |g(t)| \, dt \le M \int_0^\infty e^{(a-s)t} \, dt,$$

and this will be finite if $s > a$. Notice that the Laplace transform of g is not necessarily defined on all of $(0, \infty)$. For the moment we shall ignore this odd fact. The functions that satisfy $|g(t)| \le M e^{at}$ are said to be of **exponential growth**. We shall see that the functions we shall transform are all of exponential growth.

For emphasis, the effect of the Laplace transform on differentiation is derived again.

$$\widehat{g'}(s) = \int_0^\infty e^{-st} g'(t) \, dt = e^{-st} g(t)|_0^\infty + s \int_0^\infty e^{-st} g(t) \, dt.$$

We assume that g and g' are of exponential growth. In this case, the integrals exist (if s is large enough), and

$$e^{-st} g(t)|_0^\infty = -g(0).$$

Therefore,

$$\widehat{g'}(s) = s\hat{g}(s) - g(0).$$

Here is a theorem summarizing the effect of the transform on differentiation.

Theorem 8.1.2

Let g and g' be of exponential growth. Then

$$\widehat{g'}(s) = s\hat{g}(s) - g(0). \qquad\bullet$$

This property extends to higher derivatives. For example,

$$\widehat{g''}(s) = s\widehat{g'} - g'(0) = s(s\hat{g}(s) - g(0)) - g'(0) = s^2\hat{g}(s) - sg(0) - g'(0).$$

Note how the initial values at $t = 0$ are built into the transform. The complete generalization of this is left as an exercise.

It is important to notice that the Laplace transform is linear as we required of our machine. Indeed,

$$\mathcal{L}(af + bg)(s) = \int_0^\infty e^{-st}(af(t) + bg(t))\, dt = a\hat{f}(s) + b\hat{g}(s).$$

Another important fact is highlighted in the following theorem.

Theorem 8.1.3

The Laplace transform of continuous functions is one to one. That is, distinct continuous functions have distinct transforms. ●

This property allows us to reverse the transform machine to recover the solution to the original differential equation.

This theorem is not easy to prove, so we accept it as given. We shall have occasion to take transforms of discontinuous functions. On this wider class of functions, the Laplace transform is not precisely one to one. However, functions that have the same transform cannot differ where they are continuous. This will not bother us, and we may treat the two functions with the same transform as the same.

If $\hat{f}(s) = g(s)$, we say that $f(t)$ is the **inverse transform** of g. We shall write

$$\mathcal{L}^{-1}(g)(t) = f(t)$$

for this inverse.

Here are two conversions of differential equations into algebraic equations by the Laplace transform. Note the linearity of the equations and the linearity of the Laplace transform.

Example 8.1.4   If the Laplace transform is applied to

$$y' - 2y = 0,$$

we get

$$s\hat{y}(s) - y(0) - 2\hat{y}(s) = 0.$$

The transform of 0 is obviously 0. We can solve for $\hat{y}(s)$ to get

$$\hat{y}(s) = \frac{y(0)}{s - 2}.$$

If we knew which function had transform

$$\frac{1}{s-2},$$

we could get the solution.

We know what the solution is. It is ce^{2t}. So the following computation is to be expected:

$$\widehat{e^{2t}}(s) = \int_0^\infty e^{-st} e^{2t}\, dt = \int_0^\infty e^{(2-s)t}\, dt = \frac{1}{2-s} e^{(2-s)t}|_0^\infty = \frac{1}{s-2},$$

if $s > 2$. Thus the solution is the function (unique) whose transform is

$$\hat{y} = \frac{y(0)}{s-2}.$$

It is

$$y(t) = y(0)e^{2t}.$$

In the next example the variable s will be left out of $\hat{y}(s)$.

Example 8.1.5 We apply the Laplace transform to

$$y'' - y' + 3y = e^{2t}$$

to get

$$s^2\hat{y} - sy(0) - y'(0) - (s\hat{y} - y(0)) + 3\hat{y} = \widehat{e^{2t}}(s).$$

The transform of e^{2t} was calculated previously, so the transformed equation is

$$s^2\hat{y} - sy(0) - y'(0) - (s\hat{y} - y(0)) + 3\hat{y} = \frac{1}{s-2}.$$

Solving for $\hat{y}$ gives

$$\hat{y} = \frac{1}{(s-2)(s^2 - s + 3)} + \frac{(s-1)y(0) + y'(0)}{s^2 - s + 3}.$$

If we knew the function whose transform is the function on the right, then we would have the solution.

This introduction has shown that a linear constant-coefficient differential equation can be converted by the Laplace transform into an algebraic equation. This equation can be solved for the transformed function $\hat{y}$. If we can find the function whose transform is $\hat{y}$, the problem is solved. Clearly, finding the inverse transform of an expression is of central importance. This task is the major part of the rest of this chapter.

Linear systems of differential equations can be transformed into algebraic systems of equations in the transformed unknowns just as we have done for one equation. The reader is asked to perform this transformation in the exercises.

EXERCISES 8.1

1. Transform the following equations, and solve for $\hat{y}$.
   (a) $2y' + 3y = 4$. You will have to find the transform of 4.
   (b) $y'' + 3y' - y = 0$.

2. What is $\mathcal{L}(y^{(3)})(s)$? Generalize to $\mathcal{L}(y^{(n)})(s)$.

3. Transform $y^{(3)} - y'' + 4y = e^t$, and solve for $\hat{y}$. You will need to find the transform of e^t.

4. Apply the Laplace transform to the system
$$x' = 2x - 3y$$
$$y' = x - 4y.$$

   Solve for $\hat{x}$ and $\hat{y}$.

5. Find the Laplace transform of the following functions.
   (a) $f(t) = e^{at}$.
   (b) $f(t) = t$. You will need to integrate by parts.

6. Find the Laplace transform of the following functions.
   (a) $f(t) = t^2$. You will need to integrate by parts.

   (b) $f(t) = \sin(t)$. You will need to integrate by parts.

7. Find the Laplace transform of the following functions.
   (a) $f(t) = t^3$. You will need parts.
   (b) $f(t) = \cos(t)$. You will need parts.

8. Suppose that $\mathcal{L}(f)(s) = 1/s^2$ and $\mathcal{L}(g)(s) = 1/(s^2 + 4)$. Then what is $\mathcal{L}(3f + 2g)(s)$?

9. Suppose that $\mathcal{L}(f)(s) = 2/s^3$ and $\mathcal{L}(g)(s) = 3s/(s^2 + 9)$. Then what is $\mathcal{L}(5f - 2g)(s)$?

10. Find the Laplace transform of
$$f(t) = \begin{cases} 0 & \text{if } 0 \le t < 2, \\ 1 & \text{if } 2 \le t. \end{cases}$$

11. Find the Laplace transform of
$$f(t) = \begin{cases} t & \text{if } 0 \le t < 2, \\ -1 & \text{if } 2 \le t. \end{cases}$$

8.2 TRANSFORMS OF BASIC FUNCTIONS

In this section we shall derive the Laplace transforms of certain basic functions. It will turn out that the $\hat{y}$ that arise from transforming differential equations can be expressed in terms of sums of these basic transforms. This is the key to finding inverse transforms.

Since the Laplace transform is the integral of a product of functions, integration by parts will be central to many of the calculations that follow. There is a nice extension of the basic parts formula to repeated integrations by parts. Here is how it works.

The basic integration by parts formula is

$$\int uv' \, dt = uv - \int u'v \, dt.$$

If we set $f = u$, $g = v'$, and use g_i to denote an integral or antiderivative of g, the formula becomes

$$\int fg \, dt = fg_i - \int f'g_i \, dt.$$

If we apply this formula to $\int f'g_i \, dt$, we get

$$\int fg \, dt = fg_i - f'g_{ii} + \int f''g_{ii} \, dt.$$

This can be carried on indefinitely, and we wonder if there is an easy way to write down the parts formula repeated, say, ten times. There is! Set up two columns with f heading the first and g heading the second. In the first column, write down successive derivatives of f, in order, to the required depth. In the second column, write down successive antiderivatives of g to the same depth. To calculate the integral of the product fg, take fg_i, then subtract $f'g_{ii}$, then add $f''g_{iii}$, and so on, until the bottom row in f is next to be used. Add or subtract, as the turn dictates, the integral of the product of the bottom row. Here is the case of three repetitions of parts.

The table is as follows:

$$\begin{array}{cc} f & g \\ f' & g_i \\ f'' & g_{ii} \\ f''' & g_{iii} \end{array}$$

The integral of the product is

$$\int fg \, dt = fg_i - f'g_{ii} + f''g_{iii} - \int f'''g_{iii} \, dt.$$

We now derive the basic transform formulas as a series of examples. The results will be summarized in the table that follows the next examples.

Example 8.2.1   Let n be a nonnegative integer. We use parts to compute

$$\mathcal{L}(t^n)(s) = \int_0^\infty e^{-st}t^n \, dt.$$

The table is the result of parts n times.

$$\begin{array}{cc} t^n & e^{-st} \\ nt^{n-1} & \dfrac{-e^{-st}}{s} \\ n(n-1)t^{n-2} & \dfrac{e^{-st}}{s^2} \\ \vdots & \vdots \\ n! & \dfrac{\pm e^{-st}}{s^n} \end{array}$$

Now all integrals and terms in the parts formula are to be evaluated from 0 to ∞, so all terms of the form $e^{-st}t^k$ for $k \neq 0$ will evaluate to zero. Thus

$$\mathcal{L}(t^n)(s) = \int_0^\infty e^{-st}t^n \, dt = -\frac{n!}{s^n} \int_0^\infty e^{-st} \, dt = \frac{n!}{s^{n+1}}. \qquad \blacksquare$$

The next example shows again how useful complex numbers can be. We shall need to take the transform of complex-valued functions. The question is whether we can take transforms of complex-valued functions. The answer is that we can with no changes whatsoever. The only requirement is that the complex functions be of exponential growth as before. As with the derivative, one integrates complex-valued functions by integrating the real and imaginary parts. The reader can verify that all the rules of integrating complex functions are the same as for real functions, just as we did with differentiation. Thus integration by parts remains unchanged.

Example 8.2.2   We want the transforms $\mathcal{L}(e^{at}\sin(bt))$ and $\mathcal{L}(e^{at}\cos(bt))$. The reader will agree that the integration by parts will be a little complicated. However, if we recall the relationships

$$e^{at}\sin(bt) = \frac{e^{(a+bi)t} - e^{(a-bi)t}}{2i} \qquad \text{and} \qquad e^{at}\cos(bt) = \frac{e^{(a+bi)t} + e^{(a-bi)t}}{2},$$

and remember that the Laplace transform is linear, we can get the results that we want by transforming $e^{(a+bi)t}$ and $e^{(a-bi)t}$.

This is how it goes. Set $z = a + bi$ for brevity.

$$\mathcal{L}(e^{zt}) = \int_0^\infty e^{-st}e^{zt}\,dt = \int_0^\infty e^{-(s-z)t}\,dt.$$

But the integration here is easy, or you could use the formula derived previously with s replaced by $(s - z)$. We have

$$\mathcal{L}(e^{(a+bi)t}) = \frac{1}{(s - (a + bi))}.$$

Similarly,

$$\mathcal{L}(e^{(a-bi)t}) = \frac{1}{(s - (a - bi))}.$$

Using the linearity, we have

$$\mathcal{L}(e^{at}\sin(bt)) = \frac{1}{2i}\left[\frac{1}{(s - (a + bi))} - \frac{1}{(s - (a - bi))}\right].$$

Forming a common denominator and simplifying gives

$$\mathcal{L}(e^{at}\sin(bt)) = \frac{b}{(s - a)^2 + b^2}.$$

Similarly,

$$\mathcal{L}(e^{at}\cos(bt)) = \frac{s - a}{(s - a)^2 + b^2}. \qquad \blacksquare$$

Take note of the special cases of these formulas when $a = 0$. Also note the formula for the transform of $t^n e^{at}$ when $n = 0$. We now have the following short table of transforms.

$f(t)$	1	t	t^n	$\sin(bt)$	$\cos(bt)$	$e^{at}\sin(bt)$	$e^{at}\cos(bt)$	e^{at}
$\mathcal{L}(f)(s)$	$\frac{1}{s}$	$\frac{1}{s^2}$	$\frac{n!}{s^{n+1}}$	$\frac{b}{s^2+b^2}$	$\frac{s}{s^2+b^2}$	$\frac{b}{(s-a)^2+b^2}$	$\frac{s-a}{(s-a)^2+b^2}$	$\frac{1}{s-a}$

If you examine this table, you will notice that if $f(t)$ has transform $g(s)$ then $e^{at} f(t)$ has transform $g(s - a)$. This is a general principle called the **first shifting theorem**.

Theorem 8.2.3   (First Shifting)

If f is of exponential growth, then

$$\mathcal{L}(e^{at} f(t))(s) = \mathcal{L}(f)(s - a). \qquad \bullet$$

The proof of this theorem is very simple, so it is left to the exercises.

You will notice that we have calculated the transforms of almost all the fundamental solutions to homogeneous equations. However, certain solutions are missing. Indeed, solutions of the form $t^k e^{at} \sin(bt)$ and $t^k e^{at} \cos(bt)$ are missing. The first shifting theorem allows us to obtain the transforms of these from the transforms of $t^k \sin(bt)$ and $t^k \cos(bt)$. It is possible to use integration by parts to get recursion formulas for the latter, but they are messy to use. We shall be content computing the transform of $te^{at} \sin(bt)$.

Example 8.2.4   To get the transform of $te^{at} \sin(bt)$, we first find the transform of $t \sin(bt)$. We have

$$t \sin(bt) = \frac{te^{ibt} - te^{-ibt}}{2i}.$$

We can use the first shifting theorem on each exponential to get

$$\mathcal{L}(t \sin(bt))(s) = \frac{1}{2i}\left[\frac{1}{(s - ib)^2} - \frac{1}{(s + ib)^2}\right] = \frac{2bs}{[s^2 + b^2]^2}.$$

From this we get

$$\mathcal{L}(te^{at} \sin(bt))(s) = \frac{2b(s - a)}{[(s - a)^2 + b^2]^2}. \qquad \blacksquare$$

With the transforms already assembled, the first shifting theorem, and the linearity of the Laplace transform, we can transform very complicated expressions. Here is an example.

Example 8.2.5   Let

$$f(t) = 3t^2 e^{2t} + e^{3t} \sin(2t) - 4t^4.$$

Then the Laplace transform is

$$\hat{f}(s) = \frac{6}{(s-2)^3} + \frac{2}{(s-3)^2 + 4} - \frac{96}{s^5}.$$ ∎

We have been concerned in this section with finding the Laplace transform of relatively simple functions and expressions. This process can be reversed to find the inverse Laplace transform if the expression is not too complicated. The problem of finding inverse transforms is examined in greater depth in the next section. Here is a simple example to close this section.

Example 8.2.6   Finding the inverse Laplace transform of

$$\frac{6}{(s-4)^3} - \frac{4s}{s^2 + 25}$$

can be achieved by considering which functions had to be transformed to get the two terms. First, $6/s^3 = 3 \cdot 2/s^3$, and so this came from $3t^2$. But the term involves $(s-4)$, not just s, so we must use the first shifting theorem and include the factor e^{4t}. The second term is the transform of $4\cos(5t)$, so the inverse transform is

$$3t^2 e^{4t} - 4\cos(5t).$$ ∎

EXERCISES 8.2

1. Find the Laplace transforms of the following functions.
   (a) $\mathcal{L}(t^5)$
   (b) $\mathcal{L}(e^{at})$
   (c) $\mathcal{L}(e^{at} t^5)$
2. Find the Laplace transforms of the following functions.
   (a) $\mathcal{L}(t^4 e^{2t})$
   (b) $\mathcal{L}(te^{3t} \cos(5t))$
3. Compute $\mathcal{L}(\sin(bt))$ directly from the definition. *Hint:* Carry out integration by parts until the bottom line of the table has $\sin(bt)$ in the product. Write down the parts

formula at this depth, and solve for the unknown integral.
4. Compute $\mathcal{L}(\cos(bt))$ directly from the definition. *Hint:* Carry out integration by parts until the bottom line of the table has $\cos(bt)$ in the product. Write down the parts formula at this depth, and solve for the unknown integral.
5. What is the Laplace transform of $t^2 + te^{2t} + \sin(3t)$?
6. What is the Laplace transform of $3t^3 e^{5t} + e^{2t} + e^{4t} \sin(3t)$?
7. What function has transform $\frac{3}{s-1} + \frac{1}{s^2+1}$?
8. What function has transform $\frac{3}{s-4} + \frac{2}{s^2+4}$?
9. What function has transform $\frac{3}{s^3} + \frac{s}{s^2+1}$?

10. What function has transform $\frac{3}{(s-1)^2} + \frac{s-1}{(s-1)^2+1}$?

11. What is the inverse Laplace transform of $\frac{s}{(s-1)(s+2)}$? *Hint:* Use partial fractions to write the expression as a sum of terms whose inverse transforms can be found in the table.

12. Find the transform of $t^2 \cos(3t)$. *Hint:* Use the complex form and the first shifting theorem.

13. Find the transform of $t^2 e^{2t} \sin(t)$. *Hint:* As for Exercise 12.

14. Prove Theorem 8.2.3. *Hint:* Just write out the definition of the left side of the equation.

8.3 SOLVING LINEAR HOMOGENEOUS EQUATIONS

We are now in a position to solve second-order, linear, constant-coefficient, homogeneous equations by means of the Laplace transform. We point out again that this is not the point of the Laplace transform, for we can solve these equations practically in our heads. This section is a first step in understanding the properties and applications of the Laplace transform.

Consider the equation

$$y'' - 2y' - 3y = 0.$$

Taking the Laplace transform of both sides yields

$$s^2 \hat{y} - s y_0 - y_1 - 2(s\hat{y} - y_0) - 3\hat{y} = 0,$$

where $y_0 = y(0)$ and $y_1 = y'(0)$ are the initial conditions.

Now solve for $\hat{y}$ to get

$$\hat{y} = \frac{(s-2)y_0 + y_1}{s^2 - 2s - 3} = \frac{(s-2)y_0 + y_1}{(s+1)(s-3)}.$$

The strategy at this point is to use partial fractions to break up the right hand side into a sum of constants times terms whose inverse transforms can be read from the table. The section that follows reviews the method of partial fractions.

8.3.1 Partial Fractions

The object of partial fractions decompositions is to decompose a quotient of polynomials, $P(s)/Q(s)$, into a sum of terms of the following forms. For linear factors of $Q(s)$, the form is

$$\frac{A_1}{(s-r_i)} + \frac{A_2}{(s-r_i)^2} + \cdots + \frac{A_n}{(s-r_i)^n},$$

where $(s-r_i)^n$ is the power of the $(s-r_i)$ factor in the factorization of $Q(s)$. For irreducible quadratic factors of $Q(s)$, the form is

$$\frac{A_1 s + B_1}{(as^2 + bs + c)} + \frac{A_2 s + b_2}{(as^2 + bs + c)^2} + \cdots + \frac{A_n s + B_n}{(as^2 + bs + c)^n},$$

where $(as^2+bs+c)^n$ is the power of the irreducible quadratic factor (as^2+bs+c) in $Q(s)$.

You should recall that we must long divide first if we can, and then the remaining quotient of polynomials to which partial fractions is to be applied must have all common factors canceled out.

After the quotient has been written as a sum of the previous forms, then the constants are determined by recombining the terms of the right-hand side, writing the numerator on the right in standard form, and then equating coefficients. This yields linear equations in the constants A_i and B_i. These are then solved.

The wordiness of this description should be dispelled by the following example.

Example 8.3.1   Consider

$$\frac{s^4}{s^4 - 2s^3 + 2s^2 - 2s + 1}.$$

We can long divide, so we must. We get

$$\frac{s^4}{s^4 - 2s^3 + 2s^2 - 2s + 1} = 1 + \frac{2s^3 - 2s^2 + 2s - 1}{s^4 - 2s^3 + 2s^2 - 2s + 1}.$$

The task now is to expand

$$\frac{2s^3 - 2s^2 + 2s - 1}{s^4 - 2s^3 + 2s^2 - 2s + 1}$$

in partial fractions. We factor the denominator by noting that $(s - 1)$ is a factor. The result is

$$\frac{2s^3 - 2s^2 + 2s - 1}{s^4 - 2s^3 + 2s^2 - 2s + 1} = \frac{2s^3 - 2s^2 + 2s - 1}{(s - 1)^2(s^2 + 1)}.$$

Now $(s - 1)$ and $(s^2 + 1)$ are not factors of the numerator, so no cancellation is possible. The decomposition is

$$\frac{2s^3 - 2s^2 + 2s - 1}{s^4 - 2s^3 + 2s^2 - 2s + 1} = \frac{A}{s - 1} + \frac{B}{(s - 1)^2} + \frac{Cs + D}{s^2 + 1}.$$

Recombining and collecting like powers of s give

$$\frac{2s^3 - 2s^2 + 2s - 1}{s^4 - 2s^3 + 2s^2 - 2s + 1} = [(A + C)s^3 + (-A + B - 2C + D)s^2$$
$$+ (A + C - 2D)s + (-A + B + D)]/[s^4 - 2s^3 + 2s^2 - 2s + 1].$$

The numerators are identical, and so the coefficients of the powers of s must be the same; so we get the equations

$$
\begin{array}{rcrcrcrcr}
A & & & + & C & & & = & 2, \\
-A & + & B & - & 2C & + & D & = & -2, \\
A & & & + & C & - & 2D & = & 2, \\
-A & + & B & & & + & D & = & -1.
\end{array}
$$

We leave the reader to solve these equations. The solution is $A = 3/2$, $B = 1/2$, $C = 1/2$, and $D = 0$. Thus the complete solution to the problem is

$$
\frac{s^4}{s^4 - 2s^3 + 2s^2 - 2s + 1} = 1 + \frac{(3/2)}{s-1} + \frac{(1/2)}{(s-1)^2} + \frac{(1/2)s}{s^2 + 1}. \qquad \blacksquare
$$

8.3.2 Homogeneous Equations

Let us return to the first equation of this section:

$$
y'' - 2y' - 3y = 0.
$$

The transform of the solution was

$$
\hat{y} = \frac{(s-2)y_0 + y_1}{s^2 - 2s - 3} = \frac{(s-2)y_0 + y_1}{(s+1)(s-3)}.
$$

We now use partial fractions to break up the right-hand side. Thus

$$
\frac{(s-2)y_0 + y_1}{(s+1)(s-3)} = \frac{A}{s+1} + \frac{B}{s-3} = \frac{A(s-3) + B(s+1)}{(s+1)(s-3)}.
$$

Therefore,

$$
\begin{array}{rcrcl}
A & + & B & = & y_0, \\
-3A & + & B & = & -2y_0 + y_1.
\end{array}
$$

Then

$$
A = \frac{3y_0 - y_1}{4},
$$

and

$$
B = \frac{y_0 + y_1}{4}.
$$

Then

$$
\hat{y} = \frac{3y_0 - y_1}{4} \frac{1}{s+1} + \frac{y_0 + y_1}{4} \frac{1}{s-3},
$$

and so the solution is

$$
y(t) = \frac{3y_0 - y_1}{4} e^{-t} + \frac{y_0 + y_1}{4} e^{3t}.
$$

One more example should make the procedure clear.

Example 8.3.2   Consider

$$y'' - 2y' + 2y = 0$$

with the initial conditions $y_0 = y(0) = 1$ and $y_1 = y'(0) = 2$. Taking the Laplace transform gives

$$s^2\hat{y} - s - 2 - 2(s\hat{y} - 1) + 2\hat{y} = 0,$$

and so

$$\hat{y} = \frac{s}{s^2 - 2s + 2}.$$

Note that the roots of the denominator are complex, so the denominator cannot be factored further in the real numbers. Stop! Do not try partial fractions here because the result is already decomposed into partial fractions! If the denominator has only one factor (irreducible if quadratic), the fraction is already in partial fractions form.

The problem is that if we look in the transform table we do not find any denominator with with $s^2 - 2s + 2$ in it. If this were an integration problem, we would complete the square. That works here, too.

$$s^2 - 2s + 2 = (s - 1)^2 + 1.$$

If we get everything in terms of the unit $(s - 1)$, we have

$$\hat{y} = \frac{(s - 1) + 1}{(s - 1)^2 + 1} = \frac{s - 1}{(s - 1)^2 + 1} + \frac{1}{(s - 1)^2 + 1}.$$

Now the inverse transforms can be found in the table. The solution is

$$y(t) = e^t \cos(t) + e^t \sin(t).$$ ■

Before leaving this section you should note that the final step in solving for $\hat{y}$ is to divide through by a polynomial in s. This polynomial is, of course, the characteristic polynomial of the equation. It is also clear that the way that the characteristic polynomial factors (the eigenvalues!) has a direct effect on the nature of the solution.

EXERCISES 8.3

In Exercises 1–3, decompose the given term into partial fractions.

1. $\dfrac{s}{(s^2 - 2s + 1)(s + 2)}$

2. $\dfrac{s^2}{(s^2 + s + 1)(s - 2)}$

3. $\dfrac{s^3 - 1}{(s + 3)(s + 2)}$

4. Use the Laplace transform to solve $y'' + 3y' + 2y = 0$, where $y(0) = 2$ and $y'(0) = 3$.

5. Use the Laplace transform to find the general solution to

$$y'' - 2y' + y = 0.$$

6. Use the Laplace transform to find the solution to $y''+y = 0$, where $y(0) = 1$ and $y'(0) = 2$.

7. Use the Laplace transform to find the solution to $y''+y'+ y = 0$, where $y(0) = 1$ and $y'(0) = 2$.

8. Use the Laplace transform to solve $y'' + 2y' + y = t$, where $y(0) = 1$ and $y'(0) = -1$. Yes, it is nonhomogeneous, but you proceed exactly as before.

9. Use the Laplace transform to solve $y'' + y = \sin(t)$, where $y(0) = 1$ and $y'(0) = -1$. You will get the term $1/(s^2 + 1)^2$. To deal with this, write it as

$$\frac{1}{(s - i)^2(s + i)^2},$$

use partial fractions, and recombine using Euler's formula to get the real result.

8.4 NONHOMOGENEOUS EQUATIONS AND THE CONVOLUTION

In this section we shall see some of the effectiveness of the Laplace transform. We shall use the transform to find particular solutions to nonhomogeneous equations. We shall see that this is more efficient than previous methods. Moreover, transform methods provide an integral formula for the particular solution into which one may plug the nonhomogeneous part of the equation. In a sense, one formula fits all.

The strategy for finding a particular solution to

$$ay'' + by' + cy = g(t)$$

is as follows. First, take the initial conditions to be $y(0) = 0$ and $y'(0) = 0$. Then take the transform. In this case the initial data drop out. So

$$as^2\hat{y} + bs\hat{y} + c\hat{y} = \hat{g}(s)$$

and

$$\hat{y} = \frac{\hat{g}(s)}{as^2 + bs + c}.$$

Then use partial fraction decomposition to find the inverse transform. There is nothing new here.

Example 8.4.1   Find a particular solution to

$$y'' - 3y' + 2y = e^{2t}.$$

We have

$$\hat{y}_p(s) = \frac{1}{(s - 1)(s - 2)^2} = \frac{A}{s - 1} + \frac{B}{s - 2} + \frac{C}{(s - 2)^2}.$$

The constants are $A = 1$, $B = -1$, and $C = 1$. So the particular solution is

$$y_p(t) = e^t - e^{2t} + te^{2t}.$$

The first two terms may be absorbed in the homogeneous solution; thus the general solution can be written as

$$y(t) = te^{2t} + a_1e^t + a_2e^{2t}. \qquad \blacksquare$$

It may have occurred to you to ask what to do if it is not possible to find the Laplace transform of g. This is answered in the next section.

8.4.1 The Convolution

In finding a particular solution to

$$ay'' + by' + cy = g(t),$$

we first find the transform of g and then find the inverse transform of the product

$$\frac{1}{as^2 + bs + c} \hat{g}(s).$$

It may be hard or impossible to find a formula for the transform of g, and it may prove difficult or impossible to use partial fractions on the product. In this section we resolve these problems in a unifying way.

We are tempted to ask if the inverse transform of the product is the product of the inverse transforms. This is the same as asking if the transform of a product is the product of the transforms. If this were the case, our problem would dissolve. Unfortunately, it is false. However, there is a different kind of product, called the **convolution product**, for which the statement is true. We arrive at this product by studying the product of two transformed functions.

We have

$$\hat{f}(s)\hat{g}(s) = \int_0^\infty e^{-sx} f(x)\, dx \int_0^\infty e^{-sw} g(w)\, dw.$$

This can be written as a double integral:

$$\hat{f}(s)\hat{g}(s) = \int_0^\infty \int_0^\infty e^{-s(x+w)} f(x)g(w)\, dw\, dx.$$

Change variables by setting $w = t - x$; then

$$\hat{f}(s)\hat{g}(s) = \int_0^\infty \int_x^\infty e^{-st} f(x)g(t-x)\, dt\, dx.$$

You should note that the region of integration is the upper part of the first quadrant divided by the line $t = x$. If the order of integration is changed, then

$$\hat{f}(s)\hat{g}(s) = \int_0^\infty \int_0^t e^{-st} f(x)g(t-x)\, dx\, dt = \int_0^\infty e^{-st} \int_0^t f(x)g(t-x)\, dx\, dt.$$

But this is the Laplace transform of the function of t

$$\int_0^t f(x)g(t-x)\, dx.$$

The following definition is now called for.

Definition 8.4.2

Let $f(t)$ and $g(t)$ be functions of exponential growth. We define

$$(f \star g)(t) = \int_0^t f(x)g(t - x)\, dx.$$

The function $f \star g$ is called the convolution product of f and g or, briefly, the convolution. ●

It is easy to show that the convolution is of exponential growth, and so it has a Laplace transform. The argument leading to the definition of the convolution gives the important formula

$$\mathcal{L}(f \star g)(s) = \hat{f}(s)\hat{g}(s).$$

That is, the Laplace transform of a convolution product is the product of the transforms of the factors in the convolution.

The convolution gives an easy way to find a particular solution for the non-homogeneous equation

$$ay'' + by' + cy = g(t).$$

Take the transform with zero initial conditions to get

$$\hat{y}(s) = \frac{1}{as^2 + bs + c}\hat{g}(s).$$

Let

$$\mathcal{L}^{-1}(\frac{1}{as^2 + bs + c})(t) = f(t).$$

Then

$$y(t) = (f \star g)(t) = \int_0^t f(x)g(t - x)\, dx.$$

The function f, which is the inverse transform of the reciprocal of the characteristic polynomial, is called the **transfer function**.

Here is an example.

Example 8.4.3
Find a particular solution to

$$y'' + y = \sin(t).$$

The transfer function is

$$\mathcal{L}^{-1}\left(\frac{1}{s^2 + 1}\right) = \sin(t).$$

So a particular solution to the equation is given by

$$y_p(t) = \int_0^t \sin(x)\sin(t - x)\, dx = \frac{1}{2}\int_0^t [\cos(2x - t) - \cos(t)]\, dx.$$

So

$$y_p(t) = \frac{1}{2}[\sin(2x - t) - x\cos(t)]|_0^t = \frac{1}{2}[\sin(t) - t\cos(t)].$$

The $\sin(t)$ can be dropped since it is part of the homogeneous solution.   ∎

Here is another example in which the Laplace transform of the right-hand side is difficult or impossible to compute.

Example 8.4.4   We solve

$$y'' + 2y' + y = \ln(t + 1).$$

The transfer function is

$$\mathcal{L}^{-1}(\frac{1}{(s + 1)^2}) = te^{-t}.$$

The particular solution is

$$y_p(t) = \int_0^t xe^{-x} \ln(t - x + 1)\, dx.$$

The reader may complain that this is all well and good, but the integral cannot be evaluated. True. But we can approximate this integral for any value of t as closely as we like. Indeed, it would be easy to write a program to evaluate this integral for as many discrete values of t as we please.   ∎

An important point to note is that, for a given equation, once the transfer function has been determined, the particular solution is also determined by

$$y_p(t) = \int_0^t f(x)g(t - x)\, dx,$$

regardless of what the g might be. The program alluded to in Example 8.4.4 could be written to accept any g as input. Contrast this with the method of undetermined coefficients. In that case the method will have to be run through each time that g is changed. In this sense, one size fits all.

Here is a final example of the convolution method.

Example 8.4.5   Find a particular solution to

$$(D - 1)(D - 2)^2 y = t^2.$$

The transfer function is

$$\mathcal{L}^{-1}(\frac{1}{(s - 1)(s - 2)^2}) = \mathcal{L}^{-1}\left(\frac{1}{s - 1} + \frac{-1}{(s - 2)} + \frac{1}{(s - 2)^2}\right) = e^t - e^{2t} + te^{2t}.$$

The particular solution is

$$y_P(t) = \int_0^t (e^x - e^{2x} + xe^{2x})(t - x)^2 \, dx,$$

and after a long integration by parts we get

$$y_P(t) = -\frac{11}{8} - t - \frac{t^2}{4} + 2e^t - \frac{5}{8}e^{2t} + \frac{t}{4}e^{2t}.$$

The last three terms may be dropped since they are solutions to the homogeneous equation. ∎

EXERCISES 8.4

For the equations in Exercises 1–3, use the Laplace transform and partial fractions to find a particular solution and then write the general solution.

1. $(D^2 + 2D + 2)y = e^t$
2. $(D - 1)(D - 2)y = t^2$
3. $(D - 1)Dy = t$

For the equations in Exercises 4–6, use the convolution to find a particular solution.

4. $(D^2 + 2D + 1)y = e^t$.
5. $(D - 1)(D - 2)y = t^2$
6. $(D + 1)^2(D - 2)y = t$

7. Use the convolution to find a particular solution to

$$y'' + 2y' + y = \sqrt{t^2 + 1}.$$

You will have to leave the answer in integral form.

Find the Laplace transform of the functions in Exercises 8–11.

8. $f(t) = \int_0^t e^x(t - x) \, dx$
9. $f(t) = \int_0^t \sin(x)\cos(t - x) \, dx$
10. $f(t) = \int_0^t (e^x - 2e^{2x})(t - x)^2 \, dx$
11. $f(t) = \int_0^t x^2(t - x)^3 \, dx$
12. Prove that $f \star g = g \star f$.
13. Prove that $f \star (g \star h) = (f \star g) \star h$.

8.5   DISCONTINUOUS AND IMPULSIVE FORCING FUNCTIONS

Consider a simple mass–spring system where a mass is suspended by a spring. Suppose that there is friction and a forcing function acting on the mass. We have seen that the differential equation modeling this system is

$$my'' + cy' + ky = F(t),$$

where m is the mass, c is the friction constant, and k is the spring constant. Now consider the possibility that the force F is not continuous. For example, the forcing function might be as shown in Figure 8.1.

One approach to solving this would be to solve

$$my'' + cy' + ky = F(t)$$

to the left of 2, applying initial conditions at $t = 0$. Then find the value of the

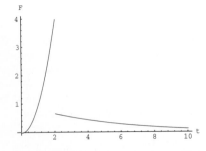

FIGURE 8.1

solution and its derivative at $t = 2$ to act as new initial conditions, and then solve

$$my'' + cy' + ky = F(t)$$

for $t > 2$. Clearly, this is a time-consuming procedure, which could be much worse if $F(t)$ is more complicated and has more discontinuities.

We shall see that the Laplace transform provides a much more elegant approach to this type of problem. However, to use the transform, we shall have to take the transform of discontinuous functions.

8.5.1 Transforms of Discontinuous Functions

We shall assume that the functions to be transformed will have only a finite number of points of discontinuity on any finite interval and that at each point of discontinuity the left and right limits of the function exist. We shall continue to assume that the functions are of exponential growth. Such functions are often said to be **piecewise continuous functions of exponential growth**.

The special discontinuous function defined next will be found useful in describing and transforming discontinuous functions.

Definition 8.5.1

The function $u_a(t)$ defined by

$$u_a(t) = \begin{cases} 0, & \text{if } t \le a, \\ 1, & \text{if } t > a. \end{cases}$$

is called a **unit step function** or the Heaviside step function.   ●

The function in Figure 8.1 is actually defined by

$$F(t) = \begin{cases} 0, & \text{if } t \le 0, \\ t^2, & \text{if } 0 < t < 2, \\ e^{-t/5}, & \text{if } 2 < t < \infty. \end{cases}$$

Using unit step functions, this can be written as

$$F(t) = [u_0(t) - u_2(t)]t^2 + u_2 e^{-t/5}.$$

Expressions of this sort can be transformed using the following theorem.

Theorem 8.5.2

$$\mathcal{L}(u_a(t)f(t - a))(s) = e^{-as}\mathcal{L}(f)(s).$$ ●

Proof

We have

$$\mathcal{L}(u_a(t)f(t-a))(s) = \int_0^\infty e^{-st} u_a(t)f(t-a)\,dt = \int_a^\infty e^{-st} f(t-a)\,dt.$$

The substitution $x = t - a$ gives

$$\mathcal{L}(u_a(t)f(t-a))(s) = \int_0^\infty e^{-s(x+a)} f(x)\,dx = e^{-as} \int_0^\infty e^{-sx} f(x)\,dx. \quad \blacklozenge$$

The function $u_a(t)f(t-a)$ is the translation of f set to zero until a is reached. This theorem is called the **second shifting theorem**.

Example 8.5.3   Find the transform of

$$F(t) = [u_0(t) - u_2(t)]t^2 + u_2 e^{-t/5}.$$

We must get the unit $t - 2$ into the expression. Now, $t = (t - 2) + 2$, so

$$\begin{aligned}
F(t) &= u_0(t)t^2 - u_2(t)[(t-2)+2]^2 + u_2(t)e^{-((t-2)+2)/5} \\
&= u_0(t)t^2 - u_2(t)(t-2)^2 - 4u_2(t)(t-2) - 4u_2(t) \\
&\quad + e^{-2/5}u_2(t)e^{-(t-2)/5}.
\end{aligned}$$

Therefore, by the theorem we have

$$\hat{F}(s) = \frac{2}{s^3} - e^{-2s}\frac{2}{s^3} - 4e^{-2s}\frac{1}{s^2} - 4e^{-2s}\frac{1}{s} + e^{-2/5}e^{-2s}\frac{1}{s-(1/5)}. \quad \blacksquare$$

Example 8.5.4   Find the inverse transform of

$$\hat{F}(s) = \frac{e^{-5s}}{(s-1)(s^2+1)}.$$

By partial fractions,

$$\hat{F}(s) = \frac{1}{2}\frac{e^{-5s}}{s-1} - \frac{1}{2}\frac{e^{-5s}s}{s^2+1} - \frac{1}{2}\frac{e^{-5s}}{s^2+1}.$$

Therefore,

$$F(t) = \frac{u_5(t)e^{(t-5)}}{2} - \frac{u_5(t)\cos(t-5)}{2} - \frac{u_5(t)\sin(t-5)}{2}. \quad \blacksquare$$

Let us try the Laplace transform on a concrete example of a mass–spring system with a discontinuous forcing function.

Example 8.5.5   Solve

$$y'' + y = F(t),$$

where

$$F(t) = \begin{cases} 0, & \text{if } t \le 0, \\ t, & \text{if } 0 < t < 10, \\ 0, & \text{if } 10 < t < \infty, \end{cases} \quad .$$

and the initial conditions are zero.

Rewrite $F(t)$ as follows:

$$\begin{aligned} F(t) &= [u_0(t) - u_{10}(t)]t = u_0(t)t - u_{10}(t)[(t-10)+10] \\ &= u_0(t)t - u_{10}(t)(t-10) - 10u_{10}(t). \end{aligned}$$

The transform of F is

$$\hat{F}(s) = \frac{1}{s^2} - \frac{e^{-10s}}{s^2} - \frac{10e^{-10s}}{s}.$$

Therefore,

$$\hat{y}(s) = \frac{\hat{F}(s)}{s^2 + 1},$$

and so

$$\hat{y}(s) = \frac{1}{s^2(s^2+1)} - \frac{e^{-10s}}{s^2(s^2+1)} - \frac{10e^{-10s}}{s(s^2+1)}.$$

The partial fractions decomposition is very simple. We get

$$y(t) = u_0(t)[t - \sin(t)] - u_{10}(t)[t - 10 - \sin(t-10)] - 10u_{10}(t)[1 - \cos(t-10)].$$

This simplifies to

$$y(t) = [u_0(t) - u_{10}(t)]t - \sin(t) + u_{10}(t)\sin(t-10) + 10u_{10}(t)\cos(t-10).$$

The term $[u_0(t) - u_{10}(t)]t$ is "on" for $0 < t < 10$ and "off" otherwise. The term $\sin(t)$ is "on" for $t > 0$, and the terms $u_{10}(t)\sin(t-10)$ and $10u_{10}(t)\cos(t-10)$ are only "on" for $t > 10$.   ■

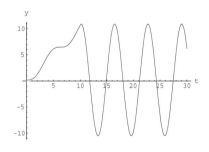

FIGURE 8.2

The graph of the solution for this example is shown in Figure 8.2.

Two remarks about this example are in order. First, notice the oscillation in the first 10 units, say seconds, of time. This is mildly surprising, since the force being applied starts at zero and is steadily increased with no oscillatory component of its own. However, a direct solution of the equation with t as the forcing function will give the same solution for the first 10 seconds. After 10 seconds the mass executes simple harmonic motion. This is also to be expected from the physics of the situation. So we see that the Laplace transform has correctly modeled this problem. No attempt will be made to prove that the Laplace transform correctly models a general mechanical system or electrical circuit with discontinuous forcing functions.

Second, this problem could have been solved by using the convolution. To use the convolution in this problem, it is convenient to note that

$$f \star g = g \star f.$$

The reason this is convenient is that

$$\int_0^t \sin(x) F(t - x) \, dx$$

is more difficult to evaluate than

$$\int_0^t F(x) \sin(t - x) \, dx.$$

In the latter we simply break the problem into two parts: $t < 10$ and $t \geq 10$. We leave it to the reader to show that the result obtained is the same as in the example.

The reader may be disturbed by one point. Clearly, the second derivative of the solution in the preceding example cannot be defined at 10. After all, the force is discontinuous there. Indeed, our method does not produce a solution to the differential equation in the strict sense in which we have defined "solution." It does, however, provide an elegant way of solving the physical problem that results in the required "piecewise solutions" pieced together correctly. In a sense, we are obtaining physical solutions that generalize our more restricted notion of a differential equation and its solution. This suggests that the mathematical notion of a differential equation and solution should be broadened. This can and has been done in what are called the theories of distributions or generalized functions.

8.5.2 Impulse Functions

Consider again our simple mass–spring system. Suppose that the mass is struck with a hammer. The force produced by the blow is sharp, but of short-duration. If the hardness of the hammer and the massive object are increased, then the duration of the blow will decrease and the maximum value of the force will increase. Let us further suppose that the hammer comes to rest at the end of the blow, thus imparting all its momentum to the mass. Such short duration forces that impart a given momentum to an object are called **impulses**. Figure 8.3 shows a diagram of idealized impulsive forces of shorter and shorter duration,

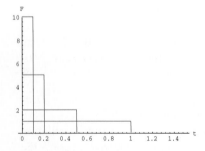

FIGURE 8.3

but having the same area under the curve. Indeed, the integral over time of a force gives the change in momentum imparted by this force. To see this, integrate the force. We have

$$\int_a^b F(t)\, dt = \int_a^b my''(t)\, dt = my'(b) - my'(a).$$

The latter is the change in momentum.

These impulses can be defined by

$$F_n(t) = \begin{cases} 0, & \text{if } t \le 0, \\ n, & \text{if } 0 < t < 1/n, \\ 0, & \text{if } 1/n < t < \infty. \end{cases}$$

What is the limit of these functions as n goes to infinity? The limit is a function that is zero everywhere except at zero, where it is infinite. This is the perfect impulse of zero duration and imparting 1-unit change in momentum to the system. But the function that we have described has zero for its integral over time, since it is zero everywhere except at zero. No! You cannot get out of it by defining $\infty 0 = 1$, because if we set up another sequence of impulses imparting 2 units of momentum you would have to conclude that $\infty 0 = 2$, and so $1 = 2$. The physics is telling us that we need a new concept here. The ordinary notion of a real-valued function cannot model our notion of a perfect impulse.

Let us use the symbol $\delta(t)$ to stand for this perfect or unit impulse. How can it be defined mathematically? We can only give a vague description of one of the ways in which it is defined. One approach is to define $\delta(t)$ to be the sequence $\{F_n(t)\}$ that led to the unit impulse in the first place. To work with this definition, if you want to perform a certain operation on $\delta(t)$, you perform it on each of the $F_n(t)$ in the sequence and take the limit as n goes to infinity.

This is how this approach works if you apply the Laplace transform to $\delta(t)$.

$$\mathcal{L}(F_n)(s) = \int_0^\infty e^{-st} F_n(t)\, dt = \int_0^{1/n} n e^{-st}\, dt = \frac{1 - e^{-s/n}}{s/n}.$$

Taking the limit as n goes to infinity yields $0/0$, so we use L'Hôpital's rule.

$$\mathcal{L}(\delta(t))(s) = \lim_{n \to \infty} \frac{1 - e^{-s/n}}{s/n} = \lim_{n \to \infty} \frac{e^{-s/n}/n^2}{1/n^2} = 1.$$

Thus the transform of $\delta(t)$ is 1.

If a unit impulse is applied to the mass–spring system, the formal equation of the dynamics is

$$my'' + cy' + ky = \delta(t).$$

Assume that the system is initially at rest. When the unit impulse is applied at $t = 0$, the mass acquires 1 unit of momentum; so its velocity at $t = 0$ instantly becomes $1/m$, while the displacement is 0. The subsequent motion is that of the homogeneous system with these initial conditions. Does the Laplace transform yield the same result as this physical argument? The answer is yes, and here is an example.

Example 8.5.6 Verify that the Laplace transform gives the same result as the physical argument for the equation

$$4y^2 + y = \delta(t).$$

We assume that the system is at rest (zero initial conditions). The transform is

$$\hat{y}(s) = \frac{1}{4s^2 + 1} = \frac{1}{2} \frac{(1/2)}{s^2 + (1/2)^2}.$$

So the solution is

$$y(t) = \frac{1}{2} \sin(t/2),$$

and the derivative is

$$y'(t) = \frac{1}{4} \cos(t/2).$$

The initial conditions satisfied by this impulse solution are those predicted by the physical argument. ∎

Because the transform of δ is 1, this suggests that

$$\mathcal{L}(\delta \star g)(s) = 1\hat{g}(s) = \hat{g}(s),$$

and so this suggests that

$$\delta \star g = g.$$

This is valid if it makes sense to take the convolution of δ with a function. It does, and we make sense out of it in the same way as we made sense out of the Laplace transform of δ. We have

$$(\delta \star g)(t) = \lim_{n \to \infty} (F_n \star g)(t) = \lim_{n \to \infty} \int_0^{1/n} ng(t - x) \, dx$$

for $t > 0$. Indeed, for $t > 0$, if n is large enough, $1/n < t$, and so we get the preceding integral. By the mean value theorem for integrals,

$$\int_0^{1/n} ng(t - x) \, dx = \frac{1}{n} ng(t - \bar{x}) = g(t - \bar{x}),$$

where $0 < \bar{x} < 1/n$. So, as n goes to infinity, the integral approaches $g(t)$, since we assume that g is continuous at t.

We often refer to δ as the **convolution identity**.

Once we know the response of a system at rest (zero initial conditions) to a unit impulse, we know the response of the system to any applied force. Indeed, the response to the impulse is the transfer function. The convolution of the transfer function with any applied force gives a particular solution. Now just throw in the homogeneous solution to get the general solution. So to discover everything one wants to know about a system, whack it with a hammer!

We conclude this section with an example illustrating the incorporation of nonzero initial data.

Example 8.5.7   Consider the equation

$$y'' - y = F(t),$$

where

$$F(t) = \begin{cases} 0, & \text{if } t \le 1, \\ t, & \text{if } 1 < t < \infty, \end{cases}$$

and $y(0) = 2$ and $y'(0) = -1$. If we are going to use partial fractions as our method of solution, we include the initial data in the usual way. Here is how it goes.

The Laplace transform of the solution uses the second shifting theorem. The result is

$$\hat{y}(s) = \frac{1}{2}\frac{1}{s-1} + \frac{3}{2}\frac{1}{s+1} - \frac{e^{-s}}{s} - \frac{e^{-s}}{s^2} + \frac{e^{-s}}{s-1},$$

so the solution is

$$y(t) = \frac{e^t}{2} + \frac{3}{2}e^{-t} - u_1(t)[t - e^{t-1}].$$

If we use the convolution, it is convenient to use it in the form

$$f \star g(t) = g \star f(t) = \int_0^t g(x)f(t-x)\,dx.$$

The transfer function is

$$f(t) = \frac{1}{2}e^t - \frac{1}{2}e^{-t},$$

so the integral is

$$y_p(t) = \frac{1}{2}\int_0^t xu_1(x)[e^{t-x} - e^{-t+x}]\,dx.$$

Because $F(t) = u_1(t)t$, we will have to consider the integral in two cases: $0 < t < 1$ and $1 < t$. In the first case, $u_1(x) = 0$, so the integral is zero. In the second case, $u_1(x) = 1$ for $x > 1$, so the integral is

$$y_p(t) = \frac{1}{2}\int_1^t x[e^{t-x} - e^{-t+x}]\,dx.$$

After two easy integrations by parts, we get

$$y_p(t) = -t + e^{t-1}.$$

The two cases can now be neatly combined as

$$y_p(t) = -u_1(t)[t - e^{t-1}].$$

The convolution approach so far has ignored the initial conditions. To deal with the initial conditions, we simply throw in the homogeneous solution to get the general solution and solve for the two constants using the initial conditions. Thus

$$y(t) = c_1 e^t + c_2 e^{-t} - u_1(t)[t - e^{t-1}].$$

The particular solution is "off" until 1 is reached, so in solving for the constants we may ignore it. We have

$$c_1 + c_2 = 2,$$
$$c_1 - c_2 = -1,$$

and so $c_1 = 1/2$ and $c_2 = 3/2$. These values yield the same solution found by partial fractions. ∎

EXERCISES 8.5

1. Solve $y'' - 3y' + 2y = F(t)$, where

$$F(t) = \begin{cases} 0, & \text{if } t \le 2, \\ 2, & \text{if } 2 < t < \infty, \end{cases}$$

and $y(0) = 1$ and $y'(0) = -1$:
   (a) By using partial fractions.
   (b) By using the convolution.

2. Solve $y'' + y = F(t)$, where

$$F(t) = \begin{cases} 0, & \text{if } t \le 2, \\ 1, & \text{if } 2 < t < 5, \\ 0, & \text{if } 5 < t < \infty, \end{cases}$$

and $y(0) = 1$ and $y'(0) = -1$:
   (a) By using partial fractions.
   (b) By using the convolution.

3. Solve $y'' + y = F(t)$, where

$$F(t) = \begin{cases} 0, & \text{if } t \le 2, \\ t^2, & \text{if } 2 < t < \infty, \end{cases}$$

and $y(0) = 1$ and $y'(0) = 2$, by the convolution method.

4. Solve $y'' + y = F(t)$, where

$$F(t) = \begin{cases} 1, & \text{if } t \le 2, \\ e^t, & \text{if } 2 < t < \infty, \end{cases}$$

and $y(0) = 1$ and $y'(0) = 2$ by the convolution method.

5. The transfer function is the solution to $ay'' + by' + cy = \delta(t)$ with $y(0) = 0$ and $y'(0) = 0$. Show that this is the same as the solution to the homogeneous equation with $y(0) = 0$ and $y'(0) = 1/a$.

6. Find the transfer function for $y'' - 3y' + 2y = F(t)$ without using partial fractions by using Exercise 5.

7. Solve $y^{(3)} - y' = u_2(t)$, where $y(0) = 0$, $y'(0) = 0$, and $y''(0) = 1$, using the convolution.

In Exercises 8-10, use the convolution to find a particular solution to the given equations.

8. $y^{(3)} + 2y'' - y' - 2y = tu_2(t)$

9. $y'' - y' - 2y = tu_5(t)$

10. $y'' + 2y' + y = t^3 u_2(t)$

11. An impulse could be applied at a later time t_0. Define a unit impulse at this later time in terms of a sequence of impulses. Denote it by $\delta(t - t_0)$. What is the Laplace transform of $\delta(t - t_0)$?

12. Solve $y'' + y = 2\delta(t-3)$, where $y(0) = 1$ and $y'(0) = 0$. Give a physical interpretation of the solution in terms of a mass on a spring.

13. Solve $2y'' + y = 4\delta(t - \pi)$, where $y(0) = 0$ and $y'(0) = 1$. Give a physical interpretation of the solution in terms of a mass on a spring.

14. Solve $5y'' + y = 4\delta(t-1)$, where $y(0) = 0$ and $y'(0) = 1$. Give a physical interpretation of the solution in terms of a mass on a spring.

8.6   LAPLACE TRANSFORMS AND SYSTEMS

The main point about the Laplace transform is that it converts linear differential equations into algebraic equations. Therefore, it is reasonable to assume that the method will be just as effective on systems of linear differential equations as it was on a single equation. Here is an example showing the method.

Example 8.6.1   Solve the following system:

$$x' = x + y + t,$$
$$y' = x - y.$$

Since we will use the Laplace transform, we must have initial conditions, so set $x(0) = 1$ and $y(0) = 0$. Applying the transform gives

$$s\hat{x} - 1 = \hat{x} + \hat{y} + \frac{1}{s^2},$$
$$s\hat{y} - 0 = \hat{x} - \hat{y}.$$

We solve these equations for $\hat{x}$. The result is

$$\hat{x}(s) = \frac{s^3 + s^2 + s + 1}{(s^2 - 2)s^2}.$$

Partial fractions yield

$$\hat{x}(s) = \frac{3(\sqrt{2}+1)}{4\sqrt{2}} \frac{1}{s - \sqrt{2}} + \frac{3(\sqrt{2}-1)}{4\sqrt{2}} \frac{1}{s + \sqrt{2}} - \frac{1/2}{s} - \frac{1/2}{s^2}.$$

Taking the inverse transform gives

$$x(t) = \frac{3(\sqrt{2}+1)}{4\sqrt{2}} e^{\sqrt{2}t} + \frac{3(\sqrt{2}-1)}{4\sqrt{2}} e^{-\sqrt{2}t} - \frac{1}{2} - \frac{1}{2}t.$$

You can solve for $y(t)$ by substitution in the first equation or by solving for $\hat{y}$ and inverting. We recommend the former in this case.   ∎

This example illustrates the method applied to a first-order system. However, it is worth observing that systems of higher-order linear equations can be dealt with using the transform without reduction to first order.

Example 8.6.2 Solve the following system.

$$D^2x + Dy = t,$$
$$(D + 1)x + y = 0.$$

For simplicity, assume that all initial conditions are zero. Taking transforms gives

$$s^2\hat{x} + s\hat{y} = \frac{1}{s^2},$$
$$(s + 1)\hat{x} + \hat{y} = 0.$$

Solving for $\hat{x}$ gives

$$\hat{x}(s) = -\frac{1}{s^3},$$

and so

$$\hat{y}(s) = \frac{s + 1}{s^3} = \frac{1}{s^2} + \frac{1}{s^3}.$$

Therefore, the solutions are

$$x(t) = -\frac{1}{2}t^2,$$

and

$$y(t) = t + \frac{1}{2}t^2. \qquad \blacksquare$$

In solving higher-order systems the required initial conditions sometimes give us pause. However, the Laplace transform tells us what the appropriate initial conditions are immediately. We will need initial values on the unknown functions and their derivatives up to one less than the highest derivative of that unknown occurring.

You may be wondering if there are equivalent notions to those of a transfer function and convolution in the case of systems. We answer this next.

8.6.1 Transfer Matrices and Matrix Convolutions

We shall consider first-order systems only. However, this is no restriction since all constant coefficient linear systems can be reduced to first-order systems. In order that the notation not get out of hand, we shall restrict our attention to 2×2 systems.

Consider the following first-order system in matrix form.

$$\begin{bmatrix} x' \\ y' \end{bmatrix} = \begin{bmatrix} a_{11} & a_{12} \\ a_{21} & a_{22} \end{bmatrix} \begin{bmatrix} x \\ y \end{bmatrix} + \begin{bmatrix} F_1(t) \\ F_2(t) \end{bmatrix}.$$

Explicitly, the equations are

$$x' - a_{11}x - a_{12}y = F_1(t),$$
$$-a_{21}x + y' - a_{22}y = F_2(t).$$

Let the initial conditions be $x(0) = x_0$ and $y(0) = y_0$. Taking the Laplace transform of the equations gives

$$s\hat{x} - x_0 - a_{11}\hat{x} - a_{12}\hat{y} = \hat{F}_1(s),$$
$$-a_{21}\hat{x} + s\hat{y} - y_0 - a_{22}\hat{y} = \hat{F}_2(s).$$

This can be rewritten in matrix form as

$$\begin{bmatrix} s - a_{11} & -a_{12} \\ -a_{21} & s - a_{22} \end{bmatrix} \begin{bmatrix} \hat{x} \\ \hat{y} \end{bmatrix} = \begin{bmatrix} \hat{F}_1(s) \\ \hat{F}_2(s) \end{bmatrix} + \begin{bmatrix} x_0 \\ y_0 \end{bmatrix}.$$

Now let $B(s) = (b_{ij}(s))$ be the inverse of the matrix

$$\begin{bmatrix} s - a_{11} & -a_{12} \\ -a_{21} & s - a_{22} \end{bmatrix}.$$

Multiplying through by $B(s)$ gives

$$\begin{bmatrix} \hat{x} \\ \hat{y} \end{bmatrix} = \begin{bmatrix} b_{11}(s) & b_{12}(s) \\ b_{21}(s) & b_{22}(s) \end{bmatrix} \begin{bmatrix} \hat{F}_1(s) \\ \hat{F}_2(s) \end{bmatrix} + \begin{bmatrix} b_{11}(s) & b_{12}(s) \\ b_{21(s)} & b_{22}(s) \end{bmatrix} \begin{bmatrix} x_0 \\ y_0 \end{bmatrix}.$$

Multiply out the matrices to get

$$\begin{bmatrix} \hat{x} \\ \hat{y} \end{bmatrix} = \begin{bmatrix} b_{11}(s)\hat{F}_1(s) + b_{12}(s)\hat{F}_2(s) \\ b_{21}(s)\hat{F}_1(s) + b_{22}(s)\hat{F}_2(s) \end{bmatrix} + \begin{bmatrix} b_{11}(s)x_0 + b_{12}(s)y_0 \\ b_{21}(s)x_0 + b_{22}(s)y_0 \end{bmatrix}.$$

Now take the inverse transforms of the equations determined by this matrix equation. The inverse transform of every product can be replaced by the equivalent convolution. All this can be summarized in the following way: Let $C(t) = (c_{ij}(t))$ be the matrix obtained from $B(s)$ by taking the inverse transform of each of its entries. To form the convolution of this matrix with a column matrix, use the convolution product as the operation, but multiply in the usual way. The solution is

$$\begin{bmatrix} x(t) \\ y(t) \end{bmatrix} = \begin{bmatrix} c_{11}(t) & c_{12}(t) \\ c_{21}(t) & c_{22}(t) \end{bmatrix} \star \begin{bmatrix} F_1(t) \\ F_2(t) \end{bmatrix} + \begin{bmatrix} c_{11}(t) & c_{12}(t) \\ c_{21}(t) & c_{22}(t) \end{bmatrix} \begin{bmatrix} x_0 \\ y_0 \end{bmatrix}.$$

The matrix $C(t)$ is called the **transfer matrix** for this system. Find the transfer matrix and the system is solved, in principle, for any inhomogeneous terms and any initial conditions. Here is an example.

Example 8.6.3 Solve the system

$$\begin{bmatrix} x' \\ y' \end{bmatrix} = \begin{bmatrix} 1 & -1 \\ -2 & 2 \end{bmatrix} \begin{bmatrix} x \\ y \end{bmatrix} + \begin{bmatrix} 1 \\ t \end{bmatrix}$$

with the initial conditions $x(0) = 1$ and $y(0) = -1$. The matrix we must invert is

$$\begin{bmatrix} s-1 & 1 \\ 2 & s-2 \end{bmatrix}.$$

The inverse is

$$\begin{bmatrix} \frac{s-2}{s(s-3)} & \frac{-1}{s(s-3)} \\ \frac{-2}{s(s-3)} & \frac{s-1}{s(s-3)} \end{bmatrix}.$$

We now take the inverse transform of each entry in this last matrix. The transfer matrix $C(t)$ is

$$\begin{bmatrix} \frac{2}{3} + \frac{1}{3}e^{3t} & \frac{1}{3} - \frac{1}{3}e^{3t} \\ \frac{2}{3} - \frac{2}{3}e^{3t} & \frac{1}{3} + \frac{2}{3}e^{3t} \end{bmatrix}.$$

The solution is given by

$$\begin{bmatrix} x(t) \\ y(t) \end{bmatrix} = \begin{bmatrix} \frac{2}{3} + \frac{1}{3}e^{3t} & \frac{1}{3} - \frac{1}{3}e^{3t} \\ \frac{2}{3} - \frac{2}{3}e^{3t} & \frac{1}{3} + \frac{2}{3}e^{3t} \end{bmatrix} \star \begin{bmatrix} 1 \\ t \end{bmatrix} + \begin{bmatrix} \frac{2}{3} + \frac{1}{3}e^{3t} & \frac{1}{3} - \frac{1}{3}e^{3t} \\ \frac{2}{3} - \frac{2}{3}e^{3t} & \frac{1}{3} + \frac{2}{3}e^{3t} \end{bmatrix} \begin{bmatrix} 1 \\ -1 \end{bmatrix}.$$

The solutions for $x(t)$ and $y(t)$ are

$$x(t) = \int_0^t \frac{2}{3} + \frac{1}{3}e^{3x} \, dx + \int_0^t (\frac{1}{3} - \frac{1}{3}e^{3x})(t-x) \, dx + (\frac{2}{3} + \frac{1}{3}e^{3t}) - (\frac{1}{3} - \frac{1}{3}e^{3t}),$$

$$y(t) = \int_0^t \frac{2}{3} - \frac{2}{3}e^{3x} \, dx + \int_0^t (\frac{1}{3} + \frac{2}{3}e^{3x})(t-x) \, dx + (\frac{2}{3} - \frac{2}{3}e^{3t}) - (\frac{1}{3} + \frac{2}{3}e^{3t}).$$

These integrals can be easily evaluated. ∎

The method illustrated in the example can be extended to first-order systems of any size. Moreover, the forcing functions do not need to be continuous, nor is it necessary to be able to find simple transforms for the forcing functions. However, for larger systems the transfer matrix can become very complicated, and the convolution integrals can become impossible to evaluate in closed form. This is not a hopeless situation. In the first case, computer algebra systems such as Mathematica and Maple can find the inverse of matrices of the type we are dealing with very effectively. In addition, these systems can find the inverse transforms of the entries in the inverted matrices. In the second case, the evaluation of the convolution integrals can be done numerically.

EXERCISES 8.6

1. Use the Laplace transform to solve the system

$$Dx + D^2y = t,$$
$$x - Dy = 0,$$

where the initial conditions are $x(0) = 0$, $y(0) = 0$, and $y'(0) = 1$.

2. Use the Laplace transform and partial fractions to solve the system

$$(D - 1)x + Dy = 0,$$
$$x - D^2y = 0,$$

where the initial conditions are $x(0) = 1$, $y(0) = 0$, and $y'(0) = 1$.

3. Use the Laplace transform to solve the system

$$Dx = -y + t,$$
$$Dy = x,$$

where the initial conditions are $x(0) = 0$ and $y(0) = 0$:

(a) By the partial fractions procedure.

(b) By the transfer matrix.

4. Use the Laplace transform and the transfer matrix to solve the system

$$Dx = 2x - y + t,$$
$$Dy = x - 1,$$

where the initial conditions are $x(0) = 1$, $y(0) = 0$, and $y'(0) = 1$.

5. Find the transfer matrix for the system

$$Dx = x - y + \sin(t),$$
$$Dy = x.$$

Write down the form of the solution in terms of the transfer matrix, the convolution, and the initial condition. Write down the convolution integrals, but do not integrate.

6. Find the transfer matrix for the system

$$Dx = x - 6y + e^t,$$
$$Dy = -2x + 2y - t.$$

Write down the form of the solution in terms of the transfer matrix, the convolution, and the initial condition. Write down the convolution integrals, but do not integrate.

7. Solve $(D^2 + 1)y = \delta(t) + t$ by reducing to a first-order system and using the transfer matrix. Take $y(0) = y_0$ and $y'(0) = y_1$ for initial conditions.

8. Solve $(D^2 + 1)y = F(t)$, where **(a)** $F(t) = \sin(t)$, **(b)** $F(t) = 3t$, and **(c)** $F(t) = 4t^3$. Do this by reducing to a first-order system and using the transfer matrix. Take $y(0) = y_0$ and $y'(0) = y_1$ for initial conditions.

9. What initial conditions at $t = 0$ will be needed to get a unique solution to the system

$$D^3x + (D - 1)y + z = e^t,$$
$$x + (D^2 + 1y) + D^2z = -t,$$
$$Dx - Dy + (D - 1)z = 0.$$

10. What initial conditions at $t = 0$ will be needed to get a unique solution to the system

$$D^4x + D^2y + z = e^t,$$
$$Dx + (D^2 + 1y) + D^3z = \sin(t),$$
$$(D^2 - 4)x - Dy + (D - 1)z = 2.$$

8.7 POLES AND QUALITATIVE BEHAVIOR

In this section we shall show how the Laplace transform can be used to give qualitative information about the behavior of solutions to constant-coefficient linear equations even when they are nonhomogeneous.

After the Laplace transform has been taken and the transform of the solution has been solved for, we get an expression of the form

$$\hat{y}(s) = \frac{F(s)}{G(s)},$$

where $G(s)$ is a polynomial. We assume that F and G have no roots in common, because if they do we divide out the common factors. We also assume that $F(s)$ is a polynomial, because if $F(s)$ contains terms of the form e^{as}, they will have come from discontinuities in the forcing function, and we shall see that the conclusions drawn in the following may not hold. The reader will recall that the next step is to factor the denominator and proceed with partial fractions. Now each real root r of $G(s)$ produces a partial fraction that, in turn, yields an exponential term of the form e^{rt} in the solution. The complex roots will be in conjugate pairs, and they will also yield exponential factors in the solution if the real part of the root is not zero. If some roots are pure imaginary, we shall see that no conclusion can be drawn, and the equation will have to be solved to see what is going on. The roots of $G(s)$ are called **poles**.

We summarize what we know so far in a theorem.

Theorem 8.7.1

Suppose, upon taking the Laplace transform of a constant coefficient linear differential equation, that the transform of the solution has the form

$$\hat{y}(s) = \frac{F(s)}{G(s)}$$

and that F and G are polynomials in lowest terms. If all the poles have negative real parts, then the solution converges to zero. If one of the poles has a positive real part, then the solution goes to infinity. If some of the poles are pure imaginary or the forcing function is discontinuous, then the poles alone do not determine the behavior of the solution. ●

The poles are complex numbers in general, so we can think of their location in the complex plane. The theorem says that if all the poles are (strictly) in the left half of the plane then the solution converges to zero. If one pole is in the right half plane, the solution must go to infinity.

The examples that follow first illustrate two applications of the theorem, and then an example of each of the exceptional cases is given.

Example 8.7.2   Consider

$$y'' + 2y' + y = e^{-2t}$$

with initial conditions $y(0) = 0$ and $y'(0) = 1$. We have

$$\hat{y}(s) = \frac{1}{(s+2)(s+1)^2} + \frac{1}{(s+1)^2} = \frac{s+3}{(s+2)(s+1)^2}.$$

The poles are in the left half of the plane, so the solution converges to zero.   ■

Example 8.7.3   Consider

$$y'' - y' - 2y = t^2$$

with initial conditions $y(0) = 1$ and $y'(0) = 0$. We have

$$\hat{y}(s) = \frac{2}{s^3(s+1)(s-2)} + \frac{s}{(s+1)(s-2)} - \frac{1}{(s+1)(s-2)}$$
$$= \frac{-s^3 + s^2 + 2}{s^3(s+1)(s-2)}.$$

This is in lowest terms and one pole is in the right half-plane, so the solution converges to infinity.   ∎

Example 8.7.4   Consider

$$y'' + y = \sin(t)$$

with initial conditions $y(0) = 0$ and $y'(0) = 0$. We have

$$\hat{y}(s) = \frac{1}{(s^2+1)^2}.$$

The poles are $\pm i$. We might be tempted to think that the solution must be bounded, but this is not so. To see this, write the denominator as a product of the complex factors.

$$\hat{y}(s) = \frac{1}{(s-i)^2(s+i)^2}.$$

The partial fractions here will introduce a factor of t into the solution. In short we have resonance.   ∎

This final example shows that if the forcing function is discontinuous then no conclusion can be drawn from the poles.

Example 8.7.5   Consider

$$y'' + 3y' + 2y = [1 - u_2(t)]e^{(t-2)}$$

with initial conditions $y(0) = 0$ and $y'(0) = 0$. We have

$$\hat{y}(s) = \frac{e^{-2}}{(s-1)(s+1)(s+2)} - \frac{e^{-2s}}{(s-1)(s+1)(s+2)}.$$

Clearly, one pole is in the right half-plane, but the solution actually converges to zero. The reason is that the forcing function is "turned off" after 2 units of time. From then on, the solution is obeying the homogeneous equation.   ∎

EXERCISES 8.7

In the exercises that follow you may or may not be able to use the theorem. Nevertheless, answer the question even if you have to carry out partial fractions. Also, where it is appropriate, give a physical interpretation in terms of your expectations as to how a mass–spring system would behave.

Determine the long-term behavior of the solution to the following initial-value problems:

1. $y'' + 3y' + 2y = 0$, with initial conditions $y(0) = 0$ and $y'(0) = 1$

2. $y'' + 3y' + 2y = e^{-t}$, with initial conditions $y(0) = 0$ and $y'(0) = 0$

3. $y'' - 4y' + 5y = 0$, with initial conditions $y(0) = 0$ and $y'(0) = 1$

4. $y'' + y = t$, with initial conditions $y(0) = 1$ and $y'(0) = 0$

5. $y'' + 3y' + 2y = \delta(t)$, with initial conditions $y(0) = 1$ and $y'(0) = 0$

6. $y'' + 3y' + 2y = [1 - u_1(t)]e^t$, with initial conditions $y(0) = 0$ and $y'(0) = 0$

7. $y'' + 3y' + 2y = [1 - u_4(t)]e^{-2t}$, with initial conditions $y(0) = 0$ and $y'(0) = 0$

8. $y'' + y = u_4(t)\sin(t)$, with initial conditions $y(0) = 0$ and $y'(0) = 0$

SUPPLEMENTARY EXERCISES FOR CHAPTER 8

These exercises will lead you through the application of the Laplace transform to periodic functions. Toward the end of these exercises you will discover an interesting and useful phenomenon.

1. Let $f(t)$ be a periodic function of period p. This means that $f(t + p) = f(t)$ for $t \geq 0$. Show that the Laplace transform of f is given by

$$\hat{f}(s) = \frac{1}{1 - e^{-ps}} \int_0^p e^{-st} f(t)\, dt.$$

Hint: Break the Laplace transform integral into an infinite sum of integrals from 0 to p, then from p to $2p$, and so on. At some point you will want to use the formula

$$\frac{1}{1 - x} = \sum_{k=0}^{\infty} x^k.$$

Apply this to $f(t) = \sin(t)$ to test the formula.
Apply the formula to the function of period 2π that is defined in one period by

$$f(t) = \begin{cases} 1, & \text{if } 0 \leq t < \pi, \\ -1, & \text{if } \pi \leq t < 2\pi. \end{cases}$$

2. Solve the initial-value problem

$$y'' + 9y = f(t),$$

$y(0) = 0$, $y'(0) = 0$, where $f(t)$ is the function of period 2π that is defined in Exercise 1. Show that the transform of $f(t)$ can be written in the form

$$\frac{1}{s}[1 - 2e^{-\pi s} + 2e^{-2\pi s} - 2e^{-3\pi s} + 2e^{-4\pi s} - + \cdots].$$

Use this to solve the problem. *Hint:* You will need to consider the solution on intervals of the form $n\pi < t < (n+1)\pi$.

3. Graph the solution in Exercise 2 on $[0, 6\pi]$ by putting together the graphs on the subintervals. Describe the dominant behavior as t gets large. Does this imply that if this were a mechanical system it would tear itself apart?

4. This strange phenomenon is due to the fact that the input square wave $f(t)$ can be regarded as an infinite sum of sines and cosines; that is,

$$f(t) = \sum_{k=0}^{\infty} [a_k \cos(kt) + b_k \sin(kt)].$$

The square wave is like a musical tone that is not pure; it is composed of many pure harmonics added together. The square wave contains a harmonic that is three times the frequency of the square wave. What is the resonance frequency of the preceding system? How does this help to explain the strange phenomenon. For more on this, consult the section on Fourier series in Chapter 9.

CHAPTER 9

PARTIAL DIFFERENTIAL EQUATIONS AND FOURIER SERIES

Up to now we have been concerned with only ordinary differential equations. In this chapter we turn to differential equations in which the unknown function has several variables. The derivatives in such differential equations are necessarily partial derivatives. Naturally, such equations are called partial differential equations. For partial differential equations there appears to be no unifying theme, like first-order systems for ordinary differential equations. Indeed, it is fair to say that partial differential equations are not nearly as well understood as ordinary differential equations. In view of this, we shall be content to study just one technique of solution that can be applied to certain equations that have proved to be important in physics and engineering.

9.1 SOME GENERAL REMARKS

For partial derivatives such as

$$\frac{\partial^2 u}{\partial x^2} \quad \text{and} \quad \frac{\partial^2 u}{\partial x \partial y},$$

we shall often write

$$u_{xx} \quad \text{and} \quad u_{xy}.$$

In defining what is meant by a solution to a partial differential equation, a possible ambiguity presents itself. Consider the equation

$$u_{xy} - u = 0.$$

It is natural to suppose that a solution to this equation is a function $u(x, y)$ of two variables such that, when the mixed partial is taken and the partial and the function inserted in the proper places in the equation, the result is an identity on some region of the x, y-plane. However, it might be the case that a function of three variables was intended for a solution. Although the context will often make clear the number of variables for a solution, it may be necessary to be explicit. Thus we can say that a solution to a partial differential equation is a function of a specified number of variables such that, if the appropriate derivatives are taken and the proper substitutions made, the result is an identity in the specified variables in some region of the space of these variables.

As an example, consider the equation

$$u_{xx} - u_{tt} = 3u.$$

We assume that solutions are of the form $u(x, t)$. The function $u(x, t) = e^{2x}e^t$ is easily seen to be a solution defined throughout the whole x, t-plane.

The next two examples illustrate an essential difference between ordinary and partial differential equations.

Example 9.1.1   Consider solutions to

$$u_x - u = 0$$

that are functions of two variables, say $u(x, y)$. Since only the derivative with respect to x appears, we can solve this by fixing y and treating the equation as ordinary. The solution is

$$u(x, y) = ce^x.$$

The constant c need only be constant with respect to x, so c can be a function of y and we still have a solution. Thus the general solution to this equation is

$$u(x, y) = c(y)e^x,$$

where $c(y)$ can be any function of y.   ∎

If the equation in this example had been an ordinary differential equation, to get a unique solution, we would only need to specify the value of u at a given value of x, for this would determine c. This is just the initial condition. However, as a partial differential equation, to get a unique solution, we need an additional condition that will specify $u(x_0, y)$ for a fixed value of $x = x_0$ and every value of y. This is needed to determine the function $c(y)$. The difference here is between the finite and the infinite. In the ordinary case, only a finite number of pieces of additional information are needed, but in the partial case the number of additional pieces of information is infinite, because we must determine $c(y)$ for each value of y. This difference is striking and it is profound. It makes the study of partial differential equations very challenging.

If we are very lucky, we may be able to solve a partial differential equation directly by integration. Here is an example. Note again the arbitrary functions that must be determined to get a unique solution.

Example 9.1.2   The equation

$$u_{xy} = x,$$

where u is defined in the plane, can be solved by integrating. First, integrate with respect to y to get

$$u_x = xy + g(x).$$

Notice the function $g(x)$, which is constant with respect to the variable of integration. From another point of view, consider

$$u_x - xy.$$

The derivative of this with respect to y is zero, so, in a rectangle at least, this must be independent of y; so it is a function of x only. Thus

$$u_x - xy = g(x).$$

Now integrate with respect to x to get

$$u(x, y) = \frac{x^2 y}{2} + \int g(x)\, dx + h(y).$$

Note that $\int g(x)\, dx$ is the antiderivative of an arbitrary function, so it is arbitrary. The solution can be written as

$$u(x, y) = \frac{x^2 y}{2} + f(x) + h(y)$$

where the functions $f(x)$ and $h(y)$ are arbitrary.   ∎

The difference between ordinary and partial differential equations can be further illustrated by considering reduction to first-order systems in both cases. For an ordinary equation such as

$$y'' - 2y' + y = x^2,$$

the procedure is simple. Set $u = y$ and $v = y'$; then we get

$$u' = v,$$
$$v' = x^2 - u + 2v.$$

Notice that the derivatives of u and v are determined by the values of u and v; so if u and v are known at a point, approximations of u and v are easily made at a nearby point. This is the basis of numerical methods in ordinary differential equations. Contrast this with the reduction of

$$u_{xx} = u_y$$

to a first-order system. We set $u = v$ and $u_x = w$. Then we get the first order system

$$v_x = w,$$

$$w_x = v_y.$$

Notice that we have not been able to express all four first partial derivatives of v and w in terms of v and w alone. Thus approximate values of v and w cannot be constructed at a neighboring point given their values at a given point, as we could in the ordinary case. Indeed, if we could, this would be equivalent to saying that a unique solution to the equation could be selected by specifying a single point. We know that initial data for partial differential equations generally have to be specified at infinitely many points. We shall see that numerical methods for partial differential equations will often require data at several points in order to approximate the solution at a new point.

These remarks should alert you to the fact that the subject of partial differential equations is vastly more subtle than that of ordinary differential equations. But you should not abandon all hope, because certain types of partial differential equations that have proved important in physics and engineering can be solved by a reasonably straightforward procedure called **separation of variables**. Here is a simple example illustrating the idea of the method.

Example 9.1.3   Consider the equation

$$u_x - u_y = 0.$$

Suppose that there is a nonzero solution of the form

$$u(x, y) = X(x)Y(y),$$

where $X(x)$ and $Y(y)$ are differentiable functions. Then we get

$$u_x - u_y = X'Y - XY' = 0.$$

Now divide through by XY to get

$$\frac{X'Y}{XY} - \frac{XY'}{XY} = \frac{X'}{X} - \frac{Y'}{Y} = 0,$$

and so

$$\frac{X'}{X} = \frac{Y'}{Y}.$$

Now the left-hand side is a function of x only, and the right-hand side is a function of y only, so both sides must be constant. So

$$\frac{X'}{X} = \frac{Y'}{Y} = \lambda.$$

From this we get the following pair of ordinary differential equations:

$$X' - \lambda X = 0,$$
$$Y' - \lambda Y = 0.$$

We have been able to trade in a partial differential equation in a function of two variables for a pair of ordinary differential equations that we can solve. The solutions are $X(x) = c_1 e^{\lambda x}$ and $Y(y) = c_2 e^{\lambda y}$. Therefore, we have

$$u(x, y) = c e^{\lambda x} e^{\lambda y} = c e^{\lambda(x+y)}.$$

You can check directly that this is a solution. We have a solution for each choice of c and of λ, so we have a lot of solutions. Furthermore, the sum of two solutions is a solution and any scalar multiple of a solution is a solution (see the exercises). So any linear combination of solutions is a solution. It will be seen in the following sections that enough solutions are produced by this method to do a lot of useful things.   ∎

Since there is nothing approaching a universal method of solution for partial differential equations, it is not surprising that individual partial differential equations often become the object of intensive study. Examples are the heat equation, wave equation, and Laplace's equation. These equations will occupy most of the remainder of this book.

EXERCISES 9.1

1. Show that $u(x, y) = e^x \sin(y)$ is a solution to $u_{xx} + u_{yy} = 0$.

2. Show that $u(x, t) = e^{-t} \cos(x)$ is a solution to $u_{xx} = u_t$.

3. Show that $u(x, t) = e^{-4t} \cos(2x)$ is a solution to $4u_{xx} = u_t$.

4. Show that $u(x, y) = \cos(x) \sin(2y)$ is a solution to $4u_{xx} - u_{yy} = 0$.

5. Show that the "operator" $L(u) = u_{xx} + u_{yy}$ is linear. That is, show that $L(au_1 + bu_2) = aL(u_1) + bL(u_2)$.

6. Find all solutions to $u_{xy} = 1$ defined in the plane.

7. Find all solutions to $u_{xy} = x$ defined in the plane.

8. Find all solutions to $u_{xx} = 1$ defined in the plane (two variables).

9. Find all solutions with $y > 0$ to $y u_{xx} = 1$ (two variables).

10. Show that, if v and w are solutions to $u_x - u_y = 0$, then so is $\alpha v + \beta w$, where α and β are constants.

In Exercises 11–14, use separation of variables to find some solutions to the given equations.

11. $u_{xx} - u_t = 0$

12. $u_{xx} - u_{tt} = 0$

13. $u_{xx} + u_{yy} = 0$

14. $x u_x - u_y = 0$

9.2 THE HEAT EQUATION, WAVE EQUATION, AND LAPLACE'S EQUATION

In this section we derive the equations that will be our principal concern for the rest of this chapter. Before doing so, it will be necessary to review Green's theorem.

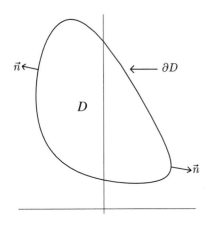

FIGURE 9.1

Let D be a region in the x, y-plane as shown in Figure 9.1. The symbol ∂D denotes the boundary curve. Suppose that

$$\vec{F}(x, y) = M(x, y)\vec{i} + N(x, y)\vec{j}$$

is a vector field defined on a region containing D and that M and N have at least continuous partials to the second order. Then Green's theorem asserts that

$$\int\int_{D} (N_x - M_y)\, dx\, dy = \int_{\partial D} M\, dx + N\, dy.$$

You will recall that the line integral on the right is evaluated by parameterizing the boundary curve by, say, $x = x(t)$ and $y = y(t)$. Then

$$\int_{\partial D} M\, dx + N\, dy = \int_a^b (Mx' + Ny')\, dt.$$

The interval $[a, b]$ is the interval of parameterization of the curve. This last integral can be written as

$$\int_a^b \vec{F} \cdot \vec{r}'\, dt,$$

where $\vec{r}(t) = x(t)\vec{i} + y(t)\vec{j}$. Note that $\vec{r}'$ is tangent to the curve.

Green's theorem can be restated in the form of a two-dimensional divergence theorem. To do this, let $\vec{F} = M(x, y)\vec{i} + N(x, y)\vec{j}$ again, and recall that the divergence of $\vec{F}$ is $\nabla \cdot \vec{F} = M_x + N_y$; then Green's theorem gives

$$\int\int_{D} \nabla \cdot \vec{F}\, dx\, dy = \int_{\partial D} -N\, dx + M\, dy.$$

But

$$\int_{\partial D} -N\, dx + M\, dy = \int_a^b (N(-x') + My')\, dt = \int_a^b \vec{F} \cdot (y'\vec{i} - x'\vec{j})\, dt.$$

The vector $y'\vec{i} - x'\vec{j}$ is at right angles to the tangent vector $x'\vec{i} + y'\vec{j}$, and so it is normal to the boundary curve. Thus, if $ds = \sqrt{(x')^2 + (y')^2}\, dt$, and $\vec{n}$ is the unit normal vector to the curve, then

$$\int\int_{D} \nabla \cdot \vec{F}\, dx\, dy = \int_{\partial D} \vec{F} \cdot \vec{n}\, ds.$$

This is the divergence version of Green's theorem.

9.2.1 The Heat Equation

Return to Figure 9.1 and imagine that the region D is a small portion of a thin homogeneous plate of, say, copper. As you know, heat will flow from regions of higher temperature to regions of lower temperature in the plate. Let $u(x, y, t)$ be the temperature at (x, y) at time t. The rate of conduction of heat across a short line segment perpendicular to the gradient of u is proportional to the magnitude of the gradient. Note that the gradient here and in the future is with respect to the space variables. The flow of heat is oppositely directed to the gradient, since heat flows from hotter to colder. If the line segment is not perpendicular to the gradient, then the flow of heat is proportional to $\nabla u \cdot \vec{n}$, where $\vec{n}$ is a unit vector perpendicular to the line segment. This flow of heat will also be proportional to the length of the little perpendicular line segment. The units for this flow of heat can be taken to be calories per second.

Suppose that $H(t)$ is the heat in the small region D of the plate. Suppose also that the specific heat of the plate is c and the area density of the plate is ρ. Recall that the specific heat, c, is the number of calories needed to raise 1 gram of the plate 1 degree Celsius. In view of this,

$$H(t) = \int \int_D c\rho u(x, y, t) \, dx \, dy.$$

The net heat flow from D is

$$\frac{dH}{dt} = \int \int_D c\rho u_t(x, y, t) \, dx \, dy,$$

and this is measured in calories per second. By the conservation of energy, this flow of heat must be equal to the net flow of heat across the boundary of D. Let ds be a very small piece of ∂D; then the flow across this piece is $\kappa \nabla u \cdot \vec{n} \, ds$, where κ is called the conductivity and $\vec{n}$ is the outward pointing unit normal to the segment ds. Thus the net flow across the boundary is

$$\int_{\partial D} \kappa \nabla u \cdot \vec{n} \, ds.$$

By Green's theorem, this is

$$\int \int_D \kappa \nabla \cdot \nabla u \, dx \, dy = \int \int_D \kappa (u_{xx} + u_{yy}) \, dx \, dy.$$

Therefore, we have

$$\int \int_D \kappa (u_{xx} + u_{yy}) \, dx \, dy = \int \int_D c\rho u_t(x, y, t) \, dx \, dy.$$

Now, if we assume that the partials are continuous and that

$$\kappa (u_{xx} + u_{yy}) \neq c\rho u_t$$

at some point, then there will be a small disk centered at this point for which

$$\kappa (u_{xx} + u_{yy}) - c\rho u_t$$

is positive on this disk or negative on this disk. If we take D to be the disk, then it follows that

$$\int\int_D \kappa(u_{xx} + u_{yy})\, dx\, dy \neq \int\int_D c\rho u_t(x, y, t)\, dx\, dy.$$

This is a contradiction, so

$$\kappa(u_{xx} + u_{yy}) = c\rho u_t$$

throughout the plate.

It is customary to combine the positive constants into one single constant a^2 and write

$$a^2[u_{xx} + u_{yy}] = u_t.$$

This is the heat equation.

It is easy to find infinitely many solutions to this equation. Indeed, if

$$u(x, y, t) = e^{(px+qy+rt)},$$

then

$$u_{xx} + u_{yy} = p^2 e^{(px+qy+rt)} + q^2 e^{(px+qy+rt)}$$

and

$$u_t = r e^{(px+qy+rt)}.$$

So we shall have a solution if

$$a^2(p^2 + q^2) = r.$$

The graph of all (p, q, r) for which this is true is a paraboloid in (p, q, r)-coordinates. For this reason, the heat equation is said to be **parabolic**.

This terminology also derives from the form of the equation itself. In the equation

$$a^2[u_{xx} + u_{yy}] - u_t = 0,$$

if you replace the partial derivatives with the corresponding powers of the variables involved and set the result equal to a constant, you get

$$a^2(x^2 + y^2) - t = c.$$

The graph of this equation is a paraboloid; hence the terminology.

The heat equation has infinitely many solutions, at least one for every point on the paraboloid. So we shall need an appropriate side condition to pin down a unique solution. The physics of the situation suggests a side condition. Suppose that we now denote the copper plate discussed above by D. Suppose also that the plate is insulated top and bottom so that all heat is transferred only through the plate and its boundary. If the plate has an initial temperature distribution $f(x, y)$ at time $t = 0$ and the temperature along the boundary is maintained at its initial values, then as time progresses the temperature distribution in the plate $u(x, y, t)$ will change as it heads toward a time-independent temperature distribution final state as $t \to \infty$. If this is repeated, it is not too hard to believe that the time evolution of the temperature distribution in the plate will follow the same development on each repetition. So the solution to

$$a^2(u_{xx} + u_{yy}) = u_t,$$

$$u(x, y, 0) = f(x, y), \quad \text{for } (x, y) \in D, \text{ and}$$

$$u(x, y, t) = f(x, y), \quad \text{for all } (x, y) \in \partial D \text{ and for all } t \in [0, \infty),$$

would appear to be unique on $D \times [0, \infty)$.

We shall give proofs of uniqueness to this problem and the ones that follow at the end of this section.

If the temperature along the boundary is maintained at 0, we say that the boundary conditions are **homogeneous**.

There are two other heat equations corresponding to one and three dimensions. They are

$$a^2 u_{xx} = u_t$$

and

$$a^2(u_{xx} + u_{yy} + u_{zz}) = u_t.$$

The physical situations that these equations model and the side conditions necessary for unique solutions will be left to the exercises.

9.2.2 The Wave Equation

Consider a drum. It consists of a frame with a membrane stretched across it. If it is struck, it vibrates. We shall develop a model of the vibration of such a drum. Figure 9.2 shows a small portion D of the membrane, and below it is a cross section of the boundary of D taken perpendicular to the boundary and at an instant in the vibration. We shall make a few simplifying assumptions as we go.

Let the vertical displacement of the membrane at (x, y) at time t be given by $u(x, y, t)$. The membrane is stretched uniformly in all directions, so the force pulling on a small element of the boundary ds is ds times the tension T. This force is directed along the hypotenuse of the triangle shown. This hypotenuse is tangent to the surface $u(x, y, t)$ and in the plane containing $\vec{n}$ and perpendicular to the (x, y)-plane. We make two assumptions here. First, we assume that the tension is great enough that the force of gravity can be ignored. Second, we

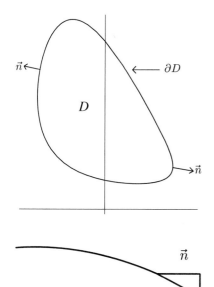

FIGURE 9.2

assume that the displacement of the membrane is so small that the horizontal component of the triangle is almost the same length as the hypotenuse. In this case the vertical component of the tension force is well approximated by

$$T \nabla u \cdot \vec{n} \, ds.$$

If we add these up around the boundary of D, we get the net vertical force acting on D, and this is

$$\int_{\partial D} T \nabla u \cdot \vec{n} \, ds.$$

Using Green's theorem again, the net vertical force is

$$\int \int_D T \nabla \cdot \nabla u \, dx \, dy.$$

On the other hand, the vertical force on a small piece of D of area $dx \, dy$ is $\rho u_{tt}(x, y, t) \, dx \, dy$, where ρ is the density of the membrane. This is simply the mass of the small piece times its acceleration. Adding these forces gives a net force of

$$\int \int_D \rho u_{tt} \, dx \, dy,$$

and this yields the equation of these forces:

$$\int \int_D \rho u_{tt} \, dx \, dy = \int \int_D T \nabla \cdot \nabla u \, dx \, dy.$$

This holds for all regions D of the membrane, so the integrands must be the same. Therefore,

$$T \nabla \cdot \nabla u = T(u_{xx} + u_{yy}) = \rho u_{tt}.$$

Combining constants, we can write

$$c^2(u_{xx} + u_{yy}) = u_{tt}.$$

This is the two-dimensional wave equation.

The related algebraic equation is

$$c^2(x^2 + y^2) - t^2 = d.$$

The graph of this latter equation in (x, y, t)-coordinates is a hyperboloid of two sheets. This equation is referred to as being **hyperbolic**.

As we did for the heat equation, we can take our cue from physics in order to find the appropriate side conditions necessary to give a unique solution to the wave equation. Let D now be the entire drumhead. If at $t = 0$ we specify the initial displacement of the drumhead by $f(x, y)$ defined on D, this will not be enough to determine the solution uniquely, since the drumhead could be given any initial velocity. However, if both an initial displacement and an initial vertical velocity of each point of the drumhead are given, then the solution will be determined. In summary, the equations

$$c^2(u_{xx} + u_{yy}) = u_{tt},$$
$$u(x, y, 0) = f(x, y), \qquad (x, y) \in D,$$
$$u_t(x, y, 0) = g(x, y), \qquad (x, y) \in D,$$
$$u(x, y, t) = 0 \qquad \text{for } x, y \in \partial D, \text{ for } t \in [0, \infty)$$

have a unique solution on $D \times [0, \infty)$.

Notice that, for the drumhead, $u(x, y, t) = 0$ for all points on the boundary and all t. We say the boundary conditions are homogeneous.

The one- and three-dimensional versions of the wave equation are

$$c^2 u_{xx} = u_{tt}$$

and

$$c^2(u_{xx} + u_{yy} + u_{zz}) = u_{tt}.$$

The physical interpretations of these equations is left to the exercises.

9.2.3 Laplace's Equation

Consider the heat equation

$$a^2(u_{xx} + u_{yy}) = u_t$$

on the region D again. If the temperature along the boundary is kept constant in time, the temperature distribution in the region will tend toward a limiting distribution as $t \to \infty$. This final state will be time independent. Let $v(x, y)$ be this limiting distribution; then, since it is independent of time,

$$v_{xx} + v_{yy} = 0$$

in D, and $v(x, y) = f(x, y)$ for $(x, y) \in \partial D$, where $f(x, y)$ is the temperature maintained on the boundary. Thus the final states are solutions to

$$u_{xx} + u_{yy} = 0 \text{ and } u(x, y) = f(x, y), \text{ for } (x, y) \in \partial D.$$

The equation

$$u_{xx} + u_{yy} = 0$$

is called **Laplace's equation**, and the linear operator defined by

$$\Delta(u) = u_{xx} + u_{yy}$$

is called the **Laplace operator** or the **Laplacian**. We describe Δ as a linear operator because it has the property

$$\Delta(c_1 u + c_2 v) = c_1 \Delta(u) + c_2 \Delta(v),$$

where u and v are any functions defined on D with second partial derivatives. We leave the simple verification to the exercises. We remind the reader that the notion of linearity is discussed in Appendix A, and it will be expanded on in Section 9.4.

The related algebraic equation is

$$x^2 + y^2 = c,$$

so you might guess that we call Laplace's equation circular. In fact, it is said to belong to the larger class of elliptic equations.

The equation and side condition

$$u_{xx} + u_{yy} = 0 \quad \text{and} \quad u(x, y) = f(x, y), \quad \text{for } (x, y) \in \partial D,$$

has a unique solution, and this equation and side condition are often called the **Dirichlet problem**. Solutions to $u_{xx} + u_{yy} = 0$ are called **harmonic functions**.

The Laplacian is a very important operator. Notice that it appears in both the heat equation and the wave equation. The Laplacian can be defined for any number of variables. We shall be particularly interested in functions satisfying

$$\Delta(u) = \lambda u$$

for some λ. These are called **eigenfunctions** of the Laplacian.

9.2.4 The Uniqueness Proofs

In this section we shall prove the uniqueness of solutions for which the side conditions are continuous. This section can be omitted without loss of continuity.

Throughout it will be assumed that D is a bounded region of the plane over which we can integrate.

Before proving uniqueness for the three equations we need to derive a useful integral identity from Green's theorem.

Recall Green's theorem. It is

$$\int\int_D \nabla \cdot \vec{f} \, dx \, dy = \int_{\partial D} \vec{f} \cdot \vec{n} \, ds,$$

where $\vec{n}$ is the outward pointing normal vector on the boundary. Observe that

$$(vu_x)_x = v_x u_x + vu_{xx}.$$

So using the same formula in y and adding, we arrive at

$$\nabla \cdot (v \nabla u) = \nabla v \cdot \nabla u + v \Delta(u).$$

Integrating, we get

$$\int\int_D v\Delta(u)\,dx\,dy = \int\int_D \nabla\cdot(v\nabla u)\,dx\,dy - \int\int_D \nabla v\cdot\nabla u\,dx\,dy.$$

Using Green's theorem on the first integral on the right, we get

$$\int\int_D v\Delta(u)\,dx\,dy = \int_{\partial D} v\nabla u\cdot\vec{n}\,ds - \int\int_D \nabla v\cdot\nabla u\,dx\,dy.$$

This is known as **Green's first identity**.

Suppose that u and v both satisfy the heat equation problem

$$a^2(u_{xx} + u_{yy}) = u_t,$$

$$u(x, y, 0) = f(x, y), \quad \text{for } (x, y) \in D, \text{ and}$$

$$u(x, y, t) = f(x, y), \quad \text{for all } (x, y) \in \partial D, \text{ and for all } t \in [0, \infty).$$

Then $w = u - v$ satisfies the heat equation and zero boundary and initial conditions. Thus

$$0 = \int\int_D (w_t - a^2\Delta(w))w\,dx\,dy$$

$$= \int\int_D [(\tfrac{1}{2}w^2)_t]\,dx\,dy - a^2\int\int_D w\Delta(w)\,dx\,dy.$$

Using Green's first identity on the second integral on the right and the fact that w is zero on the boundary give

$$0 = \int\int_D [(\tfrac{1}{2}w^2)_t]\,dx\,dy + a^2\int\int_D \nabla w\cdot\nabla w\,dx\,dy.$$

But the integral on the right is greater than or equal to zero, and the derivative with respect to t can be taken out of the first integral. Therefore,

$$\frac{d}{dt}\int\int_D \frac{1}{2}w^2\,dx\,dy \le 0.$$

Hence

$$\int\int_D \frac{1}{2}w^2\,dx\,dy$$

is nonnegative and decreasing. But, at $t = 0$, $w(x, y, 0) = 0$, so the integral is initially zero. Therefore, the integral is zero, and so the integrand, being non-negative, must be zero also. Thus $w = 0$, and $u = v$. This proves the uniqueness.

For the wave equation, assume that w satisfies the wave equation and the zero initial and boundary conditions. We shall prove that $w = 0$. As we saw previously, this is enough to prove uniqueness.

First, $0 = w_{tt} - c^2 \Delta(w)$, and so

$$0 = (w_{tt} - c^2 \Delta(w))w_t = (\frac{1}{2}w_t^2 + \frac{1}{2}c^2 ||\nabla w||^2)_t - c^2 \nabla \cdot (w_t \nabla w).$$

This can be verified by calculating the derivative with respect to t and the divergence on the right-hand side and then simplifying. Integration gives

$$\int\int_D (\frac{1}{2}w_t^2 + \frac{1}{2}c^2 ||\nabla w||^2)_t \, dx \, dy - c^2 \int\int_D \nabla \cdot (w_t \nabla w) \, dx \, dy = 0.$$

We can apply Green's theorem to the second integral to get

$$\int\int_D (\frac{1}{2}w_t^2 + \frac{1}{2}c^2 ||\nabla w||^2)_t \, dx \, dy - c^2 \int_{\partial D} (w_t \nabla w) \cdot \vec{n} \, ds = 0.$$

Since the boundary conditions are zero,

$$\int\int_D (\frac{1}{2}w_t^2 + \frac{1}{2}c^2 ||\nabla w||^2)_t \, dx \, dy = 0.$$

Taking the derivative out of the integral gives

$$\frac{d}{dt} \int\int_D (\frac{1}{2}w_t^2 + \frac{1}{2}c^2 ||\nabla w||^2) \, dx \, dy = 0,$$

and so the quantity

$$E = \int\int_D (\frac{1}{2}w_t^2 + \frac{1}{2}c^2 ||\nabla w||^2) \, dx \, dy$$

is a constant. But, at $t = 0$, $w(x, y, 0) = 0$, and $w_t(x, y, 0) = 0$ in D; so the x and y partial derivatives are zero also. Thus E is zero for $t = 0$ and hence for all t. This tells us that the partial derivatives of w are zero everywhere; hence w must be a constant. But w takes on the value zero, so w is identically zero. This proves uniqueness. This proof of uniqueness is not as much of a rabbit out of a hat as you might imagine. Physically, E is the total kinetic and potential energy of the membrane, so it is less surprising that this is a constant.

We leave the uniqueness of solutions to the Dirichlet problem to the exercises.

The preceding proofs require that w be continuous on D and on the boundary. Moreover, inside D the appropriate partial derivatives are required to be continuous and the initial data are required to be continuous. In the next sections we shall solve problems in which the boundary or initial data are not continuous at all points. This will lead to "solutions" that are not differentiable the required number of times to be a solution in the way that we have defined it. These are solutions of a more general nature. We ran into this situation with the Laplace transform and discontinuous forcing functions in Chapter 8. It is not possible to treat these more general solutions properly in this book, so we shall gloss over the matter.

EXERCISES 9.2

1. Describe the physical situation modeled by the one-dimensional heat equation. What are the side conditions that should ensure a unique solution? What is the Laplacian in this case?

2. Describe the physical situation modeled by the three-dimensional heat equation. What are the side conditions that should ensure a unique solution? What is the Laplacian in this case?

3. Describe the physical situation modeled by the one-dimensional wave equation. What are the side conditions that should ensure a unique solution?

4. Show that the Laplacian is a linear operator. Is the sum of two harmonic functions harmonic? Explain!

5. Find a derivation of the one-dimensional wave equation from a physical analysis of a vibrating stretched string.

Write a short explanation of this derivation.

6. Describe all the eigenfunctions of the one-dimensional Laplacian. That is, find all solutions to $\Delta(u) = \lambda u$. Find all eigenfunctions $u(x)$ and λ's for which $u(0) = u(2\pi) = 0$.

7. Find all one-variable harmonic functions.

8. Prove uniqueness for the one-dimensional heat equation on $[0, b]$ with the conditions $u(0, t) = u(b, t) = h(t)$, and $u(x, 0) = f(x)$.

9. Prove uniqueness for the one-dimensional Dirichlet problem. *Hint:* If w is harmonic, integrate $0 = ww''$ once by parts and take stock of the situation.

10. Prove uniqueness for the two-dimensional Dirichlet problem. *Hint:* If w is harmonic, integrate $0 = w\Delta(w)$ over D and use Green's first identity.

9.3   THE HEAT EQUATION AND INITIAL CONDITION

In this section we shall solve the one-dimensional heat equation with homogeneous boundary conditions. In doing so, we will be led to consider the representation of a function as an infinite sum of sine functions.

Consider a homogeneous rod of length b, and suppose that the physical constants are such that $a^2 = 1$. Imagine the rod on the x-axis with one end at 0 and the other at b. Assume that the rod is insulated along its length so that heat is only transferred through the rod and the ends. Assume that the temperature at both ends is held at $0°$. Therefore, the temperature distribution in the rod $u(x, t)$ satisfies

$$u_{xx} = u_t,$$

and $u(0, t) = u(b, t) = 0$ for all $t \geq 0$. Thus the boundary conditions are homogeneous. Assume also that the initial temperature distribution is given by

$$f(x) = \begin{cases} 2x, & \text{for } 0 \leq x \leq b/2, \\ b - 2(x - \frac{b}{2}), & \text{for } b/2 \leq x \leq b. \end{cases}$$

We now use **separation of variables** to solve this problem. Suppose that a solution to the equation has the form

$$u(x, t) = X(x)T(t).$$

Then

$$X''T = XT'.$$

Note that we have suppressed the variables x and t. If we divide through by XT, we get

$$\frac{X''}{X} = \frac{T'}{T} = -\lambda.$$

Now λ must be a constant because it is constant with respect to x and with respect to t. We get two equations from this:

$$\frac{X''}{X} = -\lambda$$

and

$$\frac{T'}{T} = -\lambda.$$

These equations can be written as

$$X'' + \lambda X = 0$$

and

$$T' + \lambda T = 0.$$

The strategy is to solve the equation in X first and use the side conditions to determine the choices of λ. The general solution to

$$X'' + \lambda X = 0$$

is

$$X(x) = Ae^{\sqrt{-\lambda}x} + Be^{-\sqrt{-\lambda}x}.$$

But we have the homogeneous boundary conditions $u(0, t) = u(b, t) = 0$ for all t, so, if T is not the zero function, we must have $X(0) = X(b) = 0$. This cannot happen if $\sqrt{-\lambda}$ is real. Thus λ must be a positive real number, so we set $\mu^2 = \lambda$. Then our solution becomes

$$X(x) = A\sin(\mu x) + B\cos(\mu x).$$

From $X(0) = 0$, it follows that $B = 0$. From $X(b) = 0$ it follows that

$$X(b) = A\sin(\mu b) = 0,$$

so, if the solution is not to be trivial, we must have

$$\mu b = \pi k$$

or

$$\mu = \frac{\pi k}{b}$$

for some integer k.

The temperatures at the ends of the rod have determined the choices of μ and hence the choices for λ. For each positive integer k, we get a solution

$$X_k(x) = \sin(\frac{\pi k x}{b}).$$

These functions will be multiplied by constants and added together to form linear combinations and, eventually, infinite sums. Consequently, terms corresponding to nonpositive values of k will add no new linear combinations, so we consider only positive values of k.

For each $k > 0$, we get

$$\lambda_k = \mu^2 = \frac{\pi^2 k^2}{b^2}.$$

For each of these, we solve

$$T' + \lambda_k T = 0.$$

The solution is

$$T_k(t) = Ce^{-\lambda_k t}.$$

Therefore, for each k,

$$u_k(x, t) = A_k e^{-\frac{\pi^2 k^2}{b^2} t} \sin(\frac{\pi k x}{b})$$

is a solution to the heat equation and the boundary conditions.

We can rewrite the equation in the form

$$L(u) = u_{xx} - u_t = 0.$$

Observe that if u and v satisfy this equation and the boundary conditions then

$$L(c_1 u + c_2 v) = c_1 L(u) + c_2 L(v) = 0,$$

and $c_1 u(0, t) + c_2 v(0, t) = c_1 u(b, t) + c_2 v(b, t) = 0$ for all t. Thus the linear combination $c_1 u + c_2 v$ satisfies the equation and boundary conditions. Thus any finite linear combination of the $u_k(x, t)$,

$$u(x, t) = \sum_{k=1}^{n} u_k(x, t) = A_1 e^{-\frac{\pi^2}{b^2} t} \sin(\frac{\pi x}{b}) + \cdots + A_n e^{-\frac{\pi^2 n^2}{b^2} t} \sin(\frac{\pi n x}{b}),$$

is also a solution to the heat equation and the homogeneous boundary conditions $u(0, t) = u(b, t) = 0$.

What about the condition $u(x, 0) = f(x)$? This is often called the **initial condition**. If $t = 0$, the preceding sum becomes

$$u(x, 0) = \sum_{k=1}^{n} u_k(x, 0) = A_1 \sin(\frac{\pi x}{b}) + \cdots + A_n \sin(\frac{\pi n x}{b}).$$

This cannot be equal to $f(x)$ defined at the beginning of this section, because $f(x)$ is not differentiable at $b/2$, but our sum is. However, if we allow infinite sums or series, it turns out that this initial condition can be satisfied.

Suppose that we can represent our initial condition $f(x)$ as

$$f(x) = \sum_{k=1}^{\infty} A_k \sin(\frac{\pi k x}{b}).$$

Then how can we find the A_k? Observe that

$$\int_0^b \sin(\frac{\pi k x}{b}) \sin(\frac{\pi j x}{b}) \, dx$$
$$= \frac{1}{2} \int_0^b \cos(\frac{\pi}{b}(k-j)x) - \cos(\frac{\pi}{b}(k+j)x) \, dx.$$

Here we have used the identity

$$\cos(A - B) - \cos(A + B) = 2 \sin(A) \sin(B).$$

Therefore, if $k \neq j$,

$$\int_0^b \sin(\frac{\pi k x}{b}) \sin(\frac{\pi j x}{b}) \, dx = \frac{b}{2\pi(k-j)} \sin(\frac{\pi}{b}(k-j)x)$$
$$- \frac{b}{2\pi(k+j)} \sin(\frac{\pi}{b}(k+j)x) \Big|_0^b = 0.$$

If $k = j$, then

$$\int_0^b \sin(\frac{\pi k x}{b}) \sin(\frac{\pi j x}{b}) \, dx = \int_0^b \sin^2(\frac{\pi k x}{b}) \, dx = \frac{b}{2}.$$

The relations

$$\int_0^b \sin(\frac{\pi k x}{b}) \sin(\frac{\pi j x}{b}) \, dx = 0$$

and

$$\int_0^b \sin^2(\frac{\pi k x}{b}) \, dx = \frac{b}{2}$$

are called **orthogonality relations**. We shall see such relations repeatedly in what follows.

We now multiply the series by $\sin(\frac{\pi n x}{b})$ and integrate both sides. We assume that the series can be integrated term by term. Using the orthogonality relations, the result is

$$\int_0^b f(x) \sin(\frac{\pi n x}{b}) \, dx = \sum_{k=1}^{\infty} A_k \int_0^b \sin(\frac{\pi n x}{b}) \sin(\frac{\pi k x}{b}) \, dx = \frac{b}{2} A_n.$$

Therefore, the coefficients are

$$A_n = \frac{2}{b} \int_0^b f(x) \sin(\frac{\pi n x}{b}) \, dx.$$

The A_n are called the **Fourier sine coefficients** of f.

The heat equation problem can now be finished. For concreteness sake and simplicity, set $b = 1$; then

$$A_n = 2 \int_0^1 f(x) \sin(\pi n x) \, dx$$

$$= 2 \int_0^{1/2} 2x \sin(\pi n x) \, dx + 2 \int_{1/2}^1 (1 - 2(x - 1/2)) \sin(\pi n x) \, dx.$$

The messy integration by parts required here is left to the exercises. The result is

$$A_n = \begin{cases} 0, & \text{for } n = 2k, \\ \frac{8(-1)^{k+1}}{(\pi n)^2}, & \text{for } n = 2k - 1. \end{cases}$$

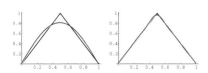

Therefore,

$$f(x) = \sum_{k=1}^{\infty} \frac{8(-1)^{k+1}}{(\pi(2k-1))^2} \sin(\pi(2k-1)x).$$

FIGURE 9.3

Figure 9.3 shows an approximation of $f(x)$ by partial sums with one and five terms.

We can now write down the solution to the problem. It is

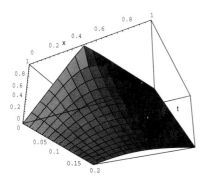

$$u(x, t) = \sum_{k=1}^{\infty} \frac{8(-1)^{k+1}}{(\pi(2k-1))^2} e^{-(\pi^2(2k-1)^2)t} \sin(\pi(2k-1)x).$$

It can be proved that, for $t > 0$, this sum can be differentiated term by term, so $u(x, t)$ is the unique solution satisfying the heat equation and the initial and boundary conditions. Figure 9.4 shows the solution as a function of x and t viewed from below. Notice how the temperature decays exponentially as t increases. Notice also the initial temperature distribution for $t = 0$.

FIGURE 9.4

We shall delve more deeply into this series method in Section 9.5. For now we shall be content to work through two more examples.

Example 9.3.1   Consider the following heat problem. Let $u_{xx} = u_t$ on $[0, 4] \times [0, \infty)$, $u(0, t) = u(4, t) = 0$ for all $t \geq 0$, and $u(x, 0) = x$ on $(0, 4)$. Notice that the boundary conditions are homogeneous and that the initial condition is discontinuous at 4. The series method will still handle this.

As before, we set

$$u(x, t) = X(x)T(t).$$

Therefore,

$$X''T = XT',$$

and, dividing by XT, we get

$$\frac{X''}{X} = \frac{T'}{T} = -\lambda$$

where λ is a constant. Thus we have

$$X'' + \lambda X = 0$$

and

$$T' + \lambda T = 0$$

exactly as before.

Exactly as before, to satisfy the homogeneous boundary conditions, we must have $\lambda = \mu^2$, $\mu = \frac{\pi k}{4}$ for $k = 1, 2, \dots$, and

$$X_k(x) = \sin(\frac{\pi k}{4}x).$$

Then, if we set

$$T_k(t) = e^{-\lambda t} = e^{-\frac{\pi^2 k^2}{16}t},$$

$$u_k(x, t) = e^{-\frac{\pi^2 k^2}{16}t} \sin(\frac{\pi k}{4}x)$$

is a solution to $u_{xx} = u_t$ and the boundary conditions. Any linear combination of these solutions

$$u(x, t) = \sum_{k=1}^{n} A_k e^{-\frac{\pi^2 k^2}{16}t} \sin(\frac{\pi k}{4}x)$$

is also a solution, because the operator $L(u) = u_{xx} - u_t$ is linear and the boundary conditions are homogeneous.

As before, this finite sum does not satisfy our initial condition $u(x, 0) = x$ on $(0, 4)$, so we turn to the infinite sum

$$u(x, t) = \sum_{k=1}^{\infty} A_k e^{-\frac{\pi^2 k^2}{16}t} \sin(\frac{\pi k}{4}x).$$

At $t = 0$,

$$u(x, 0) = x = \sum_{k=1}^{\infty} A_k \sin(\frac{\pi k}{4}x).$$

Multiply by $\sin(\frac{\pi nx}{4})$, integrate from 0 to 4, and use the orthogonality relations to get

$$A_n = \frac{2}{4} \int_0^4 x \sin(\frac{\pi nx}{4}) \, dx.$$

Use integration by parts to arrive at

$$A_n = \frac{1}{2} \int_0^4 x \sin(\frac{\pi nx}{4}) \, dx = -x \frac{2}{\pi n} \cos(\frac{\pi n}{4} x)|_0^4$$

$$+ \frac{8}{\pi^2 n^2} \sin(\frac{\pi n}{4} x)|_0^4 = \frac{8}{\pi n}(-1)^{n+1}.$$

Therefore,

$$u(x, 0) = \sum_{n=1}^{\infty} \frac{8}{\pi n}(-1)^{n+1} \sin(\frac{\pi n}{4} x).$$

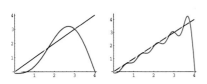

FIGURE 9.5

Figure 9.5 has two panels showing the approximation of x on $[0, 4)$ using two and ten terms.

The complete solution to the problem is

$$u(x, t) = \sum_{n=1}^{\infty} \frac{8}{\pi n}(-1)^{n+1} e^{-\frac{\pi^2 n^2}{16} t} \sin(\frac{\pi n}{4} x).$$ ∎

Example 9.3.2   Consider the following heat problem. Let $u_{xx} = u_t$ on $[-2, 2] \times [0, \infty)$, $u(-2, t) = u(2, t) = 0$ for all $t \geq 0$, and $u(x, 0) = f(x)$ on $(-2, 2)$ where

$$f(x) = \begin{cases} 1, & \text{for } -2 \leq x \leq 0, \\ x, & \text{for } 0 \leq x \leq 2. \end{cases}$$

The boundary conditions are again homogeneous.

After separating the variables we must solve

$$X'' + \lambda X = 0$$

and

$$T' + \lambda T = 0.$$

Because the boundary conditions are homogeneous, $\lambda = \mu^2$, and

$$X(x) = A \sin(\mu x) + B \cos(\mu x).$$

Using the boundary conditions gives

$$A \sin(2\mu) + B \cos(2\mu) = 0$$

and

$$-A \sin(2\mu) + B \cos(2\mu) = 0.$$

Thus

$$2B \cos(2\mu) = 0;$$

so if $B \neq 0$, then

$$2\mu = \frac{\pi}{2}(2k - 1) \qquad \text{and} \qquad \mu = \frac{\pi}{4}(2k - 1)$$

for $k = 1, 2, \ldots$. If $B = 0$, then $2\mu = \pi k$ for $k = 0, 1, \ldots$, and so

$$\mu = \frac{\pi}{2}k$$

for $k = 0, 1, \ldots$. The corresponding functions are $S_k(x) = \sin(\frac{\pi}{2}kx)$ and $C_k(x) = \cos(\frac{\pi}{4}(2k - 1)x)$. As before, we shall be forming infinite sums of these functions multiplied by constants, so nonpositive values of k will contribute nothing new to these sums.

Each $k \geq 1$ corresponds to a distinct λ. For $k = 1, 2, 3, \ldots$, we have the functions $S_k(x) = \sin(\frac{\pi}{2}kx)$ and $C_k(x) = \cos(\frac{\pi}{4}(2k - 1)x)$. We leave it as an exercise to verify that

$$\int_{-2}^{2} S_k(x)C_j(x)\,dx = 0$$

for any k and j, and

$$\int_{-2}^{2} S_k(x)S_j(x)\,dx = \int_{-2}^{2} C_k(x)C_j(x)\,dx = 0$$

if $k \neq j$. If $k = j$, we have

$$\int_{-2}^{2} \sin^2(\frac{\pi}{2}kx)\,dx = \int_{-2}^{2} \cos^2(\frac{\pi}{4}(2k - 1)x)\,dx = 2.$$

If we write

$$f(x) = \sum_{k=1}^{\infty}[A_k \sin(\frac{\pi}{2}kx) + B_k \cos(\frac{\pi}{4}(2k - 1)x)],$$

then, assuming that we can exchange integration and summation,

$$\int_{-2}^{2} f(x)S_n(x)\,dx = \sum_{k=1}^{\infty}[A_k \int_{-2}^{2} S_k(x)S_n(x)\,dx + B_k \int_{-2}^{2} C_k(x)S_n(x)\,dx].$$

Therefore,

$$A_n = \frac{1}{2} \int_{-2}^{2} f(x) S_n(x) \, dx.$$

Similarly,

$$B_n = \frac{1}{2} \int_{-2}^{2} f(x) C_n(x) \, dx.$$

Computing the integral formulas for A_n and B_n gives

$$A_n = \frac{-1 - (-1)^n}{\pi n}$$

and

$$B_n = \frac{-8}{\pi^2 (2n-1)^2} - 6 \frac{(-1)^n}{\pi (2n-1)}.$$

Finally, the solution is

$$u(x,t) = \sum_{n=1}^{\infty} \left[\frac{-1 - (-1)^n}{\pi n} e^{-\frac{\pi^2}{4} t} \sin\left(\frac{\pi}{2} n x\right) \right.$$

$$\left. + \left(\frac{-8}{\pi^2 (2n-1)^2} - 6 \frac{(-1)^n}{\pi (2n-1)} \right) e^{-\frac{\pi^2 (2n-1)^2}{4} t} \cos\left(\frac{\pi}{2} (2n-1) x\right) \right]. \quad \blacksquare$$

EXERCISES 9.3

1. Solve the problem $u_{xx} = u_t$, $u(0,t) = u(\pi, t) = 0$ for all $t \geq 0$, and $u(x,0) = \sin(x)$ for $x \in [0, \pi]$. The result should not be a surprise! Draw graphs of $u(x,t)$ as a function of x for several values of t increasing from zero until you have an animation of the solution.

2. Solve the problem $u_{xx} = u_t$, $u(0,t) = u(2\pi, t) = 0$ for all $t \geq 0$, and $u(x,0) = f(x)$ for $x \in (0, 2\pi)$, where

$$f(x) = \begin{cases} 1, & \text{for } 0 < x < \pi, \\ 0, & \text{for } \pi \leq x < 2\pi. \end{cases}$$

   Graph a partial sum of $u(x,0)$ of high enough order to clearly illustrate the approximation of the initial condition.

3. Solve the problem $u_{xx} = u_t$, $u(0,t) = u(3,t) = 0$ for all $t \geq 0$, $u(x,0) = 10$ for $x \in (0,3)$. Graph a partial sum of $u(x,0)$ of high enough order to clearly illustrate the approximation of the initial condition. Draw graphs of the corresponding approximation of $u(x,t)$ as a function of x for several values of t increasing from zero until

you have an animation of the solution.

4. Solve the problem $u_{xx} = u_t$, $u(0,t) = u(4,t) = 0$ for all $t \geq 0$, and $u(x,0) = f(x)$ for $x \in (0,4)$, where

$$f(x) = \begin{cases} 1, & \text{for } 0 < x < 2, \\ -1, & \text{for } 2 \leq x < 4. \end{cases}$$

   Graph a partial sum of $u(x,0)$ of high enough order to clearly illustrate the approximation of the initial condition.

5. Solve the problem $u_{xx} = u_t$, $u(-2,t) = u(2,t) = 0$ for all $t \geq 0$, and $u(x,0) = f(x)$ for $x \in (-2,2)$, where $f(x) = x$. Graph a partial sum of $u(x,0)$ of high enough order to clearly illustrate the approximation of the initial condition. Draw graphs of the corresponding approximation of $u(x,t)$ as a function of x for several values of t increasing from zero until you have an animation of the solution.

6. Show that $\int_{-2}^{2} S_k(x) C_j(x) \, dx = 0$ in Example 9.3.2.

7. Show that $\int_{-2}^{2} S_k(x)S_j(x)\,dx = \int_{-2}^{2} C_k(x)C_j(x)\,dx = 0$ if $k \neq j$ in Example 9.3.2.

8. Compute A_n and B_n in Example 9.3.2.

9. Compute A_n in the opening discussion of this section.

10. Solve the problem $u_{xx} = u_t$, $u(-2, t) = u(2, t) = 0$ for all $t \geq 0$, and $u(x, 0) = f(x)$ for $x \in (-2, 2)$, where

$$f(x) = \begin{cases} 1, & \text{for } -2 < x \leq 0, \\ 2, & \text{for } 0 < x \leq 2. \end{cases}$$

11. Solve the problem $u_{xx} = u_t$, $u(2, t) = u(4, t) = 0$ for all $t \geq 0$, and $u(x, 0) = x$ for $x \in [2, 4]$. *Hint:* Try translation to a more convenient location.

9.4 VECTOR SPACES AND OPERATORS

Often in the development of a subject, such as differential equations, certain themes or forms appear repeatedly. For example, the notions of linear combinations, linear independence, and linear operators have turned up frequently in our study of differential equations. When such notions appear often enough, it is difficult for mathematicians to resist defining these notions in a way that applies to all the cases. Moreover, such general definitions provide insight into the essentials of these concepts. We are now in such a situation.

9.4.1 Vector Spaces

The concept that unifies the notions mentioned previously is that of a vector space. We have repeatedly spoken of linear combinations of objects. Linear combinations of the coordinate direction vectors $\vec{\imath}$, $\vec{\jmath}$, and $\vec{k}$ provide all the vectors in space. Linear combinations of functions were employed to form general solutions to linear homogeneous differential equations in Chapter 4. Linear combinations of column vectors and solutions emerged in the solving of linear first-order systems in Chapter 5, and in this chapter linear combinations of special functions have been extended to infinite "linear combinations" of such functions in order to solve the initial condition for the heat equation. What general principle underlies these recurrent themes?

We have a set or collection of objects such that two of these objects can be added to produce a third such object. Also, each object can be multiplied by a number to produce another object in the collection. Therefore, each of our examples involves a set of objects, which we shall call vectors, together with an operation of addition on the set and an operation of scalar multiplication of the members of the set by either real or complex numbers. However, this is too general to say much. We need some axioms to define the properties of addition and scalar multiplication. This is summarized in the definition of a vector space.

Definition 9.4.1

Let F be the set of real numbers or the set of complex numbers. Let V be a nonempty set of elements together with two operations $+$ and $\cdot$ such that, for any u and v in V and r in F, $u + v$ and $r \cdot v$ are in V. We say that V is a vector space over F if the following axioms hold:

1. For all u and v in V, $u + v = v + u$.
2. For all u, v, and w in V, $u + (v + w) = (u + v) + w$.
3. There is an element 0 in V such that $u + 0 = u$ for all u in V.
4. For each u in V, there is an element v in V such that $u + v = 0$.
5. For all a and b in F and u in V, $(ab) \cdot u = a \cdot (b \cdot u)$.
6. For all a in F and all u and v in V, $a \cdot (u + v) = a \cdot u + a \cdot v$.
7. For all a and b in F and all u in V, $(a + b) \cdot u = a \cdot u + b \cdot u$.
8. For any u in V, $1 \cdot u = u$.

We call V a **vector space** over the real or complex numbers depending on whether F is the real or complex numbers. We call elements of V vectors and numbers in F **scalars**.   ●

Before giving examples of vector spaces, a few comments are in order. It is customary not to write the scalar multiplication symbol $\cdot$ in vector expressions. The vector 0 in axiom 3 is unique and is called the zero vector. In axiom 4, v can be shown to be unique, and so we write $-u$ for this vector. We call $-u$ the additive inverse of u.

The familiar algebraic properties of vectors in space can be derived from the axioms. For example, let us derive $0v = 0$. We have $0v = (0 + 0)v = 0v + 0v$. Then $0v + 0v = 0v + 0$, and adding $-(0v)$ to both sides and simplifying gives $0v = 0$. Note that you must distinguish between 0 as a number and as a vector. In the discussion of vector spaces in general, we do not use arrows or boldface to identify vectors, so you must be alert to the context. A similar proof shows that $a0 = 0$. Here both zeros are the zero vector. Other familiar properties are derived in the exercises.

Example 9.4.2   Let $\mathbf{R}^n$ and $\mathbf{C}^n$ be the sets of all n-tuples

$$(x_1, x_2, \ldots, x_n)$$

of real and complex numbers, respectively. These n-tuples are added and scalar multiplied as follows:

$$(x_1, x_2, \ldots, x_n) + (y_1, y_2, \ldots, y_n) = (x_1 + y_1, x_2 + y_2, \ldots, x_n + y_n)$$

and

$$r(x_1, x_2, \ldots, x_n) = (rx_1, rx_2, \ldots, rx_n).$$

With these operations of addition and scalar multiplication, it is easy to see that the axioms hold. For instance,

$$(x_1, x_2, \ldots, x_n) + (y_1, y_2, \ldots, y_n) = (x_1 + y_1, x_2 + y_2, \ldots, x_n + y_n)$$
$$= (y_1 + x_1, y_2 + x_2, \ldots, y_n + x_n)$$
$$= (y_1, y_2, \ldots, y_n) + (x_1, x_2, \ldots, x_n).$$

Clearly, $(0, 0, \ldots, 0)$ is the zero vector. Complete verification of the axioms is left to the exercises. It should be clear that many of the properties expressed in the axioms will follow easily from the corresponding properties of the real numbers. ∎

Example 9.4.3   The set of all 2×2 matrices with real entries is a real vector space. First, the sum of a pair of 2×2 matrices is a 2×2 matrix, as is the scalar multiple of a 2×2 matrix. Addition of matrices is done entrywise, and so addition satisfies axioms 1 and 2. The zero matrix is

$$\begin{bmatrix} 0 & 0 \\ 0 & 0 \end{bmatrix}.$$

The matrix that must be added to

$$\begin{bmatrix} a & b \\ c & d \end{bmatrix}$$

to get the zero matrix is

$$\begin{bmatrix} -a & -b \\ -c & -d \end{bmatrix},$$

so axiom 4 is satisfied. The rest of the axioms are verified just as easily.

Clearly, complex numbers could be used just as well. Furthermore, it should be clear that the set of matrices of any given dimensions forms a vector space. ∎

Example 9.4.4   Let $F(a, b)$ be the set of all functions defined on the interval (a, b) and having real values. If f and g are functions in $F(a, b)$, then we define $f + g$ in $F(a, b)$ by the usual formula for defining the sum of two functions:

$$(f + g)(t) = f(t) + g(t).$$

If r is a real number, we define rf to be the function defined by

$$(rf)(t) = rf(t).$$

With these definitions of addition and scalar multiplication, $F(a, b)$ becomes a real vector space.

We can define a similar space of complex-valued functions on (a, b). We define addition and scalar multiplication in the same way. The result is a complex vector space. ∎

Definition 9.4.5

A subspace of a vector space V is a nonempty subset W of V that is a vector space relative to the same operations of addition and scalar multiplication on V.   ●

Note carefully that if W is a subspace of V then sums and scalar multiples of vectors in W must be in W also. If a set has this property, we say it is **closed** under the operations.

We can test a subset to see if it is a subspace in a simple way. If the subset contains the zero vector and is closed under the operations, it is also a subspace. Indeed, if a subset W of the vector space V contains the zero vector and is closed under the operations of V, then W is not empty. Moreover, the axioms hold for all vectors in V, and so they hold for all vectors in W.

Example 9.4.6   Consider all vectors in $\mathbf{R}^3$ of the form $(x, 0, 0)$. This subset of $\mathbf{R}^3$ contains the zero vector, and sums and scalar products of vectors in this subset are in the subset also. Therefore, this subset is a subspace. This subspace can be thought of as the x-axis in three-dimensional space.   ■

Example 9.4.7   Consider the real-valued functions defined on (a, b) that have continuous second derivatives. Let $C^2(a, b)$ denote the set of such functions. Then $C^2(a, b)$ is a subspace of $F(a, b)$ because the function that is identically zero is in the subset, and sums and scalar multiples of twice continuously differentiable functions are twice continuously differentiable. So $C^2(a, b)$ is closed.   ■

The vector space $C^2(a, b)$ is the space in which we searched for solutions to second-order linear differential equations in Chapter 4. The vector space $\mathbf{R}^n$ played a pivotal role in the solution of $n \times n$ linear systems in Chapter 5. There the vectors were written as columns, rather than as rows or n-tuples, but it was in this space that the orbits of solutions were drawn. The space $\mathbf{C}^2$ was essential to finding eigenvectors in our search for solutions to 2×2 systems. The spaces mentioned here should be used as the reference examples for all that follows in these sections on vector spaces.

EXERCISES 9.4.1

1. Verify that all the axioms hold for the space $\mathbf{R}^2$.
2. Show that the set of all polynomials of degree less than or equal to 2 with real coefficients (or complex for that matter) is a vector space.
3. Show that the set of all polynomials of degree less than or equal to 3 with real coefficients (or complex for that matter) is a vector space.
4. Show that the set of all polynomials with real coefficients (or complex for that matter) is a vector space.
5. Is the set of real numbers a vector space? Explain!

6. Show that the set of continuous real-valued functions defined on an interval (a, b) with the usual operations of addition of functions and multiplication of functions by a real number is a vector space.

7. Find a vector space different from any discussed so far.

In exercises 8–13, you are asked to prove some basic algebraic properties of vectors from the axioms of a vector space. Thus you may only use the axioms or results you have already proved. You must not appeal to examples or familiar properties of vectors in three-dimensional space.

8. Show that in any vector space the additive identity 0 is unique. *Hint:* Suppose there are two different identities 0 and $\bar{0}$, and then use the fact that each is an identity for the other in $0 + \bar{0}$.

9. Prove that in any vector space, if $u + v_1 = 0$ and $u + v_2 = 0$, then $v_1 = v_2$. To write $v_1 = -u$ is not a proof! This exercise is a proof that the additive inverse of u is unique, and only then are we justified in using $-u$ for this inverse.

10. Prove that in any vector space $-(-u) = u$. You may assume the additive inverse of a vector v, $-v$, is unique from Exercise 9. *Hint:* What must you add to $-u$ to get zero?

11. Write out the proof of $0v = 0$ in detail pointing to the axioms used.

12. Prove that in any vector space $a0 = 0$.

13. Prove that in any vector space $(-1)u = -u$.

14. If V is a vector space, explain why the set $\{0\}$ is a subspace of V.

15. If u is a vector in a vector space V, explain why the set of all scalar multiples of u is a subspace of V.

16. If $\{v_1, v_2, v_3\}$ is a set of vectors in a vector space V, show that the set of all vectors of the form

$$x_1 v_1 + x_2 v_2 + x_3 v_3$$

is a subspace of V.

17. Describe three subspaces of $\mathbf{R}^3$. Using your visualization of three-dimensional space, describe the geometrical nature of subspaces of this space.

9.4.2 Finite and Infinite Dimensional Spaces

There is a major difference between the space $\mathbf{R}^n$ and the space $C^2(a, b)$. If v_1, $v_2, \ldots$, and v_m are vectors in a vector space V, and $c_1, c_2, \ldots$, and c_m are scalars, then

$$c_1 v_1 + c_2 v_2 + \cdots + c_m v_m$$

is called a **linear combination** of the vectors $v_1, v_2, \ldots$, and v_m. Notice that every vector in $\mathbf{R}^n$ can be written as a linear combination of a fixed finite set of vectors. For example, the vectors $(1, 0, \ldots, 0)$, $(0, 1, \ldots, 0)$, through $(0, 0, \ldots, 1)$ will suffice. However, in $C^2(a, b)$ it is impossible to write all other functions as linear combinations of a given finite set of functions. This will be proved after a little preparation. The difference between these spaces is very important, so we make a definition.

Definition 9.4.8

A vector space is said to be finite dimensional if there is a finite set of vectors in the space such that every vector in the space is a linear combination of the vectors in this finite set. We say a vector space is infinite dimensional if it is not finite dimensional. ●

If every vector in a vector space V is a linear combination of vectors in a set S, we say that S **spans** V. Thus a vector space is finite dimensional if it has a finite subset S that spans it.

Example 9.4.9   We shall show now prove that the set of vectors $\{(2, -1),$ $(3, 1), (-2, 5)\}$ spans $\mathbf{R}^2$. This means that we must show that every vector (b_1, b_2) in $\mathbf{R}^2$ can be written in the form

$$x_1(2, -1) + x_2(3, 1) + x_3(-2, 5) = (b_1, b_2).$$

But this is equivalent to being able to solve the system of linear equations

$$2x_1 + 3x_2 - 2x_3 = b_1,$$
$$-x_1 + x_2 + 5x_3 = b_2.$$

It is easy to see that these equations always have a solution (not unique). So $\{(2, -1), (3, 1), (-2, 5)\}$ is a spanning set.   ■

It is possible that one of the vectors in a spanning set is not needed because it can be written as a linear combination of the remaining spanning vectors. This is the case in the preceding example. Indeed,

$$(-2, 5) = -\frac{17}{5}(2, -1) + \frac{8}{5}(3, 1).$$

In such a case, the remaining vectors would still span the space. If all the unnecessary vectors in a spanning set have been removed, the vectors that remain have the property described in the following definition.

Definition 9.4.10

We say that a set $\{v_1, v_2, \ldots, v_n\}$ of vectors in a vector space V is linearly independent if

$$c_1 v_1 + c_2 v_2 + \cdots + c_n v_n = 0$$

implies that $c_1 = c_2 = \cdots = c_n = 0$. We say the set is linearly dependent otherwise.   ●

A useful characterization of linearly dependent sets is the following. A set of nonzero vectors $\{v_1, v_2, \ldots, v_n\}$ is linearly dependent if and only if one of the vectors is a linear combination of its predecessors. Indeed, if

$$v_i = c_1 v_1 + \cdots + c_{i-1} v_{i-1}$$

then

$$c_1 v_1 + \cdots + c_{i-1} v_{i-1} - v_i + 0 v_{i+1} + \cdots + 0 v_n = 0.$$

Thus the set is dependent. Conversely, if the set is dependent, then

$$c_1 v_1 + \cdots + c_n v_n = 0,$$

where some c_j is not zero. Let i be the rightmost subscript for which $c_i \neq 0$; then we can solve for v_i to get

$$v_i = \frac{c_1}{c_i} v_1 + \cdots + \frac{c_{i-1}}{c_i} v_{i-1}.$$

The key theorem on finite dimensional vector spaces is the following.

Theorem 9.4.11

Let V be spanned by $\{v_1, v_2, \ldots, v_n\}$, and let $\{w_1, w_2, \ldots, w_r\}$ be a linearly independent subset of V. Then $r \leq n$. ●

Proof

Let $A_1 = \{w_1, v_1, v_2, \ldots, v_n\}$. This is certainly dependent since $\{v_1, v_2, \ldots, v_n\}$ spans the space, and so w_1 must be a linear combination of these vectors. Thus some v_i is a linear combination of its predecessors. We may delete this vector from the set to get a set that still spans the space. Indeed, any vector that was a linear combination of vectors in A_1 is a linear combination of vectors in the new set by replacing any occurrence of v_i by its linear combination. To the set obtained by deleting v_i, adjoin w_2 to get $A_2 = \{w_1, w_2, \ldots\}$. This must also be dependent. Again, a vector in A_2 must be a linear combination of its predecessors, but note that it cannot be w_2 because $\{w_1, w_2, \ldots, w_r\}$ is an independent set. We delete the v vector and repeat the process. We can continue adding w's and deleting v's, but we cannot run out of v's before we have used all the w's because, if we did, one of the w's would be a linear combination of the w's now in the spanning set, and this would contradict the linear independence of $\{w_1, w_2, \ldots, w_r\}$. Thus $n \geq r$. ◆

If V is finite dimensional and $\{v_1, v_2, \ldots, v_m\}$ is a set of nonzero vectors that spans V, then it is linearly independent or dependent. If it is dependent, we delete any vector that is a linear combination of its predecessors. This process must stop with a linearly independent spanning set. Suppose that $A = \{v_1, v_2, \ldots, v_m\}$ and $B = \{w_1, w_2, \ldots, w_n\}$ are linearly independent spanning sets. Since A is independent and B spans, $m \leq n$; but B is independent and A spans, so $n \leq m$. Thus $m = n$. All linearly independent spanning sets have the same number of vectors. This motivates the following definition.

Definition 9.4.12

If V is a finite dimensional space and $\{v_1, v_2, \ldots, v_n\}$ is a linearly independent spanning set for V, we say that $\{v_1, v_2, \ldots, v_n\}$ is a basis for V. The (unique) number of vectors in a basis is called the **dimension** of the space. ●

The following theorem gives a useful summary.

Theorem 9.4.13

Let V be a finite dimensional vector space of dimension n. Then any linearly independent set of n vectors is a basis, and any spanning set of n vectors is a basis. ●

Proof

If a linearly independent set S of n vectors does not span V, there is a vector that is not a linear combination of the vectors in S. If this is added to the set, it is still independent. But this is impossible by Theorem 9.4.11.

If a spanning set of n vectors is dependent, one vector can be deleted and the remainder will still span the space. This is impossible, since the dimension is n.

◆

Example 9.4.14   Let P be the space of all polynomials of degree less than or equal to 3. This is a subspace of the space of all functions defined on the real line, so it is a vector space. Every element of P has the form

$$a_0 + a_1 x + a_2 x^2 + a_3 x^3,$$

and so P is spanned by the set of polynomials $\{1, x, x^2, x^3\}$. Moreover, the only way that a cubic polynomial can be the zero polynomial is if the coefficients of that polynomial are zero. So the set is independent. Thus $\{1, x, x^2, x^3\}$ is a basis for P. Bases are not unique. For example, you can check that $\{2, x - 1, x^2, x^3\}$ is also a basis. ∎

Example 9.4.15   Earlier it was promised to show that $C^2(a, b)$ is infinite dimensional. Suppose that it is not and that the set of functions $\{f_1, f_2, \ldots, f_n\}$ spans $C^2(a, b)$. Now consider the set of functions $\{1, x, x^2, \ldots, x^n\}$. This is a set of $n + 1$ members of $C^2(a, b)$. But this set is independent, because if

$$a_n x^n + \cdots + a_1 x + a_0 = 0$$

on the interval (a, b) then this polynomial has infinitely many roots, and the only polynomial with this property is the one with zero coefficients. So, by Theorem 9.4.11, $n + 1 \leq n$. This is impossible, so $C^2(a, b)$ is infinite dimensional. ∎

The final example of this section connects the concept of a finite dimensional vector space with the solutions to a linear nth-order homogeneous differential equation, discussed in Chapter 4.

Example 9.4.16   Consider the set S of all solutions to the equation

$$y'' - 3y' + 2y = 0.$$

Recall that, because the operator $P(D) = D^2 - 3D + 2$ is linear, linear combinations of solutions are again solutions. Thus S is a closed subset of the vector space $C^2(-\infty, \infty)$ of twice continuously differentiable functions on the real line. Obviously, the zero function is in S. So S is a subspace of $C^2(-\infty, \infty)$. A fundamental set of solutions to the equation is $\{e^t, e^{2t}\}$, and we know that every solution is a linear combination of these; so S is finite dimensional. In addition, e^{2t} cannot be written as ce^t, so, as we already know, $\{e^t, e^{2t}\}$ is linearly independent. Therefore, S is a subspace of dimension 2.

This example can be extended to any nth-order linear homogeneous differential equation to show that the set of all solutions to such an equation is an n-dimensional vector space. ■

EXERCISES 9.4.2

In Exercises 1–2, show that the given set of vectors spans $\mathbf{R}^2$ *and reduce it to a basis.*

1. $\{(1, 1), (2, -1), (3, 4)\}$

2. $\{(2, -1), (3, 1), (1, 2)\}$

3. Show that the set of vectors $\{(2, -1, 0), (3, 1, 1), (1, 2, -1), (1, 1, 1)\}$ spans $\mathbf{R}^3$ and reduce it to a basis.

4. Explain why $\{(2, -1, 0), (3, 1, 1)\}$ cannot span $\mathbf{R}^3$ without trying to solve any equations.

5. Find three different bases for $\mathbf{C}^2$, and show that they are bases. Include at least one with a vector with complex entries.

6. Find two different bases for the vector space of polynomials of degree less than or equal to 2. Explain why they are bases.

7. Show that the set $\{(1, 0, 1), (2, -1, 3), (1, 1, 2)\}$ is linearly independent in the space $\mathbf{R}^3$.

8. Show that the set $\{(1, 0, i, 2), (2, -1, 3, 0), (0, 1, 1, 2), (i, 1, 0, 3)\}$ is linearly independent in the space $\mathbf{C}^4$.

9. Formulate a way to test that a set of n vectors in $\mathbf{R}^n$ is a basis using the determinant of a matrix obtained from the vectors. *Hint:* Examine the cases provided by Exercises 7 and 8.

10. If V is an infinite dimensional space, explain why it is possible to have linearly independent sets of vectors with as many (finite) vectors in them as we like.

11. If V is a finite dimensional vector space, show that every subspace is finite dimensional. The dimension of the trivial subspace $\{0\}$ is taken to be zero. *Hint:* Consider Exercise 10.

In Exercises 12–14, find a basis for the space of solutions to the given equation and show that the vectors are linearly independent.

12. $y'' + 2y' + y = 0$

13. $y'' - 5y' + 6y = 0$

14. $y''' + y' = 0$

9.4.3   Inner Product Spaces

Finite dimensional spaces allow us to represent all vectors of the space uniquely as linear combinations of a finite set of vectors. The representation of vectors in an infinite dimensional space is done in terms of infinite sums or series, but this requires the additional structure of an inner product on the space.

We are all familiar with the dot product on the vectors in three-dimensional space. The concept can be extended to $\mathbf{R}^n$ by defining

$$(x_1, x_2, \ldots, x_n) \cdot (y_1, y_2, \ldots, y_n) = \sum_{k=1}^{n} x_k y_k.$$

In higher-dimensional spaces, the notation $v \cdot w$ is not often used. Instead, we shall use $\langle v, w \rangle$ for $v \cdot w$, and we shall refer to it as an inner product.

The following properties of this inner product are easy to verify. Let u, v and w be vectors in $\mathbf{R}^n$, and let a be a real number, then

1. $\langle u + v, w \rangle = \langle u, w \rangle + \langle v, w \rangle$,
2. $\langle au, w \rangle = a \langle u, w \rangle$,
3. $\langle u, w \rangle = \langle w, u \rangle$, and
4. $\langle u, u \rangle \geq 0$ and $\langle u, u \rangle = 0$ if and only if $u = 0$.

The last property can be used to define the length $||v||$ of a vector. We set

$$||v|| = \sqrt{\langle v, v \rangle}.$$

In $\mathbf{R}^3$ we know that two nonzero vectors are at right angles if and only if the inner or dot product of them is zero. In higher dimensions, we say that two nonzero vectors u and v are **orthogonal** if $\langle u, v \rangle = 0$. We say that a set of vectors is orthogonal if every vector in the set is orthogonal to every other vector in the set.

Certain bases for $\mathbf{R}^n$ are special in that they are orthogonal sets as well. The most familiar example is the basis $\{\vec{i}, \vec{j}, \vec{k}\}$. In $\mathbf{R}^3$ the set

$$\{(2, 0, 2), (0, 3, 0), (-1, 0, 1)\}$$

is also an orthogonal basis. Indeed, it seems likely that any orthogonal set of n nonzero vectors in $\mathbf{R}^n$ must be a basis.

Theorem 9.4.17

Suppose that $\{v_1, v_2, \ldots, v_n\}$ is an orthogonal set of vectors in $\mathbf{R}^n$. Then $\{v_1, v_2, \ldots, v_n\}$ is a basis.   ●

Proof

We show that $\{v_1, v_2, \ldots, v_n\}$ is linearly independent. Suppose that

$$c_1 v_1 + \cdots + c_n v_n = 0.$$

Then

$$0 = \langle 0, v_i \rangle = \langle c_1 v_1 + \cdots + c_n v_n, v_i \rangle$$

$$= \sum_{k=1}^{n} c_k \langle v_k, v_i \rangle = c_i \langle v_i, v_i \rangle.$$

But $\langle v_i, v_i \rangle$ is not zero, so $c_i = 0$. Thus all the coefficients are zero, and so the set is independent.   ◆

If $\{v_1, v_2, \ldots, v_n\}$ is an orthogonal basis it is easy to get the components of a vector relative to this basis. Suppose that

$$u = a_1 v_1 + \cdots + a_n v_n;$$

then

$$\langle u, v_i \rangle = \langle \sum_{k=1}^{n} a_k v_k, v_i \rangle$$

$$= \sum_{k=1}^{n} a_k \langle v_k, v_i \rangle = a_i \langle v_i, v_i \rangle.$$

Solving for a_i gives

$$a_i = \frac{\langle u, v_i \rangle}{||v_i||^2}.$$

This means that we have a representation of u in terms of the orthogonal basis and the inner product.

$$u = \frac{\langle u, v_1 \rangle}{||v_1||^2} v_1 + \cdots + \frac{\langle u, v_n \rangle}{||v_n||^2} v_n.$$

Example 9.4.18   We write $u = (2, 3, -1)$ relative to the orthogonal basis $\{(2, 0, 2), (0, 3, 0), (-1, 0, 1)\}$ in $\mathbf{R}^3$. We have

$$a_1 = \frac{\langle (2, 0, 2), (2, 3, -1) \rangle}{||(2, 0, 2)||^2} = \frac{2}{8},$$

$$a_2 = \frac{\langle (0, 3, 0), (2, 3, -1) \rangle}{||(0, 3, 0)||^2} = \frac{9}{9} = 1,$$

$$a_3 = \frac{\langle (-1, 0, 1), (2, 3, -1) \rangle}{||(-1, 0, 1)||^2} = \frac{-3}{2}.$$

Therefore,

$$u = \frac{2}{8}(2, 0, 2) + 1(0, 3, 0) + \frac{-3}{2}(-1, 0, 1).$$

It is this approach of representing vectors relative to orthogonal sets that generalizes to infinite dimensional spaces with inner products. The definition of an inner product on an infinite dimensional space is taken directly from the properties of the inner product on $\mathbf{R}^n$. We repeat them here for the sake of completeness.

Definition 9.4.19

A real vector space V is said to be an inner product space if there is an operation $\langle \cdot, \cdot \rangle$ on pairs of vectors such that, if u, v, and w are vectors in V and a is a real number, then $\langle u, v \rangle$ is a real number and

1. $\langle u + v, w \rangle = \langle u, w \rangle + \langle v, w \rangle$,
2. $\langle au, w \rangle = a\langle u, w \rangle$,
3. $\langle u, w \rangle = \langle w, u \rangle$, and
4. $\langle u, u \rangle \geq 0$ and $\langle u, u \rangle = 0$ if and only if $u = 0$.

We define the length $||v||$ of a vector by

$$||v|| = \sqrt{\langle v, v \rangle}.$$

In higher-dimensional spaces the length is usually called the **norm** of the vector. Just as in three-dimensional space, if u and v are vectors, we define the distance between them to be

$$||u - v||.$$

Two very important properties of norms are

$$||rv|| = |r|||v|| \quad \text{and} \quad ||v + w|| \leq ||v|| + ||w||.$$

The first is very easy to verify, and it is left to you. The second, called the **triangle inequality**, is more difficult to prove. We need the following theorem.

Theorem 9.4.20   (Schwarz's Inequality)

Let v and w be vectors in a real inner product space V. Then

$$|\langle v, w \rangle| \leq ||v||||w||. \qquad \bullet$$

Proof

Suppose first that $\langle v, w \rangle \geq 0$. Note that $0 \leq \langle v - w, v - w \rangle$, so

$$0 \leq \langle v - w, v - w \rangle = \langle v, v \rangle - 2\langle v, w \rangle + \langle w, w \rangle = ||v||^2 + ||w||^2 - 2\langle v, w \rangle.$$

Thus

$$2\langle v, w \rangle \leq ||v||^2 + ||w||^2,$$

but because $\langle v, w \rangle \geq 0$,

$$|\langle v, w \rangle| = \langle v, w \rangle \leq ||v||^2 + ||w||^2.$$

The case for $\langle v, w \rangle \leq 0$ is similar except that we now expand $\langle v+w, v+w \rangle$. ◆

It is now easy to get the triangle inequality. We have

$$
\begin{aligned}
||v + w||^2 &= \langle v + w, v + w \rangle = ||v||^2 + 2\langle v, w \rangle + ||w||^2 \\
&\leq ||v||^2 + 2|\langle v, w \rangle| + ||w||^2 \leq ||v||^2 + 2||v||||w|| + ||w||^2 \\
&= (||v|| + ||w||)^2.
\end{aligned}
$$

Taking the square root of both sides gives us what we want.

The concept of an orthogonal basis is similar to the one we have already discussed. Here is the definition.

Definition 9.4.21

We say that $\{v_k\}_{k=1}^{\infty}$ is an orthogonal basis for a real inner product space V if the vectors v_k belong to V, the set of vectors is orthogonal with respect to the inner product on V, and every vector u can be written in the form

$$u = \sum_{k=1}^{\infty} a_k v_k.$$

●

The infinite sum in this series demands some comment. As with most infinite series, a limit of partial sums is involved. In this case, the statement that

$$u = \sum_{k=1}^{\infty} a_k v_k$$

means that the distance between the partial sum

$$\sum_{k=1}^{n} a_k v_k$$

and the vector u approaches zero as n goes to infinity. That is,

$$\lim_{n \to \infty} \left\| \sum_{k=1}^{n} a_k v_k - u \right\| = 0.$$

A careful study of infinite dimensional inner product spaces requires more advanced methods of mathematical analysis than we can use here. The main purpose of introducing inner product spaces is to provide a unifying language in which to discuss the topics of the rest of this chapter. In view of this, we shall be careless about questions such as the convergence of series, and we shall proceed in a more formal manner. In particular, we shall assume that any operation that can be performed with a finite sum extends to infinite sums as well.

With this last comment in mind, suppose that

$$u = \sum_{k=1}^{\infty} a_k v_k,$$

where $\{v_k\}$ is an orthogonal sequence of vectors; then

$$\langle u, v_i \rangle = \langle \sum_{k=1}^{\infty} a_k v_k, v_i \rangle$$

$$= \sum_{k=1}^{\infty} a_k \langle v_k, v_i \rangle = a_i \langle v_i, v_i \rangle.$$

The last equality follows from the orthogonality, because $\langle v_k, v_i \rangle = 0$ for all k except $k = i$. Consequently,

$$a_i = \frac{\langle u, v_i \rangle}{||v_i||^2}.$$

We call the a_i the coefficients of u relative to the orthogonal sequence $\{v_i\}$. Sometimes they are called generalized Fourier coefficients, and

$$\sum_{k=1}^{\infty} a_k v_k$$

is often called a generalized Fourier series.

You may notice a similarity in form in the computation of the coefficients a_i to the computation of Fourier coefficients in the last section. This is taken up in detail in Section 9.5.

You may be wondering if there is an equivalent notion of an inner product for complex vector spaces. There is! As may be expected, the scalar product $\langle u, v \rangle$ is a complex number in the complex case, and the only axiom that we need to modify is the second. Instead of the inner product being commutative, it must satisfy

$$\langle u, v \rangle = \overline{\langle v, u \rangle},$$

where the overline indicates the conjugate of the quantity below it. Complex inner products defined in this way are often called hermitian inner products. We will not need hermitian inner product spaces, but it should be mentioned that if you become interested in quantum mechanics then complex inner product spaces are indispensable.

EXERCISES 9.4.3

1. Verify properties 1 to 4 of the inner product on $\mathbf{R}^2$.

2. Define a "product" on $\mathbf{R}^2$ by

$$\langle (x_1, x_2), (y_1, y_2) \rangle = 3x_1 y_1 + 2x_2 y_2.$$

   Show that this is an inner product.

3. Find the coefficients of $(5, 4, -2)$ relative to the orthogonal basis

$$\{(2, 0, 2), (0, 3, 0), (-1, 0, 1)\}$$

   in $\mathbf{R}^3$. Use the inner product.

4. Find the coefficients of $(4, -6)$ relative to the orthogonal basis $\{(4, 3), (-3, 4)\}$ in $\mathbf{R}^2$. Use the inner product.

5. Let P_2 be the vector space of all real polynomials of de-gree less than or equal to 2. For f and g in P_2, define

$$\langle f, g \rangle = \int_0^1 f(x)g(x)\, dx.$$

   (a) Show that $\langle f, g \rangle$ is an inner product.
   (b) Find an orthogonal basis for P_2. *Hint:* Take $f_1(x) = 1$ as the first vector. Then try to find $f_2(x) = a_0 + a_1 x$, which is orthogonal to f_1. Finally, try to find a quadratic orthogonal to the two you already have.

6. Repeat Exercise 5 for the vector space P_3 of all real polynomials of degree less than or equal to 3.

7. Consider the vector space of all real continuous functions defined on the interval $[0, \pi]$. Define an inner product on

this space by

$$\langle f, g \rangle = \int_0^\pi f(x)g(x)\, dx.$$

(a) Show that this defines an inner product on the space. Note that property 4 follows from the fact that $\int_0^\pi (f(x))^2\, dx = 0$ implies that $f(x) \equiv 0$.

(b) Show that $\{\sin(nx)\}$ is an orthogonal sequence of functions.

(c) Find the coefficients a_i of $f(x) = 1$ relative to the sequence in part b.

(d) Use a graphing facility to graph partial sums

$$\sum_{k=1}^n a_k \sin(kx)$$

for $n = 3$, $n = 5$, and $n = 10$. Describe what you see.

8. In Exercise 7, change the interval to $[0, 1]$.

(a) Show that $\{\sin(\pi nx)\}$ is an orthogonal sequence.

(b) Find the generalized Fourier series of $f(x) = x$ on $[0, 1]$.

(c) Graph several partial sums of this series, and describe what you see.

9. Consider the vector space of real continuous functions defined on $[0, 1]$. Show that

$$\langle f, g \rangle = \int_0^1 f(x)g(x)x^2\, dx$$

is an inner product on this space.

10. Consider the vector space of real continuous functions defined on $[-1, 1]$. Why does the formula

$$\langle f, g \rangle = \int_{-1}^1 f(x)g(x)x\, dx$$

not define an inner product?

9.4.4 Linear Operators

Another recurrent notion in this text has been that of a linear operator. We saw it in Chapters 4 and 5. The Laplace transform is a linear operation, and the notion of linearity surfaced again in this chapter. Now that we have the concept of a vector space, we can define what is meant by a linear operator in a unifying manner.

Before doing this, let us review the definition of a function. If A and B are sets, then by a function f from A to B we mean that f is a relation between the elements of A and those of B such that, for each $x \in A$, there is exactly one element $y \in B$ such that f relates x to y. We write $f(x) = y$. You will recall that we call A the domain of the function, and B is called the codomain. No, it is not necessarily the range of f, because the range of f is defined by

$$\text{Ran}(f) = \{f(x) \mid x \in A\}.$$

Thus the range of f is the set of all values, $f(x)$, of f, and this does not have to be all of B. Therefore, a function always consists of three parts: the domain, the codomain, and the relation between these sets. The standard notation for a function when all three of these elements are to be stated is

$$f : A \to B.$$

We say that $f : A \to B$ is a function from A to B, or we say that f maps A to B, or we say that f is a mapping from A to B.

Definition 9.4.22

Let V and W be vector spaces with the same scalars. Then a linear operator or linear transformation from V to W is a mapping $L : V \to W$ from V to W such that, for any v_1 and v_2 in V and any scalars c_1 and c_2,

$$L(c_1 v_1 + c_2 v_2) = c_1 L(v_1) + c_2 L(v_2).$$

We often abbreviate by simply saying that L is linear. ●

Example 9.4.23   Consider the vector space $\mathbf{R}^n$, where we write the vectors as columns. Let A be any $n \times n$ matrix. Define $L : \mathbf{R}^n \to \mathbf{R}^n$ by

$$L(X) = AX$$

for any column vector X. Then, by the properties of matrices,

$$L(c_1 X_1 + c_2 X_2) = A(c_1 X_1 + c_2 X_2) = c_1 A X_1 + c_2 A X_2$$
$$= c_1 L(X_1) + c_2 L(X_2).$$

Therefore, L is linear. ■

This example demonstrates that each $n \times n$ matrix defines a linear transformation from the finite dimensional space $\mathbf{R}^n$ to itself. We can symbolize this by

$$A \to L_A.$$

It is natural to ask if every linear transformation on $\mathbf{R}^n$ arises in this way. The answer is yes!

To see this, let E_i be the column vector with 1 in the ith row and zeros elsewhere. These vectors form a basis called the **standard basis**. If $L : \mathbf{R}^n \to \mathbf{R}^n$ is a linear transformation then we can write

$$L(E_1) = a_{11} E_1 + \cdots + a_{n1} E_n,$$
$$L(E_2) = a_{12} E_1 + \cdots + a_{n2} E_n,$$
$$\vdots$$
$$L(E_n) = a_{1n} E_1 + \cdots + a_{nn} E_n.$$

Let A be the matrix (a_{ij}). We show that $L(X) = AX$. Let $X = (x_1, x_2, \ldots, x_n)^t$, so X is a column. Note that

$$X = x_1 E_1 + \cdots + x_n E_n,$$

and so

$$L(X) = L(x_1 E_1 + \cdots + x_n E_n)$$

$$= x_1 L(E_1) + \cdots + x_n L(E_n)$$

$$= x_1 \sum_{k=1}^{n} a_{k1} E_k + \cdots + x_n \sum_{k=1}^{n} a_{kn} E_k.$$

Rearranging the sums gives

$$L(X) = (\sum_{k=1}^{n} a_{1k} x_k) E_1 + \cdots + (\sum_{k=1}^{n} a_{nk} x_k) E_n = AX.$$

This association of linear transformations with matrices can be done for any finite dimensional vector space, but to do it we must choose a basis as we just did. So the association is not unique. We shall not pursue this further, since we shall not need it in the sequel.

You will recall that we have used linearity more than once to show that linear combinations of solutions to homogeneous equations are also solutions. We expressed a solution to a homogeneous equation by

$$L(y) = 0,$$

where L was a linear operator. We are now in a position to describe the general principles that underlie this.

Definition 9.4.24

Let $L : V \rightarrow W$ be a linear operator. The set

$$K = \{v | L(v) = 0\}$$

is called the **kernel** or **null-space** of the operator L. ●

The kernel is a subspace of V because $0 \in K$ (why?), and it is closed under addition and scalar multiplication (why?).

Example 9.4.25 Consider the linear differential equation

$$y'' - 4y' + 3y = 0.$$

Consider the linear operator $L : C^2(R) \rightarrow C(R)$ defined by

$$L(y) = y'' - 4y' + 3y,$$

where $C^2(R)$ and $C(R)$ are the vector spaces of twice continuously differentiable functions and continuous functions on the real line, respectively. The set of solutions to the homogeneous equation is nothing but the kernel of L. From Chapter 4 we know that $\{e^t, e^{3t}\}$ is a linearly independent set of solutions and that every solution is a linear combination of these solutions. In our new language, this says that the kernel of L is a two-dimensional subspace of $C^2(R)$ with basis $\{e^t, e^{3t}\}$. . ■

This example adds the concept of the kernel to the same type of example that closed Section 9.4.2. This generalizes immediately to any nth-order linear homogeneous differential equation. The kernel of an nth-order linear differential operator has dimension n.

Example 9.4.26   The definite integral is a linear operator. Define L : $C[a, b] \to \mathbf{R}$ by

$$L(f) = \int_a^b f(x) \, dx,$$

where $C[a, b]$ is the vector space of continuous functions on $[a, b]$. The linearity property is the following familiar property of integrals:

$$\int_a^b c_1 f(x) + c_2 g(x) \, dx = c_1 \int_a^b f(x) \, dx + c_2 \int_a^b g(x) \, dx. \qquad \blacksquare$$

The Laplace transform is linear basically because integration is linear. The domain for the Laplace transform is the set of all piecewise continuous functions defined on $[0, \infty)$. That this set is a vector space is left to the exercises. The codomain is more problematical, because a Laplace transform $\hat{f}(s)$ is defined only for $s \geq a$ for some a, and this a may change from function to function. We shall skip over this subtlety.

Eigenvalues and Eigenvectors

The eigenvalues and eigenvectors of a matrix representing a first-order system played a central role in the solution of first-order linear systems in Chapter 5. They will play an important role in the rest of this chapter. Again, the concepts of a vector space and linear operator provide the unifying framework in which the notions of eigenvalue and eigenvector can be expressed.

Definition 9.4.27

Let $L : V \to W$ be a linear operator. We say that λ is an eigenvalue of L if there is a nonzero vector v in V such that

$$L(v) = \lambda v.$$

We say that v is an eigenvector of L corresponding to λ.   ●

If λ is an eigenvalue of an operator L, then the set V_λ of all vectors that satisfy $L(v) = \lambda v$ is a subspace of V. Since $L(0) = 0 = \lambda 0$, 0 is in V_λ. Also, if u and v are in V_λ, then

$$L(u + v) = L(u) + L(v) = \lambda u + \lambda v = \lambda(u + v),$$

so $u + v$ is in V_λ. Finally, if a is a scalar, then

$$L(av) = aL(v) = a\lambda v = \lambda(av),$$

so av is in V_λ. The space V_λ is the set of all eigenvectors of L corresponding to λ together with 0. This space is called the **eigensubspace** corresponding to λ.

Example 9.4.28   Consider the operator $L : \mathbf{R}^2 \to \mathbf{R}^2$ defined by $L(x, y) = (2x - 3y, -y)$. Then if (x, y) is an eigenvector, we must have

$$L(x, y) = (2x - 3y, -y) = \lambda(x, y)$$

for some eigenvalue λ. From this we get the equations

$$(2 - \lambda)x - 3y = 0$$
$$(1 + \lambda)y = 0.$$

Now, if $y \neq 0$, then $\lambda = -1$, and so $x = y$. Therefore, -1 is an eigenvalue, and the V_{-1} eigensubspace consists of all vectors of the form (x, x).

If $y = 0$, then for an eigenvector we must have $x \neq 0$. Thus $\lambda = 2$ is an eigenvalue. So V_2 consists of all vectors of the form $(x, 0)$. ∎

Example 9.4.29   Consider the matrix

$$A = \begin{bmatrix} 4 & -2 \\ 3 & -1 \end{bmatrix}.$$

Let L be the linear operator defined on $V = \mathbf{C}^2$ by $L(X) = AX$. Then λ is an eigenvalue if X is a nonzero vector such that

$$L(X) = AX = \lambda X.$$

So the eigenvalues and eigenvectors of L are precisely the eigenvalues and eigenvectors of the matrix A as defined in Chapter 5.

We can find the eigensubspaces as we did in Chapter 5. First, λ is an eigenvalue if and only if

$$AX - \lambda X = (A - \lambda I)X = 0$$

has a nonzero solution. But this is true only if the characteristic polynomial

$$P(\lambda) = \det(A - \lambda I) = \lambda^2 - 3\lambda + 2$$

is equal to zero. So the eigenvalues are 1 and 2.

We can now find V_1 by finding all solutions to

$$(A - 1I)X = 0.$$

The corresponding system is

$$3x - 2y = 0,$$
$$3x - 2y = 0.$$

The eigensubspace of 1 is spanned by the single vector

$$\begin{bmatrix} 2 \\ 3 \end{bmatrix},$$

so V_1 is a one-dimensional subspace of V. Finding V_2 is left to the reader. ∎

Many further examples of eigenvalues and eigenvectors follow in this chapter.

EXERCISES 9.4.4

1. Let P_2 be the space of polynomials of degree less than or equal to 2. Define $L : P_2 \to \mathbf{R}$ by

$$L(f) = \int_0^1 f(x)\,dx.$$

   Show that L is linear.

2. Define $L : \mathbf{R} \to \mathbf{R}$ by $L(x) = 3x$. Show that L is linear.

3. Define $L : \mathbf{R}^3 \to \mathbf{R}^2$ by $L(x, y, z) = (2x - z, 3y + z)$. Show that L is linear.

4. Define $L : \mathbf{C}^2 \to \mathbf{C}^2$ by $L(z_1, z_2) = (2z_1 + iz_2, z_1 - iz_2)$. Show that L is linear.

5. Suppose that $L_1 : V \to W$ and $L_2 : V \to W$ are linear operators. Show that $(L_1 + L_2) : V \to W$, defined by

$$(L_1 + L_2)(v) = L_1(v) + L_2(v),$$

   is linear.

6. Suppose that $L_1 : V_1 \to V_2$ and $L_2 : V_2 \to V_3$ are linear. Show that $L_2 L_1 : V_1 \to V_3$, defined by $L_2 L_1(v) = L_2(L_1(v))$ (composition), is linear.

7. Suppose that V is an inner product space. We say that the linear map $L : V \to V$ is symmetric if

$$\langle L(u), v \rangle = \langle u, L(v) \rangle$$

   for all u and v in V. If $V = \mathbf{R}^2$ and L is defined by $L(X) = AX$, that is, $L = L_A$, for a 2×2 matrix A, what condition on A will make L symmetric? Work in column form. *Hint:* What do the equations

$$\langle L(E_i), E_j \rangle = \langle E_i, L(E_j) \rangle$$

   for $i, j = 1$, or 2 say about A?

8. Let P_2 be the space of polynomials of degree 2 or less. Define $L : P_2 \to P_2$ by

$$L(a_0 + a_1 x + a_2 x^2) = a_0 + a_1 x.$$

   Find the two eigenvalues and eigensubspaces of L. *Hint:* The definition of eigenvalue and eigenvector implies that

$$a_0 + a_1 x = \lambda(a_0 + a_1 x + a_2 x^2).$$

9. Let $L : \mathbf{R}^2 \to \mathbf{R}^2$ be defined by $L(x, y) = (3x, -2y)$. Find all the eigenvalues and eigensubspaces of L.

10. Let $L : \mathbf{R}^2 \to \mathbf{R}^2$ be defined by $L(x, y) = (3x + 2y, -4y)$. Find all the eigenvalues and eigensubspaces of L.

11. Find a linear operator $L : \mathbf{R}^2 \to \mathbf{R}^2$ that has no eigenvalues. *Hint:* Find a matrix with no real eigenvalues and construct L from that.

12. Suppose that V is a complex inner product space and the operator $L : V \to V$ is symmetric, as defined in Exercise 7. Show that any eigenvalues of L must be real. *Hint:* Let v be a λ eigenvector of L. Compute $\langle L(v), v \rangle$ and $\langle v, L(v) \rangle$, and remember that $\langle u, v \rangle = \overline{\langle u, v \rangle}$.

13. Let V be the vector space of all infinitely differentiable functions defined on the interval $[0, 4]$ that are zero at the endpoints. Consider the differential operator $D^2 : V \to V$. Find all the eigenvalues and eigenvectors.

14. Let V be the vector space of all infinitely differentiable functions defined on the interval $[-2, 2]$ that are zero at the endpoints. Consider the differential operator D^2 : $V \to V$. Find all the eigenvalues and eigenvectors.

9.5 THE HEAT EQUATION REVISITED

In this section we shall use the methods developed in the last section to reexamine the solution of the heat equation given in Section 9.3. We begin by restating the problem. We have $u_{xx} = u_t$, $u(0, t) = u(b, t) = 0$ for $t \geq 0$, and $u(x, 0) = f(x)$, where

$$f(x) = \begin{cases} 2x, & \text{for } 0 \leq x \leq b/2, \\ b - 2(x - \frac{b}{2}), & \text{for } b/2 \leq x \leq b. \end{cases}$$

First notice that the boundary conditions played a central role in the solution. Indeed, the function $f(x)$ was represented as a sum of functions that satisfied these conditions. Consider the set of infinitely differentiable functions on $[0, b]$ that satisfy the boundary conditions. Because the boundary conditions are homogeneous, the sum and scalar multiple of such functions is again a function of the same type. Thus this set is a vector space. Let us denote it by V. Then V is the set of all real valued infinitely differentiable functions defined on $[0, b]$ that vanish at the endpoints of the interval.

Next we found all the solutions to

$$-X''(x) = \lambda X(x)$$

in V. That is, we found all solutions to the preceding equations that satisfied the homogeneous boundary conditions. They were $\{\sin(\frac{\pi k x}{b})\}$. Let us look at this from a different angle. The equation

$$-X''(x) = \lambda X(x)$$

can be rewritten as

$$-\frac{d^2}{dx^2} X = \lambda X.$$

The operator $\Delta = \frac{d^2}{dx^2}$ is the one-dimensional Laplace operator. On the vector space V, it is linear. That is, for X and Y in V and real numbers a and b,

$$\Delta(aX + bY) = a\Delta(X) + b\Delta(Y).$$

In solving

$$-\Delta(X) = \lambda X$$

in V we are finding the eigenvalues and eigenvectors of $-\Delta$. Eigenvectors that are functions are usually called **eigenfunctions**. The use of $-\Delta$ instead of Δ ensures that the eigenvalues are positive, and this is preferred by most.

As we saw in the last section, linear combinations of eigenvectors corresponding to a given eigenvalue are eigenvectors (or zero) of the same eigenvalue. Most often we shall have only one independent eigenvector corresponding to a given eigenvalue. That is, usually the eigensubspaces will be one dimensional. In this case the eigenvector is determined uniquely up to scalar multiples. If there should be more than one independent eigenvector corresponding to an eigenvalue, the eigenvalue is often said to be degenerate. We will deal with degenerate eigenvalues when they arise.

So far the steps are to define the space V of infinitely differentiable functions satisfying the boundary conditions and then to find the eigenvalues and eigenvectors corresponding to each eigenvalue for the Laplacian on this vector space. If λ_k is an eigenvalue with eigenvector $X_k(x)$, then, if $T_k(t)$ satisfies $T_k' = -\lambda_k T_k$, then $u_k(x, t) = X_k T_k$ satisfies

$$u_{k,xx} = X_k'' T_k = -\lambda_k X_k T_k = X_k(-\lambda_k T_k) = X_k T_k' = u_{k,t}.$$

This is a solution to the heat equation that also satisfies the boundary conditions. All that remains is to satisfy the initial condition. Since the heat equation is linear, any linear combination of the $u_k(x, t)$ will also be a solution and satisfy the boundary conditions. It turns out that, under general conditions, even infinite sums of the form

$$u(x, t) = \sum_{k=1}^{\infty} A_k u_k(x, t)$$

can be differentiated term by term, and so such infinite sums solve the heat equation and boundary conditions also. To solve the initial condition, we need

$$f(x) = u(x, 0) = \sum_{k=1}^{\infty} A_k u_k(x, 0) = \sum_{k=1}^{\infty} A_k X_k(x).$$

Notice that although $f(x)$ must satisfy the boundary conditions, $f(x)$ may not be infinitely differentiable. Indeed, $f(x)$ may not even be continuous. Thus many of the functions that we seek to represent as series do not belong to V. We must consider these functions as members of a larger vector space than V. For our purposes we can take this larger space to be the space of all piecewise continuous functions on the interval $[0, b]$. Recall that a function is piecewise continuous on an interval if it has only a finite number of discontinuities; at each discontinuity inside the interval the left- and right-hand limits exist; and if it is discontinuous at the left or right endpoint, then the right or left limit, respectively, exists. In brief, a piecewise continuous function on an interval has only a finite number of simple jump discontinuities. We shall denote this vector space by $\overline{V}$. Note that V is a subspace of this space.

The next task in our model example was to compute the A_k in the representation

$$f(x) = \sum_{k=1}^{\infty} A_k X_k(x).$$

The key to this calculation was the fact that the functions $X_k(x)$ form an orthogonal sequence relative to the inner product

$$\langle g, h \rangle = \int_0^b g(x)h(x)\, dx$$

on $\overline{V}$. Therefore, the A_k are calculated in the same way that we calculate the coefficients of any vector represented as a series relative to an orthogonal set. That is,

$$A_k = \frac{\langle f, X_k \rangle}{||X_k||^2}.$$

We can now see that the representation of $f(x)$ as a series,

$$f(x) = \sum_{k=1}^{\infty} A_k \sin(\frac{\pi k x}{b}),$$

is an example of the more general process of representing vectors in inner product spaces relative to orthogonal sequences. Before giving a final example, it is important to make a connection between the Laplacian $-\Delta$ and the orthogonality of its eigenfunctions.

9.5.1 Orthogonality of the Eigenvectors

You may ask if the orthogonality of the eigenfunctions in the sequence $\{\sin(\frac{\pi n x}{b})\}$ was an accident. The answer is no! First note that

$$\langle -\frac{d^2}{dx^2} f, g \rangle = -\int_0^b f'' g\, dx.$$

Integration by parts gives

$$\int_0^b f'' g\, dx = g(x) f'(x)|_0^b - g'(x) f(x)|_0^b + \int_0^b f g''\, dx.$$

But, because the functions vanish at the endpoints, we have

$$\langle -\frac{d^2}{dx^2} f, g \rangle = -\int_0^b f'' g\, dx = -\int_0^b f g''\, dx = \langle f, -\frac{d^2}{dx^2} g \rangle.$$

We say that $-\Delta = -\frac{d^2}{dx^2}$ is symmetric with respect to the inner product. We make the following definition.

Definition 9.5.1

If $L : V \to \overline{V}$ is a linear operator defined on a subspace V of the inner product space $\overline{V}$, we say that L is symmetric with respect to the inner product if

$$\langle L(u), v \rangle = \langle u, L(v) \rangle$$

for all vectors u and v in V. ●

Now consider any symmetric operator L on a space V. Let λ_1 and λ_2 be distinct eigenvalues of this operator with corresponding eigenvectors v_1 and v_2. Then

$$(\lambda_1 - \lambda_2)\langle v_1, v_2 \rangle = \lambda_1 \langle v_1, v_2 \rangle - \lambda_2 \langle v_1, v_2 \rangle$$
$$= \langle \lambda_1 v_1, v_2 \rangle - \langle v_1, \lambda_2 v_2 \rangle = \langle L(v_1), v_2 \rangle - \langle v_1, L(v_2) \rangle = 0.$$

But $(\lambda_1 - \lambda_2) \neq 0$, since the eigenvalues are distinct, and so

$$\langle v_1, v_2 \rangle = 0.$$

We have proved the following theorem:

Theorem 9.5.2

Let L be a symmetric operator defined on an inner product space V. Then eigenvectors corresponding to distinct eigenvalues are orthogonal.   ●

Since $\Delta = \frac{d^2}{dx^2}$ is symmetric on the space of infinitely differentiable functions on $[0, b]$ that vanish at the endpoints, the sequence $\{\sin(\frac{\pi n x}{b})\}$ is orthogonal.

Warning: It makes no sense to speak of an operator being symmetric without reference to the space on which it acts. The operator $\frac{d^2}{dx^2}$ is not symmetric in and of itself. Go back and see the crucial role that vanishing at the endpoints played.

We conclude this section with an example that reviews the points that we have made. In addition, this example introduces you to an alternative boundary condition called a **Neumann** condition.

Example 9.5.3   Consider a bar of homogeneous material on the interval $[0, 1]$. Suppose that the bar is not only insulated along its length, but also at the ends. The temperature distribution $u(x, t)$ satisfies the heat equation $a^2 u_{xx} = u_t$. We assume that $a = 1$. Since the ends are insulated also, the temperature gradient at $x = 0$ and $x = 1$ must be zero. Thus $u_x(0, t) = 0$ and $u_x(1, t) = 0$ for all $t \geq 0$. These are the Neumann boundary conditions. Neumann boundary conditions are considered further in the supplementary exercises at the end of the chapter. We also assume that the bar has an initial temperature distribution of $u(x, 0) = 4x(1 - x)$. We now solve the heat equation, reviewing all the points that we have made.

First we must identify the vector space on which the Laplacian $-\Delta$ is to be defined. The boundary conditions are that the functions must have vanishing first derivatives at the endpoints of $[0, 1]$. Therefore, we define V to be the set of all infinitely differentiable functions defined on $[0, 1]$ whose first derivatives vanish at 0 and 1. The zero function is of this type, and the sum and scalar multiple of functions of this type is again of this type. Thus V is a vector space, and

$-\Delta$ is clearly linear on this space. We take $\overline{V}$ to be the space of all piecewise continuous functions on $[0, 1]$.

We now find the eigenfunctions. That is, we solve

$$-\Delta(X) = \lambda X.$$

The form of the solution is

$$X(x) = A \cos(\mu x) + B \sin(\mu x),$$

where $\mu^2 = \lambda$. The Neumann conditions require that the derivative of this function be zero at the endpoints. Thus

$$X'(0) = -A\mu \sin(\mu 0) + B\mu \cos(\mu 0) = B\mu = 0.$$

So $B = 0$ or $\mu = 0$. If $\mu = 0$, then $X_0(x) = 1$ is an eigenfunction. If $\mu \neq 0$, then $B = 0$, and so

$$X'(1) = -A\mu \sin(\mu) = 0.$$

If we are to have a nonzero eigenfunction, we must have $A \neq 0$ and $\sin(\mu) = 0$. Hence $\mu = \pi k$, and

$$X_k(x) = \cos(\pi k x)$$

is an eigenfunction corresponding to the eigenvalue $\lambda = \pi^2 k^2$. The eigenfunctions are

$$\{1, \cos(\pi k x)\}.$$

It is left to you as an exercise to show that $-\Delta$ is symmetric on V with respect to the inner product

$$\langle f, g \rangle = \int_0^1 fg \, dx$$

by considering integration by parts. Therefore, the eigenfunctions are orthogonal.

For each eigenvalue we solve $T' + \pi^2 k^2 T = 0$ to get $T(t) = e^{-\pi^2 k^2 t}$. We now can write the form of the solution:

$$u(x, t) = A_0 + \sum_{k=1}^{\infty} A_k e^{-\pi^2 k^2 t} \cos(\pi k x).$$

For $t = 0$ we have

$$u(x, 0) = 4x(1 - x) = A_0 + \sum_{k=1}^{\infty} A_k \cos(\pi k x),$$

so $4x(1 - x)$ is represented as an orthogonal sum. We calculate the A_k as we would the coefficients in any orthogonal representation. We have

$$A_0 = \frac{\langle 4x(1 - x), 1 \rangle}{||1||^2} = \int_0^1 4x(1 - x) \, dx = \frac{2}{3}$$

and

$$A_k = \frac{\langle 4x(1-x), \cos(\pi kx) \rangle}{|| \cos(\pi kx) ||^2} = 2 \int_0^1 4x(1-x) \cos(\pi kx) \, dx$$

$$= \frac{-8(1 + (-1)^k)}{\pi^2 k^2}.$$

The complete solution is

$$u(x, t) = \frac{2}{3} + \sum_{k=1}^{\infty} \frac{-8(1 + (-1)^k)}{\pi^2 k^2} e^{-\pi^2 k^2 t} \cos(\pi kx).$$

It is well worth noticing what happens as t goes to infinity. The solution approaches 2/3. The temperature in the bar evens out to a constant temperature. This fits with our own experience. ∎

EXERCISES 9.5

1. Show that $-\Delta$ on the vector space V with Neumann conditions is symmetric.

2. Solve $u_{xx} = u_t$ on $[0, 2]$ with Neumann conditions and $u(x, 0) = x$ as initial condition. What is the final temperature?

In Exercises 3–5, assume that the inner product is

$$\langle f, g \rangle = \int_0^1 f(x)g(x) \, dx.$$

3. Is the operator $L(y) = y'' + 2y$ symmetric on the space of all infinitely differentiable functions that vanish at 0 and 1? If so, find the eigenvalues and eigenfunctions.

4. Show that the operator $L(y) = y^{(3)}$ is not symmetric on the space of all infinitely differentiable functions that vanish at 0 and 1. *Hint:* Try the functions $f(x) = x^2(x-1)$ and $g(x) = x(x-1)$.

5. Let $L(y) = y^{(4)}$. Determine minimal zero boundary conditions on the space of all infinitely differentiable functions that makes L symmetric by examining the process of integrating by parts.

In Exercises 6-8, the vector space is $\mathbf{R}^2$ with the usual dot product.

6. Define the operator L by $L(x, y) = (x+y, x+2y)$. Show that L is symmetric on $\mathbf{R}^2$ with the dot product. Find the eigenvectors, and show by direct computation that eigenvectors corresponding to distinct eigenvalues are orthogonal.

7. Define the operator L by $L(x, y) = (y, x)$. Show that L is symmetric on $\mathbf{R}^2$ with the dot product. Find the eigenvectors, and show by direct computation that eigenvectors corresponding to distinct eigenvalues are orthogonal.

8. Define the operator L by $L(x, y) = (x+y, x-y)$. Show that L is symmetric on $\mathbf{R}^2$ with the dot product. Find the eigenvectors and show by direct computation that eigenvectors corresponding to distinct eigenvalues are orthogonal.

9. Consider $L(y) = y'' + y'$.
   (a) Find a function $w(x) > 0$ such that $L(y) = \frac{1}{w(x)}(w(x)y')'$. Now show that L is symmetric if

   $$\langle f, g \rangle = \int_0^1 f(x)g(x)w(x) \, dx$$

   is the inner product on the space of twice continuously differentiable functions that vanish at the endpoints of $[0, 1]$. *Hint:* In the symmetry calculation, show that the left side and the right side are equal to the same thing.
   (b) Find the eigenvalues and eigenfunctions.

10. Look up Legendre's equation in Chapter 6.
    (a) Show that the equation can be put in the form $[(1 - x^2)y']' = -\alpha(\alpha + 1)y$. For two Legendre polynomials $P_n(x)$ and $P_m(x)$, you have $[(1 - x^2)P_n']' = -n(n + 1)P_n$ and $[(1 - x^2)P_m']' = -m(m + 1)P_m$.
    (b) Use part a to show that the Legendre polynomials

are orthogonal with respect to the inner product

$$\langle P_n, P_m \rangle = \int_{-1}^{1} P_n P_m \, dx.$$

Take the space to be the continuous functions on $[-1, 1]$.

9.6 PERIODIC FUNCTIONS AND FOURIER SERIES

You may have noticed that our series representations by sine or cosine functions extend to a periodic function beyond the interval of interest in the heat equation. This suggests that periodic functions of a very general type may be represented as series in the right inner product space.

A function f defined on the real line is periodic if there is a positive number p such that

$$f(x + p) = f(x)$$

for all x. For example, $\sin(x)$ has period 2π.

Consider the set $\overline{V}$ of all periodic functions of period p that are piecewise continuous. A function is piecewise continuous on the real line if it is piecewise continuous on every finite closed interval of the real line. The sum of such functions is again periodic with period p and piecewise continuous. Likewise, any scalar multiple is of period p and piecewise continuous. Thus $\overline{V}$ is a vector space. We define an inner product on $\overline{V}$ by

$$\langle f, g \rangle = \int_{0}^{p} f(x)g(x) \, dx.$$

Note that the integral is taken over one period. Because f and g are periodic with period p, the integral could have been taken over any interval of length p.

Consider the one-dimensional Laplacian operator $\Delta = \frac{d^2}{dx^2}$ again. Clearly, Δ is not defined on all of $\overline{V}$, for many of the functions in $\overline{V}$ are not even continuous. But Δ is defined on the subspace V of all infinitely differentiable functions of period p. On this subspace, Δ is symmetric. This follows from

$$\int_{0}^{p} f''g \, dx = g(x)f'(x)\big|_{0}^{p} - g'(x)f(x)\big|_{0}^{p} + \int_{0}^{p} fg'' \, dx$$

and the fact that the functions have period p.

To find the eigenfunctions and eigenvalues of $-\Delta$, we must solve

$$-\Delta(X) = -X'' = \lambda X,$$

where X must be in V; that is, X must be an infinitely differentiable function of period p. We must solve

$$X'' + \lambda X = 0.$$

Therefore,

$$X(x) = Ae^{\sqrt{-\lambda}x} + Be^{-\sqrt{-\lambda}x}.$$

But if the solution is to be periodic, λ cannot be negative, and so we set $\mu^2 = \lambda$. Therefore,

$$X(x) = A\sin(\mu x) + B\cos(\mu x).$$

This solution must have period p, so the choices for μ are

$$\mu = \frac{2\pi k}{p},$$

where $k = 0, 1, 2, \ldots$. Thus the eigenfunctions corresponding to $\lambda = \mu^2$ all have the form

$$X(x) = A\sin(\mu x) + B\cos(\mu x).$$

In this case we have two independent eigenfunctions corresponding to λ that generate, by taking linear combinations, all the eigenfunctions of λ.

We have found the following basic eigenfunctions:

$$\{1, \sin(\frac{2\pi k}{p}x), \cos(\frac{2\pi k}{p}x)\}$$

for $k = 1, 2, \ldots$. Since $-\Delta$ is symmetric, eigenfuctions corresponding to distinct eigenvalues are orthogonal; but what if they correspond to the same eigenvalue? In that case we have degeneracy. We have

$$\langle \sin(\frac{2\pi k}{p}x), \cos(\frac{2\pi k}{p}x)\rangle = \int_0^p \sin(\frac{2\pi k}{p}x)\cos(\frac{2\pi k}{p}x)\,dx$$

$$= \frac{p}{4\pi k}\sin^2(\frac{2\pi k}{p}x)|_0^p = 0.$$

Therefore, the sine and cosine pair corresponding to a given eigenvalue are orthogonal also.

We now show how a member of $\overline{V}$ can be represented as a series using this orthogonal basis. For definiteness, let $p = 2$. Let $f(x)$ be defined by

$$f(x) = \begin{cases} 1, & \text{for } 0 < x \le 1, \\ 0, & \text{for } 1 < x \le 2. \end{cases}$$

This is a sequence of 1-unit pulses spaced at 1-unit intervals. We write

$$f(x) = A_0 + \sum_{k=1}^{\infty} A_k\cos(\pi kx) + \sum_{k=1}^{\infty} B_k\sin(\pi kx),$$

and it remains to compute the A_k and B_k.

Now

$$\langle 1, 1\rangle = \int_0^2 1\cdot 1\,dx = 2,$$

$$\langle \sin(\pi kx), \sin(\pi kx) \rangle = \int_0^2 \sin^2(\pi kx)\, dx = \int_0^2 (1 - \cos(2\pi kx))/2\, dx = 1,$$

and, similarly,

$$\langle \cos(\pi kx), \cos(\pi kx) \rangle = 1.$$

We now use the usual formulas for computing the coefficients of a vector relative to an orthogonal family of functions. We have

$$A_0 = \frac{\langle 1, f(x) \rangle}{\langle 1, 1 \rangle} = \frac{1}{2},$$

$$A_k = \frac{\langle \cos(\pi kx), f(x) \rangle}{\langle \cos(\pi kx), \cos(\pi kx) \rangle} = \int_0^1 \cos(\pi kx)\, dx$$

$$= \frac{1}{\pi k} \sin(\pi kx)|_0^1 = 0$$

and

$$B_k = \frac{\langle \sin(\pi kx), f(x) \rangle}{\langle \sin(\pi kx), \sin(\pi kx) \rangle}$$

$$= \int_0^1 \sin(\pi kx)\, dx = -\frac{1}{\pi k} \cos(\pi kx)|_0^1 = \frac{1}{\pi k}(1 - (-1)^k).$$

Putting all this together gives

$$f(x) = \frac{1}{2} + \sum_{k=1}^{\infty} \frac{(1 - (-1)^k)}{\pi k} \sin(\pi kx).$$

Figures 9.6 and 9.7 show the approximation of $f(x)$ first with two terms of the series and then with ten terms.

The approximation can be improved on by taking more terms of the series, but it is very interesting that the little overshoots at the jump discontinuities will always remain. This is called the **Gibbs' phenomenon**, and it is further investigated in a Supplementary Exercise 1. However, this observation does raise the question of the nature of convergence of Fourier series. This is a matter that will require some discussion, so it will be presented in Section 9.8 after we have had a chance to make a further application of the method to the one-dimensional wave equation.

The orthogonal families of functions that we have studied have all arisen as eigenfunctions of the Laplacian on various spaces. This is because our motivation is the solution of partial differential equations in which the Laplacian plays a central role. However, there is nothing to prevent considering the representation of functions relative to any orthogonal family, while ignoring any connection with symmetric operators and eigenfunctions. The preceding example shows that we can represent any periodic function of period p relative to the family

$$\{1, \sin(\frac{2\pi k}{p}x), \cos(\frac{2\pi k}{p}x)\}.$$

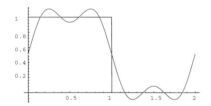

FIGURE 9.6

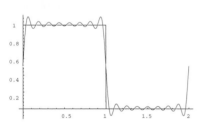

FIGURE 9.7

Let us take a few moments to review the method and give an example.

The vector space $\overline{V}$ is the space of all piecewise continuous periodic functions of period p. The inner product is

$$\langle f, g \rangle = \int_0^p f(x)g(x)\,dx,$$

and, as we have seen, the preceding family of functions is orthogonal with respect to this inner product. Given a piecewise continuous periodic function $f(x)$, we can represent it by

$$f(x) = A_0 + \sum_{k=1}^{\infty} A_k \cos(2\pi kx/p) + \sum_{k=1}^{\infty} B_k \sin(2\pi kx/p),$$

where the coefficients are computed from the usual formulas:

$$A_0 = \frac{1}{p} \int_0^p f(x)\,dx,$$

$$A_k = \frac{2}{p} \int_0^p f(x) \cos(2\pi kx/p)\,dx,$$

$$B_k = \frac{2}{p} \int_0^p f(x) \sin(2\pi kx/p)\,dx.$$

Example 9.6.1   Consider $f(x)$ of period 2 defined by $f(x) = -1$ on $[0, 1]$ and $f(x) = x$ on $[1, 2]$. Then the series is

$$f(x) =$$

$$\frac{1}{4} + \sum_{k=1}^{\infty} \frac{1 - (-1)^k}{2\pi^2 k^2} \cos(2\pi kx/2) + \sum_{k=1}^{\infty} \left(\frac{(-1)^k - 1}{\pi k} - \frac{1}{2\pi k} \right) \sin(2\pi kx/2).$$

■

The majority of series that we have considered so far have consisted of sine terms, so it is reasonable to ask if these series can be considered as special cases of the series

$$f(x) = A_0 + \sum_{k=1}^{\infty} A_k \cos(2\pi kx/p) + \sum_{k=1}^{\infty} B_k \sin(2\pi kx/p).$$

The answer is yes!

9.6.1 Even and Odd Functions

A function $f(x)$ defined on the real line is said to be **odd** if $f(-x) = -f(x)$ for all x. We say that it is **even** if $f(-x) = f(x)$. The graph of an odd function is symmetric with respect to the origin and that of an even function is symmetric with respect to the y-axis. Observe that the product of odd functions is even, and the product of even functions is even. Mixed products are odd.

Suppose that $f(x)$ is an odd periodic function with period p. Then the integrand of

$$A_k = \frac{2}{p} \int_{-p/2}^{p/2} f(x) \cos(2\pi kx/p)\, dx$$

is odd, and so the integral is zero. The same is true for A_0. Therefore, there are no cosine terms, and the series is a sine series. But there is more. Since the integrand in the formula for the B_k is even,

$$B_k = \frac{2}{p} \int_{-p/2}^{p/2} f(x) \sin(2\pi kx/p)\, dx = \frac{2}{b} \int_0^b f(x) \sin(\pi kx/b)\, dx,$$

where $b = p/2$. Moreover, for distinct k and j,

$$0 = \int_{-p/2}^{p/2} \sin(2\pi kx/p) \sin(2\pi jx/p)\, dx = 2 \int_0^b \sin(\pi kx/b) \sin(\pi jx/b)\, dx.$$

Therefore, the family $\{\sin(\pi kx/b)\}$ is orthogonal with respect to the inner product on $[0, b]$, as we have seen in discussing the Heat Equation. So the sine series is, indeed, a special case of the more general sine and cosine series. Such sine series are often called **half-range expansions**.

Perhaps the easiest way to get a sine (or cosine) series for a function $f(x)$ given on $[0, b]$ is to extend $f(x)$ as an odd (even) function to $[-b, b]$. Then extend this as a periodic function of period $p = 2b$, and use the Fourier series given previously. This way you need only recall one set of coefficient formulas. Of course, you calculate only one set of coefficients depending on whether the extension of $f(x)$ is odd or even.

Example 9.6.2   Let us derive the cosine series for the function $f(x) = x$ defined on $[0, 2]$. We extend $f(x)$ as an even function on $[-2, 2]$ with period 4. Thus on $[-2, 2]$, $f(x) = |x|$. Since it is even, we need only consider the coefficients A_k. Therefore,

$$A_0 = \frac{1}{4} \int_{-2}^2 |x|\, dx = \frac{1}{2} \int_0^2 |x|\, dx = 1$$

and

$$A_k = \frac{2}{4} \int_{-2}^2 |x| \cos(2\pi kx/4)\, dx = \int_0^2 x \cos(\pi kx/2)\, dx = \frac{-4}{(\pi k)^2}(1 - (-1)^k).$$

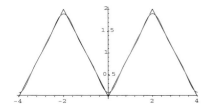

FIGURE 9.8

The even terms are zero, so

$$f(x) = 1 + \sum_{k=1}^{\infty} \frac{-8}{(\pi(2k-1))^2} \cos(\pi(2k-1)x/2).$$

Figure 9.8 shows a partial sum with three terms on the interval $[-4, 4]$. ■

EXERCISES 9.6

1. Let $f(x)$ be periodic, and let $f(x)$ be defined in one period by

$$f(x) = \begin{cases} -1, & \text{for } -3 \le x < 0, \\ 1, & \text{for } 0 \le x \le 3. \end{cases}$$

   Find the Fourier series of this function. Graph partial sums of the series.

2. Let $f(x) = x^2$ on the interval $[0, 4]$. Find the series representation of $f(x)$ relative to the eigenfunctions of $-\Delta$ that vanish at the endpoints (sines). Graph partial sums of the series.

In Exercises 3–5, let $f(x)$ be periodic, and let $f(x)$ be defined in one period by the given function. Find the Fourier series of this function. Graph partial sums of the series.

3. $f(x) = \begin{cases} x, & \text{for } -3 \le x < 0, \\ 2x, & \text{for } 0 \le x \le 3. \end{cases}$

4. $f(x) = \begin{cases} -1, & \text{for } -3 \le x < 0, \\ x, & \text{for } 0 \le x \le 3. \end{cases}$

5. $f(x) = \begin{cases} 1, & \text{for } -3 \le x < 0, \\ \sin(\pi x/3), & \text{for } 0 \le x \le 3. \end{cases}$

6. Let $f(x)$ be defined on $[0, 3]$ by

$$f(x) = \begin{cases} x, & \text{for } 0 \le x < 1, \\ 1, & \text{for } 1 \le x \le 2, \\ 3 - x, & \text{for } 2 \le x < 3. \end{cases}$$

Find the sine series of this function. Graph partial sums of the series.

7. For $f(x) = x$ defined on $[0, 1]$, find a cosine series representation by making an even extension to $[-1, 1]$ and repeating periodically with period 2. Graph partial sums and compare with $f(x)$.

8. For $f(x) = x$ defined on $[0, 3]$, find a sine series representation by making an odd extension to $[-3, 3]$ and repeating periodically with period 6. Graph partial sums and compare with $f(x)$.

9. For $f(x) = x^3$ defined on $[0, 1]$, find a cosine series representation by making an even extension to $[-1, 1]$ and repeating periodically with period 2. Graph partial sums and compare with $f(x)$.

10. For $f(x) = x^2$ defined on $[0, 3]$, find a sine series representation by making an odd extension to $[-3, 3]$ and repeating periodically with period 6. Graph partial sums and compare with $f(x)$.

11. Examine all the Fourier series in the text and those that you have computed, and make a conjecture about the convergence of a Fourier series at a point of discontinuity.

9.7 THE ONE-DIMENSIONAL WAVE EQUATION

In this section we shall apply separation of variables and the Fourier methods to the vibration of a stretched string. D'Alembert's solution of the problem will also be briefly discussed. This is done in order to make the connection between vibrations and traveling waves.

Imagine a homogeneous string stretched between the two points 0 and b on the x-axis. If $u(x, t)$ is the displacement of point x on the string at time t, the equation governing the motion of this string is the one-dimensional wave equation

$$c^2 u_{xx} = u_{tt}.$$

For a unique solution we need to specify the initial position $f(x)$ and velocity $g(x)$ of each point of the string. Also, the ends of the string are fixed, and so this gives the following side conditions:

$$u(x, 0) = f(x) \qquad \text{and} \qquad u_t(x, 0) = g(x)$$

and

$$u(0, t) = u(b, t) = 0.$$

Now let us solve this problem by separation of variables. Set

$$u(x, t) = X(x)T(t).$$

Then, as before, the separation gives

$$\frac{X''}{X} = \frac{1}{c^2} \frac{T''}{T} = -\lambda.$$

This results in the spatial eigenvalue equation

$$-\Delta(X) = \lambda X$$

and the equation

$$T'' + c^2 \lambda T = 0.$$

As before, the space for the Laplacian is the space of infinitely differentiable functions on $[0, b]$ that vanish at the endpoints. The eigenvalues for $k = 1, 2, \ldots$ are

$$\lambda_k = \mu^2 = \frac{\pi^2 k^2}{b^2},$$

and the eigenfunctions are

$$X_k(x) = \sin\left(\frac{\pi k x}{b}\right).$$

Corresponding to λ_k is the solution,

$$T_k(t) = A_k \cos\left(\frac{\pi k c t}{b}\right) + B_k \sin\left(\frac{\pi k c t}{b}\right),$$

to the equation

$$T'' + c^2 \lambda_k T = 0.$$

The function

$$u_k(x, t) = X_k(x) T_k(t)$$

satisfies the wave equation and the boundary conditions, but the initial conditions remain to be satisfied. As in the heat equation, the initial conditions are satisfied by turning to infinite series. Consider

$$u(x, t) = \sum_{k=1}^{\infty} [A_k \cos\left(\frac{\pi kct}{b}\right) + B_k \sin\left(\frac{\pi kct}{b}\right)] \sin\left(\frac{\pi kx}{b}\right).$$

For the initial displacement at $t = 0$, we have

$$u(x, 0) = f(x) = \sum_{k=1}^{\infty} A_k \sin\left(\frac{\pi kx}{b}\right).$$

The A_k are computed in the usual way. For the initial velocity, we have

$$u_t(x, t) = \sum_{k=1}^{\infty} [-A_k \frac{\pi kc}{b} \sin\left(\frac{\pi kct}{b}\right) + B_k \frac{\pi kc}{b} \cos\left(\frac{\pi kct}{b}\right)] \sin\left(\frac{\pi kx}{b}\right),$$

and so

$$u_t(x, 0) = g(x) = \sum_{k=1}^{\infty} B_k \frac{\pi kc}{b} \sin\left(\frac{\pi kx}{b}\right).$$

The B_k are found as before, except that we use $g(x)\frac{b}{\pi kc}$ instead of $g(x)$ alone in the coefficient formulas.

Example 9.7.1   Consider a string stretched between 0 and 2 on the x-axis and satisfying the equation $9u_{xx} = u_{tt}$. Assume that the boundary conditions are homogeneous. For the initial conditions, assume that $u(x, 0) = x$ on [0, 1], and $u(x, 0) = 2 - x$ on [1, 2], and $u_t(x, 0) = \sin(\pi x)$. The general form of our solution is

$$u(x, t) = \sum_{k=1}^{\infty} [A_k \cos\left(\frac{\pi 3kt}{2}\right) + B_k \sin\left(\frac{\pi 3kt}{2}\right)] \sin\left(\frac{\pi kx}{2}\right),$$

and at $t = 0$ we must satisfy

$$u(x, 0) = \sum_{k=1}^{\infty} A_k \sin\left(\frac{\pi kx}{2}\right).$$

Thus the A_k are determined by

$$A_k = \int_0^2 u(x, 0) \sin\left(\frac{\pi kx}{2}\right) dx.$$

The integration by parts yields

$$A_k = 2\frac{\sin(\frac{\pi k}{2})}{\pi^2 k^2} - 4\frac{\cos(\frac{\pi k}{2})}{\pi k}.$$

The initial velocity requires that we find the B_k from

$$u_t(x, 0) = \sin(\pi x) = \sum_{k=1}^{\infty} B_k \frac{\pi 3k}{2} \sin\left(\frac{\pi k x}{2}\right).$$

You will notice that $\sin(\pi x)$ is the eigenfunction corresponding to $k = 2$, and so it is orthogonal to all but itself. Thus the only nonzero B_k is $B_2 = 1/(3\pi)$.

Therefore, our solution is

$$u(x, t) = \frac{1}{3\pi} \sin(3\pi t) \sin(\pi x)$$

$$+ \sum_{k=1}^{\infty} [2\frac{\sin(\frac{\pi k}{2})}{\pi^2 k^2} - 4\frac{\cos(\frac{\pi k}{2})}{\pi k}] \cos\left(\frac{\pi 3k t}{2}\right) \sin\left(\frac{\pi k x}{2}\right).$$

■

When a guitar string is plucked, the string is displaced and then released. Consequently, the initial velocity is zero. The solution then reduces to the simpler form

$$u(x, t) = \sum_{k=1}^{\infty} A_k \cos\left(\frac{\pi k c t}{b}\right) \sin\left(\frac{\pi k x}{b}\right).$$

The vibration described by $u(x, t)$ is a superposition (sum) of simple vibrations $A_k \cos(\frac{\pi k c t}{b}) \sin(\frac{\pi k x}{b})$. Fix a value of x; then the simple motion of this point is a sinusoidal motion up and down with amplitude $A_k \sin(\frac{\pi k x}{b})$ and period $\frac{2b}{ck}$. For $k = 1$, the string is initially displaced as one arch of the sine function. As time progresses, the string moves toward the x-axis, crosses it, and forms into an arch of the sine function at time $t = b/c$. This motion is called the **fundamental** or **first harmonic** of the motion. Since $A_k \sin(\frac{\pi k x}{b})$ is the amplitude of the kth harmonic, if it is reflected in the x-axis, it forms an **envelope** of that simple vibration. In a sense, it is the blurred region that you would see if the string were vibrating in this simple mode. The eigenfunctions of the Laplacian are often called the **modes** of vibration. Perhaps you have seen a guitarist pluck a string while lightly touching it in the middle. The result is a tone an octave higher than a normal pluck. By touching the string in the middle, the guitarist has ensured that the coefficient A_1 is zero. Thus the vibration starts with the second harmonic, which is twice the frequency of the first. Figure 9.9 illustrates the first two modes of vibration. The amplitudes of these envelopes are, of course, greatly exaggerated.

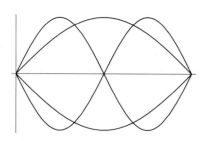

FIGURE 9.9

9.7.1 D'Alembert's Solution

You may wonder what the role of c is in the vibration. The constant c combines the physical constants of the density and tension of the string. One role of c in the solution is to effect the frequency of vibrations of the modes. The larger c is, the higher the frequencies of the vibrations. Less easy to see is the fact that c determines the speed of transmission of signals in the string.

Consider the function

$$u(x, t) = f(x - ct) + g(x + ct),$$

where f and g are twice continuously differentiable. Then

$$u_{xx}(x, t) = f''(x - ct) + g''(x + ct)$$

and

$$u_{tt}(x, t) = c^2 f''(x - ct) + c^2 g''(x + ct).$$

So u satisfies the wave equation. We can even satisfy the initial conditions by solving

$$u(x, 0) = f(x) + g(x), \qquad \text{and} \qquad u_t(x, 0) = -cf'(x) + cg'(x).$$

However, $u(x, t)$ usually does not satisfy the boundary conditions unless f and g are quite special. The function

$$u(x, t) = f(x - ct) + g(x + ct)$$

is called d'Alembert's solution to the wave equation, and it models waves in an infinite string.

D'Alembert's solution suggests taking another look at the solution

$$u(x, t) = \sum_{k=1}^{\infty} A_k \cos\left(\frac{\pi k c t}{b}\right) \sin\left(\frac{\pi k x}{b}\right).$$

By using the identity

$$\sin(A)\cos(B) = \frac{1}{2}[\sin(A + B) + \sin(A - B)],$$

we can rewrite $u(x, t)$ as follows:

$$u(x, t) = \sum_{k=1}^{\infty} \frac{A_k}{2} \sin\left(\frac{\pi k}{b}(x + ct)\right) + \sum_{k=1}^{\infty} \frac{A_k}{2} \sin\left(\frac{\pi k}{b}(x - ct)\right).$$

This is d'Alembert's form of the solution. Each sum is a periodic function that extends to the whole real line. The first function is a periodic wave traveling to the left with velocity c; the second function travels to the right with the same velocity. In a sense, the vibration of the string on $[0, b]$ can be thought of as the sum of these two traveling waves on the real line viewed only in the window $[0, b]$. This suggests that d'Alembert's approach can be used to solve the problem of the vibration of a finite string. Here is an example of this approach.

Example 9.7.2   Consider a string stretched along $[0, b]$. Suppose that the initial displacement is given by $f(x)$ and the initial velocity is zero. D'Alembert's solution has the form

$$u(x, t) = h(x - ct) + k(x + ct),$$

so

$$h(x) + k(x) = f(x)$$

and

$$-ch'(x) + ck'(x) = 0.$$

Differentiate the first relation to get

$$h'(x) + k'(x) = f'(x).$$

We can now solve for the derivatives of h and k. Indeed,

$$h'(x) = k'(x) = \frac{1}{2} f'(x).$$

Thus

$$h(x) = \frac{1}{2} f(x) + a,$$

and so

$$k(x) = \frac{1}{2} f(x) - a.$$

When these are added, a drops out, so it can be ignored.

We now have a solution that satisfies the initial conditions, but we have not faced the homogeneous boundary conditions. How can we get $u(0, t) = u(b, t) = 0$ for all t? The key is in the solution obtained previously by separation of variables. Recall that the two series in that solution define periodic functions of x of period $2b$. Moreover, each series defines an odd function. Because of these observations, we simply extend h and k from $[0, b]$ to odd periodic functions of period $2b$ on the whole real line. In view of this,

$$u(0, t) = h(-ct) + k(ct) = -h(ct) + k(ct) = 0$$

and

$$u(b, t) = h(b - ct) + k(b + ct) = h(-2b + b - ct) + k(b + ct)$$
$$= -h(b + ct) + k(b + ct) = 0.$$

We see that the boundary conditions are satisfied.   ■

9.7.2 Singular Solutions

D'Alembert's solution suggests there are "solutions" to the wave equation that do not fit the strict definition of a solution. In Example 9.7.2, suppose that the initial displacement $f(x)$ is defined by

$$f(x) = \begin{cases} 2x, & \text{for } 0 \le x \le b/2, \\ b - 2(x - \frac{b}{2}), & \text{for } b/2 \le x \le b. \end{cases}$$

This function is not differentiable at $b/2$. Such a point is called a **singularity**. Using this function in d'Alembert's approach does not, strictly speaking, give a solution of the wave equation, because the equation is not satisfied at the singularity. However, in all other respects this gives a satisfactory solution. Indeed, this solution is easily seen to be the limiting case of solutions in which the sharp corner has been smoothed out over shorter and shorter intervals about the singularity. We touched on a similar situation when considering impulses and discontinuous forcing functions in Chapter 8 and in considering uniqueness of solutions in this chapter. Both situations suggested that we need a broader definition of what a solution to a differential equation is. Such solutions can be called **singular solutions**. This has been done in the theories of distributions and generalized functions, but a introductory text on differential equations is not the place for this. Consequently, the mathematical subtleties associated with singular solutions will be ignored.

9.7.3 Separation versus D'Alembert

Finally, you may be wondering why we bother with separation of variables for the wave equation. It does seem that d'Alembert's approach is much simpler. Although this is true, d'Alembert's method does not give information about the harmonics that occur in the solution. A Fourier analysis is needed for that. Moreover, d'Alembert's method does not extend in any simple way to solutions of the wave equation in higher-dimensions where boundary conditions hold. Therefore, our use of separation of variables in the one-dimensional case can be justified as preparation for the higher-dimensional cases.

EXERCISES 9.7

Some of these exercises may be facilitated by using a computer algebra system such as Mathematica, Maple, or MatLab.

1. Use separation of variables to solve the wave equation $4u_{xx} = u_{tt}$ on $[0, 2]$ with homogeneous boundary conditions and initial conditions $u_t(x, 0) = 0$ and $u(x, 0) = \sin(\pi x)$. Describe the motion of a point x on the string. Draw, by hand, graphs of the string at a succession of times that captures the motion of the string as a whole.

2. Use separation of variables to solve the wave equation $4u_{xx} = u_{tt}$ on $[0, 2]$ with homogeneous boundary conditions and initial conditions $u(x, 0) = 0$ and $u_t(x, 0) = x(2 - x)$. Graph partial sums for several values of t. Try $t = 0, t = 0.2, t = 0.5, t = 0.8$, and $t = 1.2$ Summarize what you find out.

3. Use separation of variables to solve the wave equation $4u_{xx} = u_{tt}$ on $[0, 2]$ with homogeneous boundary conditions and initial conditions $u_t(x, 0) = 0$ and $u(x, 0) = \sin(2\pi x)$. Is this a pure mode of vibration? Draw graphs of $u(x, t)$ as a function of x for several values of t increasing from zero until you have an animation of the solution.

4. Solve $4u_{xx} = u_{tt}$ on $[0, 1]$, where the initial displacement is $u(x, 0) = \sin(\pi x)$ and the initial velocity is zero. Graph the solution for several values of t. Convert the solution to d'Alembert's form.

5. Solve $u_{xx} = u_{tt}$ on $[0, 2]$, where the initial displacement is $u(x, 0) = \sin(2\pi x)$ and the initial velocity is $u_t(x, 0) = \sin(\pi x)$. Graph the solution for several values of t. Convert the solution to d'Alembert's form.

6. Calculate the first four nonzero terms of the solution to $u_{xx} = u_{tt}$ on $[0, 2]$, where the initial displacement is

$$f(x) = \begin{cases} x, & \text{for } 0 \le x \le 1, \\ 2 - x, & \text{for } 1 \le x \le 2, \end{cases}$$

and the initial velocity is zero. Graph this partial sum for several values of t. Explain the behavior in terms of the d'Alembert traveling waves by drawing diagrams of $f(x - t)$ and $f(x + t)$ in the same coordinates for two or three values of t. In particular, how does $u(x, t) = 0$ arise in terms of traveling waves?

7. Calculate the first five nonzero terms of the solution to

$u_{xx} = u_{tt}$ on $[0, 2]$, where the initial displacement is $f(x) = x(2 - x)$ and the initial velocity is zero. Graph this partial sum for several values of t. Explain the behavior in terms of the d'Alembert traveling waves by drawing diagrams of $f(x - t)$ and $f(x + t)$ in the same coordinates for two or three values of t. In particular, how does $u(x, t) = 0$ arise in terms of traveling waves?

8. Is the initial position and velocity repeated time after time for a stretched string? Explain!

9. Use d'Alembert's approach to solve Exercise 3. Is d'Alembert's solution the same as the one in Exercise 3?

10. Use d'Alembert's approach to solve Exercise 4.

11. Use d'Alembert's approach to solve Exercise 5.

12. In Exercise 5, what is the ratio of the amplitudes of the first and third harmonics? What about the second harmonic?

13. The wave equation with air resistance for a string is $c^2 u_{xx} = u_{tt} + ru_t$. Derive the general form of the solution of this equation for a string stretched on the interval $[0, b]$. Assume that resistance is small enough that vibration is possible. Point out the factor in this solution that causes the vibration to die out.

14. Suppose that the air resistance to vibration is proportional to the square of the velocity. The equation is $c^2 u_{xx} = u_{tt} + ru_t^2$. What goes wrong with an attempt to use separation of variables on this problem? No, it is not that it is hard to solve the T equation.

9.8 THE CONVERGENCE OF SERIES

A full treatment of the convergence of Fourier series calls for a knowledge of methods from advanced calculus. Since this cannot be assumed, the treatment here is cursory and intuitive. This section can be omitted without loss of continuity, but you are encouraged to at least skim this section.

The main complication involved in the question of the nature of convergence of Fourier series is that two types of convergence are involved. These are **convergence in norm**, and **pointwise convergence**. We discuss these in turn.

If $\{v_k\}$ is an orthogonal sequence in an inner product space $\overline{V}$, then the statement

$$u = \sum_{k=1}^{\infty} a_k v_k$$

means that the "distance"

$$\left\| u - \sum_{k=1}^{n} a_k v_k \right\|$$

between u and the partial sum of the series $\sum_{k=1}^{n} a_k v_k$ can be made as small as we please by choosing n large enough. We can express this by

$$u = \lim_{n \to \infty} \sum_{k=1}^{n} a_k v_k.$$

We say the partial sums converge to u in norm.

Consider the specific case where $\overline{V}$ is the space of piecewise continuous functions on $[0, 2\pi]$. An orthogonal sequence is given by

$$\{\sin(kx)\}.$$

Suppose that $f(x)$ is represented as a Fourier series relative to this orthogonal sequence. Then

$$f(x) = \sum_{k=1}^{\infty} A_k \sin(kx),$$

but what does this mean? If convergence in norm is meant, then

$$\int_0^{2\pi} |f(x) - \sum_{k=1}^{n} A_k \sin(kx)|^2 \, dx = ||f - \sum_{k=1}^{n} A_k \sin(kx)||^2$$

can be made as small as we please by choosing n large enough. Notice that the partial sum is considered close to f if this integral is made small. Above all, notice that this criterion of closeness between the partial sum and f says nothing about whether the value $f(x)$ and the partial sum $\sum_{k=1}^{n} A_k \sin(kx)$ evaluated at x are close. Indeed, for a given value of x we can redefine the value of $f(x)$ to any new value without changing the integral. Roughly, a single point x has no length, and so altering the function at this point does not affect the integral.

If the partial sums converge to $f(x)$ for a given value of x, this is called **pointwise convergence** at x. More precisely, the partial sums converge pointwise to $f(x)$ at x if

$$|f(x) - \sum_{k=1}^{n} A_k \sin(kx)|$$

can be made as small as we please by choosing n large enough. We say that the partial sums converge pointwise on a given set of real numbers if the partial sums converge pointwise at every point of that set.

We have observed that norm convergence does not imply pointwise convergence at any particular point. However, our experience indicates that, for a given function f, pointwise convergence is taking place for most of the points in the domain of f. Indeed, experience indicates that the partial sums converge pointwise at the points of continuity of f. At jump discontinuities of f, the partial sums converge to the mean of the jump. Figure 9.10 shows a partial sum approximation of a "square wave" with period 2π. Observe the features dis-

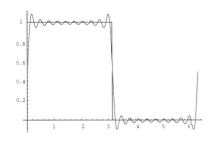

FIGURE 9.10

cussed so far. If you use higher-order partial sums (see the exercises), you will see that they are converging pointwise at any value of x in $(0, \pi)$ or $(\pi, 2\pi)$. At the jump discontinuities, the sums converge to 0.5. The only disturbing thing is the Gibbs phenomenon mentioned earlier. These "ears" next to the jump discontinuities do not go away as the partial sums are made larger. However, they do become narrower; so for any fixed x in the open intervals where the wave is continuous, the Gibbs "ears" will eventually contract enough to uncover x. In view of this, we still have pointwise convergence on these open intervals. The Gibbs Phenomenon is investigated in the supplementary exercises.

For the Fourier series of periodic functions represented by sine and cosine series, the basic theorem on pointwise convergence is the following:

Theorem 9.8.1

If f is a piecewise continuous periodic function on the real line and f' is also piecewise continuous, then the corresponding Fourier series converges pointwise at every point. If x is a point of continuity of f, then the series converges to $f(x)$, and if x is a point of discontinuity of f, then the series converges to the average of the left and right limits of f at x. ●

EXERCISES 9.8

1. Let $f(x) = x^2$. Then $\int_0^2 f(x)\,dx = 8/3$. Suppose that we redefine f by setting $f(1) = 4$ and $f(x) = x^2$ for $x \neq 1$. What is the value of $\int_0^2 f(x)\,dx$? What point does this illustrate in norm convergence of Fourier series?

2. Let f be a periodic function defined in one period by $f(x) = x$ for x in $[0, 1]$. Find the Fourier series of f. Draw the graphs of f and several partial sums of the Fourier series. Describe what you see in light of the theorem of this section.

3. Let f be a periodic function defined in one period by $f(x) = 1$ for x in $[0, 1]$ and $f(x) = -1$ for x in $[1, 2]$. Find the Fourier series of f. Draw the graphs of f and several partial sums of the Fourier series. Describe what you see in light of the theorem of this section.

4. Let f be a periodic function defined in one period by $f(x) = 2$ for x in $[0, 1]$ and $f(x) = 1$ for x in $[1, 2]$. To what values does the Fourier series converge at $x = 1$ and $x = 0.5$?

5. Let f be a periodic function defined in one period by $f(x) = x^2$ for x in $[0, 1]$ and $f(x) = 0$ for x in $[1, 2]$. To what values does the Fourier series converge at $x = 1$ and $x = 0.5$?

6. This problem gives a way to compute π. Consider the periodic function f defined in one period by $f(x) = -1$ for x in $[-\pi, 0]$ and $f(x) = 1$ for x in $[0, \pi]$. Compute the Fourier series. To what does it converge at $\pi/2$? Use this to get a series for π.

9.9 THE TWO-DIMENSIONAL WAVE EQUATION

In this section we apply the method of separation of variables to two drums. One is a rectangular drum and the other is circular.

9.9.1 A Rectangular Drum

Consider a rectangular drum with the drumhead being the rectangle $D = [0, a] \times [0, b]$ in x,y-coordinates. If $u(x, y, t)$ is the vertical displacement of the membrane at time t, we have seen that u satisfies the two-dimensional wave equation

$$c^2[u_{xx} + u_{yy}] = u_{tt}.$$

The boundary conditions are that the membrane does not move along the boundary, so $u(x, y, t) = 0$ for all (x, y) on the boundary and for all $t \geq 0$. The initial conditions specify the initial displacement and velocity, so we are given

$$u(x, y, 0) = f(x, y) \text{ and } u_t(x, y, 0) = g(x, y)$$

for all $(x, y) \in D$.

We solve this equation by again separating the spatial and time parts. We set

$$u(x, y, t) = S(x, y)T(t).$$

If we set $-\Delta(S) = -[S_{xx} + S_{yy}]$, then we have

$$\frac{\Delta(S)}{S} = \frac{1}{c^2}\frac{T''}{T} = -\lambda.$$

As before, we solve the spatial eigenvalue problem

$$-\Delta(S) = \lambda S$$

first.

In this case the space V is the space of all functions of two variables that vanish on the boundary of D and have partial derivatives of all orders. The inner product is defined by

$$\langle f, g \rangle = \int\int_D f(x, y)g(x, y)\, dx\, dy.$$

We leave it to the exercises to show that $-\Delta$ is symmetric on this space.

The equation

$$-\Delta(S) = \lambda S$$

is solved by separation of variables. Let

$$S(x, y) = X(x)Y(y).$$

Then

$$\frac{X''}{X} + \frac{Y''}{Y} = -\lambda,$$

so

$$\frac{X''}{X} = -\frac{Y''}{Y} - \lambda = -\mu.$$

Here μ is again a constant. Therefore, we must solve

$$X'' + \mu X = 0 \quad \text{and} \quad Y'' + (\lambda - \mu)Y = 0.$$

Now $X(0) = X(a) = Y(0) = Y(b) = 0$ from the boundary conditions, so

$$\sqrt{\mu} = \frac{\pi j}{a}$$

and

$$X_j(x) = \sin\left(\frac{\pi j x}{a}\right).$$

To satisfy the boundary conditions for Y, we must have $\lambda > \mu$. In which case

$$\sqrt{\lambda - \mu} = \frac{\pi k}{b},$$

and

$$Y_k(y) = \sin\left(\frac{\pi k y}{b}\right).$$

Furthermore,

$$\lambda_{jk} = \frac{\pi^2 j^2}{a^2} + \frac{\pi^2 k^2}{b^2},$$

so for a given j and k we have the eigenfunction

$$S_{jk}(x, y) = \sin\left(\frac{\pi j x}{a}\right) \sin\left(\frac{\pi k y}{b}\right).$$

Notice that it could happen that some of the λ_{jk} are the same, so there could be more than one independent eigenfunction corresponding to a given eigenvalue. This certainly happens if $a = b$. The eigenfunctions corresponding to distinct eigenvalues are orthogonal since they are eigenfunctions of a symmetric operator. In fact, it is very easy to check that the S_{jk} are orthogonal for distinct pairs (j, k) by direct integration. This is left as an exercise.

Solutions to the wave equation for each j and k are provided by

$$u_{jk}(x, y, t) = [A_{jk} \cos(c\sqrt{\lambda_{jk}}t) + B_{jk} \sin(c\sqrt{\lambda_{jk}}t)] \sin\left(\frac{\pi j x}{a}\right) \sin\left(\frac{\pi k y}{b}\right),$$

so the general form of the solution is

$$u(x, y, t) =$$

$$\sum_{k=1}^{\infty} \sum_{j=1}^{\infty} [A_{jk} \cos(c\sqrt{\lambda_{jk}}t) + B_{jk} \sin(c\sqrt{\lambda_{jk}}t)] \sin\left(\frac{\pi j x}{a}\right) \sin\left(\frac{\pi k y}{b}\right).$$

To satisfy the initial conditions, we must find the A_{jk} in

$$u(x, y, 0) = f(x, y) = \sum_{j=1}^{\infty} \sum_{k=1}^{\infty} A_{jk} \sin\left(\frac{\pi j x}{a}\right) \sin\left(\frac{\pi k y}{b}\right)$$

and find the B_{jk} in

$$u_t(x, y, 0) = g(x, y) = \sum_{j=1}^{\infty} \sum_{k=1}^{\infty} B_{jk} c \sqrt{\lambda_{jk}} \sin\left(\frac{\pi j x}{a}\right) \sin\left(\frac{\pi k y}{b}\right).$$

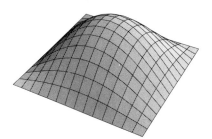

FIGURE 9.11

But this is the same as for any orthogonal basis. Indeed,

$$\langle S_{jk}, S_{jk} \rangle = \int_0^a \sin^2\left(\frac{\pi j x}{a}\right) dx \int_0^b \sin^2\left(\frac{\pi k y}{b}\right) dy = \frac{ab}{4},$$

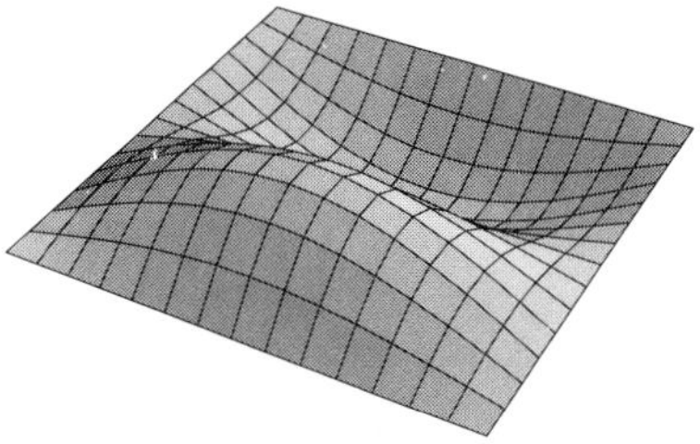

and so

$$A_{jk} = \frac{4}{ab} \langle f, S_{jk} \rangle.$$

Similarly,

$$B_{jk} = \frac{4}{abc\sqrt{\lambda_{jk}}} \langle g, S_{jk} \rangle.$$

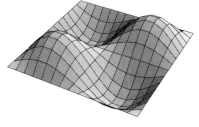

FIGURE 9.12

Like the one-dimensional wave equation, solutions here are sums of fundamental modes of vibration. But, unlike the one-dimensional case, the frequency of each mode is not necessarily an integer multiple of a base frequency. Indeed, the frequencies are determined by

$$c\sqrt{\lambda_{jk}} = c\sqrt{\frac{\pi^2 j^2}{a^2} + \frac{\pi^2 k^2}{b^2}},$$

and even if $a = b$, the majority of the frequencies will not be in integer ratio to one another. Figures 9.11, 9.12, and 9.13 show the initial displacements for the modes corresponding to $j = k = 1$, $j = 1$ and $k = 2$, and $j = k = 2$. If there is no initial velocity, points on these surfaces oscillate up and down with amplitude determined by the initial displacement of the point on the surface.

FIGURE 9.13

EXERCISES 9.9.1

1. Suppose that a drum is in the shape of the square $[0, 2] \times [0, 2]$. Suppose the initial velocity is zero and the initial displacement is $f(x, y) = \sin(\pi x) \sin(\pi y)$. Assume that the wave equation is $u_{xx} = u_{tt}$. Find the solution by separation of variables. Graph the solution in order for $t = 0$ to $t = 1$ in steps of 0.1. The result is an animation of the motion of the drumhead.

2. Suppose that a drum is in the shape of the rectangle $[0, 4] \times [0, 2]$. Suppose the initial velocity is zero and the initial displacement is $f(x, y) = \sin(\pi x) \sin^2(\pi y)$. Assume that the wave equation is $u_{xx} = u_{tt}$. Find the so-

lution by separation of variables. Take the partial sum out to $k = 7$, say, and graph the partial sum in order for $t = 0$ to $t = 0.2$ in steps of 0.01. The result is an animation of the motion of the drumhead.

3. Suppose that a drum is in the shape of the rectangle $[0, 4] \times [0, 2]$. The initial velocity is zero and the initial displacement is $f(x, y) = \sin^2(\pi x) \sin^2(\pi y)$. Assume that the wave equation is $u_{xx} = u_{tt}$. Find the solution by separation of variables. Graph a sufficiently high order partial sum for a sequence of values of t so that a reasonable animation of the motion of the drum head is achieved.

4. Suppose that a drum is in the shape of the square $[0, 2] \times [0, 2]$. The initial velocity is zero and the initial displacement is $f(x, y) = x(2 - x)y(2 - y)$. Assume that the wave equation is $4u_{xx} = u_{tt}$. Find the solution by separation of variables. Graph a sufficiently high order partial sum for a sequence of values of t so that a reasonable animation of the motion of the drum head is achieved.

5. Is periodic vibration possible for a square drum? Explain!

6. For a drum of shape $[0, 4] \times [0, 2]$, draw the possible modes of vibration for the first two frequencies.

7. Is it possible for a square drum to have more than one mode of vibration of a given frequency? Explain!

8. Show by direct calculation that $-\Delta$ is symmetric on the space of infinitely differentiable functions on a rectangle with homogeneous boundary conditions.

9. Show that the eigenfunctions of $-\Delta$ on the space of infinitely differentiable functions on a rectangle with homogeneous boundary conditions are orthogonal.

10. Drag due to air resistance is easily introduced for the vibrating drum. If we assume that the drag on a small piece of the membrane is proportional to the area and the velocity of the small piece, then the force on this piece is $ru_t(x, y, t)\Delta A$, where ΔA is the area of the piece, $u_t(x, y, t)$ is the velocity of the piece, and $r > 0$ is the proportionality constant. Go back to the derivation of the wave equation for the drum and show that the preceding assumption leads to the equation

$$c^2 \Delta u = u_{tt} + ru_t.$$

9.9.2 The Circular Drum

Consider a circular drum of radius 1 unit. So we assume that D is defined by

$$D = \{(x, y) | x^2 + y^2 \le 1\}.$$

If $u(x, y, t)$ is the vertical displacement of the membrane at (x, y) at time t, then u satisfies the wave equation. Just as for the rectangular drum, we assume that the boundary conditions are zero and that the initial displacement and velocity are given. The plan of solution is the same as before.

We separate the spatial and time parts, so $u(x, y, t) = S(x, y)T(t)$. Once again we must find the eigenvalues and eigenfunctions of $-\Delta$, but now it is for functions on D that vanish on the boundary and are differentiable to all orders in the partials. As for the rectangle, the inner product on this space is integration with respect to $dx\,dy$. The Laplacian is symmetric as usual. In fact, we can show that the Laplacian is symmetric on any domain D with the standard integral inner product.

Recall Green's first identity. It is

$$\int\int_D v\Delta(u)\,dx\,dy = \int_{\partial D} v\nabla u \cdot \vec{n}\,ds - \int\int_D \nabla v \cdot \nabla u\,dx\,dy.$$

If we assume that the functions u and v vanish on the boundary of D we have

$$\int\int_D v\Delta(u)\,dx\,dy = -\int\int_D \nabla v \cdot \nabla u\,dx\,dy.$$

Exchanging u and v shows that

$$\int\int_D v\Delta(u)\,dx\,dy = \int\int_D \Delta(v)u\,dx\,dy.$$

This shows that Δ is symmetric on D with the usual inner product and homogeneous boundary conditions.

This calculation also shows that the eigenvalues of $-\Delta$ must be positive. Indeed, if $-\Delta(f) = \lambda f$, then set $u = v = f$ to get

$$\langle-\Delta(f), f\rangle = \int\int_D -\Delta(f)f\,dx\,dy$$
$$= \int\int_D \nabla f \cdot \nabla f\,dx\,dy.$$

Now ∇f cannot be zero in the disk D because, if it were, the directional derivative would be zero in D, and f would have to be constant. But f has to be zero on the boundary, so f would have to be zero. However, f is an eigenfunction, and so it is not zero. Since ∇f is not zero, the last integral must be greater than zero. So we have

$$0 < \langle-\Delta(f), f\rangle = \langle\lambda f, f\rangle$$
$$= \lambda\langle f, f\rangle.$$

The last inner product is the square of the norm of f, so it is positive. Thus $\lambda > 0$.

The fact that D is a circle rather than a rectangle makes the problem of finding the eigenfunctions more difficult. It is perhaps not surprising that it is beneficial to switch to polar coordinates.

Recall that the equations for changing from polar to rectangular coordinates are

$$x = r\cos(\theta),$$
$$y = r\sin(\theta).$$

Let $f(x, y)$ be a function on D in rectangular coordinates; then

$$g(r, \theta) = f(r\cos(\theta), r\sin(\theta))$$

is the corresponding function in polar coordinates. By the chain rule, we have

$$g_r = f_x\cos(\theta) + f_y\sin(\theta),$$
$$g_\theta = -f_x r\sin(\theta) + f_y r\cos(\theta).$$

Solving these equations for f_x and f_y yields

$$f_x = \cos(\theta)g_r - \frac{\sin(\theta)}{r}g_\theta,$$

$$f_y = \sin(\theta)g_r + \frac{\cos(\theta)}{r}g_\theta.$$

This may be rephrased in operator notation as follows:

$$\frac{\partial}{\partial x} = \cos(\theta)\frac{\partial}{\partial r} - \frac{\sin(\theta)}{r}\frac{\partial}{\partial \theta},$$

$$\frac{\partial}{\partial y} = \sin(\theta)\frac{\partial}{\partial r} + \frac{\cos(\theta)}{r}\frac{\partial}{\partial \theta}.$$

The meaning of this is that to calculate $f_x(x, y)$ we apply the operator on the right to $g(r, \theta)$, where (r, θ) corresponds to (x, y). To get the second derivative, do this twice. So the operator corresponding to $\frac{\partial^2}{\partial x^2}$ is

$$[\cos(\theta)\frac{\partial}{\partial r} - \frac{\sin(\theta)}{r}\frac{\partial}{\partial \theta}]^2.$$

When this is expanded, the resulting operator is

$$\frac{\partial^2}{\partial x^2} = \cos^2(\theta)\frac{\partial^2}{\partial r^2} - 2\frac{\sin(\theta)\cos(\theta)}{r}\frac{\partial^2}{\partial r\partial\theta}$$

$$+ \frac{\sin^2(\theta)}{r^2}\frac{\partial^2}{\partial\theta^2} + \frac{\sin(\theta)\cos(\theta)}{r^2}\frac{\partial}{\partial\theta} + \frac{\sin^2(\theta)}{r}\frac{\partial}{\partial r}.$$

Similarly,

$$\frac{\partial^2}{\partial y^2} = \sin^2(\theta)\frac{\partial^2}{\partial r^2} + 2\frac{\sin(\theta)\cos(\theta)}{r}\frac{\partial^2}{\partial r\partial\theta}$$

$$+ \frac{\cos^2(\theta)}{r^2}\frac{\partial^2}{\partial\theta^2} - \frac{\sin(\theta)\cos(\theta)}{r^2}\frac{\partial}{\partial\theta} + \frac{\cos^2(\theta)}{r}\frac{\partial}{\partial r}.$$

If we add these operators, we get the polar form of the Laplacian:

$$\Delta_{r,\theta} = \frac{\partial^2}{\partial r^2} + \frac{1}{r}\frac{\partial}{\partial r} + \frac{1}{r^2}\frac{\partial^2}{\partial\theta^2}.$$

Let $f(x, y)$ be an eigenfunction for the Laplacian Δ on the unit disk with homogeneous boundary conditions. Assume that the eigenvalue is λ. The corresponding polar function is $g(r, \theta)$. The domain for this function is the rectangle $R = [0, 1] \times [0, 2\pi]$, and $g(r, 0) = g(r, 2\pi)$ for all $r \in [0, 1]$ and $g(0, \theta) = f(0, 0)$ for all θ. The homogeneous boundary conditions become $g(1, \theta) = 0$. Also, $g(r, \theta)$ satisfies

$$\Delta_{r,\theta}g(r, \theta) = \lambda g(r, \theta)$$

on $(0, 1] \times [0, 2\pi]$. Note that we must exclude $r = 0$.

Conversely, if $g(r, \theta)$ satisfies all the preceding conditions, the function $f(x, y)$ corresponding to $g(r, \theta)$ satisfies the homogeneous boundary condition on the unit disk, and it also satisfies

$$\Delta f(x, y) = \lambda f(x, y),$$

except possibly at the origin. It can be shown that $f(x, y)$ satisfies the preceding equation throughout the unit disk. Therefore, the polar coordinate transformation provides a one-to-one correspondence between the eigenfunctions and eigenvalues of the Laplacian on the disk and the eigenfunctions and eigenvalues of the polar Laplacian. Because of this correspondence, we shall complete the analysis in polar coordinates.

The polar Laplacian is symmetric on this space provided that we integrate in polar coordinates. Indeed, the change-of-variables formula gives

$$\int\int_R \Delta_{r,\theta} f(r\cos(\theta), r\sin(\theta)) g(r\cos(\theta), r\sin(\theta)) r \, dr \, d\theta$$

$$= \int\int_D \Delta(f) g \, dx \, dy$$

$$= \int\int_D f \Delta(g) \, dx \, dy$$

$$= \int\int_R f(r\cos(\theta), r\sin(\theta)) \Delta_{r,\theta} g(r\cos(\theta), r\sin(\theta)) r \, dr \, d\theta.$$

We now find the eigenfunctions of the negative of the polar Laplacian by separating the variables. Let

$$S(r, \theta) = R(r)\Theta(\theta).$$

Then

$$\frac{R''}{R} + \frac{1}{r}\frac{R'}{R} + \frac{1}{r^2}\frac{\Theta''}{\Theta} = -\lambda,$$

and so

$$\frac{\Theta''}{\Theta} = -r^2\lambda - r^2\frac{R''}{R} - r\frac{R'}{R}.$$

Therefore,

$$\frac{\Theta''}{\Theta} = -\gamma$$

must be constant. We are led to the two equations

$$\Theta'' + \gamma\Theta = 0,$$

and

$$R'' + \frac{1}{r}R' + (\lambda - \frac{\gamma}{r^2})R = 0.$$

The periodic condition on Θ requires that

$$\Theta(\theta) = A_n \cos(n\theta) + B_n \sin(n\theta),$$

where $n^2 = \gamma$ and $n = 0, 1, 2, \ldots$. Thus the family of eigenfunctions here is $\{\cos(n\theta), \sin(n\theta)\}$. The equation in R can be rewritten as

$$r^2 R'' + r R' + (\lambda r^2 - n^2) R = 0.$$

Remember that λ is positive; therefore, we can make the change of variables $t = \sqrt{\lambda} r$ and set

$$y(t) = R(r) = R(t/\sqrt{\lambda}).$$

With this substitution we get the equation

$$t^2 y'' + t y' + (t^2 - n^2) y = 0.$$

This is Bessel's equation of order n, which was solved in Chapter 6. Since the drum membrane must be continuous throughout the region, we are only interested in solutions that are bounded at $r = 0$. Therefore, we consider only the Bessel functions of the first kind,

$$J_n(t).$$

As a function of r, we have the solutions

$$R_n(r) = J_n(\sqrt{\lambda} r).$$

We must not forget the boundary condition, which is

$$R_n(1) = J_n(\sqrt{\lambda}) = 0.$$

Thus $\sqrt{\lambda}$ must be one of the zeros of J_n. In Chapter 6 we saw that J_n has an infinite sequence of zeros. We denote the corresponding sequence of λ's by $\{\lambda_{nk}\}$. We have the double-indexed family

$$J_n(\sqrt{\lambda_{nk}} r).$$

We have the following eigenfunctions for the polar Laplacian:

$$\{J_n(\sqrt{\lambda_{nk}} r) \cos(n\theta),\ J_n(\sqrt{\lambda_{nk}} r) \sin(n\theta)\}.$$

The form of the general solution is

$$u(r, \theta, t) = \sum_{n=0, k=1}^{\infty} [A_{nk} \cos(\sqrt{\lambda_{nk}} ct) + B_{nk} \sin(\sqrt{\lambda_{nk}} ct)] J_n(\sqrt{\lambda_{nk}} r) \cos(n\theta)$$

$$+ \sum_{n=0, k=1}^{\infty} [C_{nk} \cos(\sqrt{\lambda_{nk}} ct) + D_{nk} \sin(\sqrt{\lambda_{nk}} ct)] J_n(\sqrt{\lambda_{nk}} r) \sin(n\theta).$$

This is rather complicated. To reduce the complication, let us consider the initial conditions where the drum is pressed down at the center and then released from rest. The initial conditions are

$$u(r, \theta, 0) = f(r) \quad \text{and} \quad u_t(r, \theta, 0) = 0.$$

The condition of zero initial velocity simplifies things to

$$u(r, \theta, t) = \sum_{n=0, k=1}^{\infty} [A_{nk} \cos(\sqrt{\lambda_{nk}} ct) J_n(\sqrt{\lambda_{nk}} r) \cos(n\theta)$$
$$+ C_{nk} \cos(\sqrt{\lambda_{nk}} ct) J_n(\sqrt{\lambda_{nk}} r) \sin(n\theta)].$$

But $u(r, \theta, 0) = f(r)$, so $u(r, \theta, 0)$ is independent of θ, and $u_\theta(r, \theta, 0) = 0$, and the series reduces to

$$u(r, \theta, t) = \sum_{k=1}^{\infty} A_{0k} \cos(\sqrt{\lambda_{0k}} ct) J_0(\sqrt{\lambda_{0k}} r).$$

To solve the initial condition

$$u(r, \theta, 0) = f(r) = \sum_{k=1}^{\infty} A_{0k} J_0(\sqrt{\lambda_{0k}} r),$$

we need to compute the A_{0k}. To do this, as we have done before, we need an inner product space in which the functions $J_0(\sqrt{\lambda_{0k}} r)$ form an orthogonal sequence. We know that the functions

$$\{J_n(\sqrt{\lambda_{nk}} r) \cos(n\theta), \ J_n(\sqrt{\lambda_{nk}} r) \sin(n\theta)\}$$

are orthogonal with respect to the inner product

$$\langle f, g \rangle = \int_0^1 \int_0^{2\pi} f(r, \theta) g(r, \theta) r \, d\theta \, dr$$

because they are eigenfunctions of the polar Laplacian. But the functions

$$J_0(\sqrt{\lambda_{0k}} r)$$

are members of this orthogonal family, so

$$\langle J_0(\sqrt{\lambda_{0k}} r), J_0(\sqrt{\lambda_{0j}} r) \rangle = \int_0^1 \int_0^{2\pi} J_0(\sqrt{\lambda_{0k}} r) J_0(\sqrt{\lambda_{0j}} r) r \, d\theta \, dr$$
$$= 2\pi \int_0^1 J_0(\sqrt{\lambda_{0k}} r) J_0(\sqrt{\lambda_{0j}} r) r \, dr = 0$$

for $k \neq j$. Therefore, the functions $J_0(\sqrt{\lambda_{0j}}r)$ are orthogonal with respect to the inner product

$$\langle f, g \rangle = \int_0^1 f(r)g(r)r\,dr.$$

In summary, the vector space $\overline{V}$ is the space of continuous functions on $[0, 1]$ equipped with the previous inner product. The computation of the coefficients is performed in the usual way in this inner product space. Nice formulas for the coefficients cannot be found, but numerical methods will approximate the coefficients as closely as desired.

Notice again that the modes of vibration are not at simple multiples of a base frequency. Again, the vibration of a drum is not periodic in general.

EXERCISES 9.9.2

1. Is periodic vibration possible for a circular drum? Explain!

2. For the circular drum in the text, draw crosssections of the first three modes of vibration where the initial conditions are

$$u(r, \theta, 0) = f(r) \text{ and } u_t(r, \theta, 0) = 0.$$

   Hint: Look at the graph of J_0.

3. Consider a circular drum of radius b with initial conditions

$$u(r, \theta, 0) = f(r) \text{ and } u_t(r, \theta, 0) = 0.$$

   Derive the solution, and express the coefficients in terms of $f(r)$ and the appropriate inner product.

4. Consider a circular drum of radius 1 with initial conditions

$$u(r, \theta, 0) = J_0(\sqrt{\lambda_{01}}r) \text{ and } u_t(r, \theta, 0) = 0.$$

   Write down the solution. Explain!

5. Consider a circular drum of radius 1 with initial conditions

$$u(r, \theta, 0) = 2J_0(\sqrt{\lambda_{01}}r) + 3J_0(\sqrt{\lambda_{05}}r)$$

and

$$u_t(r, \theta, 0) = 0.$$

   Write down the solution. Explain!

6. What is $\sqrt{\lambda_{01}}$? Use any approach you like to approximate $\sqrt{\lambda_{01}}$ to one decimal place. Explain your approach briefly.

7. What is $\sqrt{\lambda_{11}}$? Use any approach you like to approximate $\sqrt{\lambda_{11}}$ to one decimal place. Explain your approach briefly.

8. Briefly explain why it is reasonable to say that the vibration of a guitar string is harmonious, but that of a drum is not.

9. Why was symmetry essential to establishing the orthogonality of the eigenfunctions of the polar Laplacian? *Hint:* Can you establish the orthogonality by direct integration as we did originally in the heat equation?

9.10 LAPLACE'S EQUATION

Up to now, we have dealt only with homogeneous boundary conditions. Suppose that, in the heat equation for a plate occupying a region D in the x, y-plane, the temperature of the boundary of D is not maintained at zero, but at some temperature $h(x, y)$, where (x, y) is on the boundary of D. Physically, it is reasonable to expect that as time goes to infinity the temperature distribution $u(x, y, t)$ in the plate will reach a steady state $v(x, y)$. At the steady state, $v_t = 0$, and so

$$v_{xx} + v_{yy} = 0$$

and

$$v(x, y) = h(x, y)$$

on the boundary of D. The equation $v_{xx} + v_{yy} = 0$ is called **Laplace's equation**, and the problem of solving $v_{xx} + v_{yy} = 0$ and $v(x, y) = h(x, y)$ for (x, y) on the boundary of D is called the **Dirichlet problem**. As you may have guessed, solving this problem will allow us to solve the heat equation with inhomogeneous boundary conditions. It is not so easy to see that this will also permit the solution of the wave equation with inhomogeneous conditions. We shall see how this is done in this section. Laplace's equation has wide application in physics and engineering. In particular, Laplace's equation has important applications in electro-magnetism and potential theory. Solutions to Laplace's equation in one, two, or three (or more!) dimensions are called **harmonic functions**.

The uniqueness of solutions to the Dirichlet problem was established in an earlier section. It is harder to show in general that solutions to the Dirichlet problem exist, so we shall be content with constructing solutions in special cases.

9.10.1 The Dirichlet Problem in a Rectangle

Let D be the rectangle $[0, a] \times [0, b]$. We shall assume that the boundary conditions are specified by $f_1(x)$ on the bottom, $f_2(y)$ on the right, $f_3(x)$ on the top, and $f_4(y)$ on the left. It will be easier to break this problem up into four separate problems. In the first, $f_1(x)$ specifies the boundary condition on the bottom, and we assume that the other edges have zero boundary conditions. We repeat this for each edge. If u^1, u^2, u^3, and u^4 are the corresponding solutions, a moment's reflection shows that

$$u = u^1 + u^2 + u^3 + u^4$$

satisfies the original Dirichlet problem. We solve each subproblem by the method of separation of variables as usual.

Set

$$u^1(x, y) = X(x)Y(y).$$

Then separating variables gives

$$\frac{X''}{X} + \frac{Y''}{Y} = 0,$$

and so

$$\frac{X''}{X} = -\frac{Y''}{Y} = -\lambda.$$

Therefore, we have the equations

$$X'' + \lambda X = 0 \qquad \text{and} \qquad Y'' - \lambda Y = 0.$$

Now, if u^1 is to satisfy the homogeneous conditions, $X(0) = X(a) = 0$. These are the familiar homogeneous conditions for the eigenfunctions of the one-dimensional Laplacian, so the eigenfunctions are

$$X_k(x) = \sin(\sqrt{\lambda_k}x),$$

where

$$\lambda_k = \frac{\pi^2 k^2}{a^2}.$$

The general solution of the equation in Y is

$$Y_k(y) = A_k e^{\sqrt{\lambda_k}y} + B_k e^{-\sqrt{\lambda_k}y}.$$

The condition $Y(b) = 0$ requires that

$$A_k e^{\sqrt{\lambda_k}b} = -B_k e^{-\sqrt{\lambda_k}b}$$

and therefore that

$$B_k = -A_k e^{2\sqrt{\lambda_k}b}.$$

Hence

$$Y_k(y) = A_k e^{\sqrt{\lambda_k}y} - A_k e^{2\sqrt{\lambda_k}b} e^{-\sqrt{\lambda_k}y}.$$

The series solution then is

$$u^1(x, y) = \sum_{k=1}^{\infty} A_k [e^{\sqrt{\lambda_k}y} - e^{2\sqrt{\lambda_k}b} e^{-\sqrt{\lambda_k}y}] \sin(\sqrt{\lambda_k}x).$$

This equation satisfies the homogeneous boundary conditions, so it remains to satisfy the the condition on the bottom edge. We have

$$u^1(x, 0) = f_1(x) = \sum_{k=1}^{\infty} A_k [1 - e^{2\sqrt{\lambda_k}b}] \sin(\sqrt{\lambda_k}x).$$

The A_k are calculated from the inner product formulas

$$A_k [1 - e^{2\sqrt{\lambda_k}b}] = \frac{\langle f_1, X_k \rangle}{\langle X_k, X_k \rangle}.$$

The same analysis yields the following three formulas:

$$u^2(x, y) = \sum_{k=1}^{\infty} B_k[e^{\sqrt{\gamma_k}x} - e^{-\sqrt{\gamma_k}x}]\sin(\sqrt{\gamma_k}y),$$

$$u^3(x, y) = \sum_{k=1}^{\infty} C_k[e^{\sqrt{\lambda_k}y} - e^{-\sqrt{\lambda_k}y}]\sin(\sqrt{\lambda_k}x),$$

$$u^4(x, y) = \sum_{k=1}^{\infty} D_k[e^{\sqrt{\gamma_k}x} - e^{2\sqrt{\gamma_k}a}e^{-\sqrt{\gamma_k}x}]\sin(\sqrt{\gamma_k}y).$$

The coefficients are computed as usual.

The final solution is

$$u(x, y) = u^1(x, y) + u^2(x, y) + u^3(x, y) + u^4(x, y).$$

This solution is harmonic in the rectangle, and it satisfies the boundary conditions.

Example 9.10.1   We solve the Dirichlet problem on the rectangle $[0, 1] \times [0, 2]$, where $f_3(x) = 2\sin(\pi x) - 4\sin(3\pi x)$ and the values on the other edges are zero.

Set $u^3(x, y) = XY$. Then we must solve

$$X'' + \lambda X = 0 \quad \text{and} \quad Y'' - \lambda Y = 0.$$

You should think about why the plus and minus signs in these equations are in the positions that they are. Solving the first equation and applying $X(0) = X(1) = 0$ gives $\lambda_k = \pi^2 k^2$ and

$$X_k(x) = \sin(\pi k x).$$

The general solution for Y_k is

$$Y_k(y) = A_k e^{\pi k y} + B_k e^{-\pi k y}.$$

But $Y_k(0) = 0$, so $B_k = -A_k$. Therefore,

$$Y_k(y) = A_k[e^{\pi k y} - e^{-\pi k y}],$$

and so the general form of the solution is

$$u^3(x, y) = \sum_{k=1}^{\infty} A_k[e^{\pi k y} - e^{-\pi k y}]\sin(\pi k x).$$

Now we must satisfy the boundary condition on the top edge of the rectangle. Thus

$$u^3(x, 2) = f_3(x) = 2\sin(\pi x) - 4\sin(3\pi x) = \sum_{k=1}^{\infty} A_k[e^{2\pi k} - e^{-2\pi k}]\sin(\pi k x).$$

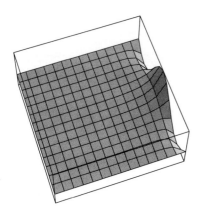

FIGURE 9.14

It follows immediately that $A_1[e^{2\pi} - e^{-2\pi}] = 2$, $A_3[e^{6\pi} - e^{-6\pi}] = -4$, and $A_k[e^{2\pi k} - e^{-2\pi k}] = 0$ for k not equal to 1 or 3. Thus the solution is

$$u^3(x, y) = \frac{2}{e^{2\pi} - e^{-2\pi}}[e^{\pi y} - e^{-\pi y}]\sin(\pi x)$$

$$- \frac{4}{e^{6\pi} - e^{-6\pi}}[e^{\pi 3y} - e^{-\pi 3y}]\sin(3\pi x).$$

Figure 9.14 shows the graph of this solution. ∎

9.10.2 The Dirichlet Problem for the Circle

Assume that D is a circular region of radius 1 centered at the origin. As with the circular drum, we convert to polar coordinates, so the problem in polar coordinates is

$$\Delta_{r,\theta}u(r, \theta) = \left[\frac{\partial^2}{\partial r^2} + \frac{1}{r}\frac{\partial}{\partial r} + \frac{1}{r^2}\frac{\partial^2}{\partial \theta^2}\right]u(r, \theta) = 0,$$

and $u(1, \theta) = f(\theta)$.

We shall solve this by separation of variables. Set $u(r, \theta) = R(r)\Theta(\theta)$. Then we have

$$R''\Theta + \frac{1}{r}R'\Theta + \frac{1}{r^2}\Theta'' = 0.$$

Multiplying by r^2 and dividing by $R\Theta$ gives

$$\frac{r^2 R''}{R} + \frac{r R'}{R} = -\frac{\Theta''}{\Theta} = \lambda.$$

Now

$$\Theta'' + \lambda\Theta = 0,$$

and since $\Theta(0) = \Theta(2\pi)$, we have the eigenfunctions

$$\Theta(\theta) = A_k \cos(k\theta) + B_k \sin(k\theta),$$

where $\lambda_k = k^2$. Using this in the equation for R, we get

$$r^2 R'' + r R' - k^2 R = 0.$$

This equation is called an **Euler equation**, and there is an easy way to solve it.

Set $r = e^t$ and $y(t) = R(e^t)$. Then $y'(t) = e^t R'(e^t)$ and $y''(t) = (e^t)^2 R''(e^t)$. So solutions to the Euler equation can be found by finding the solutions to the equation

$$y'' + y' - k^2 y = 0$$

and setting $R(r) = y(\ln(r))$. The roots of the characteristic polynomial for y are

$$\gamma_k = \frac{-1 + \sqrt{1 + 4k^2}}{2} \quad \text{and} \quad \overline{\gamma}_k = \frac{-1 - \sqrt{1 + 4k^2}}{2}.$$

Therefore, the general solution is

$$y(t) = C_k e^{\gamma_k t} + D_k e^{\overline{\gamma}_k t},$$

and so

$$R_k = C_k r^{\gamma_k} + D_k r^{\overline{\gamma}_k}.$$

The $\overline{\gamma}_k$ are negative, and so that part of the solution may be rejected, since our solutions must be bounded at the origin. Therefore, each function

$$u_k(r, \theta) = r^{\gamma_k}[A_k \cos(k\theta) + B_k \sin(k\theta)]$$

satisfies the polar Laplacian. The series

$$u(r, \theta) = A_0 + \sum_{k=1}^{\infty} r^{\gamma_k}[A_k \cos(k\theta) + B_k \sin(k\theta)]$$

satisfies Laplace's equation, and the coefficients can be calculated from

$$u(1, \theta) = A_0 + \sum_{k=1}^{\infty}[A_k \cos(k\theta) + B_k \sin(k\theta)]$$

in the usual manner.

9.10.3 Inhomogeneous Boundary Conditions

Now that we have some familiarity with the Dirichlet problem, we can use it to solve the heat and wave equations with inhomogeneous boundary conditions. Consider the heat equation on a region D. Suppose that we require $u(x, y, t) = h(x, y)$ for all (x, y) on the boundary of D. This means that the boundary of the region is to be maintained at the temperature $h(x, y)$ at each point along the boundary. Suppose that $v(x, y)$ is the solution to the Dirichlet problem, with $h(x, y)$ given on the boundary, and that the initial condition is $u(x, y, 0) = f(x, y)$ in D. Now consider the solution $w(x, y, t)$ to the heat equation with initial condition

$$w(x, y, 0) = f(x, y) - v(x, y)$$

and homogeneous boundary conditions. Then we claim that

$$u(x, y, t) = v(x, y) + w(x, y, t)$$

is a solution to the inhomogeneous problem. Certainly, u satisfies the heat equation. On the boundary,

$$u(x, y, t) = h(x, y) + 0 = h(x, y),$$

and the initial condition is

$$u(x, y, 0) = v(x, y) + w(x, y, 0) = v(x, y) + f(x, y) - v(x, y) = f(x, y).$$

Thus u satisfies the inhomogeneous problem. Notice that this is very much like the "particular plus homogeneous" solution to nonhomogeneous linear ordinary differential equations. The same method applies to the wave equation with inhomogeneous boundary conditions.

Here is an example in which the wave equation with inhomogeneous boundary conditions is solved.

Example 9.10.2   We solve $u_{xx} = u_{tt}$ on $[0, 1]$, where $u(0, t) = 1, u(1, t) = 2$, $u(x, 0) = \sin(\pi x/2) + 1$, and $u_t(x, 0) = 0$.

First, we solve the corresponding Dirichlet problem. If $v''(x) = 0$, then $v(x) = ax + b$. But $v(0) = 1$ and $v(1) = 2$, and so $v(x) = x + 1$.

The solution to the problem is of the form $u(x, t) = v(x) + w(x, t)$, where $w(x, t)$ satisfies the wave equation, homogeneous boundary conditions, and the initial conditions $w(x, 0) = \sin(\pi x/2) + 1 - (x + 1) = \sin(\pi x/2) - x$ and $w_t(x, 0) = u_t(x, 0) = 0$. We solve for $w(x, t)$.

The general form of the solution is

$$w(x, t) = \sum_{k=1}^{\infty} A_k \cos(\pi k t) \sin(\pi k x),$$

and the initial condition requires that

$$w(x, 0) = \sum_{k=1}^{\infty} A_k \sin(\pi k x).$$

Calculating the coefficients gives

$$w(x, t) = \sum_{k=1}^{\infty} \frac{(-1)^{k+1}}{k(4k^2 - 1)\pi} \cos(\pi k t) \sin(\pi k x).$$

Therefore, the solution to the original problem is

$$u(x, t) = 1 + x + \sum_{k=1}^{\infty} \frac{(-1)^{k+1}}{k(4k^2 - 1)\pi} \cos(\pi k t) \sin(\pi k x). \qquad \blacksquare$$

EXERCISES 9.10

1. Solve the Dirichlet problem on [0, 2], where $u(0) = -1$ and $u(2) = 3$.

2. Solve the Dirichlet problem on [−2, 2], where $u(−2) = 2$ and $u(2) = -3$.

3. Solve the Dirichlet problem on the unit square, where $f_1(x) = \sin(4\pi x)$ and the rest of the boundary values are zero.

4. Solve the Dirichlet problem on the unit square, where $f_2(y) = \sin(\pi y) + 3\sin(5\pi y)$ and the rest of the boundary values are zero. Check your solution by direct calculation.

5. Solve the Dirichlet problem on the rectangle $[0, 2] \times [0, 3]$, where $f_1(x) = \sin(2\pi x)$, $f_3(x) = 3\sin(\pi x) - 2\sin(4\pi x)$, and the rest of the boundary values are zero.

6. Solve the Dirichlet problem on the rectangle $[0, 2] \times [0, 3]$, where $f_1(x) = \sin(2\pi x)$, $f_2(x) = 3\sin(\pi y) - \sin(2\pi y)$, and the rest of the boundary values are zero.

7. Solve the Dirichlet problem on the rectangle $[0, 2] \times [0, 3]$, where $f_1(x) = 1$, $f_2(y) = 3$, $f_3(x) = x$, and $f_4(y) = -1$.

8. Solve the Dirichlet problem for the unit circle, where $u(1, \theta) = \sin(\theta) + 3\cos(2\theta)$.

9. Solve the Dirichlet problem for the unit circle, where $u(1, \theta) = -2\sin(\theta) + 5\cos(\theta)$.

10. Solve the Dirichlet problem for the unit circle, where $u(1, \theta) = 1$ for $\theta \in [0, \pi)$ and $u(1, \theta) = -1$ for $\theta \in [\pi, 2\pi)$.

11. Solve the heat equation on [0, 3], when the initial temperature is zero along the rod, but the endpoints are at −2 at the left and 5 at the right. Assume $u_{xx} = u_t$.

12. Solve the heat equation $u_{xx} = u_t$ on [0, 4], when the initial temperature along the rod is given by $u(x, 0) = x$, but the endpoints are at −4 at the left and 6 at the right.

13. Solve $u_{xx} = u_{tt}$ on [0, 2], when the boundary conditions are $u(0, t) = 2$ and $u(2, t) = 3$. The initial displacement is $u(x, 0) = \cos(\pi x/4) + x + 1$, and the initial velocity is zero.

14. Solve the heat equation $u_{xx} + u_{yy} = u_t$ on the unit square when the boundary temperatures are $f_1(x) = \sin(\pi x)$, $f_2(y) = 0$, $f_3(x) = 0$, and $f_4(y) = 0$ and the initial temperature of the plate is zero. The two-dimensional heat equation is treated in the same way as the two-dimensional wave equation. This problem requires a lengthy integration, so a computer algebra system is recommended for this task.

SUPPLEMENTARY EXERCISES FOR CHAPTER 9

1. **Gibbs Phenomenon**. Expand the function

$$f(x) = \begin{cases} 1, & \text{for } 0 \le x \le \pi, \\ -1, & \text{for } \pi < x \le 2\pi \end{cases}$$

as a sine series. For larger and larger partial sums, study the overshoot behavior near the jump discontinuity. Roughly, what percentage of the jump is the sum of the overshoots both top and bottom? What happens to the width of the overshoot region as the partial sum gets larger? Repeat this for the following:

$$f(x) = \begin{cases} x, & \text{for } 0 \le x \le \pi, \\ x - 2\pi, & \text{for } \pi < x \le 2\pi, \end{cases}$$

and

$$f(x) = \begin{cases} x^2, & \text{for } 0 \le x \le 1, \\ -1, & \text{for } 1 < x \le 2. \end{cases}$$

Summarize your observations in a conjecture about the Gibbs phenomenon. The use of a computer algebra system such as Mathematica or Maple could be helpful.

2. **Neumann Conditions**. The side conditions that we have used in this chapter are by no means the only ones possible. In this exercise you will be introduced to the Neumann conditions.

(a) Consider the heat equation $u_{xx} = u_t$ for a copper bar on [0, a]. Instead of fixing the temperature at the ends of the bar, we insulate the ends as well as the length of the bar. Since no heat can flow from the ends of the bar, the temperature gradient at the ends must be zero. Thus $u_x(0, t) = u_x(a, t) = 0$. This is an example of a Neumann condition. If $u(x, 0) = f(x)$ is the initial temperature distribution, find the general form of the solution. Explain what happens as $t \to \infty$.

(b) Consider Laplace's equation in the plane region D. The Neumann condition for this problem is to specify the directional derivative of the solution in the outward pointing normal direction at each point on the boundary of D. Physically, this amounts to specifying the heat flow from (or into) the plate D at each point along the boundary. If a solution to Laplace's equation can be considered an equilibrium temperature distribution, then the net flow of heat from the plate must be zero. Prove this mathematically by using Green's first identity with $v = 0$. Is the solution to a valid Neumann problem unique? Explain.

(c) Consider a plate in the form of the unit square. Suppose that the plate is completely insulated. If the initial temperature distribution is $u(x, y, 0) = xy$, what is the final equilibrium temperature?

CHAPTER 10

THE FINITE DIFFERENCES METHOD

The subject of numerical approximations to partial differential equations is vast and subtle. Unlike numerical methods in ordinary differential equations, there is no algorithm like Runge–Kutta that can be applied to a very wide variety of problems. Just as the method of separation of variables in the last chapter had to be tailored to the specific problem, so do numerical methods for partial differential equations. In this chapter we shall study the method of finite differences. This approach is simple in concept, but the application of this concept to a particular problem can lead to algorithms with surprising properties.

The first two sections of this chapter trace the application of the finite difference method to one problem. This single problem illustrates the main features of the finite differences method and points to a surprising possibility. In succeeding sections the method will be applied to the familiar heat, wave, and Laplace equations, but, in addition, the method will be applied to nonlinear and nonconstant-coefficient equations. These applications point to the usefulness of the method and some of its difficulties.

10.1 FINITE DIFFERENCE APPROXIMATIONS

Finite differences are approximations of derivatives. Recall the definition of the derivative. It is

$$u'(x) = \lim_{\Delta x \to 0} \frac{u(x + \Delta x) - u(x)}{\Delta x}.$$

This means that

$$\frac{u(x + \Delta x) - u(x)}{\Delta x}$$

can provide an approximation of $u'(x)$. Of course it is not clear how good an approximation this might be. To this end, recall Taylor's theorem.

Theorem 10.1.1 (Taylor)

Let u have $n + 1$ continuous derivatives on the interval $(x - r, x + r)$. Then for Δx such that $x + \Delta x$ is in $(x - r, x + r)$ there is a number z in between x and $x + \Delta x$ such that

$$u(x + \Delta x) = u(x) + \frac{1}{1!}u'(x)\Delta x + \cdots + \frac{1}{n!}u^{(n)}(x)\Delta x^n + \frac{u^{(n+1)}(z)\Delta x^{n+1}}{(n + 1)!}.$$

●

Now, if $u^{(n+1)}$ is bounded , then

$$\left| \frac{u^{(n+1)}(z)\Delta x^{n+1}}{(n + 1)!} \right| \le M|\Delta x|^{n+1}$$

for some positive number M. In this case we say that the expression

$$\frac{u^{(n+1)}(z)\Delta x^{n+1}}{(n + 1)!}$$

is "big O of Δx^{n+1}", and we write

$$u(x + \Delta x) = u(x) + \frac{1}{1!}u'(x)\Delta x + \cdots + \frac{1}{n!}u^{(n)}(x)\Delta x^n + O(\Delta x^{n+1}).$$

Explicitly,

$$O(\Delta x^{n+1}) = u(x + \Delta x) - u(x) - \frac{1}{1!}u'(x)\Delta x - \cdots - \frac{1}{n!}u^{(n)}(x)\Delta x^n.$$

Here is a simple example.

Example 10.1.2　Let $x = 1$ and $u(x) = 3 + 5x - 2x^2$. Then

$$O(\Delta x^2) = u(1 + \Delta x) - 6 - \Delta x$$
$$= 3 + 5(1 + \Delta x) - 2(1 + \Delta x)^2 - 6 - \Delta x = -2\Delta x^2. \qquad ■$$

If u is twice continuously differentiable on a closed interval $[a, b]$ and x and $x + \Delta x$ are in (a, b), then

$$u(x + \Delta x) = u(x) + u'(x)\Delta x + O(\Delta x^2).$$

Therefore,

$$u'(x) = \frac{u(x + \Delta x) - u(x)}{\Delta x} + O(\Delta x).$$

We can say that the difference quotient approximates the derivative with an error term $O(\Delta x)$. Thus the magnitude of the error is smaller than $M|\Delta x|$ for some constant M.

These considerations extend to functions of more than one variable. In most cases, Δx will be positive. Assuming this and sufficient differentiability of u in the region of interest, we can write

$$u(x + \Delta x, t) = u(x, t) + u_x(x, t)\Delta x + O(\Delta x^2),$$

$$u(x - \Delta x, t) = u(x, t) - u_x(x, t)\Delta x + O(\Delta x^2),$$

$$u(x + \Delta x, t) = u(x, t) + u_x(x, t)\Delta x + \frac{1}{2}u_{xx}(x, t)\Delta x^2 + O(\Delta x^3),$$

and

$$u(x - \Delta x, t) = u(x, t) - u_x(x, t)\Delta x + \frac{1}{2}u_{xx}(x, t)\Delta x^2 + O(\Delta x^3).$$

Recall again that $O(\Delta x^3)$ is a quantity bounded by a constant times Δx^3. We approximate the partial derivative $u_x(x, t)$ in three ways:

$$u_x(x, t) = \frac{u(x + \Delta x, t) - u(x, t)}{\Delta x} + O(\Delta x),$$

$$u_x(x, t) = \frac{u(x, t) - u(x - \Delta x, t)}{\Delta x} + O(\Delta x),$$

and subtracting gives

$$u_x(x, t) = \frac{u(x + \Delta x, t) - u(x - \Delta x, t)}{2\Delta x} + O(\Delta x^2).$$

The first is called the **forward difference**, the second is called the **backward difference**, and the third is called the **centered difference**.

Clearly, a little briefer notation would be a benefit. In a typical problem we shall divide intervals $[a, b]$ and $[c, d]$ for the x and t variables into equal parts of lengths Δx and Δt, respectively. We shall write

$$u_j^k = u(a + j\Delta x, c + k\Delta t).$$

With this notation, the forward difference is

$$u_{x,j}^k = \frac{u_{j+1}^k - u_j^k}{\Delta x}.$$

The other differences are similar. The centered second difference for the second derivative is

$$u_{xx}(a + j\Delta x, c + k\Delta t) = \frac{u_{j+1}^k - 2u_j^k + u_{j-1}^k}{\Delta x^2} + O(\Delta x^2).$$

This is obtained by adding the previous Taylor expansions. Similar formulas for u_t and u_{tt} are obtained in the same way.

Higher degrees of accuracy can be obtained as follows. Let $h = \Delta x$. Then

$$u(x+h) = u(x) + u'(x)h + \frac{1}{2}u''(x)h^2 + \frac{1}{6}u'''(x)h^3 + \frac{1}{24}u^{(4)}(x)h^4 + O(h^5),$$

$$u(x-h) = u(x) - u'(x)h + \frac{1}{2}u''(x)h^2 - \frac{1}{6}u'''(x)h^3 + \frac{1}{24}u^{(4)}(x)h^4 + O(h^5),$$

$$u(x+2h) = u(x) + 2u'(x)h + 2u''(x)h^2 + \frac{4}{3}u'''(x)h^3 + \frac{2}{3}u^{(4)}(x)h^4 + O(h^5),$$

and

$$u(x-2h) = u(x) - 2u'(x)h + 2u''(x)h^2 - \frac{4}{3}u'''(x)h^3 + \frac{2}{3}u^{(4)}(x)h^4 + O(h^5).$$

Subtracting the second equation from the first and the fourth from the third gives

$$u(x+h) - u(x-h) = 2u'(x)h + \frac{1}{3}u'''(x)h^3 + O(h^5)$$

and

$$u(x+2h) - u(x-2h) = 4u'(x)h + \frac{8}{3}u'''(x)h^3 + O(h^5).$$

The derivative $u'''(x)$ can be eliminated, and the remaining equation can be solved for $u'(x)$. The result is

$$u'(x) = \frac{1}{12h}[u(x-2h) - 8u(x-h) + 8u(x+h) - u(x+2h)] + O(h^4).$$

The price to be paid is the need for higher continuous derivatives on u. The preceding formulas also yield a finite difference formula for the third derivative. This is left to the exercises.

EXERCISES 10.1

1. If $u(x) = 3 + 2x - 7x^2$, use the forward, backward, and centered differences to approximate $u'(2)$ with $\Delta x = 0.1$. Compare this with the true value.

2. If $u(x) = 3 + 5x - x^3$, use the forward, backward, and centered differences to approximate $u'(1)$ with $\Delta x = 0.1$. Compare this with the true value.

3. If $u(x) = \sin(x)$, use the forward, backward, and centered differences to approximate $u'(\pi/4)$ with $\Delta x = 0.2$. Compare this with the true value.

4. If $u(x) = e^x$, use the forward, backward, and centered differences to approximate $u'(1)$ with $\Delta x = 0.1$. Compare this with the true value.

5. If $u(x) = \ln(x)$, use the forward, backward, and centered differences to approximate $u'(1)$ with $\Delta x = 0.2$. Compare this with the true value.

6. If $u(x) = 3 + 5x - x^3$ is written as a Taylor expansion out to the second degree, the remainder is $O(\Delta x^3)$. Find this remainder term explicitly if the center of expansion

is $x = 1$.

7. If $u(x) = 3 + 2x^2 - 4x^4$ is written as a Taylor expansion out to the second degree, the remainder is $O(\Delta x^3)$. Find this remainder term explicitly if the center of expansion is $x = 1$.

8. Compute the centered difference approximation to $u'(2)$, where $u(x) = x^2$ and $\Delta x = 0.2$. Compare with the true value. Explain this using the Taylor expansion! It is not an accident!

9. Compute the centered second difference for $u''(1)$, where $u(x) = x + x^3$ and $\Delta x = 0.2$. Compare this with the true value.

10. Derive the difference formula for $u'''(x)$.

11. Explain why $O(h^5) + O(h^5) = O(h^5)$ makes sense.

10.2 AN EXAMPLE

In this section we shall try to apply forward, backward, and centered differences to a simple, first-order, partial differential equation. This will demonstrate the major features and difficulties of applying finite differences.

10.2.1 A Forward Method (Explicit)

Consider the problem

$$u_x - u_t = u \text{ and } u(x, 0) = \sin(2\pi x).$$

You can easily check that

$$u(x, t) = \sin(2\pi(x + t))e^{-t}$$

is a solution by differentiating and substituting. We shall now approximate this solution by finite differences on the square $[0, 1] \times [0, 1]$.

The forward procedure for this equation begins with replacing the derivatives with their forward difference approximations. We have

$$\frac{v_{j+1}^k - v_j^k}{\Delta x} - \frac{v_j^{k+1} - v_j^k}{\Delta t} = v_j^k.$$

We shall use u to denote the true solution and v for the values calculated in the approximation algorithm. Next solve for v_j^{k+1} to get

$$v_j^{k+1} = \frac{\Delta t}{\Delta x}(v_{j+1}^k - v_j^k) - \Delta t v_j^k + v_j^k = (1 - \frac{\Delta t}{\Delta x} - \Delta t)v_j^k + \frac{\Delta t}{\Delta x}v_{j+1}^k.$$

This formula gives the value of the approximations at $(j\Delta x, (k+1)\Delta t)$ in terms of the values at the immediately preceding "time", $(j\Delta x, k\Delta t)$. Notice that to calculate v_j^{k+1} we need to know v_{j+1}^k. This means that we always need one more term calculated in the preceding k line than are to be calculated in the $k + 1$ line. Thus, if we divide the x interval into m steps and the t interval into n steps, we shall need to start with v_j^0 computed for at least $j = 0$ to $j = m + n$. Of course, these are computed from the initial condition, which is in fact defined on the whole real line.

For brevity, let $s = (1 - \frac{\Delta t}{\Delta x} - \Delta t)$ and $d = \frac{\Delta t}{\Delta x}$. We now proceed as follows. Compute

$$v_0^1 = sv_0^0 + dv_1^0.$$

The data on the right are supplied by the initial condition. Now compute

$$v_1^1 = sv_1^0 + dv_2^0.$$

This is also computed from the initial data. Continue until all the v_j^1 have been computed out to $j = m + n - 1$. Now repeat the process for v_j^2 for $j = 0$ to $j = m + n - 2$. Since for each step in the process we compute the data points for the next level in the t variable from the preceding level, this process is often called "marching in time". We continue to march in time until $(k + 1) = n$ and the end of the time interval has been reached.

CAS Implementation

The following is a schematic form of an implementation of the algorithm of this example for a computer algebra system such as one of the Three M's.

$m = 20$;
$n = 20$;
$\Delta x = 1/m$;
$\Delta t = 1/n$
For $j = 0$ to $m + n$ do
$v(j, 0) = \sin(2\pi j \Delta x)$;
For $k = 0$ to $n - 1$ do
For $j = 0$ to $m + n - k$ do
$v(j, k + 1) = (1 - \Delta t/\Delta x - \Delta t)v(j, k) + (\Delta t/\Delta x)v(j + 1, k)$;
For $j = 0$ to m do
For $k = 0$ to n do
Print($v(j, k)$);
For $j = 0$ to m do
For $k = 0$ to n do
Plot3D($v(j, k)$);

The following table of data is taken from this routine.

Δx	Δt	$u(0.2, 0.5)$	$v(0.2, 0.5)$	$u(0.5, 0.5)$	$v(0.5, 0.5)$
$1/10$	$1/10$	-0.5768	-0.6626	0	0.2080
$1/20$	$1/10$	-0.5768	-1.0490	0	0.1495
$1/10$	$1/20$	-0.5768	-0.3593	0	0.0618
$1/20$	$1/20$	-0.5768	-0.6081	0	0.0993
$1/40$	$1/20$	-0.5768	-0.7760	0	0.0937
$1/20$	$1/40$	-0.5768	-0.4578	0	0.0382
$1/40$	$1/40$	-0.5768	-0.5901	0	0.0486

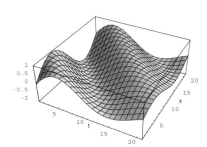

FIGURE 10.1

Note that $u(0.2, 0.5)$ and $u(0.5, 0.5)$ are the true values and $v(0.2, 0.5)$ and $v(0.5, 0.5)$ are the approximations. The data suggest two things. First, the rate of convergence, if the algorithm is converging at all, is fairly slow. Second, the data indicates some sensitivity to the ratio $\Delta t / \Delta x$. Generally, the algorithm seems to do a little better with the smaller ratio rather than the larger.

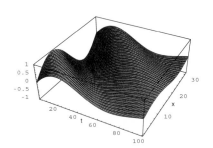

FIGURE 10.2

Most revealing are the following three graphics taken from the same routine. Figure 10.1 shows the approximate solution on the unit square when the number of subdivisions for both x and t is 20. Then comes a shock. Figure 10.2 shows a further refinement of the subdivisions with 100 subdivisions for x and 30 for t. The errors are now accumulating explosively, and the approximation is worthless. Finally, Figure 10.3 shows the output with 30 subdivisions for x and 100 subdivisions for t. Clearly, the algorithm is sensitive to the ratio $\Delta t / \Delta x$. This will be a recurrent theme in the following sections, and to understand it, we shall need to examine the way in which errors propagate.

Error Analysis

We begin by estimating the error made in one step of the algorithm. Let u_j^{k+1} be the true value at the lattice point $(j \Delta x, (k+1)\Delta t)$, and let v_j^{k+1} be the computed approximation. Then the one-step error is

$$u_j^{k+1} - v_j^{k+1} = u_j^{k+1} - \left[\frac{\Delta t}{\Delta x}(v_{j+1}^k - v_j^k) - \Delta t v_j^k + v_j^k \right].$$

Since we are concerned with the one-step error, we assume that the $v_j^k = u_j^k$, that is, we assume that the preceding data are accurate. Using the Taylor expansion for u_j^{k+1}, we have

$$u_j^{k+1} - v_j^{k+1} = u_j^k + u_t(j \Delta x, k \Delta t)\Delta t$$
$$+ O(\Delta t^2) - \left[\frac{\Delta t}{\Delta x}(u_{j+1}^k - u_j^k) - \Delta t u_j^k + u_j^k \right].$$

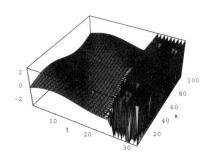

FIGURE 10.3

Now use the differential equation to replace u_t. Thus

$$u_j^{k+1} - v_j^{k+1} = u_j^k + [u_x(j\Delta x, k\Delta t) - u_j^k]\Delta t$$
$$+ O(\Delta t^2) - \left[\frac{\Delta t}{\Delta x}(u_{j+1}^k - u_j^k) - \Delta t u_j^k + u_j^k \right].$$

Canceling gives

$$u_j^{k+1} - v_j^{k+1} = u_x(j\Delta x, k\Delta t)\Delta t + O(\Delta t^2) - \frac{\Delta t}{\Delta x}(u_{j+1}^k - u_j^k).$$

Using the forward difference for u_x gives

$$u_j^{k+1} - v_j^{k+1} = \frac{u_{j+1}^k - u_j^k}{\Delta x}\Delta t + O(\Delta x)\Delta t + O(\Delta t^2) - \frac{\Delta t}{\Delta x}(u_{j+1}^k - u_j^k).$$

Finally, this simplifies to

$$u_j^{k+1} - v_j^{k+1} = O(\Delta x)\Delta t + O(\Delta t^2).$$

Therefore,

$$|u_j^{k+1} - v_j^{k+1}| \le M_1\Delta t \Delta x + M_2 \Delta t^2$$

for some positive constants M_1 and M_2. This is an estimate of the one-step error. It is quadratic in Δt and Δx.

Now let us turn to the cumulative error. Let $c_j^k = u_j^k - v_j^k$. This is the error between the true value and the computed value at the point (j, k). This is called the **cumulative error**. A recursive formula for the c_j^k can be obtained as follows.

$$c_j^{k+1} = u_j^{k+1} - v_j^{k+1} = u_j^{k+1} - [sv_j^k + dv_{j+1}^k].$$

But $v_j^k = u_j^k - c_j^k$, and so

$$c_j^{k+1} = u_j^{k+1} - [s(u_j^k - c_j^k) + d(u_{j+1}^k - c_{j+1}^k)].$$

Collecting terms gives

$$c_j^{k+1} = [sc_j^k + dc_{j+1}^k] + u_j^{k+1} - [su_j^k + du_{j+1}^k].$$

Notice that the difference of the last two terms is the local one-step error, which we denote by e_j^{k+1}. Thus

$$c_j^{k+1} = sc_j^k + dc_{j+1}^k + e_j^{k+1}.$$

This formula can be used to recursively compute the c_j^k in terms of c_j^0 and the one-step errors. This is how it goes. Assume that the absolute value of the one-step errors is everywhere less than E. Then

$$|c_j^1| \le |s||c_j^0| + |d||c_{j+1}^0| + E.$$

The cumulative errors c_j^0 and c_{j+1}^0 are both zero, since they are the errors in the initial data, which we assume are accurate. Thus

$$|c_j^1| \le E.$$

Next

$$|c_j^2| \le |s||c_j^1| + |d||c_{j+1}^1| + E \le (|s| + |d|)E + E.$$

At the next level we have

$$|c_j^3| \le |s||c_j^2| + |d||c_{j+1}^2| + E \le (|s| + |d|)^2 E + (|s| + |d|)E + E.$$

The general formula is

$$|c_j^p| \le (|s| + |d|)^{p-1} E + (|s| + |d|)^{p-2} E + \cdots + (|s| + |d|)E + E$$

$$= E \sum_{k=0}^{p-1} (|s| + |d|)^k.$$

The sum is a partial sum of a geometric series. This can be bounded by the sum of the series if the series converges, and this will happen if $(|s| + |d|) < 1$. Note that if $s > 0$ then $(|s| + |d|) = s + d = 1 - \Delta t < 1$. In this case we have

$$|c_j^p| \le E \sum_{k=0}^{\infty} (1 - \Delta t)^k = \frac{E}{\Delta t}.$$

Thus the one-step error estimate yields the global error estimate

$$|c_j^p| \le \frac{M_1 \Delta t \Delta x + M_2 \Delta t^2}{\Delta t} = M_1 \Delta x + M_2 \Delta t.$$

Given that $s > 0$, the global error will go to zero with a rate that is first order in Δx and Δt. This is rather slow as the table of data indicated. If $(|s| + |d|) \ge 1$, we lose our estimate of the cumulative or global error, and this opens the door to the possibility that we could make Δx and Δt smaller and smaller but fail to have a converging algorithm. We shall see that this is the case with the heat and wave equations.

The Domain of Influence

It is worth looking at the propagation of errors from a more intuitive point of view. Each new value is calculated from two values from the preceding row, and these are calculated from their predecessors, and so on, back to the initial data. The set of all points (j, k) that plays a role in computing a term is called the **domain of influence** of that term. For the term v_j^3, the domain of influence is shown in Figure 10.4. Since the bottom row is the initial data, there is no error there. In the next row up, the error at each point is at most the maximum one-step error E. At the next step, each value is computed from two predecessors, so

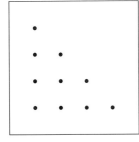

FIGURE 10.4

the errors could combine to give an error of $2E$ for each. At the last level, these errors could combine to give an error of $4E$. This is a worst-case scenario, and it describes an explosive propagation of errors. As we have seen, if $s > 0$ and $(s + d) < 1$, then the errors can partially cancel and we have control over the global error.

10.2.2 Other Difference Methods

Of course, other differences could be tried. We shall attempt to apply the backward and centered differences. The effort will not be successful, but there is a moral.

The backward difference formula is

$$\frac{v_j^k - v_{j-1}^k}{\Delta x} - \frac{v_j^k - v_j^{k-1}}{\Delta t} = v_j^k.$$

This can be rearranged to give

$$\frac{\Delta t}{\Delta x} v_{j-1}^k + (1 - \frac{\Delta t}{\Delta x} + \Delta t) v_j^k = v_j^{k-1}.$$

Notice that now it is v_j^{k-1} on the right that is known and it is v_{j-1}^k and v_j^k that are to be computed. The succeeding terms are only implicitly defined in terms of their predecessors. For this reason the method is called **implicit**.

Notice that to get to the next level we need to solve for $j = 1$ to $j = m$. Therefore, we need to solve m equations in $m + 1$ unknowns. In fact, to do this for each k, we need equations for each of the v_0^k. This amounts to requiring boundary data for $x = 0$. It is an exercise to show that the solution to our example is uniquely determined by the initial data on the x-axis. Hence data cannot be specified independently on the t-axis. In short, the backward method is not appropriate for this problem. However, this attempt does suggest that the backward method might be appropriate for problems with different initial or boundary conditions.

Consider the centered difference approach. We get the difference equations

$$\frac{v_{j+1}^k - v_{j-1}^k}{2\Delta x} - \frac{v_j^{k+1} - v_j^{k-1}}{2\Delta t} = v_j^k.$$

If we fix (j, k), then v_j^k is given in terms of values at points immediately north, south, east, and west of the point (j, k). This suggests that centered differences may be suited to problems where the initial data surround a region such as in the case of the Dirichlet problem.

Consider the region shown in Figure 10.5. There are seven interior points. For each of these there is the corresponding difference equation expressing this interior point in terms of the "satellite" points around it. This means that there are

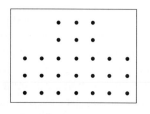

FIGURE 10.5

seven equations in the seven unknown values at the interior points. These equations will include some values from the boundary points, and so if the boundary values are given, the equations can be solved to get the values at the interior points. Our example is not an equation in which boundary data surrounding a region are given, and so centered differences are not applicable to this problem.

The moral of these attempts to apply backward and centered differences is that the choice of difference method must match the problem.

EXERCISES 10.2

1. Compute v_1^1 and v_1^2 in the forward algorithm of this section when there are four subdivisions in x and four in t.

2. Repeat Exercise 1, except use $u(x, 0) = x^2$ as the initial condition.

3. Implement the appropriate finite difference algorithm with graphical output in a CAS such as one of the Three M's. Apply it to the problem $u_x - u_t = u$, where $u(x, 0) = \cos(\pi x)$ on the (x, t) square $[0, 2] \times [0, 3]$. Experiment to see if you can get the algorithm to fail. Report!

4. Implement the appropriate finite difference algorithm with graphical output in a CAS such as one of the Three M's. Apply it to the problem $u_x - 2u_t = 0$, where $u(x, 0) = x$ on the (x, t) square $[0, 1] \times [0, 1]$. Experiment to find a ratio $\Delta t / \Delta x$ for which the algorithm appears to be stable under refinement of the step sizes. Find a ratio for which it is unstable if you can. Report!

5. Implement the appropriate finite difference algorithm with graphical output in a CAS such as one of the Three M's. Apply it to the problem $u_x - 2u_t = 3u$, where $u(x, 0) = x$ on the (x, t) square $[0, 1] \times [0, 1]$. Experiment to find a ratio $\Delta t / \Delta x$ for which the algorithm appears to be stable under refinement of the step sizes. Find a ratio for which it is unstable if you can. Report!

Find the forward difference algorithm for the equations in Exercises 6–10.

6. $3u_x - 2u_t = 0$

7. $4u_x - u_t = u$

8. $4u_x + 3u_t = u$

9. $u_x + u_t = u^2$

10. $u_x + u_t - u = x^2$

For Exercises 11 and 12, find the backward difference algorithm for the equation, and explain why this is refered to as an implicit method.

11. $4u_x - u_t = u$

12. $u_x + u_t = u$

For Exercises 13 and 14, find the centered difference algorithm for the equation, and explain why this is refered to as an implicit method.

13. $4u_x - u_t = u$

14. $4u_x + 3u_t = u$

15. Solve the equation $u_x - u_t = u$ as follows. First change variables by setting $\bar{x} = x - t$ and $\bar{t} = x + t$. Define $w(\bar{x}, \bar{t}) = u(x, t)$. Show that u satisfies $u_x - u_t = u$ if and only if $2w_{\bar{x}} = w$. Find the general solution to this equation. Use this to give $u(x, t)$ and apply the initial condition.

16. In view of Exercise 15, does it make sense to specify initial conditions on the x and t axes for the equation $u_x - u_t = u$? Explain!

17. Briefly explain in your own words why the backward method is not suitable for the example of this section.

10.3 THE HEAT AND WAVE EQUATIONS

In this section we shall apply the forward and centered second differences to the heat and wave equations.

10.3.1 The Heat Equation

The method of finite differences will first be applied to the heat equation in the rectangle $[0, b] \times [0, t_0]$. Recall that the problem is to solve

$$u_t = a^2 u_{xx},$$

where the initial and boundary conditions are $u(x, 0) = f(x)$ and $u(0, t) = u(b, t) = 0$.

The rectangle $[0, b] \times [0, t_0]$ is divided into $m \times n$ subrectangles. The derivatives are replaced by the corresponding differences. Recall that we use u for the true solution and v for the values of the algorithm. The result is

$$\frac{v_j^{k+1} - v_j^k}{\Delta t} = a^2 \frac{v_{j+1}^k - 2v_j^k + v_{j-1}^k}{\Delta x^2}.$$

A little algebra leads to

$$v_j^{k+1} = \frac{a^2 \Delta t}{\Delta x^2} [v_{j+1}^k - 2v_j^k + v_{j-1}^k] + v_j^k.$$

This formula allows us to compute by "marching in time." Note that the next time value at j is computed from the previous time values at $j - 1$, j, and $j + 1$. If $[0, b]$ is divided into m subdivisions, what happens when $j = 0$ or $j = m$? Do we have to obtain data from outside the interval $[0, b]$, as we did in Section 10.2? No, the boundary conditions tell us what the values of v_0^k and v_m^k are for all k, so we need only apply the formula for $j = 1$ to $j = m - 1$.

If you have been observant, you may have noticed that the algorithm will still work, with minor modifications, if the boundary data are not homogeneous. Indeed, the boundary data could even be time dependent. Investigation of this will be left to the exercises.

CAS Implementation

The following is a schematic for the programming of the algorithm in a CAS, such as one of the Three M's. Of course, you fill in the '?'.
$xo = ?;$
$to = ?;$
$a = ?;$
$f(x) = ?;$
$m = ?;$
$n = ?;$
$\Delta x = xo/m;$
$\Delta t = to/n;$
$s = a^2 \Delta t / \Delta x^2;$
For $j = 0$ to m do
$v_j^0 = f(j\Delta x);$

For $k = 0$ to n do
$v_0^k = 0$;
$v_m^k = 0$;
For $k = 0$ to $n - 1$ do
For $j = 1$ to $m - 1$ do
$v_j^{k+1} = sv_{j-1}^k + (1 - 2s)v_j^k + sv_{j+1}^k$;
For $k = 0$ to n do
For $j = 0$ to m do
$\{\text{Print}(v_j^k)$;

$\text{Plot3D}(v_j^k); \}$ In the following examples we employ an implementation of the algorithm. Notice again the disastrous results if the ratio of Δt to Δx is not suitable. We shall see in the error analysis that it is the quantity

$$s = \frac{a^2 \Delta t}{\Delta x^2}$$

that we need to pay particular attention to.

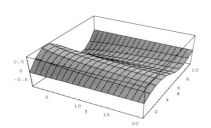

FIGURE 10.6

Example 10.3.1   We can graph the output data v_j^k from the routine described above to get a three-dimensional plot. Figure 10.6 shows the plot of the boundary value problem $u_t = 0.5u_{xx}$, $u(x, 0) = \sin(\pi x/5)$ on $[0, 10]$, and $u(0, t) = u(10, t) = 0$. The range on t is $[0, 20]$. The number of subdivisions for x is 10 and for t it is 20 giving a value of 0.25 for s. The tick marks in the horizontal directions are the step numbers in each direction.

This image is what we would expect to see if the approximation was good. We see the initial sine temperature distribution decaying away to zero as time progresses. Figure 10.7 shows the result with the number of subdivisions for x equal to 60 and 10 for t. In this case, $s = 18$. The result is that errors accumulate explosively. ∎

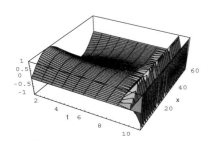

FIGURE 10.7

Example 10.3.2   Consider $u_t = u_{xx}$, $u(x, 0) = \sin(x)$ on $[0, \pi]$ with homogeneous boundary conditions. The unique solution to this simple problem is

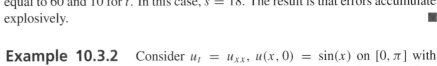

$$u(x, t) = e^{-t} \sin(x).$$

This time we use the algorithm to produce numerical data. By way of illustration, let us choose 10 subdivisions of $[0, \pi]$ and 25 subdivisions of $[0, 1]$. The true value at the point $(1.5708, 0.52)$ is 0.594521, and the approximation at that point is 0.590819. However, if we use 40 subdivisions on the x-axis and 20 subdivisions on the t-axis, the algorithm with an s value of about 8 becomes wildly unstable with computed values in the millions, where the solution is not greater than 1. On the other hand, further refinement of the mesh while keeping s less than 0.5 produces approximations that appear to be converging. Indeed, with 20 subdivisions on the x-axis and 100 on the t-axis, the approximate value at the point $(1.5708, 0.52)$ is now 0.593. ∎

The dependence of the stability and instability of the algorithm on the quantity s is explained in the error analysis that follows. It is shown that the approximation converges to the true solution provided that the subdivisions are refined while maintaining $s \le 1/2$. The error analysis can be omitted without loss of continuity.

Error Analysis (Optional)

Recall that the one-step error is $e_j^{k+1} = u_j^{k+1} - v_j^{k+1}$, and so

$$e_j^{k+1} = u_j^{k+1} - \left[\frac{a^2 \Delta t}{\Delta x^2} [u_{j+1}^k - 2u_j^k + u_{j-1}^k] + u_j^k \right].$$

Replacing the second difference yields

$$e_j^{k+1} = u_j^{k+1} - a^2 \Delta t (u_{xx,j}^k + O(\Delta x^2)) - u_j^k.$$

Exchange the space derivative for the time derivative to get

$$e_j^{k+1} = u_j^{k+1} - \Delta t (u_{t,j}^k + O(\Delta x^2)) - u_j^k.$$

Replace the time derivative with its forward difference equivalent to get

$$e_j^{k+1} = u_j^{k+1} - \Delta t \left(\frac{u_j^{k+1} - u_j^k}{\Delta t} + O(\Delta t) + O(\Delta x^2) \right) - u_j^k.$$

Simplifying leads to

$$e_j^{k+1} = \Delta t O(\Delta t) + \Delta t O(\Delta x^2).$$

Assuming that the solution has continuous second derivatives, the maximum one-step error E satisfies

$$E \le M_1 \Delta t \Delta x^2 + M_2 \Delta t^2.$$

For the cumulative error, it will be useful to set $s = a^2 \Delta t / \Delta x^2$. Thus

$$v_j^{k+1} = s v_{j-1}^k + (1 - 2s) v_j^k + s v_{j+1}^k.$$

Following the same steps as in the example of Section 10.2, it is easy to show that

$$c_j^{k+1} = s c_{j-1}^k + (1 - 2s) c_j^k + s c_{j+1}^k + e_j^{k+1}.$$

Therefore,

$$|c_j^{k+1}| \le |s||c_{j-1}^k| + |1 - 2s||c_j^k| + |s||c_{j+1}^k| + E.$$

Starting at $k = 0$, we have the initial data, and so $c_j^0 = 0$. Thus

$$|c_j^1| \le E.$$

Then

$$|c_j^2| \le |s|E + |1 - 2s|E + |s|E + E.$$

This will get complicated from here if we do not use a simplifying assumption. If we choose the mesh so that

$$s \le \frac{1}{2},$$

then we get

$$|c_j^2| \le E + E = 2E.$$

The third step is

$$|c_j^3| \le |s|2E + |1 - 2s|2E + |s|2E + E = 3E.$$

If there are n time steps, then the worst the cumulative error can be is

$$|c_j^k| \le nE \le M_1 n \Delta t \Delta x^2 + M_2 n \Delta t^2.$$

But $n \Delta t$ is the length of the time interval t_0, so

$$|c_j^k| \le t_0 M_1 \Delta x^2 + t_0 M_2 \Delta t.$$

This goes to zero as the mesh goes to zero. But remember that the mesh must go to zero while satisfying the condition that $s \le 1/2$. Under this condition the approximation converges to the solution.

10.3.2 The Wave Equation

We shall use centered second differences to generate an algorithm to solve

$$c^2 u_{xx} = u_{tt},$$

where

$$u(0, t) = u(b, t) = u_t(0, t) = u_t(b, t) = 0,$$

and

$$u(x, 0) = f(x) \text{ and } u_t(x, 0) = g(x)$$

on $[0, b]$. We fix a time interval $[0, t_0]$ as before.

The difference equation is

$$\frac{v_j^{k+1} - 2v_j^k + v_j^{k-1}}{\Delta t^2} = c^2 \frac{v_{j+1}^k - 2v_j^k + v_{j-1}^k}{\Delta x^2}.$$

If we set $s = c^2 \Delta t^2/\Delta x^2$ and solve for v_j^{k+1}, we get

$$v_j^{k+1} = sv_{j-1}^k + 2(1-s)v_j^k + sv_{j+1}^k - v_j^{k-1}.$$

Notice that to calculate v_j^{k+1} you have to go back two steps in time. In other words, the algorithm requires the two preceding rows to get the next row. We shall need two rows to start with. We have the first, since $u(x,0) = f(x)$ gives us the v_j^0, but what about the v_j^1? Here is one approach to this step.

We have the forward difference

$$\frac{u_j^1 - u_j^0}{\Delta t} = u_t(j\Delta x, 0) + \frac{\Delta t}{2}u_{tt}(j\Delta x, 0) + O(\Delta t^2).$$

But u satisfies the wave equation, so

$$\frac{u_j^1 - u_j^0}{\Delta t} = u_t(j\Delta x, 0) + \frac{c^2\Delta t}{2}u_{xx}(j\Delta x, 0) + O(\Delta t^2).$$

We use the centered second difference on u_{xx} and the initial data to get

$$\frac{u_j^1 - u_j^0}{\Delta t} = g_j + \frac{c^2\Delta t}{2}\left[\frac{f_{j+1} - 2f_j + f_{j-1}}{\Delta x^2} + O(\Delta x^2)\right] + O(\Delta t^2).$$

Solving for u_j^1 gives

$$u_j^1 = f_j + \Delta t g_j + \frac{c^2\Delta t^2}{2\Delta x^2}[f_{j+1} - 2f_j + f_{j-1}] + O(\Delta t^2\Delta x^2 + \Delta t^2).$$

Our approximation is

$$v_j^1 = f_j + \Delta t g_j + \frac{c^2\Delta t}{2\Delta x^2}[f_{j+1} - 2f_j + f_{j-1}].$$

Also note that

$$u_j^1 - v_j^1 = O(\Delta t^2\Delta x^2 + \Delta t^3).$$

We can use the physical interpretation of the wave equation to predict the effect of the quantity

$$s = \frac{c^2\Delta t^2}{\Delta x^2}$$

on the convergence of the approximation. Recall that, in $u_{tt} = c^2u_{xx}$, c can be interpreted as the speed of transmission of a pulse along a stretched string. In the numerical approximation, data cannot travel to the next point on the x-axis until one time step has been taken. So the speed of transmission of data is at most $\Delta x/\Delta t$. If this is not at least as great as c, the numerical method cannot hope to "keep up" with the transmission of the true wave. Therefore, if the approximation is to have any success, we must have $\Delta x/\Delta t \leq c$. This means that we must have

$$s = \frac{c^2\Delta t^2}{\Delta x^2} \leq 1.$$

CAS Implementation

The algorithm for the wave equation just developed can be implemented in the following schematic form. Again, you fill in the question marks.

The intervals for x and t are $[0, a]$ and $[0, b]$, c is the combined constants of the string, and m and n are the subdivisions for the x and t intervals, respectively. The functions $f(x)$ and $g(x)$ are the initial displacement and velocity.

$a = ?;$
$b = ?;$
$c = ?;$
$m = ?;$
$n = ?;$
$\Delta x = a/m;$
$\Delta t = b/n;$
$s = c^2(\Delta t/\Delta x)^2;$
For $k = 0$ to n do
$v_0^k = 0;$
$v_m^k = 0;$
For $j = 1$ to $m - 1$ do
$v_j^0 = f(jdx);$
For $j = 1$ to $m - 1$ do
$v_j^1 = f(jdx) + dtg(jdx) + s(f((j+1)dx) - 2f(jdx) + f((j-1)dx))/2;$
For $j = 1$ to $m - 1$ do
For $k = 1$ to $n - 1$ do
$v_j^{k+1} = sv_{j-1}^k + 2(1-s)v_j^k + sv_{j+1}^k - v_j^{k-1};$
For $j = 0$ to m do
For $k = 0$ to n do
Print(v_j^k);

As with the heat equation, we can add three-dimensional graphing of the data generated by the routine.

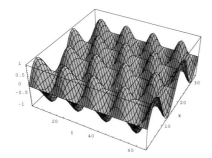

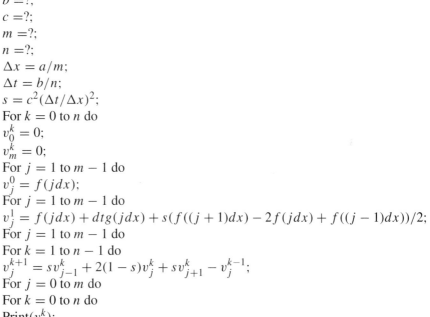

FIGURE 10.8

Example 10.3.3   Figure 10.8 shows the approximating surface to the solution to the wave equation $u_{tt} = 4u_{xx}$ with initial conditions $u(x, 0) = \sin(4\pi x)$ and $u_t(x, 0) = 0$ on $[0, 1]$ and homogeneous boundary conditions. The time interval is $[0, 1]$, and 32 subdivisions were used for x and 64 for t. Thus $s = 1$.

A slice of the surface taken parallel to the left vertical plane gives a snapshot of the string at an instant of time. Slices taken perpendicular to the left wall and the horizontal plane give graphs of the motion of a point on the string as a function of time. The approximation would appear to be very good. The motion does appear to correspond to the simple mode of vibration that the initial data require.

Figure 10.9 shows the behavior of the algorithm when the number of divisions on the x-axis has been changed to 36. In this case, $s = 1.27$, and the algorithm is not approximating the solution because errors are accumulating in a compounding fashion.

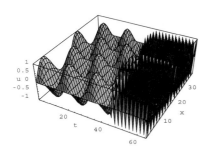

FIGURE 10.9

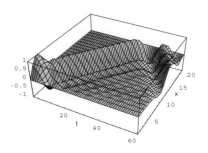

FIGURE 10.10

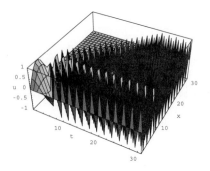

FIGURE 10.11

Example 10.3.4 This example shows a three-dimensional view of a pulse transmitted along the string. We apply the algorithm to $u_{tt} = 0.25u_{xx}$ with initial conditions $u(x, 0) = \sin(\pi x)$ for x in $[0, 1]$ and $x = 0$ elsewhere, and $u_t(x, 0) = 0$ on $[0, 4]$. The time interval is $[0, 12]$. You can verify that $s < 1$, and the algorithm appears to be giving reasonable results.

In Figure 10.10 you can see the initial displacement at $t = 0$. In your mind's eye, take cross-sections perpendicular to the t-axis. You can see the wave followed by ripples as it moves along the string. You can also see what happens when the wave reaches the end of the string. The wave is reflected and turned upside down. Figure 10.11 shows the results where $s > 1$. Again, the algorithm has become unstable and useless. ∎

Continued experimentation lends strong evidence that the approximation converges to the true solution if $s \leq 1$, and if $s > 1$, the algorithm becomes unstable. The reasons for this are discussed in the optional error analysis section that follows.

Error Analysis (Optional)

The ordinary one-step error is found in the usual way. It is left as an exercise. The result is

$$e_j^{k+1} = O(\Delta t^4 + \Delta t^2 \Delta x^2).$$

We shall now analyze the cumulative errors c_j^k. We shall show that if $s = 1$ then the approximation converges to the true solution. In the case that $s < 1$, the approximation also converges, and this can be deduced from the case $s = 1$. This is left to the supplementary exercises.

The usual argument shows that, for $s = 1$,

$$c_j^{k+1} = c_{j-1}^k + c_{j+1}^k - c_j^{k-1} + e_j^{k+1},$$

where e_j^{k+1} is the one-step error. We now get c_j^{k+1} in terms of the starting data by repeated back substitution. Here is how it goes.

$$c_{j-1}^k = c_{j-2}^{k-1} + c_j^{k-1} - c_{j-1}^{k-2} + e_{j-1}^k,$$

and

$$c_{j+1}^k = c_j^{k-1} + c_{j+2}^{k-1} - c_{j+1}^{k-2} + e_{j+1}^k.$$

Therefore,

$$c_j^{k+1} = c_{j-2}^{k-1} + c_j^{k-1} + c_{j+2}^{k-1} - c_{j+1}^{k-2} - c_{j-1}^{k-2} + 3 \text{ error terms.}$$

The three error terms are the one-step errors. These have absolute value less than the maximum one-step error E provided that we have not yet reached row 1. The errors c_j^1 will be discussed soon. Using the basic formula on c_{j-2}^{k-1}, c_j^{k-1}, and c_{j+2}^{k-1}, we get

$$c_j^{k+1} = c_{j-3}^{k-2} + c_{j-1}^{k-2} + c_{j+1}^{k-2} + c_{j+3}^{k-2} - c_{j-2}^{k-3} - c_j^{k-3} - c_{j+2}^{k-3} + 6 \text{ error terms.}$$

The bottom will be reached in k steps. Of course, if any subscript is equal to 0 or to m, the point is located on the boundary, and so the cumulative error for those points is zero, and those terms can be discarded. Recall that the c_j^0 are all zero, since the initial data are assumed to be accurate. The result at the bottom is

$$c_j^{k+1} = c_{j-k}^1 + c_{j-k+2}^1 + \cdots + c_{j+k}^1 + \frac{k(k+1)}{2} \text{ error terms.}$$

Notice that the number of c_i^1 terms is at most $k+1$. Recall the one-step error and that

$$c_i^1 = O(\Delta t^2 \Delta x^2 + \Delta t^3),$$

and so

$$|c_j^{k+1}| \le nO(\Delta t^2 \Delta x^2 + \Delta t^3) + \frac{n(n+1)}{2} O(\Delta t^4 + \Delta t^2 \Delta x^2).$$

However, $n\Delta t = t_0$, and so

$$|c_j^{k+1}| \le O(\Delta t \Delta x^2 + \Delta t^2) + O(\Delta t^2 + \Delta x^2).$$

Therefore, the approximation converges to the true solution for $s = 1$. As we have said, the same is true for $s < 1$.

EXERCISES 10.3

1. Consider the heat equation $u_t = u_{xx}$ on the unit square $[0, 1] \times [0, 1]$. Assume homogeneous boundary conditions, and let $u(x, 0) = \sin(\pi x)$. Using four subdivisions on the x-axis and $s = 1/2$, compute v_1^1 and v_1^2. *Hint:* You only need to calculate values in the domain of influence.

2. Consider the heat equation $u_t = u_{xx}$ on the unit square $[0, 1] \times [0, 1]$. Assume homogeneous boundary conditions, and let $u(x, 0) = x - x^2$. Using four subdivisions on the x-axis and $s = 1/2$, compute v_1^1 and v_1^2. *Hint:* You can save computation by finding the domain of influence.

3. Consider the heat equation $u_t = u_{xx}$ on the unit square $[0, 1] \times [0, 1]$. Assume that $u(0, t) = 1$ and $u(1, t) = 2$, and let $u(x, 0) = x - x^2$. Using four subdivisions on the x-axis and $s = 1/2$, compute v_1^1 and v_1^2.

4. Consider the heat equation $u_t = u_{xx}$ on the unit square $[0, 1] \times [0, 1]$. Assume that $u(0, t) = t$ and $u(1, t) = 2$,

and let $u(x, 0) = x - x^2$. Using four subdivisions on the x-axis and $s = 1/2$, compute v_2^1 and v_2^2.

5. Consider the heat equation $u_t = u_{xx}$ on the unit square $[0, 1] \times [0, 1]$. Assume that $u(0, t) = t$ and $u(1, t) = t^2$, and let $u(x, 0) = x^3 - x$. Using four subdivisions on the x-axis and $s = 1/2$, compute v_2^1 and v_2^2.

6. Find v_2^2 for the wave equation $u_{tt} = u_{xx}$ with homogeneous boundary conditions, $u(x, 0) = \sin(x)$, and $u_t(x, 0) = 0$. Do this on the rectangle $[0, \pi] \times [0, 1]$ with four subdivisions on a side. Is s acceptable? Compare with the true solution. *Hint:* You can save computation by finding the domain of influence.

7. Find v_3^3 for the wave equation $u_{tt} = 4u_{xx}$ on $[0, 1] \times [0, 1]$ with homogeneous boundary conditions, $u(x, 0) = x - x^2$, and $u_t(x, 0) = 0$. Use eight subdivisions on the x side and sixteen on the t side. Is s acceptable? You only

need to calculate values in the domain of influence.

8. Find v_4^3 for the wave equation $u_{tt} = 4u_{xx}$ on $[0, 1] \times [0, 1]$ with homogeneous boundary conditions, $u(x, 0) = 0$, and $u_t(x, 0) = \sin(\pi x)$. Use eight subdivisions on the x side and sixteen on the t side. Is s acceptable? Remember, you only need to calculate values in the domain of influence.

9. Implement the finite difference approximation of solutions to the heat equation in the CAS of your choice. Make sure to provide graphical output. Apply it to the problem $u_t = u_{xx}$, where $u(x, 0) = \sin(3\pi x)$ on $[0, 1]$ and the boundary conditions are homogeneous. Assume that the time interval is $[0, 1]$. Experiment with different step ratios. Be sure to create a disaster.

10. Apply your program in Exercise 9 to the problem $u_t = u_{xx}$, where $u(x, 0) = 4x(1 - x)$ on $[0, 1]$ and the boundary conditions are homogeneous. Assume that the time

interval is $[0, 3]$. Experiment with different step ratios. Be sure to create a disaster.

11. Implement the finite difference approximation of solutions to the wave equation in the CAS of your choice. Make sure to provide graphical output. Apply it to the boundary value problem in Exercise 6. Experiment with different step ratios. Comment on the results.

12. Apply your program for the wave equation to the problem in exercise 7. Experiment with different step ratios. Comment on the results.

13. Derive the one-step error for the wave equation. Remember, in the one-step error we assume that the preceding data are accurate.

14. Show that for $s = 1$ the cumulative errors satisfy

$$c_j^{k+1} = c_{j-1}^k + c_{j+1}^k - c_j^{k-1} + e_j^{k+1}.$$

10.4 A BACKWARD METHOD FOR THE HEAT EQUATION

In the last section we used forward methods on both the heat and wave equations. In this section, we will apply a backward difference method to the heat equation, and we shall discover through examples that the method does not suffer from the instability of the forward methods. We shall give a brief explanation of the instability and stability of these methods in the last section of this chapter.

Recall that the backward difference has the form

$$\frac{v_j^k - v_j^{k-1}}{\Delta t}.$$

So, if we use the backward difference for u_t and the centered second difference for u_{xx}, then the difference equation for the equation $u_t = a^2 u_{xx}$ is

$$\frac{v_j^k - v_j^{k-1}}{\Delta t} = a^2 \frac{v_{j+1}^k - 2v_j^k + v_{j-1}^k}{\Delta x^2}.$$

If we set $s = a^2 \Delta t / \Delta x^2$, we can write

$$(1 + 2s)v_j^k - sv_{j+1}^k - sv_{j-1}^k = v_j^{k-1}. \qquad (*)$$

We assume that the boundary conditions are homogeneous. Now fix k, and assume that we know the values v_j^{k-1} for $j = 1, \ldots, m - 1$ (of course, $v_0^{k-1} = v_m^{k-1} = 0$ because of the homogeneous boundary conditions). Then $(*)$ defines the following $(m - 1)$ linear equations in the $(m - 1)$ unknowns v_j^k.

$$(1 + 2s)v_1^k - sv_2^k + 0v_3^k + \cdots + 0v_{m-1}^k = v_1^{k-1},$$

$$-sv_1^k + (1+2s)v_2^k - sv_3^k + \cdots + 0v_{m-1}^k = v_2^{k-1},$$

$$\vdots$$

$$0v_1^k + 0v_2^k + \cdots - sv_{m-2}^k + (1+2s)v_{m-1}^k = v_{m-1}^{k-1}.$$

We can express this system of linear equations in matrix form if we set $v^k = (v_1^k, v_2^k, \ldots, v_{m-2}^k, v_{m-1}^k)^t$; then we can write

$$Bv^k = v^{k-1},$$

where

$$B = \begin{bmatrix} (1+2s) & -s & 0 & 0 & \cdots & 0 & 0 \\ -s & (1+2s) & -s & 0 & \cdots & 0 & 0 \\ 0 & -s & (1+2s) & -s & \cdots & 0 & 0 \\ & & & \vdots & & & \\ 0 & 0 & 0 & 0 & \cdots & (1+2s) & -s \\ 0 & 0 & 0 & 0 & \cdots & -s & (1+2s) \end{bmatrix}.$$

The special form of this matrix is called tridiagonal. Notice that the method is implicit because we must solve $Bv^k = v^{k-1}$ to get to the next time level.

It can be shown that the tridiagonal matrix B is invertible. Thus the algorithm can be implemented through

$$v^k = B^{-1}v^{k-1}$$

for $k = 1, 2, \ldots$. Thus the implementation will require the entry of the initial data, the boundary data, the matrix B, and the inversion of this matrix. The schematic CAS routine to do this follows.

CAS Implementation

To implement this backward algorithm in a computer algebra system, we need to enter the interval for x, the number of subdivisions m for x, the number of time steps n, and the value of s. We can start with

$a = 2$;
$m = 10$;
$n = 10$;
$s = 1$;
$dx = a/m$;

Here, dx is the increment in x.

Next, we need to define the matrix B. This is not hard because the matrix is tridiagonal. As an array, something like the following will do.

For $j = 1$ to $m - 1$ do
For $k = 1$ to $m - 1$ do

$\{B[j, j] = (1 + 2s);$
$B[j, j + 1] = -s;$
$B[j + 1, j] = -s;$
if $j + 1 < k$ then
$B[j, k] = 0;$
if $k < j - 1$ then
$B[j, k] = 0\};$

In most CAS's finding B^{-1} is a simple command, so we assume that we have B^{-1}. The next step is to compute the initial data vector from the initial condition $u(x, 0) = f(x)$. This is easily done with
$f(x) = ?;$
$v[0] = \text{array}(f(j * dx), j = 1 \text{ to } m - 1);$

We can generate the data vectors at future time steps by

For $k = 1$ to n do
$v[k] = B^{-1}v[k - 1];$

We must remember that the boundary conditions are homogeneous, so all that remains is to define the data points along the edges of the region to be zero. If our final array to be graphed is C, then we can easily set $C[j, k] = v[k][j]$ for $k = 1$ to n and for $j = 1$ to $m - 1$. For the rest, we define $C[0, k] = C[m, k] = 0$ for $k = 0$ to n. Then the two-dimensional array C can be plotted in three dimensions.

Example 10.4.1 Consider the equation $u_t = u_{xx}$ with homogeneous boundary conditions and $u(x, 0) = \sin(\pi x)$ on the interval $[0, 1]$. Take the time interval to be $[0, 1]$ also. Consider four subdivisions on both intervals. We shall compute v^1 and v^2.

First we find s. We have $s = 1\Delta t / \Delta x^2 = 0.25 / 0.625 = 4$. Then

$$B = \begin{bmatrix} 9 & -4 & 0 \\ -4 & 9 & -4 \\ 0 & -4 & 9 \end{bmatrix}.$$

It is easy to compute that

$$B^{-1} = \begin{bmatrix} \frac{65}{441} & \frac{36}{441} & \frac{16}{441} \\ \frac{36}{441} & \frac{81}{441} & \frac{36}{441} \\ \frac{16}{441} & -\frac{36}{441} & \frac{65}{441} \end{bmatrix}.$$

The initial vector is
$$v^0 = (0.0137, 1, 0.0137)^t.$$

Thus
$$v^1 = B^{-1}v^0 = (0.0841, 0.1859, 0.0841)^t.$$

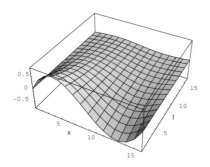

FIGURE 10.12

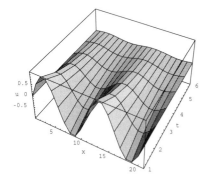

FIGURE 10.13

Likewise

$$v^2 = B^{-1}v^1.$$

Example 10.4.2   We approximate the solution to $u_t = u_{xx}$, where $u(x, 0)$ $= 2x(x - 1)(x - 2)$ on the interval $[0, 2]$. Figure 10.12 shows the result were $s = 1$, $m = 15$, and $n = 15$. Observe that $s = a^2 \Delta t / \Delta x^2$, and so $\Delta t = \Delta x^2 = (2/15)^2 \equiv 0.0177$. So the time interval covered is about 0.266.

　　　If you experiment with different values of s, m, and n, you will find that you are not able to provoke the kind of disaster that was possible with the forward method. The algorithm appears to be stable.   ■

Example 10.4.3   Figure 10.13 shows the approximation to the solution to the heat equation with homogeneous boundary conditions and initial condition $u(x, 0) = \sin(4\pi x)$ on the interval $[0, 1]$. We used 20 subdivisions of the interval, and we moved forward in time by six steps. We used $s = 2$ for this image. However, experimenting with other values still could not cause instability.   ■

　　　It is reasonable to conjecture that this backward method is not sensitive to the value of s. This is indeed the case, and an explanation of this stability will be given at the end of the chapter.

EXERCISES 10.4

1. For the problem $u_t = u_{xx}$, $u(x, 0) = \sin(\pi x)$ on $[0, 1]$, and homogeneous boundary conditions, use the backward method to compute v^1 and v^2, where $m = 3$. Use $s = 1$ in these calculations.

2. For the problem $u_t = u_{xx}$, $u(x, 0) = 2x(x - 1)$ on $[0, 1]$, and homogeneous boundary conditions, use the backward method to compute v^1 and v^2 where $m = 3$. Use $s = 1$ in these calculations.

3. For the problem $u_t = u_{xx}$, $u(x, 0) = \sin(\pi x)$ on $[0, 1]$, and homogeneous boundary conditions, use the backward method to compute v^1 and v^2, where $m = 3$. Use $s = 2$ in these calculations.

4. For the problem $u_t = u_{xx}$, $u(x, 0) = 2x(x - 1)$ on $[0, 1]$, and homogeneous boundary conditions, use the backward method to compute v^1 and v^2, where $m = 3$. Use $s = 4$ in these calculations.

5. Implement the backward algorithm in your favorite CAS.

6. Get graphical output of the approximations to Exercise 1 when $m = 20$ and the time interval is $[0, 1]$. Do this for $s = 1$, $s = 5$, and $s = 0.5$.

7. Get graphical output of the approximations to Exercise 2 when $m = 15$ and the time interval is $[0, 2]$. Do this for $s = 1$, $s = 5$, and $s = 0.5$.

8. Get graphical output for the problem $u_t = 4u_{xx}$, $u(x, 0) = \sin(2\pi x)$ on $[0, 1]$, and homogeneous boundary conditions. Use a time interval of $[0, 4]$

10.5 VARIABLE COEFFICIENT AND NONLINEAR EXAMPLES

The heat and wave equations of the last sections have analytic solutions through the method of separation of variables, so one would not normally apply numerical methods. However, the heat and wave equations provided familiar examples through which the method of finite differences could be discussed. In this section we shall discuss two variants of the heat equation and one variant of the wave equation that do not lend themselves to solution by separation of variables.

In deriving the heat equation

$$u_t = a^2 u_{xx},$$

we lumped the density, specific heat, and conductivity into the single constant a^2. This assumes that the rod is homogeneous; but if it is not, then a^2 is no longer a constant. In this case the equation would take the form

$$u_t = a(x)u_{xx},$$

where $a(x)$ is a positive function of position along the rod. Perhaps it is not impossible to approach the solution through separation of variables, but it would not be easy. Therefore, we try our method of finite differences.

Given the same boundary and initial conditions as for the constant coefficient heat equation, it can be shown that the solution is still unique. In view of the physical interpretation of the equation, this is plausible. So at least we have a unique solution to try to approximate. The finite difference scheme is a very simple modification of the one for the heat equation. Instead of the constant a^2, we must include the function $a(x)$ discretely by $a_j = a(j\Delta x)$. The forward difference scheme is

$$v_j^{k+1} = a_j \frac{\Delta t}{(\Delta x)^2}[v_{j+1}^k - 2v_j^k + v_{j-1}^k] + v_j^k.$$

The computer algebra routine for the heat equation can be easily modified to accommodate this change.

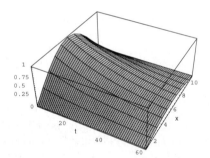

FIGURE 10.14

Example 10.5.1 In this example we attempt to approximate $u_t = a(x)u_{xx}$, where $a(x) = 1 - 0.5\sin(x)$ and $u(x, 0) = \sin(x)$ on $[0, \pi]$. The time interval is $[0, 3]$. We assume homogeneous boundary conditions.

Figure 10.14 shows the approximation with 10 subdivisions for x and 60 for t. However, consider Figure 10.15. Here we have used 20 subdivisions for x and 20 for t. The result is an explosive disaster. The first approximation was done with a small ratio of $\frac{\Delta t}{(\Delta x)^2}$, whereas this ratio was much larger for the second attempted approximation. Since the function $a(x)$ oscillated below 1, it was hoped that behavior similar to that of the heat equation with $a^2 = 1$ might occur. This seems to be the case.

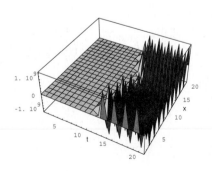

FIGURE 10.15

However, the moral of this example is that, in many applications of numerical methods, it is impractical or impossible to prove an error estimate from the step sizes. Worse is the fact that further refinement of the steps may lead to disastrous results in the case of partial differential equations, because some unknown required relationship between Δx and Δt has been breached. Engineers must approach the use of numerical methods in partial differential equations with a strong intuition about what they are looking for. In the case in hand, the first figure shows a behavior that is to be expected. The temperature should die away in the manner shown. The second figure is completely unbelievable given the physical problem.   ∎

Our second example is again a minor modification of the heat equation. The heated rod in the heat problem may be homogeneous so that the physical parameters of the rod do not vary with position, but this does not mean that they could not vary with temperature. In this case we could have an equation of the form

$$u_t = a(u)u_{xx},$$

where $a(u)$ is a positive function of the temperature. This new equation is nonlinear, and so the method of separation of variables is ruled out. We must use numerical methods.

Again, it is a very simple thing to modify the computer algebra routine for the heat equation to accommodate this new equation.

Example 10.5.2   In this example we attempt to approximate $u_t = u^2 u_{xx}$, where $u(x, 0) = \sin(2x)$ on $[0, \pi]$ and the time interval is $[0, 2]$. We assume homogeneous boundary conditions.

Figure 10.16 shows the approximation where the number of subdivisions for x is 10 and the number for t is 20. The behavior here seems consistent with physical expectations. Figure 10.17 shows the approximation where the number of subdivisions for x has been increased to 20. Something suspicious is emerging. Look at that roughening of the surface. This suggests some growing instability. Figure 10.18 shows the attempted approximation with the number of subdivisions for x increased to 23. The algorithm has blown up.   ∎

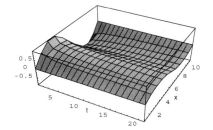

FIGURE 10.16

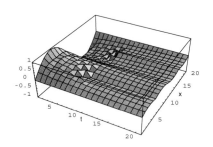

FIGURE 10.17

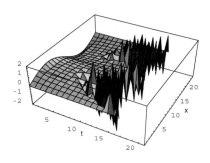

FIGURE 10.18

The lesson of these two examples is that we should experiment with various ratios of Δx to Δt until we find a stable configuration that will then let us refine the the subdivisions while maintaining the ratio. If we attempt to apply the backward method to the last example, we will be faced with solving a system of nonlinear equations. Solutions of systems of nonlinear equations can present profound difficulties, and so the application of the backward method to nonlinear problems may have only limited use. The problem of solving a nonlinear equation can even arise in the forward method, as the next example shows.

The one-dimensional wave equation ignores the possibility of drag on the vibrating string. If we include drag by assuming that it is proportional to the velocity of the string, we get

$$u_{tt} + du_t = c^2 u_{xx}.$$

However, this equation is linear, and the method of separation of variables applies easily here. On the other hand, if drag is proportional to the cube of velocity, the equation is

$$u_{tt} + d(u_t)^3 = c^2 u_{xx},$$

and this equation is nonlinear. Separation of variables will not work here, so we again turn to numerical methods.

For this equation the finite difference equation is

$$\frac{v_j^{k+1} - 2v_j^k + v_j^{k-1}}{\Delta t^2} + d\left(\frac{v_j^{k+1} - v_j^k}{\Delta t}\right)^3 = c^2\left[\frac{v_{j+1}^k - 2v_j^k + v_{j-1}^k}{\Delta x^2}\right].$$

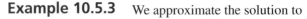

At this point we normally solved for v_j^{k+1} and proceeded to march in time. However, now we cannot easily solve for v_j^{k+1} because it is contained in a cubed term. We must solve for it by some means, and it is most natural to employ a root-solving numerical method. Most computer algebra systems have packaged facilities for doing this. Thus, in the computer algebra routine, we replace the direct computation of v_j^{k+1} by a root-finding method and then set v_j^{k+1} equal to the result.

Before giving an example of the approximation, notice that the physical situation suggests the existence and uniqueness of a solution satisfying the same boundary and initial conditions as for the original wave equation.

Example 10.5.3   We approximate the solution to

$$u_{tt} + (u_t)^3 = u_{xx},$$

where the initial condition is $u(x, 0) = 4x(1 - x)$ and $u_t(x, 0) = 0$ on $[0, 1]$. The time interval is $[0, 3]$. The boundary conditions are homogeneous.

Since the equation is modeling the vibration of a string, we know that the speed of data transmission must be at least as great as the speed of transmission of signals along the string. In this example, this means that we need $\Delta t / \Delta x \le 1$. Figure 10.19 shows the result of running the algorithm with this condition satisfied. The image corresponds to what we would expect on physical grounds. The amplitude of oscillation of a point on the string initially decreases very rapidly. This is because the drag is great for large-amplitude oscillations. But as the amplitude becomes small, the velocity decreases also, and the drag for velocities less than 1 is very small because the cube of a number smaller than 1 is even smaller. Figure 10.20 shows what happens when we use a speed of data transmission that is much smaller than the physical transmission speed. The numerical output has no relation to the problem.   ∎

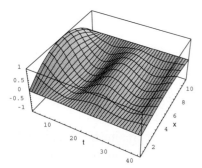

FIGURE 10.19

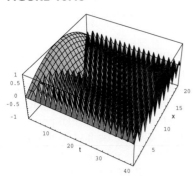

FIGURE 10.20

EXERCISES 10.5

1. Modify your program for the heat equation to solve $u_t = \frac{0.25}{x^2+1}u_{xx}$, where $u(x, 0) = \sin(2\pi x)$ on $[0, 1]$. Assume that the boundary conditions are homogeneous and the time interval is $[0, 1]$. Experiment with step ratios, and get what you believe is a good approximation of the solution. Find a step ratio that causes failure of the algorithm.

2. Modify your program for the heat equation to solve $u_t = \frac{0.2}{x^2+1}u_{xx}$, where $u(x, 0) = 8x(2-x)$ on $[0, 2]$. Assume that the boundary conditions are homogeneous and the time interval is $[0, 3]$. Experiment with step ratios, and get what you believe is a good approximation of the solution. Find a step ratio that causes failure of the algorithm.

3. Modify your program for the heat equation to solve $u_t = u^4 u_{xx}$, where $u(x, 0) = \sin(3\pi x)$ on $[0, 1]$. Assume that the boundary conditions are homogeneous and the time interval is $[0, 4]$. Experiment with step ratios, and get what you believe is a good approximation of the solution. Find a step ratio that causes failure of the algorithm if you can.

4. Modify your program for the heat equation to solve $u_t =$

$(u^2 + 1)u_{xx}$, where $u(x, 0) = \sin(4\pi x)$ on $[0, 1]$. Assume that the boundary conditions are homogeneous and the time interval is $[0, 4]$. Experiment with step ratios, and get what you believe is a good approximation of the solution. Find a step ratio that causes failure of the algorithm.

5. Modify your program for the wave equation to solve $u_{tt} + (u_t)^3 = 2u_{xx}$, where $u(x, 0) = \sin(5\pi x)$ and $u_t(x, 0) = 0$ on $[0, 1]$. Assume that the boundary conditions are homogeneous and the time interval is $[0, 4]$. Experiment with step ratios, and get what you believe is a good approximation of the solution. Find a step ratio that causes failure of the algorithm.

6. Modify your program for the wave equation to solve $u_{tt} + u_t|u_t| = u_{xx}$, where $u(x, 0) = \sin(\pi x)$ and $u_t(x, 0) = 0$ on $[0, 1]$. Assume that the boundary conditions are homogeneous and the time interval is $[0, 4]$. Experiment with step ratios, and get what you believe is a good approximation of the solution. Comment on the results. Note, you may have to write $|u| = \sqrt{u^2}$.

10.6 LAPLACE'S EQUATION

In this section we shall approximate solutions to the Dirichlet problem. Since this is a boundary value problem of a second-order equation, it is not surprising that we use the centered second differences. If D is the region where $u_{xx} + u_{yy} = 0$ and $u(x, y) = f(x, y)$ on the boundary ∂D of D, then we cover D with a rectangular grid of points. Take all the points that lie in D. This set of points divides into two sets: the interior grid points which are those points that are surrounded on the north, south, east, and west, and the grid points that are not interior. The points that are not interior points will be called **boundary points**, just as in the continuous problem. Note that for reasonable regions D and a fine enough grid the boundary grid points will be close to the boundary of D, and so the boundary values of the approximation can be computed (approximately) from $f(x, y)$. Thus we assume that the values at the grid boundary points are known.

The task is to compute the approximations to the values of the solution at the interior points. With each interior point (j, k) we associate the difference equation

$$\frac{v_{j+1,k} - 2v_{j,k} + v_{j-1,k}}{\Delta x^2} + \frac{v_{j,k+1} - 2v_{j,k} + v_{j,k-1}}{\Delta y^2} = 0,$$

which is centered at the point (j, k). Note that we use subscripts for both space variables. If there are n interior points, then we have n equations in n unknowns. Of course, some of these equations will include known values from the boundary.

It very much simplifies matters to use a square grid where $\Delta x = \Delta y$. In this case we can write the difference equation in the form

$$v_{j,k} = \frac{1}{4}[v_{j+1,k} + v_{j,k+1} + v_{j-1,k} + v_{j,k-1}].$$

Thus the central point is just the average of its surrounding satellite points. This has an important consequence called the **maximum/minimum principle**. We claim that the maximum or minimum value of the $v_{j,k}$ cannot occur at an interior point unless the $v_{j,k}$ are constant on all points. Suppose not. Then at some point (j, k), $v_{j,k}$ is strictly greater (less than) than at least one of its surrounding satellite values. But $v_{j,k}$ is the average of these values. This is impossible. The maximum/minimum principle implies that the solution to the system of interior difference equations is unique. Assume that $v_{j,k}$ and $w_{j,k}$ are two solutions. Then both satisfy the boundary values, and so $v_{j,k} - w_{j,k}$ satisfies the (linear) difference equations and zero boundary values. Now the maximum and minimum values for $v_{j,k} - w_{j,k}$ can only occur on the boundary, so these values must be zero. Thus $v_{j,k} - w_{j,k} = 0$, and the solution is unique. This method is implicit and has a unique solution.

Here is an example showing the boundary values and the equations corresponding to the interior points.

Example 10.6.1 Label the points of the region in Figure 10.21 starting from the lower left at $(0, 0)$. We assume that the points are equally spaced.

The known boundary values are $v_{0,0}$, $v_{1,0}$, $v_{2,0}$, $v_{3,0}$, $v_{4,0}$, $v_{4,1}$, $v_{4,2}$, $v_{3,3}$, $v_{2,3}$, $v_{1,2}$, $v_{0,2}$, and $v_{0,1}$. The equations are

$$\frac{v_{2,1} - 2v_{1,1} + v_{0,1}}{h^2} + \frac{v_{1,2} - 2v_{1,1} + v_{1,0}}{h^2} = 0,$$

$$\frac{v_{3,1} - 2v_{2,1} + v_{1,1}}{h^2} + \frac{v_{2,2} - 2v_{2,1} + v_{2,0}}{h^2} = 0,$$

$$\frac{v_{4,1} - 2v_{3,1} + v_{2,1}}{h^2} + \frac{v_{3,2} - 2v_{3,1} + v_{3,0}}{h^2} = 0,$$

$$\frac{v_{2,2} - 2v_{1,2} + v_{0,2}}{h^2} + \frac{v_{1,3} - 2v_{1,2} + v_{1,1}}{h^2} = 0,$$

$$\frac{v_{3,2} - 2v_{2,2} + v_{1,2}}{h^2} + \frac{v_{2,3} - 2v_{2,2} + v_{2,1}}{h^2} = 0,$$

and

$$\frac{v_{4,2} - 2v_{3,2} + v_{2,2}}{h^2} + \frac{v_{3,3} - 2v_{3,2} + v_{3,1}}{h^2} = 0.$$

The factor h^2 can be divided out. Also notice that some of the boundary values are not used. ∎

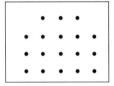

FIGURE 10.21

The algorithm for solving the Dirichlet problem numerically that we have just described does converge to the true solution. The error analysis requires a different approach from the one we have employed on the heat and wave equations. This analysis may also be omitted, and it is postponed to the end of the section.

Clearly, the selection and solution of the interior difference equations are a major tasks, which are more complicated the more irregular the shape of the region D. For a simple region such as a rectangle, the interior points and equations are easily identified, but writing down the equations can still be cumbersome.

Example 10.6.2   Consider the square $[0, 3] \times [0, 3]$ with three subdivisions on each side. The interior values are $v_{1,1}$, $v_{2,1}$, $v_{1,2}$, and $v_{2,2}$. Assume that the boundary values are given by $\sin(\pi x/3)$ on the bottom edge, by $\sin(\pi y/3)$ on the right edge, and by zero on the other edges. Thus the boundary values are $v_{0,0} = v_{0,1} = v_{0,2} = v_{0,3} = v_{1,3} = v_{2,3} = v_{3,3} = v_{3,0} = 0$, $v_{1,0} = v_{3,1} = 0.8660$, and $v_{2,0} = v_{3,2} = 0.8660$.

The four interior equations are

$$v_{1,1} = \frac{v_{2,1} + v_{0,1} + v_{1,2} + v_{1,0}}{4} = \frac{v_{2,1} + v_{1,2} + 0.8660}{4},$$

$$v_{2,1} = \frac{v_{3,1} + v_{1,1} + v_{2,2} + v_{2,0}}{4} = \frac{0.8660 + v_{1,1} + v_{2,2}}{4},$$

$$v_{1,2} = \frac{v_{2,2} + v_{0,2} + v_{1,3} + v_{1,1}}{4} = \frac{v_{2,2} + v_{1,1}}{4},$$

and

$$v_{2,2} = \frac{v_{3,2} + v_{1,2} + v_{2,3} + v_{2,1}}{4} = \frac{0.8660 + v_{1,2} + v_{2,1}}{4}.$$

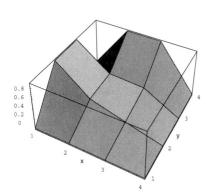

FIGURE 10.22

Figure 10.22 shows the solution presented as a surface. This image was created using a computer algebra system to solve the interior equations and to set the boundary values. The graphic is the result of a surface plot of the computed data.

Recall that we can think of the solution to this problem as the long-term steady-state solution to the heat equation

$$u_t = u_{xx} + u_{yy},$$

so the solution may be thought of as the static temperature distribution in a square plate, given the prescribed temperatures along the edges. The approximation is consistent with physical expectation. However, there is clearly room for improvement. ∎

An obvious approach to improving the result of Example 10.6.2 is to include more subdivisions, but this will rapidly increase the number of interior equations to be written down and solved. This can become too much of a burden. We need a method that is much more easily programmable. The key to this is the observation that the solution to the Dirichlet problem can be thought of as the limiting case of the solution to the heat equation

$$u_t = u_{xx} + u_{yy}$$

as t goes to infinity. The difference equation is

$$\frac{v_{j,k}^{n+1} - v_{j,k}^n}{\Delta t} = \frac{v_{j+1,k}^n - 2v_{j,k}^n + v_{j-1,k}^n}{\Delta x^2} + \frac{v_{j,k+1}^n - 2v_{j,k}^n + v_{j,k-1}^n}{\Delta x^2}.$$

It is left to the exercises to show that if $\Delta t = \Delta x^2/4$ the difference equation reduces to

$$v_{j,k}^{n+1} = \frac{1}{4}[v_{j+1,k}^n + v_{j,k+1}^n + v_{j-1,k}^n + v_{j,k-1}^n].$$

This scheme is used in the following way. We start with any reasonable choice for the values $\{v_{j,k}^1\}$ as long as they satisfy the boundary data. Then for each (j, k) we compute $v_{j,k}^2$ from

$$v_{j,k}^2 = \frac{1}{4}[v_{j+1,k}^1 + v_{j,k+1}^1 + v_{j-1,k}^1 + v_{j,k-1}^1].$$

This is marching in time in the usual way. We continue in this fashion to a large value of n. This corresponds to a large value of t in the heat problem, and so the $\{v_{j,k}^n\}$ should be close to those for the steady state. This approach is called the **Jacobi method**. Like the Euler method, the Jacobi method is not used in practice because it converges so slowly. There are modifications of the Jacobi method that converge much faster, but we shall not pursue them here. The reader is directed to [2] for further information.

Example 10.6.3 Let us apply the Jacobi method to Example 10.6.2. Recall that we have the Laplacian on the square $[0, 3] \times [0, 3]$. We assume that the boundary values are given by $\sin(\pi x/3)$ on the bottom edge, by $\sin(\pi y/3)$ on the right edge, and by zero on the other edges. This determines the v_{jk}^1 values on the boundary, but we must choose values in the interior to get started. A good choice is to set the interior values to zero. This is the equivalent in the heat problem of setting the initial condition to zero, though the boundary conditions are not homogeneous.

The algorithm can be implemented with a few simple "do loops," and this is left to the exercises. Figure 10.23 shows the image obtained by making 24 subdivisions on a side and setting the n value to 15. The result is a marked improvement and is probably very good, since the image did not change much in going from 12 subdivisions a side and 10 for n to the final values. ∎

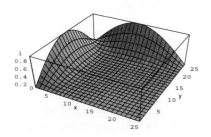

FIGURE 10.23

10.6.1 Error Analysis (Optional)

The error analysis for the approximation of the Dirichlet problem, being implicit, is different from what we have seen before. Since the method is implicit, the notion of a one-step error does not apply. In a sense to be made clear, the error must be dealt with "all at once." To this end, we introduce the following terminology.

Let G be a finite set of equally spaced grid points such as in Figure 10.15. Let I be the set of interior points of G, and let B be the set of boundary points of G. Thus $G = I \cup B$. We can call G a grid.

We make the following definition.

Definition 10.6.4

If G is a grid, a grid function V is a real-valued function defined on G. Thus $V : G \rightarrow \mathbf{R}$. ●

The terms v_j^k are values of a grid function. But, since our focus is going to shift to the grid function as a whole, we shall use the function notation $V(x_j, y_k) = v_j^k$. When no confusion can arise, we shall write $V(j, k) = V(x_j, y_k)$.

The left-hand side of the difference version of Laplace's equation can be viewed as defining an operator on grid functions. We define the discrete Laplace operator L_G on grid functions on G by

$$L_G(V)(j, k) = V(j, k)$$

for all points (j, k) in B, and

$$L_G(V)(j, k) = \frac{V(j-1, k) - 2V(j, k) + V(j+1, k)}{h^2}$$
$$+ \frac{V(j, k-1) - 2V(j, k) + V(j, k+1)}{h^2}$$

for all (j, k) in I. This is a linear operator. That is, for real numbers r_1 and r_2 and grid functions U and V, we have

$$L_G(r_1 U + r_2 V) = r_1 L_G(U) + r_2 L_G(V).$$

The following theorem is pivotal in the error analysis.

Theorem 10.6.5   (Maximum/Minimum Principle)

Let $G = I \cup B$ be a grid and V a grid function on G. If

$$L_G(V)(j, k) \geq 0 \quad \text{for} \quad (j, k) \in I,$$

then

$$\max\{V(j, k) | (j, k) \in I\} \leq \max\{V(j, k) | (j, k) \in B\},$$

and if

$$L_G(V)(j, k) \leq 0 \quad \text{for} \quad (j, k) \in I,$$

then

$$\min\{V(j, k) | (j, k) \in I\} \geq \min\{V(j, k) | (j, k) \in B\}. \qquad \bullet$$

Proof

We give the proof only for a square grid where $\Delta x = \Delta t = h$. For a rectangular grid, the proof is a little more complicated, and it may be found in [5].

Assume that $L_G(V)(j, k) \geq 0$ on the interior. Multiplying by h^2 gives

$$V(j-1, k) - 2V(j, k) + V(j+1, k) + V(j, k-1) - 2V(j, k) + V(j, k+1) \geq 0.$$

Solving for $V(j, k)$, we get

$$V(j, k) \leq [V(j-1, k) + V(j+1, k) + V(j, k-1) + V(j, k+1)]/4.$$

Now suppose that the interior maximum occurs at (j, k), and that this is strictly larger than the values on the boundary. If this is the case, then

$$[V(j-1, k) + V(j+1, k) + V(j, k-1) + V(j, k+1)]/4 \leq V(j, k),$$

and so

$$V(j, k) = [V(j-1, k) + V(j+1, k) + V(j, k-1) + V(j, k+1)]/4.$$

Now $V(j, k)$ is greater than or equal to all the terms in the sum on the right. This is impossible unless $V(j, k)$ is actually equal to each of the terms in the sum on the right. So the value at each interior point is equal to its satellite values. So $V(j, k)$ must be equal to a boundary value by moving out until a boundary point is included as a satellite point. This is a contradiction. The other part is similar. ◆

This theorem implies that the solution to the approximating system of equations must be unique. Indeed, if grid functions U and V satisfy the difference equations and the same boundary values, then

$$L_G(U - V) = 0$$

in G. But then the maximum and minimum of $U - V$ must be taken on the boundary of G. But there $U - V = 0$, since the two grid functions satisfy the same boundary values. Thus $U - V = 0$ throughout G, so U and V are the same grid functions.

The next theorem is all that we need to get the error estimate.

Theorem 10.6.6

Let V be a grid function on a grid $G = I \cup B$. Then there is a number a such that

$$\max\{|V(x_j, y_k)| \mid (x_j, y_k) \in I\} \leq$$

$$\max\{|V(x_j, y_k)| \mid (x_j, y_k) \in B\} + \frac{a^2}{2}\max\{|L_G(V)(x_j, y_k)| \mid (x_j, y_k) \in I\}. \bullet$$

Proof

Let $\phi(x, y) = x^2/2$. Let a be the magnitude of the x-coordinate of the point in G having the greatest magnitude. Then, for all $(x, y) \in G$,

$$\phi(x, y) \leq \frac{a^2}{2} \quad \text{and} \quad L_G(\phi)(x, y) = 1$$

in G. Define

$$K = \max\{|L_G(V)(x, y)| \mid (x, y) \in I\},$$
$$V^+(x, y) = V(x, y) + K\phi(x, y),$$

and

$$V^-(x, y) = -V(x, y) + K\phi(x, y).$$

Then

$$L_G(V^+)(x, y) = L_G(V)(x, y) + KL_G(\phi)(x, y) = L_G(V)(x, y) + K \geq 0.$$

Likewise,

$$L_G(V^-)(x, y) \geq 0.$$

Applying the first conclusion of the maximum/minimum principle we get

$$V^+(x, y) \leq \max\{V^+(x, y) \mid (x, y) \in B\}$$
$$= \max\{V(x, y) + K\phi(x, y) \mid (x, y) \in B\}$$
$$\leq \max\{V(x, y) \mid (x, y) \in B\} + K\frac{a^2}{2}.$$

Likewise,

$$V^-(x, y) \leq \max\{-V(x, y) \mid (x, y) \in B\} + K\frac{a^2}{2}.$$

From the definition of V^+ and V^- and the fact that $\phi \geq 0$, it follows that

$$V(x, y) \leq V^+(x, y) \quad \text{and} \quad -V(x, y) \leq V^-(x, y).$$

Therefore,

$$V(x, y) \leq \max\{V(x, y) \mid (x, y) \in B\} + K\frac{a^2}{2}$$

$$\leq \max\{|V(x, y)| \mid (x, y) \in B\} + K\frac{a^2}{2},$$

and

$$-V(x, y) \leq \max\{-V(x, y) \mid (x, y) \in B\} + K\frac{a^2}{2}$$

$$\leq \max\{|V(x, y)| \mid (x, y) \in B\} + K\frac{a^2}{2}.$$

Finally, we have

$$\max\{|V(x_j, y_k)| \mid (x_j, y_k) \in I\} \leq \max\{|V(x_j, y_k)| \mid (x_j, y_k) \in B\}$$

$$+ \frac{a^2}{2}\max\{|L_G(V)(x_j, y_k)| \mid (x_j, y_k) \in I\}. \blacklozenge$$

We can now get the error bound. Let u be the true solution. Let V be a grid function that is a solution to the approximation equations. That is, assume that $L_G(V)(x_j, y_k) = 0$ in I. Note that u restricted to G is also a grid function, and it follows immediately from the centered second difference formulas that $L_G(u)(x_j, y_k) = O(\Delta x^2 + \Delta y^2)$. We now apply the preceding inequality to $u - V$ while recalling that $u - V$ is as small as we please at the boundary points if the grid is fine enough. Thus

$$\max\{|u(x_j, y_k) - V(x_j, y_k)| \mid (x_j, y_k) \in I\}$$

$$\leq \max\{|u(x_j, y_k) - V(x_j, y_k)| \mid (x_j, y_k) \in B\} + \frac{a^2}{2}O(\Delta x^2 + \Delta y^2).$$

This implies that V approaches u as the mesh of the grid is refined.

The error estimate that we have derived places no restriction on the grid as was the case with the heat and wave equations The implicit method that we have derived for Laplace's equation is called unconditionally stable.

EXERCISES 10.6

For Exercises 1–4, prepare routines in a CAS to solve the interior equations of the Dirichlet problem and to implement the Jacobi method. Be sure to arrange for graphical output.

1. Consider the Dirichlet problem on the square $[0, \pi] \times [0, \pi]$, where the boundary values are $\sin(x)$ top and bottom and $\sin(y)$ left and right. Using three equal subdivisions on a side, write down the system of equations for the interior points. Be sure to evaluate the boundary values. Use your CAS to solve the equations and display the result as a surface. Use the Jacobi method to obtain more refined results.

2. Consider the Dirichlet problem on the square $[0, 1] \times [0, 1]$, where the boundary values are $\sin(\pi x)$ top and bottom and zero on the left and right. Using three equal subdivisions on a side, write down the system of equations for the interior points. Be sure to evaluate the boundary values. Use your CAS to solve the equations and display the result as a surface. Use the Jacobi method to obtain more refined results.

3. Consider the Dirichlet problem on the square $[0, 1] \times [0, 1]$, where the boundary values are $4x(1 - x)$ top and bottom and zero on the left and right. Using four equal subdivisions on a side, write down the system of equations for the interior points. Be sure to evaluate the boundary values. Use your CAS to solve the equations and display the result as a surface. Use the Jacobi method to obtain more refined results.

4. Consider the Dirichlet problem on the square $[0, 2] \times [0, 2]$, where the boundary values are $4x(2 - x)$ top and bottom and $\sin(\pi y)$ on the left and right. Using four equal subdivisions on a side, write down the system of equations for the interior points. Be sure to evaluate the boundary values. Use your CAS to solve the equations and display the result as a surface. Use the Jacobi method to obtain more refined results.

5. Consider the Dirichlet problem on the rectangle $[0, 2] \times [0, 3]$ where the boundary conditions are homogeneous.
   (a) What grids can be used that subdivide the region into squares?
   (b) What is V where $L_G(V) = 0$ and why?

6. Consider the Dirichlet problem on the rectangle $[0, 4] \times [0, 5]$ where the boundary conditions are 1 on each edge. For any grid, what is V where $L_G(V) = 0$? Explain!

7. Consider the Dirichlet problem on the square $[0, \pi] \times [0, 1]$ where the boundary values are $\sin(x)$ top and bottom and zero on the left and right. Using three subdivisions on a side, write down the system of equations for the interior points. Be sure to evaluate the boundary values. Note that the grid is rectangular.

8. Suppose that u satisfies the Dirichlet problem in a rectangle and that a rectangular grid is used. Show that, at any point in the interior of the grid G, $L_G(u)(x, y) = O(\Delta x^2 + \Delta y^2)$.

9. Show that, if $\Delta t = \Delta x^2 / 4$, the difference equation for the two-dimensional heat equation reduces to

$$v_{j,k}^{n+1} = \frac{1}{4}[v_{j+1,k}^n + v_{j,k+1}^n + v_{j-1,k}^n + v_{j,k-1}^n].$$

10.7 STABILITY

We have seen that the forward methods that we have used exhibit instability for certain values of the parameter s. On the other hand, the backward method applied to the heat equation proved to be stable. To gain insight into this, we shall formulate both the forward and backward methods for the heat equation in matrix form.

We begin by reformulating the forward algorithm for the heat equation in matrix form. The basic equation describing marching in time is

$$v_j^{k+1} = \frac{a^2 \Delta t}{\Delta x^2}[v_{j+1}^k - 2v_j^k + v_{j-1}^k] + v_j^k.$$

If we set $s = a^2 \Delta t / \Delta x^2$, then we can write

$$v_j^{k+1} = sv_{j-1}^k + (1 - 2s)v_j^k + sv_{j+1}^k.$$

We assume that the boundary conditions are homogeneous. Let

$$v^k = (v_1^k, v_2^k, \ldots, v_{m-2}^k, v_{m-1}^k)^t$$

be the data at the kth time step with m subdivisions written in vector form. Recall that the t means transpose, so the vector is to be regarded as a column. Remember that $v_0^{k+1} = v_m^{k+1} = 0$, and so the the remaining data for the $k+1$ time step can be obtained from v^k by the matrix equation

$$v^{k+1} = Av^k,$$

where

$$A = \begin{bmatrix} (1-2s) & s & 0 & 0 & \cdots & 0 & 0 \\ s & (1-2s) & s & 0 & \cdots & 0 & 0 \\ 0 & s & (1-2s) & s & \cdots & 0 & 0 \\ & & & \vdots & & & \\ 0 & 0 & 0 & 0 & \cdots & (1-2s) & s \\ 0 & 0 & 0 & 0 & \cdots & s & (1-2s) \end{bmatrix}.$$

This $(m-1) \times (m-1)$ matrix is said to be tridiagonal because of its form.

In summary, we can say that the matrix form of the forward algorithm gives us the data in vector form at the $(k+1)$st time step by applying the matrix A to the vector data at the kth time step. So if v^0 is the vector of initial data, then

$$v^k = A^k v^0$$

is the vector of data at the kth time step.

Recall that for $s > 1/2$ the algorithm could blow up. The matrix form allows for a more pointed analysis of this phenomenon. Suppose that the v^k represents the data generated by the algorithm with no round-off errors, so it is the mathematical data that the algorithm defines. To see how errors can propagate up the time steps, let e^0 be the error in measuring the initial data, so

$$w^0 = v^0 + e^0$$

is the vector to which the algorithm is applied. Then the error at level 1 is

$$e^1 = w^1 - v^1 = A(v^0 + e^0) - v^1 = Ae^0.$$

At the next step we have

$$e^2 = w^2 - v^2 = A(v^1 + e^1) - v^2 = A^2 e^0.$$

In general,

$$e^k = A^k e^0.$$

A measure of the magnitude of the error is given by the norm of the vector; thus

$$||A^k e^0|| = ||e^k||$$

describes the propagation of error as the algorithm is repeatedly applied. It is reasonable to describe the algorithm as **stable** if the error does not get larger from step to step. Indeed, we define the algorithm to be **stable** if

$$||A^k e^0|| \leq ||e^0||$$

for all error vectors e^0 and all k. We have seen that the algorithm can be unstable for $s > 1/2$. In fact, it can be shown that the algorithm is stable only if $s \leq 1/2$. The proof of this requires the introduction of the spectral radius and the computation of the eigenvalues of the matrix A. This is not appropriate here, so we refer you to [2] and [7].

Recall that we applied a backward method to the heat problem by using the backward difference for u_t and the centered second difference for u_{xx}. We have

$$\frac{v_j^k - v_j^{k-1}}{\Delta t} = a^2 \frac{v_{j+1}^k - 2v_j^k + v_{j-1}^k}{\Delta x^2}.$$

If we set $s = a^2 \Delta t / \Delta x^2$, we can write

$$(1 + 2s)v_j^k - sv_{j+1}^k - sv_{j-1}^k = v_j^{k-1} \qquad (*)$$

Again, we can express the system of linear equations defined by $(*)$ in matrix form by setting $v^k = (v_1^k, v_2^k, \ldots, v_{m-2}^k, v_{m-1}^k)^t$. Then we can write

$$Bv^k = v^{k-1},$$

where

$$B = \begin{bmatrix} (1+2s) & -s & 0 & 0 & \cdots & 0 & 0 \\ -s & (1+2s) & -s & 0 & \cdots & 0 & 0 \\ 0 & -s & (1+2s) & -s & \cdots & 0 & 0 \\ & & & \vdots & & & \\ 0 & 0 & 0 & 0 & \cdots & (1+2s) & -s \\ 0 & 0 & 0 & 0 & \cdots & -s & (1+2s) \end{bmatrix}.$$

It can be proved that, for any vector v and any k,

$$||(B^{-1})^k v|| \leq ||v||.$$

By definition, this means that the algorithm is stable and that errors cannot grow as they propagate.

In either the forward or backward case, if the algorithm is stable, the approximation generated converges to the true solution. Let us focus on a stable case of the forward algorithm. Then

$$||Av|| \leq ||v||$$

for any vector v.

Recall that we defined the one-step error to be

$$u_j^{k+1} - v_j^{k+1} = e_j^{k+1},$$

where we assume that $v_j^k = u_j^k$, because we are assuming that the data at the last step are accurate. If we write the data in vector form, we have

$$e^{k+1} = u^{k+1} - Au^k.$$

For the cumulative error, we have

$$c^{k+1} = u^{k+1} - v^{k+1} = Au^k + e^{k+1} - Av^k$$
$$= Ac^k + e^{k+1}.$$

Using the triangle inequality for norms, we have

$$||c^{k+1}|| = ||Ac^k + e^{k+1}|| \le ||Ac^k|| + ||e^{k+1}||.$$

Recall that the one-step error is bounded by

$$E \le M_1 \Delta t \Delta x^2 + M_2 \Delta t^2$$

in the rectangle of our approximation. Therefore,

$$||e^k|| \le E \le M_1 \Delta t \Delta x^2 + M_2 \Delta t^2$$

in the rectangle. Now $||c^0|| = 0$ because we assume that the initial data are accurate. Then

$$||c^1|| \le ||Ac^0|| + E = E.$$

But then

$$||c^2|| \le ||Ac^1|| + E \le ||c^1|| + E \le 2E.$$

Consider one more step and the conclusion should be clear.

$$||c^3|| \le ||Ac^2|| + E \le ||c^2|| + E \le 3E.$$

Thus the cumulative error satisfies

$$||c^k|| \le kE.$$

But if $[0, t_0]$ is the time interval for the approximation and we use n subdivisions, then $\Delta t = t_0/n$. Thus

$$||c^k|| \le kE \le k(M_1 \Delta t \Delta x^2 + M_2 \Delta t^2) \le n(M_1 \Delta t \Delta x^2 + M_2 \Delta t^2)$$
$$= M_1 t_0 \Delta x^2 + M_2 t_0 \Delta t.$$

Therefore, the cumulative error goes to zero as the mesh is refined provided stability is maintained.

SUPPLEMENTARY EXERCISES FOR CHAPTER 10

1. Work out an algorithm for the two-dimensional heat equation in the unit square. Make an error analysis. Is any restriction on the grid used?

2. Work out an algorithm for the two-dimensional wave equation in the unit square. Make an error analysis. Is any restriction on the grid used?

3. Show how the error analysis for the one-dimensional wave equation with $s < 1$ can be reduced to the $s = 1$ case. *Hint:* Try a change of scale on the t-axis.

4. Work out an algorithm for the two-dimensional heat equation in the unit circle. Make an error analysis. Is any restriction on the grid used? How do you propose to handle the boundary values?

APPENDIX A

LINEAR SYSTEMS, MATRICES, AND DETERMINANTS

This appendix and Section 9.4 cover topics in linear algebra that may be used as lectures or as review, as the instructor or reader finds necessary. Exercise sets are also provided, so this appendix and Section 9.4 may be considered as supplementary material for the text.

A.1 SOLUTION OF SYSTEMS OF EQUATIONS

The central problem of this section is to decide when and how a system of equations of the form

$$a_{11}x_1 + a_{12}x_2 + \cdots + a_{1n}x_n = b_1$$
$$a_{21}x_1 + a_{22}x_2 + \cdots + a_{2n}x_n = b_2$$
$$\vdots$$
$$a_{m1}x_1 + a_{m2}x_2 + \cdots + a_{mn}x_n = b_m$$

can be solved. Such a system is called an $m \times n$ system of linear equations. The system is said to be homogeneous if all the b_i are zero. The a_{ij} are called the coefficients.

The method of solution is as follows. If all the coefficients a_{i1} in the first column of coefficients are zero, we move on to the second column. If not, we choose an equation for which the first coefficient is not zero. We exchange it with the first equation and then divide through by the nonzero coefficient. This makes the first coefficient of the first equation 1. We now multiply this new equation by the appropriate numbers and subtract from the equations below it to get zero terms in the first places of all the remaining equations. It is most important to note that if $\{x_1, x_2, \dots, x_n\}$ solves the original system then it also solves the system produced by the procedure described, and vice versa.

We now move on to the second column. If all the coefficients in the second column below the first equation are zero, we move on to the third column. If not, we again choose an equation below the first with a nonzero coefficient in the second column. We exchange this with the second equation and divide through this equation to get a 1 for the coefficient in the second column. We multiply and subtract the second equation from those above and below to get zero coefficients in the second column, except for the 1 in the second row and column. We now continue this procedure until all columns containing the variables have been treated. If there is any equation in which all the variable coefficients are zero, we move it below those with nonzero coefficients. The result is called an **echelon form**.

Again, it is most important to recognize that the echelon form system of equations that results from this process has exactly the same solutions as the system that we started with. Moreover, the echelon form tells all that we want to know about the solutions of the original equations.

A considerable notational economy is effected if we delete the variables x_i, the addition operations $+$, and the equalities. What is left is called the **augmented matrix** of the system. The operations described previously can still be applied to the augmented matrix to get what is called the **echelon form matrix** of the system. Notice that the equations can be written down at any stage in the process, so nothing is lost in this economy. The array of numbers that we get, if the right-hand column in the augmented matrix is deleted, is called the **matrix of coefficients** of the system or the **coefficient matrix**.

Example A.1.1   We solve

$$2x + 2y - z = 2,$$
$$x + y + 2z = 0,$$
$$0x + 0y - 3z = 1.$$

Here is the sequence of augmented matrices in the reduction to echelon form.

$$\begin{bmatrix} 2 & 2 & -1 & 2 \\ 1 & 1 & 2 & 0 \\ 0 & 0 & -3 & 1 \end{bmatrix} \rightarrow \begin{bmatrix} 1 & 1 & 2 & 0 \\ 2 & 2 & -1 & 2 \\ 0 & 0 & -3 & 1 \end{bmatrix} \rightarrow \begin{bmatrix} 1 & 1 & 2 & 0 \\ 0 & 0 & -5 & 2 \\ 0 & 0 & -3 & 1 \end{bmatrix}$$

$$\rightarrow \begin{bmatrix} 1 & 1 & 0 & 2/3 \\ 0 & 0 & 0 & 1/3 \\ 0 & 0 & 1 & -1/3 \end{bmatrix}.$$

The middle row of the last matrix gives the equation $0x + 0y + 0z = 1/3$, so in this case there are no solutions.   ∎

The operations that are used on the rows of the matrix in the reduction process are called **row operations**. There are three of them:

1. Rows may be exchanged.
2. A row may be multiplied by a nonzero number.
3. Any row may be multiplied by any number and added to any other row.

The possible echelon forms are as follows. As in the example, a row could consist of zeros except for the last. In this case the corresponding equation would assert that 0 is equal to a nonzero number. Thus the equation is false, and the echelon system can have no solutions. Therefore, the original system has no solutions. Now assume that we do not have such false equations; then the rows with zeros up to the last entry have zero in the last entry as well. We call such rows **zero rows**. If a column of coefficients of one of the variables is all zeros, then that variable can have any value, and so the number of solutions is infinite. Finally, consider the number of leading 1s in the nonzero rows. There can be no more than the number of columns in the coefficient matrix, since as you move down you must move to the right in echelon form. If the number of leading 1s is exactly the number of columns in the coefficient matrix, then there is exactly one solution to the corresponding system, which is found by reading off the last column in the augmented matrix down to the nth row. If there are fewer 1s, then we start finding solutions by back substituting. That is, we start with the last nonzero equation and solve for the variable that has the leading coefficient of 1 in terms of the variables to the right, if any. If there are variables to the right, they can assume any values, and so the set of solutions must be infinite. If there are no variables to the right, we move up to the next equation and repeat the process. Eventually, either there is a column of zeros or we must encounter an equation with a variable to the right; otherwise, the number of leading 1s must equal the number of columns of the coefficient matrix.

The process is called row reduction to echelon form, and the echelon form tells us whether we have no solutions, exactly one solution, or infinitely many solutions. The following examples illustrate the procedure.

Example A.1.2   Consider the system

$$0x_1 + x_2 + 2x_3 + 0x_4 = 1,$$
$$x_1 + x_2 - x_3 - x_4 = 2,$$
$$x_1 + x_2 + x_3 + x_4 = -1.$$

The augmented matrix and reduction follow. Several row operations have been carried out at each stage.

$$\begin{bmatrix} 0 & 1 & 2 & 0 & 1 \\ 1 & 1 & -1 & -1 & 2 \\ 1 & 1 & 1 & 1 & -1 \end{bmatrix} \rightarrow \begin{bmatrix} 1 & 1 & -1 & -1 & 2 \\ 0 & 1 & 2 & 0 & 1 \\ 0 & 0 & 2 & 2 & -3 \end{bmatrix}$$

$$\rightarrow \begin{bmatrix} 1 & 0 & -3 & -1 & 1 \\ 0 & 1 & 2 & 0 & 1 \\ 0 & 0 & 1 & 1 & -3/2 \end{bmatrix} \rightarrow \begin{bmatrix} 1 & 0 & 0 & 2 & -7/2 \\ 0 & 1 & 0 & -2 & 4 \\ 0 & 0 & 1 & 1 & -3/2 \end{bmatrix}.$$

This system has infinitely many solutions. In fact, we can back substitute to express the dependent variables (those with leading coefficient 1) in terms of independent variables as follows:

$$x_3 = -3/2 - x_4,$$
$$x_2 = 4 + 2x_4,$$
$$x_1 = -7/2 - 2x_4.$$

Infinitely many solutions are generated by assigning values to x_4. ∎

Example A.1.3   We solve the system

$$2x_1 + x_2 = 1,$$
$$3x_1 - x_2 = 0,$$
$$2x_1 - 4x_2 = -2.$$

$$\begin{bmatrix} 2 & 1 & 1 \\ 3 & -1 & 0 \\ 2 & -4 & -2 \end{bmatrix} \rightarrow \begin{bmatrix} 3 & -1 & 0 \\ 2 & 1 & 1 \\ 2 & -4 & -2 \end{bmatrix}$$

$$\rightarrow \begin{bmatrix} 1 & -2 & -1 \\ 2 & 1 & 1 \\ 2 & -4 & -2 \end{bmatrix} \rightarrow \begin{bmatrix} 1 & -2 & -1 \\ 0 & 5 & 3 \\ 0 & 0 & 0 \end{bmatrix}$$

$$\rightarrow \begin{bmatrix} 1 & -2 & -1 \\ 0 & 1 & 3/5 \\ 0 & 0 & 0 \end{bmatrix} \rightarrow \begin{bmatrix} 1 & 0 & 1/5 \\ 0 & 1 & 3/5 \\ 0 & 0 & 0 \end{bmatrix}.$$

The last row is a zero row and there are as many leading 1s as columns in the coefficient matrix, so there is a unique solution. The solution is $x_1 = 1/5$ and $x_2 = 3/5$. ∎

EXERCISES A.1

Use row reduction to echelon form to solve Exercises 1–4. Express solutions in terms of independent variables where appropriate.

1. $2x_1 + x_2 + x_3 = 1,$
$3x_1 - x_2 - x_3 = 0,$
$2x_1 - 4x_2 + 3x_3 = -2.$

2. $x_1 - x_2 + x_3 = 1,$
$3x_1 + x_2 - 3x_3 = 0,$
$2x_1 + 0x_2 - 2x_3 = -2.$

3. $2x_1 + x_2 + x_3 + x_4 = 1,$
$3x_1 - x_2 - x_3 - x_4 = 0,$
$x_1 - 4x_2 + 3x_3 + 2x4 = -2.$

4. $2x_1 + x_2 + x_3 = 1,$
$1x_1 - 2x_2 - x_3 = 0,$
$2x_1 - 4x_2 + 3x_3 = -2,$
$4x_1 + 2x_2 + 2x_3 = 2.$

5. You have probably noticed that you do not need to get zeros above the leading 1 in order to solve. Demonstrate this by repeating Exercises 1 and 2.

A.2 MATRICES, INVERSES, AND DETERMINANTS

In this section, the determinant of a matrix is introduced and used as a criterion for deciding when a system of n linear equations in n unknowns has a unique solution and when a square matrix has an inverse. As a bonus, we get Cramer's rule.

The basic operations on matrices were introduced in Chapter 5. These are repeated here for ease of reference.

A matrix is a rectangular array of numbers. The general form of a matrix is

$$\begin{bmatrix} a_{11} & a_{12} & \cdots & a_{1n} \\ a_{21} & a_{22} & \cdots & a_{2n} \\ & & \vdots & \\ a_{m1} & a_{m2} & \cdots & a_{mn} \end{bmatrix}.$$

Such a matrix is said to be $m \times n$ since it has m rows and n columns.

Here is an example of a 4×3:

$$\begin{bmatrix} 2 & -3 & 5 \\ 0 & 1 & 4 \\ -2 & 3 & 7 \\ 1 & 1 & -6 \end{bmatrix}.$$

Matrices are often symbolized by expressions of the form

$$(a_{ij})_{m \times n}.$$

For example,

$$((-1)^{i+j})_{4 \times 3} = \begin{bmatrix} 1 & -1 & 1 \\ -1 & 1 & -1 \\ 1 & -1 & 1 \\ -1 & 1 & -1 \end{bmatrix}.$$

This notation is useful in defining the three basic operations that can be performed on matrices: addition, multiplication, and multiplication of a matrix by a scalar. This is how they are defined. Matrices are added as follows:

$$(a_{ij})_{m \times n} + (b_{ij})_{m \times n} = (a_{ij} + b_{ij})_{m \times n}.$$

To add two matrices, simply add the entries in a given location. Notice that one can only add matrices of the same dimensions.

The matrix product is defined by

$$(a_{ij})_{m \times n}(b_{ij})_{n \times p} = \left(\sum_{k=1}^{n} a_{ik}b_{kj}\right)_{m \times p}.$$

The matrix product is more complicated. To get the ij entry in the product matrix take the ith row of the first matrix and lay it against the jth column of the second matrix; then multiply the numbers that are adjacent and add the products. Here is an example

$$\begin{bmatrix} 2 & -3 & 5 \\ 0 & 1 & 4 \\ -2 & 3 & 7 \\ 1 & 1 & -6 \end{bmatrix} \begin{bmatrix} 1 & -2 \\ 0 & 1 \\ -2 & 4 \end{bmatrix} = \begin{bmatrix} -8 & 13 \\ -8 & 17 \\ -16 & 35 \\ 13 & -25 \end{bmatrix}.$$

Note that in the multiplication of matrices the column number of the first matrix must match the row number of the second. The order of the factors here cannot be reversed, because the dimensions do not match up to perform the multiplication. Even if the factors in the product can be reversed, there is no guarantee that the products will be the same. For example,

$$\begin{bmatrix} 2 & -3 \\ 1 & 1 \end{bmatrix} \begin{bmatrix} 1 & -2 \\ 1 & 2 \end{bmatrix} = \begin{bmatrix} -1 & -10 \\ 2 & 0 \end{bmatrix},$$

and

$$\begin{bmatrix} 1 & -2 \\ 1 & 2 \end{bmatrix} \begin{bmatrix} 2 & -3 \\ 1 & 1 \end{bmatrix} = \begin{bmatrix} 0 & -5 \\ 4 & -1 \end{bmatrix}.$$

We say that matrix multiplication is not commutative.

Multiplication by a scalar is defined by

$$r(a_{ij}) = (ra_{ij}).$$

To multiply by a scalar, simply multiply every entry in the matrix by the scalar. Note that we may drop the dimensions from the matrix symbol when it is not needed or is obvious from the context.

A matrix consisting of all zeros is called a zero matrix and is denoted by 0.

A square ($n \times n$) matrix that has 1s down the diagonal from the a_{11} position to the a_{nn} position (called the main diagonal) and 0s elsewhere is called the $n \times n$ **identity matrix**. The reader can quickly verify that the product of the identity matrix with any matrix of the correct dimension for multiplying leaves that matrix unchanged. The identity matrix is a little like the number 1 in the real number system. We use I to denote an identity matrix. Here is a 3×3 identity matrix:

$$I = \begin{bmatrix} 1 & 0 & 0 \\ 0 & 1 & 0 \\ 0 & 0 & 1 \end{bmatrix}.$$

If A and B are $n \times n$ matrices we say that B is an **inverse matrix** of A if

$$AB = BA = I.$$

For a given matrix A, the inverse matrix B, if it exists, is unique. In this case we use the notation $B = A^{-1}$. It is not true that every nonzero square matrix has an inverse. Indeed, the matrix

$$\begin{bmatrix} 1 & 0 \\ 0 & 0 \end{bmatrix}$$

has no inverse, because, if it had, we would have

$$\begin{bmatrix} 1 & 0 \\ 0 & 0 \end{bmatrix} \begin{bmatrix} a & b \\ c & d \end{bmatrix} = \begin{bmatrix} a & b \\ 0 & 0 \end{bmatrix} = \begin{bmatrix} 1 & 0 \\ 0 & 1 \end{bmatrix}.$$

The rules of matrix algebra are not much different from the algebra of numbers. There are two notable exceptions. First, multiplication is not commutative and, second, many nonzero matrices do not have inverses. Here are some of the rules that can be easily proved by appealing to the definitions of the matrix operations. We assume that the dimensions of the matrices are appropriate for the operations. Let A, B, and C be matrices and r and s scalars.

1. $A + B = B + A$ (addition commutes)
2. $A + (B + C) = (A + B) + C$ (associative law of addition)
3. For any matrix A, there is a matrix $-A$ such that $A + (-A) = 0$
4. $A(BC) = (AB)C$ (associative law of multiplication)
5. $r(sA) = (rs)A$ (associative law of scalars)
6. $(r + s)A = rA + sA$ (distributive law)
7. $r(A + B) = rA + rB$ (distributive law)

Matrices can be used to express systems of linear equations in a very succinct form. Consider a general $m \times n$ system

$$a_{11}x_1 + a_{12}x_2 + \cdots + a_{1n}x_n = b_1,$$
$$a_{21}x_1 + a_{22}x_2 + \cdots + a_{2n}x_n = b_2,$$
$$\vdots$$
$$a_{m1}x_1 + a_{m2}x_2 + \cdots + a_{mn}x_n = b_m.$$

Let $A = (a_{ij})$ be the matrix of coefficients, and let X and B be the matrices defined by

$$X = \begin{bmatrix} x_1 \\ \vdots \\ x_n \end{bmatrix}, \qquad B = \begin{bmatrix} b_1 \\ \vdots \\ b_m \end{bmatrix}.$$

Then the preceding system of equation is most economically expressed by

$$AX = B.$$

We call A the coefficient matrix of the system.

A.2.1 Elementary Matrices and Inverses

An elementary matrix is a matrix obtained from the identity by applying one row operation.

Example A.2.1 The following are elementary matrices.

$$\begin{bmatrix} 0 & 1 & 0 \\ 1 & 0 & 0 \\ 0 & 0 & 1 \end{bmatrix} \qquad \begin{bmatrix} 1 & 2 & 0 \\ 0 & 1 & 0 \\ 0 & 0 & 1 \end{bmatrix} \qquad \begin{bmatrix} 1 & 0 & 0 \\ 0 & 1 & 0 \\ 0 & 0 & -3 \end{bmatrix}. \qquad \blacksquare$$

If we multiply A on the left by an elementary matrix, the result is the same as if we applied the corresponding row operation directly to A. Now each elementary matrix has an elementary inverse. For example, if E is the elementary matrix obtained from the identity by, say, multiplying the second row by 2 and adding it to the first, then the elementary matrix F obtained by multiplying the second row of the identity by -2 and adding to the first row is the inverse of E. This is because FE has the effect of multiplying the second row in E by -2 and adding it to the first row of E. But this takes E back to the identity. The same argument can be applied to EF.

Suppose that A is an $n \times n$ matrix that can be row reduced to the identity. Let $\{E_1, E_2, \ldots, E_k\}$ be the elementary matrices whose row operations reduced A to the identity. Then

$$E_k E_{k-1} \cdots E_1 A = I.$$

But since each E_i has an inverse,

$$A = E_1^{-1} E_2^{-1} \cdots E_k^{-1}.$$

Now, if C and D are matrices of the same dimension and each has an inverse, then CD has inverse $D^{-1}C^{-1}$. So the inverse of A is

$$E_k E_{k-1} \cdots E_1.$$

This last observation tells us how to find the inverse of a matrix A if it has one. Simply apply the row operations to the identity that were used to reduce A to the identity. Here is an example.

Example A.2.2   Let

$$A = \begin{bmatrix} 3 & 1 \\ 4 & 1 \end{bmatrix}.$$

We place the identity matrix to the right of A and row reduce A to the identity.

$$\begin{bmatrix} 3 & 1 & 1 & 0 \\ 4 & 1 & 0 & 1 \end{bmatrix} \rightarrow \begin{bmatrix} 3 & 1 & 1 & 0 \\ 1 & 0 & -1 & 1 \end{bmatrix}$$

$$\rightarrow \begin{bmatrix} 1 & 0 & -1 & 1 \\ 3 & 1 & 1 & 0 \end{bmatrix} \rightarrow \begin{bmatrix} 1 & 0 & -1 & 1 \\ 0 & 1 & 4 & -3 \end{bmatrix}.$$

Then

$$A^{-1} = \begin{bmatrix} -1 & 1 \\ 4 & -3 \end{bmatrix}. \qquad \blacksquare$$

We have shown that, if a square matrix A can be row reduced to the identity, it has an inverse given by the product of the elementary matrices of the row operations used. Conversely, if A has an inverse, then the system of which A is the coefficient matrix can be row reduced to the identity. To see this, remember that the system can be written

$$AX = B.$$

So if A has an inverse, then

$$X = A^{-1}B$$

is the unique solution to the system. But the system only has a unique solution if the coefficient matrix of the system can be row reduced to the identity.

Observe that the homogeneous $n \times n$ system

$$AX = 0$$

has the unique solution $X = 0$ if and only if A has an inverse. Note that if A does not have an inverse then the echelon form of A cannot be the identity. Since the system is homogeneous, there cannot be the case of a zero left-hand side being equal to a nonzero right-hand side, so the only alternative is that there are independent variables in the solution. Thus there are infinitely many solutions. We have proved the following theorem.

Theorem A.2.3

A square matrix A has an inverse if and only if A can be row reduced to the identity, if and only if $AX = 0$ has only $X = 0$ for its solution. Moreover, if A does not have an inverse, then $AX = 0$ has infinitely many solutions. $\bullet$

A.2.2 Determinants

To define the notion of the determinant of a matrix, we need the concept of a permutation of a list of numbers, $\{1, 2, \ldots, n\}$. A permutation of this list is simply a rearrangement of this list. For example, $\{2, 3, 1\}$ is a permutation of $\{1, 2, 3\}$. For $\{1, 2, \ldots, n\}$ there are $n!$ different permutations, so for $\{1, 2, 3\}$ there are 6 permutations. Another way to think of a permutation is as a one-to-one function from $\{1, 2, \ldots, n\}$ to $\{1, 2, \ldots, n\}$. Such a function is completely described by listing its values in order. Thus, if σ is the permutation $\{2, 3, 1\}$ then $\sigma(1) = 2$, $\sigma(2) = 3$, and $\sigma(3) = 1$.

Each permutation of a list can be defined to be even or odd as follows. If $\{a_1, a_2, \ldots, a_n\}$ is a permutation of $\{1, 2, \ldots, n\}$, it is even if it takes an even number of pairwise exchanges to return the permutation to the form $\{1, 2, \ldots, n\}$; it is odd otherwise. It is true that the number of exchanges (called **transpositions**) needed to return to increasing order is always even or odd, no matter in what order the transpositions are performed, but we shall not prove this.

The permutation $\{2, 3, 1\}$ is even whereas $\{2, 3, 4, 1\}$ is odd.

Let σ be a permutation. We define $\text{sgn}(\sigma) = 1$ if σ is even, and $\text{sgn}(\sigma) = -1$ if σ is odd. The function sgn is called the **signum** function.

Let S_n stand for the set of all the permutations of $\{1, 2, \ldots, n\}$.

Definition A.2.4

Let $A = (a_{ij})$ be an $n \times n$ matrix. We define the determinant of A to be the number

$$\det(A) = \sum_{\sigma \in S_n} \text{sgn}(\sigma) a_{1\sigma(1)} a_{2\sigma(2)} \cdots a_{n\sigma(n)}. \qquad \bullet$$

Here is the definition written out in full for the 3×3 case. Let $A = (a_{ij})$; then

$$\det(A) = a_{11}a_{22}a_{33} - a_{12}a_{21}a_{33} - a_{13}a_{22}a_{31}$$
$$- a_{11}a_{23}a_{32} + a_{12}a_{23}a_{31} + a_{13}a_{21}a_{32}.$$

If we collect the terms that contain a_{11}, those that contain a_{12}, and those that contain a_{13}, we get

$$\det(A) = a_{11}(a_{22}a_{33} - a_{23}a_{32}) - a_{12}(a_{21}a_{33} - a_{23}a_{31}) + a_{13}(a_{21}a_{32} - a_{22}a_{31}).$$

This is the familiar expansion of a 3×3 determinant by the top row. Indeed, this grouping can be done in the general case for any row or column, and a proof by induction on the dimension of the matrix would establish the rule for expanding determinants by columns or rows in general.

Expansion of determinants by rows or columns is called **expansion by minors**. We describe the process in a little more detail. If A is a square matrix, then the (i, j) **minor** is the matrix obtain by deleting the ith row and jth column. The (i, j) **cofactor** is

$$(-1)^{i+j} \det(M_{ij}),$$

where M_{ij} is the (i, j) minor of A. All this amounts to is assigning a sign to $\det(M_{ij})$ according to the following rule. Imagine a matrix of plus and minus signs where there is a plus in the upper-left corner and the rest of the signs alternate as you go across and down. Thus the (i, j) cofactor is $\det(M_{ij})$ with a minus sign if there is a minus sign in the (i, j) position. For a matrix A, let us denote the (i, j) cofactor by A_{ij}. Now we can write the row and column expansions by minors as follows:

$$\det(A) = \sum_{j=1}^{n} a_{kj} A_{kj}$$

is expansion by the kth row, and

$$\det(A) = \sum_{i=1}^{n} a_{ik} A_{ik}$$

is expansion by the kth column.

Definition A.2.5

Let $A = (a_{ij})$ be an $n \times n$ matrix. The transpose of A, written A^t, is the matrix $A^t = (b_{ij})$, where $a_{ij} = b_{ji}$ for all i and j.   ●

The transpose of a matrix is simply obtained by reflection about the main diagonal.

It is useful to note that the transpose of a product of square matrices is the product of the transposes in reverse order. That is, $(AB)^t = B^t A^t$. The proof of this is obtained directly by writing down the definition of the entries in the transpose of the product and the product of the transposes and comparing. This is left to the exercises.

In calculating the determinant of the transpose, all the products that appear in the determinant of A appear in A^t. Moreover, the odd or even nature of the permutation is unchanged in this switch. Therefore,

$$\det(A) = \det(A^t).$$

We now discuss the effect of the row operations on determinants.

If a row is multiplied by any constant, then expansion by the minors of that row shows immediately that the determinant has been multiplied by that constant.

It two rows are interchanged, then the determinant changes sign. An interchange of two rows in A produces an interchange of two columns in the transpose. But the interchange of two columns changes the sign of the determinant of a matrix. This is obvious since every even permutation becomes an odd one, and vice versa. But $\det(A) = \det(A^t)$, and so the interchange of two rows changes the sign also.

If two rows are the same, then the determinant is zero. This follows by realizing that if these two rows are switched the matrix is the same, but its sign has changed. Only zero is equal to its negative.

Finally, if a row is multiplied by a constant and added to another the determinant is unchanged. This requires a little algebra. For concreteness sake, let us multiply the second row by c and add it to the first. The determinant of this new matrix is

$$\sum_{\sigma \in S_n} \text{sgn}(\sigma)[a_{1\sigma(1)} + ca_{2\sigma(1)}]a_{2\sigma(2)} \cdots a_{n\sigma(n)}.$$

This equals

$$\sum_{\sigma \in S_n} \text{sgn}(\sigma)a_{1\sigma(1)}a_{2\sigma(2)} \cdots a_{n\sigma(n)} + c \sum_{\sigma \in S_n} \text{sgn}(\sigma)a_{2\sigma(1)}a_{2\sigma(2)} \cdots a_{n\sigma(n)}.$$

But the last summation in this expression is the determinant of a matrix with the first and second rows the same, so it is zero. The remaining term is the determinant of the original matrix.

Since a matrix has an inverse precisely when it can be row reduced to the identity, a matrix has an inverse if and only if its determinant is not zero.

Let us summarize this in a theorem.

Theorem A.2.6

Let A be an $n \times n$ matrix. Then

1. $\det(A^t) = \det(A)$.
2. If two rows are the same, then $\det(A) = 0$.
3. If B is obtained from A by interchanging two rows, then $\det(B) = -\det(A)$.
4. If B is obtained from A by multiplying a row by c, then $\det(B) = c \det(A)$.
5. If B is obtained from A by multiplying one row by a constant and adding it to another, then $\det(B) = \det(A)$.
6. A has an inverse if and only if $\det(A) \neq 0$.
7. A has an inverse if and only if A^t has an inverse.   ●

Observe that, since $\det(A^t) = \det(A)$, what has been said about row operations and determinants can be said about the corresponding column operations.

An immediate corollary of this theorem is the computation of determinants of the elementary matrices. The elementary matrices are obtained from the identity by row operations. The identity has determinant equal to 1. If the elementary matrix is obtained by interchanging two rows, the determinant is -1. If a row is multiplied by c, the determinant is c. If the operation is to multiply and add, then the determinant is 1.

Theorem A.2.7

Let A and B be $n \times n$ matrices. Then

$$\det(AB) = \det(A)\det(B).$$ ●

Proof

If B does not have an inverse, then $\det(B) = 0$. But if B does not have an inverse, then neither does AB. To see this, note that the equation $BX = 0$ has infinitely many solutions, but then so does $ABX = 0$. Thus AB has no inverse. But then

$$\det(AB) = 0 = \det(A)0 = \det(A)\det(B).$$

If A does not have an inverse, then A^t does not also. So $(AB)^t = B^t A^t$ does not have an inverse, by the preceding reasoning. Thus AB has no inverse. Therefore,

$$\det(AB) = 0 = 0\det(B) = \det(A)\det(B).$$

Suppose that A has an inverse. Then $A = E_1 E_2 \cdots E_r$, where the E_i are elementary matrices. Let E be any elementary matrix. Then $\det(EB) = \det(E)\det(B)$. For example, if E was obtained by interchanging two rows, then EB is the matrix obtained by interchanging the two rows of B. Therefore, $\det(EB) = -\det(B)$. But $\det(E) = -1$, so $\det(EB) = -\det(B) = \det(E)\det(B)$. If E is the matrix that multiplies B by c, then $\det(EB) = c\det(B) = \det(E)\det(B)$. The reader can check the remaining case. Since $\det(EB) = \det(E)\det(B)$, it follows that

$$
\begin{aligned}
\det(AB) &= \det(E_1 E_2 \cdots E_r B) \\
&= \det(E_1)\det(E_2)\cdots\det(E_r)\det(B) \\
&= \det(E_1 E_2 \cdots E_r)\det(B) \\
&= \det(A)\det(B).
\end{aligned}
$$ ◆

An alternative means of calculating an inverse matrix employs determinants. To describe this, we need to consider the expansion of a determinant by minors or cofactors again. The expansion is

$$\sum_{j=1}^{n} a_{kj} A_{kj} = \det(A).$$

If we consider the sum

$$\sum_{j=1}^{n} a_{ij} A_{kj},$$

this would be the same as the expansion of the determinant of the matrix in which the kth row is also the ith row. But the determinant of a matrix with two rows the same is zero, so

$$\sum_{j=1}^{n} a_{ij} A_{kj} = 0.$$

These two sums can be viewed as the calculation of entries in a certain product. In fact, the product is

$$A(A_{ij})^t,$$

so the product is A times the transpose of the matrix of cofactors. According to the two sums, the off-diagonal terms of the product are all zero, and the diagonal terms are $\det(A)$. Thus the product is $\det(A)I$. Therefore,

$$A(A_{ij})^t = \det(A)I,$$

and so if $\det(A) \neq 0$ then

$$A\frac{1}{\det(A)}(A_{ij})^t = I.$$

Thus

$$A^{-1} = \frac{1}{\det(A)}(A_{ij})^t.$$

So we can say that the inverse of A is the transpose of the matrix of cofactors of A divided by the determinant of A.

A.2.3 Cramer's Rule

Cramer's rule follows immediately from the cofactor representation of the inverse of A. If A is the coefficient matrix of an $n \times n$ system $AX = B$, then this system has a unique solution if A has an inverse, and

$$X = A^{-1}B = \frac{1}{\det(A)}(A_{ij})^t B$$

is that solution. Thus

$$x_k = \frac{\sum_{j=1}^{n} A_{jk} b_j}{\det(A)}.$$

But the numerator is precisely the expansion of the determinant of the matrix A with the kth column replaced by B. This is Cramer's rule.

Example A.2.8   We solve

$$2x_1 - x_2 = 2$$
$$x_1 + 3x_2 = -4$$

by Cramer's rule. We have

$$x_1 = \frac{\det\left(\begin{bmatrix} 2 & -1 \\ -4 & 3 \end{bmatrix}\right)}{\det\left(\begin{bmatrix} 2 & -1 \\ 1 & 3 \end{bmatrix}\right)} = \frac{10}{7}$$

and

$$x_2 = \frac{\det\left(\begin{bmatrix} 2 & 2 \\ 1 & -4 \end{bmatrix}\right)}{\det\left(\begin{bmatrix} 2 & -1 \\ 1 & 3 \end{bmatrix}\right)} = \frac{-6}{7}.$$ ∎

EXERCISES A.2

1. Add the matrices, and multiply the matrices in both orders $A = \begin{bmatrix} 3 & 2 \\ -1 & 3 \end{bmatrix}$ and $B = \begin{bmatrix} 2 & 5 \\ 0 & 3 \end{bmatrix}$.

2. Add the matrices, and multiply the matrices in both orders $A = \begin{bmatrix} 3 & 2 & 2 \\ -1 & 3 & 5 \\ 2 & 1 & -4 \end{bmatrix}$ and $B = \begin{bmatrix} 2 & 5 & 2 \\ 0 & 3 & -2 \\ 3 & -1 & 1 \end{bmatrix}$.

3. Find the inverse of the matrix $A = \begin{bmatrix} 3 & 2 \\ -1 & 3 \end{bmatrix}$ two ways.

4. Find the inverse of the matrix $A = \begin{bmatrix} 3 & 2 & 2 \\ -1 & 3 & 5 \\ 2 & 1 & -4 \end{bmatrix}$ two ways.

In Exercises 5–7, solve the system by finding the inverse matrix and by Cramer's Rule

5. $2x_1 + x_2 = 1$
   $1x_1 - 2x_2 = 0$

6. $2x_1 + x_2 + x_3 = 1$
   $1x_1 - 2x_2 - x_3 = 0$
   $2x_1 - 4x_2 + 3x_3 = -2$
   $4x_1 + 2x_2 + 2x_3 = 2$

7. $x_1 + x_2 - x_3 = 2$
   $-x_1 - 2x_2 - x_3 = 0$
   $2x_1 + 3x_2 + x_3 = -2$
   $4x_1 + 2x_2 + 2x_3 = 1$

THE TWO-VARIABLE TAYLOR THEOREM

Taylor's theorem for a function of one variable is

Theorem   (Taylor)

Let f have $n+1$ continuous derivatives on the interval $(a-r, a+r)$. Then for x in $(a - r, a + r)$ there is a number z in between x and a such that

$$f(x) =$$
$$f(a) + \frac{1}{1!} f'(a)(x - a) + \cdots + \frac{1}{n!} f^{(n)}(a)(x - a)^n + \frac{f^{(n+1)}(z)(x - a)^{n+1}}{(n + 1)!}.$$

●

Let $g(x, y)$ be a function of two variables with continuous partial derivatives up to order $n + 1$ in a disk about (x, y). We want to approximate $g(x + \Delta x, y + \Delta y)$ with a two-variable polynomial in the variables Δx and Δy. The parameterization of the line from (x, y) to $(x + \Delta x, y + \Delta y)$ is

$$\overline{x} = x + t\Delta x,$$
$$\overline{y} = y + t\Delta y.$$

The interval of parameterization is $[0, 1]$.

Now consider the function

$$f(t) = g(x + t\Delta x, y + t\Delta y).$$

We apply Taylor's theorem for one variable to $f(1)$ centered at 0. We have

$$f(1) = f(0) + \frac{f'(0)}{1!} 1 + \frac{f''(0)}{2!} 1^2 + \cdots + \frac{f^{(n)}(0)}{n!} 1^n + \frac{f^{(n+1)}(z)}{(n + 1)!} 1^{n+1},$$

where z is between 0 and 1. But $f(1) = g(x + \Delta x, y + \Delta y)$ and $f(0) = g(x, y)$. Moreover, by the chain rule, we have

$$f^{(k)}(0) = \sum_{j=0}^{k} \binom{k}{j} \frac{\partial^k g}{\partial x^{k-j} \partial y^j}(x, y) \Delta x^{k-j} \Delta y^j.$$

Therefore,

$$g(x + \Delta x, y + \Delta y) =$$

$$g(x, y) + \frac{\partial g}{\partial x}(x, y)\Delta x + \frac{\partial g}{\partial y}(x, y)\Delta y$$

$$+ \frac{1}{2!} [\frac{\partial^2 g}{\partial x^2}(x, y)\Delta x^2 + 2\frac{\partial^2 g}{\partial x \partial y}(x, y)\Delta x \Delta y + \frac{\partial^2 g}{\partial y^2}(x, y)\Delta y^2]$$

$$+ \cdots + \frac{1}{n!} \sum_{j=0}^{n} \binom{n}{j} \frac{\partial^n g}{\partial x^{n-j} \partial y^j}(x, y)\Delta x^{n-j} \Delta y^j$$

$$+ \frac{1}{(n+1)!} \sum_{j=0}^{n+1} \binom{n+1}{j} \frac{\partial^{n+1} g}{\partial x^{n+1-j} \partial y^j}(x_0, y_0)\Delta x^{n+1-j} \Delta y^j,$$

where (x_0, y_0) is the point on the line corresponding to $t = z$.

The last term is the remainder. If the $(n + 1)$st partial derivatives are continuous on the disk about (x, y), then this remainder will be of order $O(\Delta x^{n+1} + \Delta x^n \Delta y + \cdots + \Delta y^{n+1})$.

APPENDIX C

THE EXISTENCE AND UNIQUENESS THEOREM

This appendix is devoted to an outline of the proof of the existence and uniqueness theorem. The only thing missing from the proof is a justification of the interchange of limits and integration. For this, consult any advanced calculus text on the subject of uniform convergence and the Weierstrass M-test.

Consider the initial-value problem

$$y' = f(x, y) \text{ and } y(x_0) = y_0.$$

Recall that we assume that f and $\partial f / \partial y$ are continuous in some rectangle containing the initial point (x_0, y_0), say $R = [x_0 - r_1, x_0 + r_1] \times [y_0 - r_2, y_0 + r_2]$. We note two consequences of this assumption. First, there is a constant M such that

$$|f(x, y)| \leq M$$

on R. Second, by the mean-value theorem in the variable y, we have

$$|f(x, y_1) - f(x, y_2)| = |\frac{\partial f}{\partial y}(x, z)(y_1 - y_2)| \leq L|y_1 - y_2|,$$

where z is between y_1 and y_2 and L is a bound on $\partial f / \partial y$ on R.

Observe that if $y(x)$ satisfies the "integral equation"

$$y(x) = y_0 + \int_{x_0}^{x} f(t, y(t)) \, dt,$$

then $y(x)$ satisfies the initial-value problem. Thus the strategy is to solve this integral equation instead. The approach we use is called **Picard's method**. First, let $y_0(x) = y_0$, so this is a constant function. Now define

$$y_1(x) = y_0 + \int_{x_0}^{x} f(t, y_0(t)) \, dt.$$

405

Next define

$$y_2(x) = y_0 + \int_{x_0}^{x} f(t, y_1(t)) \, dt.$$

We continue in this recursive fashion by defining

$$y_n(x) = y_0 + \int_{x_0}^{x} f(t, y_{n-1}(t)) \, dt.$$

Now consider the differences $|y_n(x) - y_{n-1}(x)|$ recursively. To get the latter inequalities, consider $x > x_0$ and then $x_0 < x$. First,

$$|y_1(x) - y_0| \leq \int_{x_0}^{x} |f(t, y_0)| \, dt \leq M|x - x_0|$$

since $|f|$ is bounded by M. Next,

$$|y_2(x) - y_1(x)| \leq \int_{x_0}^{x} |f(t, y_1(t)) - f(t, y_0(t))| \, dt \leq \int_{x_0}^{x} L|y_1(t) - y_0(t)| \, dt$$

by the bound L, and so

$$|y_2(x) - y_1(x)| \leq \int_{x_0}^{x} LM|t - x_0| \, dt = LM|x - x_0|^2/2.$$

There is a subtlety here. Our bounds only work if the functions defined still lie in R. We will show that they do if x is close enough to x_0 at the end of the argument. Continuing,

$$|y_3(x) - y_2(x)| \leq \int_{x_0}^{x} |f(t, y_1(t)) - f(t, y_0(t))| \, dt \leq L^2 M|x - x_0|^3/3!,$$

and, in general,

$$|y_n(x) - y_{n-1}(x)| \leq \frac{M}{L}[L|x - x_0|]^n/n!.$$

The series

$$\sum_{k=1}^{\infty} \frac{M}{L}[L|x - x_0|]^n/n!$$

converges absolutely for all x by the ratio test.

The telescoping series

$$\sum_{k=1}^{\infty} (y_k(x) - y_{k-1}(x))$$

converges absolutely by comparison with the preceding series. Therefore,

$$y_n(x) - y_0 = \sum_{k=1}^{n} (y_k(x) - y_{k-1}(x))$$

converges as n goes to infinity. Thus $\lim_{n \to \infty} y_n(x) = y(x)$ exists if x is close enough to x_0. The convergence is, in fact, uniform, and this is where the advanced calculus comes in. The uniform convergence and continuity of f allow the limit to be taken inside the integral in the following:

$$y(x) = \lim_{n \to \infty} y_n(x) = y_0 + \lim_{n \to \infty} \int_{x_0}^{x} f(t, y_n(t)) \, dt = \int_{x_0}^{x} f(t, y(t)) \, dt.$$

Thus $y(x)$ satisfies the integral equation, and so it satisfies the initial-value problem.

We still need to see that everything stays inside R. Recall that

$$y_n(x) = y_0 + \int_{x_0}^{x} f(t, y_{n-1}(t)) \, dt,$$

and so

$$|y_n(x) - y_0| \leq \int_{x_0}^{x} |f(t, y_{n-1}(t))| \, dt.$$

Now, if the graph of $y_{n-1}(t)$ lies in R, then

$$|y_n(x) - y_0| \leq |x - x_0| M.$$

Therefore, the graph of $y_n(x)$ is in R provided that

$$|x - x_0| M \leq r_2 \quad \text{and} \quad |x - x_0| \leq r_1.$$

Thus we only need to choose $h = \min\{r_1, r_2/M\}$ and $|x - x_0| < h$ in order for everything to stay in R. This is where the h comes from!

Uniqueness is proved by getting the exponential bound on the difference between two solutions with neighboring initial conditions. Let $y_1(x)$ and $y_2(x)$ be solutions to $y' = f(x, y)$. Let $t = x - x_0$ and

$$g(t) = (y_1(t + x_0) - y_2(t + x_0))^2.$$

Then

$$g'(t) = 2(y_1(t + x_0) - y_2(t + x_0))(y_1'(t + x_0) - y_2'(t + x_0)),$$

but remembering that $y_1(x)$ and $y_2(x)$ are solutions gives

$$g'(t) = 2[f(t, y_1(t + x_0)) - f(t, y_2(t + x_0))](y_1(t + x_0) - y_2(t + x_0)).$$

But we know that

$$|f(t, y_1(t + x_0)) - f(t, y_2(t + x_0))| \le L|y_1(t + x_0) - y_2(t + x_0)|,$$

and so

$$-L|y_1(t + x_0) - y_2(t + x_0)| \le f(t, y_1(t + x_0)) - f(t, y_2(t + x_0))$$
$$\le L|y_1(t + x_0) - y_2(t + x_0)|.$$

Using this and the fact that $|y_1(t+x_0) - y_2(t+x_0)| = \pm(y_1(t+x_0) - y_2(t+x_0))$ yields

$$g'(t) \le 2L(y_1(t + x_0) - y_2(t + x_0))^2 = 2Lg(t).$$

Thus $g'(t) - 2Lg(t) \le 0$, and multiplying through by e^{-2Lt} gives

$$g'(t)e^{-2Lt} - 2Le^{-2Lt}g(t) = [e^{-2Lt}g(t)]' \le 0.$$

Therefore, $e^{-2Lt}g(t)$ is a decreasing function, and so for $t \ge 0$, $e^{-2Lt}g(t) \le g(0) = (y_1(x_0) - y_2(x_0))$. But this means that

$$(y_1(t + x_0) - y_2(t + x_0))^2 \le e^{2L(x-x_0)}(y_1(x_0) - y_2(x_0))^2.$$

By setting $x = t + x_0$ and taking square roots, we get

$$|y_1(x) - y_2(x)| \le e^{L(x-x_0)}|y_1(x_0) - y_2(x_0)|.$$

If we set $t = x_0 - x$ and repeat the argument for $t \le 0$, we get

$$|y_1(x) - y_2(x)| \le e^{L(x_0-x)}|y_1(x_0) - y_2(x_0)|$$

and, combined, we have

$$|y_1(x) - y_2(x)| \le e^{L|x-x_0|}|y_1(x_0) - y_2(x_0)|.$$

Therefore, if the initial conditions are equal, the right hand side is zero, so the solutions must be the same.

We conclude with two remarks. By now it should be clear that it is not the continuity of $\partial f/\partial y$ that really matters; it is the Lipschitz condition

$$|f(x, y_1) - f(x, y_2)| \le L|y_1 - y_2|$$

that is needed; hence the uniqueness of solutions to $y' = |y|$ in the exercises of Section 2.1.

The proofs given here can be extended with almost no change to first-order systems by writing them in vector form and replacing absolute values with the lengths of vectors.

APPENDIX **D**

MATHEMATICA, MAPLE, AND MATLAB

This appendix provides guidance to readers who wish to develop the skill of writing routines and programs in one or more of the Three M's: Mathematica, Maple or MatLab. In the following, most of the software packages used in this book are discussed, and the necessary Three M's commands and coding to implement them is developed. By the time you reach routines that are not discussed here, you should be ready to go out on your own.

In the sections that follow, notice that the language expressions and commands to be executed are written in plain type.

D.1 GRAPHING

The three problems presented in elementary graphing are to define a function, call the plotting facility to plot it, and then set the dimensions of the plot in the plotting facility.

D.1.1 Mathematica

In Mathematica, functions can be defined as follows.

```
f[x_] = x^2;
```

Notice the low dash following the x in f[x_]. This is Mathematica's way of identifying the free variable. Also notice the semicolon. If we did not include it, upon execution of the line the function definition would be printed out as output. So including the semicolon suppresses the output of that line to the screen.

The plot function is as follows:

```
Plot[f[x],{x,-2,2}];
```

All functions enclose their arguments with square brackets. Note that the semicolon does not suppress output. This is because Plot is a kind of print command. Note that the *x* range of the plot is automatically to be included in the call to the Plot function. For the *y* range, we must use the Mathematica option or substitution statement of the form `Option -> data` . Here is how it works for setting the *y* range.

```
Plot[f[x], {x,-2,2}, PlotRange -> {-5,5}]
```

You can use options to set the color of the graph.

```
Plot[f[x], {x,-2,2}, PlotRange -> {-5,5},
PlotStyle -> Hue[0]]
```

The function Hue[] takes arguments in the range [0,1]. You should experiment to see the effect.

A call to plot multiple functions with different colors could be

```
Plot[{f[x],g[x]}, {x,-2,2}, PlotRange -> {-5,5},
PlotStyle ->{Hue[0],Hue[.5]}
```

Finally, you may find Mathematica's habit of not preserving scales on the axes annoying. This calls for another option.

```
Plot[{f[x],g[x]}, {x,-2,2}, PlotRange -> {-5,5},
PlotStyle -> {Hue[0],Hue[.5]}, AspectRatio -> Automatic]
```

Note that virtually all Mathematica commands and functions are capitalized. This includes just about every noun, even if it is only part of a larger word.

D.1.2 Maple

Input into a Maple worksheet is marked by the > prompt. We shall assume that you are entering all your expressions into a Maple input cell headed by such a prompt.

Function input in Maple is quite mathematical. To define a function f of one variable x, we input

```
f := x -> x^2;
```

Note that Maple displays input in red where we are using plain type for input. Try the function entry just made. Note that the output repeats the function definition that we entered. Now enter

```
f(2);
```

```
f(2):
```

The difference should be clear. A line must be terminated by either ";" or ":". The semicolon returns output to the screen and the colon suppresses it.

Plotting is performed by calling the plot() function in the form plot(f(x),x range,y range,option). Try this:

```
plot(f(x),x=-2..2,y=-4..4,color=red);
```

An alternative form is

```
plot(f,-2..2,-4..4,color=blue);
```

To plot two functions, try

```
plot([f(x),g(x)],x=-2..2,y=-4..4,color=[red,blue]);
```

Virtually all resident functions in Maple are in lowercase.

D.1.3 MatLab

MatLab has a very different flavor from Mathematica and Maple. This is because it is not, strictly, a computer algebra system. MatLab executes procedure calls at a command line prompt symbolized by >> or EDU>> for the student version. There are basically two things that you can do at the prompt: make an assignment such as x = 3 or execute a function/procedure. In either case, the execution is performed by pressing the carriage return. If the prompt entry is terminated by a semicolon, then the output to the screen is suppressed.

Another feature of MatLab that distinguishes it from other systems is that virtually all data are held in the form of matrices. If you execute

```
>> x = 3
```

and then execute the function

```
size(x)
```

the result is ans = 1 1. This tells us that the matrix x is 1×1. Try size(5) just for emphasis on this point. That numbers are 1×1 matrices does not affect the usual arithmetic computations.

Arithmetic:

The arithmetic operations are the usual ones:

```
^, *,
/, +,-.
```

The precedence of these operations is the order shown. To force a different order of operations, the parentheses "(" and ")" are used.
Execute

```
>> 3*5
```

and

```
>> 3*5-10
```

Because most data are held in the form of matrices, matrices and matrix operations play an important role.

Matrices

A row matrix or vector is entered as follows:
Execute

```
>> [1,2,3]
```

To define a matrix enter the rows separated by semicolons. Execute

```
>>A=[1,2,3;-1,0,4]
```

To access the entries in A, we type A(i,j). When executed, this gives the ith row and jth column entry in A. Execute

```
>> A(1,2), A(2,3)
```

Note the comma separator for multiple executions.
You can define a matrix by defining its entries as follows. Execute

```
>> B(1,1)=-1; B(1,2)=0; B(2,1)=3; B(2,2)=-4;
```

```
>> B
```

Note that to suppress the output of each entry we separate with a semicolon.
For matrix multiplication, the inner dimensions must match. Try

```
>>A*B
```

```
>>B*A
```

Scalar matrix multiplication is illustrated by

```
>> 2*A
```

The command for the transpose of a matrix is

```
>> A'
```

For matrix addition the matrices must have the same dimensions. Matrix addition is an example of an entry-by-entry operation. Others include multiplication and exponentiation. These entry-by-entry operations are performed by `.*` and `.^`, respectively. For example, `A.*B` gives the matrix whose entries are obtained by multiplying the corresponding entries of A and B. Naturally, for this the matrices must have the same dimensions. Execute

```
>>A.^2
```

All the resident functions are matrix "smart" in the sense that they map the function over each entry in the matrix to which the function is applied. Execute

```
>> sin(A)
```

The resident functions do not capitalize the first letter of the call. Similarly, the ratio of the circumference of a circle to the diameter is pi, not Pi. Try

```
>> pi
```

M-files and Functions

Any function that is to be called from the prompt is defined in a plain text file called an M-file. Here is the plain text that defines a function called Input(x).

```
function y=Input(x)

y=x.^2;
```

Type this into a plain text file and save it as the file named Input.m. Notice that the name of the file is the same as the function name with the extension ".m". In this way the function `Input(x) = x.^2` is defined. Note that the power is ready to accept matrices in place of x. It is matrix smart, and this is very important in graphing.

TO USE Input.m **IT IS IMPERATIVE THAT THE FOLDER THAT IT IS IN BE IN THE FILE PATH OF MATLAB!** To do this just open MatLab by double clicking the file Input.m. Alternatively, set the file path from the File menu in MatLab. Now execute

Input(2)

The MatLab plot facility takes sets of "x" coordinates and sets of "y" coordinates and draws line segments between the points so created. Execute

```
plot([1,2,3],[0,-1,6])
```

The plot function plots "x" values against "y" values. To plot $f(x) = x^2$, all we do is construct a list of "x" values, feed this to Input(x), and then plot these two lists one against the other. Remember that we made Input(x) matrix smart, so if you feed it a list, it will return a list. A list of numbers 0.1 unit apart is constructed by the following command:

```
x=-2:0.1:2
```

Yes, we should have used a semicolon to suppress that output.

Now apply Input() to this list to create a list of squares y, and then plot x against y.

```
y=Input(x);
```

```
plot(x,y)
```

To force plot() to set the plot dimensions to those you desire, use:

```
axis([-4,4,-5,5]);
```

Now, if you want to plot y=x^2 in those coordinates, you have to tell MatLab to hold the plotting frame for both setting the coordinates and the plot. This is done using the "hold" command. Be sure you have constructed the lists x and y. Try the following:

```
hold on, axis([-4,4,-5,5]), plot(x,y)
```

Notice how a series of commands can be executed in sequence by setting them out on the command line separated by commas.

We change the color of a plot by adding an option as follows:

```
plot(x,y,'r');
```

Notice the quotes for the character "r".

Clearly, all this could get very tiresome if we have many plots to make. It would be nice if we could bundle all these commands into one single function or procedure. This can easily be done, and this is where M-files come in again. Create the following M-file and save it as Graph.m.

```
function  Graph(lft,rt,dn,up,c);
hold on;
axis([lft,rt,dn,up]);
a=(rt-lft)/100;
t=lft:a:rt;
plot([lft,rt],[0,0],'k')
plot([0,0],[dn,up],'k')
if nargin > 4
   plot(t,Input(t),c)
else
   plot(t,Input(t))
end
hold off;
```

This is how this simple function works. First define a function in your Input.m file and SAVE IT. For example, enter y=x.^3. At the >> prompt, enter Graph(-4,4,-5,5,'r') and execute it. Upon execution, "hold" is set to "on"; the graphing frame is called with the correct ranges. Next, the list t is created using 100 subdivisions from left to right, and horizontal and vertical axes are drawn in black. Finally, the graph is drawn. However, observe the conditional "if...else...end". The variable "nargin" is a MatLab variable to hold the number of arguments in the function Graph() being executed. If nargin > 4, you have specified a color and `plot(t,Input(t),c)` is performed; if not, `plot(t,Input(t))` is executed. Finally, the hold is turned off.

D.2 FIELD&SOLUTION

In this section we show how the Three M's can be used to generate an inclination field and solutions through initial conditions and then present all of this in a frame of the desired dimensions.

D.2.1 Mathematica

The field package that we shall call actually draws representations of fields of the form

$$\vec{F}(x, y) = g_1(x, y)\vec{i} + g_2(x, y)\vec{j}.$$

To apply this to equations of the form

$$y' = f(x, y),$$

we simply set $g_1(x, y) = 1$ and plot

$$\vec{F}(x, y) = \vec{i} + f(x, y)\vec{j}.$$

The vectors of such a field have the correct slopes to form a slope field of $f(x, y)$.

We must first open the package before the function defined in that package can be used. To do this, we use the import operator <<. We open the folder Graphics and call the PlotField package by running

```
<< Graphics'PlotField'
```

Be sure to note the details of this call. Note the back quotes about the package to be called.

Once we have called the package, we run the vector field function as any other function. The call is

```
PlotVectorField[{1,x-y},{x,-6,6,.5},{y,-4,4,.5}]
```

This plots the field of $f(x, y) = x - y$ in the window $[-6, 6] \times [-4, 4]$ at half-unit increments in the x and y directions.

To solve a differential equation of the form $y' = f(x, y)$, we use the general form

```
NDSolve[{y'[x]==f(x,y[x]),y[xo]==yo},y[x],{z,lft,rt}].
```

Note carefully the use of "==" for equations as opposed to "=" for assignments. Here is an example to run. Do not use a semicolon because we need to see the output.

```
sol = NDSolve[{y'[x]==x-y,y[0]==1},y[x],{x,-6,6}]
```

The output, stored in `sol`, is

```
{{y[x] -> InterpolatingFunction[{-6,6},<>][x]}}
```

We need to know a little about Mathematica's substitution rules to understand the use of this output. Mathematica allows for the substitution of one expression in another by the construct `exp1/. exp2 -> sub`. Here you must understand that `exp1` contains `exp2` as a subexpression. Then the construct says that `sub` is to be substituted for the occurrences of `exp2` in `exp1`. Try this:

```
a*x+a /. a->2
```

Expressions of the form `a -> 2` are called substitution rules.

Now we can plot the solution to the differential equation with the call

```
Plot[y[x]/.sol,{x,-6,6}]
```

Mathematica seems to ignore the fact that the substitution rule is two sets deep in `sol`.

Finally, it would be nice to put this all together in a simple routine. To do this, we need to display the graphics together in the same image; we use `Show[]`. Execute

```
<< Graphics'PlotField'
F = PlotVectorField[{1,x-y},{x,-6,6,.5},{y,-4,4,.5},
DisplayFunction->Identity]
sol = NDSolve[{y'[x]==x-y,y[0]==1},y[x],{x,-6,6}];
P = Plot[y[x]/.sol,{x,-6,6},DisplayFunction->Identity]
Show[F,P,PlotRange->{{-6,6},{-4,4}},Axes->True,
DisplayFunction->$DisplayFunction]
```

The function `Show[]` is the graphics equivalent of a print command.
```
Show[]
```
can take most of the options that `Plot[]` can. One of these options is
```
DisplayFunction->Identity
```
which suppresses the graphics output. In `Show[]` we use
```
DisplayFunction->$DisplayFunction
```
to restore the output. The option `Axes->True` tells `Show[]` to display axes.

As an exercise, you should modify the preceding code to handle a second, and perhaps a third, initial condition, and it would also be a help if the window dimensions were set at the beginning of the notebook.

D.2.2 Maple

To create a Field&Solution graphic for the equation $y' = f(x, y)$, we need to do three things: plot the field of $f(x, y)$, solve the equation in a numerical sense and plot it, and then display the two graphics together.

The field drawing function is a part of the "plots" package, so we must import the package at the start of the Maple session, or at least before it is used. This is done using the `with` call. Type the following into a fresh Maple worksheet.

```
> with(plots);
```

Note that if you use ";" instead of ":" you will get a listing of the functions in the plots package. Among these we find `fieldplot()`, which is the one that we want. This function plots vector fields of the form

$$\vec{F}(x, y) = g_1(x, y)\vec{i} + g_2(x, y)\vec{j}.$$

To apply this to equations of the form

$$y' = f(x, y),$$

we simply set $g_1(x, y) = 1$ and plot

$$\vec{F}(x, y) = \vec{i} + f(x, y)\vec{j}.$$

The vectors of such a field have the correct slopes to form a slope field of $f(x, y)$.
A typical call is

```
> fieldplot([1,x-y],x=-6..6,y=-4..4,grid=[10,10]);
```

The `grid` option allows control over the fineness of the field drawn. Experiment to see the effect.

To solve the equation, we need Maple's differentiation function. There are actually two, but we will only use one here. To differentiate an expression `f(x)`, we make the call `diff(f(x),x)`. Try the following:

```
> f:=x->x^3-7*x;
 diff(f(x),x);
```

Now try the following call:

```
> sol:=dsolve({diff(y(x),x)=(x-y(x))^4,y(0)=0},
y(x),type=numeric);
```

Note that the output is a Maple procedure called `sol`. We can use this directly in the function `odeplot()` to plot our numerical solution. Try

```
> odeplot(sol,[x,y(x)],-1..1);
```

We now need to display these two plots together. Type the following:

```
> p1:=fieldplot([1,x-y],x=-6..6,y=-4..4,grid=[10,10]):
  sol:=dsolve({diff(y(x),x)=(x-y(x))^4,y(0)=0},y(x),
  type=numeric):
  p2:=odeplot(sol,[x,y(x)],-6..6):
  display([p1,p2],view=[-6..6,-4..4],scaling=CONSTRAINED);
```

The `scaling` option ensures that the x and y axes are scaled the same.

As an exercise, you should now try to create a Field&Solution worksheet in which you need only enter the equation and the window for the field and solution once. Also, modify the worksheet to handle two initial conditions.

D.2.3 MatLab

We need to do three things to implement a Field&Solution routine for an equation of the form $y' = f(x, y)$: draw the slope field of the equation, draw the solution, and then display these together. As you know, the latter is done with the "hold on" command.

First create a folder called Field&Solution. We need to input the function $f(x, y)$, so we first create an Input.m file in the folder as follows. Open the MatLab editor by clicking File/New/M-file. Now type the function definition

```
function z=Input(x,y);

z=x-y;
```

Save this in the folder Field&Solution with the name Input.m.

We need to create a field plotting function. All we will need to give such a function as arguments is the window dimensions and the fineness lattice factor. Type in and save the following. Be sure to note the ellipsis in the long plot function. This is needed if you wrap text.

```
function  Field(win,n);

 hold on;
 axis([win(1),win(2),win(3),win(4)]);
 plot([win(1),win(2)],[0,0],'k')
 plot([0,0],[win(3),win(4)],'k')
 if n >0
 for i=win(1):1/n:win(2)
 for j=win(3):1/n:win(4)
 plot([i,i+(1/(2*n*sqrt(1+(Input(i,j))^2)))],/...
 [j,j+(Input(i,j)(2*n*sqrt(1+(Input(i,j))^2)))],'k')
 end
 end
 end
```

The window dimensions win must be entered as a row vector, say [-6,6,-4,4]. We make several additional comments. First, the hold on ensures that all plots are drawn in the same window. Second, the axis command sets the window dimensions. The two plots that follow draw the axes in the window in black. Third, the if n > 0 is a safety check to see that a proper lattice factor has been entered. Fourth, the two for loops and the plot draw line segments of the correct length and slope at the lattice points determined by n. Note the creation of the i and j lists for this purpose.

To run this function, you must set the path to your folder. Do this by opening Set Path in the file menu. Click browse in the dialog box and find your folder and open it. This sets the current path. Now type

```
>> Field([-6,6,-4,4],2);
```

MatLab has a built-in differential equation solver called ode45. The call for this function takes the form [t,x] = ode45('Input',[a,b],yo). The function $f(x, y)$ defining the differential equation is defined in the file Input.m, hence the first argument. The second argument is the interval of the solution with initial value at a. The initial value is yo. We will deal with solutions to the left in a moment. The function returns a list of two lists t and x, which form the coordinates of points of the approximation to the solution. Try the following commands.

```
>> hold on;
>> Field([-6,6,-4,4],2);
>> [t,x] = ode45('Input',[0,6],2);
>> plot(t,x);
```

To get a plot to the left, just use
```
    [t,x] = ode45('Input',[0,-6],2);.
```
Now try combining both to get a plot to the left and right.

To plot multiple solutions, just add additional groups of the form

```
>> [t,x] = ode45('Input',[0,6],yo);
>> plot(t,x,c);
>> [t,x] = ode45('Input',[0,-6],yo);
>> plot(t,x,c);
```

The "c" is to be replaced with the desired color.

D.3 ERGRAPHICAL

This package allows Euler's method and the Runge–Kutta method to be compared to each other and to what may be considered a good approximation to the solution.

D.3.1 Mathematica

For this package we will construct our own field-drawing routine. The idea is simple. At each lattice point use $f(x, y)$ to compute the slope of the field segment and then draw a short line of that slope. To do this, we shall need three new functions from Mathematica: Do[], ListPlot[], and Table[]. Do[] is Mathematica's "do loop," and it allows multiple loops within one call of the function. ListPlot[] plots a list of points, and, if an option is applied, it will draw line segments between the points in the order of the list. In our case this will consist of two points to be joined. Finally, Table[] is a function used to construct arrays.

Here is the form of an array construction using Table[]. Type the following in a new notebook and run it.

```
T = Table[P[i,j],{i,1,5},{j,1,7}]
T[[1,2]]
T[[3,6]]
```

It should be clear how entries in the table are accessed. We are now ready to examine the code that creates the Graphics object that is the field. Type the following into a fresh notebook.

```
lft = -6;
rt = 6;
dn = -4;
up = 4;
n = 2;
a = 0;
b = 4;
yo = 1;
h = 0.1;

f[x_,y_] = x-y;
```

```
Do[p[i,j]=ListPlot[{{i,j},{i+(1
/(2n*Sqrt[0.01 + 1 + (f[i,j])^2]))
,j+(f[i,j]/(2n*Sqrt[0.01+1+(f[i,j])^2]))}},
PlotJoined->True, DisplayFunction -> Identity],
{i,lft,rt,1/n},{j,dn,up,1/n}];

F=Table[p[i,j],{i,lft,rt,1/n},{j,dn,up,1/n}];
```

The entries from `lft` to `h` provide variables for the window dimensions, the lattice spacing, the left and right range of the interval of solution, the initial value, and the step size. We give these variable names so that we need enter them only once in our program. Of course, `f[x_,y_] = x-y` is the function definition. Next comes the heart of the matter, the "do loop."

The structure of a do loop is `Do[S[i,j],{i,a,b,r},{j,c,d,s}]`, where `S[i,j]` is a Mathematica function depending on `i` and `j`. These functions are then executed as `i` and `j` increment over the ranges shown with steps of `r` and `s`, respectively. We will not worry about the order in which this is done. The reader is referred to the Mathematica handbook for more details on the "do loop." In the case we have before us, the function to be executed at each iteration is `ListPlot[]`, which creates a field line segment at (i, j) and assigns it to the variable `p[i,j]`.

The function `Show[]` takes sets of graphics elements as an argument, and so we must form our line segments into a set. This is the task of `Table[]`.

We use `Show[]` to display the field. The call is

```
Show[F,DisplayFunction->$DisplayFunction,
PlotRange->{{lft,rt},{dn,up}},
AspectRatio->Automatic,Frame->True,AxesLabel->{x,y}]
```

Next we use Mathematica's `NDSolve[]` to draw what we may take as the graph of the true solution. This you can copy from your Field&Solution notebook. The only changes to make are to insert `f[x_,y_]` for the function and `lft` and `rt` for the left/right range for x.

```
sol = NDSolve[{y'[x]==f[x,y],y[a]==yo},y[x], {x,left,rt}];
P1=Plot[y[x]/.sol,{x,lft,rt},
 DisplayFunction->Identity];
```

Next comes the code for Euler's method.

```
m=(b-a)/h;
x[0]=a;
y[0]=yo;
Do[x[i]=x[0]+i*h;
y[i+1]=y[i]+h*f[x[i],y[i]],{i,0,m}];
P2=ListPlot[Table[{x[i],y[i]},{i,0,m}],
PlotJoined->True,DisplayFunction -> Identity,
PlotStyle -> {Hue[.7]}];
```

In this case, we create a set of points using `Table[]`. These points are then joined in order by `ListPlot[]`. This creates a blue polygonal curve, which is Euler's approximation.

Finally, we leave the creation of the Runge–Kutta algorithm to the reader. If you follow the lead of the Euler algorithm, this should not present a difficulty. The output should be a `ListPlot[]` named P3.

The plots can be displayed with

```
Show[{F,P1,P2,P3},DisplayFunction->$DisplayFunction,
PlotRange->{{lft,rt},{dn,up}},
AspectRatio->Automatic,Frame->True,AxesLabel->{x,y}]
```

Plots that you do not want can be omitted from the list of plots to be shown.

D.3.2 Maple

The ERGaphical package introduces the use of Maple's `Table()` and `array` procedures.

We begin with assignments to variables that define the function, the window dimensions, the interval of solution, the initial value, the field lattice factor, and the step size.

```
f := (x,y)->x-y:
lft := -6:
rt := 6:
dn := -4:
up := 4:
a := 0:
b := 2:
yo := 1:
n := 2:
h := 0.1:
```

The following code draws the field.

```
>with(plots):
 A:=table():
 for i from lft by 1/n to 1.2*rt do
 for j from dn by 1/n to 1.2*up do
 A[i,j]:=[[i,j],[i+(1/(2*n*sqrt(1+(f(i,j))^2))),
 j+(f(i,j)/(2*n*sqrt(1+(f(i,j))^2)))]]:
 od:
 od:
 L:=convert(A,set):
 i:='i':
 j:='j':
 F:=plot(L,lft..rt,dn..up,color=black):
```

The assignment `A:=table()` in the code creates a table data type with the name `A`. The table is then filled with pairs of points that represent the line segments of the field. Here two nested "for" loops are employed. Note the syntax for beginning and ending the loops. The table is then converted to a set of pairs of points, which the `plot()` function then joins with black line segments and saves as a graphics structure called `F`. The assignments `i:='i':` and `j:='j':` clear these variables. This is just precautionary to avoid possible clashes in later use of these variables.

Next we add the code that draws what we may consider to be a good approximation of the solution.

```
> sol:=dsolve({diff(z(x),x)=f(x,z(x)),z(a)=yo},
z(x), numeric):
 P1:=odeplot(sol,[x,z(x)],a..b,color=black):
```

To this is added the Euler and Runge–Kutta methods. Here is the code implementing Euler's method. We leave the implementation of the Runge–Kutta method to the reader.

```
> m:=round((b-a)/h):
x:=array(0..m+1):
y:=array(0..m+1):
x[0]:=a:
y[0]:=yo:
E:=[[x[0],y[0]]]:
for i  from 1 to m do
x[i]:=a+i*h:
y[i]:=y[i-1]+h*f(x[i-1],y[i-1]):
E:=[op(E),[x[i],y[i]]]:
od:
P2:=plot(E,lft..rt,dn..up,color=blue):
```

Note the construction of the arrays x and y. These are sequences indexed from 0 to m+1. Note the way in which a member of the sequence is accessed. Thus x[i] is the value corresponding to i. The function op(E) returns the set of elements or operands in E. Thus the line E:=[op(E),[x[i],y[i]]]: adjoins the next point to E.

We display the graphics that we have created by the call

```
display(F,P1,P2);
```

We can add the graphic P3 generated by the Runge–Kutta algorithm to the display or remove others as desired.

D.3.3 MatLab

MatLab requires very little to implement ERGraphical. Create a new folder and name it ERGraphical. Copy into this folder the Input.m and Field.m files. All we now need to create are the Euler.m and Runge.m files defining these algorithms. Here is the Euler routine. The Runge–Kutta routine is left to the reader.

```
function Euler(a,b,yo,h);
m = floor((b-a)/h);
tout(1)=a;
yout(1)=yo;
for i=1:1:m
  tout(i+1)=a+i*h;
  yout(i+1)=yout(i)+h*Input(tout(i),yout(i));
end
plot(tout,yout,'b');
```

Note the direct construction of the sequences `tout` and `yout`. These define the Euler approximation points.

Remember to use `hold on` to perform all graphing in the same frame. A typical run of this package might be

```
>> hold on;
>> Field([-6,6,-4,4],2);
>> [t,x] = ode45('Input',[0,6],2);
>> plot(t,x);
>> Euler(0,6,2,0.5);
```

D.4 ERNUMERICAL

The goal of ERNumerical is to apply the Euler and Runge–Kutta methods to the equation $y' = f(x, y)$ and print out the results. The algorithms are the same as for ERGraphical. The only difference is that we need to learn how to print out the results. Consequently, the completion of the task is left to the reader.

D.4.1 Mathematica

The Mathematica print function can print a quoted string or numerical values or both. This allows us to format printed output very easily. Try the following:

```
x = 5;
 Print["The value of x  =   ",x];
```

Now try

```
Clear[x];
 Do[x[i]=i,{i,1,5}];
 Do[Print["x[i] = ",x[i]],{i,1,5}];
```

Note the `Clear[x]` command. Mathematica remembers the values of each variable and so, unless we clear it, using x in `x[i]` will cause a conflict.

Now that you know how the `Print[]` command works you should have no trouble completing a notebook to print out the data from the Euler and Runge-Kutta methods.

D.4.2 Maple

The Maple print function `lprint()` prints back quoted expressions and numerical data on a line. Try

```
> x := 5:
 lprint('The value of x = ',x);
```

Now try

```
> for i from 1 to 5 do
 x[i] := i:
 od:
 for i from 1 to 5 do
 lprint('x[',i,'] = ',x[i]);
 od;
```

This should be enough for you to complete the task of writing a worksheet to print out the results of applying the Euler and Runge–Kutta algorithms.

D.4.3 MatLab

The only difference between ERNumerical and ERGraphical is that data are output numerically rather than graphically. So to implement the ERNumerical package in MatLab we must learn how to print out data. We shall use a somewhat crude but simple and effective way of doing this.

Open MatLab and, at the prompt, type in a list as shown and press return.

```
>> x = [1,2,3]
```

Now run

```
>> x'
```

Note that `x'` is the transpose of x and it prints out as a column. This is the key to printing output for ERNumerical. As an example of multiple columns, try

```
>> x = [1,2,3]; y = [4,5,6];
>> x_____y = [x',y']
```

Crude but effective.

Now write an M-file to define a function `ERNum(a,b,yo,h)`. This file should collect the subdivision points and values for the Euler and Runge–Kutta methods in three lists, say, `tout`, `xout`, and `yout`. Then your output line might read `t_____Euler_____Runge = [tout',xout',yout']`.

D.5 2X2SYSTEM

The package 2x2System must draw the field and orbits of a 2x2 system of first-order equations and be able to draw the component solutions. In Mathematica and Maple, we will only employ built-in functions to draw the fields; otherwise, we will construct our own routines.

D.5.1 Mathematica

Open a new notebook and enter all the input data that you will need, as follows:

```
f[t_,x_,y_] = y;
g[t_,x_,y_] = -x;
lft = -6;
rt = 6;
dn = -4;
up = 4;
a = 0;
b = 7;
xo = 0;
yo = 3;
h = 0.1;
```

Now call the PlotField graphics package and the field plot function in a separate input cell by

```
<< Graphics'PlotField';
F = PlotVectorField[{f[0,x,y],g[0,x,y]},
{x,-lft,rt,.5},{y,dn,up,.5}];
```

This must be in a separate cell, because it can only be run if the field is autonomous. Also note that we enter 0 for t in the field functions because these functions must not contain t as a variable in the call to PlotVectorField.

The following code creates the plot of the Euler data. Note the use of Table[] to get a set of points to be plotted by ListPlot[] and joined.

```
t[0] = a;
x[0] = xo;
y[0] = yo;
n=(b-a)/h;
Do[t[i]=a+i*h;
x[i+1]=x[i]+h*f[t[i],x[i],y[i]];
y[i+1]=y[i]+h*g[t[i],x[i],y[i]],{i,0,n-1}]
T1=Table[{x[i],y[i]},{i,0,n-1}];
```

```
P1=ListPlot[T1,PlotRange->{{lft,rt},{dn,up}},
PlotJoined->True,
DisplayFunction->Identity];
```

The code that creates the Runge–Kutta plot P2 is left to you. You should plot the output in red. Be very careful to introduce new notation for the variables in the Runge–Kutta algorithm. You do not want to overwrite data that you created in the Euler algorithm. Try rx[i], and so on.

We can now display our plots with

```
Show[{F,P1,P2},DisplayFunction->$DisplayFunction,
Axes->True];
```

The component functions can be plotted easily by creating tables of points and plotting them as we have just done. For example, the plot of $x(t)$ is achieved by

```
T2=Table[{t[i],rx[i]},{i,0,n-1}];
P3=ListPlot[T2,PlotRange->{{lft,rt},{dn,up}},PlotJoined->True,
DisplayFunction->Identity];
Show[{P3},DisplayFunction->$DisplayFunction,
Axes->True];
```

The plot of $y(t)$ is almost identical.

D.5.2 Maple

Open a new worksheet and enter all the input data tha you will need as follows:

```
> f:=(t,x,y)-> y:
g:=(t,x,y)-> -x:
lft := -6:
rt := 6:
dn := -4:
up := 4:
a := 0:
b := 7:
xo := 0:
yo := 3:
h := 0.1:
```

In the next input cell, call the plots package and filedplot(), as we did in Field&Solution.

```
>with(plots):
 F:=fieldplot([f(0,x,y),g(0,x,y)],x=lft..rt,y=dn..up,
 grid=[10,10]);
```

Note that t is set to 0 in the field functions because `fieldplot()` should be called only on autonomous systems, so this draws the field at $t = 0$.

The code that follows implements the Euler method. Notice the declaration of the arrays. Recall that `E:=[op(E),[x[i],y[i]]]` `op(E)` extracts the entries in E as a list and then the next term in the list can be adjoined to form the new list. Remember that `plot()` plots the points in a list and joins them.

```
> m:=round((b-a)/h):
 t:=array(0..m+1):
 x:=array(0..m+1):
 y:=array(0..m+1):
 t[0]:=a:
 x[0]:=xo:
 y[0]:=yo:
 E:=[[x[0],y[0]]]:
 for i  from 1 to m do
 t[i]:=a+i*h:
 x[i]:=x[i-1]+h*f(t[i-1],x[i-1],y[i-1]):
 y[i]:=y[i-1]+h*g(t[i-1],x[i-1],y[i-1]):
 E:=[op(E),[x[i],y[i]]]:
 od:
 P1:=plot(E,lft..rt,dn..up,color=blue):
```

The two plots may be displayed in the usual way.

We leave the Runge–Kutta algorithm to you. You should use new notation, such as `rx[i]` and `ry[i]` in Runge–Kutta to avoid possible conflicts with the data in Euler. The `t[i]` can remain the same.

The Runge–Kutta component solutions can be plotted easily. Here is the $x(t)$ component.

```
> E:=[[t[0],rx[0]]]:
 for i  from 1 to m do
 E:=[op(E),[t[i],rx[i]]]:
 od:
 P3:=plot(E,lft..rt,dn..up,color=blue):
```

The plot of $y(t)$ is left to you.

D.5.3 MatLab

MatLab does not have a resident field-drawing routine, so we shall have to make our own. The procedure is no different in principle from the method we used in Field&Solution. All we need to do is add arrowheads to the direction line segments. If you look at the following Field.m M-file, you will quickly see what is going on. But first we must make a two-function Input.m file.

```
function fun=Input(t,x,y);

fun(1)=t*y;
fun(2)=-x+t;
```

Note carefully how MatLab defines a pair of functions under the single call to Input().

Here is the field file.

```
function  Field(win,n);

hold on;
axis([win(1),win(2),win(3),win(4)]);
plot([win(1),win(2)],[0,0],'k')
plot([0,0],[win(3),win(4)],'k')
if n >0
for i=win(1):1/n:win(2)
for j=win(3):1/n:win(4)
fun=Input(0,i,j);
 plot([i,i+fun(1)/...
        (1.8*n*sqrt(0.01 + (fun(1))^2 + ...
        (fun(2))^2)),i+fun(1)/...
        (1.8*n*sqrt(0.01 + (fun(1))^2 + ...
        (fun(2))^2))+(fun(2)-1.7*fun(1))/...
        (7*n*sqrt(0.01+(fun(1))^2+ ...
        (fun(2))^2)),i+fun(1)/...
        (1.8*n*sqrt(0.01 + (fun(1))^2 + ...
        (fun(2))^2)),i+fun(1)/...
        (1.8*n*sqrt(0.01 + (fun(1))^2 + ...
        (fun(2))^2))+(-fun(2)-1.7*fun(1))/...
        (7*n*sqrt(0.01+(fun(1))^2+(fun(2))^2))],...
      [j,j+fun(2)/(1.8*n*sqrt(0.01+(fun(1))^2+ ...
        (fun(2))^2)),j+fun(2)/...
        (1.8*n*sqrt(0.01+(fun(1))^2+ ...
        (fun(2))^2))+(-fun(1)-1.7*fun(2))/...
        (7*n*sqrt(0.01 + (fun(1))^2 + ...
        (fun(2))^2)),j+fun(2)/...
```

```
            (1.8*n*sqrt(0.01+(fun(1))^2+...
            (fun(2))^2)),j+fun(2)/...
            (1.8*n*sqrt(0.01+(fun(1))^2+(fun(2))^2))+ ...
            (fun(1)-1.7*fun(2))/...
           (7*n*sqrt(0.01 + (fun(1))^2 + (fun(2))^2))],'k')


    end
    end
    end
```

Here is the M-file for the Euler function.

```
function Euler(a,b,xo,yo,h);
m = floor((b-a)/h);
tout(1)=a;
xout(1)=xo;
yout(1)=yo;
for i=1:1:m
  fun=Input(tout(i),xout(i),yout(i));
  tout(i+1)=a+i*h;
  xout(i+1)=xout(i)+h*fun(1);
  yout(i+1)=yout(i)+h*fun(2);
end
plot(xout,yout,'b');
```

You can easily write your own Runge.m file.

Remember that you can easily force coordinate ranges on your plot by the call axis([lft,rt,dn,up]).

D.6 2X2NUMERICAL

The task here is to write a package that prints out the data from the Runge-Kutta algorithm. You have all the tools that you need for this so the task is left to you.

D.7 FOURIER SERIES

The following packages allow a partial sum of a Fourier series to be compared with its function. The function must be defined over one period on $[0, p]$. In each package the unit step function U is provided. The unit step function is 0 to the left of 0 and 1 to the right. This allows for the definition of a wide array of piecewise continuous functions.

D.7.1 Mathematica

The code is provided here in its entirety, but you should take note of the integration and summation calls.

```
U[x_] = If[x<0,0,1];

(*Enter the desired period*)
 p = 2;
(*Enter the desired function*)
 f[x_] := (U[x-1]-U[x])+ U[x-1]*x;
(*Enter the degree of the partial sum*)
 m = 10;

A[0] =NIntegrate[f[x],{x,0,p},
AccuracyGoal->Automatic]/p;
Do[ A[n]=2*NIntegrate[f[x]*Cos[2*Pi n x/p],{x,0,p},
AccuracyGoal->Automatic]/p;
B[n] = 2*NIntegrate[f[x]*Sin[2*Pi nx/p],
{x,0,p}, AccuracyGoal->Automatic]/p, {n,1,m}]
g[x_] =A[0]+Sum[A[n]*Cos[2 Pi n x/p],{n,1,m}]+
Sum[B[n]*Sin[2 Pi nx/p],
{n,1,m}];
Plot[{f[x],g[x]},{x,0, p},AspectRatio->Automatic]
```

D.7.2 Maple

The package is provided in its entirety. Note the opening procedure definition that defines the unit step function U.

```
>  U:=proc(x)
if x<0 then
RETURN(0):
else
RETURN(1):
fi:
end:

#Enter the desired period.
p:=2:
#Enter the desired function defined on [0,p].
f:=x->x^2;
#Enter the order of the partial sum.
m:=5:
```

```
A:=array(0..m):
B:=array(0..m):
C:=array(1..m):
E:=array(1..m):
A[0]:=evalf(int(f,0..p)/p):
for i from 1 to m do
C[i]:=x->f(x)*cos(2*Pi*i*x/p):
A[i]:=2*evalf(int(C[i],0..p))/p:
E[i]:=x->f(x)*sin(2*Pi*i*x/p):
B[i]:=2*evalf(int(E[i],0..p))/p:
od:
i:='i':
g:=x->A[0]+sum(A[i]*cos(2*Pi*i*x/p),i=1..m)+
sum(B[i]*sin(2*Pi*i*x/p),i=1..m):
plot([f,g],0..p);
```

D.7.3 MatLab

The Fourier Series package requires that we supply the input function defined in the Input.m file. This often entails defining a piecewise continuous function such as a square wave or sawtooth. To this end, the unit step function U(x) is defined to be 0 if x is less than 0 and to be 1 if x is greater than one. You might think that a definition such as

```
function y=U(x);
 if x<0
 y=0;
 else
 y=1;
 end
```

should do the trick, but this will not work. You have to remember that x will be a row vector or list. In that case, MatLab will say "yes" to x<0 only if every entry in the list is less than zero. Surprisingly, < in MatLab is an operator, and the call x<0 actually creates a new list in which the entries are zeros or ones according as the entry in x is greater than or equal to zero or not. The correct way to define U(x) is as follows:

```
function y=U(x)

 y= x>0;
```

Now this can be used in the definition of input functions, but you must remember to use "matrix smart" operations. Here is a simple example in which the input function is defined to be x on [0, 1] and zero elsewhere.

```
function y=Input(x)

y=(U(x)-U(x-1)).*x;
```

The Fourier function performs two tasks. It computes numerically the Fourier coefficients to as high an order as desired, and then it plots the original function and the selected partial sum of the Fourier series in the same frame and for two periods. Clearly, we must tell Fourier what the period is and what the order of the partial sum is to be. The base format is `Fourier(p,m)`, where p is the period and m is the order of the partial sum. `Fourier` does allow a third variable, which is the number of subdivisions to use for the Simpson's rule integration routine that computes the coefficients. We will comment further on this after the program has been listed.

```
function   Fourier(p,m,n);

if nargin <3
n=50;
end
k=2*n;

Ao=Input(0)*cos(0)+Input(p);
for i=1:n
Ao=Ao+4*Input(p*(2*i-1)/k);
end
for i=1:n-1
Ao=Ao+2*Input(p*(2*i)/k);
end
Ao=p*Ao/(3*p*k);

for j=1:m
A(j)=Input(0)*cos(0)+Input(p)*cos(2*pi*j);
for i=1:n
A(j)=A(j)+4*Input(p*(2*i-1)/k)* ...
cos(2*pi*j*(2*i-1)/(k));
end
for i=1:n-1
A(j)=A(j)+2*Input(p*(2*i)/k)*cos(2*pi*j*(2*i)/(k));
end
A(j)=p*A(j)/(3*k); A(j)=2*A(j)/p;
end


for j=1:m
```

```
B(j)=Input(0)*cos(0)+Input(p)*sin(2*pi*j);
for i=1:n
B(j)=B(j)+4*Input(p*(2*i-1)/k)* ...
sin(2*pi*j*(2*i-1)/(k));
end
for i=1:n-1
B(j)=B(j)+2*Input(p*(2*i)/k)*sin(2*pi*j*(2*i)/(k));
end
B(j)=p*B(j)/(3*k);
B(j)=2*B(j)/p;
end

 a=p/300;
 x1=0:a:p;
 x2=p:a:2*p;
 x=0:a:2*p;
 y1=Input(x1);
 y2=Input(x2-p);
 z=Ao;
 for j=1:m
 z=z+A(j)*cos(2*pi*j*x/p)+B(j)*sin(2*pi*j*x/p);
 end
 hold on
 plot(x1,y1,'b')
 plot(x2,y2,'b')
 plot(x,z,'r')
 hold off
```

The default number of subdivisions for Simpson's rule is k=2*50. By overriding the default you can enter k=2*n. Notice that this is even, as required by this method. If you want partial sums of order greater than 10, you will probably want to increase the number of subdivisions, because the higher-order coefficients involve integrands that are oscillating rapidly, so numerical accuracy is at risk.

ANSWERS AND HINTS TO ODD-NUMBERED EXERCISES

CHAPTER 1

1. $y = e^x$, $y' = e^x$, and $y'' = e^x$, so $y'' - 2y' + y = e^x - 2e^x + e^x = 0$.

3. $y = (1 - 2x)^{-1/2}$ and $y' = (1 - 2x)^{-3/2}$, so $y' - y^3 = 0$.

5. $y' = 1/(2y)$ has solution $y = \sqrt{x}$ for $x > 0$.

7. $P' = a(P - P^2)$.

9. $u_1' = e^x - 2e^{2x} = u_2$. Also, $u_2' = e^x - 4e^{2x}$, and $-2u_1 + 3u_2 = -2e^x + 2e^{2x} + 3e^e - 6e^{2x} = e^x - 4e^{2x}$.

11. Set $u_1 = y$, $u_2 = y'$, and $u_3 = y''$. Then

$$u_1' = u_2$$
$$u_2' = u_3$$
$$u_3' = \sin(x)u_1 - u_3.$$

13. Set $u_1 = y$ and $u_2 = y'$. Then

$$u_1' = u_2$$
$$u_2' = (e^x - 3^x u_1 + 2xu_2)/3.$$

15. Set $u_1 = y$, $u_2 = y'$, $u_3 = y''$, and $u_4 = y^{(3)}$. Then

$$u_1' = u_2$$
$$u_2' = u_3$$
$$u_3' = u_4$$
$$u_4' = e^{-x}[\cos(x) + x + u_1 + 2u_3].$$

17. If y satisfies the second-order equation and $u_1 = y$ and $u_2 = y'$, then $\{u_1, u_2\}$ satisfies the system. Conversely,

if $\{u_1, u_2\}$ satisfies the system, then $y = u_1$ satisfies the second-order equation.

19. a. and C. b. and B. c. and A.

CHAPTER 2

Section 2.1, p. 15

1. $f(x, y) = x - y^2$ and $\partial f/\partial y = -2y$ are continuous, so solutions cannot touch without being identical.

3. No! $f(x, y) = x^3 - y$ and $\partial f/\partial y = 3x^2 - 1$ are continuous in the window, so if solutions merge, they must be identical.

5. No. The solution has a vertical asymptote at $x = 1$.

7. The solution does not appear to be defined for all x in $[-6, 6]$. The solution is asymptotic to the negative x-axis, and there appears to be an asymptote to the right of the y-axis between 2 and 3.

9. No, f and $\partial f/\partial y$ are continuous, so, by Theorem 2.1.2, solutions cannot touch.

11. The graph is U-shaped, and there appear to be asymptotes at about $x = \pm 1.5$.

13. Draw curves through the initial conditions passing through the field tangentially.

15. A solution to the equation $y' = x + y$ is a function $\phi(x)$ defined on an interval (a, b) such that $\phi'(x) = x + \phi(x)$ is an identity on (a, b). A solution passing through an initial condition (x_0, y_0) is said to be a unique solution passing through that point if there is no other solution through the

437

initial point that is different from the first solution on some common interval of definition of the two solutions.

17. There are multiple solutions through the same point, so, since f is continuous, $\partial f/\partial y$ must be discontinuous.

19. Since $f(x, y)$ is continuous and the solutions cross, $\partial f/\partial y$ must be discontinuous at points in the window.

21. There is no constant solution since $y' > 0$. All solutions are strictly increasing.

23. If $f(x, -y) = -f(x, y)$, the field is symmetric with respect to the x-axis. The reflection of a solution across the x-axis is again a solution.

25. Suppose that $\phi(x)$ is a solution. Set $\psi(x) = -\phi(x)$. Then

$$\psi'(x) = -\phi'(x) = -f(x, \phi(x))$$
$$= f(x, -\phi(x)) = f(x, \psi(x)).$$

So $\psi(x)$ is also a solution.

Section 2.2, p. 21

1. *Euler*: $x_1 = 0.5$, $y_1 = 2$. $x_2 = 1$, $y_2 = 1.90$. *Runge–Kutta*: $x_1 = 0.5$, $k_1 = 0$, $k_2 = -0.1$, $k_3 = -0.988$, $k_4 = -0.195$, $y_1 = 1.951$. $x_2 = 1$, $k_1 = -0.195$, $k_2 = -0.285$, $k_3 = -0.282$, $k_4 = -0.362$, $y_2 = 1.810$.

3. *Euler*: $k_1 = 3$, $x_1 = 0.25$, $y_1 = 3.75$, $k_1 = 4.$, $x_2 = 0.5$, $y_2 = 4.75$. *Runge–Kutta*: $k_1 = 3$, $k_2 = 3.5$, $k_3 = 3.5625$, $k_4 = 4.14062$, $x_1 = 0.25$, $y_1 = 3.88607$, $k_1 = 4.13607$, $k_2 = 4.77808$, $k_3 = 4.85833$, $k_4 = 5.60065$, $x_2 = 0.5$, $y_2 = 5.0948$.

5. *Euler*: $x_1 = 1.1$, $y_1 = 2.6$. *Runge–Kutta*: $x_1 = 1.1$, $k_1 = 6$, $k_2 = 7.705$, $k_3 = 8.194$, $k_4 = 11.050$, $y_1 = 2.814$.

7. As h gets smaller the Runge–Kutta method converges more rapidly

9. Try $f(x, y) = x^2/3$. Use a lattice factor of 1, interval of $[-2, 6]$, and $y_0 = -3$. You will not "hit" every field line segment, but it gives a good indication.

11. Try $f(x, y) = 1$. Then $y' = 1$. In one step there is no error in either method. In Euler, $y_{i+1} = y_i + h$, which is the new value on the solution $y = x + c$. In Runge–Kutta, $k_1 = k_2 = k_3 = k_4 = 1$, and so $y_{i+1} = y_i + h(6)/6 = y_i + h$.

13. *Runge–Kutta*: 1.6487210, 1.6487212, the rest are the same. The value 1.6487212 is probably accurate because of the stability upon refinement of the step size.

15. *Runge–Kutta*: 0.63212160, 0.63212062, 0.63212056, 0.63212055. We should be confident in 0.632121 because this corrected value is stable.

17. There is an asymptote at $x = 2$. The values at 1 grow, but from the data alone it is not clear what the value of the

solution is. Near asymptotes, numerical data are suspect.

19. **(c)** The first case winds up following the x-axis. The second crosses the axis.

(d) The explanation is that there are multiple solutions through points on the x-axis. In the second case, the second point in the method is across the x-axis, and so the approximation follows the solution above the x-axis rather than the x-axis as in the former case.

(e) Yes. Even good computers have round-off error, and so, depending on the round-off, different results could be obtained.

21. The numerical data goes to ∞ before getting to 5. Numerical methods are not to be used with blind faith in the data that they put out. Numerical methods can produce erroneous data, even for relatively simple equations.

Section 2.3.1, p. 29

1. $y = e^x$. No, no solutions are lost because the general solution is $y = Ae^x$ and $y \equiv 0$ is included.

3. $y = \tan(x^2/2)$ is the solution.

5. $y = -1/(x^3 - (1/4))$. The solution is defined on $x < (1/4)^{1/3}$. Yes, $y \equiv 0$.

7. $y = \sin^{-1}(x^2/2)$.

9. $y = \dfrac{2e^{x^2/2}}{1 - 2e^{x^2/2}}$.

11. $y^4 + y^2 - x^2 = 1$. The solution is the lower half of the "hyperbola."

13. $\sin(y) + y^2 - \sin(x) - x^2 = \pi^2$. The solution is the lower portion of the curve.

15. $\sin(3y)/3 + \cos(2x)/2 = 1/2$. The solution is the lower part of the oval at the origin.

17. The equation is $2\ln|y| - y = x - 2\ln|x| + c$. This reduces to $e^{-(x+y)}x^2y^2 = A$. In the first quadrant the curve is closed. The solution is that part of the curve in the first quadrant passing through $(2, 1)$ that is a function.

19. $y = x^3$. No, $\partial f/\partial y$ is not continuous.

21. $y = x \ln(x) + x$.

23. All solutions with positive initial conditions different from the carrying capacity increase or decrease to the carrying capacity.

25. Yes. Positive populations should not become negative, and populations should not go to infinity as $t \to \infty$.

27. **(a)** All solutions with positive initial conditions are asymptotic to the line $y = b$. Thus all populations tend to this limiting population.

(b) Try the equation $y' = y(5 + \sin(t) - y)$, for example. Here t is the independent variable representing time.

Section 2.3.3, p. 35

1. $y = -\frac{1}{4} + \frac{x}{2} + 2.75e^{-2x-2}$.

3. $y = 3e^{-x^2}$.

5. $y = 3x^3 e^{-x} + Cx^2 e^{-x}$.

7. $y = e^x/x + C/x$.

9. $y = \sqrt{1 + 3e^{-2x}}$.

11. $y = \left[e^{2x^2/3} \int_0^x -\frac{2}{3} e^{-2t^2/3}, dt + e^{2x^2/3} \right]^{-3/2}$.

13. Approximately 0.03 second.

15. The equation is $Ly' + Ry = V_0$. The solution is $y = \frac{V_0}{R} + Ke^{-Rt/L}$.

17. $A(t) = 3(200 + t) - \frac{580 \times 200^2}{(200+t)^2}$.

19. $v(t) = \sqrt{32} \frac{e^{2\sqrt{32}t} - 1}{e^{2\sqrt{32}t} + 1}$.
    The terminal velocity is $\sqrt{32}$ ft/sec.

21. $A = A_0 e^{rt/100}$. Time is $t = 100 \ln(2)/r$, and the rate is approximately 6.9%.

23. The number of poachers is not likely to be a constant. The birth rate of the elephants is likely to be affected by the poachers, the weather, and other factors.

25. Neglecting friction, the boat will accelerate from rest until it approaches the velocity of the wind W asymptotically. This is much like an object warming up in an oven. Thus a provisional model could be given by $dV/dt = a(W - V)$. This is the same as assuming that the force on the boat due to the wind is proportional to the difference between the wind and boat speeds. Thus we could write $mdV/dt = a(W - V)$. To include friction on the skates, we could write $mdV/dt = a(W - V) - cV$.

Section 2.3.4, p. 39

1. Exact. $(x - y)^2 = 4$. The solution is $y = x + 2$.

3. Not exact.

5. Exact. $(x^2 + y^2)^2 - 3x^2 y + y^3 = 0$. This is a three-petal rose. The solution extends from just to the right of $(\sqrt{3}/2, 1/2)$ to halfway down the left half of the bottom petal.

7. Exact. $x^2 y - xy + y^3 = 1$. The solution is the whole curve.

9. Exact. The first step is $f(x, y) = xy^4 - x^3 y + g(y)$. The equation is $xy^4 - x^3 y + 5y^2 = 5$. The "middle curve."

11. $y = c/x$.

13. In trying to find $g(y)$, terms involving x do not drop out.

15. *Solution*: $y' = -1/f(x, y)$.

17. Ellipses $x^2 + y^2/2 = c$ and parabolas $y^2 = kx$.

19. We solve $y' = -1/y$. The trajectories are $y^2 = -2x + c$.

21. The function whose gradient is the field is $f(x, y) = $

$(1 + x^4 + y^2)/10$. The field is orthogonal to the level curves of this function. So we need to find the orthogonal trajectories to these level curves. We must solve $y' = -10/(1 + x^4 + y^2)$. This would seem to have no easy analytic solution, so we use Field&Solution to view the field and a few solution curves. The general shape of the flow is a reversed integral sign!

Section 2.4, p. 43

1. Solutions decrease on $(-\infty, -3)$, increase on $(-3, 0)$, decrease on $(0, 2)$, and increase on $(2, \infty)$. So 2 and -3 are unstable, and 0 is stable.

3. Solutions increase on $(0, \pi)$, decrease on $(\pi, 2\pi)$, increase on $(2\pi, 3\pi)$, and so on. The stable critical points are the odd multiples of π.

5. Solutions increase on $(-\infty, -2)$, decrease on $(-2, 1)$, and increase on $(1, \infty)$, so -2 is stable and 1 is unstable.

7. The only critical point is 1, and it is unstable.

9. Below 100 solutions go to zero. Above 100 solutions go to 1000.

11. $P' = (P - a)^2(P - b)$ is one choice.

13. $y' = (x^2 + 1)y(y - 1)$ will work.

15. The arrows point in to a stable point, and at least one arrow points out for an unstable point.

17. The critical points are at odd multiples of $\pi/2$. $\pi/2$ is stable, $3\pi/2$ is unstable, and so on.

Section 2.5, p. 46

1. $y = -x - 1 + Ce^x$. $|\phi_1(x) - \phi_2(x)| = e^x|y_1 - y_2|$. Yes, if $y_0 = -1$ then $C = 0$ and $y = -x - 1$. Any other initial condition gives a solution containing e^x.

3. This equation is linear.

5. (a) $y = Ae^{x^2}$.

   (c) $|\phi_1(x) - \phi_2(x)| = e^{x^2}|y_1 - y_2|$.

   (d) On $[-1, 1] \times [-1, 1]$, $e^{x^2} = e^{x \cdot x} \le e^{1 \cdot |x|}$, so $L = 1$ will do.

7. With a bit of experimentation you can get the y-coordinates as close as four or five decimal places.

CHAPTER 3

Section 3.1, p. 54

1. Every solution has the form $x = c_1 e^{2t}$ and $y = c_2 e^t$. For each initial point there is only one choice of c_1 and c_2, so there exists only one solution through each initial point. This is consistent with the conclusions of the theorem.

3. The solution is $x = -1/(e^t - 2)$ and $y = e^t$. This is not defined for all t. Yes, some solutions are defined for all t. Theorem 3.1.1 guarantees a unique solution through each point, but does not guarantee that it will be defined for all t. The derivation of this solution shows that it is the only solution through the initial point, as the theorem predicts.

5. The solution is $x = \frac{4}{e}e^{e^t} - 3$ and $y = 3e^t$.

7. Yes! Since the system is not assumed to be autonomous, it is perfectly possible for the orbit of a solution to return to a point going in a different direction, because the field vector at that point may have changed direction.

9. One solution is $x = e^t$ and $y = (\frac{3}{5}e^t - \frac{3}{5})^{5/3}$. Another solution is $x = e^t$ and $y \equiv 0$. No, one partial derivative is not continuous.

11. At $(0, 0)$ the field vector $\vec{F}(x, y) = f(x, y)\vec{\imath} + g(x, y)\vec{\jmath}$ is zero. So $x(t) \equiv 0$ and $y(t) \equiv 0$ is the unique solution through $(0, 0)$.

13. The three functions and their partials with respect to the three dependent variables must be continuous in a block of the form $[a, b] \times [c_1, d_1] \times [c_2, d_2] \times [c_3, d_3]$.

15. The difference is that the graph of a solution is a curve in (t, x, y) coordinate space, and the corresponding orbit is the projection of this into the xy plane. If the system is written in the vector form $\vec{R}'(t) = \vec{F}(\vec{R})$, then the orbit of the solution $\vec{R}(t)$ is the range of $\vec{R}(t)$.

17. The vectors drawn by 2 × 2System are all of the same length because the field has been normalized, but the vectors drawn by hand are not all of the same length and have the actual length determined by the field. Directions are unchanged.

19. Same as Exercise 17.

Section 3.2, p. 58

1. Use the software provided.

3. Use the software provided.

5. When the orbit returns to the crossing point, the field vector has changed direction, thus allowing crossing at an angle. The solution is a kind of helix winding about the t-axis.

7. No! The orbit crosses at an angle.

9. The solutions appear to all be periodic with the same period of approximately 6.3.

11. The data fit the formula $2\pi/\sqrt{a}$.

13. $y(6) = 2$, because the solution returns to a point and the system is autonomous, so the solution is periodic.

15. With initial condition $(1, 0)$ the period is approxi-

mately 3.4. With an initial condition of $(2, 0)$ the period is about 4.2. Yes!

Section 3.3, p. 62

1. *Euler:* $t_1 = 3$, $x_1 = 7$, $y_1 = 2$. $t_2 = 5$, $x_2 = 17$, $y_2 = 6$.
   Runge–Kutta: $t_1 = 3$, $p_1 = 3$, $q_1 = 0$, $p_2 = 4$, $q_2 = 0$, $p_3 = 4$, $q_3 = -1$, $p_4 = 3$, $q_4 = 0$, $x_1 = 8.333$, $y_1 = 1.333$. $t_2 = 5$, $p_1 = 4.3333$, $q_1 = 0.66667$, $p_2 = 6$, $q_2 = 3.3333$, $p_3 = 8.66667$, $q_3 = 1.66667$, $p_4 = 9.66667$, $q_4 = -0.66667$, $x_2 = 22.7778$, $y_2 = 4.66667$.

3. *Euler:* $t_1 = 0.5$, $x_1 = 1.5$, $y_1 = 1$. $t_2 = 1$, $x_2 = 2.25$, $y_2 = 1.375$.
   Runge–Kutta: $t_1 = 0.5$, $p_1 = 1.0$, $q_1 = 0$, $p_2 = 1.25$, $q_2 = 0.3125$, $p_3 = 1.41235$, $q_3 = 0.32813$, $p_4 = 1.85504$, $q_4 = 0.85309$, $x_1 = 1.6817$, $y_1 = 1.1779$. $t_2 = 1$, $p_1 = 1.88736$, $q_1 = 0.84082$, $p_2 = 2.67673$, $q_2 = 1.61551$, $p_3 = 3.25159$, $q_3 = 1.76312$, $p_4 = 5.24122$, $q_4 = 3.30744$, $x_2 = 3.2637$, $y_2 = 2.0865$.

5. *Euler:* $t_1 = 2.1$, $x_1 = 2.2$, $y_1 = 1.4$. $t_2 = 2.2$, $x_2 = 2.508$, $y_2 = 1.862$.
   Runge–Kutta: $t_1 = 2.1$, $p_1 = 2$, $q_1 = 4$, $p_2 = 2.52$, $q_2 = 4.305$, $p_3 = 2.5836$, $q_3 = 4.3583$, $p_4 = 3.2426$, $q_4 = 4.7426$, $x_1 = 2.2575$, $y_1 = 1.4345$. $t_2 = 2.2$, $p_1 = 3.2384$, $q_1 = 4.7408$, $p_2 = 4.0441$, $q_2 = 5.2017$, $p_3 = 4.1682$, $q_3 = 5.2884$, $p_4 = 5.2505$, $q_4 = 5.8835$, $x_2 = 2.6727$, $y_2 = 1.9612$.

7. With step $h = 0.1$, the package gives $x(2) = -4.688$ and $y(2) = 3.158$. The true values are the same when rounded to three decimal places.

9. $u' = v$,
   $v' = -u - v$.
   $h = 0.5$, $y(1) = 0.53395$. $h = 0.2$, $y(1) = 0.5335$. $h = 0.1$, $y(1) = 0.5335$. Corrected to four decimal places, the digits are stable for even smaller steps.

11. $u' = v$,
    $v' = \sin(t) + tu - t^2v$.
    $h = 0.5$, $y(2) = 2.51$. $h = 0.1$, $y(2) = 2.50$. $h = 0.05$, $y(2) = 2.50$. Corrected to two decimal places, the digits are stable for even smaller steps.

13. $h = 0.5$, $y(2) = 4.24759$, $h = 0.1$, $y(2) = 4.20322$, $h = 0.05$, $y(2) = 4.20303$, $h = 0.01$, $y(2) = 4.20302$. To four decimal places, 4.2030 is likely accurate.

15. The solution goes to infinity within the interval $[0, 1]$ of t. No, the orbit goes to infinity.

17. $t_{k+1} = t_k + h,$

$x_{k+1} = x_k + hf_1(t_k, x_k, y_k),$

$y_{k+1} = y_k + hf_2(t_k, x_k, y_k),$

$z_{k+1} = z_k + hf_3(t_k, x_k, y_k).$

19.

$$p_{1k} = hf_1(t_k, x_k, y_k, z_k),$$

$$q_{1k} = hf_2(t_k, x_k, y_k, z_k),$$

$$r_{1k} = hf_3(t_k, x_k, y_k, z_k),$$

$$p_{2k} = hf_1(t_k + \frac{h}{2}, x_k + \frac{p_{1k}}{2}, y_k + \frac{q_{1k}}{2}, z_k + \frac{r_{1k}}{2}),$$

$$q_{2k} = hf_2(t_k + \frac{h}{2}, x_k + \frac{p_{1k}}{2}, y_k + \frac{q_{1k}}{2}, z_k + \frac{r_{1k}}{2}),$$

$$r_{2k} = hf_3(t_k + \frac{h}{2}, x_k + \frac{p_{1k}}{2}, y_k + \frac{q_{1k}}{2}, z_k + \frac{r_{1k}}{2}),$$

$$p_{3k} = hf_1(t_k + \frac{h}{2}, x_k + \frac{p_{2k}}{2}, y_k + \frac{q_{2k}}{2}, z_k + \frac{r_{2k}}{2}),$$

$$q_{3k} = hf_2(t_k + \frac{h}{2}, x_k + \frac{p_{2k}}{2}, y_k + \frac{q_{2k}}{2}, z_k + \frac{r_{2k}}{2}),$$

$$r_{3k} = hf_3(t_k + \frac{h}{2}, x_k + \frac{p_{2k}}{2}, y_k + \frac{q_{2k}}{2}, z_k + \frac{r_{2k}}{2}),$$

$$p_{4k} = hf_1(t_k + h, x_k + p_{3k}, y_k + q_{3k}, z_k + r_{3k}),$$

$$q_{4k} = hf_2(t_k + h, x_k + p_{3k}, y_k + q_{3k}, z_k + r_{3k}),$$

$$r_{4k} = hf_3(t_k + h, x_k + p_{3k}, y_k + q_{3k}, z_k + r_{3k}),$$

$$t_{k+1} = t_k + h,$$

$$x_{k+1} = x_k + [p_{1k} + 2p_{2k} + 2p_{3k} + p_{4k}]/6,$$

$$y_{k+1} = y_k + [q_{1k} + 2q_{2k} + 2q_{3k} + q_{4k}]/6,$$

$$z_{k+1} = z_k + [r_{1k} + 2r_{2k} + 2r_{3k} + r_{4k}]/6.$$

21. The terms $4^t(x^2 + y^2 - 2)$ and $30^t(x^2 + y^2 - 2)$ cause the circular orbit of radius $\sqrt{2}$ to be very unstable. Any divergence from this orbit introduces a strong radial component to the field.

Section 3.4, p. 69

1. $(0, 0)$ is unstable.

3. $(0, 0)$ is unstable.

5. $(0, 0)$ is asymptotically stable, $(2, 1)$ is unstable.

7. The orbits satisfy $x^2 + y^2 = C$. So $(0, 0)$ is stable, but not asymptotically.

9. The orbits satisfy $y^3 - x^3 = C$. The origin is unstable.

11. The critical points are $(0, 0)$, $(0, 6)$, $(4, 0)$, and $(2, 4)$. The point $(2, 4)$ is the only stable point, and it is asymptotically stable. The species coexist.

13. Species x drives out species y.

15. The factor of x in the equation for x' and y in that of y'. The axes contain any orbits starting in the axes.

17. (a) The only critical point in the first quadrant is $(2, 3)$.

(b) Solutions spiral in to the critical point. The populations approach $x = 2$ and $y = 3$.

(c) No! The x-axis cannot be crossed because of the factor y in the equation for y'. If $x = 0$ then $x' = 2$, so the solution is moving to the right.

19. The helpful predators are wiped out, and the pests increase in population.

Section 3.5, p. 73

1. (c) The initial condition $(8, 0)$ means that the pendulum has been rotated through 2π before being set in oscillation. For $(0, 3)$, the initial velocity is high enough for the pendulum to go "over the top."

3. 2π.

5. We use the change of variable $\theta = -x$ to get

$$\int_{-\alpha}^{0} 1/\sqrt{2(\cos(\theta) - \cos(-\alpha))} \, d\theta$$

$$= \int_{\alpha}^{0} -1/\sqrt{2(\cos(-x) - \cos(\alpha))} \, dx$$

$$= \int_{0}^{\alpha} 1/\sqrt{2(\cos(x) - \cos(\alpha))} \, dx.$$

7. The orbits are the graphs of $x^2 + y^2 = c$. $dx/dt = y = \sqrt{c - x^2}$, and so $dt/dx = 1/\sqrt{c - x^2}$. So the period is

$$p = 4 \int_{0}^{\sqrt{c}} 1/\sqrt{c - x^2} \, dx = 4 \sin^{-1}(x/\sqrt{c})|_{0}^{\sqrt{c}} = 2\pi.$$

Section 3.6, p. 77

1. The only critical point is $(0, 0)$. The only periodic orbit is the circle of radius 2, and this is a limit cycle. The period is about 6.2.

3. The only critical point is $(2, 0)$. There is one limit cycle about the point $(2, 0)$. The period is about 6.25.

5. Basically, the field is composed of a term at right angles to the radial vector and a term that is radial or antiradial, depending on the size of $\sqrt{x^2 + y^2}$. Thus the periodic orbits are $\sqrt{x^2 + y^2} = \pi k$, and of these the odd ones are limit cycles because the radial part of the field points out inside and in outside.

7. The period depends on c.

9. The orbits cannot escape because on the boundary the direction of motion is into the region between the two curves. There is also no critical point between the two curves. Therefore, there must be a limit cycle between the two curves.

CHAPTER 4

Section 4.2, p. 87

1. The functions e^t and te^t are solutions by direct substitution. The determinant is e^{2t}, which is not zero for any t. $y = 2e^t - 3te^t$.

3. The functions $\sin(t)$ and $\cos(t)$ are solutions by direct substitution. The Wronskian of these functions is -1, which is not zero for any t. $y = (\sqrt{3} - 3)/2 \sin(t) + (1 - 3\sqrt{3})/2 \cos(t)$.

5. The functions t and t^3 are solutions for $t > 0$ by direct substitution. The determinant is $2t^3$, which is not zero for any $t > 0$. $y = 3t - 2t^3$.

7. The functions t and $t \ln(t)$ are solutions for $t > 0$ by direct substitution. The determinant is t, which is not zero for any $t > 0$. $y = -t + 3t \ln(t)$.

9. The functions 1, e^t, and te^t are solutions for all t by direct substitution. The determinant is e^{2t}, which is not zero for any t. $y = 5 - 3e^t + 2te^t$.

11. The identity $c_1 + c_2t + c_3t^2 = 0$ implies that $c_1 = c_2 = c_3 = 0$.

13. $c_1t + c_2(t^2 - 2) + c_3(t^3 - t) = 0$ implies that $-2c_2 + (c_1 - c_3)t + c_2t^2 + c_3t^3 = 0$. Thus the coefficients of -2, t, t^2, and t^3 are zero. So $c_1 = c_2 = c_3 = 0$, and so $c_1 = 0$ also.

15. $-2t + t^2 - (t^2 - 2t) = 0$.

17. $1 - \sin^2(t) - \cos^2(t) = 0$.

19. If $c_1t^2 + c_2t|t| = 0$, then evaluating at 1 and -1 shows that $c_1 = c_2 = 0$. These functions cannot be solutions to a second-order linear homogeneous equation!

Section 4.3.2, p. 91

1. The fundamental set is $\{e^t, e^{-4t}\}$. The Wronskian is $-5e^{-3t}$. The solution is $y = 2e^t/5 + 3e^{-4t}/5$.

3. The fundamental set is $\{e^{-t}, e^t, e^{3t}\}$. The Wronskian is $16e^{3t}$. The solution is $y = 11e^{-t}/8 - e^t/4 - e^{3t}/8$.

5. The fundamental set of solutions is $\{1, e^{-t}, e^{3t}\}$. The Wronskian is $-12e^{2t}$. The solution is $y = 2 - e^{-t}$.

7. The general solution is $y = c_1e^{(1+\sqrt{7})t} + c_2e^{(1-\sqrt{7})t}$.

9. $y = c_1e^{-t} + c_2e^{3t}$.

11. $y = c_1 + c_2e^{-3t} + c_3e^{3t}$.

13. We have only one root. We need a fundamental set of two solutions.

15. There are no real roots. The roots are $\pm i$. Yes, $(e^{it} + e^{-it})/2$ and $(e^{it} - e^{-it})/2i$.

Section 4.3.3, p. 93

1. In either order you get $4t^3 - 9t^2 + 6t + 6\cos(2t)$.

3. $D^2 - 5D + 4 = (D - 1)(D - 4)$.

5. $D^2 + D + 1 = (D - (-\frac{1}{2} + \frac{\sqrt{3}}{2}i))(D - (-\frac{1}{2} - \frac{\sqrt{3}}{2}i))$.

7. $D^2 + 3D + 2 = (D + 1)(D + 2)$.

9. $(D - t^3)(D + t)f = f'' + f + tf' - t^3f' - t^4f$, and $(D + t)(D - t^3)f = f'' - 3t^2f - t^3f' + tf' - t^4f$. These are not the same for all f.

Section 4.3.4, p. 96

1. $y = -\frac{4}{\sqrt{7}}e^{t/4}\sin(\sqrt{7}t/4)$.

3. $y = -e^{t/2}\cos(\sqrt{11}t/2) + \frac{5}{\sqrt{11}}e^{t/2}\sin(\sqrt{11}t/2)$.

5. $y = 2\cos(2t) + \sin(2t)$.

7. $y = c_1e^{-t}\sin(2t) + c_2e^{-t}\cos(2t)$.

9. $y = c_1 + c_2e^{-2t}$.

11. $y = c_1 + c_2t + c_3t^2 + c_4\cos(t) + c_5\sin(t) + c_6t\cos(t) + c_7t\sin(t)$.

13. $y = c_1e^{-t/2}\cos(\sqrt{3}t/2) + c_2e^{-t/2}\sin(\sqrt{3}t/2) + c_3te^{-t/2}\cos(\sqrt{3}t/2) + c_4te^{-t/2}\sin(\sqrt{3}t/2)$.

15. $y = -\frac{25}{27} + 16t/9 + t^2/3 - 2e^{-3t}/27$.

17. $y = -3e^{-3t}/8 + 3e^t/8 - 3te^{-3t}/8 - te^t/8$.

Section 4.4.1, p. 103

1. $y = 2 + 2\sin(t) - \cos(t)$.

3. $y = -7/108 - t/18 - t^2/6 - 449e^{-3t}/675 - 2te^{-3t}/5 - 27e^{2t}/100$.

5. $y = -7t - 3t^2 - t^3 - 8 + 9e^t$.

7. $y = \frac{3}{10}\sin(t) + \frac{1}{10}\cos(t) + c_1e^{-t} + c_2e^{-2t}$.

9. $y = -\cos(t) + c_1e^{-t/2}\cos(\sqrt{3}t/2) + c_2e^{-t/2}\sin(\sqrt{3}t/2)$.

11. $y = -\sin(t)/2 + c_1e^{-t} + c_2e^t$.

13. $y = -2 + t^2 + c_1e^{-t/2}\cos(\sqrt{3}t/2) + c_2e^{-t/2}\sin(\sqrt{3}t/2)$.

15. $y = 3te^{2t}/16 - t^3/24 + c_1 + c_2t + c_3e^{-2t} + c_4e^{2t}$.

Section 4.4.2, p. 106

1. $y = e^{3t}/20 + c_1e^{-2t} + c_2e^{-t}$.

3. The particular solution is $\psi(t) = \sin(t)\ln|\sec(t) + \tan(t)| - 1$.

5. $y = \sin^3(t)/2 + \cos(t)[\sin(2t)/4 - t/2] + (\pi/2 - 1)\cos(t)$.

7. $y = t^4/3 + c_1t + c_2t^3$.

9. Divide through by 2 first. $y = e^{3t}/32 + c_1e^{-t} + c_2te^{-t}$.

11. The particular solution is $\psi(t) = e^{-t}/4 - te^{-t}/2$.

13. $y = \dfrac{1}{3}\sin(3t)\displaystyle\int_0^t f(x)\cos(3x)\,dx$

$\qquad - \dfrac{1}{3}\cos(3t)\displaystyle\int_0^t f(x)\sin(3x)\,dx$

$\qquad + c_1\sin(3t) + c_2\cos(3t).$

15. You will need to set

$$u_1'\phi_1 + u_2'\phi_2 + u_3'\phi_3 = 0,$$
$$u_1'\phi_1' + u_2'\phi_2' + u_3'\phi_3' = 0, \text{ and}$$
$$u_1'\phi_1'' + u_2'\phi_2'' + u_3'\phi_3'' = b(t)$$

in turn at each differentiation.

Section 4.5, p. 114

1. The roots are $(-1 - \sqrt{31})/4$, and the solution is

$$y(t) = \frac{20}{\sqrt{31}}e^{-t/4}\sin(\sqrt{31}t/4).$$

3. The solution is $y(t) = \frac{1}{2}e^{-t/4}\cos(\sqrt{15}t/4) + \frac{3}{10}\sqrt{15}e^{-t/4}\sin(\sqrt{15}t/4)$.

5. $r_1 = -3/2 - \sqrt{5}/2$ and $r_2 = -3/2 + \sqrt{5}/2$. Then $-c_1/c_2 < 0$. The system is overdamped, and there is no crossing.

7. $r_1 = -2$ and $r_2 = -1/2$. Then $-c_1/c_2 < 1$. The system is overdamped, and there is no crossing.

9. $r = -1$. Then $-c_1/c_2 > 0$. The system is critically damped, and there is one crossing.

11. The t-axis is crossed every time the orbit crosses the "y" or "velocity" axis.

13. The resonant frequency is $\omega_r = 0.707$. The response ratio is 0.204.

15. The resonant frequency is $\omega_r = 1.4$. The response ratio is 7.07.

17. The resonant frequency is $\omega_r = 2.24$. The response ratio is 22.36.

19. The solution is $y(t) = -\frac{2}{19}\sin(10t) - \frac{20}{171}\sin(9t) - \cos(9t)$.

21. The frequency is $\sqrt{500}/2\pi$ cycles per second.

23. **(a)** The resonant frequency is very close to 50. The response curve is very sharply peaked at 50.

(b) The steady state has a frequency between 8 and 9 cycles per sec. $50/(2\pi)$, between 8 and 9.

(c) The steady state is virtually the same as in part b.

(d) The steady state is tiny in comparison with part b.

(e) The term $\sin(50t)$ has a frequency very close to the resonant frequency, so the response is much greater than the response to $\sin(60t)$. Thus, if the latter is removed, there is little difference, but if the fomer is removed, there is hardly any response since the driving frequency is well away from the peak on the response curve.

(f) If we tune a circuit so that it resonates at the frequency of the station that we want, then the circuit will give a much greater response than to neighboring stations. Thus the desired station will be heard over the neighbors.

CHAPTER 5

Section 5.1, p. 130

1. $A + B = \begin{bmatrix} 5 & 7 \\ -1 & 6 \end{bmatrix}$, $AB = \begin{bmatrix} 6 & 21 \\ -2 & 4 \end{bmatrix}$, and $BA = \begin{bmatrix} 1 & 19 \\ -3 & 9 \end{bmatrix}$

3. **(a)** $A'(t) = \begin{bmatrix} 3 & 2t & 0 \\ -3e^{3t} & 2 & 0 \\ 4t^3 & \cos(t) & -8t \end{bmatrix}$.

(b) $B'(t) = \begin{bmatrix} 0 & 2t & 3t^2 \\ 5e^{5t} & -1 & 10t \\ 4t^3 & 1 & -3t^2 \end{bmatrix}$.

5. $\begin{bmatrix} x' \\ y' \end{bmatrix} = \begin{bmatrix} 3 & 4 \\ -1 & 2 \end{bmatrix}\begin{bmatrix} x \\ y \end{bmatrix}$.

7. If $(c_{ij}) = (I_{ij})(a_{ij})$, then, by definition of the matrix product, $c_{ij} = \sum_{k=0}^{n} I_{ik}a_{kj}$. But for the identity matrix $I_{ik} = 1$ only if $i = k$, and it is 0 otherwise. So $c_{ij} = I_{ii}a_{ij} = a_{ij}$.

9. Solve

$$c_1 + 3c_2 = 0,$$
$$c_1 + c_2 = 0.$$

The result is $c_1 = c_2 = 0$, so the vectors are independent.

11. Solve

$$-c_1 + 2c_2 = 0,$$
$$2c_1 + c_2 = 0.$$

The result is $c_1 = c_2 = 0$, so the vectors are independent.

13. The equations

$$c_1 + 3c_2 - 2c_3 = 0,$$
$$c_1 + 3c_2 - c_3 = 0,$$
$$2c_1 + 6c_2 + 3c_3 = 0$$

have a nontrivial solution, so the vectors are dependent.

15. If $v_i = c_1 v_1 + \cdots + c_n v_n$, where there is no v_i term on the right, then

$$c_1 v_1 + \cdots + (-1)v_i + \cdots + c_n v_n = 0.$$

But this is a nonzero linear combination equal to zero, so the set is dependent.

17. The eigenvalues are 0 and 4. Corresponding eigenvectors are $(-1, 2)$ and $(1, 2)$.

19. The eigenvalues are -4 and -1. $\{(-\sqrt{2}, 1), (1/\sqrt{2}, 1)\}$ is an independent set.

21. The only eigenvalue is 2. The only independent eigenvector is $(-1, 1)$.

23. The matrix of the first-order system is $\begin{bmatrix} 0 & 1 \\ -2 & 3 \end{bmatrix}$. The characteristic polynomial of this matrix is $r^2 - 3r + 2$, and this is the same for the original equation.

Section 5.2, p. 137

1. The general solution is

$$X(t) = c_1 \begin{bmatrix} -1 \\ 1 \end{bmatrix} e^{2t} + c_2 \begin{bmatrix} 1 \\ 2 \end{bmatrix} e^{5t}.$$

The particular solution is $X(t) = \begin{bmatrix} 1 \\ 2 \end{bmatrix} e^{5t}$. The origin is unstable. There are two straight-line orbits containing the eigenvectors.

3. The general solution is

$$X(t) = c_1 \begin{bmatrix} -1 \\ 1 \end{bmatrix} e^{-2t} + c_2 \begin{bmatrix} -2 \\ 3 \end{bmatrix} e^{-t}.$$

The origin is asymptotically stable. There are two straight-line orbits containing the eigenvectors.

5. The general solution is

$$X(t) = e^{-t/2} c_1 \begin{bmatrix} -\frac{1}{2}\cos(\sqrt{3}t/2) - \frac{\sqrt{3}}{6}\sin(\sqrt{3}t/2) \\ \cos(\sqrt{3}t/2) \end{bmatrix}$$

$$+ c_2 \begin{bmatrix} \frac{1}{2}\sin(\sqrt{3}t/2) - \frac{\sqrt{3}}{6}\cos(\sqrt{3}t/2) \\ \sin(\sqrt{3}t/2) \end{bmatrix}.$$

The solutions spiral in to the origin, so the origin is asymptotically stable. There are no straight orbits.

7. The general solution is

$$X(t) = c_1 \begin{bmatrix} 1 \\ 1 \end{bmatrix} e^{-t} + c_2 \left(\begin{bmatrix} 1 \\ 1 \end{bmatrix} t e^{-t} + \begin{bmatrix} 0 \\ 1/3 \end{bmatrix} e^{-t} \right).$$

There is one straight-line orbit corresponding to the only independent eigenvector. Because of the negative exponentials, the origin is asymptotically stable.

9. The eigenvalues are 0 and 4. Corresponding eigenvectors are $(1, -2)$ and $(1, 2)$. The general solution is

$$X(t) = c_1 \begin{bmatrix} 1 \\ -2 \end{bmatrix} + c_2 \begin{bmatrix} 1 \\ 2 \end{bmatrix} e^{4t}.$$

There is one straight-line orbit corresponding to $(1, 2)$. There is a line of single-point orbits.

11. If the real parts of the eigenvalues are negative, the origin is asymptotically stable.

13. If one eigenvalue is positive, the origin is unstable.

15. The general solution is

$$X(t) = c_1 \begin{bmatrix} -2 \\ -2 \\ 3 \end{bmatrix} e^{t} + c_2 \begin{bmatrix} 0 \\ -1 \\ 1 \end{bmatrix} e^{2t} + c_3 \begin{bmatrix} 0 \\ 0 \\ 1 \end{bmatrix} e^{3t}.$$

17. Let $(x_0 + x_1 i, y_0 + y_1 i)$ be the eigenvector corresponding to the eigenvalue $\lambda + \mu i$. There is a common factor of $e^{\lambda t}$, so this may be factored out. Now combine

$$\begin{bmatrix} x_0 + x_1 i \\ y_0 + y_1 i \end{bmatrix} (\cos(\mu t) + i \sin(\mu t))$$

$$+ \begin{bmatrix} x_0 - x_1 i \\ y_0 - y_1 i \end{bmatrix} (\cos(\mu t) - i \sin(\mu t))$$

as a single vector, and then divide by 2. In the case where we subtract, divide by $2i$.

19. The system is

$$x' = -x/10 + y/30,$$
$$y' = x/10 - y/12.$$

The solution is $x(t) = 20(3e^{-3t/20} + 4e^{-t/30})/7$ and $y(t) = -90e^{-3t/20}/7 + 160e^{-t/30}/7$.

21. (a) The system is

$$x' = -x/100 + y/100,$$
$$y' = x/100 - y/100.$$

(b) The eigenvalues are 0 and -1/50. The eigenvectors are $(1, 1)$ and $(-1, 1)$. The general form of the solution is $X(t) = c_1(1, 1) + c_2(-1, 1)e^{-t/50}$.

(c) The orbits are straight lines perpendicular to the line $y = x$. Solutions converge to this line as time increases. This is consistent with intuition, since we expect the solution to approach a uniform density in both tanks.

Section 5.3, p. 150

1. $e^{At} = \begin{bmatrix} e^{3y} & 0 \\ 0 & e^{3t} \end{bmatrix}$.

3. $e^{At} = \begin{bmatrix} (2e^t - te^t)/2 & te^t/2 \\ -te^t/2 & (2e^t + te^t)/2 \end{bmatrix}$.

5. $e^{At} = \begin{bmatrix} \cos(2t) + \sin(2t)/2 & 5\sin(2t)/2 \\ -\sin(2t)/2 & \cos(2t) - \sin(2t)/2 \end{bmatrix}$.

7. $e^{At} = \begin{bmatrix} 3e^{-2t} - 2e^{-t} & 2e^{-2t} - 2e^{-t} \\ -3e^{-2t} + 3e^{-t} & -2e^{-2t} + 3e^{-t} \end{bmatrix}$.

9. If the eigenvalues have negative real parts, the solutions converge to the origin. There is at least one straight orbit for each real eigenvalue. If an eigenvalue is positive, then at least some orbits go to infinity.

11. $X(t) =$

$\begin{bmatrix} \dfrac{e^{(-2-\sqrt{2})t/50} + e^{(-2+\sqrt{2})t/50}}{2} & \dfrac{e^{(-2+\sqrt{2})t/50} - e^{(-2-\sqrt{2})t/50}}{2\sqrt{2}} \\ \dfrac{e^{(-2+\sqrt{2})t/50} - e^{(-5-\sqrt{2})t/50}}{\sqrt{2}} & \dfrac{e^{(-2-\sqrt{2})t/50} + e^{(-2+\sqrt{2})t/50}}{2} \end{bmatrix} \begin{bmatrix} 60 \\ 25 \end{bmatrix}$.

13. $X(t) = \begin{bmatrix} e^{3t} & 0 & 0 \\ 2te^{3t} & e^{3t} & 0 \\ 0 & 0 & e^{-t} \end{bmatrix} \begin{bmatrix} x_0 \\ y_0 \\ z_0 \end{bmatrix}$.

15. (a) The system is

$$x' = -k_1 x + k_2 y,$$
$$y' = k_1 x - k_2 y.$$

The matrix is

$$\begin{bmatrix} -k_1 & k_2 \\ k_1 & -k_2 \end{bmatrix}.$$

(b) The first is

$$\begin{bmatrix} 1/2 + e^{-2t}/2 & 1/2 - e^{-2t}/2 \\ 1/2 - e^{-2t}/2 & 1/2 + e^{-2t}/2 \end{bmatrix},$$

and the second is

$$\begin{bmatrix} 2/3 + e^{-3t}/3 & 2/3 - 2e^{-3t}/3 \\ 1/3 - e^{-3t}/3 & 1/3 + 2e^{-3t}/3 \end{bmatrix}.$$

17. (a) The matrix is

$$A = \begin{bmatrix} -k_1 & 0 & k_3 \\ k_1 & -k_2 & 0 \\ 0 & k_2 & -k_3 \end{bmatrix}.$$

(b) The first row of the first exponential matrix is $1/3 + 2e^{-3t/2}\cos(\sqrt{3}t/2)/3$, $1/3 - e^{-3t/2}\cos(\sqrt{3}t/2)/3 -$

$e^{-3t/2}\sin(\sqrt{3}t/2)/\sqrt{3}$, and
$1/3 - e^{-3t/2}\cos(\sqrt{3}t/2)/3 + e^{-3t/2}\sin(\sqrt{3}t/2)/\sqrt{3}$.
The remaining rows contain similar sin and cos terms. The solutions oscillate as they converge to a steady state.

19. $e^{At} = \begin{bmatrix} e^{2t}(-1 + 2e^t) & 2e^{2t}(1 - e^t) \\ e^{2t}(-1 + e^t) & e^{2t}(2 - e^t) \end{bmatrix}$.
The solution is

$$X(t) = \begin{bmatrix} 1/36 - e^t - t/6 \\ (5 - 54e^t + 6t)/36 \end{bmatrix} + e^{At} \begin{bmatrix} x_0 \\ y_0 \end{bmatrix}.$$

Section 5.4, p. 155

1. The eigenvalues are 2 and 4, so the origin is unstable.

3. The eigenvalues are 1 and -2, so the origin is unstable.

5. The eigenvalues are $1 \pm i$, so the origin is unstable.

7. The eigenvlaues are $\pm\sqrt{5}$, so the origin is unstable.

9. A solution is $X(t) = c \begin{bmatrix} 0 \\ 0 \\ 1 \end{bmatrix} e^{3t}$, so there are orbits starting as close to the origin as desired and going to infinity.

11. The number 2 is an eigenvalue. The vector $(1, 2, 1)$ is an eigenvector of 2.

13. There is one real eigenvalue and two independent eigenvectors.

15. There is one real eigenvalue and one independent eigenvector.

17. If 0 is an eigenvalue, we have $AX = 0$ for some $X \neq 0$. So X is a critical point, as is every scalar multiple of X.

19. The matrix cannot have dimension 3 because there would have to be a real eigenvalue.

Section 5.5, p. 159

1. The two periods are 2π and $2\pi/\sqrt{3}$.

3. $x_1' = x_2$

$$x_2' = -\frac{k_1 + k_2}{m_1}x_1 + \frac{k_2}{m_1}x_3$$

$$x_3' = x_4$$

$$x_4' = \frac{k_2}{m_2}x_1 - \frac{k_2 + k_3}{m_2}x_3 + \frac{k_3}{m_2}x_5$$

$$x_5' = x_6$$

$$x_6' = \frac{k_3}{m_3}x_3 - \frac{k_3 + k_4}{m_3}x_5.$$

Section 5.6, p. 164

1. The matrix of the linearization is $\begin{bmatrix} 2 & -1 \\ 0 & 3 \end{bmatrix}$. One eigenvalue is positive, so the origin is unstable.

3. The only critical point is the origin. The linearization is
$\begin{bmatrix} 1 & 0 \\ 1 & 1 \end{bmatrix}$, so the origin is unstable.

5. The matrix of the linearization is $\begin{bmatrix} 2 & -1 \\ -1 & 1 \end{bmatrix}$, and the eigenvalues are positive, so the origin is unstable.

7. For $(0.1, 0)$, it is approximately $t = 48$. For $(0.01, 0)$, the time seems infinite.

9. For $(0.1, 0)$, it takes $t = 99/2$, and for $(0.01, 0)$, it takes $t = 9999/2$.

CHAPTER 6

Section 6.1.1, p. 169

1. $|x - 1| < 1/2$. The interval is $(1/2, 3/2)$.

3. $(-\infty, \infty)$.

5. $f'(x) = \frac{1}{1+1} + \frac{2x}{4+1} + \frac{3x^2}{9+1} + \cdots$. $f'(x) = \sum_{k=1}^{\infty} \frac{kx^{k-1}}{k^2+1}$.

7. $f'(x) = \frac{2^3 x}{1} + \frac{2^3 3x^2}{2} + \cdots$,
$$f'(x) = \sum_{k=2}^{\infty} \frac{2^k k x^{k-1}}{k-1}.$$

9. **(a)** For $x_0 = 0$, $f(x) = -1 + 2x - 3x^2 + x^3$. For $x_0 = 1$, $f(x) = -1 - \frac{1}{1!}(x-1) + \frac{0}{2!}(x-1)^2 + \frac{6}{3!}(x-1)^3$.

   (b) For $x_0 = 0$, $f(x) = \sum_{k=0}^{\infty}(-1)^k \frac{x^{2k+1}}{(2k+1)!}$. For $x_0 = 1$, $f(x) = \sin(1) + \frac{\cos(1)}{1!}(x-1) - \frac{\sin(1)}{2!}(x-1)^2 - \frac{\cos(1)}{3!}(x-1)^3 + \frac{\sin(1)}{4!}(x-1)^4 + \cdots$.

11. For $x_0 = 0$, $f(x) = -x - 3x^2 + x^3$. For $x_0 = 3$, $f(x) = -3 + 8(x-3) + 14(x-3)^2/2 + 6(x-3)^3/6$.

13. The product is $2 + x + 4x^2 + 4x^3 + 4x^4 + 4x^5 + \cdots$.

15. $x + 3x^2 + \frac{11}{2}x^3 + \frac{49}{6}x^4 + \cdots$.

17. We find that the derivative of the series for f and that for f' are the same, so $f(x)$ satisfies $y' = y$. Also, $f(0) = 1$. But the same is true for e^x, and so by uniqueness $f(x) = e^x$.

Section 6.1.2, p. 180

1. $y(x) \approx 1 + 2x - \frac{1}{12}x^4 - \frac{1}{10}x^5 + \frac{1}{672}x^8$. The fifth and eigth partial sums seem to agree fairly well on $(-1.5, 1.5)$.

3. $y(x) \approx 1 - x + \frac{1}{2}x^2 + \frac{1}{6}x^3 + \frac{1}{12}x^4 - \frac{3}{40}x^5 + \frac{1}{180}x^6$. The solution seems reasonably stable on $(-1.2, 1)$.

5. $y(x) \approx 2 - (x-1) - (x-1)^2/2 - 2(x-1)^3/3 - 5(x-1)^4/24$.

7. $y(x) \approx 1 + (x-2) - 5(x-2)^2 + 5(x-2)^3/6 + 19(x-2)^4/6$.

9. $y(x) = 1 + 2x + x^3/6 + x^4/6 + \cdots$.

11. $y(x) \approx 1 + 2x - x^2/2 + x^3/3 + x^5/120$.

13. $y = y_0[1 + \sum_{k=1}^{\infty}(-1)^k \frac{x^{2k}}{1 \cdot 3 \cdot 5 \cdots (2k-1)}]$
$+ y_1[x + \sum_{k=1}^{\infty}(-1)^k \frac{x^{2k+1}}{2 \cdot 4 \cdot 6 \cdots (2k)}]$.
If $y_1 = 0$, solutions are even; if $y_0 = 0$, solutions are odd.

15. $P_0(x) = 1$, $P_1(x) = x$, $P_2(x) = -[1 - 3x^2]/2$, $P_3(x) = -[3x - 5x^3]/2$, and $P_4(x) = [3 - 30x^2 + 35x^4]/8$.

17. The solution out to the sixth order is
$$y(x) \approx 1 - x + x^2/2 - x^3/6 + x^4/24 - x^5/120 + x^6/720.$$
The next term is $-x^7/5040$, so by the alternating series test $y(1)$ can be computed from the preceding with error less than $1/5040$.

19. A partial sum of a series solution is a polynomial in t. So, as t goes to infinity, the partial sum must go to infinity or minus infinity, but the solution goes to zero.

Section 6.2, p. 185

1. $C(x) = \sum_{k=0}^{\infty}(-1)^k \frac{x^{2k}}{(2k)!}$. Use the ratio test to show convergence.

3. If $t = p$ is the period and the orbit is the unit circle, then the arc length of the circle is 2π, so
$$2\pi = \int_0^p \sqrt{(v')^2 + (-u')^2}\, dt = p.$$

5. **(a)** $f(x) = \sum_{k=0}^{\infty}(-1)^k \frac{2^k x^{2k+1}}{k!(2k+1)}$. Use the ratio test.

   (b) $f'(x) = \sum_{k=0}^{\infty}(-1)^k \frac{2^k x^{2k}}{k!} = e^{-2x^2}$.

   (c) $f(x) = \int_0^x e^{-2t^2}\, dt$.

   (d) Make the substitution $v = y'$ to get the equation $v' + 4xv = 0$. This is linear, and the solution is $v = e^{-2x^2}$. Then $y(x) = \int_0^x e^{-2t^2}\, dt$.

7. Two solutions to the same initial-value problem must be equal.

9. Solutions to the same initial-value problem are unique.

11. $\frac{1}{2^n n!} \frac{d^n}{dx^n}[(x^2 - 1)^n] = \frac{1}{2^n n!} \frac{d^n}{dx^n} \sum_{m=0}^{n} \binom{n}{m}(-1)^k x^{2n-2m}$.
Differentiating n times gives
$$\frac{1}{2^n n!} \sum_{m=0}^{[n/2]}(-1)^k \frac{n!(2n-2m)(2n-2m-1)\cdots(n-2m)}{m!(n-m)!} x^{n-2m},$$
but this reduces to the form of the Legendre polynomial derived in this section.

13. The basis functions are

$$\psi_1(x) = 1 - \sum_{k=1}^{\infty} \frac{\alpha^2(2^2-\alpha^2)(4^2-\alpha^2)\cdots((2k-2)^2-\alpha^2)}{(2k)!} x^{2k}$$

and

$$\psi_2(x) = x + \sum_{k=2}^{\infty} \frac{(1-\alpha^2)(3^2-\alpha^2)(5^2-\alpha^2)\cdots((2k-3)^2-\alpha^2)}{(2k-1)!} x^{2k-1}.$$

Clearly, if α is an integer, one series terminates, giving a polynomial.

Section 6.3, p. 192

1. $y_1(x) = x[1 + x^2/5 + x^4/30 + \cdots]$

and $y_2(x) = \sqrt{x}[1 + x^2/6 + 5x^4/168 + \cdots]$.

3. $y_1(x) = x[1 + 4x/3 + 16x^2/15 + 64x^3/105 + \cdots]$

and $y_2(x) = \sqrt{x}[1 + 2x + 2x^2 + 4x^3/3 + \cdots]$.

5. $c_n = -\dfrac{c_{n-1}}{(r+n-1)(2r+2n-1)}$.   The general solution is

$$y(x) = Ax \sum_{n=0}^{\infty} (-1)^n \frac{x^n}{n!3\cdot5\cdot7\cdots(2n+1)}$$

$$+ B\sqrt{x} \sum_{n=0}^{\infty} (-1)^n \frac{x^n}{n!1\cdot3\cdot5\cdots(2n-1)}.$$

7. $y_1(x) = x^{-1}\sum_{n=0}^{\infty}(-1)^n \frac{x^n}{(n!)^2}$.   The root is repeated, so there is no second root to try to apply the recusion to.

9. $J_1(x) = x \sum_{n=0}^{\infty}(-1)^n \frac{x^{2n}}{2^{2n}(n!)^2(n+1)}$.

11. $J_3(x) = x^3 \sum_{n=0}^{\infty}(-1)^n \frac{x^{2n}}{2^{2n+3}n!(n+3)!}$.

15. Let the conjugate roots be $r_1 = a + bi$ and $r_2 = a - bi$. The form of the solutions is

$$y(x) = |x|^{r_i} \sum_{n=0}^{\infty} c_n x^n,$$

where

$$c_n(r_1) = -\frac{\sum_{k=0}^{n-1}[a_{n-k}(r_1+k)c_k(r_1) + b_{n-k}c_k(r_1)]}{n(n+2bi)}$$

and

$$c_n(r_2) = -\frac{\sum_{k=0}^{n-1}[a_{n-k}(r_2+k)c_k(r_2) + b_{n-k}c_k(r_2)]}{n(n-2bi)}.$$

Starting with $c_0 = 1$, each succeeding coefficient in the first solution is clearly the conjugate of the corresponding coefficient in the second solution.

Section 6.4, p. 196

1. The roots are $r_1 = 3$ and $r_2 = -2$. The first solution is

$$y_1 = x^3 \sum_{n=0}^{\infty} (-1)^n \frac{120}{n!(n+5)!} x^n.$$

For the second solution, $n_0 = 5$, and $c_5(-2) = 1/2880$. So

$$y_2 = \frac{1}{2880} y_1(x) \ln(x) + x^{-2}[1 - x + x^2/24 + \cdots].$$

3. $c_0(r) = r+1$, so the derivative is 1. $c_2(r) = -1/[(r+3)]$. Take the derivative of this and evaluate at -1 to get 1/4. Repeat to the required order.

5. Try $x^2y'' + x(1+x)y' - y = 0$.

CHAPTER 7

Section 7.1, p. 203

1. The only bifurcation point is $a = 0$. If $a = 0$, every point is critical, and if $a \neq 0$, only $y = 0$ is critical.

3. If $a = 0$, there is only one critical point, but if $a \neq 0$, there are two. So $a = 0$ is the only bifurcation point.

5. For $a = 0$ the orbits are circles. For other values of a there are orbits that go to infinity, so $a = 0$ is a bifurcation point. The circle of radius 3 centered at the origin divides the orbit structure into two regions.

7. There is only one critical point, $(0,0)$. For $a = 0$ the orbits are circles. For $a \neq 0$ the solutions spiral in or out as can be seen by computing eigenvalues.

9. Yes! Plot the critical points in xya-coordinates. For example, the system

$$x' = y(a - y),$$
$$y' = x(a - x)$$

has the a-axis and the line $x = a$, $y = a$ for sets of critical points. There is a bifurcation from two to one and back to two critical points as a passes through the origin.

11. The equation is $y' = y(2 - y) - a$. The critical points are the solutions to $y^2 - 2y + a = 0$. The solutions are $y = (2 \pm \sqrt{4 - 4a})/2$. If $a = 0$, the equilibrium number of fish is 2 or 0. As we start harvesting, these two critical points move toward 1, with the higher value being stable. As a passes 1, the critical points vanish and the population of fish heads for extinction. The diagram is the parabola $a = -y^2 + 2y$. This parabola lies to the left of $a = 1$, so, for values of a bigger than 1, y' is negative.

13. Same as part 11 with numbers changed.

Section 7.2, p. 208

1. $\phi(t, y) = ye^t$. $(e^3, 2e^3)$.

3. $\phi(t, y) = 5/3 + (y - 5/3)e^{-3t}$. $(5/3 - 2/5e^{-3}, 5/3 + 1/5e^{-3})$.

5. $\phi(t, x, y) = (xe^t, ye^{-t} + x(e^t/2 - e^{-t}/2))$. The center of the unit disk remains fixed, it is squashed along the y-axis, and it is stretched a great deal along the approximate direction of $y = x/2$.

7. $\phi(t, x, y) = 4x/5e^{-3t} - 2y/5e^{-3t} + x/5e^{2t} + 2y/5e^{2t}, -2x/5e^{-3t} + y/5e^{-3t} + 2x/5e^{2t} + 4y/5e^{2t})$. The center of the disk moves off to the "northeast." During this motion, the disk becomes elongated in the direction of motion since the flow lines converge in this direction.

9. The divergence is 4, so $A'(t) = \int_{A(t)} 4 \, dx \, dy = 4A(t)$. Thus $A(t) = A_0 e^{4t}$. The area expands exponentially.

Section 7.3, p. 213

1. $|f(t, y_1) - f(t, y_2)| = |4y_1 - 4y_2| = 4|y_1 - y_2|$, so a Lipschitz constant is 4. The general solution is $y = ce^{4t}$, so

$$|y_1(t) - y_2(t)| = |y_1 e^{4t} - y_2 e^{4t}| \le e^{4t}|y_1 - y_2|,$$

as predicted by the theorem.

3. $|f(t, y_1) - f(t, y_2)| = |3t^2 y_1 - 3t^2 y_2| = 3t^2|y_1 - y_2| \le 48|y_1 - y_2|$, so a Lipschitz constant is 48. The general solution is $y = ce^{t^3}$, so

$$|y_1(t) - y_2(t)| = |y_1 e^{t^3} - y_2 e^{t^3}| \le e^{t^3}|y_1 - y_2|.$$

But $e^{t^3} \le e^{48|t|}$ on $(-4, 4)$, so the theorem is verified.

5.

$$\|\vec{F}(t, x_1, y_1) - \vec{F}(t, x_2, y_2)\|$$
$$= \|(x_1 - x_2 + y_2 - y_1)\vec{i} + (x_1 - x_2 + y_1 - y_2)\vec{j}\|$$
$$= \sqrt{2}\|(x_1 - x_2)\vec{i} + (y_1 - y_2)\vec{j}\|.$$

Therefore, the Lipschitz constant is $\sqrt{2}$. Experimenting with various intervals of t and measuring between the endpoints of the orbits confirm the theorem.

7. (a) $|y_1^2 - y_2^2| = |(y_1 + y_2)(y_1 - y_2)| \le 4|y_1 - y_2|$, because $|y_1 + y_2| \le 4$ in the rectangle.

(b) The general solution is $y = -1/(t + c)$. The two solutions are $y_1 = -1/(t - 1)$ and $y_2 = -1/(t - 10/9)$. Then $y_1 - y_2 = \frac{1}{9(t-1)(t-10/9)}$.

(c) The maximum that t can be without the solutions exiting the rectangle is 1/2. So the maximum that the difference can be is 4/11. This is much less than what the theorem allows.

9. From Exercise 8 we have a Lipschitz constant L. Thus $|y_1(t) - y_2(t)| \le e^{L|t - t_0|}|y_1(t_0) - y_2(t_0)|$. If the initial conditions are equal, then the left-hand side of the inequality must be zero, so the solutions are equal.

Section 7.4, p. 217

1. No, the orbits are circles, and so there is no subset that is approached asymptotically.

3. The eigenvalues are -1 and 2. The corresponding eigenvectros are $(1,0)$ and $(1,3)$. Thus all solutions converge asymptotically to the line containing the vector $(1,3)$.

5. It is the plane defined by the eigenvectors of the positive eigenvalues.

7. No, the system

$$x' = 2x + y,$$
$$y' = -y$$

has divergence equal to 1, but there is a straight-line attractor.

9. It is the straight line parameterized by $x = \frac{11}{4} - \frac{3}{2}s + \frac{1}{2}t^2$, $y = -\frac{3}{2} + s$, and $t = s$.

Section 7.5, p. 222

1. The initial conditions $(0, 2.07)$ and $(0, 2.08)$ appear to do the job, but different machines may get different results; it is enough to illustrate the sensitivity.

3. The solution with initial condition $(0, 1.4)$ orbits the origin, the solution with initial condition $(0, 1.5)$ goes into a long-term rotation, but the solution with initial condition $(0, 1.505)$ falls into orbiting $(2\pi, 0)$.

5. Chaotic behavior occurs at about $a = 0.34$.

7.

$$x' = y,$$
$$y' = -y + x - x^3.$$

The critical points are $(0, 0, (1, 0)$, and $(-1, 0)$. The first is unstable and the other two are stable. The first equilibrium position is with the rod straight up. The others correspond to the ball sagging over to one side or the other.

9. It is easy to think that the component functions of the solution still have period 6, but if you look very closely you will see that the wave form of the first half is not quite like the second half. The change is more obvious in the orbits.

11. A generic form of the loop is something like

```
n=100;
a=2;
x[0]=b;
for(i=0,n,i++)
x[i+1]=f(x[i]);
for(i=0,n,i++)
plot(x[i]);
```

At about $a = 3.6$, the behavior appears to switch from lengthening periodic behavior to chaotic behavior.

Section 7.6, p. 228

1. When $b < 1$, there is only one critical point. For $b > 1$, bifurcation has occurred and there are now three critical points.

3. Initially, the solutions spiral in to the critical points P_1 and P_2. But for $b > 24$ a strange attractor emerges.

5. Subtract λ from the main diagonal entries and compute the determinant. This is facilitated by a computer algebra system.

7. They do approach closed orbits. The first appears to make one circuit, but the second comes around twice before repeating. The period of the second should be roughly twice that of the first.

9. The period doubling shows up as an alternation of higher and lower peaks.

CHAPTER 8

Section 8.1, p. 235

1. (a) $\hat{y} = (4 + 2sy(0))/(2s^2 + 3s)$.

  (b) $\hat{y} = (sy(0) + y'(0) + 3y(0))/(s^2 + 3s - 1)$.

3. $\hat{y} = \frac{1}{(s-1)(s^3 - s^2 + 4)} + \frac{s^2 y(0) + s y'(0) + y''(0) - s y(0) - y'(0)}{s^3 - s^2 + 4}$.

5. (a) $\hat{f}(s) = 1/(s - a)$.

  (b) $\hat{f}(s) = 1/s^2$.

7. (a) $\hat{f}(s) = 3!/s^4$.

  (b) $\hat{f}(s) = s/(s^2 + 1)$.

9. $\mathcal{L}(5f - 2g)(s) = 10/s^3 - 6s/(s^2 + 9)$.

11. $\hat{f}(s) = \frac{-3e^{-2s}}{s} + \frac{1 - e^{-2s}}{s^2}$.

Section 8.2, p. 239

1. (a) $5!/s^6$.

  (b) $1/(s - a)$.

  (c) $5!/(s - a)^6$.

3. The parts table is

$$\begin{array}{ll} \sin(bt) & e^{-st} \\ b\cos(bt) & -e^{-st}/s \\ -b^2\sin(bt) & e^{-st}/s^2 \end{array}$$

The partial solution for the integral is

$$\frac{s^2 + b^2}{s^2} \int_0^\infty e^{-st} \sin(bt)\, dt = \frac{b}{s^2}.$$

Solving this gives the result.

5. $2/s^3 + 1/(s - 2)^2 + 3/(s^2 + 9)$.

7. $3e^t + \sin(t)$.

9. $3t^2/2 + \cos(t)$.

11. $\frac{s}{(s-1)(s+2)} = \frac{1}{3}\frac{1}{s-1} + \frac{2}{3}\frac{1}{s+2}$.

Therefore, the inverse transform is $e^t/3 + 2e^{-2t}/3$.

13. $(6(s - 2)^2 - 2)/((s - 2)^2 + 1)^3)$.

Section 8.3, p. 243

1. $\frac{2/9}{(s-1)} + \frac{1/3}{(s-1)^2} - \frac{2/9}{(s+2)}$.

3. $-5 + s - \frac{9}{s+2} + \frac{28}{s+3}$.

5. We have $\hat{y} = \frac{y_0}{s-1} - \frac{y_0 - y_1}{(s-1)^2}$, so $y(t) = y_0 e^t - (y_0 - y_1)te^t$.

7. We have $\hat{y} = \frac{5/2}{(s+1/2)^2 + 3/4} + \frac{s+1/2}{(s+1/2)^2 + 3/4}$, so $y(t) = \frac{5}{\sqrt{3}}e^{-t/2}\sin(\frac{\sqrt{3}}{2}t) + e^{-t/2}\cos(\frac{\sqrt{3}}{2}t)$.

9. We have $\hat{y} = -\frac{1}{s^2+1} + \frac{s}{s^2+1} + \frac{1}{(s^2+1)^2}$. Expand the last term using partial fractions factored over the complex numbers in the same way that you do for real linear factors. Now combine to get a real result. We finally get

$$y(t) = -\frac{1}{2}\sin(t) + \cos(t) - \frac{t}{2}\cos(t).$$

Section 8.4, p. 248

1. $\hat{y}_p(s) = \frac{1}{5}\frac{1}{s-1} - \frac{1}{5}\frac{s+3}{s^2+2s+2}$.

The last term can be dropped since it will yield solutions to the homogeneous equation. Hence

$$y(t) = \frac{1}{5}e^t + c_1 e^{-t}\sin(t) + c_2 e^{-t}\cos(t).$$

3. $\hat{y}_p(s) = \frac{-1}{s} - \frac{1}{s^2} - \frac{1}{s^3} + \frac{1}{s-1}$.

We can drop the first and last terms because they yield homogeneous solutions. Hence

$$y(t) = -t - \frac{1}{2}t^2 + c_1 + c_2 e^t.$$

5. $y_p(t) = \int_0^t (e^{2x} - e^x)(t - x)^2\, dx = -2e^t + e^{2t}/4 + \frac{7 + 6t + 2t^2}{4}$.

7. $y_p(t) = \int_0^t xe^{-x}\sqrt{(t - x)^2 + 1}\, dx$.

9. $\hat{f}(s) = \frac{1}{s^2+1}\frac{s}{s^2+1}$.

11. $\hat{f}(s) = 12/s^7$.

13. $f \star (g \star h)(t) = \int_0^t \int_0^{t-x} f(x)h(y)g(t - x - y)dy\,dx$.
Change the order of integration and use Exercise 10.

Section 8.5, p. 256

1. (a) The partial fractions are

$$\hat{y} = \frac{3}{s-1} - \frac{2}{s-2} + \frac{e^{-2s}}{s-2} - \frac{2e^{-2s}}{s-1} + \frac{e^{-2s}}{s}.$$

The solution is $y(t) = 3e^t - 2e^{2t} + u_2(t)[e^{2(t-2)} - 2e^{t-2} + 1]$.

(b) The transfer function is $f(t) = e^{2t} - e^t$. The convolution is

$$y_p(t) = \int_0^t 2u_2(x)[e^{2(t-x)} - e^{t-x}]\,dx.$$

The solution is

$$y(t) = 3e^t - 2e^{2t} + u_2(t)[1 + e^{2(t-2)} - 2e^{t-2}].$$

3. $y_p(t) = \int_0^t u_2(x)x^2 \sin(t - x)\,dx$.
Break the integration into the cases $0 < t < 2$ and $2 < t$.
In the first interval, $y_p(t) = 0$. In the second, integrate by parts, and then the two cases can be combined as

$$y_p(t) = u_2(t)[-2 + t^2 - 2\cos(t - 2) + 4\sin(t - 2)].$$

Add the homogeneous solution and use the initial conditions to complete the solution.

5. The transform of the transfer function is $\hat{f}(s) = 1/(as^2 + bs + c)$. The transform of the homogeneous solution is obtained by solving

$$a(s^2\hat{y} - 1/a) + bs\hat{y} + c\hat{y} = 0.$$

The result is $\hat{y} = 1/(as^2 + bs + c)$. The transforms are the same, so the inverse transforms are the same.

7. The transfer function is $f(t) = -1 + e^t/2 + e^{-t}/2$. Then

$$y_p(t) = \int_0^t u_2(x)[-1 + \frac{e^{t-x}}{2} + \frac{e^{-(t-x)}}{2}]\,dx.$$

Thus,

$$y_p(t) = u_2(t)[2 - t + \frac{e^{t-2}}{2} - \frac{e^{-(t-2)}}{2}].$$

The complete solution is

$$y(t) = -1 + \frac{e^t}{2} + \frac{e^{-t}}{2} + y_p(t).$$

9. $y_p(t) = u_5(t)[-5/12 + t/6 - 4e^{-(t-5)}/3 + 11e^{2(t-5)}/12]$.

11. $F_n(t) = n[u_{t_0}(t) - u_{t_0+1/n}]$.

$$\mathcal{L}(F_n) = e^{-t_0 s}\frac{e^{s/n} - 1}{1/n}.$$

Take the limit as $n \to \infty$ to get $e^{-t_0 s}$.

13. $y(t) = \frac{1}{\sqrt{2}}\sin(\sqrt{2}t) + \sqrt{2}u_\pi(t)\sin(\sqrt{2}(t - \pi))$.
For $t < \pi$, the motion is of an undriven system. At $t = \pi$, the system absorbs an impulse imparting 4 units of momentum to the mass. The velocity is increased by 2 at that instant. The motion continues with these initial conditions.

Section 8.6, p. 261

1. $x = t^2/4 + 1/2$, and $y = t^3/12 + t/2$.

3. (a) $x = 1 - \cos(t)$, and $y = t - \sin(t)$.

(b) The transfer matrix and convolution is
$\begin{bmatrix} \cos(t) & -\sin(t) \\ \sin(t) & \cos(t) \end{bmatrix} \star \begin{bmatrix} t \\ 0 \end{bmatrix}$. The convolution integrals are $t \star \cos(t) = \int_0^t (t - x)\cos(x)\,dx$ and
$t \star \sin(t) = \int_0^t (t - x)\sin(x)\,dx$. The solutions are the same as in part (a).

5. The transfer matrix is $C(t) =$

$$\begin{bmatrix} e^{t/2}\cos(\sqrt{3}t/2) + \frac{1}{\sqrt{3}}e^{t/2}\sin(\sqrt{3}t/2) & -e^{t/2}\sin(\sqrt{3}t/2) \\ e^{t/2}\sin(\sqrt{3}t/2) & e^{t/2}\cos(\sqrt{3}t/2) - \frac{1}{\sqrt{3}}e^{t/2}\sin(\sqrt{3}t/2) \end{bmatrix}$$

and the solution is

$$\begin{bmatrix} x \\ y \end{bmatrix} = C(t) \star \begin{bmatrix} \sin(t) \\ 0 \end{bmatrix} + C(t)\begin{bmatrix} 2 \\ 1 \end{bmatrix}.$$

The integrals are

$$\int_0^t \sin(t - x)[e^{x/2}\cos(\sqrt{3}x/2) + \frac{1}{\sqrt{3}}e^{x/2}\sin(\sqrt{3}x/2)]\,dx$$

and

$$\int_0^t \sin(t - x)e^{x/2}\sin(\sqrt{3}x/2)\,dx.$$

7. $y(t) = t + y_0\cos(t) + y_1\sin(t)$.

9. $x(0), x'(0), x''(0), y(0), y'(0), z(0),$ and $z'(0)$.

Section 8.7, p. 264

1. The poles are at -1 and -2, so the solution decays to zero. This undriven mass–spring system has friction, so solutions must die away to zero.

3. The poles are in the right half-plane, so the solution goes to infinity.

5. The poles are in the left half-plane, so the solution goes to zero. As a mass-spring system, the system receives a unit of momentum at $t = 0$, but the system has friction, so the motion dies away to zero.

7. The forcing function "turns off" for $t > 4$, so, because there is friction, the solution decays to zero.

CHAPTER 9

Section 9.1, p. 269

1. We have $e^x \sin(y) - e^x \sin(y) = 0$.

3. Show that $u(x, t) = e^{-4t} \cos(2x)$ is a solution to $4u_{xx} = u_t$.
   Solution: $u_{xx} = -e^{-4t} 4 \cos(2x)$, and $u_t = -4e^{-4t} \cos(2x)$.

5. $L(au + bv) = (au + bv)_{xx} + (au + bv)_{yy} = au_{xx} + bv_{xx} + au_{yy} + bv_{yy} = au_{xx} + au_{yy} + bv_{xx} + bv_{yy} = aL(u) + bL(v)$.

7. Integrating with respect to x gives $u_y = x^2/2 + f(y)$; hence $u = x^2 y/2 + \int f(y)\, dy + g(x)$.

9. $u_{xx} = 1/y$, so $u_x = x/y + g(y)$, and so $u = x^2/(2y) + xg(y) + h(y)$.

11. Set $u(x, t) = X(x)T(t)$. The separation gives $X''/X = T'/T = \lambda$. The equations are $X'' - \lambda X = 0$ and $T' - \lambda T = 0$. Solutions have the form $u(x, t) = e^{\lambda t}[Ae^{\sqrt{\lambda}x} + Be^{-\sqrt{\lambda}x}]$ if λ is positive. If λ is negative, we get $e^{\lambda t}[A \sin(\sqrt{-\lambda}x) + B \cos(\sqrt{-\lambda}x)]$.

13. The separated equations are $X'' + \lambda X = 0$ and $Y'' - \lambda Y = 0$. For $\lambda > 0$ some solutions are $u(x, t) = (A \sin(\sqrt{\lambda}x) + B \cos(\sqrt{\lambda}x))[Ce^{\sqrt{\lambda}t} + De^{\sqrt{\lambda}t}]$.

Section 9.2, p. 279

1. The one-dimensional heat equation models the time-dependent distribution of temperature in a thin heat-conducting rod that is insulated along its length so that heat may only be transfered along the rod and through the ends. The side conditions are the initial temperature distribution in the rod $u(x, 0) = f(x)$ and the temperatures at which the ends are maintained, $u(0, t) = T_0$ and $u(b, t) = T_1$. The Laplacian is d^2/dx^2.

3. The one-dimensional wave equation models the vibration of a stretched string. Reasonable side conditions are the initial displacement and velocity of each point of the string at $t = 0$ and requiring the ends of the string to be fixed. These conditions are $u(x, 0) = f(x)$, $u_t(x, 0) = g(x)$, $u(0, t) = u(b, t) = 0$, and $u_t(0, t) = u_t(b, t) = 0$.

5. Let the tension in the string be T, and assume that the displacement at x and time t is $u(x, t)$. Also assume that the tension is large enough that gravity may be ignored and that the displacement is small. Consider a portion of the string from x to $x + \Delta x$ at time t. The vertical components of the forces on the ends of the segment are well approximated by $Tu_x(x + \Delta x, t)$ on the right and $-Tu_x(x, t)$ on the left. The net force must be equal to the change in momentum of the segment of the string, so

$$T(u_x(x + \Delta x, t) - u_x(x, t))$$
$$= \int_x^{x+\Delta x} \rho u_{tt}(x, t)\, dx = \rho u_{tt}(z, t)\Delta x$$

where ρ is the density of the string and z is between x and $x + \Delta x$. Dividing by Δx and taking the limit yield the wave equation.

7. The one-variable harmonic functions are the solutions to $u_{xx} = 0$, and these are $u = ax + b$.

9. We assume that $w'' = 0$ on $[0, b]$ and $w(0) = w(b) = 0$.
   Thus $\int_0^b ww''\, dx = 0$. So $\int_0^b w'w'\, dx = 0$, and so $w'(x) = 0$ on $[0, b]$. Therefore, w is a constant; but then it must be zero because of the values at the ends.

Section 9.3, p. 287

1. $u(x, t) = e^{-t} \sin(x)$.

3. $u(x, t) = \sum_{k=1}^{\infty} \frac{40}{\pi(2k-1)} e^{-\pi^2 (2k-1)^2 t/4} \sin(\pi(2k - 1)x/3)$.

5. There are no cosine terms. $A_k = \frac{-4(-1)^k}{\pi k}$, so

$$u(x, t) = \sum_{k=1}^{\infty} \frac{-4(-1)^k}{\pi k} e^{-\pi^2 k^2 t/4} \sin(\pi kx/2).$$

7. We have

$$\int_{-2}^{2} \sin(\pi kx/2) \sin(\pi jx/2)\, dx = \frac{1}{2} \int_{-2}^{2} \cos(\pi(k + j)x/2)$$
$$- \cos(\pi(k - j)x/2)\, dx.$$

Integrate and evaluate to get zero. The other identity is similar.

9. $A_n = 2[\int_0^{1/2} 2x \sin(\pi nx)\, dx + \int_{1/2}^{1} (2 - 2x) \sin(\pi nx)\, dx]$.
   Applying parts gives

$$\int_a^b x \sin(\pi nx)\, dx = -\frac{1}{\pi n} \cos(\pi nx) + \frac{1}{\pi^2 n^2} \sin(\pi nx)\Big|_a^b.$$

Apply this formula with the appropriate integration limits to get the result.

11. Solve $u_{xx} = u_t$, $u(0, t) = u(2, t) = 0$ for all $t \geq 0$, and $u(x, 0) = x + 2$ for $x \in [0, 2]$, and then translate the solution to the right by 2. The solution is

$$u(x, t) = \sum_{k=1}^{\infty} \frac{4}{\pi k}[1 - 2(-1)^k]e^{-\pi^2 k^2 t/4} \sin(\pi kx/2).$$

Section 9.4.1, p. 291

1. We indicate a few of the verifications. For Axiom 1, $(x_1, x_2) + (y_1, y_2) = (x_1 + y_1, x_2 + y_2) = (y_1 + x_1, y_2 + x_2) = (y_1, y_2) + (x_1, x_2)$. For Axiom 3, $(x, y) + (0, 0) = (x + 0, y + 0) = (x, y)$. For Axiom 9, $1(x, y) = (1x, 1y) = (x, y)$.

3. Note that the sum and scalar multiple of a polynomial of degree 3 or less is a polynomial of the same kind. Verifying the axioms is a straightforward consequence of the properties of polynomials. For instance, Axioms 1 and 2 are true because addition of polynomials is commutative and associative. The zero polynomial is the zero of this vector space. Axiom 3 is satisfied, because if $P(x)$ is any polynomial then $P(x) + (-P(x)) = 0$, and so on.

5. Yes, it is a real vector space. The sum and product of real numbers is a real number. Addition and multiplication of real numbers satisfy the axioms.

7. Consider all real linear combinations of the functions $\sin(t)$ and $\cos(t)$. Clearly, the sum and scalar product of such linear combinations is a linear combination. The axioms are easily verified.

9. Suppose that $u + v_1 = 0$ and $u + v_2 = 0$. Then $u + v_1 = u + v_2$. Axiom 4 says that we have a vector v such that $u + v = v + u = 0$. So $v + (u + v_1) = v + (u + v_2)$, and so $(v + u) + v_1 = (v + u) + v_2$ by Axiom 2. But $v + u = 0$, and so $0 + v_1 = 0 + v_2$. Thus $v_1 = v_2$.

11. $0 + 0 = 0$ is a property of real numbers. Thus $0v = (0 + 0)v$. But $(0 + 0)v = 0v + 0v$ by Axiom 7. So $0v = 0v + 0v$. Now add $-0v$ to both sides to get $-0v + 0v = -0v + (0v + 0v)$. So, by Axioms 4 and 2, $0 = -0v + (0v + 0v) = (-0v + 0v) + 0v$. Again, by Axiom 4, $0 = 0 + 0v$, and so by Axiom 3, $0 = 0v$.

13. $u + (-1)u = 1u + (-1)u = (1 + (-1))u$ by Axiom 7. Thus $u + (-1)u = 0u = 0$ by Exercise 11. But by Exercise 9 the additive inverse of a vector is unique, so $(-1)u$ must be that inverse, so $(-1)u = -u$.

15. It contains 0, and it is closed under addition and scalar multiplication.

17. The subspaces are $\{0\}$, any straight line through the origin,

any plane through the origin, and the whole space.

Section 9.4.2, p. 296

1. Reduction of the system

$$x + 2y + 3z = b_1,$$
$$x - y + 4z = b_2$$

shows that it can always be solved for x, y, and z. Thus there is a linear combination of the vectors in the set equal to (b_1, b_2). The set $\{(1, 1), (2, -1)\}$ is linearly independent, so it is a basis of $\mathbf{R}^2$.

3. There are many ways to do this. One is row reduction of the system corresponding to $x_1(2, -1, 0) + x_2(3, 1, 1) + x_3(1, 2, -1) + x_4(1, 1, 1) = (b_1, b_2, b_3)$. It is easier to observe that the subset $\{(2, -1, 0), (1, 2, -1), (1, 1, 1)\}$ is independent in a three-dimensional space, so it is a basis; so it and the larger set must span.

5. Obviously, $\{(1, 0), (0, 1)\}$ is independent, so it is a basis. The same can be said for $\{(i, 0), (0, i)\}$. It is easy to check that $\{(2, 1), (1, 2)\}$ is independent, and hence a basis.

7. Show that the only solution to

$$c_1(1, 0, 1) + c_2(2, -1, 3) + c_3(1, 1, 2) = (0, 0, 0)$$

is $c_1 = c_2 = c_3 = 0$ by solving the corresponding system of equations for c_1, c_2, and c_3.

9. If the vectors in the set are transposed to columns, the matrix that you get when these vectors are used as the columns is the matrix of coefficients in the homogeneous system of equations that derives from the definition of independence. The c's will be zero if and only if the determinant of the coefficient matrix is not zero. Thus the set is independent if and only if the determinant of the matrix composed of these vectors as rows or columns is not zero.

11. Suppose that there is an infinite dimensional subspace. Then there must be an independent set of vectors of number greater than the dimension of the whole space that is finite. This is impossible, since independent sets always have a number of vectors less than or equal to the dimension of the space.

13. A basis is $\{e^{2t}, e^{3t}\}$. Clearly, the Wronskian at, say, $t = 0$ is not zero, so the set is independent.

Section 9.4.3, p. 301

1. (a) $\langle(x_1, x_2) + (y_1, y_2), (z_1, z_2)\rangle = \langle(x_1 + y_1, x_2 + y_2), (z_1, z_2)\rangle = (x_1 + y_1)z_1 + (x_2 + y_2)z_2 = x_1 z_1 + x_2 z_2 + y_1 z_1 + y_2 z_2 = \langle(x_1, x_2), (z_1, z_2)\rangle + \langle(y_1, y_2), (z_1, z_2)\rangle$.

(b) $\langle a(x_1, x_2), (y_1, y_2)\rangle = \langle(ax_1, ax_2), (y_1, y_2)\rangle =$

$$ax_1 y_1 + ax_2 y_2 = a(x_1 y_1 + x_2 y_2) =$$
$$a\langle(x_1, x_2), (y_1, y_2)\rangle.$$

(c) $\langle(x_1, x_2), (y_1, y_2)\rangle = x_1 y_1 + x_2 y_2 = y_1 x_1 + y_2 x_2 = \langle(y_1, y_2), (x_1, x_2)\rangle.$

(d) $\langle(x_1, x_2), (x_1, x_2)\rangle = x_1^2 + x_2^2 \geq 0$, and the product equals zero only if $(x_1, x_2) = (0, 0)$.

3. $(5, 4, -2) = a_1(2, 0, 2) + a_2(0, 3, 0) + a_3(-1, 0, 1)$. $a_1 = 6/8$, $a_2 = 12/9$, and $a_3 = -7/2$.

5. (a) Check each of the four properties of an inner product. For example, $\langle f + g, h \rangle = \int_0^1 (f(x) + g(x))h(x)\,dx = \int_0^1 (f(x)h(x) + g(x)h(x))\,dx = \int_0^1 f(x)h(x)\,dx + \int_0^1 g(x)h(x)\,dx = \langle f, h \rangle + \langle g, h \rangle$, and $\langle f, f \rangle = \int_0^1 f(x)f(x)\,dx = \int_0^1 (a + bx + cx^2)^2\,dx \geq 0$. By direct calculation, this is zero only if $f(x)$ is the zero polynomial.

(b) Set $f_1(x) = 1$. We want $\int_0^1 1(a+bx)\,dx = a+b/2 = 0$, so choose $a = 1$ and $b = -2$. Thus $f_2(x) = 1 - 2x$ works. We require that $\int_0^1 1(a + bx + cx^2)\,dx = 0$ and $\int_0^1 (1 - 2x)(a + bx + cx^2)\,dx = 0$. Therefore, we need $6a + 3b + 2c = 0$ and $24a - 2b + c = 0$. Choose $c = -1$. Then $a = 1/12$ and $b = 1/2$.

7. (a) Checking properties 1 through 4 is routine. For instance, $\langle af, g \rangle = \int_0^\pi af(x)g(x)\,dx = a\int_0^\pi f(x)g(x)\,dx = a\langle f, g \rangle.$

(b) We have $\langle \sin(mx), \sin(nx) \rangle = \int_0^\pi \sin(mx)\sin(nx)\,dx$. If $m \neq n$, then it is easy to show that the integral is zero.

(c) Compute $a_i = \langle 1, \sin(ix) \rangle / \|\sin(ix)\|^2$. We get $a_i = 2(1 - (-1)^i)/(\pi i)$.

(d) Better approximations to $f(x) = 1$ on $[0, \pi]$.

9. It is routine to check properties 1 through 4. For instance,

$$\langle af, g \rangle = \int_0^1 af(x)g(x)x^2\,dx$$

$$= a \int_0^1 f(x)g(x)x^2\,dx$$

$$= a\langle f, g \rangle,$$

and

$$\langle f, g \rangle = \int_0^1 f(x)g(x)x^2\,dx$$

$$= \int_0^1 g(x)f(x)x^2\,dx$$

$$= \langle f, g \rangle.$$

Section 9.4.4, p. 307

1. $L(af + bg) = \int_0^1 af(x) + bg(x)\,dx = a\int_0^1 f(x)\,dx + b\int_0^1 g(x)\,dx = aL(f) + bL(g).$

3. $L(a(x_1, y_1, z_1) + b(x_2, y_2, z_2)) = L((ax_1 + bx_2, ay_1 + by_2, az_1 + bz_2)) = (2(ax_1 + bx_2) - (az_1 + bz_2), 3(ay_1 + by_2) + (az_1 + bz_2))$. Collecting up the terms in a and b gives $L(a(x_1, y_1, z_1) + b(x_2, y_2, z_2)) = a(2x_1 - z_1, 3y_1 + z_1) + b(2x_2 - z_2, 3y_2 + z_2) = aL((x_1, y_1, z_1)) + bL((x_2, y_2, z_2)).$

5. $(L_1 + L_2)(au + bv) = L_1(au + bv) + L_2(au + bv) = a(L_1(u) + L_2(u)) + b(L_1(v) + L_2(v)) = a(L_1 + L_2)(u) + b(L_1 + L_2)(v).$

7. We have $\langle L(E_i), E_j \rangle = a_{ji}$ and $\langle E_i, L(E_j) \rangle = a_{ij}$. Thus $a_{ij} = a_{ji}$. We say the matrix is symmetric.

9. We must solve $L(x, y) = (3x, -2y) = \lambda(x, y)$, so $\lambda x = 3x$, and $\lambda y = -2y$, and x or y is not zero. Thus λ is 3 or -2. The 3 eigensubspace is spanned by $(1, 0)$ and the -2 eigensubspace is spanned by $(0, 1)$.

11. The matix $A = \begin{bmatrix} 0 & 1 \\ -1 & 0 \end{bmatrix}$ has eigenvalues $\pm i$. Define $L(X) = AX$.

13. We must solve $D^2 u = \lambda u$, where $u(0) = u(4) = 0$. The solution is $u(x) = Ae^{\sqrt{\lambda}} + Be^{-\sqrt{\lambda}}$. But the endpoint conditions can only be satisfied if the exponentials are complex; that is, λ must be negative. So set $\mu^2 = -\lambda$. Then the general solution is $u(x) = A\sin(\mu x) + B\cos(\mu x)$. To satisfy the endpoint conditions, we must have $B = 0$ and $\mu = \frac{\pi k}{4}$. Thus the eigenvalues are $\lambda = -(\frac{\pi k}{4})^2$ and the corresponding eigenvectors are $\sin(\pi kx/4)$.

Section 9.5, p. 313

1. This is the same as the symmetry of $-\Delta$ on the space of infinitely differentiable functions that vanish at the endpoints. The only difference is that the derivatives vanish now. Integration by parts gives

$$\int_0^b f''g\,dx = g(x)f'(x)|_0^b - g'(x)f(x)|_0^b + \int_0^b fg''\,dx.$$

Therefore,

$$\langle -\frac{d^2}{dx^2}f, g \rangle = -\int_0^b f''g\,dx$$

$$= -\int_0^b fg''\,dx$$

$$= \langle f, -\frac{d^2}{dx^2}g \rangle.$$

3. Yes! $\langle Lf, g \rangle = \int_0^1 (f'' + 2f)g\,dx = gf'|_0^1 - g'f|_0^1 + \int_0^1 fg'' + 2fg\,dx = \langle f, Lg \rangle$. For the eigenfunctions, solve $Ly = \lambda y$; that is, $y'' + (2 - \lambda)y = 0$. The eigenvalues are $\lambda = 2 - \pi^2 k^2$, and the eigenfunctions are $\sin(\pi k x)$, where $k = 1, 2, \ldots$.

5. The boundary conditions $f(0) = f'(0) = f(1) = f'(1) = g(0) = g'(0) = g(1) = g'(1) = 0$ will do.

7. $\langle L(x, y), (u, v) \rangle = \langle (y, x), (u, v) \rangle = uy + xv = \langle (x, y), L(u, v) \rangle$.
Eigenvectors are $(-1, 1)$ and $(1, 1)$. These are obviously orthogonal.

9. (a) We require that $\frac{w'}{w} = 1$ because we need $y'' + y' = \frac{1}{w(x)}(w(x)y')'$. Thus $w = e^x$ will do. Now calculate $\langle Lf, g \rangle$ and $\langle f, Lg \rangle$ relative to the inner product $\langle f, g \rangle = \int_0^1 f(x)g(x)e^x\,dx$.

(b) The eigenvalues are $(-1 - 4\pi^2 k^2)/4$, and the eigenfunctions are $e^{-x/2} \sin(\pi k x)$, where $k = 1, 2, \ldots$.

Section 9.6, p. 319

1. The basis of eigenfunctions is $\{1, \sin(2\pi k/6), \cos(2\pi k/6)\}$. There are no cosine terms. The series is $f(x) =$
$$\sum_{k=1}^{\infty} \frac{4}{\pi(2k-1)} \sin\left(\frac{\pi(2k-1)x}{3}\right).$$

3. The series is
$$f(x) = \frac{3}{4} + \sum_{k=1}^{\infty} 6\frac{\pi k \cos(\pi k/2) - \sin^2(\pi k/2)}{(\pi k)^2} \cos\left(\frac{\pi k x}{3}\right)$$
$$- \frac{9}{\pi k}(-1)^k \sin\left(\frac{\pi k x}{3}\right).$$

5. The series is
$$f(x) = \frac{3\pi + 6}{6\pi}$$
$$+ \sum_{k=1}^{\infty} \frac{-1 + (-1)^k}{\pi(k^2 - 1)} \cos(2\pi k x/6) + \frac{-1 + (-1)^k}{\pi k} \sin(2\pi k x/6).$$

7. $1/2 + \sum_{k=1}^{\infty} \frac{2[(-1)^k - 1]}{\pi^2 k^2} \cos(\pi k x)$.

9. $f(x) = 1/4 + \sum_{k=1}^{\infty} [\frac{12 + (-1)^k(-12 + 6(\pi k)^2)}{\pi^4 k^4}] \cos(\pi k x)$.

11. The series appears to converge to the mean of the jump discontinuity.

Section 9.7, p. 325

1. $u(x, t) = \cos(2\pi t) \sin(\pi x)$. A point x on the string executes simple harmonic motion with amplitude $\sin(\pi x)$ and period 1. You see one period of a sine curve whose amplitude diminishes to zero and then grows to the negative of the starting curve. The motion repeats.

3. $u(x, t) = \cos(4\pi t) \sin(2\pi x)$. Yes!

5. $u(x, t) = \cos(\pi t) \sin(\pi x) = \frac{1}{2} \sin(\pi(x-t)) + \frac{1}{2} \sin(\pi(x+t))$.

7. $u(x, t) = \sum_{k=1}^{\infty} \frac{32}{\pi^3(2k-1)^3} \cos((2k-1)\pi t/2) \sin((2k-1)\pi x/2)$.
The d'Alembert solution is $u(x, t) = f(x - t)/2 + f(x + t)/2$. The function $f(x)$ is extended as an odd periodic function with period 4. As the first wave moves to the right and the second to the left, they sum to give the behavior seen. In particular, when each has moved 1/4 of a period, the sum is zero.

9. Using an identity: $u(x, t) = [\sin(2\pi(x - 2t)) + \sin(2\pi(x + 2t))]/2 = \cos(4\pi t) \sin(2\pi x)$. Yes!

11. $u(x, t) = [f(x - t) + f(x + t)]/2$. Here $f(x)$ is extended as an odd periodic function with period 4.

13. The roots in the T equation take the form $-r/2 \pm \omega_k i$. The form of the solution is $u(x, t) = \sum_{k=1}^{\infty} [A_k e^{-rt/2} \sin(\omega_k t) + B_k e^{-rt/2} \cos(\omega_k t)] \sin(\pi k x/a)$. The exponentials cause the solution to die away as time increases.

Section 9.8, p. 328

1. $\int_0^2 f(x)\,dx$ is still 8/3. A Fourier series can converge in norm to the given function f, but this does not mean it will converge pointwise to f at each point.

3. The series converges pointwise to $f(x)$ at each point x for which f is continuous. At $x = 1$ the series converges to 1/2.

5. 0.5 and 0.25.

Section 9.9.1, p. 331

1. $u(x, y, t) = \cos(\sqrt{2}\pi t) \sin(\pi x) \sin(\pi y)$.

3. The integrals are
$$A_{jk}$$
$$= \frac{1}{2} \int_0^4 \sin^2(\pi x) \sin(\pi j x/4)\,dx \int_0^2 \sin^2(\pi y) \sin(\pi k y/2)\,dy$$
$$= \frac{(64 - 64\cos(\pi j))(16 - 16\cos(\pi k))}{\pi j(j^2 - 64)\pi k(k^2 - 16)}.$$

For $j = 8$ or $k = 4$, $A_{jk} = 0$. We have
$$u(x, y, t) = \sum_{j=1, k=1, j \neq 8, k \neq 4}^{\infty} \frac{(64 - 64\cos(\pi j))(16 - 16\cos(\pi k))}{\pi j(j^2 - 64)\pi k(k^2 - 16)}$$
$$\cos(\sqrt{\lambda_{jk}}t) \sin(\pi j x/2) \sin(\pi k y/2),$$
where $\lambda_{jk} = (\pi^2 j^2/16 + \pi^2 k^2/4)$.

5. Yes! Choose an eigenfunction for the initial displacement and the initial velocity equal to zero; then $u(x, y, t) = A_{jk} \cos(c\sqrt{\lambda_{jk}}t) \sin(\pi jx/a) \sin(\pi ky/b)$.

7. Yes! The frequency is determined by $\sqrt{j^2 + k^2}$, and so we could have the $j = 2, k = 3$ and $j = 3, k = 2$ modes, for example.

9. The eigenfunctions are $X_{jk} = \sin(\pi jx/a) \sin(\pi ky/b)$. Also,

$$\langle X_{jk}, X_{pq} \rangle$$
$$= \int_0^a \sin(\tfrac{\pi jx}{a}) \sin(\tfrac{\pi px}{a}) \, dx \int_0^b \sin(\tfrac{\pi ky}{b}) \sin(\tfrac{\pi qy}{b}) \, dy.$$

Recall from the one-dimensional case that $\{\sin(\pi jx/a\}$ and $\{\sin(\pi ky/b)\}$ are orthogonal families on the respective intervals. So $\langle X_{jk}, X_{pq} \rangle = 0$ if $(j, k) \neq (p, q)$.

Section 9.9.2, p. 338

1. Yes! Assume that $u(r, \theta, 0) = J_0(\sqrt{\lambda_{01}}r)$ and $u_t(r\theta, 0) = 0$. Thus $u(r, \theta, t) = \cos(c\sqrt{\lambda_{01}}t)J_0(\sqrt{\lambda_{01}}r)$. Here $\sqrt{\lambda_{01}}$ is the first zero of J_0.

3. Repeat the derivation in the text, paying attention to where b comes in.

5. The initial data determine that $A_{01} = 2$ and $A_{05} = 3$ and all the rest are zero, so $u(r, \theta, t) = 2\cos(\sqrt{\lambda_{01}}ct)J_0(\sqrt{\lambda_{01}}r) + 3\cos(\sqrt{\lambda_{05}}ct)J_0(\sqrt{\lambda_{05}}r)$.

7. $\sqrt{\lambda_{11}}$ is the first zero of J_1. Using one of the Three M's, the approximate value is 3.8.

9. The problem is that we have no formulas for the integrals of the Bessel functions in terms of familiar functions.

Section 9.10, p. 345

1. $u(x) = 2x - 1$.

3.

$$u^1(x, y) = \frac{e^{4\pi y} - e^{8\pi}e^{-4\pi y}}{1 - e^{8\pi}} \sin(4\pi x).$$

5.

$$u^1(x, y) = 3\frac{e^{2\pi y} - e^{12\pi}e^{-2\pi y}}{1 - e^{12\pi}} \sin(2\pi x),$$

$$\text{and } u^3(x, y) = \frac{e^{\pi y} - e^{-\pi y}}{e^{3\pi} - e^{-3\pi}} \sin(\pi x)$$

$$- 2\frac{e^{4\pi y} - e^{-4\pi y}}{e^{12\pi} - e^{-12\pi}} \sin(4\pi x).$$

The solution is $u(x, y) = u^1(x, y) + u^3(x, y)$.

7. $u^1 = \sum_{k=1}^{\infty} \frac{2[1-(-1)^k]}{\pi k[1-e^{3\pi k}]} (e^{\pi ky/2} - e^{3\pi k}e^{-\pi ky/2}) \sin(\pi kx/2)$.

$u^2 = \sum_{k=1}^{\infty} \frac{6[1-(-1)^k]}{\pi k[e^{2\pi k/3}-e^{-2\pi k/3}]} (e^{\pi kx/3} - e^{-\pi kx/3}) \sin(\pi ky/3)$.

$u^3 = \sum_{k=1}^{\infty} \frac{-4(-1)^k[e^{\pi ky/2}-e^{-\pi ky/2}]}{\pi k[e^{3\pi k/2}-e^{-3\pi k/2}]} \sin(\pi kx/2)$.

$u^4 = \sum_{k=1}^{\infty} \frac{6[(-1)^k-1]}{\pi k[1-e^{4\pi k/3}]} (e^{\pi kx/3} - e^{4\pi k/3}e^{-\pi kx/3}) \sin(\pi ky/3)$.

The solution is $u(x, y) = u^1(x, y) + u^2(x, y) + u^3(x, y) + u^4(x, y)$.

9. $u(r, \theta) = 5r^{(-1+\sqrt{5})/2} \cos(\theta) + -2r^{(-1+\sqrt{5})/2} \sin(\theta)$.

11. $u(x, t) = 7x/2 - 2 + \sum_{k=1}^{\infty} \frac{6+15(-1)^k}{\pi k} e^{-\pi^2 k^2 t/9} \sin(\pi kx/3)$.

13. $u(x, t) = x/2 + 2 + \sum_{k=1}^{\infty} \frac{-2}{\pi k(1-4k^2)} \cos(\pi kt/2) \sin(\pi kx/2)$.

CHAPTER 10

Section 10.1, p. 350

1. $u'(2) = -26$. The forward difference is -26.7, the backward difference is -25.3, and the centered difference is -26.

3. $u'(\pi/4) = 0.707$. The forward difference is 0.632, the backward difference is 0.773, and the centered difference is 0.702.

5. $u'(1) = 1$. The forward difference is 0.912, the backward difference is 1.116, and the centered difference is 1.014.

7. $O(\Delta x^3) = (-16 - 4\Delta x)\Delta x^3$.

9. Both are 6.

11. $O(h^5) \leq M|h|^5$. Given two such terms, $O(h^5) + O(h^5) \leq M|h|^5 + N|h|^5 = (M + N)|h|^5$.

Section 10.2, p. 357

1. $v_1^1 = -0.25, v_1^2 = -0.9375$.

3. A ratio of approximately 25 caused the algorithm to fail. In general, if $\Delta t/\Delta x$ is large, the algorithm tends to be unstable.

5. The finite difference scheme is $v_j^{k+1} = \Delta t(v_{j+1}^k - v_j^k)/(2\Delta x) - 3\Delta t v_j^k/2 + v_j^k$. Instability could be seen for a ratio of 40 and 200 subdivisions on the x-axis.

7. $v_j^{k+1} = \frac{4\Delta t}{\Delta x}(v_{j+1}^k - v_j^k - \Delta t v_j^k + v_j^k$.

9. $v_j^{k+1} = \Delta t(v_j^k)^2 + v_j^k + \frac{\Delta t}{\Delta x}v_j^k - \frac{\Delta t}{\Delta x}v_{j+1}^k$.

11. The equation is $(4/\Delta x - 1 - 1/\Delta t)v_j^k - (4/\Delta x)v_{j-1}^k = -v_j^k/\Delta x$. The succeeding time row terms are not computed explicitly from the preceding row, but are defined as unknowns in a system of equations.

13. The difference equation is

$$4\frac{v_{j+1}^k - v_{j-1}^k}{\Delta x} - \frac{v_j^{k+1} - v_j^{k-1}}{\Delta t} = v_j^k.$$

15. The chain rule gives $u_x = w_{\bar{x}} + w_{\bar{t}}$ and $u_t = -w_{\bar{x}} + w_{\bar{t}}$. Subtract to get $2w_{\bar{x}}(\bar{x}, \bar{t}) = u_x - u_t = u(x, t) = w(\bar{x}, \bar{t})$. This argument reverses. Now $w(\bar{x}, \bar{t}) = c(\bar{t})e^{\bar{x}/2}$, where $c(\bar{t})$ is an arbitrary function of $\bar{t}$. So $u(x, t) = c(x + t)e^{(x-t)/2}$. Now use the initial condition $u(x, 0) = \sin(20x)$.

17. We have the values v_j^0 for $j = 0$ to $j = m$ from the initial condition. To find the v_j^1, we must solve $\frac{\Delta t}{\Delta x}v_{j-1}^1 + (1 - \frac{\Delta t}{\Delta x} + \Delta t)v_j^1 = v_j^0$ for $j = 1$ to $j = m$. If we have v_0^1, then the rest of the v_j^1 are easily computed. But this means that we must have initial data on the t-axis, and this cannot be specified consistently unless the solution is already known.

Section 10.3, p. 365

1. $v_1^1 = 0.5$, $v_1^2 = 0.3536$.

3. $v_1^1 = 0.6250$, $v_1^2 = 0.5938$.

5. $v_2^1 = -0.2813$, $v_2^2 = -0.1875$.

7. Yes, $s = 1$. $v_3^3 = 0.09375$.

9. The three arches of $\sin(3\pi x)$ rapidly decay to zero as time increases. Disaster seems to strike for any s with $s > 1/2$.

11. The initial arch of the sin is in the process of flattening out as time progresses. It is not hard to get the algorithm to blow up for values of s greater than 2, say.

13. $u_j^{k+1} - v_j^{k+1} = u_j^{k+1} - su_{j-1}^k - 2(1-s)u_j^k - su_{j+1}^k + u_j^{k-1} = u_j^{k+1} - 2u_j^k + u_j^{k-1} - s(u_{j+1}^k - 2u_j^k + u_{j-1}^k) = \Delta t^2 u_{tt} + \Delta t^2 O(\Delta t^2) - c^2\Delta t^2[u_{xx} + O(\Delta x^2)] = O(\Delta t^4 + \Delta t^2 \Delta x^2)$.

Section 10.4, p. 369

1. $v^1 = (0.433013, 0.433013)^t$ and

$v^2 = (0.216506, 0.216506)^t$.

3. $v^1 = (0.2887, 0.2887)^t$ and $v^2 = (0.09623, 0.09623)^t$.

7. Note that the algorithm seems to be stable for each s.

Section 10.5, p. 373

1. The algorithm fails for 10 subdivisions on a side. The algorithm seems stable for s values less than 0.5.

3. It is quite hard to get a stable result. Ten subdivisions for x and 200 for t seem to work. Instability is the order of the day. Sensitivity to the step ratio can severely limit the practical application of the forward method.

5. With $\Delta t/\Delta x \leq 1$, the algorithm is stable as expected. The sine mode decays as time progresses, as expected. If we choose $\Delta t/\Delta x > 1$, it is easy to get the algorithm to fail.

Section 10.6, p. 380

1. The boundary values are $v_0^0 = v_3^0 = v_0^3 = v_3^3 = 0$ and $v_1^0 = v_1^3 = v_2^0 = v_2^3 = v_0^1 = v_3^1 = v_0^2 = v_3^2 = \sqrt{3}/2$. The equations are

$$v_0^1 - 2v_1^1 + v_2^1 + v_1^2 - 2v_1^1 + v_1^0 = 0,$$
$$v_1^1 - 2v_2^1 + v_3^1 + v_2^2 - 2v_2^1 + v_2^0 = 0,$$
$$v_1^2 - 2v_2^2 + v_3^2 + v_2^3 - 2v_2^2 + v_2^1 = 0,$$
$$v_0^2 - 2v_1^2 + v_2^2 + v_1^3 - 2v_1^2 + v_1^1 = 0.$$

3. Follow Exercise 1.

5. (a) $h = 1/n$ for n an integer.

(b) $V \equiv 0$ because the max and min must be taken on the boundary where the values are zero.

7. The boundary values are $v_0^0 = v_3^0 = v_0^3 = v_0^1 = v_0^2 = v_3^1 = v_3^2 = v_3^3 = 0$ and $v_1^0 = v_2^0 = v_1^3 = v_2^3 = \sqrt{3}/2$. The first equation is

$$\frac{v_0^1 - 2v_1^1 + v_2^1}{(\pi/3)^2} + \frac{v_1^2 - 2v_1^1 + v_1^0}{1/9} = 0.$$

There are three more centered at $(2, 1)$, $(2, 2)$, and $(1, 2)$.

9. Multiply through by Δt and simplify.

BIBLIOGRAPHY

Cited References

[1] William E. Boyce and Richard C. DiPrima, *Elementary Differential Equations and Boundary Value Problems*, Wiley, New York, 1992.

[2] Richard L. Burden and J. Douglas Faires, *Numerical Analysis*, Prindle, Weber, & Schmidt—Kent, Boston, 1989.

[3] Vladimir I. Arnol'd, *Ordinary Differential Equations*, Springer-Verlag, Berlin, Heidelberg, London, et al., 1992.

[4] Garrett Birkhoff and Saunders Mac Lane, *A Survey of Modern Algebra*, Macmillan, New York, 1959.

[5] Eugene Isaacson and Herbert Bishop Keller, *Analysis of Numerical Methods*, Dover, New York 1966.

[6] Hubert Kennedy, *Selected works of Giuseppe Peano*, University of Toronto Press, Toronto, Canada, 1973.

[7] G. D. Smith, *Numerical solution of partial differential equations, Finite Differences Methods*, Oxford University Press, New York, 1978.

Suggested Reading

Arnol'd, Vladimir I., *Ordinary Differential Equations*, Springer-Verlag, Berlin, Heidelberg, London, et al., 1992.

Blanchard, Paul, Robert L. Devaney, and Glen R. Hall, *Differential Equations*, Prindle, Weber, & Schmidt, Boston, 1996

Borrelli, Robert L., and Courtney S. Coleman, *Differential Equations – A Modeling Approach*, Prentice Hall, Upper Saddle River, NJ, 1987.

Boyce, William E., and Richard C. DiPrima, *Elementary Differential Equations and Boundary Value Problems*, Wiley, New York, 1992.

Burden, Richard L., and J. Douglas Faires, *Numerical Analysis*, Prindle, Weber, & Schmidt–Kent, Boston, 1989.

Edwards, C. H., and David Penney, *Elementary Differential Equations*, Prentice Hall, Upper Saddle River, NJ, 2000.

Smith, G. D., *Numerical Solution of Partial Differential Equations – Finite Difference Methods*, Oxford University Press, New York, 1978.

Strauss, Walter A., *Partial Differential Equations – An Introduction*, Wiley, New York, 1992.

Williamson, Richard E., *An Introduction to Differential Equations and Dynamical Systems*, McGraw-Hill, New York, 1997.

INDEX

Symbols
2×2 linear systems, 131

A
adding matrices, 118, 392
analytic method, 6
analytic methods of solution, 23
annihilator, 98
asymptotically stable, 66
autonomous, 40, 54, 64

B
backward method, 366
basic theorem, 209
beating, 114
Bernoulli equations, 31
bifurcation, 199
bifurcation and numerical methods, 202
bifurcation diagram, 200

C
Cayley-Hamilton theorem, 147
center, 154
chaos, 223
characteristic polynomial, 124

circuit, 3
circular drum, 332
closed, 291
cofactor, 397
column vector, 120
competing species, 68
complex eigenvalues, 133
complex-valued functions, 88
constant coefficient, 79, 88
convergence of series, 326
convolution, 245, 246
convolution identity, 254
Cramer's rule, 83, 400
critical points, 40, 65
critically damped, 110

D
D'Alembert's solution, 323
defined implicitly, 25
degenerate, 309
dependence of solutions on initial conditions, 44
derivative of a matrix, 121
direction field, 12
Dirichlet problem, 339
Dirichlet problem for the circle, 342
Dirichlet problem in a rectangle, 339
discontinuous and impulsive forcing functions, 248
discretization error, 60

E,
eigenvalue, 91, 124, 305
eigenvector, 305
elementary matrices and inverses, 394
elephant, 26
equilibrium point, 40
error analysis, 377
essential singularity, 186
Euler's method, 17, 58
even, 318
exact, 37
exact equations, 36
existence, 6
existence and uniqueness for systems, 50
expansion by minors, 396
exponential growth, 232

F
famous functions, 181
finite and infinite dimensional spaces, 292
finite difference approximations, 347
first kind, 189
flow, 203, 204
flow lines, 205
forward method, 351
Fourier series, 314
Fourier sine coefficients, 283
fundamental set, 83

G
graphical, 6

H
half-range, 318
hanging cable, 4
hard and soft springs, 116
heat and wave equation, 357
heat equation, 279
heat equation revisited, 308
higher order linear equations, 79

homogeneous, 79, 122
homogeneous equations, 27
hyperbolic, 274

I
identity matrix, 119, 392
improved Euler, 19
impulse functions, 252
inclination field, 12
indicial polynomial, 188
inhomogeneous boundary conditions, 343
initial condition, 12
inner product spaces, 296
integer difference of roots, 194
inverse transform, 233

J
Jacobi method, 376

L
Laplace transforms and systems, 257
Laplace's equation, 338, 373
Laplacian, 276
Legendre polynomials, 180
Legendre's equation, 179
limit cycles, 74
linear, 82, 122
linear combination, 82, 123, 292
linear equations, 30
linear homogeneous equations, 80
linear independence, 85
linear operators, 302
linear systems, matrices, and determinants, 387
linearity, 82
linearization of 2×2 Systems, 159
Liouville's theorem, 206
Lipschitz condition, 210

M

mathematical models, 25
matrices, 118
matrix, 118, 391
matrix algebra, 120
matrix exponential function, 138
matrix operations and definitions, 118
matrix product, 118, 392
matrix valued functions, 121
maximal, 15
maximum/minimum principle, 374
method of Frobenius, 187
minor, 397
mixture problem, 33

N

Neumann condition, 311
Newton's law of cooling, 27
Newton's second law, 3
node, 154
nonhomogeneous equations, 97
nonhomogeneous equations and the convolution, 244
nonlinear examples, 370
norm, 299
normalized, 54
nullclines, 66
numerical methods, 7, 17

O

odd, 318
one-dimensional wave equation, 319
operator, 81
operator notation, 92
orbit crossing and periodic solutions, 56
order, 1
orthogonal, 297
orthogonal trajectories, 40
overdamped, 109

P

parabolic, 272
parachute jump, 34
partial fractions, 240
pendulum, 70
periodically driven pendulum, 218
phase plane, 9
piecewise continuous, 249
Poincaré return map, 220
pointwise convergence, 327
poles, 262
poles and qualitative behavior, 261
power series, 167
power series method, 166

Q

qualitative behavior, 64
qualitative behavior of systems, 151

R

real roots, 89
rectangular drum, 329
recursion relation, 173
reduction to first order, 7
regular singular point, 186
regular singular points, 186
removable singularity, 186
repeated and complex roots, 93
repeated eigenvalues, 135
repeated roots, 193
resonance, 112
resonant frequency, 112
review of vectors, 48
Rodrigues's formula, 185
Runge-Kutta, 20, 58, 60

S

saddle, 154
scalar multiple of a matrix, 119, 392
separable, 23

separation of variables, 23
series methods, 166
signum, 396
singular solutions, 325
singularity, 186
solution, 2, 6
solution of systems of equations, 387
solutions to first-order systems, 48
solving linear homogeneous equations, 240
some results on the Lorenz system, 224
some simple attractors, 213
spiral point, 154
stability, 151, 381
stable, 41, 66, 383
step size, 17
system, 6
systems, 9
systems as vector equations, 53

T
Taylor coefficients, 168
The Laplace Transform, 230
transfer function, 246
transfer matrices and matrix convolutions, 258
transforms of discontinuous functions, 249

triangle inequality, 299
tunnel diode, 75
two-dimensional wave equation, 328

U
underdamped, 110
undetermined coefficients, 98
uniqueness, 7
unit step function, 249

V
van der Pol, 78
variation of parameters, 103
vector spaces, 288
vibration, 107

W
Wronskian, 83

Z
zero matrix, 119, 392

Table of Integrals (continued)

30. $\int \cos au \cos bu \, du = \dfrac{\sin(a-b)u}{2(a-b)} + \dfrac{\sin(a+b)u}{2(a+b)} + C \qquad$ if $a^2 \neq b^2$

31. $\int \sin au \cos bu \, du = -\dfrac{\cos(a-b)u}{2(a-b)} - \dfrac{\cos(a+b)u}{2(a+b)} + C \qquad$ if $a^2 \neq b^2$

32. $\int \sin^n u \, du = -\dfrac{1}{n} \sin^{n-1} u \cos u + \dfrac{n-1}{n} \int \sin^{n-2} u \, du$

33. $\int \cos^n u \, du = \dfrac{1}{n} \cos^{n-1} u \sin u + \dfrac{n-1}{n} \int \cos^{n-2} u \, du$

34. $\int \tan^n u \, du = \dfrac{1}{n-1} \tan^{n-1} u - \int \tan^{n-2} u \, du \qquad$ if $n \neq 1$

35. $\int \cot^n u \, du = -\dfrac{1}{n-1} \cot^{n-1} u - \int \cot^{n-2} u \, du \qquad$ if $n \neq 1$

36. $\int \sec^n u \, du = \dfrac{1}{n-1} \sec^{n-2} u \tan u + \dfrac{n-2}{n-1} \int \sec^{n-2} u \, du \qquad$ if $n \neq 1$

37. $\int \csc^n u \, du = -\dfrac{1}{n-1} \csc^{n-2} u \cot u + \dfrac{n-2}{n-1} \int \csc^{n-2} u \, du \qquad$ if $n \neq 1$

38. $\int u \sin u \, du = \sin u - u \cos u + C$

39. $\int u \cos u \, du = \cos u + u \sin u + C$

40. $\int u^n \sin u \, du = -u^n \cos u + n \int u^{n-1} \cos u \, du$

41. $\int u^n \cos u \, du = u^n \sin u - n \int u^{n-1} \sin u \, du$

FORMS INVOLVING $\sqrt{u^2 \pm a^2}$

42. $\int \sqrt{u^2 \pm a^2} \, du = \dfrac{u}{2}\sqrt{u^2 \pm a^2} \pm \dfrac{a^2}{2} \ln|u + \sqrt{u^2 \pm a^2}| + C$

43. $\int \dfrac{du}{\sqrt{u^2 \pm a^2}} = \ln|u + \sqrt{u^2 \pm a^2}| + C$

FORMS INVOLVING $\sqrt{a^2 - u^2}$

44. $\int \sqrt{a^2 - u^2} \, du = \dfrac{u}{2}\sqrt{a^2 - u^2} + \dfrac{a^2}{2} \sin^{-1} \dfrac{u}{a} + C$

45. $\int \dfrac{\sqrt{a^2 - u^2}}{u} \, du = \sqrt{a^2 - u^2} - a \ln\left|\dfrac{a + \sqrt{a^2 - u^2}}{u}\right| + C$